DWORKI

AND HIS CRITICS

PHILOSOPHERS AND THEIR CRITICS

General Editor: Ernest Lepore

Philosophy is an interactive enterprise. Much of it is carried out in dialogue as theories and ideas are presented and subsequently refined in the crucible of close scrutiny. The purpose of this series is to reconstruct this vital interplay among thinkers. Each book consists of a temporary assessment of an important living philosopher's work. A collection of essays written by an interdisciplinary group of critics addressing the substantial theses of the philosopher's corpus opens each volume. In the last section, the philosopher responds to his or her critics, clarifies crucial points of the discussion, or updates his or her doctrines.

DWORKIN

AND HIS CRITICS

with replies by Dworkin

Edited by
Justine Burley

Blackwell
Publishing

BLACKWELL PUBLISHING
350 Main Street, Malden, MA 02148-5020, USA
108 Cowley Road, Oxford OX4 1JF, UK
550 Swanston Street, Carlton, Victoria 3053, Australia

First published 2004 by Blackwell Publishing Ltd

Library of Congress Cataloging-in-Publication Data

Dworkin and his critics : with replies by Dworkin / edited by Justine Burley.
p. cm. — (Philosophers and their critics ; 11)
Includes bibliographical references and index.
ISBN 0-631-19765-6 (alk. paper)—ISBN 0-631-19766-4 (pbk. : alk. paper)
1. Dworkin, Ronald William. 2. Social ethics. 3. Social justice. 4. Equality.
5. Right to life. 6. Right to die. I. Dworkin, R. M. II. Burley, Justine. III. Series.

HM665.D86 2004
303.3′72′01—dc22
2004003078

A catalogue record for this title is available from the British Library.

Set in 10/12pt Ehrhardt
by SNP Best-set Typesetter Ltd., Hong Kong
Printed and bound in the United Kingdom
by MPG Books Ltd, Bodmin, Cornwall

For further information on
Blackwell Publishing, visit our website:
http://www.blackwellpublishing.com

This book is dedicated to my father who was the first to instruct me that constant critical evaluation, of even the best views, is a valuable exercise.

Contents

Notes on Contributors

RICHARD J. ARNESON is Professor of Philosophy at the University of California, San Diego, where he was chair from 1992–6. He has held visiting professor appointments at the University of California, Davis and at Yale University, and been Visiting Fellow at Australian National University. He works on political and moral philosophy. His recent work explores how ideas of personal responsibility might be integrated into a liberal egalitarian theory of justice and how to interpret "welfare" in a welfarist version of liberal egalitarian justice. He has also written about the prospects for consequentialism in moral theory.

JUSTINE BURLEY is Adjunct Associate Professor, National University of Singapore. Prior to this appointment she was Simon Fellow in the Department of Government, University of Manchester, UK, and a lecturer at the University of Oxford for nine years. In addition to *Ronald Dworkin and His Critics*, she is editor (with John Harris) of *A Companion to Genethics* (2000) and *The Genetic Revolution and Human Rights* (1999). She is currently working on a monograph entitled *Genetic Justice*.

PAULA CASAL is a lecturer in the School of Politics, International Relations and the Environment at Keele University, UK. Her current research focuses on contemporary egalitarian theories of justice, but she has published papers on a variety of subjects, including analytical Marxism, animal rights, environmentalism, and multiculturalism. She is an associate editor of the journal *Politics, Philosophy and Economics*.

MATTHEW CLAYTON is Lecturer in Political Philosophy, University of Warwick, UK. He is editor (with A. Williams) of *The Ideal of Equality* (2000). He works on toleration, equality, medical ethics, and philosophy of education.

G. A. COHEN was educated at McGill and Oxford Universities where he obtained, respectively, the degrees of B.A. in Philosophy and Politics and B.Phil. in Philosophy. For 22 years he was a lecturer and then a reader in Philosophy at University College London. In 1985 he became Chichele Professor of Social and Political Theory and a Fellow of All Souls, Oxford. Professor Cohen is the author of *Karl Marx's Theory of History: A Defense* (1978; expanded edition, 2000), *History, Labor, and Freedom* (1988), *Self-Ownership, Freedom, and Equality* (1995), and *If You're an Egalitarian, How Come You're So Rich?* (2000). He has given lectures all over the world, including the Tanner Lectures at Stanford University in 1991 and the Gifford Lectures at Edinburgh University in 1996. He was made a Fellow of the British Academy in 1985.

MIRIAM COHEN CHRISTOFIDIS is currently a lecturer in Philosophy at University College London. She is registered for a D.Phil. at Oxford University. She works in moral and political philosophy.

LESLIE GREEN is a professor at the Osgoode Hall Law School and in the Department of Philosophy, York University, Toronto. His publications include *The Authority of the State* (1988) and many articles in legal and political theory.

LESLEY A. JACOBS is Associate Professor and Director of the Law & Society Program at York University, Toronto. His books include *Rights and Deprivation* (1993), *The Democratic Vision of Politics* (1997), *Pursuing Equal Opportunities: The Theory and Practice of Egalitarian Justice* (2003), and the forthcoming *Canadian Health Care: Values, Rights, Law.*

F. M. KAMM is Professor of Philosophy, Professor of Medicine (Bioethics), and Law School Affiliated Faculty, New York University, and Visiting Professor of Philosophy and Public Policy, Harvard University. She is the author of *Creation and Abortion* (1992), *Morality, Mortality*, vols. 1 and 2 (1993, 1996), and of numerous articles on normative ethical theory and practical ethics.

WILL KYMLICKA is a professor of philosophy at Queen's University, Ontario, and a visiting professor in the Nationalism Studies program at the Central European University in Budapest. He is the author of *Liberalism, Community, and Culture* (1989), *Contemporary Political Philosophy* (1990; 2nd edn. 2002), *Multicultural Citizenship* (1995), *Finding Our Way: Rethinking Ethnocultural Relations in Canada* (1998), and *Politics in the Vernacular: Nationalism, Multiculturalism, Citizenship* (2001). He is also the editor of *Justice in Political Philosophy* (1992), and *The Rights of Minority Cultures* (1995), and coeditor of *Ethnicity and Group Rights* (1997), *Citizenship in Diverse Societies* (2000), *Alternative Conceptions of Civil Society* (2001), and *Can Liberal Pluralism Be Exported?* (2001).

MICHAEL OTSUKA is a reader in philosophy at University College London. He has published articles in the areas of political philosophy, normative ethics, and moral responsibility and is the author of a defense of left-libertarianism entitled *Libertarianism Without Inequality* (2003).

GERALD J. POSTEMA is Cary C. Boshamer Professor of Philosophy and Professor of Law at the University of North Carolina. He is author of *Bentham and the Common Law Tradition* (1986/1989) and editor of *Racism and the Law* (1997), *Rationality, Conventions, and the Law* (1998), *Philosophy and the Law of Torts* (2001), and of two volumes of critical essays on Bentham, *Jeremy Bentham: Moral, Political, and Legal Philosophy* (2002).

ERIC RAKOWSKI is Professor of Law at the University of California at Berkeley (Boalt Hall School of Law). He has written widely on abortion, euthanasia, health care rationing, and the permissibility of killing some to save more lives. *Equal Justice* (1991) sets forth his egalitarian, opportunity-based theory of distributive justice.

JOSEPH RAZ is Professor of the Philosophy of Law, Oxford University and Fellow of Balliol College, Oxford as well as Visiting Professor, Columbia University School of Law. His publications include *Practical Reason and Norms* (2nd edn., 1990), *The Authority of Law* (1979), *The Morality of Freedom* (1986) and *Ethics in the Public Domain* (1995).

SEANA VALENTINE SHIFFRIN is Professor of Law and Associate Professor of Philosophy at the University of California, Los Angeles. She holds a D.Phil. in Philosophy from the University of Oxford and a law degree from Harvard University. While her research interests span a range of topics in moral and political philosophy she is particularly interested in those concerning procreation as well as the end of life. Professor Shiffrin is currently developing a theory of the special moral significance of harm.

PHILIPPE VAN PARIJS is Professor of Economic and Social Ethics at the Catholic University of Louvain, Belgium. He is the editor of *Arguing for Basic Income* (1992) and the author of *Evolutionary Explanation in the Social Sciences* (1981), *Marxism Recycled* (1993), and *Real Freedom for All* (1995). In 1997/8 he held visiting appointments at All Souls College, Oxford and Yale University.

JEREMY WALDRON is Maurice and Hilda Friedman Professor of Law and Director of the Center for Law and Philosophy at Columbia University, New York. His most recent books are *The Dignity of Legislation, Law and Disagreement* (1999) and *God, Locke, and Equality* (2002). He is presently working on a compilation of readings on "the rule of law."

ANDREW WILLIAMS is a lecturer in Philosophy and Politics at the University of Reading, UK. He is coeditor of *The Ideal of Equality* (2000) and *Real Libertarianism Assessed* (2003), and he is an associate editor of *Politics, Philosophy and Economics*.

Acknowledgments

The completion of this volume was long in coming. Thanks are therefore due first and foremost to the contributors, especially to Ronald Dworkin, for bearing with me. All involved were positively heroic in the face of protracted delay. I wish also to extend a warm thank you to Jeff Dean, Acquisitions Editor for Philosophy at Blackwell, whose firm guidance helped move the project to completion. Thanks are also due to Nirit Simon, Assistant Editor for Philosophy at Blackwell, for her assistance with all book production matters. Jenny Roberts, the copy-editor of *Ronald Dworkin and His Critics*, much improved the book, and was a pleasure to work with. Finally, I am grateful to C. L. Ten and to Stephen Guest for their help in compiling the extensive bibliography of Professor Dworkin's work.

Introduction

Ronald Dworkin and His Critics is a celebration of the work of one of the leading minds of the twentieth century. Professor Dworkin's sophisticated appreciation of the relationship between moral, legal, and political philosophy, and of the mutual dependence of these three branches of inquiry and practical controversy, is unrivaled by his contemporaries. Indeed, the depth and scope of Ronald Dworkin's scholarship invites favorable comparison with the theories of past masters which display artful command of ideas from diverse intellectual quarters.

"Celebration" might seem an odd choice of term to describe a book comprising 17 *critical* essays. But the choice is an apt one for the simple reason that criticism is not best understood as a negative exercise. It is, in fact, quite the opposite. Disagreement is one of the most fruitful ways in which people work to make a better world. The hope we all have for moral progress, and for improvements in other important areas of our lives, depends crucially on sustained critical evaluation of *all* views. This, famously, was Socrates' observation, and later, again famously, Mill's. We gain from questioning not just opinions and attitudes we regard as being deeply misguided, but also views that strike us as mostly right, or right for the wrong reasons, and even norms we are convinced provide authoritative guidance on difficult issues. *Ronald Dworkin and His Critics* contains analysis that reflects all of these critical stances toward the subject matter.

The volume is divided into five parts. Part I focuses on discussion of Dworkin's account of political morality which *A Matter of Principle*, and the more recently published collection of essays, *Sovereign Virtue*, both explore. Part II examines a number of policy debates relating to Dworkin's conception of liberal egalitarian justice, hence to the two texts just mentioned. Part III treats the central issues of *Life's Dominion*, which also receive coverage in *Freedom's Law*. Part IV explores key aspects of Dworkin's legal theory as articulated in *Taking Rights Seriously* and in *Law's Empire*. A rough summary of the disagreements raised by Dworkin's critics, now follows.

Dworkin and His Critics takes as its starting point discussion (chapters 1–3) a pair of essays that originally formed part of a series of articles all beginning with the title question: "What is Equality?" It will be useful to set the scene by sketching briefly the content of these two seminal contributions to political philosophy. In "Equality of Welfare," Dworkin launches a multipronged attack on welfare egalitarianism, considering and rejecting in turn *success*, *conscious state*, and *objective* versions of it. Three objections are leveled at welfarism so understood. The first is that there is no one dimension of life that we all value fundamentally and equally. The second is that welfarism is self-defeating: assessment of whether inequalities in the distribution of welfare obtain necessarily involves recourse to a theory of fair shares which, being independent of equality of welfare, requires the latter's abandonment. Dworkin's third main antiwelfarist argument is that welfare egalitarianism cannot avoid catering to "expensive tastes." On the basis of these three objections and supporting argumentation, Dworkin concludes that we have strong reasons to reject welfarist approaches to equality.

In "What is Equality? Part 2: Equality of Resources," Dworkin argues for an alternative conception of equality to that of welfarism – equality of resources. Dworkin thinks that we should prefer his theory to any welfarist conception because it offers relatively robust distributive principles, and is faithful to the liberal notion that individuals should be allowed to decide for themselves, within certain parameters, which aspects of life hold value. In context, the theory may be regarded as the linchpin of a more ambitious project in which Dworkin aims to provide "a unified account of equality and responsibility."

Equality of resources promotes an economic structure that is sensitive to individuals' choices (or personality) and insensitive to unchosen differences between their mental and physical capacities, including talent levels (personal resources or circumstances). Two necessary conditions of an equal distribution of resources are freedom from envy and true opportunity costs. To illustrate how a distribution could meet the first of these conditions, Dworkin takes recourse to the market device of a hypothetical auction. The auction device is complemented by a liberty/constraint system to guarantee the second condition. An ideal equal distribution of resources is said to obtain when, following an auction in which available resources are offered up in the most abstract form possible and in other conditions conducive to authentic preference, no one would prefer any resource bundle successfully bid for by others to their own. This formulation of ideal resource equality takes no account of differences in people's natural endowments. How might ideal equality be approximated in the light of these?

Postauction wealth holdings will become progressively unequal owing both to different choices people have made and to unchosen relative differences in their natural capacities – state of health and levels of talent. Resource egalitarianism does not permit the state to redistribute wealth to mitigate inequalities that are traceable to "personality," that is, to lifestyle choices, preferences, tastes, and so forth, with which an agent identifies (choice). But it does mandate compensation to people whose resource shortfalls are traceable to "brute bad luck" (chance) like genetic-based disease. In a society governed by equality of resources, what an individual is compensated for, and by how much, is modeled on the results of the appropriate hypothetical insurance scheme. There are two principal schemes: one is geared to deal with health-related misfortune, the other with morally relevant differences in talent between individuals. Respectively these schemes are designed to be as sensitive as possible to individual choices about which aspects of health and occupation matter most. Through hypothetical insurance models Dworkin seeks to translate welfarist concerns into the language of money, and to introduce individual responsibility for whether and how measures are taken to alleviate inequalities in wealth that are not traceable to choice. The above discussion informs real world practice with respect to wealth distribution in a variety of ways, including the endorsement of progressive taxation and state-run health insurance.

The personality/circumstance distinction drawn by Dworkin in equality of resources circumscribes personal and collective responsibility and is, he tells us, the backbone of our wider ethics and morality. Its prominence in Dworkin's account of political morality has been the subject of much theoretical wrangling and is the subject of chapter 1.

G. A. Cohen in "Expensive Taste Rides Again" reaffirms his allegiance to a position he calls "equality of access to advantage," a position of which welfare is a part, and which endorses government compensation for expensive tastes. The chapter, ambitious in scope and rife with detailed argument, declares a refutation of Dworkin's resourcist conception of equality, and mounts a defense of Cohen's access view (throughout the chapter, but particularly in sections XI through coda XII, as well as in the appendix). For Cohen, the importance of the expensive tastes issue is not confined to the debate over which conception of equality is most attractive, important as that may be. It is also relevant to the more general and much bigger question of whether or not the marketplace is a just forum (section VII). The first three sections of the chapter set the stage; Cohen clarifies distinctions and terms, specifically Dworkin's broad criticisms of welfarism, and the phrase "expensive taste," and offers a reformulation of his own approach. In sections IV and V where he assesses various of Dworkin's arguments against compensation for expensive tastes, Cohen aims principally to undermine Dworkin's main objection, and, strikingly, to demonstrate that Dworkin has quietly performed a "U-turn" on the justice of such compensation. The thrust of Cohen's chapter as a whole, however, is not to cast Dworkin as friendly about the issue, rather it is to present Dworkin as a misguided egalitarian whose conception of equality misses completely, and unfairly, an important element of human well-being.

Miriam Cohen Christofides, in chapter 2, also finds fault with Dworkin's theory of equality for failing to live up to its egalitarian aims, namely the elimination of inequalities in wealth stemming from differences between individuals' talent levels. Her central contention is that Dworkin assigns an unacceptably greater weight to the interests of individuals who are more talented. She supports this first by taking issue with Dworkin's claims that the talented would envy the untalented in a talent auction, and that such a scheme would lead to the slavery of the talented in particular. Cohen Christofides then objects to Dworkin's view that maintaining a lower level of insurance premiums (which has the consequence of lower levels of compensation to the untalented) is necessary both to avoid the enslavement of the talented, and to avoid failure of the envy test. Here she argues that the enslavement of the untalented under the proposed lower premium arrangement is just as likely a possibility as enslavement of the more talented under a higher premium. In addition, Dworkin's own solution to the problem presented by unequal talents results in the failure of the envy test. He cannot therefore, Cohen Christofides stresses, plausibly argue that we should prefer a strategy that restricts insurance premiums for the untalented on the grounds that if we didn't, the envy test would not be met. Cohen Christofides wraps up her assault on Dworkin's treatment of talent by pointing out that Dworkin supplies no solid argumentation for favoring his hypothetical insurance scheme over the talent auction.

Philippe Van Parijs, in chapter 3, provides a comprehensive examination of what it means to give *due weight* to the claims of people who suffer deficits in their natural endowments. His specific questions are: does justice require deviation from an equal distribution of external endowments (as that is specified by Van Parijs) to take account of differences in talent? If so, how? Unlike the two thinkers just discussed, Van Parijs's conception of political morality shares Dworkin's theoretical slant. However, he argues that his view, "undominated diversity," which he pits against Dworkin's theory of equality throughout the chapter, does a better job of respecting the central tenets of Dworkin's approach than do Dworkin's own proposals. Van Parijs's inquiry is part of a broader endeavor, that of devising a plausible conception of distributive justice that takes diversity of talent into account. It also forms part of a long-term project in which he attempts to determine and justify the conditions under which an unconditional basic income would be granted to everyone.

Chapter 4 shifts the focus of discussion to the relationship between liberty and equality. In the third essay in Dworkin's "What is Equality" series, reprinted in *Sovereign Virtue* under the same title, "The Place of Liberty," Dworkin argues that certain liberal rights are *constitutive* elements of equality rather than independent considerations that conflict with it. The crux of his view is that a system of baseline rights is *required*, if market procedures (like the auction) are to legitimize outcomes. Michael Otsuka's chapter focuses on demonstrating that Dworkin's various attempts to reconcile liberty and equality are unsuccessful. Otsuka begins by challenging Dworkin's presupposition of the *compossibility* of the envy test and the realization of the principle of abstraction. Necessary to Dworkin's account of ideal equality is a maximally sensitive liberty/constraint system, which he derives from the "principle of abstraction." According to this principle, resources in the initial auction must be offered in as abstract a form as possible to afford the greatest flexibility possible in the matching of bids to plans and preferences. Otsuka notes that the abstraction principle condemns any laws constraining gift-giving. This is a problem, Otsuka argues, because the bestowal of gifts frustrates the envy test by allowing some recipients to become wealthier than others. Moreover, Dworkin's proposal that gifts should be regulated by a tax modeled on hypothetical insurance does not wholly avoid frustration of the envy test. Furthermore, and importantly, Dworkin's more recent response to the problem undermines his reconciliation project. Dworkin now thinks that two *competing* egalitarian demands are relevant to gift-giving: the first is provided by the envy test, the second by the principle of abstraction. Otsuka argues that this compromise between the envy test and the principle of abstraction *prevents* the reconciliation of the two values of liberty and equality. All Dworkin's "reconciliation" amounts to is "a demonstration that the conflict between liberty and equality is a competition intermixed with cooperation, which takes place wholly within the boundaries of distributive equality, rather than a conflict between equality and the external demand of liberty."

Following the publication of the "What is Equality?" series, Dworkin sought to cement his liberal egalitarianism in ethical foundations. Up until his "Foundations of Liberal Equality," which appears under the title of "Equality and the Good Life" in *Sovereign Virtue*, the focus of Dworkin's political theory had been on establishing an account of the "right" principles of justice – not the "good." The general failure on the part of liberals to furnish an account of the good life in their theories has elicited harsh criticism from postmodernists, perfectionists, conservatives, and communitarians. Dworkin answers the general criticism by introducing his *challenge model* of the good life. On this model, the critical value of a life is evaluated not in terms of its objective *impact* in the world, but in terms of the Aristotelian notion of a skillful performance. One reason to prefer this model to that of impact is that it allows that events, achievements, and experiences can have ethical value even when that value resides *within* lives.

Two parameters are central to the challenge model: justice and ethical integrity. Dworkin embraces the Platonic thesis that living well is living justly. He regards justice as specifying what an appropriate challenge involves, and also what the appropriate response to that challenge might be. The liberal state may therefore permissibly enforce justice. The second parameter of the good life, ethical integrity – the idea that the kind of life individuals lead should accord with their *own* convictions about the kind of life they ought to be leading – does not, in most cases, support state paternalism. This is because a life cannot be improved by forcing individuals to pursue a course of action or hold beliefs that they do not endorse. Thus neutrality, which Dworkin previously regarded as axiomatic to political morality, becomes in "Foundations ..." a theorem. Government is neutral in operation but not neutral in terms of avoiding appeal to abstract claims about the good.

Chapters 5 and 6 take Dworkin to task on this development in his political thought. In chapter 5, Richard Arneson complains that the counterfoil to the challenge model, the model of impact, is so effete that it has little comparative value. In addition, Arneson contends that Dworkin's challenge model confuses the ideas of "an admirable life and a choice-worthy . . . life." In the light of this confusion, even were the challenge model to support Dworkin's liberal egalitarianism, he argues that the support would be worthless because the challenge model is unsatisfactory. Arneson, a proponent of equal opportunity for welfare, further argues that the challenge model offers no compelling reason to endorse equality of resources. It says nothing to dissuade us from the view that the theory is misguided because it prohibits conferring benefits on an individual when doing so imposes no costs on others. Arneson also argues that Dworkin is wrong in supposing that the challenge model supports the idea that distributive justice should be resource-oriented and not welfare-oriented. This is because when the challenge model is properly conceived it is utterly irrelevant to the resources/welfare issue. Lastly, Arneson presses for the rejection of Dworkin's view of liberal tolerance on the grounds that it is extremely illiberal.

Matthew Clayton pushes Dworkin on the issues of neutrality and ethical integrity from a different angle, in chapter 6. Clayton asks whether Dworkin's rejection of state paternalism can plausibly be extended to support his liberal position with respect to the "sacred." As I elaborate in more detail below when introducing Part III of this volume, Dworkin understands disputes over abortion as being fundamentally disagreements about the *detached* value of life's sanctity – where detached connotes the idea that no one's interests or rights are at stake. Dworkin defends a neutral position on virtually all matters of detached value, including abortion. Taking the case of abortion as his example, Clayton seeks to demonstrate that it is far from clear why the ideal of ethical integrity is sufficient to settle the question of abortion. He argues that Dworkin offers no reason for why respect for life's impersonal value should not also figure as a parameter of well-being. If justice may be enforced politically, even though people disagree about the best interpretation of justice for a free and equal society, why cannot the sacredness of life, which people also disagree about, likewise be enforced at the level of political morality? Clayton insists that Dworkin needs to supply an account of why the ideal of ethical integrity with respect to detached values trumps our reasons to protect those values at a deeper philosophical level, in his account of political morality.

Part II of *Ronald Dworkin and His Critics* contains discussion of a range of policy matters. The first of these is Will Kymlicka's theoretical exploration of cultural structures, and language and group rights. Kymlicka's chapter 7 references a plethora of real world examples, to provide detailed analysis of a response made by Dworkin to the general communitarian objection, to wit, that liberals neglect the social preconditions that make possible freedom of choice. Kymlicka charges that Dworkin's writings on cultural structures have implications for both liberal theory and government policy that Dworkin has ignored, and moreover that these raise serious challenges to liberal constitutionalism as that traditionally is conceived of. He identifies three questions raised by Dworkin's remarks concerning the relationship between individual choice and cultural structures:

> (1) how do we individuate cultural structures?; (2) is individual choice tied to membership in one's *own* culture, or is it sufficient for people to have access to some or other culture?; and (3) what if a culture is structured so as to preclude individual choice, for example, if it assigns a specific role or way of life, and prohibits any questioning or revising of that role?

Kymlicka demonstrates that while Dworkin's own suggested answers are attractive they are by no means uncontroversial. In addition, Kymlicka argues that Dworkin's account leads naturally to a liberal justification of *group rights* – an implication he doubts Dworkin would be happy to accept. This is because if choice requires culture, and culture requires language, then developing a just language policy would seem to be one of the first priorities of liberal theory. Yet, Kymlicka complains, Dworkin has never engaged with the issue of language rights.

In chapter 8, Lesley Jacobs explores the issue of universal access to health care in relation to Dworkin's liberal egalitarianism. Dworkin has made two contributions to public debate over how health care should be distributed: "Justice in the Distribution of Heath Care" and "Will Clinton's Plan Be Fair?," reprinted with amendments as chapter 8 of *Sovereign Virtue*. Social decisions about health care spending should, according to Dworkin, be a function of what individuals would in just circumstances spend. On Dworkin's account, assuming an initial just distribution of resources, and also that information has been made available about the effectiveness and costs of various health care options, all individuals must be responsible for deciding for themselves what the relative importance of heath care is to other goods. Thus Dworkin's insurance approach is a reflection of his idea that health care distribution must be "ambition-sensitive." The emphasis on individual choice allows him to treat social choices about health care spending as an aggregate of individual choices and also makes individuals directly responsible for health.

Jacobs' core claim is that Dworkin's approach to equality, in particular the feature of ambition sensitivity, is not compatible with a policy of universal access to health care. Universal access requires in-kind transfers, argues Jacobs, whereas Dworkin's entire theory is geared toward cash compensation for resource shortfalls relating to health. Recall that a necessary condition of an initial ideal equal distribution of resources is that the resources that go up for auction should be offered in the most abstract form possible. Jacobs observes that the principle of abstraction demanding this appears to proscribe all policies, including any health care policy, that are not as sensitive as possible to the plans and preferences of individuals. Therefore, Jacobs argues, Dworkin's *prima facie* commitment to cash transfers that flows from ambition sensitivity supplies strong grounds for the view that there is general incompatibility between the requirement of ambition sensitivity in his theory and the use of in-kind transfers in the real world. Jacobs considers three possible egalitarian grounds, which might be drafted in to support in-kind transfers: efficiency, externalities, and superficial paternalism. None of these, he argues, are capable of justifying the sort of in-kind distribution involved in the provision of universal access.

Paula Casal and Andrew Williams address in chapter 9 an issue that has been underexplored both by Dworkin and the literature on procreative justice, namely the effects that procreative decisions can have on third parties. To start on their answer of how equality of resources would deal with this issue they, along with Dworkin, assume that individuals have the legal right to determine the size of their families. Then they proceed, drawing from discussions in economics, to identify that having children can generate two kinds of effects: positive and negative externalities. Following from there, they examine and reject the suggestion that for reasons of fairness the costs of reproduction should be shared by parents and nonparents who benefit from the public good of additional children. Finally, they argue that when overpopulation threatens, resource egalitarianism ideally demands that parents bear the costs of their actions. Casal and Williams conclude by favoring an asymmetric approach to cope with the third party effects of procreation. If parents produce a public good, there is no reason from justice (as fairness) to require that that activity be subsidized. However, when procreation threatens a public bad, justice (as equality of resources) requires parents to be taxed when they have children.

In "Playing God, Genes, Clones, and Luck," reprinted as chapter 13 in *Sovereign Virtue*, Dworkin advances the striking claims that recent developments in genetics threaten to undermine a large chunk of our ethics and morality, and therefore to pitch us into moral free-fall. As noted above, the chance/choice distinction sets the parameters of personal and collective responsibility in Dworkin's conception of political morality. The possibility of controlling the genetic fate of our offspring afforded by human reproductive cloning and genetic engineering would seem to weaken the force of that distinction. This has implications for current ethical views regarding the right to reproductive freedom and the liberal precept of bodily integrity, the critical moral background in Dworkin's theory that informs these practices, and also for Dworkin's analysis of how the effects of brute bad luck on lives might be checked. The contention I develop and defend in chapter 10 is that Dworkin's moral free-fall hypothesis is motivated by recognition that much of his *own theory* is compromised by new facts from genetic science, and so, if anyone, it is him, not us, confronting a crisis in morals. I first cast doubt on Dworkin's idea that simply being aware of the power to control the sort of people who come to exist, is psychologically destabilizing. Dworkin only thinks it is, I argue, because the centerpiece of his normative account of equality and responsibility relies so heavily on the idea that people may be fairly held responsible for the lives they make against a background of social luck – in an age of biological control, what traditionally was regarded as genetic luck is now better characterized as social luck. I then examine two areas of morality: procreative freedom and distributive justice, to make clear that while the "new genetics" does pose challenges to our ethics and morality, familiar approaches in moral and political philosophy can cope with these challenges, hence moral free-fall is not imminent. Dworkin promotes his conception of ethical individualism to guide policy in the future world he considers. I argue that this conception is not so much a solution as it is part of the problem. In endorsing the idea that people may act on most of their detached ideas of what gives meaning and value to human life, I suggest Dworkin's theory is ill-equipped to cope with all those cases in which people eschew technologies that would secure for their offspring some species-typical normal functioning. Moreover, I suggest both that government should promote such a standard, and that Dworkin's theory cannot, at least not comfortably. In the final subsection of my chapter I bring to light the implications for Dworkin's egalitarian theory of genetic fate being controllable, the main of which concerns his hypothetical insurance scheme. This scheme is rendered virtually impotent in a world in which parents have the power to control procreative outcomes; in practice, Dworkin's liberal egalitarianism becomes the uncomfortable bedfellow of libertarianism.

Some of the theoretical features of Dworkin's approach to morality touched on in chapters 6 and 10 figure prominently in discussion in Part III of *Ronald Dworkin and His Critics*. Part III concentrates on *Life's Dominion*, in which Dworkin examines two debates that have galvanized the public in many countries: abortion and euthanasia. Dworkin suggests that the debates over these issues have been unhelpfully conceptualized as arguments over rights conflicts. He proposes that controversies on these issues have the character of detached value – they do not relate directly to the interests of individuals – and are therefore properly likened to *essentially religious* disputes about the intrinsic value of human life. Once the kind of disagreement driving people's views on abortion and euthanasia is recognized, it becomes apparent what sort of stance government should adopt with respect to both issues. The liberal position on the freedoms of expression and religious worship is that it is impermissible for the state to direct individuals' views about why life has value, how much value, and how best to respect that value, and also for the state to protect that value. In the cases of abortion and euthanasia the subject of controversy is the intrinsic value of human life; the state must therefore remain neutral in the way required of it with respect to freedoms of expression and religious worship.

In chapter 11, Seana Valentine Shiffrin examines Dworkin's views about respect for and control over autonomy at the end of life. She focuses on Dworkin's argument for the implementation of advance directives that specify what treatment should be given to the permanently demented. The reasons justifying respect of the fully competent adults *do not*, Valentine Shiffrin argues, justify extending that autonomous control over self-regarding life and death decisions to include control over what should happen to themselves if they become permanently demented. She also charges that Dworkin's conception of autonomy is flawed and that it leads him to disregard the autonomy that demented individuals may be capable of. Finally, she argues that Dworkin's analysis of the duty of beneficence we have to demented people neither does nor can emerge from a neutral stance toward the sacred.

Frances Kamm, in chapter 12, considers Dworkin's views on the moral and legal problems posed by abortion and physician-assisted suicide. Kamm raises numerous objections to and questions about various distinctions and arguments that Dworkin advocates. In keeping with Kamm's own structure, my survey of her "reservations" concentrates first on Dworkin's ideas in *Life's Dominion*, and then on the subject matter of "The Philosophers' Brief on Assisted Suicide," of which Dworkin is a coauthor. As noted in our outline of chapter 6, and also immediately above, Dworkin understands the controversy over abortion as being about the intrinsic value of human life, and thus he recommends a neutral stance on the part of the state toward abortion. Kamm begins by asking whether Dworkin really has a theory of the intrinsic value of life, and concludes that he has a theory of the *extrinsic, but noninstrumental*, value of life. Second, Kamm doubts that the value of life changes in its cause the way Dworkin describes – a fetus conceived by rape, she thinks, has no less intrinsic value just because its life started in the frustration of the woman's life who carries it. Third, Kamm argues that examples are available that show, contra Dworkin, that the intrinsic value of life can be incremental. Fourth, Kamm doubts that Dworkin's use of "inviolability" is correct: his notion of the sacred does not involve inviolability as commonly understood, and it appears to mean merely that a bad thing occurs when something dies or is destroyed. She also maintains that it is misleading to call an entity "sacred" if one thinks only that something bad happens when it is destroyed. Fifth, Kamm tests the implications of Dworkin's "investment waste thesis" and finds it wanting on two main grounds. First she argues that determining how bad the death of a fetus is has more to do with the quality of its properties than investment in the fetus. Then she objects to the idea that an assessment of the relative importance of abortion to two different women should hinge on the extent to which investment in them is paid off.

Kamm's sixth query about Dworkin's approach to abortion raises a number of powerful objections to the idea that the existence of conflicts between values is sufficient to account for the permissibility of abortion. I mention only one such conflict here. Kamm notes that Dworkin considers women to possess both intrinsic nonincremental value (INOV) as well as interests and rights. Fetuses, by contrast, have only INOV. Why is it that when the preservation of a fetus interferes with the rights and interests of a woman, Dworkin favors the dominance of legal rights and interests rather than argue that fetal destruction is an essentially religious matter? Kamm's penultimate area of objection is that Dworkin is mistaken in arguing that views about the intrinsic value of life are fundamentally religious and not *philosophical*. Moral philosophy after all deals not just with interests but also with the sacred. Furthermore, Kamm has the sense that Dworkin employs the term "religious" to connote an area of discourse not subject to rational proof, thereby hiving it off from political debate. In the final section of this part of Kamm's chapter, she takes issue with Dworkin's view that abortion would be impermissible were the fetus a person. Kamm suggests that it is a mistake to argue that: "(1) Either the fetus is a person or it is not a person. (2) It would be permissible to abort it if it is a person. (3) It would be permissible to abort it if it is not a person. (4) Hence, it is permissible to abort it." It is a mistake to argue in this way Kamm says, because even were (2) true of a fetus that was always a person, it may not be true of a fetus who develops into a person.

On the basis of the aforementioned and other arguments, Kamm suggests an alternative to Dworkin's view, before she moves on to discuss euthanasia. In "The Philosophers' Brief on Assisted Suicide," Dworkin et al. argue that if it is permissible to terminate or withhold medical treatment with the intention that the patient die, it is permissible, when a patient consents, to assist in killing with the intention that the patient die. It is impossible to do justice to Kamm's counterarguments here; I shall mention only the bare bones of them. Two reasons offered by Dworkin et al. in support of their proassisted suicide position are that (1) there is no intrinsic moral difference between killing and letting die; and (2) individuals have the right to make decisions of fundamental importance to their own lives, and whether to be killed or let die could be a means of facilitating such choices. With respect to the first of these reasons Kamm concentrates on developing two objections at length, relating respectively to acts/omissions versus killing/letting die, and killing/letting die versus intending/foreseeing death. She broadly agrees with Dworkin et al. in the first area, and offers examples that serve to refine the issues at stake. Kamm's chief counterclaim to the second is that we cannot *always* move from the permissibility of letting the patient die when intending that patient's death, to the permissibility of assisted suicide that involves patients killing themselves. Kamm then moves from the case-based arguments in "The Philosophers' Brief on Assisted Suicide" to the theoretical argument Dworkin et al. advance in favor of physician-assisted suicide. This is the argument that patients have the right to self-determination in areas involving deep-seated moral conviction about their own lives. From this, Kamm argues, they deduce a right to determine when and how they will die. Does this theory endorse, Kamm asks, the permissibility of killing a patient in cases where a person gives important reasons other than terminal illness for wanting to die? If so, it is too broad. Kamm then presents three alternative views to those of the authors of "The Philosophers' Brief on Assisted Suicide" before she concludes with a four-stage argument that supports the idea, against Dworkin et al., that doctors have a *duty* to assist suicide.

Eric Rakowski, in chapter 13, carries yet further discussion of abortion and suicide. Rakowski's critique concentrates on Dworkin's claim that the debates over abortion and euthanasia debates are best conceptualized as disputes about an essentially "religious" notion, the intrinsic value of human life. Although Dworkin's approach to these issues has the attractive feature of courting practical compromise, Rakowski denies that his *reductio* strategy is persuasive. It simply does not capture many of the true reasons people disagree with these practices. When people oppose abortion and euthanasia, he claims, they commonly do so on moral philosophical and not religious grounds. For example, with respect to abortion, opposition is often based on a conception of personal identity and the importance of physical or mental continuity, and concern for the future that an entity might have. The wrongness of suicide and euthanasia is thought to rest on views of what makes a life valuable, the force of advance directives, and of whether personal identity continues when an individual's mental faculties undergo dramatic change. There are also other sources of opposition to abortion, euthanasia, and suicide that properly command the attention of lawmakers, such as concerns about unfavorable consequences on health care professionals and wider society, and the exploitation of innocents.

Rakowski insists that Dworkin's distinction between intrinsic values and personal interests fails to define relevant spheres of legislation with ample breadth. In Rakowski's view, the real (and difficult) issues for law-makers are the force of a fetus's or psychologically altered person's claims (whatever they may be), whether paternalistic constraints are compelling, and the perils to third-party interests, relative to the loss of personal autonomy and experienced hardships to mothers or the ailing elderly if their freedom to shape their future were limited in some way. Rakowski concedes that many of these issues may well be intractable. But, in arriving at his conclusion, Rakowski found no reason from Dworkin to set them aside. In the cause of social compromise, Dworkin has shirked the responsibility of engaging directly with a host of issues, due consideration of which is fundamental to the development of adequate state policies and laws governing abortion, euthanasia, and suicide.

The final part of *Ronald Dworkin and His Critics* provides coverage of Dworkin's legal philosophy – the area in which he first gained prominence. The first three essays in Part IV are edited versions of previously published pieces, selected for their penetrating insight into key features of Dworkin's legal theory, namely political obligation, coherence, and integrity. The final contribution is a new essay by Jeremy Waldron which conducts a sweep of Dworkin's legal thought as argued for in *Taking Rights Seriously* and *Law's Empire*, and posits a novel interpretation of Dworkin's rule of law thesis.

In chapter 14 Green takes up Ronald Dworkin's challenge to skeptics about political obligation to "either deny all associative obligations or show why political obligation cannot be associative." Green's subject is the second part of this challenge. He advances numerous arguments to show that Dworkin's account of both associative obligations and political obligation fails. Green also develops an account of consent theory which he argues can accommodate the social dimension of political life, although this is not intended to demonstrate that every citizen has an obligation to obey the law.

In chapter 15, Joseph Raz examines Dworkin's views on integrity and coherence. For Raz, any theory of law that diminishes the doctrine of authority and the role of politics is problematic. He objects *in principle* to *any* doctrine that requires the courts to adjudicate disputes on the assumption that the law speaks with one voice. Raz's chapter is devoted to exploring the role of *coherence explanations* of law and integrity in Dworkin's *Law's Empire*. After surveying various passages from the text, he attributes to Dworkin the following position: "the law consists of those principles of justice and fairness and procedural due process that provide the best (i.e., morally best) set of sound principles capable of explaining the legal decisions taken throughout the history of the polity in question." This is not a coherence explanation of either law or integrity. Raz considers three objections to his reading of Dworkin. The first relates to Dworkin's references to "constructive interpretation" that imply coherence. The second objection he considers is that since integrity is only one component of law and adjudication, the fact that integrity in adjudication is not committed to coherence does not demonstrate that it is not necessary to base either the law or adjudication on a set of principles exhibiting tight coherence. And the third objection is that it is unfair to ignore the general feel of *Law's Empire*, which indicates that coherence is to be striven for. Raz rebuts each of these objections in turn and concludes that there is nothing in *Law's Empire* to require an endorsement of any presumption in favor of coherence.

Integrity receives sustained treatment by Gerald Postema in chapter 16. Unlike Raz, Postema agrees with Dworkin that integrity is an important value of political morality. But he is also in agreement with skeptics that a compelling case for integrity has yet to be made. Postema attempts to construct such a case. He draws on Dworkin's writings on integrity, but his conception departs from Dworkin's and, where they agree, his arguments sometimes assume a different form from Dworkin's. The first point of disagreement between the two is that Postema objects to Dworkin's notion that the attitude of integrity is a "protestant attitude that makes each citizen responsible for imagining what his society's public commitments to principles are, and what these commitments require in new circumstances." Dworkin's "protestant" attitude misses out, argues Postema, the interactive public character of the practical reasoning demanded by integrity. For Postema, the community only achieves integrity when it acts as a community from a coherent vision of justice. Second, Postema argues that integrity is hollow if it does not balance *respect* for past practice with the more critical attitude of *regret*. Dworkin's notion of integrity does not rule this out, but Postema claims that his interpretive project loses sight of the dimension of regret. Integrity requires that we take responsibility for the whole past, not just agreeable aspects of it. Postema's defense of integrity focuses on its political and historical character; it links to justice and fidelity, two fundamental values that integrity serves. Dworkin insists that integrity is an independent value of political morality, that it is distinct from justice and fairness. Postema disagrees: integrity, he argues, is justice in "political workclothes." Taking a cue from Waldron, Postema argues that integrity is called forth when members of a community want justice, but disagree about what justice requires. In such cases, integrity will help to assist in the forging of a common conception of justice, and the institutions that conform to it. Postema goes on to argue at some length that the most fundamental reason to pursue a common conception of justice is that it is required by the *structural features of justice itself*. He then links integrity with *fidelity*. His thesis is that fidelity assumes the form of integrity in "a community bound to pursue justice in the circumstances of integrity." Finally, he defends the view that the law offers a natural means by which to seek justice in the manner integrity prescribes.

In chapter 17, Jeremy Waldron departs from the critical approach adopted by those preceding him in Part IV, and instead elects to probe Dworkin's jurisprudence with a view to unearthing the true character of Dworkin's conception of the rule of law. Is his conception purely objectivist or is it also proceduralist? If it is the latter, in what way(s)? The thesis Waldron defends in his chapter is that there is substantial proceduralist element in Ronald Dworkin's conception of the rule of law, and moreover that this element is ascendant over the objectivist component. To help establish his thesis Waldron seeks to demonstrate that when Dworkin responds to his legal positivist adversaries he does so not with an objectivist but with a version of the proceduralist conception of the rule of law; Dworkin has all along been running with his objectivist conception only when it agrees with the proceduralist; and when confronted with a choice Dworkin is just as likely to embrace a conception of the rule of law that stresses commitment to certain procedures as he is to embrace a conception that is open to any political procedures provided they reach the right result.

In the closing chapter and part of *Ronald Dworkin and His Critics*, Professor Dworkin has the last word. Of the many matters raised in the volume – some highlighted above, others identified by Dworkin as commanding more of his immediate attention – Dworkin finds plenty to say. Certain objections leveled at Dworkin's work may, in this volume, have taken their final breath. Of others, it is likely that protracted debate will ensue. Whatever the fate of individual arguments, the elegance, skill, and majesty of Professor Dworkin's rebuttals further reinforce the notion that reasoned debate is an essential prerequisite for us to be confident that our views are well placed. The importance of Ronald Dworkin's scholarship to the intellectual fabric of our day is considerable, and there is little doubt many of his ideas will endure the test of repeated scrutiny, long into the future. This book, if it meets only the modest aim of sharpening debate, will dignify that legacy.

Revised in the autumn of 2003
Justine Burley

Part I

Equality, Liberty, and the Good Life

1

Expensive Taste Rides Again

G. A. Cohen

Swiss researchers say an eating disorder associated with right anterior brain lesions can turn people with average food preferences into passionate culinary aficionados. "Gourmand syndrome" seems to affect a small percentage of patients with focal lesions involving cortical areas, basal ganglia, or limbic structures. Patients have persistent cravings for fine foods, explain researchers Marianne Regard (University Hospital, Zurich) and Theodor Landis (Hôpital Cantonal Universitaire de Genève, Geneva).

723 patients with known or suspected single cerebral lesions were studied by Regard and Landis. 36 had gourmand syndrome; of these, 34 had a lesion in the right anterior region. The study was initiated after the authors noted altered eating behavior in two patients with right hemisphere hemorrhagic lesions. The first patient was a political journalist described as an average eater. During hospitalization, his diary was filled with references to food and dining. After discharge, he gave up his old job and became a successful fine-dining columnist. The second patient was an athletic businessman who "preferred a tennis match to a fine dinner." While in hospital, he fantasized about dining in a certain well-known restaurant, which he proceeded to do the day after discharge.

(Marilynn Larkin, "Eating Passion Unleashed by Brain Lesions,"
The Lancet, May 31, 1997, p. 1607).

The present paper is a reply to "Equality and Capability,"[1] in which Ronald Dworkin responded to some of the criticisms of his work that I made in "On the Currency of Egalitarian Justice."[2]

The first two sections of the paper are clarificatory. Section I distinguishes two broad criticisms of equality of welfare that Dworkin has developed, one surrounding the indeterminacy of the concept of welfare and one surrounding the problem of expensive taste. I express sympathy with the first criticism, and I argue that the second one must be assessed in abstraction from the first. Section II explains what the phrase "expensive taste" means within the present debate. It is vital that it does not mean, here, what it ordinarily means. Confusion of its ordinary meaning with the meaning that it bears here produces a false understanding of the point of disagreement between Dworkin and me about expensive taste.

Section III states the view of expensive taste that I defended in "On the Currency," but it also articulates a significant revision of that view, one that makes my present position in one respect more distant from Dworkin's than it was in 1989. Section IV discusses brute taste, that is, taste that is not guided by judgment. I claim that Dworkin has now abandoned his 1981 refusal to compensate for expensive brute taste, albeit without acknowledging that he has done so.

Section V refutes the principal argument that Dworkin deploys against compensation for expensive judgmental taste. That argument rejects the claim that uncompensated (and relevantly involuntary) expensive taste represents an injustice, on the ground that the stated claim requires people to conceive themselves as alienated from their own personalities. I show that no such bizarre self-conception follows from the mooted claim. Section VI scouts some further arguments that Dworkin brings against compensation for expensive taste.

Section VII refutes Dworkin's charge that equality of opportunity for welfare offers a "buzzes and ticks" picture of human well-being, according to which people have reason to care about two things only: pleasurable experiences, no matter what occasions them; and satisfying their desires, no matter what the objects of those desires happen to be.

Section VIII explains why the dispute about expensive taste matters: it bears deeply on the justice of the market process. The section also explores the consequences that equality of opportunity for welfare has for state action. Section IX shows, against Dworkin's claims to the contrary, that neither my view – which is not equality of opportunity for welfare – nor equality of opportunity for welfare proper, collapses into equality of welfare.

Section X offers a fragment of a taxonomy that distinguishes contrasting degrees of control that people display over the acquisition and the persistence of their tastes. The taxonomy bears against one premise in Dworkin's argument that equality of opportunity for welfare collapses into equality of welfare. Section XI reviews, and rejects, various arguments, only one of which is Dworkin's, for not compensating for expensive tastes.

A coda (section XII) comments briefly on wider aspects of the "Equality of what?" question[3] and the Appendix reconstructs, and refutes, a variant of the "alienation" argument against compensation for expensive taste whose substance is due to Matthew Clayton and Andrew Williams.

Before I proceed to business, I wish to point out that, although Dworkin treats me, for (legitimate) convenience, as a proponent of equality of opportunity for welfare, I *rejected* equality of opportunity for welfare in "On the Currency." I affirmed not equality of opportunity for welfare, but equality of access to advantage,[4] under an understanding of "advantage" in which welfare, in various of its forms, is only a proper part of it. Welfare is, in my view, no more than a part of advantage because, as Dworkin has taught us, egalitarians are moved to eliminate disadvantages that are not reducible to welfare deficits. But I also think, against Dworkin, that welfare is a part of advantage because egalitarians are (equally legitimately) moved to compensate for the very fact that some people's welfare is lower than others. But the indicated simplifying treatment of my position by Dworkin will not matter in the present paper except in section X below, and even there it won't matter very much. For the most part, I am happy, and it is also convenient for *me*, to accept, heuristically, the role of champion of equality of opportunity for welfare, for the restricted purpose of confronting the argument that is central to Dworkin's polemic against me, and which is addressed in section V.

A word about what will be meant by the sentence-form "*x* represents an injustice" here. It will not mean "*x* represents an injustice that ought to be rectified by the state." (No one should in any case think that that's what "*x* represents an injustice" *ordinarily* means: the words "that ought to be rectified by the state" surely *add* meaning to the phrase that they expand.) It will mean, more elementarily, that the world is less than fully just by virtue of the presence of *x* in it. So, to be as clear as possible, if, in the sequel, I say such things as "compensation is required by egalitarian justice," I mean: for there to be egalitarian distributive justice, there must be compensation; and not: there must (unconditionally) be compensation, because of the (unoverridable and always implementable) requirements of egalitarian distributive justice.

I

Dworkin's "Equality of Welfare"[5] criticizes equality of welfare as a reading of the form of equality that is demanded by equal concern, but it does so on at least two quite distinct grounds. The first ground of objection to equality of welfare can be called "the indeterminacy objection." It says that any tendency to embrace equality of welfare depends on lack of clarity with respect to what *kind* of welfare *equality* of welfare is to be understood as an equality *of*: whenever we try to specify the *kind* of welfare that people are to be equal in, we soon find ourselves formulating a plainly unacceptable view. So, for example, a degree of what Dworkin calls *overall success* may appear attractive as the relevant reading of welfare, but not when we consider the case of people whose judgments of what constitutes overall success are either extravagant or extraordinarily modest. That case inclines us to favor the alternative reading of welfare that Dworkin calls *relative success*, but relative success loses its shine when we realize that people may achieve a high degree of relative success simply because they set their sights low. Summing up the lesson of this first line of criticism, Dworkin says that ". . . welfare has gained whatever appeal it has precisely by remaining abstract and therefore ambiguous: the ideal loses its appeal whenever a particular conception of welfare is specified, which presumably explains why those who defend it rarely attempt any such specification" (p. 285).[6]

Dworkin's second and entirely distinct ground of objection to equality of welfare is that it mandates provision for expensive tastes: the objection is that it is unfair to impose the cost of satisfying a given person's expensive taste on other people.

In "On the Currency" I criticized the expensive taste objection to equality of welfare, but I said little about the indeterminacy objection, beyond crediting Dworkin with a "masterful exposé of ambiguities in the concept of welfare" (p. 921, fn. 4). So let me say, as I should have said in "Currency," that, in my view, the indeterminacy objection is extremely powerful. But, however strong or weak the indeterminacy objection to equality of welfare may be, the point I am here concerned to make is that the expensive taste objection requires assessment in its own properly separate terms. To test that objection against cases, we need to fix what we mean by "welfare," in a given case, which is not to say that we must mean one thing only by it, across all cases. We can discuss expensive *preference*, or expensive *rational* preference, or expensive *enjoyable mental state*, or expensive *subsets* of goods that appear on a correct "objective list" of what is worthwhile in life. Whether or not, as Dworkin rather improbably suggests, the *whole* appeal of the welfare metric depends on its indeterminacy,[7] I believe that people find the expensive taste objection more powerful when particular examples of expensive taste are underspecified with respect to what "welfare" is to mean in the description of the example. When we fix what welfare is, in a given example, we clarify and thereby strengthen the case for affirming that there can be injustice when and because people's resource bundles do not compensate for the fact that (a certain form of) welfare that is cheap for some is expensive for others.

II

To say that someone has expensive tastes, in the present meaning of the phrase, which is its meaning in Dworkin's article on "Equality of Welfare," is to say that that person "need[s] more income" than others do "simply to achieve the same level of [some form of] welfare as those with less expensive tastes" (p. 48), be that form of welfare satisfaction of preference, or self-development, or good experience, or whatever other form of welfare is brought into view. But the ordinary understanding of the expression "expensive tastes" does not match the technical Dworkin-meaning that I just stated, and, to the extent that resonances from the ordinary meaning of the phrase continue to occupy the mind, the issue of whether uncompensated expensive tastes represent an injustice risks being clouded.

Ordinarily, when we say that people have expensive tastes, we have in mind the lifestyle that they *actually* live, one characterized by fine-textile clothes, caviar, posh furniture, and so on. But their *actual* pattern of consumption may show not that their tastes are expensive in the *required* sense, but just that their bank balance is large. Nor is expensive taste in the required sense necessarily exhibited by someone who is not *willing* to *settle* for a lesser satisfaction, for example, for hamburger instead of steak. For that is a matter not of the structure of such people's taste or preference as such, but, precisely, of their will. It is a matter of the *policy* that they adopt when seeking to satisfy their tastes.

A person's tastes are expensive in the required sense if and only if, as I have explained, they are such that it costs more to provide that person than to provide others with given levels of satisfaction or fulfillment. People who insist on expensive cigars and fine wines are not *eo ipso* possessed of expensive tastes, in the required sense. For they may thereby be insisting on a higher level of fulfillment than the norm. In the present acceptation, people have expensive tastes if, for example, ordinary cigars and cheap wine that give pleasure to most people leave them cold, and they can get something like that pleasure (and, *ex hypothesi*, *not* a greater one) only with Havana cigars and Margaux.[8] People's expensive tastes, here, are a matter neither of their behavior nor of their will but of their constitution. They are a matter of what they are satisfied *by*, not of what they are satisfied *with*. (It does not prejudice the integrity of that distinction that it is often difficult to discern which limb of it applies, nor even that there may be cases with respect to which there is no "fact of the matter" to discern.)

An expensive taste, then, is a dispositional characteristic: not a disposition to action, like the disposition to choose steak rather than hamburger, but, to stay with that example, the disposition to get from steak only what others get from something as cheap as hamburger. Expensive tastes, in the specified sense, militate against, because they reduce the opportunity for, a fulfilling life. For any given income you are worse off in terms of satisfaction or fulfillment if you have expensive tastes.

So: do not picture people who consume steak and thereby get premium-level satisfaction and nevertheless present its cost as an injustice. People like that, who whine that their tastes are expensive in the ordinary sense of the phrase, give expensive taste in the appropriately technical sense a bad name that it doesn't deserve. Instead, picture people who consume hamburger but fail to get ordinary satisfaction from it and who present the high price they have to pay for the steak that would bring them up to mere par as an injustice.

Now, someone who loves cheap wine may hate ordinary cigars, and someone who is satisfied by ordinary cigars may need Margaux for ordinary-level wine pleasure. More generally, each person's satisfaction function will likely be an amalgam of cheap and expensive tastes, and few may have expensive tastes in an aggregate sense, when one considers the vast variety of commodities that are available to people. That fact is relevant to practical politics. It is certainly a reason for not worrying too much, in many practical contexts,[9] about compensating people for expensive tastes, particularly in the light of the invasiveness of the procedures that would sometimes have to be set in train to discover how cheap or expensive (in the *required* sense) a given person's tastes are. But the self-same fact is irrelevant to the philosophical question, which is whether or not, *ceteris paribus*, an expensive taste warrants compensation. Dworkin rejects compensation for expensive tastes as a matter of *principle*, not on the grounds that a principle that might dictate their compensation is never *in fact* satisfied (because everyone can find *some* reasonably priced things that satisfy them as much as other people are satisfied by things that they find unsatisfying). I criticize Dworkin's principled position. Expensive tastes may be peripheral to the *practice* of justice, but the concept of expensive taste nevertheless raises questions at the heart of the *theory* of justice.

III

Dworkin believes that expensive tastes do not warrant compensation, from an egalitarian point of view. Against that, I said the following (p. 923, and cf. p. 920):

> I distinguish among expensive tastes according to whether or not their bearer can reasonably be held responsible for them. There are those which he could not have helped forming and/or could not now unform, and then there are those for which, by contrast, he can be held responsible, because he could have forestalled them and/or because he could now unlearn them.

I now want to improve that statement, in two respects. I want to improve the *formulation* of its first sentence, but I also want to enter a *substantial* correction to the second sentence, one that also affects how the first sentence is to be understood.

The improvement as to formulation expands the first sentence by deleting "them" and adding "the fact that her tastes are expensive." It is, as I made abundantly clear elsewhere in "Currency,"[10] precisely *that* fact for which the question of responsibility is crucial.

Secondly, and more substantively, the statement needs improvement because it confuses a *general* criterion for deciding whether people should pay for their expensive tastes, which is described in the (now amended) first sentence of the statement, with a more *specific* criterion, described in its second sentence, and one that I now think is appropriate only to a subset of expensive tastes.

Let me explain. While the first sentence applies, so I think, to *all* expensive tastes, the second, which specifies the first *entirely* in terms of choice and will, is appropriate, I belatedly see, only in the case of tastes that do not embody judgments of valuation, and that I shall call *brute* tastes, such as my own liking for Diet Coke, which embodies no particular *approval* of it. With respect to tastes that *are* informed by valuational judgment,[11] we can still ask whether their bearers could have avoided developing them or could be asked to rid themselves of them, and the answers will be variously relevant, but I no longer think that the mere fact that people chose to develop and/or could now school themselves out of an expensive judgmental taste means that they should pick up the tab for it, and that is *precisely* because they *did* and *do* identify with it, and therefore cannot *reasonably* be expected to have not developed it or to rid themselves of it.[12] So what Dworkin gives as a reason for *withholding* compensation – the subjects' approving identification with their expensive tastes – is something that I regard as a reason for offering it, since, where identification *is* present, it is, standardly,[13] the agents' very bad luck that a preference with which they strongly identify happens to be expensive, and to expect them to forgo or to restrict satisfaction of that preference (because it is expensive) is, therefore, to ask them to accept an alienation from what is deep in them.[14] Accordingly, the significant revision of my view of expensive taste that I offer here renders my position more different from Dworkin's than it was in 1989.

Let me, then, set forth the flagship statement in its revised form:

> I distinguish among expensive tastes according to whether or not their bearers can reasonably be held responsible for the fact that their tastes are expensive. There are those that they could not have helped forming and/or could not now unform without violating their own judgment, and then there are those for whose cost, by contrast, they can be held responsible, because they could have forestalled their development, and/or because they could now quite readily unlearn them, without violating their own judgment.

The result, I acknowledge, is hardly a determinate theory, as opposed to a sketch for constructing one, but, incomplete as it is, the statement will do for present purposes.

IV

I return to expensive *judgmental* taste in section V. But first I want to say something about brute taste, the taste that does not track a judgment of the value of its object.

In his 1981 articles Dworkin set himself against compensation for *all* tastes, whether brute or judgmental, other than those pathological ones which qualify as such because their bearer would prefer not to have them.[15] "Equality of resources," he said, "offers no . . . reason for correcting for the contingencies that determine how expensive or frustrating someone's preferences turn out to be" (p. 69). And that went for such brute expensive tastes as (suppose in a given case it is a brute one) a desire for plovers' eggs belonging to someone cursed with a propensity to find chickens' eggs disgusting. The only qualification on this rigor was signaled by this footnote: "See, however, the discussion of handicaps below, which recognizes that certain kinds of preferences, which people wish they did not have, may call for compensation as handicaps" (p. 478, fn. 4). The footnote implies that compensation is in order *only* when people disidentify with (that is, wish they did not have) their own tastes.

Now people who find chickens' eggs disgusting may not regret having that reaction *as such*: they might even approve of it. If they wish that they did not have it, that is probably because the alternative to which the reaction drives them, namely, plovers' eggs, are so expensive. But that hardly qualifies their desire for plovers' eggs as a *craving*, either in the ordinary sense of that word or as Dworkin intended his use of it. And if regretting the special expense that one of my tastes imposes on me *did* make that taste a craving, then virtually *all* expensive tastes would attract compensation[16] under this widened understanding of Dworkin's compensate-for-cravings proviso.

To motivate my counterview, which is that *all* appropriately involuntary brute expensive tastes warrant compensation, suppose that there are only two edible things on Dworkin's island,[17] eggs and fish. Eggs are abundant, but fish are scarce. Consequently, fish are expensive and eggs are very cheap. Most people love eggs, but Harry hates them. Most people mostly eat eggs, reserving fish for special occasions, and they consequently have plenty of clamshells left to pay for other things, such as shelter, clothing, recreation, and so forth. Unlike them, Harry has a tough choice, which is between regularly eating fish and therefore having little of anything else, and eating lots of eggs, at the cost of gagging when he nourishes himself. We may suppose that it is because of how his taste buds work that he gags, although we could equally well suppose that he gags because eggs remind him of his mother, whom he (perhaps rightly) could not bear. What we rule out is that he gags because he judges eggs to be an inferior sort of food: he has nothing against eating eggs, except that they make him gag. Although the example is stylized and peculiar, it stands here for the unpeculiar phenomenon of different people (through no fault, or merit, of their own) finding the same consumables differentially satisfying, and therefore being differentially placed with respect to what they can get out of life with a given income. And, in my view, that phenomenon explodes the pretension of Dworkin's auction to being an engine of distributive justice. It shows that equality of resources should give way to equality of opportunity for welfare, because identical quantities of resources are capable of satisfying people to different degrees, since people are made differently, both naturally and socially, not only (a fact to which Dworkin is sensitive) in their capacities to produce, but also (the fact to which he is insensitive) in their capacities to obtain fulfillment.

Relative to his 1981 auction treatment of taste, chapter 7 of *Sovereign Virtue* represents a remarkable and consequential U-turn. For, although he does not acknowledge this, Dworkin has *in effect* given up completely on brute taste, and now defends noncompensation for judgmental taste only. Under a regime of compensation for brute expensive tastes, people impose the costs of servicing their tastes on other people in just the way they were not supposed to do (except in the case of cravings). Yet what Dworkin says in *Sovereign Virtue* (2000, p. 288) about the person who finds his tap water repugnantly sour is entirely generalizable:

> Suppose someone cannot stand the taste of ordinary water from the tap – it tastes unbearably sour to him – and he therefore chooses to buy more expensive bottled water. It is true that he has a choice whether or not to do that. But he did not choose to have the property – a special sensory reaction – that made the choice not to do so distasteful. That physiological condition is his bad luck, and he should therefore be compensated for his misfortune: he should be given extra resource [sic] so that he will not be worse off buying bottled water than others are who make do with tap water.

But there is no relevant difference between finding tap water sour and finding (hens') eggs disgusting. And if, as Dworkin says, "[t]he unfortunate man whose tap water tastes sour would prefer not to have that disability: his condition is a handicap, and equality of resources would regard it as such . . ." (p. 291), then that can *only* be because bottled water is expensive, so that what he regrets is that he has an expensive taste, and it is to precisely *that* object of regret that equality (here misnamed "of resources") is responding. If the water drinker is handicapped, then so is Harry the egg hater. But then – this is why I called Dworkin's U-turn consequential – Dworkin's market treatment of goods that supply brute satisfaction falls to the (in my view morally superior) principle: to each according to what they need for their satisfaction. In the huge domain of brute taste, market prices cease to embody justice. The scope of Dworkin's auction shrivels.

Note that one may identify with a preference (by which I here mean, roughly, be glad that one has it), disidentify with it (by which I here mean, roughly, wish that one did not have it), or possess neither attitude. In Dworkin (1981) you pay for your preference *unless you disidentify with it*, in which case it qualifies as a handicapping craving. But in Dworkin (2000) you pay for your preference *if you identify with it*, and not if you neither identify nor disidentify with it, this last being the condition of typical haters of tap water and hens' eggs.[18] And, as I said, that greatly reduces the writ of the market.

Let me now deal with another of Dworkin's responses to a "Currency" discussion of a case of brute taste. I argued (pp. 918ff.) that Dworkin could not countenance compensation for nondisabling pain, for pain, that is, that does not prevent people from pursuing their plans, since such pain constitutes no resource deficit. Dworkin responds (p. 297) that,

> everyone would agree that a decent life, whatever its other features, is one that is free from serious and enduring physical or mental pain or discomfort, and having a physical or mental infirmity or condition that makes pain or depression or discomfort inescapable without expensive medicine or clothing is therefore an evident and straightforward handicap.

And he draws this lesson: "If the community gives someone money for medicine to relieve pain, it does so not in order to make his welfare or well-being equal to anyone else's, but because his physical constitution handicaps his ability to lead the life he wishes to lead" (p. 491, fn. 11).

In my view, the quoted formulations run together two contrasts that must be kept apart for the sake of a proper assessment of the impact of what is here said on the matter in dispute. There is the contrast between, on the one hand, making a person's "welfare or well-being *equal* to anyone else's," with the emphasis on *equal*, and, on the other hand, ensuring that a person achieves a decent level of life, *however* that level is to be measured. That contrast is not material to the present dispute. The contrast that bears here is, rather, between aiming at remedying a deficiency in welfare, and aiming at remedying a deficiency in something else.[19] And on this, the only relevant count, what Dworkin says is ineffective. You do not turn a welfare consideration into a resource consideration by appealing to the fact that the source of the illfare in question is a person's physical constitution. What is claimed to be compensation for resource deficit is *not* compensation for welfare deficit in another guise when resources are valued independently of their bearer's particular wishes, which is how the market values them. But we get the stated mere guise when "resources" of physical constitution are treated as handicapping a person's "ability to lead the life he wishes to lead," and *that* means, *ex hypothesi*, in the relevant context, nothing more than that he wishes to lead a life without the deleterious welfare effects of that constitution. If I say that people should be compensated for desiring fine foods, and Dworkin responds that they should be compensated for the constitution that makes them want them,[20] then he disagrees with me in appearance only. Nor is it any kind of reply to my objection that people would *insure* against serious pain (p. 297): a deficit doesn't count as a resource deficit just because people would insure against it.[21]

For the rest of this paper I ignore the large concession documented here and I treat chapter 7 of *Sovereign Virtue* as a full defense of Dworkin's original view. For he continues to criticize my position as though he has not made the stated concession, and I have said what I wanted to say about that concession here.

V

Let us now focus on expensive judgmental taste, with respect to which Dworkin undoubtedly stands his ground. He continues to hold that costly judgmental preferences warrant no subsidy when they constitute, as they normally do, preferences with which the agent identifies, preferences, that is, which the agent would not wish to lack. Dworkin thinks, in my view falsely, that it is of the nature of preferences that they do not relevantly reflect choice,[22] so he does not think that compensation for expensive preferences is out of order *because* they have a *chosen* character. It is, rather, because to demand compensation for an expensive judgmental preference is to treat it as a burden or a disability, and therefore to repudiate it, which is not something that a person whose preference is informed by a judgment that endorses the value of its object can in general coherently do. To my urging that expensive preference may be relevantly unchosen bad luck, Dworkin replies that although it is indeed unchosen, the agents cannot regard it as a piece of bad luck for which they should be compensated, on pain of incoherently repudiating their own personality, on pain of confessing to a most bizarre alienation from themselves.

But this move is entirely unpersuasive, since the relevant bad luck does not lie in the mere *having* of the preference. As I tried to make clear in "On the Currency" (see again endnote 10), the person regards the relevant taste as bad luck *only* in the light of its price. And people can certainly without any self-misrepresentation or incoherence ask for compensation for (what might be, in every relevant sense) the *circumstance* that their taste is expensive. Whether or not it is weird to regret one's preference for reading certain kinds of books (that *happen* to be expensive),[23] there is nothing weird or self-alienating in regretting precisely this: that the kinds one wants to read are expensive. Accordingly, so many of us think, libraries should not charge people more who borrow more expensive books, since people cannot reasonably be held responsible for the property of the object of their book preference that it is expensive. Perhaps the stated antimarket policy, which does compensate for expensive taste, is mistaken, but it is no argument against it that library readers must represent themselves as dissociated from their own taste if they support such a policy. That is no argument against the antimarket policy, for the simple reason that no such dissociation is in fact displayed.

The bulk of Dworkin's reply to me, and the whole of his extended allegory of "buzzes and ticks,"[24] misrepresents me as supposing that the person with an expensive taste that raises a case for compensation regrets having the taste, rather than merely that it is expensive.

Towards the end of his reply to me, Dworkin does bring that critical distinction to the fore, when he reports what he importantly misdescribes as a "new argument" (p. 298) that I put against equality of resources:

> Cohen's final objection to equality of resources . . . says that *even* if people cannot sensibly claim that they have suffered bad luck in *having* the tastes and ambitions that they do, they can certainly claim that they have suffered bad luck when, in virtue of other people's competing tastes and ambitions, what they want is expensive. (p. 297, emphases added)

But Dworkin's "even if" is out of place, for I never say that people might be thought to suffer bad luck *just* in having the tastes that are in fact expensive. The regret I had in mind was wholly and solely that their tastes are *expensive*: perhaps I was not always explicit about that because I so took it for granted that price is the proper object of their regret. I did not say, and would never say, for example, that it is the *very fact* that he likes photography that is a burden to Paul (p. 925). The locus of his burden is the entirely different fact that photography is an *expensive* hobby. Accordingly, what Dworkin calls my "final objection" is not, as he represents it, a *distinct* objection. It is my central objection to Dworkin's unwillingness to compensate for expensive tastes: that they may be tastes that we cannot reasonably expect their bearers to shed and that plunge them in what is straightforwardly the *circumstance* that satisfying their tastes is expensive, and regret about this circumstance is transparently coherent.

Consider this passage:

> It would strike us as bizarre for someone to say that he should be pitied, or compensated by his fellow citizens, because he had the bad luck to have decided that he should help his friends in

need, or that Mozart is more intriguing than hip-hop, or that a life well lived includes foreign travel. (p. 290)

It might indeed be absurd for Mozart-lovers to regard their love for Mozart as *itself* bad luck. But there is nothing absurd, there is no dissociation from their own personality, when they express regret that Mozart CDs are more expensive than Madonna CDs. What Mozart-lovers or opera-lovers (p. 292) regret is not that their whole personality affirms their love of Mozart or of opera, but that what their whole personality (*legitimately*) affirms is expensive. Nor need anyone regret "loyalty to his friends" (p. 291), as such. What they may regret is that the friends have moved to Scotland, so that the exercise of loyalty to them costs so much more in time and money than it would if they were still in London: if they think some rail travel should be subsidized for this sort of reason, it remains false that they are repudiating, or affecting to repudiate, their own convictions, any more than bereaved air travelers repudiate their desire to show solidarity with their loved ones when they request and accept the low ticket price that some airlines charge for last-minute bookings to attend funerals.

Although "complex tastes are" indeed "interwoven with judgments of endorsement and approval" (p. 291), it simply doesn't follow that those judgments are prejudiced or denied by a request for, or an offer of, subsidy for the cost of satisfying complex tastes. A taste for reading art books rather than dime novels is, as tastes go, pretty complex, but one might think, with no trace of self-alienation, that one should not pay extra because it costs more for the library to stock art books than it does for it to stock dime novels. The art book lover *is* unfairly handicapped if libraries charge readers according to the market cost of what they read, and that is one good reason[25] why libraries, in the real world, subsidize tastes for expensive books by charging a uniform entrance fee, be it zero or some positive amount. It is precisely because lovers of art books quite reasonably *do* identify with their expensive book preference, it is because they cannot reasonably be expected to divest themselves of it, that the relevant readers have a case for support, regardless of whether they could have avoided or could now divest themselves of that preference.[26]

So it is no reason to deny support that the claimants in question identify with their preferences. But I do not say the polar opposite of what Dworkin does: I do not say that wherever there is an expensive identification, there is a case for support. And, as I have already acknowledged, I was certainly wrong, in "Currency," to distinguish the cases merely according to presence and absence of will, although I think they do count. It may, for example, also be important in our response to the art book lovers, that their preference runs to books that merely *happen* to be expensive, that they do not, be it noted, prefer them for Louis-like snobbish reasons[27] that justify less sympathy.

I would add that the unsubsidized art book lovers might or might not prefer, all things (including prices) considered, to have other preferences over books: that will depend on many things, including the size of their bank balance and how they *now* rate being relatively poor but reading what they *now* like to read against the comforts of a less literate solvency.[28] (There is an intensity of dissatisfaction that Socrates might suffer that might well make him, or, at any rate me, prefer to be a satisfied pig.) But in either case, that is, whatever their preferences across their preferences may be, it is no reason for charging them more that they must misrepresent themselves as alienated from their preference if they ask to pay less, since no such misrepresentation is required.

Suppose that the members of a minority group appeal to the local municipality for funds to sustain a recreation center, be it because they are very poor or because they happen to believe that such things should be paid for by the state: the motive and justifiability, all things considered, of their request are not in point here. Dworkin must say, what is preposterous, that they thereby distance themselves from their own culture and/or that they show a preference for lacking that culture, all things considered. And things stand no differently, as far as alienation is concerned, with respect to less cultural expensive preference, whether or not justice calls for compensation in *either* instance.

I must point out that when I say that compensation for expensive taste is warranted, I do not mean that the state should establish a comprehensive program to provide it, since epistemic and practical obstacles rule that out: see, further, section IX below. I mean, instead, that, absent compensation, an injustice obtains,[29] one, however, that, so I have just implied, it may be unwise in many cases to seek to eradicate, because it may be hard to identify, and hard and/or invasive to treat. So I am not saying that people's trips to their friends, or their practice of helping others, or their love of Mozart, *should* be subsidized. For all that I have argued here, there might be (as I am sure there are) excellent reasons for not doing so. But Dworkin's alienation reason is not one of them.

VI

I must now reply to Dworkin's objections to what he misnames my "new argument" (p. 298). But, before I reply to them, let me say that it is noteworthy, it is, indeed, of the first importance, that those objections abandon the "alienation" motif that frames Dworkin's earlier discussion in chapter 7 of *Sovereign Virtue*. And that confirms, what I have already urged, the utter irrelevance of the alienation motif for our dispute. If Dworkin had thought it relevant against what he describes as (merely) my "final objection," but what is in fact, simply my objection, he would have continued to press the alienation motif. But he did not continue to press it. So it isn't relevant to what is called my "final objection." So it isn't relevant at all, since what Dworkin calls my "final objection" *is* my objection.

In response to my objection, Dworkin (p. 298) invokes an analogy with politics:

> The mix of personal ambitions, attitudes, and preferences that I find in my community, or the overall state of the world's resources, is not in itself either fair or unfair to me; on the contrary, that mix is among the facts that fix what it is fair or unfair for me to do or to have. This is plain in politics: it would be absurd for me to claim unfairness or injustice in the fact that so few others share my tastes in civic architecture or my views on foreign policy that I am on the losing side of every vote on these matters.

I cannot disagree with Dworkin's insistence that what it is fair for me to have depends on the condition both of other people and of the world: what follows "on the contrary" is undeniable, and the dispute concerns not its truth but the right way to respect that truth, be it equality of resources, equality of welfare, or something else. But an unadjusted market that reflects the relevant "mix" may nevertheless be unfair to me, even if the mix *itself* isn't. (If one added people's *talents* to the "mix," then Dworkin would readily agree with that.) So "on the contrary" in the first sentence of the exhibited paragraph proposes a false contrast.

Dworkin's substantive point is carried by his second sentence, which presents the analogy with voting, an analogy that may not be fully appropriate, but which I accept for the sake of argument. Let me then point out that, if Dworkin were right in what he says here about voting, then there would be no problem of the permanent minority in politics, and no need to write constitutions that constrain the ambit of majority decision. Note, further, that in a polity that displays a rift in architectural taste, a Palladian majority that cares about justice might defer to a Gothic-loving minority and allow some civic architecture to be Gothic,[30] and it might also, in the same spirit, legislate subsidies on books that only a minority desire and whose market price is therefore inordinately high. *Even if* a majority could *legitimately* deny a minority its recreation center, or the books it likes, there would still be a case for saying that it was thereby acting oppressively. The majority would then not be paying the social cost of its choice, which, on any sensible conception of social cost, must include the deprivation visited on members of the minority.[31] And there is indeed no relevant difference, here, between being at the short end of the electoral process and being at the short end of the market process. Dworkin's analogy with politics therefore suggests the opposite of what he wants it to suggest. The injustices visited on minorities by an oppressively majoritarian *state* are matched by the different sorts of constraint that *market* processes impose on people's opportunities to secure what they value, of which I shall say more in section VIII below.

Will Kymlicka points out that "the viability of [some minority] societal cultures may be undermined by economic and political decisions made by the majority. They could be outbid or outvoted on resources and policies that are crucial to the survival of their societal cultures."[32]

And that is also true of those who have a minority taste in non- (or less) cultural (in the relevantly ethnic sense) aspects of life, such as for old-fashioned local shopping, or countrysides with hedges, or vegan food, and so on. The survival of *their* preferred ways may also be subject to threat from majority preference, whether that threat expresses itself politically or more anonymously, through the market.

Dworkin also claims (p. 298) that my "final objection" undermines any prospect I may cherish of distinguishing between tastes for which compensation is in order and tastes for which compensation is not in order:

> This argument, if successful, would certainly undermine my claim that expensive tastes should not entitle anyone to extra resource. But it would also, on its own, sweep away Cohen's own distinction between equality of opportunity for welfare and plain equality of welfare. Even if we accepted his claim that some people, like Louis, have chosen their own champagne tastes, we would also have to concede that such people have not chosen that these tastes be expensive: They can sensibly complain that it is their bad luck that, in virtue of the scarcity of soil of the right kind and orientation, champagne is more expensive than beer. Indeed everyone, no matter how cheap his tastes and ambitions are to satisfy, can complain that it is his bad luck that other people's tastes, or the fortunes of supply and demand, are not such that his own tastes would be cheaper still.

Louis *may* not have chosen *that* his tastes be expensive: whether that is so depends on details in the structure of his snobbery that are not disclosed to us in "Equality of Welfare." But he is said by Dworkin to have chosen to develop tastes that he knew would be expensive,[33] his reason for having done so being something at least closely related to their expense. And that is a perfectly natural reason for hesitating to compensate him. It is *not* mere bad luck that *his* tastes are expensive, since it is true *ex hypothesi* that he could have avoided expensive tastes, and it is significant that his reason for developing them relates to their expensiveness.

Let me also respond to the final sentence of the quoted paragraph above. It is irrelevant whether or not it constitutes bad luck that my tastes, though cheap, are more expensive than they would be if supply of and/or demand for their objects were different. What matters here is bad luck that raises an issue of justice, and identifying *such* luck requires a comparison with the luck that *other* people have, which goes unrepresented in Dworkin's parting sentence. What matters is whether I have the bad luck to be saddled with tastes that are *more* expensive to satisfy than, on the whole, other people's tastes are.

Before we proceed further, let me sum up the polemical position. Dworkin's central argument[34] runs as follows.

(1) Harry genuinely prefers expensive A to cheap B.
∴ (2) He cannot honestly repudiate that preference.
But (3) To ask for help in satisfying a preference is to regard it as a handicap, and, therefore, to distance oneself from it in a fashion that implies repudiation.
∴ (4) Harry cannot coherently ask for such help.
∴ (5) We should not supply such help.[35]

My main objection to this argument is that, whatever may be said about the inference from (1) to (2), premise (3) is false, for reasons that were laid out in section V. At one point (see the exposition of "strategy 2" on p. 937) I *conjectured* that one might wish to challenge the inference from (4) to (5), as a means of handling a peculiar sort of preference, one, that is, whose high cost is *welcomed* by its bearer. But I expressly favored a different solution[36] to that problematic preference than the one that denies the inference from (4) to (5). At p. 295 Dworkin misdescribes the unaffirmed conjecture as something that I affirm. But even if I had affirmed it, and was not merely raising it as one of three alternative treatments of a peculiar sort of example, each of which struck me as deserving of consideration, the thought in question would be independent of our main disagreement, which concerns expensive preferences whose expensiveness their bearer indeed regrets.

VII

I turn to what Dworkin calls "buzzes" and "ticks," buzzes being episodes of experiential enjoyment *as such* and ticks being satisfactions of preference *as such*, that is, considered independently of, respectively, the source of the enjoyment and the object of the preference. Dworkin thinks that I am committed to believing that buzzes and/or ticks are what people do or should care about, to the extent that I think that egalitarians should be concerned about each of experiential enjoyment and preference satisfaction, as such.

Dworkin is right that it is an insane metaphysic of the person that gives buzzes and ticks the stated centrality. But I am not committed to that metaphysic, and it is interesting that, in "Equality of Welfare," Dworkin did not accuse believers in the eponymous ideal of trafficking in that metaphysic. (The passage quoted in endnote 40 shows that he could not, in all consistency, have made that accusation.)

The reason why egalitarians whose metric is or includes welfare are committed to no such metaphysic is that welfare, *even* buzz-and-tick-defined, might be a good metric of just equality even if it isn't the right metric by which to run one's life. Thomas Scanlon points out that other people can aim at my well-being *as such* in a way that I do not myself aim at it: I aim at its constituents, and normally, moreover, not *as* (prospective) constituents of my well-being, but as what they specifically are, as such (this particular career, that holiday, this chocolate bar, etc.).[37] And the egalitarian distributor can, like Scanlon's other people, aim at ensuring equality within a dimension that is not the dimension in which people's primary[38] aims are located.

The buzz/ticks parody of my view has whatever properly intellectual force it does through being a representation of some such argument as the following:

(1) Sensible human beings don't care exclusively or even centrally about buzzes and ticks as such.
(2) The egalitarian distributor must distribute according to what sensible people care about, as such.
∴ (3) The egalitarian distributor should not have regard to buzzes and ticks as such.

The first premise of that argument, one with which I agree, is beautifully set out by Dworkin. But the second premise, which is also required, isn't mentioned in "Equality and Capability," and Scanlon's point shows that it is a false premise. It is, moreover, a premise that Dworkin himself must reject, since his egalitarian distributor distributes according to a metric of resources, and, as Dworkin well realizes, balanced people do not care about *resources* as such.[39] During Oxford seminars in the late 1980s Amartya Sen used to object to equality of resources on the ground that resources are not what people care about. Dworkin used to respond (e.g., on June 1, 1987) by rightly denying premise (2) above.[40]

A final point, on buzzes, ticks, and judgment. Some utilitarians, and many economists, underestimate the role of judgment in desire: they are deserving butts of Dworkin's "buzz/tick" parody. Dworkin rightly emphasizes the role of judgment in desire, but he also undoubtedly overestimates it. The idea that the thrill that one gets from jazz is "predicated on [the] judgment . . . that good jazz is wonderful" (p. 293) is bizarre. I get a kick from certain works of rock and roll that I consider to be pretty worthless. Endorsement of the objects of desire doesn't run so far across the map as Dworkin appears to believe.

Where judgment endorses a desire, a regret about the cost of one's desire doesn't undermine that judgment, because the regret attaches to *that* cost. And where, as in my rock and roll case, there is no endorsement by judgment, where a pure "buzz" is indeed in question, the idea that asking for it to be subsidized involves some sort of unrealistic "dissociation from personality" (p. 290) is a manifest nonstarter.

VIII

For all that I have said, it may seem peculiar that a person, that is, me, whom most people would account more radically egalitarian than Dworkin is, should be tender, where Dworkin is tough, towards those who have expensive tastes. And, independently of which *side* I am on in this dispute, it might also seem odd that I should have spent so much time and energy on what might seem to be such an unimportant issue.

The answer to the first puzzlement follows from the clarification given in section II above of what an expensive taste, *here*, is: expensive tastes, in the unordinary meaning of the phrase that operates here, militate against the quality of a person's life. Typically, if not always, they generate an involuntary welfare deficit, and it is not peculiar that a radical egalitarian should be exercised by involuntary welfare deficits.

But why – I turn here to the second puzzlement – should I concern myself with what might nevertheless seem to be so tiny an issue? The answer is that it is not a tiny issue at all: the correct assessment of the justice of the market is at stake here. Dworkin regards market process as integral to the specification of what distributive justice is:[41] it is his endorsement of the market that enforces his rejection of the claims of expensive taste.[42] Egalitarians like me, by contrast, see the market as at best a mere brute luck machine, and are correspondingly obliged to highlight the misfortune of those who are saddled with expensive tastes.

To see why I disagree with Dworkin about the justice of the market, consider, once again, a library that subsidizes some at the (money) expense of others by charging the same rate per borrowed book regardless of which book, be it cheap or expensive, a member borrows. There are, as I have acknowledged (see endnote 25), reasons for a uniform entry price that are not telling here, such as an aversion to the pettiness, and costs, of setting individual rates for books and keeping detailed accounts. But I think that a distinct good reason is that which books people find fulfilling is not a matter of people's choices, but of their culturally and socially developed constitutions. It is, of course, a matter of choice, if anything is, that some members borrow expensive art books when they could have borrowed inexpensive novels. But it would not normally reflect relevant exercises of their will that novels fail to engage their powers in the way that art books do. When, as is usual, libraries charge the same price to all comers, few regard those who choose expensive books as taking unfair advantage of the subsidy on them. Egalitarians believe that there is a fairness case for one price, and more generally, for nonmarket pricing of *many* activities that people pursue, the ground for a uniform and therefore redistributive price being relevantly unchosen or otherwise defensible variations in the cost of satisfying people's tastes and fulfilling their aspirations. The distributive norm that I favor takes part of its inspiration from the socialist slogan, "To each according to their needs – according, that is, to what they need for fulfillment in life," which is an antimarket slogan. Need satisfaction, thus capaciously understood, is a major element within what I have called "advantage."

When there are charges for use according to cost, then some are unfairly penalized for expensive tastes that they could not, and cannot, help having, or, more generally,[43] that they cannot reasonably be expected not to pursue: that is the case against market allocation here. Because of the vagaries and variations of preference, markets do not deliver justice, but that is not to say that there exists a practicable alternative that does so. To see that, let us distinguish between general and special subsidies: *general* subsidies reduce the cost of a given good to *all* comers, and therefore not only to those whose taste for that good is in the relevant way expensive; *special* subsidies are to those particular consumers of a given good whose taste for it is expensive. Now, special subsidies are in most cases multiply impractical. For one thing, it would almost certainly be impossible for the state to determine which tastes reflect disqualifying choice and which do not. For another, it could not easily determine whether a person, as that person is now constituted, *needs* more resources than others do, for comparable effect or, on the contrary, simply *demands* more satisfaction than they do from life.[44] If, moreover, the state could indeed determine such things, it could do so only through a monstrous invasion of privacy that would not be justified, in my view, by the contemplated particular gain in egalitarian justice. What our tastes, *as individuals*, are, and how we got them, should, therefore, largely not be the state's business. (Note that library subsidies target groups, not individuals as such.)

But while individual subsidies are not on, general subsidies are, like the market, insensitive to individual variations in levels of fulfillment. So we produce some injustice whether we leave the market alone or interfere with it in a generally subsidizing way. If we wish to serve justice as well as we reasonably can, then we have to try to guess when taste differences make general subsidy *more* just than market upshots, and in some cases, such as that of libraries, my guess is that justice is indeed better served by our actual practice of subsidy: it is less insensitive to individual need than the market is. If we fix in our minds the form of welfare that we are supposing the library delivers, be it reading enjoyment, or preference fulfillment, or self-development, then the case for a general subsidy seems to me to be overwhelming. We must not be misled, inappropriately, by vagueness about what "welfare" might mean here: we must not let the expensive taste objection to equality of welfare ride piggyback on the indeterminacy objection (see section I above). (The library example is importantly different from a case where someone needs expensive cigars to get what others get from cheap ones, for we may suppose that everyone prefers expensive to cheap cigars, whereas people differ not only in the degrees of satisfaction – or whatever – that they get from different books but also in their preference orderings over them. Partly for that reason, the library case is the appropriate model for how to treat different, and differentially expensive, cultural needs.[45])

Dworkin does not himself believe in pure *laissez-faire*, since he thinks that, so far as possible, people should be compensated for handicaps and for poor earning capacity before they enter the market. But he thinks that the market produces justice insofar as its prices reflect the play of people's tastes and ambitions. So he claims[46] that his auction produces stainless justice, when people differ only in their (comprehensively unrepudiated) tastes, but not in their capacities, whereas I believe that, for example, it is unjust if I have to pay more for figs than you do for apples simply because few people like figs and many like apples – always assuming that you get from apples more or less what I get from figs. In my view, markets can "produce" justice only in the Pickwickian sense that they do so when in some unattainable possible world they are so comprehensively rigged that they induce a distribution that qualifies as just for reasons that have nothing to do with how market prices form.

In sum: Dworkin believes that the market constitutes its results as just when pretrading assets are suitably equalized, where that equalization is blind to differences of taste, but I believe that, while market results may be more or less just, the market plays no part in the *constitution* of justice, precisely because it is blind to how well it satisfies different tastes and aspirations.

Some will baulk at the idea that what is claimed to be a demand of justice is not something that the state, or, indeed, any other agent, is in a position to deliver. I cannot here defend the methodology that allows such a result. But it merits comment that Dworkin could not (and, so I believe, would not) object to my position on any such methodological basis. For he himself believes that egalitarian justice justifies compensation for expensive tastes whose bearer is disposed to repudiate them, and he can no more infer, in all due realism, that the state should comprehensively see to such compensation than I can realistically propose that it compensate with precision for unrepudiated expensive taste whose cost their bearer cannot reasonably be asked to shoulder.

Although I agree with Dworkin that the state cannot put particular individuals' tastes on its agenda, our reasons for that common stance could not be more different. For it is false, on my view, that people's (unrepudiated) tastes are not the state's business *because* it is reasonable to expect them to take responsibility for those tastes, no matter how they came to have them, and no matter what they can do about them now. Instead, they must perforce pick up the tab for them because they cannot reasonably be the state's business.

IX

Dworkin writes (p. 286):

> One group of critics – I shall use G. A. Cohen's version as representative – proposes that citizens should be equal, not in the welfare they achieve, but in the opportunity that each has to achieve welfare. As we shall see, that supposedly different ideal turns out to be equality of welfare under another name.

What we come to see, according to Dworkin, is that no one really *chooses* their tastes or preferences, and, so his argument continues, since equality of opportunity for welfare differs from equality of welfare only because the former refuses to compensate for certain tastes (chosen ones) that the latter compensates, it follows that there turns out to be no difference between the two positions.

There are two objections (1 and 2 below) to the claim that equality of opportunity for welfare collapses into equality of welfare for the stated reason. They are also objections to the claim that *my* view (equal access to advantage) collapses into that. And there is a third reason (3 below) for objecting to the claim that my view in particular collapses into equality of welfare.

1   P does not become q "under another name" because r is true and the conjunction of p and r implies q (the relevant values of those variables here are, respectively, *there should be equality of opportunity for welfare* (p), *there should be equality of welfare* (q), and *people never really choose their tastes* (r)). It is a matter of principle for equality of opportunity for welfare that tastes are compensated for only if and when and because they are (to put it crudely) not chosen, however often (including never) they are *in fact* chosen, and equality of welfare denies that principle. That deep difference of principle would survive even if it should turn out that all tastes are unchosen: we would still be faced with "a distinct political ideal" (p. 289), or, at any rate, a distinct conception of justice.

2   We *can*, as I shall show in section X, distinguish relevantly different *degrees* of care and choice in preference formation. To be sure, we never quite simply *choose* a preference or a taste, in the way that we choose actions: preferences, unlike actions, and like all the things that aren't actions, are not immediately subject to the will. But there remain more nuanced things to be said about preference and the will.

3   *I* am not, in any case, a proponent of equality of opportunity for welfare, but, rather, of equality of access to advantage, according to which there should be equality of opportunity not for welfare alone but for a vector which includes that, *and* resources, *and* need satisfaction, and, perhaps, other advantages. And that makes my own view proof against the mooted collapse. *Even if* no tastes were affected by the will, even if 2 above were false, my view would remain trebly removed from equality of welfare: first, for the reason given in 1 above; second, because I do not think welfare is the only element that belongs in an egalitarian metric; and finally because there would *still* be scope for distribution-affecting choice, on my view (as, of course, on Dworkin's, but not according to plain equality of welfare), with respect to things *other* than preferences.

X

I now take up the task laid down two paragraphs back, that of showing that some preferences reflect more will than others do, in a way that bears on justice. But before I do so, I wish to reiterate and emphasize that any disagreement that Dworkin and I may have concerning the dynamics of preference formation is quite surplus to my disagreement with him about whether preferences that fall outside the governance of the will should be compensated. Even if we agreed that preferences never do in a relevant way reflect will, our root *normative* disagreement would persist.

I say that some preferences reflect will *more* than others do: I do not say that any preferences are (just like that) *chosen*. That would contradict the nature of preference. It is conceptually excluded that we should (just) *choose* our preferences (as opposed to the objects that they prompt us to pursue). But we can devote more or less control to the development of our preferences, and be differentially responsible for their cost as a result.

Consider, for example, Shirley, who relishes hamburger and steak in the same different degrees that the rest of us do. She knows that if she eats steak all the time it will lose its special zing and become no more satisfying than hamburger is. But for a while there will be extra pleasure, and Shirley's resources are ample enough for her to embark on the stated course: indeed, she has it in mind occasionally to buy super-duper steak once ordinary steak has come to taste, for her, like hamburger does now. She is warned that the temporary gains she contemplates will be nullified if her income drops, and she is aware that there is some chance that it will.[47] But she embraces that risk, and, in the event, her income does happen to drop, so that she is landed with an expensive taste that is difficult for her to satisfy. Her predicament cannot plausibly be represented as a matter of mere bad luck, and we should be as reluctant to compensate her as we are to compensate losing gamblers who gambled with their eyes open.

Unlike Shirley, Dworkin's Louis (Bourbon) does not gamble on getting *more* welfare at the cost of developing an expensive taste. On the contrary: he "sets out deliberately to cultivate some taste or ambition he does not now have, but which will be expensive in the sense that once it has been cultivated he will not have as much welfare . . . as he had before unless he acquires more wealth" (p. 49). Louis originally, perhaps, hates caviar, but, being attracted to it because of its snob value, he trains himself to like it. That is an entirely coherent, even somewhat familiar, story, and, so it seems to me, justice should look less kindly on the proposition that he be sold caviar at a discount than on the proposition that Louisa, who came by the same taste inadvertently, should be given that discount.

It may, however, be unfair to characterize what Dworkin calls Louis's "taste for refined tastes" as a piece of snobbery. Perhaps he is moved by a certain more admirable ideal of consumption. If so, then my own disposition would be to treat him more indulgently (see section III above).

So we may indeed distinguish between tastes for whose cost we hold people responsible because they could readily and reasonably have avoided developing them or could now be reasonably expected to develop cheaper ones (which means: learn to gain an ordinary degree of satisfaction from cheaper things), and tastes where responsibility is relevantly absent and/or where judgment is relevantly present and where compensation is therefore required by egalitarian justice. To be sure, you might find it unrealistic, and in any case likely to be special pleading, for people to say that they just *cannot* get from hamburger what others get from it (as opposed to that they are unwilling to *settle* for a lesser satisfaction). But the epistemic – and even conceptual problems[48] – that arise here do not affect the content of justice.

Sometimes no relevant choice obtained or obtains. If you were brought up on baseball, you did not deliberately develop a taste for it, and it may be impossible for you to come to enjoy cricket, irrespective of any judgments you may now make about the comparative value of those sports. But in other cases, nothing similar is true.

Suppose that I am hypnotized into an expensive taste, and, for good measure, into the endorsement of the value of its object that, so Dworkin thinks, puts it beyond the reach of legitimate compensation. It seems to me plain that it would offend against egalitarian justice to deny me the extra means that are required to satisfy it (although, *ex hypothesi*, it is not a Dworkin-compensable "obsession," or "craving":[49] an endorsing judgment obtains). But, importantly, that is merely an extreme case, at the far end of a continuum of absence and presence of will in taste formation, rather than something that in no way resembles ordinary processes of the genesis of preference and desire.

In responding to my claim, illustrated above, that preferences vary with respect to how much they represent will, Dworkin has not expressly addressed the motif of schooling oneself out of an expensive taste. But he has addressed the issue of responsibility for acquiring a taste in the first place. He has remarked that "people who deliberately cultivate tastes do so out of opinions they did not in the pertinent sense cultivate but had."[50] That remark is supposed to upset my insistence on the distinction, and its importance for justice, between tastes for which people can, and ones for which they cannot, be held responsible. But I do not think that Dworkin's remark, whatever truth may lie in it, does upset the required distinction.

It would do so only if it were generally true that responsibility for the consequences of a choice requires responsibility for the (always more or less constraining) situation in which it is made, and we normally suppose no such thing. Of course we do not choose out of the blue to develop our tastes, but it does not follow, and it is false, that we never have a significant choice with respect to whether or not we develop them. When any sort of choice of anything occurs, we normally modulate any resulting assignment of responsibility according to the character of the alternatives that the chooser had, and I believe that we can proceed in that fashion here. Louis chooses to develop a certain taste in the light of a "taste for refined tastes." That makes him a very special case, but set that aside. The feature to focus on here is that he indeed chooses a certain course of action, that of developing a certain taste, in the light of a (further) taste. Dworkin thinks that people choose *courses of action* in the light of their tastes, yet he also thinks that, despite *that* unchosen background to their choices, they may reasonably be held responsible for (some of) the consequences of those actions. I treat Louis's choosing to develop an expensive taste, in the light of a further taste, in precisely that fashion.

You do not escape responsibility for the costs of your choice by virtue of the mere fact that you made that choice *against a choice-affecting background*. But *also*, the mere fact that you made a choice, and could have chosen otherwise (for example, not to buy that steak), no more shows that subsidy is out of order than does the *mere* fact that you could have chosen not to buy that wheelchair show that subsidy is out of order. In each case facts in the background to the choice, facts about degrees of control, and about the cost of alternatives, affect the proper allocation of responsibility for the consequences of the choice.

My strategy has been to propose a reckoning of presence and absence of responsibility for the costs of expensive taste that in material part imitates our quotidian treatment of responsibility in more familiar domains. It is false that the only relevant questions about choice and responsibility are whether or not something (an action, a preference) is, simply, *chosen* (that is, *tout court*), and that the only relevant upshot is whether the agent is responsible, *tout court*.

Here, as elsewhere, we make judgments of *degree* of responsibility, and they are based on *graded* and *shaded* judgments about choice. It always bears on the matter of responsibility that a person chose a certain course, but it is also always pertinent how *genuine* that choice was (see p. 934) *and* how constraining the circumstances were in which it was made. The genuineness of a choice is a function of the chooser's knowledge, self-possession, and so forth. And the point about constraining circumstances is illustrated by the case of the juvenile delinquent from a deprived background who undoubtedly chose to commit the crime, but our response to whom is conditioned by knowledge of what the criminal's alternatives were, and of how, for example, they differed from that of someone from the middle class, who had, as we say, many advantages. For a relevantly comparable contrast in the domain of expensive taste formation, consider the difference between someone who would have had to make a special effort to avoid developing a dependence on steak and someone whose taste for hamburger was ensured by the unavailability of steak.[51]

It is, of course, an extremely complex question what the shape of the function is which, in our ordinary thought, takes us from data about what lies inside and outside of a choice to an assignment of (some degree) of responsibility for its consequences: I cannot discuss that here (or anywhere else). But nothing says that we cannot operate that function (which has more than two values) for the case of expensive choice and the taste that lies behind it. To be sure, it may be that it is only in unusual cases of taste formation that responsibility, on quotidian criteria, is in order. And it may also be true that the quotidian criteria which I have applied to the special case of taste and choice disintegrate, in the general case, under metaphysical interrogation. But I need not say that people *are*, in general, responsible for their expensive tastes. And if, indeed, we never are, whether because the metaphysics of the will says that we are responsible for nothing, or for more particular reasons, then, on my view, they *always* constitute a complaint, from the point of view of distributive justice. The final *judgment* of justice depends on the facts of responsibility, but the ultimate *principle* of justice (compensate if and only if it is not reasonable to hold disadvantaged people responsible for their plight) is independent of those facts.[52]

XI

I close with brief comments on several arguments to be found in the literature for regarding expensive tastes as outside the scope of compensatory justice.

> Argument (1): Since people choose which tastes to pursue, they have the opportunity to pursue others, and there is therefore no call to subsidize their expensive tastes.[53]

Argument (1) confuses the truth that you decide what tastes to pursue (that is, what objects of taste to acquire) with the falsehood (in the general case) that you decide what tastes to have. Different lifestyles are (within situational constraints) indeed chosen, but the preferences guiding those choices are not usually commensurately subject to the agent's control, and this has implications for justice.

Argument (1) is attributed to Dworkin by Kymlicka, among others, and with some textual basis: Dworkin offers noncongruent formulations on this matter, some of which more than suggest argument (1). (See pp. 927–31 for substantiation of that noncongruency claim.) But argument (1) is not Dworkin's considered position, which is that tastes are substantially unchosen – their bearer has little discretion with respect to their development – but that, for argument (4)-type reasons (the fact, barring special cases, that they are not repudiated) they should not be subsidized.

Argument (2): To subsidize some tastes, and, therefore, tax others would be to violate that neutrality across conceptions of the good which it is the duty of liberal states to maintain.

Richard Arneson has shown that argument (2) misapplies the concept of neutrality.[54] The policy of equality of opportunity for welfare is thoroughly neutral, even though it allows subsidy to those whose welfare costs more because of the structure of their tastes.

Argument (3): Whether or not you choose your tastes, it is part of your proper responsibility as an adult to cope with them. They are a private, not a public matter.

Argument (3) is suggested by this passage in Rawls's *Political Liberalism*:

. . . that we can take responsibility for our ends is part of what free citizens may expect of one another. Taking responsibility for our tastes and preferences, whether or not they have arisen from our actual choices, is a special case of that responsibility. As citizens with realized moral powers, this is something we must learn to deal with. . . . We don't say that because the preferences arose from upbringing and not from choice that [sic] society owes us compensation. Rather, it is a normal part of being human to cope with the preferences our upbringing leaves us with.[55]

But to the extent that this contention differs from argument (1), it is nothing but an appeal to popular opinion. People no doubt do think about the matter as Rawls says they do, but no justification of that familiar way of thinking is provided here. Why is the misfortune of expensive taste an essentially private matter when the misfortune of expensive mobility is not?

In my view, the Rawls passage gets things backward. The right argument says: it is extremely difficult and/or unacceptably intrusive to determine whether people's tastes are expensive *and* how much they are responsible for them; therefore the state cannot and/or should not seek to make determinations of that sort; therefore people must (on the whole) take responsibility for the costs of their tastes. But Rawls propounds the opposite argument, which says that *because* it is right to hold people responsible for their tastes, the state should not intervene here. (Compare the last paragraph of section VIII above).

Argument (4): It is incoherent for people with (at any rate judgmental) expensive tastes to represent them as handicaps or disadvantages that warrant subsidy. They would thereby be repudiating as a burden what they *ex hypothesi* affirm as a desideratum.

Argument (4), which is put by Dworkin, depends, I have argued, on failure to make pertinent distinctions. Those who need expensive things for satisfaction would not, indeed, normally regard their very desire for them as a handicap. What handicaps them is that they are expensive. And no repudiation of their desire for them, or dissociation from their own personality, attaches to their representation of that as a handicapping circumstance.

XII Coda

I have not in this essay argued positively for the view that I set out in "On the Currency," nor indeed, except in small part, for the (somewhat sketchy) descendant view which replaces it and which is described in section III above. What I have principally done is to refute one argument against equality of (opportunity for) welfare, namely, the expensive taste argument, and *pari passu*, to support one argument against equality of resources: that it is unfair to people who cannot reasonably be expected to pay the cost of satisfying their own expensive tastes.

I close with some remarks about the architectonic of Dworkin's magisterial 1981 diptych. It is of great importance to the apparent success of his case that he examines equality of welfare *first*. It is undoubtedly comprehensively demolished, in any *single one* of its interpretations,[56] so that the way then appears clear to propose equality of resources as an alternative. But the latter is not argued for positively, and it is also not subjected to the same test by counterexample that equality of welfare faced. And if one urges against equality of resources that people who are equal in resources will frequently be unequal in welfare in ways that look unfair, then Dworkin rules the objection out on the ground that equality of welfare has *already* been refuted.

But if that latter move appears sound, then that is only because of the *order* in which the competing equalities were examined. If Dworkin had considered equality of resources *first*, it would have faced counterexamples that could not be dismissed simply because of their welfarist character. (Note that the force of a welfare-inspired objection to equality of resources does not depend on an affirmation of (unqualified) *equality* of (opportunity for) welfare.)

It is because welfare equality can lead to crazy resource results and resource equality can lead to crazy welfare results that I was moved to float a pluralistic answer to the "Equality of What?" question. That question may be misframed, because, for example, distributive justice comes in uncombinable "spheres."[57] But *if*, what I increasingly doubt, Sen[58] and Dworkin's question, is sound, then I remain confident that a heterogeneous plurality is the answer.[59]

Appendix

In parallel efforts, Matthew Clayton and Andrew Williams have sought to refurbish the "endorsing judgment" objection to compensation for expensive taste.[60] Their argument, here reconstucted, stepwise, by me, can be stated with respect to the case of Paul and Fred (p. 923). Paul's unchosen recreational taste is for expensive photography, while Fred's is for inexpensive fishing. As I understand the Clayton/Williams argument, it has, when rendered fully explicit, four premises and a validly derived conclusion:

(1) Paul merits compensation only if he can ask Fred for compensation.
(2) Paul cannot ask Fred for compensation unless he thinks himself worse off than Fred.[61]
(3) Paul cannot think himself worse off than Fred unless he would rather be in Fred's shoes.[62]
(4) But Paul would not rather be in Fred's shoes. He does not want to love fishing rather than photography.
∴ Paul cannot ask Fred for compensation.

I shall not reject premise (1). I believe that it is false *at most* in the peculiar cases typified by Scanlon's suffering-welcoming worshiper,[63] and perhaps also in cases where people's false beliefs prejudice their welfare but at the same time make it incoherent for them to request relief. But such are not the cases that induce the disagreement between Dworkin and me.

"Worse off" in premise (2) is underspecified. It is true only if we add, at the end: worse off in some justice-sensitive respect. But the argument requires that we add: worse off, all things considered, since that is how "worse off" in premise (3) must be read. But when (2) is read in the required fashion, equality of resources itself contradicts (2). Underresourced people need not think, when demanding the compensation that Dworkin licenses, that they are all things considered worse off than relevant others. They need be worse off only in resources terms.[64] And Dworkin has no monopoly on the idea that you can be worse off precisely in the justice-sensitive respect without thinking yourself worse off *tout court*. There is a certain sort of welfare in which Paul is deficient: he fulfills his leisure needs less well that Fred does,[65] but he need not think himself comprehensively worse off even if in other respects he is on a par with Fred. If Dworkin's continuity test indeed implies premise (2),[66] under the "all things considered" interpretations of (2) that the Clayton/Williams argument requires, then so much the worse for the continuity test.

The very "shoes" metaphor that is used to formulate premise (3) exposes the falsehood of that premise. I can think myself better off in my shoes than I would be in yours while nevertheless thinking myself worse off in mine than you are in yours: yours fit your feet better than mine do. To speak without metaphor, (3) is relevantly false because I can think myself better off with my preferences ill-satisfied than I would be with your preferences well-satisfied. An important example of this structure of preference is provided by Justine Burley:

> . . . when it comes to reproductive capacities for example, the greater financial burdens imposed on women by virtue of their unique biological endowments probably will not be compensated on Dworkin's view. A woman's complaint is only deemed legitimate if there is penis envy, as it were. If she affirms her possession of female reproductive capacities, if, that is, she affirms the fact that she is a woman, we cannot say that there is any injustice along Dworkinian lines when *actually* there is. To demand that a woman *want to be a man* to support compensation is simply ridiculous.[67]

Finally, premise (4) is not always true. As I noted in sections V and VII, Paul can care *both* about the source of his satisfaction (he prefers it to be photography rather than fishing) *and* about the extent of his satisfaction. They are both, plainly, desiderata, and he can trade them off against each other (without thereby showing himself to be a buzz or a tick addict). Differently put: there is value *both* in pursuing what is more valuable *and* in getting whatever it is one pursues – one might have to add: as long as it has *some* value; but that wouldn't affect my argument against (4). And Paul might be sufficiently exercised by that second value that he indeed prefers to be in Fred's shoes.

Acknowledgements

I am grateful to Daniel Attas, John Baker, Alex Callinicos, Miriam Cohen Christofidis, Michèle Cohen, Ronald Dworkin, Cécile Fabre, Kerah Gordon-Solmon, Will Kymlicka, Michael Otsuka, Derek Parfit, John Roemer, Hillel Steiner, Zofia Stemplowska, Peter Vallentyne, Andrew Williams, Bernard Williams, and Erik Wright for helpful discussion. Some of the text in sections II, IV,

VIII, and IX of this chapter provide a modified version of pp. 83–8 of my "Expensive Tastes and Multiculturalism," in R. Bhargava, A. K. Bagchi, and R. Sudarshan (eds.), *Multiculturalism, Liberalism, and Democracy* (New Delhi: Oxford University Press, 1999), which is available on request from me.

Notes

1   Which is chapter 7 of Ronald Dworkin's *Sovereign Virtue* (Cambridge, MA: Harvard University Press, 2000). All pure page references in the present chapter are either to that book or to my "On the Currency": see the next endnote.

2   *Ethics*, vol. 99, 1989, pp. 906–44. Unless otherwise stated, all citations of my work in the present chapter are to that article. All such citations begin with the number "9," and are there unconfusable with citations of *Sovereign Virtue*.

3   Or, as I sometimes think it should be designated, "The 'Equality of What!?!' question."

4   There is a fleeting acknowledgement of that distinction by Dworkin at p. 289: he did not dwell on it because he rightly judged that it is substantially irrelevant to our principal disagreement and also because, as he has argued forcefully (but not to me convincingly) in a private communication, it is, in his view, an unsustainable distinction.

5   Originally published in *Philosophy and Public Affairs*, vol. 10, 1981, pp. 185–246, and reproduced as chapter 1 of *Sovereign Virtue*.

6   One good consequence of the publication in 1981 of "Equality of Welfare" is that a lot of hard work has since been devoted to such specification.

7   I believe that anything that can plausibly be considered welfare (enjoyment, preference-satisfaction, the objective value of a life, and maybe etcetera) is something that egalitarians have reason to care about, and that that also helps to explain the illusion that equality of (some undifferentiated) welfare supplies the right metric of equality. (The pluralism of equality of access to advantage embraces all the welfares that there are, and also nonwelfare advantages. For more on that pluralism, see the final paragraph of section XII).

8   I infer that Margaux is an unordinary wine because it is the one that David Niven ordinarily drank: see his various memoirs.

9   But not all. Under Dworkin's characterization of expensive taste (see the first paragraph of this section) a person who is burdened with an expensive taste needs more resources to reach the same level of welfare as another. But people may be afflicted by expensive taste not because given commodities provide them with smaller *increments* of welfare but because they are generally miserable. A wide menu of commodities is unlikely to extinguish their welfare deficits.

10   "A typical unrich bearer of an expensive musical taste would regard it as a piece of bad luck *not that he has the taste itself but that it happens to be expensive* (I emphasize those words because, simple as the distinction they formulate may be, it is one that undermines a lot of Dworkin's rhetoric about expensive tastes) . . . He can take responsibility for the taste, for his personality being that way, while reasonably denying responsibility for needing a lot of resources to satisfy it." (p. 927).

11   I take the distinction between the two types of taste (but not the word "brute," in this use of it) from Dworkin: see, e.g., pp. 290–1, and for more extended discussion, where they are called "volitional" and "critical" tastes, see pp. 216ff., 242ff.

12   I am here influenced by Terry Price's penetrating criticism of my "On the Currency" in section III of his "Egalitarian Justice, Luck, and the Costs of Chosen Ends," *American Philosophical Quarterly*, vol. 36, 1999, pp. 267–78. As Price points out, it might have been just someone's "bad luck that those preferences that he believed he ought to cultivate turned out to be [and might have happened to be from the start – G. A. C.] expensive preferences" (p. 272): thereby "the successful pursuit of the projects he finds important (and, so, *chose* to pursue), unlike the successful pursuit of the chosen projects of others, is frustrated by factors completely beyond his control" (p. 271).

13 That is, barring the special case where people *welcome* the fact that their taste is expensive – see pp. 937–8.

14 For a particularly compelling illustration of this point, see the quotation from Justine Burley at the end of this paper.

15 Dworkin calls such tastes "cravings": see pp. 81–3, and my response at pp. 925–7.

16 The exceptional case was mentioned in endnote 13 above.

17 The island, and the auction that occurs on it, are described at pp. 65ff.

18 That is, once we set aside as *ultra vires* their wish not to have the tastes they do *because* they are expensive: see the third paragraph of the present section.

19 In Susan Hurley's terms, we are here disputing the *currency* of distribution, not its *pattern*. See her *Justice, Luck, and Knowledge* (Cambridge, MA: Harvard University Press, 2003), chapter 6. Examples of the former are resources, welfare, capabilities, and so on. Examples of the latter are equality, "sufficiency," and maximin. (It might be thought curious that Dworkin, who is not a sufficientarian, but a relational egalitarian, should here introduce an element of sufficiency into his view, but that, as I said, is not the matter in issue between us).

20 For example, for the state of their cerebral cortices, rather than for "gourmand syndrome" as such: see the epigraph to this chapter.

21 Bernard Williams suggested to me (personal communication, December 4, 2002) that the relevant difference between handicaps (ordinarily so called) and satisfaction-reducing expensive tastes might be "between giving up or not getting something nice as opposed to having to put up with or being subjected to something nasty." I think that there is a lot of plausibility in that, but it is not a thought that a *relational* egalitarian like Dworkin can exploit in the present polemic, since equalizing, as opposed to providing some sort of sufficiency, or a decent level of life, is indifferent to any distinction that may obtain between the less pleasant and the more nasty.

22 See p. 289. I take up this disagreement in section XI.

23 I use parentheses to mark off a feature of the books that plays no role in the preference for them under specification here.

24 For more on which, see section VII.

25 There are no doubt other reasons for the policy: perhaps we charge no or low fees to everyone for the perfectionist reason that we approve of education; or we charge the same fee to all for the sake of administrative simplicity; or low fees have a public good justification (because educated people are a boon to others); and so on. But what requires focus here is what we should think of a library that resolved to charge according to the book's cost: would we not regard that as, *inter* whatever *alia*, *unfair*?

26 I here apply the revision in my view that I described in section III.

27 See section VI.

28 Dworkin himself points out (p. 30) that people might prefer pursuing preferences for what they judge to be inferior things that they are likely to fulfill to pursuing preferences whose objects they regard as superior.

29 See the final paragraph of the introductory section above.

30 A punctiliously fair-minded Palladian majority might make half the architecture Gothic, so that everyone sees what they like half the time.

31 Dworkin represents the auction, and the market more generally, as inducing the result that what I pay for the elements in my bundle represents the costs to others of my choices. And so it may do, in *money* (or clamshell) terms. But the intuitive force of the idea arguably depends on an interpretation of cost in *welfare* terms. If so, Dworkin is not entitled to invoke that intuitive force.

32 *Multicultural Citizenship* (Oxford: Oxford University Press, 1995), p. 109.

33 It is not I but Dworkin who says that Louis "sets out deliberately to cultivate" champagne tastes (p. 49: the point receives special emphasis on p. 50). Accordingly, "even if we accepted," in the third sentence of the text quoted above, is out of order: "*deliberately* cultivated expensive taste" denotes no invention of mine.

34 He also has some subsidiary arguments, to which I have just replied, against my *real* (and misnamed
    "new") argument, to wit, the analogy with majority voting, the "self-undermining" claim, and a par-
    ticular spin on "luck."
35 See the Appendix for a variant understanding of Dworkin's argument which merits independent con-
    sideration.
36 Namely, "strategy 3":

> This final strategy is to revise the view I have defended, as follows. Instead of saying, "compensate for
> disadvantages which are not traceable to the subject's choice," say, "compensate for disadvantages which
> are not traceable to the subject's choice *and* which the subject would choose not to suffer from." The
> revisionary element is the second clause. In the revised view, choice appears at two levels, actual and coun-
> terfactual. (p. 937).

37 See his *What We Owe to Each Other* (Cambridge, MA: Harvard University Press, 1999), chapter 3,
    section IV.
38 The qualification "primary" is necessary because it is reasonable to suppose that people commonly (thus
    I do, even if Socrates didn't: see p. 12 above) *also* have some second-order concern as to whether or not
    their preferences *whatever they may be* are satisfied. You don't have to believe any ridiculous buzz/tick
    metaphysic to appreciate that measured truth.
39 See the contemptuous reference to preoccupation with "bank account wealth" at p. 107.
40 Cf. pp. 19–20: "We may believe that genuine equality requires that people be made equal in their success
    (or enjoyment) without believing that essential well-being, properly understood, is just a matter of
    success (or enjoyment)."
41 "[T]he idea of an economic market, as a device for setting prices for a vast variety of goods and
    services, must be at the center of any attractive theoretical development of equality of resources"
    (p. 66).
42 I ignore, once again, Dworkin's (effective) volte-face on brute tastes: see section IV.
43 See section III.
44 I invoke here the will/constitution distinction that I made at p. 6 above.
45 Which is a topic that I explore in "Expensive Tastes and Multiculturalism," op. cit.
46 Or claimed: see the discussion in section IV.
47 Compare and contrast Richard Arneson's person who voluntarily cultivates "a preference for spending
    [her] leisure hours driving about in [her] car at a time when gas is cheap, when it is unforeseeable that
    the price of gas will later skyrocket" ("Liberalism, Distributive Subjectivism, and Equal Opportunity
    for Welfare," *Philosophy and Public Affairs*, vol. 19, 1990, pp. 159–94; quote p. 186.)
48 See the end of third paragraph of section II.
49 See the beginning of section IV.
50 Text of Oxford seminar talk, January 24, 1994, and cf. p. 289.
51 It might be objected that I here support a reactionary view to the effect that people whose tastes are
    cheap, people who get satisfaction from modest things, should not be permitted, or, at any rate encour-
    aged, to expand their horizons: the Etonian steak lover gets his steak because he needs it, but the street
    boy is condemned to eternal hamburger. My reply to the objection is that different dimensions of justice
    tell against one another here. It is indeed an injustice that A's scope for development is worse than B's,
    but it remains an independent injustice if A has the good fortune, lacking to B, of access to cheap
    contentment.
52 See, further, my "Facts and Principles," *Philosophy and Public Affairs*, vol. 31(3), 2003. If, as I think he
    does, Dworkin means, by "determinism," "hard determinism," then I agree with him that "we all reject
    determinism, all the time," but I do not think that our affirmation or rejection of hard determinism has
    any bearing at the deepest level of *normative* philosophy. (The quotation from Dworkin appears at p.
    107 of his "Sovereign Virtue Revisited," *Ethics*, vol. 113, 2002, pp. 106–43, and see ibid., pp. 118–19
    for evidence that he means "hard determinism" in particular (whether or not he thinks that soft deter-

minism is coherent). For my own rejection of hard determinism, see p. 76, fn. 14 of my "Why not Socialism?," in Edward Broadbent (ed.), *Democratic Equality* (Toronto: University of Toronto Press, 2001, pp. 58–78).

53 I discern argument (1) at p. 369 of John Rawls's "Social Unity and Primary Goods," in his *Collected Papers* (Cambridge, MA: Harvard University Press, 1999). See my p. 913 *et circa*, for discussion of the Rawls text.

54 See his "Liberalism, Distributive Subjectivism, and Equal Opportunity for Welfare," op. cit.

55 *Political Liberalism* (New York: Columbia University Press, 1993), p. 185.

56 Dworkin also rejects an "ecumenical" view under which egalitarianism has regard to *several* types of welfare (pp. 47–8). I do not find his reasons for rejecting it cogent, but saying why would take us too far afield.

57 Cf. Michael Walzer, *Spheres of Justice* (New York: Basic Books, 1983). Note that a belief that the goods that figure in distributive justice cannot be aggregated implies neither Walzer's particular differentiation of such goods nor his relativizing view that goods count as such in virtue of "social meanings."

58 Amartya Sen, "Equality of What?" in Sterling McMurrin (ed.), *The Tanner Lectures on Human Values*, vol. 1 (Cambridge, UK: Cambridge University Press, 1980).

59 I expressed doubt at p. 921 about my own answer to the question, because of its awkward pluralism. I remain uncertain as to whether that pluralism is sustainable, and, hence, whether the Sen/Dworkin question *is* sound. A tentative defense of the pluralism is available in a document called "Afterword to chapters XI and XII," which I can supply on request.

60 Matthew Clayton, "The Resources of Liberal Equality," *Imprints*, vol. 5(1), 2000, pp. 63–84; Andrew Williams, "Equality for the Ambitious," *Philosophical Quarterly*, vol. 53 (208), 2002, pp. 377–89.

61 Williams: "the basic idea underlying the continuity test is that a political community should regard certain conditions as disadvantaging some of its members only if those members' own views about what it is to live well also imply that those conditions disadvantage them" (p. 387). Cf. Clayton, op. cit., p. 77.

62 Clayton: ". . . an individual can plausibly claim that she is less advantaged than another in virtue of having a physical impairment or taste only if she would prefer to have the other's physical resources or taste" (op. cit., p. 75; cf. Williams, op. cit., p. 379).

63 See pp. 937–8. Williams focuses too much on this bizarre example: Paul/Fred is the significant case.

64 Recall Dworkin's refutation of Sen's objection to equality of resources: see p. 16 above.

65 *Even if* – what need not be true: see the comment below on premise (4) – he prefers having those needs and having them less well satisfied than having Fred's needs, better satisfied.

66 See endnote 61 above.

67 Justine Burley, private communication, May 1995.

2

Talent, Slavery, and Envy

Miriam Cohen Christofidis

Many egalitarians are, I believe, unjustifiably biased towards the interests of the talented. The general goal of these egalitarians is to eliminate those inequalities that derive from morally arbitrary factors, by improving the position of the worst off. And they include, among these arbitrary factors, the distribution of natural talents. But in developing their theories, they do not remain true to those beliefs, since they give to the talented various unfair advantages.

Such an objection has been made by Ronald Dworkin against John Rawls's theory of justice. Rawls famously argued that, given the arbitrary nature of the natural lottery, egalitarians should aim to redistribute the benefits that talents bring. Dworkin objects that Rawls's theory fails to achieve this goal since it is not endowment-insensitive:[1] there is no compensation for those who suffer undeserved natural disadvantages. Unlike Rawls, Dworkin insists that there should be such compensation. But, as I shall argue here, Dworkin's own theory fails to achieve this goal. He assigns an unacceptably higher weight to the interests of those who are more talented, both when he rejects a form of redistribution because it would lead to what he calls "slavery of the talented," and when he favors a distributive regime that violates his "envy test" for equality by having the untalented envy the talented, even though he rejects more egalitarian regimes on the ground that they violate the envy test because they have the talented envying the untalented.

A division of resources is unequal, Dworkin says, if anyone would prefer someone else's bundle of resources to his or her own: this is his "envy test" criterion for equality. In the first section of this paper, I criticize Dworkin's claim that the talented would envy the untalented in a "talent auction" and that such a scheme would lead to the slavery of the talented in particular. In section II, I look at some ways in which the talent auction is underdescribed and comment on the results for the talented under different descriptions of it. In section III, I discuss Dworkin's alternative to the talent auction – his insurance scheme. I argue that there is no justification for Dworkin's view that maintaining a lower level of insurance premiums, and, consequently, of payouts to the untalented, is necessary in order to protect the talented from slavery, and so to avoid failure of the envy test. This is because (1) the untalented are as much at risk of being "enslaved" by such a move as are the talented under high premium levels, and (2) Dworkin's own solution (as he acknowledges, himself) results in a failure of the envy test, therefore he has no grounds for preferring lower premiums on the basis that under higher insurance premiums the envy test would fail because the talented would envy the untalented. Moreover, and more damagingly, he has established no grounds for preferring the hypothetical insurance scheme to the talent auction. I conclude that Dworkin's deviation from the "envy test" criterion results in an inequality between the talented and the untalented which cannot be justified in egalitarian terms.[2]

To achieve the desired "envy-free" result, Dworkin designs an auction in which immigrants bid for all the assets on an island, using an initial and equal endowment of clamshells which is distributed to them. (The clamshells are worthless except as a means of bidding for the island's resources.) If the auction works efficiently, and if everyone has equal talents and equal luck, then the result of the auction will be equality, in the stated sense: that is to say, no one will prefer anyone else's bundle. (If someone did envy another's bundle then the auction could be run again until the result was envy-free.) This result will also be Pareto-efficient: no one could be made better off without someone else being made worse off. However, the unequal distribution of natural endowments (i.e., abilities, talents, and other attributes such as beauty) that can be used to make money, leads to inequalities that are not rectified by the auction, and that is unacceptable to Dworkin from the standpoint of justice.

As stated above, Dworkin wants to improve on Rawls's theory: he seeks a more endowment-insensitive account of distributive justice. He thinks, as does Rawls, that natural endowments are arbitrary from a moral point of view. But Dworkin thinks that natural inequalities of endowment, including differences in ability that would produce differences in income, should be compensated for, whereas Rawls does not think of justice in terms of compensation: the difference principle is not aimed at balancing compensation. Dworkin also thinks that differences in income that reflect differences in preference and choice should not be reduced: a fair distribution should be "ambition-sensitive." We can make sense of this in terms of the envy test: I can prefer the talent bundle of someone who is born much more talented than myself, but I manifestly cannot prefer the talent bundle of someone whose bundle is the same as mine. True, in virtue of working hard, that person might be able to afford to have nice things, things that I would like to have, but, *ex hypothesi*, I too was equally able to work hard, and thereby acquire those things, so I cannot reasonably object to *this* inequality between us.

Dworkin attempts to respect the requirements of both ambition sensitivity and endowment insensitivity. To satisfy the second requirement, he treats physical and mental abilities (considered, initially, in themselves, that is, apart from their role in production) as part of a person's bundle of resources. To compensate for shortfalls in such abilities, for example physical and mental defects, Dworkin proposes an insurance mechanism,[3] which is intended to have the effect that cases of disadvantage are a matter of option luck rather than brute luck.[4]

We can agree that if all people had an equal risk of suffering some catastrophe that would leave them handicapped, and if everyone knew what its probability was and had the opportunity to insure against that risk, then any handicaps that ensued would not upset equality of resources. The envy test would be satisfied. However, even with such an insurance policy in place, equality of resources would be disturbed by production and trade, since people vary in their income-producing talents. To use Dworkin's example (p. 304), if an immigrant is especially proficient at producing tomatoes, he might trade his surplus for more than anyone else could acquire, in which case others will envy, or prefer to have, his bundle of resources, and the envy test will fail, for people of low talent will envy those with more. So Dworkin has to find a way of preventing inequalities in talent from upsetting equality of resources. Eventually he does so through an extension of the insurance scheme originally designed to cope with what he calls "handicaps" (the term being used in a technical sense). But I would now like to criticize Dworkin's dismissal of an alternative solution to the problem of talent inequality.

I

The rejected proposal is that the labor of the islanders themselves be included in the set of resources to be auctioned. I shall call this "the labor auction." The proposal involves each person bidding for the right to control part or all of his or her own labor and that of others. Everyone would then have an equal opportunity to purchase the right to control the special skills of particularly talented islanders and so, too, the benefits of having those skills. As a result, so Dworkin says, "except in unusual cases, since people begin with equal resources for bidding, each agent would bid enough to secure his own labor" (p. 311). In that case each person would lose the number of clamshells from his or her bundle which corresponds to what he or she could produce, and inequality of talent would thereby be neutralized. I shall return to a discussion of this claim below.

Dworkin dismisses the suggested labor-auction solution because, as he writes: "[T]he principle that people should not be penalized for talent is part of the same principle we relied on in rejecting the apparently opposite idea, that people should be allowed to retain the benefits of superior talent. The envy test forbids both of these results" (p. 312). But we need to see why Dworkin thinks that the labor auction fails the envy test. He says that the result of the auction would be

> that each would have to spend his life in close to the commercially most profitable manner he could, or, at least if he is talented, suffer some very serious deprivation if he did not. For since Adrian, for example, is able to produce prodigious income from farming, others would be willing to bid a large amount to have the right to his labor and the vegetables thereof, and if he outbids them, but chooses to write indifferent poetry instead of farming full time, he will then have spent a large part of his initial endowment on a right that will bring him little financial benefit. This is indeed the slavery of the talented. (pp. 311–12)

For example, Dworkin claims (p. 312) that "if talented Adrian is required to purchase leisure time or the right to a less productive occupation at the cost of other resources, then Adrian will envy Claude's package" (Claude being an untalented person). Adrian will envy Claude, Dworkin claims, because Adrian will be a slave.

What Dworkin calls "slavery," however, should actually be called *restricted choice*. A situation in which someone has to choose between being very poor and being a slave is a situation of severely restricted choice, but the fact that the options are so dire does not mean that such a person is *already* a slave. It might be objected that Dworkin is really only talking about the talented being slaves *to their talents* and not being slaves *simpliciter*. But that would support my point that they are not really slaves. Dworkin is using the term "slavery" loosely if it is only meant to apply to a relation between the talented and certain aspects of their lives. If this is what he means, then the accusation that the labor auction results in slavery loses the force that Dworkin needs it to have in order to justify the special treatment that he gives to the talented, since being a slave to one's talents is not obviously unjust, whereas being a slave *simpliciter* is. Having suggested that Dworkin's "slavery" terminology is misused, I shall, for the greater part of this paper, adopt that terminology: "slavery" will mean "severely restricted choice."

Dworkin's dismissal of the proposal to throw labor into the auction is not, I shall argue, well founded. To begin with, it is unclear why Dworkin believes that the fact that Adrian will have spent a large portion of his initial endowment on a right that will bring him little financial benefit is a criticism of the proposal in question. Whereas having to work at one's most profitable occupation to avoid serious deprivation is clearly bad, it is not clearly bad, in this context, that Adrian would get little financial benefit from self-purchase, or that he would not have the opportunity to write indifferent poetry without sacrificing financial benefit. It is important to remember that Dworkin's egalitarian concern is not with how the process of redistribution might treat people differently. Rather it is with the question of whether or not that process renders people's circumstances equal. Accordingly, if the talented are disadvantaged in that process, that is only bad if they end up worse off than the less talented. We are trying, after all, to avoid inequalities between Adrian and Claude that would cause failure of the envy test. It is to be expected, therefore, that in order to make Claude better off the scheme will make Adrian worse off than he would otherwise have been.

Secondly, we had not been led to think that Dworkin believes that people should get financial benefit from some sort of right of self-ownership.[5] In other words, the middle sentence of the extract above ("For since Adrian . . . financial benefit") has no evaluative force as a criticism of the labor auction unless we already believe that it is wrong that, though people spend a large part of their initial endowment, they get little financial gain. What Dworkin should instead be concerned with is whether Adrian would *then* have the same amount of resources as Claude, with abilities included among the resources. We can tell whether that is so, in the relevant sense, from the envy test. The envy test applies to the amount of resources that people come to have. It does not apply to the procedure by which the redistribution against talent inequalities occurs, or to comparisons between people's conditions before and after that procedure has been applied, which *should*, for Dworkin, be irrelevant.

Thirdly, I have suggested that, on the basis of what Dworkin actually says, it is not clear either that the talented would suffer slavery in the labor auction or that they would envy the untalented for any other reason. Naturally, Dworkin does not need to show that every talented islander would envy every untalented one, in order to claim that the labor auction is unfair to the talented. Nor is it enough for him to show that one talented person would envy some untalented people under some circumstances in the labor auction. In very few interesting cases would the envy test be passed completely, and Dworkin himself allows that there may be no distributions under which it would be passed. Therefore, for the test to be useful, we need to make more complex assessments of how it would apply to different policy proposals. For example, we need to look at how many people of either group envy other people, and how much ground there is for their envy. This complicates the envy test criterion in a way that Dworkin does not acknowledge that it should be complicated. However, although it is harder to assess the results of the more complicated test, such assessment would be much more valuable and interesting for an egalitarian. Furthermore, we face such complications if we want to assess the relative merits of the labor auction and the insurance mechanism. In its simple Dworkinian form, the test is violated in both. I shall discuss these issues in further detail below. At present, and as a partial contribution to envy test assessment of the labor auction, I shall suggest that if we fill out Dworkin's labor-auction scenario, then we can indeed identify *a* way in which Adrian will necessarily be worse off than Claude if labor is thrown into the auction. But we must bear in mind that, to show that the hypothetical auction with the labor auction is not the best egalitarian distribution available, it does not suffice to show that all or even most of the talented would always envy the untalented in the labor auction.

I shall present some figures to illustrate why Dworkin might think that Adrian will envy Claude. Adrian and Claude each have 100 clamshells to spend per day.[6] The highest someone would be prepared to pay for Adrian's labor is 80 shells. This means that Adrian will have to pay 80 if he wants to own himself, after which he would be left with only 20. Suppose also that Claude's value to the highest bidder is 30 shells. Consequently, for him to own himself he has to pay 30. He can own himself and still be left with 70. Now imagine that the cost of avoiding what Dworkin calls "serious deprivation" is 90, so that the situation is as follows:[7]

	Claude	Adrian
Shell value of ability to other people	30	80
Shells in hand after self-purchase	70	20
Shells required to avoid serious deprivation	90	90
Shell value of what they must produce to avoid serious deprivation	20	70

From this chart we can work out what Adrian and Claude will be able to produce, respectively, per hour of labor, on the reasonable assumption that each can work the same number of hours per day. Let us suppose that each can work eight hours. It would follow that Claude can produce three and three-quarter units of shell value per hour, and Adrian 10, so that Claude must work five and one-third hours a day and Adrian seven hours a day to avoid serious deprivation. It is, moreover, a fact that whatever values we put into such a chart, as long as Adrian is worth more than Claude he will have to work more hours in order to reach subsistence level than Claude will.[8] And there is indeed a relation between the number of hours one is required to work and occupational choice. If someone has to work more hours or earn more money, they have less occupational choice.

Now, Dworkin's claim is that Adrian will have to work at his most lucrative occupation to avoid serious deprivation and Claude will not. But, although, as we have seen, Adrian will have to work more hours than Claude, so that he will have fewer hours of leisure, he will not *necessarily* have to "spend his life in close to the most commercially profitable manner he could" since he does still have some free time, which means that he might be able to take a less productive, but preferred occupation, if he works more hours. Of course the amount of free time that either would have would be affected by the figures that go into the equation. In the present case there is not much free time for Adrian. But the difference in the amounts of free time the two have is not significant enough to constitute a difference between being enslaved (and/or being forced) or not.

I am in the course of demonstrating that, under the figures given in the example above, it is unclear that Adrian will envy Claude. I remarked above that in an assessment of the envy test one needs to show more than that some people will envy others under certain circumstances and in certain ways. One needs to show how many people would envy how many other people and what the basis of that envy is. Accordingly, it is not enough for Dworkin to show that some, or even all, of the talented would envy some or all of the untalented under a range of plausible cases. He needs to show that there is not an equally plausible range of cases in which the envy goes the other way around. And even if he can show that, he still needs to show that the number of talented people who envy the untalented in the labor auction, and the strength of the ground for their doing so, lead to a more serious failure of the envy test than any other possible solutions to inequality do.

There are some cases in which, undeniably, a talented person would envy a less talented one. Imagine John who, like Adrian, wants to write indifferent poetry (assume they have exactly the same preferences). But John does not have a highly valued talent. So John does not have to spend as much of his initial endowment as Adrian does. Adrian now envies John's bundle because of his (Adrian's) natural endowment.

This is a clear case in Dworkin's favor. It is an example where the person with more talent would indeed envy the person with less talent. And this case would certainly need to be included in the kind of assessment I have suggested is necessary to evaluate the relative failures of the envy test under different systems. In this paper, the particularly interesting comparison is between the failure of the envy test in the labor auction and its failure under the insurance mechanism. So we would need to ask how likely it would be that people with different talents would have exactly the same preferences, how common those cases would be, what the intensity of the envy would be in those cases, what the envy derives from, and so on. I am not making a claim about the results of such an assessment. I am suggesting merely that, although cases where the talented would envy the untalented in the labor auction support Dworkin, they do not settle any of the important contested issues.

As we have seen, Dworkin is unclear as to what the slavery claim exactly depends on. He does not cite the conclusion drawn from the equation, namely that Adrian will always have to work more hours than Claude to avoid serious deprivation, as his reason for saying that Adrian will be enslaved if labor is thrown into the auction. My chart does, however, support his claim that Adrian will envy Claude's bundle. But it does not prove it, and to affirm the desired conclusion on this basis would be too swift. First, it is not obvious that it is less likely that Claude will have to work at his most lucrative occupation to avoid serious deprivation, although it is true that if he does he will have to do so for fewer hours than the number Adrian has to work at his for. So the alleged asymmetry in their situations is not there. Secondly, even if Claude does not have to work at his most lucrative occupation, it is not obvious that Adrian will envy Claude's (whole) package. For that would require the assumption that the only possible object of envy in the bundle is the number of hours that one is required to work, or, in other words, how much leisure time is available to a person. But, as we shall see, there are other relevant aspects of their bundles that we have not yet considered.

We might ask how much the comparative situations of the untalented and the talented would change if we varied the values of the variables in the chart that I have constructed. These variables are: the shell value of Adrian's labor, that of Claude's, the level needed in order to avoid serious deprivation, and the number of shells had in the beginning. The results of varying the first two variables are quite clear. The more Adrian is worth, the more hours he will have to work in order to avoid serious deprivation, and the same goes for Claude. The only point of interest for the envy test is the gap between the two of them. The level needed to avoid serious deprivation is a very important variable. Using the figures in my chart we can see that if we make the level of resources required to avoid serious deprivation high, then the talented will have to work nearly all their hours to avoid serious deprivation, but the untalented will then only have to work marginally fewer hours to avoid serious deprivation and, before we make conjectures about envy, we must keep in mind other values, such as the appealingness of different sets of occupational choices. It is important, in this connection, that the difference between the number of hours they must each work to avoid serious deprivation is relatively small by comparison with that huge difference in their earning power. Considering the common association between talent and a fulfilling occupation, it is questionable whether the bonus to those like Claude of having to work slightly less time will often outweigh the huge difference in talent. It may be objected that Adrian might not want to be a farmer but wants instead to write indifferent poetry, so he does not see being a farmer as a fulfilling occupation. However, it is unclear that there is any kind of society where someone would make a living out of writing indifferent poetry. Granted, farming may not be fulfilling, but it is still more fulfilling than scaring crows, which might be what Claude's most lucrative occupation is. The point is that, for relevant comparisons, we must keep in mind what the occupations would be in the bundles. Writing indifferent poetry would never be a lucrative occupation, it would only be something a very untalented person would have time to do, and we need to ask how plausible it is that Adrian would prefer the situation of that untalented person. It is true that not all talent-requiring occupations are fulfilling but they are likely to be more fulfilling than nontalent-requiring occupations (as opposed to pastimes).

As the level of resources required to avoid serious deprivation gets lower, life becomes freer for both. There will be a point where the talented have to work a little but the untalented do not have to work at all because they have enough resources left after the auction to avoid serious deprivation without working. But, where the talented only have to work very little, they might value their work, and therefore prefer working to having the choice not to work at all. (Remember that for the talented to envy the untalented they must prefer to have the talents *and* the choices of the untalented.) Given certain assumptions, to which I shall return below, the most extreme figures that could occupy the variables in the chart will be where Adrian is worth 100 shells to everybody and Claude is worth none. In that case, if the level needed to avoid serious deprivation is 100, then Adrian will have to work all his hours to survive and Claude will not have to work at all. But Claude would have to be severely disabled, and Adrian as talented as possible, for these figures to hold. Who would envy whose package in that case? The answer is at best unclear.

It might be objected that it is illegitimate to count the fulfillingness of an occupation as significant within a resource theory of equality, and that I therefore cannot invoke it in order to show that Adrian might not envy Claude. But it is Dworkin who includes occupation in the bundle of resources, and it is unclear how occupation can be an object of envy if we are not allowed to consider the fulfillingness of occupations.[9] To exclude which occupations are available would be arbitrary, in that such a circumstance is surely relevant for the envy test. Including it, however, does seem to take us into the territory of welfare. That might be a problem for a theory that purports to be purely resourcist, but I shall not discuss this point further here. For the purposes of this chapter, I shall assume that Dworkin needs to include occupation in the bundle and that comparisons of fulfillingness of occupations are therefore necessarily involved when bundles are compared for the purposes of a properly complicated envy test.

We can next note that if both Adrian and Claude enjoy their work and like income they will each work for eight hours a day. If they both do this then they will both get the same amount above serious deprivation, namely, 10 extra. Then the only difference would be that they pass the level of serious deprivation at different times, Adrian only after seven hours and Claude after five and one-third. But this seems entirely insignificant if, as is true, they both end up in the same condition in the end. If we both want to get to the cinema and both of our journeys (as a result of different modes of transport and different distances) take half an hour, I will not envy you because you pass the postbox sooner than I do, unless I am so mean-minded that I care that you *would* have reached the postbox sooner *if* we had both wanted only to post letters.

The position is more complicated when Adrian and Claude do not both want to work for 10 hours. It is true that if all they want to do is work as little as possible, then Claude is better off, but we cannot assume that such is always (or even ever) the case. They would only want that in the highly specific and unusual cases where neither cares *what* kind of work he does. For example, if I want to get to the cinema in time for the film which starts in one hour, I may prefer to count envelopes for one hour than to do two hours of interesting legal work on a law case, but that is because in this special case the leisure activity has special weight and the occupations are temporary anyway. A lifetime of five and one-third hours a day of counting envelopes is not obviously preferable to seven a day of being a lawyer. So Adrian may not envy Claude's bundle, even though

Claude has a few extra hours a day for leisure, given what the occupations available to Claude may be.

It might be said that I have missed the point because it is not Claude's free hours that Adrian envies but the fact that they enable him to have occupational choice. Let us therefore examine that different suggestion.

For Claude to end up with occupational choice in contrast to Adrian, there must be something available to Claude which is less remunerative than his most lucrative occupation. Imagine that Claude's most lucrative occupation is acting as a scarecrow, which he hates doing because it is so tedious. There simply may not be anything else less remunerative available to him for him to be able to avoid that job entirely, so that he has to do that for n hours, whereas Adrian is, say, a concert pianist for n + m hours. It is, again, not obvious that Adrian will envy Claude's package, which includes occupation, especially in the light of the fact that Claude may be able to do very little in his free time anyway. He may not be able to write even indifferent poetry.

Now imagine that there is something less remunerative than scaring crows (but remunerative enough) available to Claude, for example, looking at the ocean to check for invaders. Claude might find this more boring still, but whether he does or does not, it is unlikely that Adrian will envy him, and even if Claude did prefer looking at the ocean, his range of options is so undesirable that the occupational choice he is presented with is still not one that Adrian is likely to envy. The point is that occupational choice, just as such, is not worth so much that any amount of it out-weighs whatever may be the direness of the options it provides.[10]

II

Leaving aside the particulars of the chart, I would now like to raise two further points about the description of the auction. This section assesses the plausibility of including labor in the auction independently from Dworkin's criticisms of doing so. The first point concerns Dworkin's claim that "except in unusual cases, since people begin with equal resources for bidding, each agent would bid enough to secure his own labor" (p. 311). Now the fact that people begin with equal resources does not in itself entail that all agents would be able to bid enough to secure their own labor. For that to be true, it is also necessary that each person would be able to afford to do so, and the fact that everyone has the same number of clamshells does not establish that. If they get 100 clamshells per day, then those who can produce more than 100 clamshells' worth of resources per day would not be able to buy themselves (unless they were allowed to pay less than they were worth). So Dworkin has not shown that people would even be *able* to purchase their own labor, let alone that they actually would do so, even though the structure of the quoted sentence implies that he thinks he has shown that.

As these remarks suggest, Dworkin's description of the labor auction is simplified in a way that avoids certain important issues. Dworkin unjustifiably assumes, what is false, that purchasing oneself will almost always be possible: his wording implies that he assumes that, since he says that people will be able to self-purchase *because* everyone starts with the same number of clamshells. One of two conditions must hold for Dworkin's unjustified assumption to be true: first, it must be the case that no one's labor can be worth more than the number of clamshells he or she has to bid with. The second condition is that coalitions of purchasers are not allowed, so that a person cannot be outbid by a coalition. If it were the case both that a person's labor could be worth more than 100 clamshells, and that coalitions were allowed, then it would be false that all people could buy their own labor.

It might be asked why this is important, since all thought experiments restrict circumstances in an artificial way. But the implications of Dworkin's restriction are relevant to the assessment of including labor in the auction. The first suggestion, that no one is worth more than the number of clamshells each immigrant has, is entirely implausible. The idea that we can arbitrarily fix the value of goods so that people can afford them is economically infeasible. Why might someone not be worth 300 shells? (Imagine that Wilt Chamberlain or Pablo Picasso is one of the immigrants.) Still, we might accept that people can be worth more than 100 clamshells but that only a total of 100 clamshells can be bid for any one person's labor. Yet if we admit that, and maintain a prohibition on purchaser coalitions, then the talented will be able to buy themselves at a rate, namely 100, which is much lower than what they are worth, and so can earn, namely 300, and then the auction will dramatically fail to redistribute. The only way around the problem is to say that in the auction scenario people are not worth more than 100 clamshells but that ducks the real and serious problem for egalitarians of how to redistribute against massively differential earning power.

If coalitions are allowed, then people would not necessarily be able to buy their own labor. If we accept that some people are bound to be worth more than 100 clamshells, then those very talented people really will be slaves since they will have no possibility of buying their labor and all of their labor will be directed by a coalition of others. The empirically plausible possibility that the labor of some talented people will be worth more clamshells than they start out with shows that Dworkin restricts his proposal in a way that avoids a serious problem. If we accept what Dworkin says about people buying their own labor, then the way in which the proposal is artificial happens to protect the interests of the talented, since unless we claim, implausibly, that no one could be worth more than 100 clamshells, the very talented will do extra specially well out of the situation. If the two required conditions did not obtain, then, if someone's labor was worth an enormous amount, and coalitions were allowed, then that person would not be able to outbid all coalitions in order to own his or her own labor. The only options for such people would be partial or full (genuine) slavery: it would be partial if they joined a coalition that bought their labor. So the disjunction of the two conditions is needed both to protect the talented from slavery and to prevent them from being extravagantly well off.

Stating that most people will be buying their own labor simply avoids problems that are raised by including labor in the auction. If we are going to reject labor in the auction, we need a proper description of how it would work. Without an answer to the questions about coalitions and value of labor, we cannot make an assessment of whether the talented, or anyone else for that matter, would be enslaved. As I have said, some solutions make the talented much better off than others, and fail to redistribute. Other solutions seem to end in actual slavery. But this will be because they *cannot* buy their labor, and not that they can but have to pay a high price for it. Dworkin's claim that the talented would be enslaved under the labor auction is importantly different from my own. I suggest that under certain conditions the talented would be enslaved, namely, when they could not afford to buy their own labor because their labor costs more than the number of clamshells they have. Dworkin denies these conditions hold. Therefore our claims about the possibility of enslavement of the talented are importantly different. Dworkin says that the talented will be slaves precisely because they *will* buy their labor and will have to pay a lot for it. I do not think that Dworkin is deliberately trying to protect the talented when he assumes that they can buy themselves, but that is the result of the two conditions his assumption relies on. It is interesting to note, however, that a similar result, namely that the talented are protected, is achieved in his own hypothetical insurance scheme. Dworkin argues that it would be irrational to insure against not being able to earn at very high levels of income. He also argues that everyone would insure at the same level. The result of this is that the very talented are able to pay insurance premiums lower than the amount at which they can earn. In effect they have the kind of surplus of access to resources that I have claimed they would have if they were worth 300 clamshells but only had to pay 100 to own their own labor. I return to this point in section III.

To sum up what we have seen thus far: it is not at all clear that, in the example of the chart, and other plausible ones, there will be a tendency for the talented to envy the untalented. Dworkin cannot reject the proposal to throw labor into the auction on the grounds he does, namely, failure of the envy test, in the case of the talented, without making the comparisons I have suggested need to be included in an assessment of the envy test. To make a correct assessment of where the envy test criterion would not be satisfied we need to include not only occupation in the bundle, but also the parties' preferences across leisure time, rewarding career, and monetary resources. Depending on the relative weight given to each of these, the outcome of the envy test will be different. Dworkin gives special weight to the fact that the talented will get little financial reward from self-purchase and we can infer that if he addressed my chart, he would find it particularly objectionable that the talented would have to work for more hours than the untalented in order to avoid serious deprivation. But these special concerns reflect an entirely unwarranted special interest in the outcome for the talented, as against that for the untalented.

Furthermore, even if Dworkin thought that the result of a comprehensive assessment which took into account how many people envy how many others, and how much, was that some or all of the talented would, on the whole, envy some or all of the untalented, he could still not conclude that the labor auction should be rejected on grounds of failure of the envy test, in advance of comparisons with failures of the envy test under alternative systems. I have argued that Dworkin is mistaken that the talented would necessarily envy the untalented if labor were included in the auction (since the talented do not necessarily do worse from such an inclusion once we consider factors other than the number of hours of work required to ensure subsistence). However, even if I am wrong about that, it is not clear that Dworkin can reject the addition of labor to the auction on the basis that its addition would cause a violation of the envy test since the envy test is also violated by Dworkin's final insurance scheme.

The aforementioned criticisms of the basis of Dworkin's rejection of the proposal to throw labor into the auction might be countered if there were a valid assumption that the talented *should* always end up better off than the untalented, so that we might agree with Dworkin that we cannot permit the situation where Adrian spends "a large part of his initial endowment on a right [to write indifferent poetry] that will bring him little financial benefit." But this assumption would have to be justified by Dworkin, and it does not seem that there could be a justification of it that was consistent with his egalitarianism. If, moreover, there were this assumption, then the envy test would lose its role and the system would be endowment-sensitive.

Dworkin's underlying concern for Adrian, or, more generally, for the talented, highlights a failing on his part, as an advocate of equality of resources. If we are aiming at such equality what is important is what people can get, in the way of resources (including occupation), from their talents. We should not be concerned with whether there are ways people would like to live their lives, other than the ones best suited to their talents, without paying a penalty in terms of resources. Indeed, that would be a welfarist response unavailable to Dworkin. The fact that Adrian would prefer to have another lifestyle, but would not have the resources to get one, is not a basis open to the egalitarian of resources for an objection to the distribution that results from includ-ing labor in the auction.

It might be argued that Dworkin gives special treatment to the talented to avoid Pareto-inefficiency (or "leveling-down") objections. Equality can be inefficient when the only way to achieve it is by reducing the best off to the level of the worst off, with no benefit to the worst off. And the envy test is a strong requirement, since it entails that no one may envy what others have even if that means throwing some resources away.[11] But, although its propensity to level down may present a difficulty for Dworkin's theory, I do not think that that is his motivation for giving special treatment to the talented. Firstly, Dworkin thinks that, because of the market system that he invokes, the results he endorses will in fact be Pareto-efficient. Secondly, although the leveling down objection is indeed a powerful one, one cannot assume that Dworkin would give up values such as endowment insensitivity and satisfaction of the envy test, because of that objection: it is at least a question worth asking which of these values is to be respected more. I think that Dworkin's concern is about what he perceives as the possible slavery of the talented, as such. The remarkable thing is that he does not see the analogous danger for the less talented.

III

Having excluded the labor auction solution to the problem of inequality of talent, Dworkin goes on to suggest his own solution, which is an extension of the insurance scheme for handicaps. In developing his solution, Dworkin once again shows special concern that the talented not be made "slaves" to their talents.

Dworkin says that just as you would insure against bad brute luck, you would insure against not being able to earn at a certain percentile.[12] But, he says, it would be irrational to insure against not earning a very high salary (call it a "movie star" salary). For, if it turned out that you did have the ability to earn such a salary, you would then be a slave to your talents. You would have to work as a movie star in order to pay your insurance premium even if you would strongly prefer to work at something else, which attracted a lower salary.[13] So, he says, it will be rational to insure at a level lower than movie star level.[14] He claims, moreover, that, as the premiums go down, these special welfare disadvantages disappear, so that insuring at a lower level does not involve the same risks of people's being slaves to their talents that movie star level insurance does (pp. 319–20). So Dworkin protects the talented from the risk of what he calls "slavery" by arguing for the rationality of insuring at a lower level, which, he says, has no analogous risks for anybody.[15]

But it is unlikely that the talented will be put in any worse situation by an insurance premium that makes them work at their full capacity than the less talented will be put in by an insurance policy that makes them work at *their* full capacity (even though that capacity is smaller). Dworkin's special attention to the talented is, therefore, once again, unjustified.

Dworkin does argue that the special welfare disadvantages disappear as the premium drops, but his argument is not persuasive. He says that if the level of insurance is at, say, the 30th per-centile, then anyone who can earn at this level, and so has to pay the premium, is likely to have "the talents to earn at a higher level, and so would retain a considerable freedom of choice about the character of work, and the mix of work and labor and the additional consumption, that he prefers" (p. 322).[16] But, as Dworkin himself admits (in using the term "likely"), it is clear that some who can earn at the 30th percentile will not be able to earn at a higher level, and, so

I believe, they will be "enslaved" in the way the talented are when insurance is at a higher level: it is simply untrue that there are no analogous risks for (other) people once the premium drops. There is no reason to think that there would be fewer people in the position Dworkin describes as enslavement when a lower premium is in place than are in that position with higher premiums, which affect those with very high talent. Accordingly, the envy test would still fail, and on more than one count. First, the enslaved (who would now be in the middle range of talent) would envy the set of nonslaves (which would include both the very talented and those with less talent than those in the middle range). Secondly, the untalented (who include those in the middle range) would envy the talented, who would have more choices, because of the lower premiums.

Dworkin also says that welfare disadvantages diminish as the insured level drops because there is a greater variety of jobs at a lower level than at a higher one (p. 322). His thought is that although people who are not very talented may be forced to work at their full capacity, there are lots of jobs at that level, so that they will still face a substantial choice, whereas at the talented level there are not so many jobs and there is therefore less choice. But this seems empirically unjustified. There are surely levels of salary at which there are a greater variety of occupations than there is at lower levels. Furthermore, even if there is a variety of jobs at a given salary level, why should we assume that someone who can do one of them could do any of them? This assumption is implicit in Dworkin's treatment of the untalented, but absent in his treatment of the talented. Yet Dworkin does nothing to show that there is this systematic difference with respect to freedom in the situations of the talented and the untalented, under the appropriately different assumptions about insurance levels.

What Dworkin goes on to say represents more accurately his reason for the differential treatment that he gives, although it is a reason that shows, once again, that he is interested in protecting the welfare of some more than that of others. He says that even if those who are less talented have to work flat out, and have no choice of work, their situation is very little worse than it would have been had they taken out no insurance, that they are not much differently enslaved by their talent if they insure and have to pay the premium than they would have been enslaved by their lack of talent if they had not insured (pp. 322–3). But the point of the insurance scheme was to reduce the inequalities that would exist in its absence. To say that it does not matter if the untalented are not on an equal level with the talented or if they are enslaved by their lack of talent, since their situation would have been similar if they had not insured, seems, therefore, to negate the whole purpose of the project.

In the end, Dworkin justifies a lack of choice and a type of "enslavement" for the untalented, whereas he would not countenance analogous conditions for the talented. The point of interest here is not so much whether either class is truly enslaved, but whether there is any justification for the unequal treatment that Dworkin provides for them.

Under Dworkin's preferred insurance system, the talents of the talented allow them to have more choices. Accordingly, the envy test will be violated because the untalented will envy the position of the talented. Not only does this lead to a violation of the envy test, but, as Dworkin realizes, it also means that the distribution lacks endowment insensitivity, which was one of Dworkin's main aims, particularly in presenting his theory as an improvement on the Rawlsian model. The distribution is endowment-sensitive because the untalented end up with fewer choices because of their lack of talent: that, in turn, is what would cause them to envy the talented. Dworkin permits this because, he says, any alternative would result in what he thinks of as the slavery of the talented. But, even if he were right about that, his conclusion – rejection of high pay-offs for the untalented – would be unjustified, since the envy test is also violated by the scheme that Dworkin himself proposes.

Dworkin seems to recognize that the untalented may have preferences for as much leisure or wealth as is made available by the market to the talented, and so the only way to explain his special treatment of the talented is that he must think that the untalented are expecting there to be bundles that do not exist, that is, bundles in which people's naturally low talent does not result in their having fewer resources and a less rewarding occupation than the talented have. Dworkin set out to achieve an endowment-insensitive distribution of resources, yet his final distribution is endowment-sensitive. It is the failure to avert the assumption that being talented rightly goes with having access to a privileged position both in terms of status and in terms of the range of options available to them in the society that leads to this result.

We saw earlier that Dworkin ruled out including labor in the auction because, he said, including it would violate the envy test. Now we have seen that his own solution does not satisfy the envy test and that, in fact, he thinks that no solution would do so. It seems, therefore, as I have suggested, that he is unjustified in rejecting the proposal to include labor in the auction on the basis of its alleged violation of the envy test, since his own proposal can also be rejected on the same basis. If, moreover, the slavery of the talented is rejected for some reason *other* than the envy test, then the envy test does not posses the weight that Dworkin claims it should have in an egalitarian theory.

It is interesting to note that the violation of the envy test, which Dworkin takes to justify ruling out an auction for labor, is a violation in which the talented envy the untalented, whereas the violation in the insurance scheme that he recommends is one where the untalented envy the talented. I have said that Dworkin is wrong to characterize the violation of the envy test in the auction in the way he does. He is wrong to claim that including labor in the auction would lead to the slavery of the talented, and consequently to the envy (in general) of the untalented by the talented. However, since he does take the violation to be that the talented would envy the untalented, and it is on the basis of this alleged violation that he rejects the proposal to throw labor into the auction, it is unclear why, as an egalitarian, he would favor a violation resulting in the untalented envying the talented over the converse, which would be the result of his proposed hypothetical insurance scheme. It is hard to see why a theory that purports to be egalitarian takes such particular account of the preferences of the more fortunate.

Dworkin might answer this point by saying that the violation of the envy test in the auction case involves slavery, whereas that of the insurance scheme does not. That is, those who envy in the auction are the talented and they are envious because they are enslaved and the untalented are not, whereas the enviers in the hypothetical insurance scheme are the untalented and they envy the talented because their choices and opportunities for resources are more restricted than those of the talented. But, since what Dworkin is talking about in the auction is, I have argued, not real slavery, but rather just such restricted choice, the suggested distinction cannot work to distinguish the cases.

An interesting question would be whether most of the talented in the labor auction would envy the untalented in the hypothetical insurance scheme. And, furthermore, if the talented in the auction would indeed envy the untalented in the hypothetical insurance scheme, whether the ground for that envy would be as strong as the untalented's envy of the talented in the hypothetical insurance scheme. Answering such questions might be regarded by Dworkin as a way of deciding which scheme is worse. Since I do not myself agree that failures of the envy test in the labor auction would generally be ones where the talented are the enviers, I do not think that the talented in the labor auction would envy the untalented in the insurance scheme. If that is so, and we use the envy test in a properly comprehensive way, the labor auction would seem to beat the insurance scheme.

My conclusions are, then, these: Dworkin is wrong to think that the talented are specially vulnerable to slavery. We have seen that in applying the envy test, both in the labor auction and in the hypothetical insurance scheme, his argument for that alleged vulnerability is unsuccessful. Dworkin's assumptions and aims are genuinely egalitarian and morally plausible. But I have argued that he does not remain true to those aims when faced with the problem of the burdens equality would impose on the talented. He is biased, if unconsciously, in favor of the talented. By virtue of the concessions that he makes to the talented, Dworkin's theory, in the end, recommends a society not far from one like our own.[17] After the attractively egalitarian start, this is a disappointing result.

Acknowledgement

I am very grateful to Derek Parfit who read and criticized several drafts of this paper. I also wish to thank Justine Burley, G. A. Cohen, Sarah Cohen, Cécile Fabre, Veronique Munoz-Darde, Michael Otsuka, Peter Vallentyne, Robert van der Veen, Andrew Williams, and Jonathan Wolff, for helpful discussions and criticisms.

Notes

1   Ronald Dworkin, "What is Equality? Part 2: Equality of Resources," *Philosophy and Public Affairs*, vol. 10(4), 1981, pp. 283–345. All page references in text are to this work.
2   I think that the "envy test" that Dworkin employs is in principle in direct conflict with Pareto efficiency. I say "in principle" because some satisfactions of the envy test may be compatible with Pareto efficiency, but there are others, under conditions of indivisibility of goods, which are not. I shall discuss that conflict only briefly in this paper since it is not directly related to my main criticism of Dworkin here.
3   Strictly, a taxation system that imitates such a mechanism, but there is no room or need to deal with that complication here, beyond what is said in fn. 17.
4

> [The] difference between brute luck and option luck is that option luck is a matter of how deliberate and calculated gambles turn out – whether someone gains or loses through accepting an isolated risk he or she should have anticipated and might have declined. Brute luck is a matter of how risks fall out that are not in that sense direct gambles. (Dworkin, "Equality of Resources," op. cit., p. 293)

5   See ibid., p. 312 (where he expressly rejects the thesis of self-ownership).
6   For simplicity, I use daily figures: imagine that the labor auction is rerun each morning. But an annual or lifetime auction would have the same results.
7   Note that in the figures I have used there is a big gap between what the talented need to produce to live and what the untalented need to produce. I have not chosen an example that makes the position of the talented easy.
8   I am indebted to Robert van der Veen for providing me with a proof of this generalization.
9   Referring to the fulfillingness of occupations is no more illegitimately welfarist than referring to a normal preference for subtle wine over cheap wine.

10 It is generally accepted in the literature that Dworkin is correct about his slavery of the talented claim. I have argued that he is not. Stuart White argues for an alternative scheme which he calls "The Egalitarian Earnings Subsidy Scheme" (*British Journal of Political Science*, vol. 29, 1999, pp. 601–22), which, so he claims, avoids the slavery of the talented objection. I will not asses that scheme in this paper. I note, however, that both White's endorsement of the objection to the labor auction and his claim that his scheme avoids the objection only hold if the sole things that matter are leisure and income.

11 This problem would not arise in Dworkin's initial auction scenario where, *ex hypothesi*, all the goods are divisible, either physically or in ownership shares. But it may well be a problem for a real world satisfaction of the envy test.

12 X earns at the nth percentile if and only if $(100 - n)\%$ of the population earn more than X does.

13 Note that Dworkin is worried about high insurance premiums because he thinks that they would enslave the talented. His move away from high insurance premiums cannot be based on a Rawlsian worry about incentives since there is no problem of motivating people to do something that they are forced to do. (If the premiums were very high, then the talented would be forced to work at lucrative occupations.) Accordingly, an incentive problem cannot be what explains Dworkin's preferential treatment of the talented, as it does with Rawls. The "slavery" problem is to do with justice and freedom, not efficiency.

   The high insurance premium level which Dworkin says would be rejected would also achieve a Pareto-efficient system. So once again the treatment of the talented cannot be based on the demands of Pareto efficiency. The problem with the system in its original description is, then, so Dworkin thinks, that the talented would be enslaved and that the envy test would therefore fail. By lowering the insurance premium level Dworkin takes himself, I think wrongly, to have avoided such problems.

14 In exposition of this point, Will Kymlicka writes that if the insurance premium were high then "[t]he insurance scheme would cease to be a constraint which the talented could reasonably be expected to recognise in deciding how to live their lives, but would rather become the determining factor in their lives. Their talents would be a liability that restricted their options, rather than a resource which expanded their options" (Will Kymlicka, *Contemporary Political Philosophy* (Oxford: Oxford University Press, 1990), p. 80). It will be clear by now that I think that neither of these points is persuasive against high insurance levels. First, the idea of reasonable expectation is context-relative and it is precisely the context for expectations which is under discussion here. Secondly, egalitarians have no moral grounds for objecting to a system in which talents do not expand options.

15 There is a technical reason why it may be irrational to insure at a very high level. Since it is assumed that everyone insures at the same level, if everyone insures at a very high level then most people would receive a pay-off, which means that the pay-off would be very low. But this has nothing to do with Dworkin's claim that the talented will be enslaved. What it does show is that the insurance scheme is not a very good system, in terms of giving people what justice requires that they should have, since what they get would depend on contingencies such as how risk-averse or risk-loving people are. Such contingencies would militate against achieving what Dworkin originally set out to achieve, which was actually to compensate people for their disabilities or lack of earning power, since the amount of insurance received would be independent of how much was needed to count as genuine compensation. I want to leave these particular problems aside, and concentrate on the way that Dworkin describes the insurance scenario, in relation to the notion of the slavery of the talented.

16 "labor" should be "leisure" here.

17 This is especially true in the light of the fact that when the insurance mechanism is imitated by the tax system, taxation will be on actual income and not on ability. This is both because of problems of knowing what people's abilities are, and because of not wholly unrelated problems of moral hazard. But, as a result, the talented do not need to work at any occupation they do not want to, and therefore the redistribution of (or compensation for) levels of talent that Dworkin achieves is unimpressive. The effect of this is that the talented have a lot of choice because if they do not want to pay a lot of tax they simply take a job with a lower income or they work less. Under progressive taxation systems some people do in fact think that it is not worth taking a job with more money because the tax will be too high to be worth it. Similar choices are clearly not open to the untalented.

3

Equality of Resources Versus Undominated Diversity

Philippe Van Parijs

The inhabitants of Polypolis form a motley community. They greatly differ from one another in both their tastes, in particular their income/leisure trade-offs, and their internal endowments or talents, that is, the capacities they have received from either nature or upbringing.[1] At the beginning of the present inquiry, external endowments have just been distributed among Polypolitans in a way that would be fair if all had identical talents. I shall here assume without argument that this fair distribution consists in distributing whatever has been received by the present generation of Polypolitans from either nature or previous generations in such a way as to maximin the competitive value of what each is given or, equivalently, in giving each, at the highest sustainable level, an equal unconditional grant which enables them to acquire all goods at their competitive value.[2] The question I shall be dealing with is simple enough: does justice require that one should deviate from this equal distribution of external endowments in order to take account of differences in talents – and if so, how?

By tackling this question, I shall attempt to contribute to a notoriously tricky aspect of liberal conceptions of justice, an aspect to which Ronald Dworkin has paid more sustained attention than most and to which he has made a more original and elaborate contribution than anyone. What does it mean to give due weight to the claims of the handicapped, of the poorly talented, of those with a lesser endowment of "natural primary goods"? Against a background I largely share with Dworkin, I shall discuss and reject his own specific answer to this question, and then formulate my own proposal, inspired by Bruce Ackerman's notion of undominated genetic diversity, and consistent, I believe, with the central tenets of Dworkin's own approach – indeed more consistent than his own proposal with his crucial requirement that people should not be rewarded for having expensive tastes.

This inquiry does not only fit into the very broad collective effort towards an adequate theory of distributive justice that takes talent diversity into account. It also fits into a more specific endeavor in which I have been engaged for some time: the attempt to determine under what conditions granting everyone an unconditional basic income can be ethically justified.[3] From this angle, the present chapter addresses head on a powerful challenge. Is it not obvious from the start that anyone seriously concerned with talent inequalities will have to reject anything like a universal system of transfers, and favor instead – at least on a first best level – a highly differentiated system of taxes and subsidies? This may seem obvious, but it is not true – so at least I shall argue. For under appropriate conditions to be specified below, the answer I offer to the question of distributive justice in Polypolis is fully consistent with granting everyone an unconditional income.

The most salient features of the background I shall take for granted in this chapter – and which I share with Dworkin, Sen, Ackerman, Cohen, and others – can be described as follows. First, contra pure entitlement theorists, justice bears a close relationship to substantive equality.[4] Secondly, for equalization of the relevant "substance" to make any sense, some appropriate metric must be found. This metric can neither be defined in terms of goods, nor in terms of welfare. A goods metric is too high up the causal chain: goods equalization would catch too little. A welfare metric is too low down the causal chain: welfare equalization would catch too much. Somewhat less elliptically, welfare equalization would wrongly neutralize the impact on welfare of expensive tastes. Those who develop, or fail to keep under check, a desire for expensive goods, would be rewarded for this fact – they would be given a larger share of goods than those with less expensive tastes. What goods equalization wrongly leaves out, on the other hand, is the fact that equal amounts of goods give people with different talents different opportunities for pursuing whatever they might value in life.[5] Against this background, our task is clear, at least in broad outline. The criterion of distributive justice we are after must take us beyond goods equalization – being a disabled person, for example, must give rise to a special claim on grounds of justice – but not as far as welfare equalization – having expensive tastes, for example, does not entitle one to getting more than others. This is, however, only a rough characterization of the task ahead. For any adequate solution to the problem it consists in addressing will have to meet additional desiderata. These will not be specified from the start,[6] but will emerge from the discussion of counterexamples to a number of existing and potential proposals.

I The Extended Auction

A first proposal that is worth exploring consists in a straightforward extension of the intellectual device that Dworkin himself plausibly uses in the case of external endowments.[7] In his famous parable, the identically talented immigrants landing on the desert island are each given a fair share of the resources they find on the island if they are given what they have bid for with equal amounts of clamshells in a perfectly competitive auction. If the immigrants now possess unequal talents, could we not just add these, on a par with fancy pebbles and banana trees, to the aggregate up for bids in the auction? All participants in the auction would bid for their own talents (simply to enjoy them, or to put them to some productive use) or other people's talents (to put them to their most productive use and cash in the proceeds), in the same way as they bid for goods. Nothing but the initial check – the equal number of clamshells – can be used to buy all these goods, which the auctioneer allocates to the highest bidder when all checks have been committed in their owners' best interest.[8] No doubt, a fair amount of intellectual gymnastics is needed to figure out exactly what skills are for sale (only "talents," i.e., those that have been "given" to their holder, genetically or otherwise) as well as to imagine how one person's talents could be jointly owned by several people. But the exercise is not fundamentally different from the one that has to be performed in the case of external endowments. What are the implications?

What are now being auctioned off are people's talents, and hence their command over their own time. If people want to retain command over them – which they can be safely assumed to do – they have to outbid anyone else who might be interested in using them.[9] For those without any valuable talent, this is a great advantage. They will be able to appropriate their own time very cheaply, thus enabling them to gain access to more external resources than was the case when only external resources were being auctioned. For those with highly productive talents, on the other hand, the reverse is the case. They may well have to spend the whole of their check buying their own time – indeed, more than their check, thereby running a debt that they will have to pay back with the income their talents will enable them to earn. The most straightforward institutional expression of this procedure consists in supplementing whatever follows from our criterion for the fair distribution of external resources, with a highly differentiated tax-and-transfer system, in sharp contrast to universal systems such as a negative income tax or a basic income. Assuming away, for the moment, any informational problem, such a system consists in identifying the maximum earning power associated with each person's internal endowment, in granting all people with below average talents (measured by the corresponding earning power) a lump-sum subsidy driving their earning power up to the average, and in imposing on all people with above average talents a lump-sum tax driving their earning power down to the average.[10]

The criterion of justice thus proposed for Polypolis, where talents are different, is fully consistent with, indeed a natural generalization of, what is being assumed to be appropriate when talents are identical. The earning power associated with identical internal endowments is, of course, equal for all. Hence, there is then no deviation from the average to be compensated by means of lump-sum transfers or taxes, and the whole procedure reduces to its external endowment component. In the course of the generalization, however, something has been lost. With identical talents, the auction procedure guaranteed the satisfaction of a criterion of envy-freeness: the outcome was necessarily such that no one preferred the bundle attributed to anyone else to the one they themselves ended up with. In Polypolis, where both tastes and talents diverge, no such guarantee can be given. To understand why, briefly consider the case of Johnson and Jackson, identically talented except for the fact that Johnson is an exceptional runner, whereas Jackson is an amazing singer. If it so happens that there is nothing in life Johnson would like as much as having a great voice, while Jackson's strongest ambition is to win a race, each will envy the other's internal endowment. And no transfer of external endowments – no combination of lump-sum taxes and subsidies – will enable us to get rid of all envy, for any such transfer from Johnson to Jackson will only alleviate Jackson's envy at the expense of aggravating Johnson's, and the other way around.[11] This fact will prove of great importance further on, but it must be acknowledged that equity theorists have, in a sense, managed to get around it by introducing a different criterion of envy-freeness which can be guaranteed to be satisfied by the outcome of the auction even in a Polypolitan context. A distribution is said to be *income-fair* if no one envies the implicit income of any other agent. Johnson's *implicit income* is the competitive value of the consumption bundle accessible to him, including his leisure, evaluated by the maximum competitive wage he could earn, given his abilities. The outcome of the comprehensive auction described above is necessarily income-fair in this sense.[12]

II Working in the Peep Show, Flirting in the Square

There is no doubt that this approach provides a way of performing the task mentioned at the outset. By equalizing maximum earning power or implicit income, it avoids the goods metric's insensitivity to the plight of the handicapped: those with poor abilities will have their earning power propped up to the average. And it does so in a way that avoids the welfare metric's sensitivity to the tastes of the person concerned: true, how much your talents are worth depends on which services are in demand, and hence on everyone's tastes, but whether you possess expensive tastes does not affect in any way what you are entitled to by virtue of the criterion that is being proposed. What people are owed or owe, if earning power is to be equalized, is determined by their talents and left unaffected by their tastes. Thus, the requirements enshrined in the formulation of that task would seem to be satisfied, and we may be tempted to conclude that the system of differentiated taxes and subsidies implied by the equalization of earning power is what justice demands in Polypolis. This would be too rash, however, for the proposal under consideration has two exceedingly unwelcome implications. To understand them, let us turn to Lonely and her sibling Lovely.[13] Regarding taste, both siblings are identical. In particular, they both care comparatively little for a high income, while attaching great importance to the enjoyment of free time. Regarding talent, they are identically mediocre in all respects except one: unlike Lonely, Lovely is truly ravishing.

Let us first suppose that the Polypolitans' tastes (and the available technology) are such that Lovely's gorgeous looks enable her to earn a handsome income by displaying them in a peep show. Understandably, however, she hates that job – as would her sibling if she were given it. How do the siblings fare under the talent egalitarianism sketched above? Lonely cannot complain. Because of her below-average talents, she is further granted a lump-sum subsidy that raises her earning power to the average level. Given her strong desire for leisure (whether used for sunbathing, praying, or campaigning), she has decided to live off this reasonably high income and forgo any additional income she could earn by renting out her modest talents. Lovely is far less fortunate. Her fabulous earning power means that she is forced to pay as a lump-sum tax an amount of money that she could not possibly earn in any occupation other than daily performance in the peep show. Far from being able to indulge in the same leisurely life pattern as her sibling, she is forced to devote a large chunk of her time – not all of it, but enough to pay the tax and subsist – doing a job she thoroughly hates. Is this not frightfully unfair to Lovely, indeed a form of slavery incompatible with any ideal of justice that pays at least minimum attention to freedom?

Secondly, suppose that for whatever reason there is no peep show in Polypolis, nor indeed, more generally, any way of making money out of one's looks. The two siblings are now indistinguishable as far as the auction is concerned, and they will both be entitled (owing to their feebly valued talents) to the same lump-sum subsidy. But Lonely is ugly, while Lovely is gorgeous. And while Lovely has a great time flirting in the square, Lonely sadly sits on a lonely bench and occasionally overhears a bad joke about her spotty face and funny nose. Surely, a procedure which treats them alike does not really equalize the resources they are endowed with in order to pursue whatever they regard as valuable. Good looks may matter a great deal even if they do not add a penny to one's earning power. By reducing the talents to be equalized to those affecting a person's earning power, is the auction approach not unacceptably harsh on Lonely, in this second version of our example, and blatantly at odds with our commitment to give everyone the greatest real freedom to do whatever they might want to do, and not just to make money?

III   Insurance Behind a Veil of Ignorance

The two implications thus illustrated by Lonely and Lovely constitute fatal objections to the extended auction. The first of them is closely related to the reason Ronald Dworkin offers for rejecting the extended auction as an appropriate general interpretation of his principle of equality of resources.[14] That he should be bothered by it is not obvious at once. After all, he is not committed to equalizing Lonely's and Lovely's welfare. And resources, as measured by the (competitively determined) cost to others of one's appropriating them, are distributed in spotlessly egalitarian fashion. True, Lovely has less leisure than Lonely. But then her leisure is far more valuable as an asset for the community as a whole (or at least the subset of it that consists in peep show customers), though not necessarily as a source of enjoyment for herself. As Roemer points out,[15] the taste that talented people have for the use of their own leisure can be construed as a form of expensive taste. Moreover, Dworkin does not want to object to the extended auction on the ground that people such as Lovely are treated like things, or that their self-ownership is violated, for such objections rely "on the idea of pre-political entitlement based on something other than equality" and is "inconsistent with the premise of the scheme of equality of resources" under consideration.[16]

Dworkin articulates his dissatisfaction with this implication of the extended auction by pointing out that it fails to meet the envy test relevant to the resource-egalitarian ideal he tries to express. Just as one must "require that no one have less income simply in consequence of less native talent"[17] – the whole point of the extended auction – one must also require that no one be forced to have less leisure in consequence of more native talent. Failing to do so would mean an unwarranted bias in the understanding of resources. If it could be assumed that people cared for nothing apart from collecting as high an income as possible, it would be legitimate to conflate resources and earning power, as the auction does. Once leisure-lovers such as our two siblings are brought into the picture, this can no longer be legitimate.[18]

We must, therefore, try to imagine some other device, which would get rid of this bias. One possibility Dworkin invites us to consider is as follows. Ask everyone to ignore the particular internal endowment they have, while bearing in mind their particular conception of the good life as well as the distribution of all features of internal endowments in the relevant population, and ask them to say for how much they would insure against the presence or absence of any particular feature. The more important a feature is to individuals (given their conception of the good life), the greater the compensation they will receive in case they turn out not to have it. But the level of the premium they will have to pay (sensibly at a rate increasing with their earning power) increases as the compensation level goes up and will therefore impose a ceiling on the latter. As we shall see shortly, this is not yet the scheme on which Dworkin settles. But it is worth examining, as it clearly holds a promise of meeting both objections illustrated by Lonely and Lovely. If Lovely wants to make sure she won't be stuck in the peep show, she will just have to keep the amount for which she insures at a low level. And if being attractive matters a lot to Lonely, regardless of any pecuniary consequences, then she will have to make sure she gets a handsome compensation in case she turns out to be ugly – whether to pay for cosmetic surgery or to enable her to do more of the things for which beauty is unnecessary. Such a scheme obviously raises the practical difficulty of detecting the true importance Lonely and Lovely attach to the talents they do not possess: it is in their interest to peep through the veil and pretend they attach the greatest importance to everything they happen to lack. But we can leave this practical difficulty aside, for the proposal is defective for reasons that would apply – as we shall see – even if its implementation were straightforward.

In one of the most thorough discussions of Dworkin's approach, John Roemer considers and rejects the insurance scheme just sketched.[19] To start with, the latter has a number of embarrassing implications. For example, like the extended auction (in section I above), it "appears to overcompensate those whose bad luck we wished to repair": the talented become worse off than the untalented. Moreover, though introduced in order to soften the fate of the talented (relative to the extended auction), the insurance scheme makes the talented worse off than under the extended auction scheme.[20] However, these claims crucially depend on the assumption that each agent "agrees to make payments to or to receive payments from others, depending on which state of the world occurs, in such a way as to maximize his expected utility over the various states of the world." Roemer recognizes that "the expected-utility model of behavior, and therefore in particular of insurance-taking behavior, has been challenged in recent years."[21] And he further concedes that "Dworkin does not propose this kind of insurance (which economists consider to be rational insurance), but rather a minimum floor insurance policy where a person insures himself not to maximize expected utility, but to guarantee some minimum income. Dworkin does not describe in a sufficiently precise way how his catastrophe insurance is defined."[22]

The obvious alternative conjecture, which Roemer does not consider, is that Dworkin's agents want to maximize not expected utility but minimum utility. Maximin makes a lot of sense when what is at issue is not one of the many decisions that you have to take in the course of your life, but the one big decision that determines how much will be put at your disposal to conduct the whole of your life. The case for expected-utility maximization is compelling when there is a long run to think about. But it falls apart when the coin is tossed only once.[23] In the first-best world considered here, such maximin welfare insurance (with known tastes but unknown talents) yields equal welfare in all circumstances with given tastes.[24] Both of Roemer's embarrassing specific implications mentioned above are then avoided: when this criterion is used instead of utility maximization, the talented cannot become worse off than the untalented (with the same tastes), nor worse off than under the tough deal they got out of the extended auction.

When interpreted in this more charitable way, the insurance scheme is immune to the fire of Roemer's muskets. But it does not seem capable of escaping his heavy artillery. Roemer does not rest content with pointing out embarrassing implications. He also establishes a general impossibility claim to the effect that "there is no mechanism which distributes transferable resources in a way which resource egalitarianism requires, except one: the mechanism that allocates resources to equalize welfare."[25] If this claim is valid, and actually says what it seems to say, then there is no way in which our task, as characterized above, can ever be completed, and this insurance scheme, like any other scheme that does not end up equalizing welfare, is bound to violate at least one of the plausible desiderata that make up the requirements of resource egalitarianism. One of these, the axiom of consistency, stipulates that as one extends equalization to a new type of resource, those who have few of these resources are not made worse off as a result. Innocuous though it seems, this requirement is question-begging. If resources are defined as anything that may affect one's welfare, including the "tastes" which, jointly with a person's objective situation, determine a person's level of welfare, then this axiom directly entails the demand that people with expensive tastes should not be penalized. If instead one makes a sharp distinction between people's endowments – what is given to them, without their bearing any responsibility for having or lacking them – and their tastes or ambitions, which they can legitimately be held responsible for, then this axiom no longer does such a thorough job. As Roemer recognizes in fine, one can avoid the reduction of equality of resources to equality of welfare, even at a first-best level of analysis, if one succeeds in "formulat[ing] criteria for differentiating those aspects of a person which constitute his resources from those which constitute his preferences."[26]

However, once this conceptual distinction is made, it is not impossible in principle (though not easy in practice) to draw a meaningful boundary – at least for anyone who does not hold a determinist position.[27] Factors that do not qualify as endowments can then prevent equality of resources from collapsing into equality of welfare, thereby blocking the compensation of expensive tastes. Once the relevant boundary is drawn, the hypothetical insurance scheme described above and attributed by Roemer to Dworkin no longer has the consequence that one should tax the cheerful and subsidize the morose up to the point where they will all be equally (un)happy. Given the background assumptions – including the interpersonal comparability of welfare levels – people with identical tastes will, whatever their talents, end up with the same welfare. But people with different tastes will not.

IV Dworkin's Hybrid Scheme

The hypothetical insurance scheme thus salvaged from Roemer's critique is worth pondering about, and I shall return to it shortly. But, as already mentioned, it does not coincide with Dworkin's own proposal. The basic reason why he rejects it is that it relies on the possibility of abstracting from the talents one possesses without also abstracting from tastes one only possesses because of the possession of these very talents. Someone without a musical ear, for example, is unlikely to find music of great importance. This difficulty can be avoided, Dworkin suggests, by adopting a slightly different hypothetical insurance scheme, in which insurance takers know both their tastes and their talents, but not the latter's economic rent, that is, how highly the services of these talents happen to be priced on the market.[28] From behind this somewhat thinner veil of ignorance, everyone chooses the height of the earning power that they want to have guaranteed to themselves. If the earning power associated to their talents turns out to be lower, they are given a lump-sum subsidy (the net-of-premium benefit from the insurance is positive). If it turns out to be higher, they have to pay a lump-sum tax (the net-of-premium benefit is negative).

Does this more complex scheme handle the two difficulties illustrated by Lonely and Lovely (in section II)? Let us examine, first of all, whether it gets Lovely out of the peep show. In a society whose members are exclusively concerned with income, risk-averse people will insure at the highest possible level, and all will end up with average earning power – exactly as they did with the extended auction. But Polypolis is not such a society. Lonely and Lovely, in particular, are anxious to secure as much leisure as possible, subject to earning a subsistence income. Risk-averse people with tastes for leisure and income similar to theirs will not maximin their potential income, but minimax the number of hours they will have to work in order to gain subsistence. If the grant received as a share of external endowments falls short of subsistence, each sibling will opt for an insurance scheme that distributes lump-sum subsidies and taxes in such a way that she will have to work the same number of hours in order to reach the subsistence level, whatever the maximum earning power her talents happen to be associated with. Instead of Lonely being able to spend all her time on her favorite leisure activities (because of receiving more than subsistence income as a lump-sum subsidy), while Lovely had to work nearly full time at the peep show (because of the lump-sum tax absorbing, say, 95 percent of her fabulous earning power), as was the case with the extended auction, both siblings now have to work for, say, 15 hours a week on their most lucrative activity – say, knitting sweaters in one case, appearing in the peep show in the other.[29]

Of course, Lovely may still envy her sibling because she would rather knit than strip. But the relevant envy test may be said to be met in the sense that no one has less leisure in consequence of more native talent, any more than "less income simply in consequence of less native talent." Moreover, in this modified insurance scheme, just as in the previous one, the most defensible general decision rule is not the maximinning of earning power or leisure, but rather the max-iminning of utility from both work and income. The extent to which the various available jobs are judged attractive by the people concerned would then automatically be taken into account, and such a scheme would only generate the same outcome as the extended auction, so hard on Lovely, if people's utility coincided with their income – precisely the assumption under which this outcome would no longer look unfair.

Thus, the thin-veil hypothetical insurance scheme proposed by Dworkin is just as effective as the thick-veil scheme examined before in tackling the first of our two difficulties. But it is hopeless at dealing with the second one. The extended auction was not only unsatisfactory because of its toughness with Lovely stuck in the peep show, but also because of its toughness with Lonely left alone on the bench. But unlike the first insurance scheme, Dworkin's modified one similarly ignores all talents that are not reflected in a higher potential income, and will therefore be just as callous to Lonely as the extended auction was. This is, no doubt, the underlying reason why Dworkin only proposes this thin-veil insurance scheme for lucrative talents and combines it with a thick-veil scheme for "ordinary handicaps." In the case of such handicaps, people are assumed to take an insurance as in the first scheme, knowing what tastes they have, but not whether or not they possess the talents whose absence constitutes a handicap. Thus, if Lonely's ugliness is absolutely horrendous, it will presumably qualify as a handicap, and thereby entitle Lonely to a significant compensation.

V   Four Objections to Dworkin

This hybrid scheme, Dworkin's final proposal,[30] raises a number of difficulties. He himself mentions as its main defect the fact that envy will persist. After receiving due compensation in accordance with the scheme, an unemployed person is still most likely to envy the circumstances of a film star whose skills are in high demand and therefore command a far higher income, even after the payment of the premium.[31] However, this can only occur if people are not assumed to adopt a maximin criterion in taking their insurance decisions.[32] If they do – as I have argued (see section III above) can sensibly be assumed in matters of justice – people will still end up with unequal earning powers (like Lonely and Lovely in the first of our two situations), but the scheme will alter these inequalities in such a way that all possible internal endowments will be equivalent to each person, and hence that any welfare difference that may subsist between people can be ascribed to their tastes, not to their talents.

There are, however, three further objections which apply even to the maximin version of the insurance scheme. First, in the case of inequalities that do not involve handicaps, an arbitrary bias subsists between lucrative and nonlucrative talents. If Lovely's earning power is inferior to Lonely's, while Lonely's flirting power is inferior to Lovely's, Dworkin's scheme legitimates a transfer from Lonely to Lovely to compensate for the latter's inferior earning power, but will do nothing to correct Lonely's symmetric inferiority in flirting power. Why this bias? Why this privilege to those aspects of our internal endowments that are, or can be, marketed, as opposed to those that are not or cannot be, whether for physical or social reasons?[33]

Secondly, the status of the key distinction between ordinary handicaps and the lack of specific talents remains problematic. The plausible intuition behind it is that there are general talents (say, sight) that everyone firmly values, whether or not one possesses them. Unlike the desire for specific talents (say, the ability to play the oboe), therefore, the desire for general talents can safely be assumed not to be determined by one's particular internal endowment. Hence, abstracting from this endowment does not force us to abstract from that desire, and the first insurance scheme considered above can make sense: one can meaningfully insure with known tastes against the unknown lack of such general talents, that is, against handicaps. The trouble is that *how much* one cares about the absence of general talents is not independent of the specific tastes one has, nor there-fore of the particular talents that may have helped generate these tastes. Having one's left hand paralyzed no doubt counts as a handicap, but how much one will want to insure it for behind the veil of ignorance will heavily depend on whether, for example, one has developed, as a conse-quence of possessing some more specific talents, a powerful passion for playing the piano. Hence if the initial insurance scheme is deemed unsuitable for the lack of specific talents, it must also be deemed unsuitable for handicaps, and consistency requires that the fall-back solution – Dworkin's insurance scheme with known talents but unknown earning power – should apply across the board. Tough luck for Lonely: however ugly she is, as long as her potential income is not affected by her ugliness, no compensation whatever will be forthcoming. No relevant distinction can be made between handicaps and other lacks of talents that would soften the sharp asymmetry between lucrative and nonlucrative talents. The second of our two difficulties remains therefore totally unsolved.

Given the cumulative effect of these two objections, one may well be inclined to reexamine the case for abandoning the thick veil of ignorance in favor of a thinner one. There is little promise in denying that people's preferences, their conceptions of what is important in life, are often deeply affected by the talents they happen to possess. But one could argue that it does not follow – at the level of abstraction at which the whole exercise is pitched – that it is impossible to abstract from the latter without abstracting from the former. The fact that I would not be A had it not been for my being B, does not entail that I could not conceivably know that I am A without also knowing that I am B. However, returning to the thick-veil scheme would not get us out of trouble, because there is a final objection to Dworkin's hybrid scheme that applies just as much to both a pure thin-veil scheme and to a pure thick-veil scheme.

Whatever the variant chosen, the counterfactual insurance scheme can be impugned on the ground that it raises a particular version of the expensive taste problem, and hence fails to accom-plish the task that we set ourselves at the start. True, the scheme does not amount, as pointed out earlier (in section III), to equalizing welfare. It does not condone an unfair transfer of endow-ments from the cheerful to the morose. But it does amount to giving unequal external endow-ments to people with identical talents, because of their different tastes. Suppose you and I have identical internal endowments, including a pathetic disposition for playing the oboe. I am stub-bornly sticking to the ambition of becoming a brilliant oboe player, whether for its own sake or because of the fortune I believe I could earn that way. You instead have wisely shifted your aspi-rations to table soccer, which we are both far more gifted for. Under the thin-veil variant of the scheme or under Dworkin's hybrid variant, I shall be entitled to compensation to the extent that being a brilliant oboe player would affect my earning power, whereas you will not. Under the thick-veil variant, I shall be entitled to compensation even if no money whatever can be made by playing the oboe. In all three variants, therefore, we find again the implication it was one of our main objectives to avoid. Compared to you, I have an expensive taste whose cost it is right that I should bear. It is not right that you should be penalized, relatively speaking, for having adjusted your ambitions to your circumstances.

What all three variants of the scheme enable you to do, in effect, is fictitiously to insure against your taste for playing the oboe turning out to be costly, due to the absence of a matching talent. The scheme does not generate equality of welfare because, although it allows you to insure against the lack of talents with given tastes, it does not enable you to insure against your having a taste for doing things requiring a talent that happens to be scarce in the relevant population.[34] Under the proposed scheme, those with a taste for playing the oboe will have access to a level of welfare

lower than that accessible to those who have instead (*ceteris paribus*) a taste for another activity –
say, whistling – whose exercise requires the use of more widespread talents. Though you won't
be worse off because of the talents you (do not) possess, you may be worse off because of the
tastes you have. The scheme, therefore, only generates a limited, taste-sensitive equality of welfare.
But this does not prevent it from being vulnerable to the expensive taste objection, since it gives
more or less compensation, as we have seen, depending on people's tastes.[35] It therefore fails to
live up to the requirements of the task described at the outset.

To this objection – the only one I have mentioned which applies to all three variants of the
scheme – one may want to reply that this differential compensation according to tastes is all right,
being the outcome of what Dworkin calls option luck.[36] An insurance scheme is like a lottery. If
you play and lose, you cannot complain that you are unfairly treated compared to your sister who
played and won, or to your brother who abstained. Fairness requires equality *ex ante* – which is
guaranteed in the scheme by access to the same insurance possibilities and the hiding of actual
talents – but not equality *ex post* – the outcome of the insurance scheme may give people with
identical internal endowments unequal external endowments. But surely this reply misrepresents
the status of the insurance scheme. The taste-sensitive inegalitarian outcome could be characterized and legitimized as option luck only if it were the consequence of insurance choices actually
made by the people involved. But of course it is not, the insurance being a purely fictitious thought
experiment designed to provide us with a determinate criterion for correcting inequalities of
talents. And once it is viewed as such, the taste-sensitiveness of the distribution of external endowments comes out as what it truly is: a blatant departure from the principle that people should be
held responsible for their preferences and hence cannot legitimately expect to get more than others
identically talented because of the mismatch there happens to be between their talents and their
tastes.

It may of course be the case that we are being too fussy, and that, in the context of unequal
talents, there simply is no criterion that can meet simultaneously all our desiderata.[37] I do not
believe so, and I shall present in the next section an alternative criterion that does seem to do the
trick. Before doing so, however, one final remark about Dworkin's stimulating approach. We have
seen above why his criterion for the equality of external endowments could not be generalized
into the extended auction to cover internal endowments as well. But should we not ask the converse question? What prevents his criterion for the equality of internal endowments from applying to external endowments as well? In other words, instead of adding people's talents to the goods
they have received in order for the whole lot to be evaluated at competitive prices, why do we not
add their gifts and bequests to their talents in order for the whole lot to be subjected to the insurance scheme? In the simplest variant, this would mean that people would be asked to retain their
tastes – for the intrinsic enjoyment of specific external and internal endowments as well as for the
instrumental enjoyment of these endowments through the purchasing power they confer – but to
ignore how large their endowments are and what they consist of. They can then take insurance in
such a way that their getting the worst external and internal endowment, given their tastes, would
give rise to the highest compensation, while their getting their best endowment would make them
liable to the heaviest tax. However, this does not really yield a scheme different from the one we
have been considering so far. If one opts, as before, for a maximin criterion – and given a number
of mild assumptions, such as nonsatiation in external endowments – the global insurance scheme
thus constructed leads to equalizing the value of external endowments in the special case of identical talents, that is, to the criterion here taken for granted at the stage at which differences in
internal endowments are ignored. This observation shows the coherence of Dworkin's treatment

of external and internal endowments: his treatment of the latter is a generalization of his treatment of the former, though not the most obvious one. At the same time, it shows that our negative conclusion about the counterfactual insurance schemes has not been reached at the cost of ignoring their most general version, to which the above discussion is no less relevant.

VI Ackerman Generalized

Before considering a final proposal, let us first go back a few steps. Both the extended auction with which we started this discussion and, as we have just seen, Dworkin's insurance scheme, can be seen as generalizations of the approach adopted in the case of external endowments (see section I). The latter was chosen as the most plausible way of avoiding the ubiquitous indeterminacy that would arise if one restricted oneself to the following formulation: one person enjoys less freedom than another if the set of options open to the former is a proper subset of the set of options open to the latter. The opportunity cost metric proposed seemed ethically far more meaningful, in particular, than a physicalist metric of spatiotemporal possibilities, and unlike a metric of potential welfare, it does not systematically reward expensive tastes. But now that this metric too has proved inadequate in a context of unequal talents, it is worth going back to the very weak notion of equality as the absence of a strict inclusion of one person's option set in another person's. Those inclined to discard this suggestion straightaway on the ground of its being excessively inegalitarian should pause to reflect on the following two considerations. First, the criterion of noninclusion would operate on the background of a strongly egalitarian distribution of external endowments. Secondly, it could be sensibly improved, and made significantly more demanding, by interpreting options as possibilities of access to some worthwhile existence, or as equipment for some sensible conception of the good life – where what is "worthwhile" or "sensible" is decided by its actually being sustained in the society considered.

The latter suggestion amounts to proposing a criterion of justice in matters of internal endowments that can be viewed as a generalization of an idea put forward by Bruce Ackerman in the context of genetic engineering.[38] As Ackerman uses it himself, "dominated diversity" applies to genetic features only. But the notion generalizes naturally to all talents or aspects of a person's internal endowment, as the latter has been understood so far, including features that are due to accidents (whether antenatal or postnatal) or to a person's family or social environment. A's internal endowment (a vector of talents) *dominates* B's internal endowment if and only if all people (given their own conception of the good life) would prefer to have the former than the latter.[39] If there were a boundless variety of conceptions of the good life, such dominance could only occur if A were superior to B in all respects (that is, in each component of the vector), and hence hardly ever: a blind and deaf paraplegic may still have nicer hair than some or be better than others at arithmetic, which would be deemed sufficient to make for a more favorable endowment by at least one person, given that person's conception of the good life. If people's conceptions of life display a convergence on the relative importance given to the various components of the vector, however, what will be required for dominance to obtain will fall far short of superiority for each feature.[40] At the limit, if the only thing people care about is the ability to curl their tongues, superiority along this dimension entails dominance, however poorly one performs in all other dimensions of life.

This criterion is of central importance, according to Ackerman, not only to formulate a consistent liberal position in matters of genetic engineering – which need not detain us here[41] – but also, in case genetic engineering is not used or fails, to determine who owes compensation to whom because of a better internal endowment. Here is Ackerman's formula:

> Pick any two people out of the population. Compare their genetic endowments. In principle, two – and only two – conclusions are possible. Either A genetically dominates B and B may properly demand compensatory assistance; or A and B stand in a relation of undominated equality, and B gains no relief – no matter how envious of A's talents he may be.[42]

The precise criterion that emerges roughly coincides with the standard distinction between the "normal" and the "handicapped." For any "normal" person X, although it will be very easy for each of the members of a large community to name one person he or she regards as better endowed than X, it is very unlikely that there will be any single person whom all would regard as better endowed than X. For any "handicapped" person Y, on the other hand, although it will still be possible to find people whom some, indeed all, regard as less well endowed than Y, it will be easy to find people whom all would regard as better endowed.[43] On Ackerman's criterion, therefore, it is very unlikely that any normal person will be entitled to any compensation, while all the "handicapped" will be entitled to compensation from some other (less) "handicapped" and from many (not necessarily all) "normal" persons.

How can this criterion be handled in practice? As Ackerman points out, one will have to start by marking out broad categories dominated by a large number of their fellows. But how much compensation is owed by the "dominators" to the "dominated"? Minimally, one must make sure that the "dominated" do not get a worse deal than others in other respects, material wealth or education for example.[44] Beyond that, all Ackerman says, and claims that can be said, is that in at least one other respect they must be given at least somewhat more than their "dominators." However, a more precise suggestion comes up naturally. We have assumed, in our initial characterization of Polypolis, that people had been given the highest sustainable basic income, and that this was what justice required, had they all been equally talented. One could then uniformly reduce this equal amount given to all, and use the amount thus saved as compensation to the "handicapped" (possibly used to build up the latter's internal resources: say, money for an eye operation). This procedure stops as soon as, for each pair of *comprehensive* – that is, internal-cum-external – endowments, there is at least one person who prefers either endowment to the other.[45] Whether this happens before the uniform external endowment given to all is driven down to zero – and hence whether the condition of undominated diversity could be satisfied without introducing lump-sum taxes – is an empirical matter. It depends on the frequency of malformations and accidents, on the wealth of the society concerned, and, last, but not least, on the diversity of the conceptions of the good life.[46]

Once again, we seem to have completed our task. Like the extended auction and the various counterfactual insurance schemes considered, the procedure thus sketched recognizes the fact that it would be unfair to distribute external endowments irrespective of people's internal endowment. At the same time, like the extended auction but unlike the counterfactual insurance schemes, it does not give more or less compensation depending on the tastes that two identically talented people happen to have. How does it fare with the two difficulties on which the extended auction faltered? Can it simultaneously avoid enslaving the talented (the peep show) and paying privileged attention to lucrative talents (the bench in the square)?

On the first issue, Lovely and her likes are undoubtedly better protected against any disadvantage they may owe to their talents than was the case with the extended auction. If the society consisted only of people with the same talents as Lonely and Lovely and if the external resources made available to each of them from the outside (say, from nature), were sufficient to cover subsistence, there would be no redistribution whatever from leisure-loving Lovelies to equally leisure-loving Lonelies, however high the former's earning power. If instead some work is needed to reach subsistence, some redistribution from those with access to quicker ways of earning the required income will be in order – unless working in a peep show is regarded by all as lexically worse (that is, worse no matter how well paid) than earning one's living by knitting. But this will never reach the point where the Lovelies would prefer the Lonelies' fate to their own, since it is only as long as everyone prefers Lovely's situation to Lonely's that redistribution is warranted.

It is, however, important to recognize that the pattern of transfers that maximizes basic income subject to the constraint of undominated diversity is generally not the only one (if there is one) that satisfies the latter. Instead of diminishing everyone's basic income in favor of those with dominated internal endowments, up to the point where no comprehensive endowment is dominated any longer, one could carry on up to, for example, the far more distant point where distributing any further to those with dominated internal endowments would begin to involve dominance of the others' comprehensive endowments. Stopping the process *as soon as* at least one person starts preferring the fate of the handicapped seems no more legitimate than stopping it *just before everyone* prefers it, or indeed anywhere in between. The second extreme possibility is just as consistent as the first one with equality of endowments, conceived as undominated diversity. If it were adopted, we would of course be stuck with the slavery of the talented. Assuming there is at least one person in Lovely's society who has no other concern than earning as much money as possible, she would then be faced with a heavy lump-sum tax that will force her to work for long hours in the peep show, no matter how much she loathes the job.[47] Undominated diversity, however, is not a principle I propose as a full characterization of distributive justice, but as a component of such a characterization that enters as a constraint on the maximization of everyone's basic income.

Secondly, does the scheme grant any privilege to inequalities in lucrative talents? Clearly not. Whether for lucrative or nonlucrative talents, only "handicaps," that is, unanimously recognized overall disadvantages, are allowed compensation. As far as lucrative talents are concerned, these disadvantages need not take the form of one or more major identifiable defects, such as blindness or paraplegia. They can simply consist in the inability to make ends meet, due to a modest endowment for those features whose services happen to be in demand on the market.[48] In a rich society with a substantial (highest sustainable) basic income, this case may never occur. But in a poor society, where both the wage rate for the unskilled and the highest sustainable level of basic income are low, this case will often occur. In order to fund the required transfers, one may then have to drive the basic income down to zero. Indeed, one would have to drive it into negative figures (in the form of a lump-sum tax) unless one wanted to prevent this by imposing some constraint of self-ownership. Beyond the unanimously recognized necessities, however, the fact that someone is bad at earning money does not justify any targeted transfer at all on the basis of our criterion of undominated diversity, providing of course (as is likely in a heterogeneous society) that all those better than that person at making money are worse than him or her in at least one other respect that is judged decisive by at least one person.

Before considering some objections, it may be illuminating to relate the present approach to the notion of envy-freeness closely related to our criterion for the fair distribution of external endowments. What is required by the Dworkin–Varian criterion of envy-freeness over external endowments is that there is no pair of people such that one prefers the other person's endowment to his or her own. What undominated diversity requires is only that there be no pair of people

such that *all prefer* one person's endowment to the other's. As mentioned earlier, the first criterion is generally impossible to satisfy, as soon as endowments are understood to include internal
features: someone with Lonely's endowments and an overwhelming drive for income will envy
Lovely's endowment as long as they have the same external endowment, but Lovely will envy that
person's comprehensive endowment as soon as one tries (however inadequately) to reduce this
envy with some compensating transfer of external resources. The second criterion – undominated
diversity – can be viewed against this background as replacing envy-freeness by *potential envy-
freeness* and thereby avoiding the general impossibility just mentioned. For comprehensive endowments to be distributed in a fair fashion, it is no longer required that no one should envy anyone
else's endowment, but only that no one should envy anyone else's endowment under at least one
available preference schedule (that can vary for each pair-wise comparison). In other words, the
partial ordering given by the intersection of all the individual orderings of the various comprehensive endowments is taken to provide a characterization of unfairness.[49]

VII   Not Enough Redistribution?

In this light, let us first consider the objection that our criterion justifies far too little redistribution. It is enough for one eccentric person to consider blindness a blessing for compensation to
the blind to cease to be required. To tackle this challenge, one should begin by stressing that the
relevant preference schedules must be genuine and somehow available to the people concerned.
For redistribution from the A-endowed to the B-endowed to stop, it is not enough for someone
to declare, or even to believe, that B is just as good as A. It can only stop when it is true that at
least one person who knows and understands all the consequences of having B rather than A,
judges in the light of his or her conception of a good life that B is no worse than A. Some of the
eccentric people one may have in mind can no doubt be disqualified on the ground that they do
not understand what they are talking about. If any are left, they are likely to belong to isolated
subsocieties, whose cultural world is unavailable to others (this is precisely why these regard them
as eccentric), and hence whose preference schedules cannot be viewed as generally available.[50] If
these two conditions are met, that is, if there is no problem with either understanding or availability – and if, therefore, there is no such eccentricity left – there is nothing shocking, it seems
to me, in discontinuing redistribution.

Cannot one then object, secondly, that the proposed solution, even if it is acceptable in general,
does not fit the case in which the only person whose tastes prevent dominance from occurring is
precisely the person whose endowment is found worse by everyone else, typically a person afflicted
by a handicap and attempting to come to terms with that situation by adjusting his or her preferences. Along with welfare egalitarianism, undominated diversity seems to have the unwelcome
consequence of penalizing people with adaptive tastes. One amendment worth contemplating is
to exclude a person's own preferences from the pair-wise comparisons that are relevant to the criterion. But this would clearly be a bad move. To start with, it would allow people with identical
handicaps to be entitled to different levels of compensation – an implication that was decisive in
the rejection of Dworkin's scheme. For a particularly perverse illustration of this implication,
imagine two people, one of them the single atheist in a community, who lacks a feature – say, comfortable knees – that is required to perform some essential religious practice – say, spending hours
praying. The suggested amendment bizarrely implies that the atheist, who does not care at
all about the lack of this feature, would receive compensation, while the believer, who is made

bitterly miserable by this incapacity, would receive nothing.[51] Furthermore, the suggested amendment would generally fail to block the penalization of adaptive tastes, for the simple reason that one can usually expect a number of similarly situated people to have developed similar tastes. Hence, the adaptive tastes of some others would prevent redistribution to each of them.

One might wish to deal with both objections to the suggested amendment by requiring that one should discount not only the preferences of the person who risks losing entitlement to compensation because of adaptive tastes, but those of all the people who share that person's objective situation. However, the hopelessness of this strategy becomes blatant as soon as one realizes the difficulty of meaningfully characterizing "similar situations" when comparisons need to range over comprehensive endowments that are points in multidimensional continua. Hence the following suggestion. Why not stick to the simple criterion of undominated diversity without either the original or the modified amendment? Having an unusual pattern of preferences that happens to be (or has become) well suited to one's particular set of capacities and handicaps can then legitimately disqualify people for compensation they would otherwise be entitled to. But what is wrong with this? One must of course make sure that the preferences are genuine, that they do not rest on delusion, and are consistent with full information and understanding. This should take care of the cases in which "penalizing" adaptive preferences is uncontroversially counterintuitive. Beyond this, ignoring some people's preferences would amount to not giving them the equal respect they deserve.

Another objection to the effect that undominated diversity does not justify enough redistribution stresses the relevance of features of people's situations that do not belong to their comprehensive endowment. To illustrate, suppose, first, that people have identical talents, equally valuable external endowments, and the same preferences, including a strong attachment to the place where they grew up, but that the cost of living happens to be far higher (for reasons that are of no intrinsic value to the people concerned) in some places than others and hence that some people can satisfy their desire to keep living in their birthplace only at the expense of a lower standard of living. Secondly, suppose that people have identical talents, equally valuable external endowments, and the same preferences, including a strong sense of duty towards their elderly relatives that imposes strong constraints on what they can do with their lives, but that some of them have elderly relatives and others not. In either example, there is no dominated diversity among comprehensive endowments. Yet one cannot say "it is up to the people who feel hard up to adopt another preference schedule available in the community," for there is none, since all preferences are assumed identical. This suggests that envy-freeness and undominated diversity should rather be defined over "situations" (in a sense that encompasses but reaches beyond external and internal endowments), as suggested in fact by Tinbergen in the first known formulation of the concept of envy-freeness.[52] In both our examples, undominated diversity would then justify granting unequally valuable external endowments to identically talented people as a way of compensating disadvantages in objective situations more broadly construed. But here again, preference diversity will soon block the need for compensation: it is enough that one of the community's members should not give a damn about living close to his or her birthplace or about assisting elderly relatives, for the ground for special compensation to disappear.[53]

Thus my general strategy for tackling the objection that undominated diversity does not require enough redistribution consists in stressing that the preferences involved must be both genuine and available. It is worth stressing that in so doing I am rejecting at least three alternative strategies one might think of. One consists in viewing endowments not as means for pursuing what it is possible for people to believe to be a good life, but rather as means for pursuing what we know to be a good life. The latter may not be conceived in a very homogeneous way and may therefore also fall short of providing a complete ordering.[54] Yet it could be restrictive enough to allow for redistribution despite the presence of odd preference profiles that would block it if the criterion of undominated diversity were adopted. Adopting this first strategy, however, would amount to "thickening" one's conception of the good beyond the equal respect assumption, one of the core liberal presuppositions I share with Dworkin or Ackerman.

The second strategy upholds this assumption, but weakens the requirement that redistribution is only warranted when there is unanimous agreement that one endowment is superior to another. Why not be content with, say, a two-thirds majority? In most cases, this suggestion too would get rid of the difficulty presented for undominated diversity by the possibility of eccentric or adaptive preferences. But it raises fatal difficulties of its own. First, it opens the possibility of cycles closely analogous to those exemplified by Condorcet's paradox: there may be a majority preferring A's endowment to B's, another majority preferring B's to C's, and yet another preferring C's to A's. In that case, one would need to redistribute from A to B, and even more from B to C, thereby making the majority preference of C over A even stronger than it was. With unrestricted preference profiles, only unanimity guarantees that such cycles, which make the criterion useless, do not occur. Secondly and more fundamentally, the sheer number of people holding a particular conception of the good cannot really be relevant. What matters, as explained above, is whether people could feasibly adopt – and hence could fairly be held responsible for failing to adopt – a view by reference to which their endowment would be no worse than the one to which it is being compared. This is what availability (in any number) in the person's community is meant to provide a (roughly) sufficient condition for.

The third strategy consists in turning to the variant of the welfarist approach that comes closest to the approach that is being proposed here. It is presented and defended under the heading of equal opportunity for welfare in various papers by Richard Arneson.[55] The key question to ask, when considering this alternative criterion, is whether tastes are supposed to be malleable or given. If they are supposed to be fully malleable, everyone can be blissful with any endowment, and all endowments become equivalent. If instead tastes are given, the untalented with a taste for playing the oboe will have a lesser opportunity for welfare, and will therefore be entitled to a compensation to which an identically talented person with no such taste will not be entitled. In order to avoid the dilemma between bliss in all cases and the rewarding of expensive tastes, one can sensibly restrict malleability to "accessible" preference schedules, that is, to tastes one has the capacity, though not necessarily the desire, to acquire. Equality of opportunity for welfare is then achieved if the expected level of welfare under the best suited of accessible preference schedules is equal for all (presumably taking the cost of taste alteration into account). The dilemma is avoided, since (1) owing to the limits on accessibility, not all endowments yield the same opportunity for welfare, and (2) if two people have the same talents, including the same grip on their tastes, equal opportunity for welfare treats them identically, irrespective of their current tastes.

This comes quite close to undominated diversity as clarified above – so close that one may wonder whether any difference is left.[56] Since the criteria of accessibility (as used to reinterpret equal opportunity for welfare) and of availability (as used to clarify undominated diversity) are practically equivalent, where can the difference be? Consider a society with two categories of people: some with a taste for a quiet, undemanding life – call them hippies – and others with great ambitions – call them yuppies. The hippies have talents slightly better adapted to a quiet life than the yuppies, and the yuppies possess talents far better suited to their own ambitions than the hippies. Yet, with given tastes, the hippies' opportunity for welfare or preference satisfaction (on any nontautological interpretation) is far superior to the yuppies', precisely because of their lesser "ambitions." Neither category, however, would like to swap its situation (talents plus tastes) with that of the other if it could: in a hippie's view, a yuppie's life is sheer nonsense, while in a yuppie's view, a hippie's life is pure mediocrity. Against the background of this story, let us contrast the implications of undominated diversity and equal opportunity for welfare under two different factual assumptions.

Suppose first that tastes are not malleable: people are stuck with them, and the inability to change them is therefore a feature of their internal endowment. As we have assumed that there was no envy – and hence a fortiori no dominated diversity – in terms of overall situations, undominated diversity does not require any transfer. But as we have assumed differences in the expected levels of preference satisfaction, equal opportunity for welfare does require a large compensatory transfer, curiously perhaps from the less talented hippies to the more talented yuppies, to enable these to satisfy their tastes to the same extent as the hippies satisfy theirs. (This would hold even if the yuppies had talents better suited not just to their own, but also to the hippies' lifestyle.) There is nothing counterintuitive about the latter implication, one might argue, if one thinks about it as compensation for an addiction. But the notion of an addiction conflates two things: an addiction is a taste one cannot (easily) get rid of, and it is a taste one does not identify with, one that can be an obstacle to the pursuit of one's fundamental aims. In our example, however, only the first feature was assumed. If the second feature were too, envy-freeness may no longer obtain and, if it does not, undominated diversity is likely to join equal opportunity for welfare in justifying a transfer to the addicted yuppies. If the second feature is not present, however, that is, if the yuppies are stuck with their ambitious tastes, but would not want to get rid of them anyway, all things considered, if they were not, then what is it that justifies a transfer from the less talented hippies to the more talented yuppies, as equal opportunity for welfare, unlike undominated diversity, would recommend? It can only be the (illiberal) view that there is only one thing that matters or should matter to people, or to the distribution of resources among them, namely (opportunity for) welfare or preference satisfaction.

Let us now suppose, secondly, that each category could adopt (at negligible cost) the other category's tastes. People's particular tastes (or their inability to change them) could then no longer be regarded as a fixed feature of their internal endowment. Undominated diversity will again, though for a distinct reason – the absence of envy, with current preferences, over the bundles of talents (not over the overall situations) – fail to require any transfer. Equal opportunity for welfare, on the other hand, will again justify a transfer from those less well equipped for an ambitious life (the hippies) to those better equipped for it (the yuppies), though this time only to the extent required to equip the latter as well as the former for an undemanding life, and thereby giving them the same opportunity for welfare under the most favorable set of tastes. (In this case, unlike the first one, the transfer would go the other way if the yuppies were better equipped for both types of life.) Such a transfer would be justified, from the standpoint of equal opportunity for welfare, even if the yuppies looked down upon the mediocre life of the hippies and would never avail themselves of this possibility of pursuing happiness. Why? The answer, once again, can only be that all that matters or should matter, whatever people think about it, is (opportunity for) welfare or preference satisfaction. If this monistic view of the good is abandoned, undominated diversity is the obvious alternative.[57]

VIII   Too Much Redistribution?

Let us now turn to the symmetric objection. Far from implying too little redistribution, is it not the case that undominated diversity justifies too much of it? One reason may be that, in recommending redistribution when it does, it is being inconsistent with the expensive taste argument used against Dworkin's and other proposals (see section IV). If we say, as we have done, that those with a taste but no gift for playing the oboe must not make others bear the cost of this unfortunate taste, should we not also say that blind people with a taste for seeing, or deaf people with a taste for hearing, must similarly be made to bear the full cost of the tastes they happen to have? The formulation just given highlights the intuition behind the criterion that is being offered. Compensation between two people stops when potential envy-freeness starts, when the repertoire of available preference schedules is such that neither endowment is unanimously preferred to the other. The fact that everyone prefers endowment A to endowment B provides highly plausible ground for considering that people endowed with B must not be held responsible for persistently preferring A to B. They cannot reasonably be expected to adopt a preference no one has. This is why blind or deaf people can safely count on significant levels of compensation.[58] But if this is the underlying intuition, we must, of course, be careful to pick an adequate definition of the relevant community. The inability to make an effective use of one's fists, to afford a pilgrimage to Mecca, or to match the colors of one's clothes may count as "handicaps" to be compensated if a pretty homogeneous cultural group is taken as the relevant community, but not if a large, diverse, pluralist society is selected instead. The nature of customs, and the degree to which they are shared, thus enter the determination of what counts as adequate compensation according to the criterion that is here being offered.[59] In a society such as ours, with real exit possibilities from homogeneous groups and ubiquitous mass media spreading the awareness of diverse conceptions of the good life, the relevant universe of preference schedules is very large.[60]

There is a second reason why one might think that the proposed criterion leads to an excessive level of redistribution. Is not the strict satisfaction of undominated diversity likely to require the unreasonable sacrifice of much real freedom on the part of most members of the community?[61] True, in a society with a wide diversity of conceptions of the good life, the level of redistribution required to meet undominated diversity is far less than the level that would be required to achieve equality of welfare, for example, or equality of resources in the sense of the extended auction. As soon as one person genuinely finds an initially dominated endowment at least as good as that of the contributors to the redistribution scheme, redistribution can stop. But clearly, some people may be so badly handicapped that even massive transfers from the rest of society would hardly make their situation more attractive, and would therefore still fail to meet the criterion.

In order to deal adequately with this objection, undominated diversity must be qualified in two ways. First, once sustainability is brought into the picture, it is not the simple version of the criterion that provides a legitimate constraint, but a leximin variant of it. If the impact of the taxes and transfers required to sustainably maintain undominated diversity is such that everyone would gain from keeping some pattern of dominance in place, a sensible conception of justice will obviously recommend that the latter be tolerated.[62] Secondly, the priority of undominated diversity must not be understood in rigid fashion. "Mild" violations of it can be admitted if they prevent "considerable" losses for the rest of society. Hence, before reaching the point where further redistribution to the badly handicapped becomes counterproductive in absolute terms (taking dynamic effects into account), it may be legitimate to stop it because very large further transfers would only produce a hardly noticeable improvement in the beneficiary's situation. These two qualifications should go a long way towards meeting Sen's concern that "aggregative considerations" including – but not reducing to – Pareto optimality, should be brought into the picture and soften undominated diversity's exclusively distributive concern,[63] or Arneson's objection that there are significant nonegalitarian values by which egalitarian concerns should sometimes be overridden.[64]

Thus clarified and qualified, the requirement of undominated diversity remains an important constraint. In all circumstances, it will reduce significantly the highest sustainable level of basic income, and in some circumstances, it will drive this level down to zero.[65] But it does not seem unreasonable to believe, bearing in mind the qualifications that have just been made, that under the conditions that now prevail in advanced industrial societies, the highest sustainable basic income consistent with both formal freedom and undominated diversity can confidently be expected to be quite substantial, indeed to exceed what is there unanimously considered as belonging to the bare necessities. In a society that is not only sufficiently diverse (which makes dominance less frequent for "subjective" reasons), but also sufficiently healthy (which makes dominance less frequent for "objective" reasons) and sufficiently affluent (which drives up the average external endowment), a small minority of "handicapped" people will be entitled to differentiated transfers, but all, including the majority consisting of "normal" people, will remain entitled to a substantial basic income.[66]

To some, this very fact may constitute a further and possibly decisive argument against undominated diversity and in favor of such alternatives as Dworkin's equality of resources. But to others it may not. Indeed, it may powerfully boost the practical motivation for taking undominated diversity seriously as a central component of any consistent liberal conception of distributive justice.[67]

Acknowledgement

For stimulating critical comments, I am very grateful to Bruce Ackerman, Richard Arneson, Christian Arnsperger, Vicky Barham, Brian Barry, David Copp, Ronald Dworkin, Marc Fleurbaey, Louis Gevers, Jean Hampton, Dan Hausman, Guy Perez, John Roemer, Erik Schokkaert, Amartya Sen, Bernard Stainier, Robert Sugden, and Erik Wright, even though several of them will probably judge that the present version persists in what they regard as a wrong direction. A longer version of this chapter forms chapter 3 of my *Real Freedom for All* (Oxford: Oxford University Press, 1995).

Notes

1   I use the term "capacities" (and hence "talents") in a broad sense that covers both capacities to function and capacities for welfare. See G. A. Cohen, "On the Currency of Egalitarian Justice," *Ethics*, vol. 99, 1989, pp. 918–19. I prefer to use the term "endowments" where others might have used, for example, "resources," "opportunities," or "capacities" to stress the restriction to what people have been "given," whether at the start or later on, whether intentionally or unwittingly, whether in the form of external goods and purchasing power or as bodily and mental features.

2   This assumption is both argued for and qualified in my *Real Freedom For All*, op. cit., chs. 2 and 4. It is sufficiently close conceptually to Doworkin's own conception of fairness in the distribution of external resources to provide a convenient background assumption for the present discussion, even though

the radically broader way in which I interpret external resources leads to quite different policy implications.

3   See esp. Van Parijs (ed.), *Arguing for Basic Income, Ethical Foundations for a Radical Reform* (London: Verso, 1992), and ibid.

4   "Bears a close relationship to" and not "amounts to," because I do not want to rule out that a maximin or leximin criterion should be favored over strict equality.

5   This aspect of the background is spelled out by Amartya Sen, for example, in his critique of "commodity fetishism," "Equality of What?" in A. Sen (ed.), *Choice, Welfare and Measurement* (Oxford: Blackwell, 1982), pp. 353–69; *Commodities and Capabilities* (Amsterdam: North-Holland, 1985), p. 28.

6   As in John Roemer's "Equality of Talent," *Economics and Philosophy*, vol. 1, 1985, pp. 151–87, and his "Equality of Resources Implies Equality of Welfare," *Quarterly Journal of Economics*, vol. 101, 1986, pp. 751–84. Or as in Marc Fleurbaey's axiomatic treatment in his "L'absence d'envie dans une problématique post welfariste," *Recherches Economiques de Louvain*, vol. 60, 1994, pp. 9–42, to which I return below.

7   Ronald Dworkin, "What is Equality? Part II: Equality of Resources," *Philosophy and Public Affairs*, vol. 10, 1981, pp. 283–345. For an anticipation of this aspect of Dworkin's conception of distributive justice, including his parable of a postshipwreck auction, see François Huet's *Le règne social du christianisme* (Paris, Firmin Didot, 1853), pp. 258–9.

8   Equivalently, one can imagine that each of the n Polypolitans is given, in the form of a tradable share, $1/n$ of each external good and of each person's talents.

9   We could equivalently model the problem in such a way that some people would not bother to buy all their own leisure and would rather abandon some of it to other people, who would allocate it to its most productive use (or sell it to firms that would do so), since they would anyway do exactly the same with it if they had bought it themselves.

10 Or, equivalently, as giving everyone a grant matching the per capita value of all endowments, while taxing at a rate of 100 percent those who happen to hold those endowments. Akerlof points out some advantages that such a system of "tagged" transfers possesses over a negative income tax system, without claiming that the overall balance of advantages is in its favor. G. A. Akerlof, "The Economics of 'Tagging' as Applied to the Optimal Income Tax, Welfare Programs, and Manpower Planning," in G. A. Akerlof, *An Economic Theorist's Book of Tales* (Cambridge, UK: Cambridge University Press, 1984), pp. 45–68.

11 If talents were identical, this difficulty would not arise, because there would be no reason to depart from equality of external endowments. Nor would it arise if tastes were identical, for if both care for racing and not for singing, the good runner will have to compensate the good singer up to the point where both will feel equivalence is reached. Classic formulations of the nature of the problem and how it might be tackled can be found in E. Pazner and D. Schmeidler, "A Difficulty in the Concept of Fairness," *Review of Economic Studies*, vol. 41, 1974, pp. 441–3; and H. Varian "Distributive Justice, Welfare Economics and the Theory of Fairness," in F. Hahn and M. Hollis (eds.), *Philosophy and Economic Theory* (Oxford: Oxford University Press 1979), pp. 152–3.

12 Provided of course the abilities in relation to which people's implicit incomes are defined coincide with the received "talents" that are supposed to be up for bids in the auction. This is taken for granted by Varian in his discussion of Dworkin's "Equality of Resources." However, the market price of people's leisure, i.e. the earning power associated with their current abilities, does not generally coincide with the earning power associated with their talents, i.e. to that part or aspect of their abilities which has been "given" to them. At first sight, the latter seems necessarily inferior to the former, since it concern a subset or incipient stage of abilities. But the opposite is the case. For in the context of the auction, the counterfactual earning power that must be equalized is not the one associated to people's talents if they had been left undeveloped, but the one associated to those same talents when developed and used in the most productive fashion. It is all people's maximally developed potential, given their internal endowment, that must be equalized. See Varian, "Dworkin on Equality of Resources," *Economics and Philosophy*, vol. 1, 1985, esp. pp. 111–13.

13 In this sentence and the rest of the discussion of this example, "she" and "her" are used as abbreviations for "he or she" and "his or her".

14 Lonely and Lovely resemble Dworkin's Deborah and Ernest in relevant respects. The second objection does not play such a central role in Dworkin's motivation for his own proposal, even though its relevance is implicitly acknowledged in the fact that Dworkin finds it necessary (as we shall see in section V) to introduce a separate device for dealing with handicaps, whether or not these affect people's productive abilities. See "Equality of Resources," op. cit., p. 312.

15 J. Roemer, "Equality of Talent," *Economics and Philosophy*, vol. 1, 1985, p. 165.

16 Dworkin, "Equality of Resources," op. cit., p. 312.

17 Ibid., p. 327.

18 Dworkin suggests three further arguments for discarding the extended auction that I find less convincing. First, he points out that we are not "able to find some way of identifying, in any person's wealth at any particular time, the component traceable to different talents as distinguished from different ambitions" (ibid., p. 313). However, a similar problem arises, and is assumed to be solved, in the case of external resources. People's ambitions do not leave external any more than internal resources unimproved and combine them all together to generate their wealth. This does not in principle prevent the counterfactual auction from yielding a competitive price for either. Secondly, Dworkin stresses the "reciprocal influence that talents and ambitions exercise on each other" (ibid.). But similarly, while your ambitions determine which external resources you will bid for, if any, in the auction, the external resources you actually possess will affect your ambitions (you'll want to become a botanist because of the many flowers in the garden of the family house you have inherited). True, there is a difference. Unlike your external resources, you cannot (much?) help having the talents you actually have. And it makes, therefore, little sense to ask yourself what your preferences might have been without them when bidding for the various resources, whereas it does make some sense to abstract from the external resources actually allotted to you. But this does not prevent the auction from applying to talents. All it requires is that the bidders should be able to say, given their preferences (which they have in part because of the internal – but also the external – resources they possess in the real world) how much they would give for the opportunity to possess, use, and develop the various sorts of talents. Thirdly, one rough way of describing the auction for external resources consists in viewing it as a counterfactual determination of what people's incomes would be if they had been allocated the same amount of these resources. But, Dworkin (ibid., p. 314) points out, it is impossible to determine, for each person, what "income he would have had if, counterfactually, talents for production had all been equal." And even if we do not agree with him that "in a world in which everyone could play sexy roles in films with equal authority, there would probably be no . . . films," it must be recognized that trying to imagine what the distribution of income (or earning power) would look like in such a world is a hopeless business. What is required in the auction (for both internal and external resources), however, is not that everyone should possess (either before or after) an equal amount of each resource, but an equal tradable title to each resource. The counterfactual exercise remains rather adventurous. But it is not meaningless. It is, as it happens, exactly the sort of exercise in terms of which Roemer in his *A General Theory of Exploitation and Class* (Cambridge, MA: Harvard University Press, 1982) defines his notions of capitalist (external resources) and socialist (internal resources) exploitation (see § 5.7).

19 J. Roemer, "Equality of Talent," op. cit., pp. 151–87; "Equality of Resources Implies Equality of Welfare," op. cit.

20 J. Roemer, "Equality of Talent,"op. cit., p. 173.

21 Ibid., p. 159.

22 Ibid., p. 175.

23 This argument discussed for example, by Thomas C. Grey ("The First Virtue," *Stanford Law Review*, vol. 25, 1973, pp. 317–20), is in my view the best defense of a maximin principle against Harsanyi-like original-position utilitarians. Rawls himself insists that he has never claimed that maximin was adequate in all circumstances of risk or uncertainty: "The only question is whether given the highly special, indeed unique, conditions of the original position, the maximin rule is a useful heuristic rule of thumb

for the parties to use to organize their deliberations" (John Rawls, *Justice as Fairness. A Restatement* (Cambridge, MA: Harvard University Press, 2001), p. 97, fn. 19). Roemer ("Equality of Talent," op. cit., p. 165) must have come close to seeing the strength of this point when contrasting the case where people want to insure against fluctuation of their skill level and the case where "after the die is cast, each person will be either of high or of low skill for his whole life."

24   I assume, for simplicity's sake, that we are in a certain world. Tastes being given, each endowment is associated with one level of welfare. If uncertain events were allowed to disturb this simple association, the most natural extension would consist of evaluating each endowment by the level of welfare it would yield under the worst possible circumstances.

25   See Roemer's "Equality of Talent," op. cit., pp. 175–6; and his "Equality of Resources Implies Equality of Welfare," op. cit.

26   Roemer's "Equality of Talent," op. cit., pp. 179–80. As meticulously shown by Cohen, Dworkin is not always clear as to whether his central distinction is one of identity versus circumstances, capacities versus preferences, or choice versus (brute) luck. But I believe what he says can consistently be reconstructed along the lines sketched here. See § 4 of Cohen's "On the Currency," op. cit.

27   Alexander and Schwarzchild similarly reject Roemer's critique of Dworkin because of its deterministic presuppositions. See § IIIC in L. Alexander and Larry M. Schwarzschild "Liberalism, Neutrality, and Equality of Welfare vs. Equality of Resources," *Philosophy and Public Affairs*, vol. 16, 1987, pp. 85–110.

28   "Equality of Resources," op. cit., pp. 316–18, 324–5.

29   Note that this implies that risk-averse people interested in maximum leisure subject to subsistence will choose a level of coverage (in terms of *earning power*) that *exceeds* the subsistence level. Otherwise, they would end up having to work nearly full time in order to reach subsistence with very poor talents, while having to work far less with abundant talents.

30   In the formulation of Dworkin ("Equality of Resources," op. cit.), not altered nor qualified in Dworkin's later writings on equality.

31   "Equality of Resources," op. cit., p. 329.

32   At least in a certain world. Under uncertainty, on the other hand, there is no reason why luck should systematically lead the film star to be be envied rather than to envy.

33   This might provide a fair reconstruction of what Sen presents as his central criticism of Dworkin's approach:

> Indeed, to see the interpersonal variations of the mappings from resources to capabilities as due only to handicaps of some people is to underestimate the general nature of the problem. As was already mentioned, depending on our body size, metabolism, temperament, social conditions, etc., the translation of resources into the ability to do things does vary substantially from person to person and from community to community, and to ignore this is to miss out on an important general dimension of moral concern. (A. Sen, "Rights and Capabilities," op. cit., p. 323.)

To be fair to Dworkin, one must concede that his concern with the equalization of capabilities does not boil down to a compensation for handicaps. But to the extent that he actually goes beyond such compensation, he does so in a biased way, by completely ignoring any "ability to do things" (of the type Sen has in mind) that is not matched by an ability to make money.

34   Dworkin ("Equality of Resources," op. cit., p. 302) forcefully argues against a conception that would allow for insurance against tastes leading to a less-than-average level of welfare: if one abstracts from one's tastes, how could one possibly decide how much to insure for?

35   More formally, it fails Fleurbaey's strict pair-wise compensation test, which requires two people to receive equal external endowments if their internal endowments are identical. See §4 of his "L'absence d'envie." A different formulation of basically the same objection can be found in E. Rakowski, *Equal Justice* (Oxford: Oxford University Press, 1991), pp. 135–7.

36   Dworkin, "Equality of Resources," op. cit., p. 293.

37 In §4 of his "L'absence d'envie," Fleurbaey shows, for example, that there is no criterion that can meet simultaneously the condition of strict pair-wise compensation that has just been shown to be violated by Dworkin's proposals and a condition of "full pair-wise compensation" which requires that two people with identical preference schedules should achieve the same level of welfare. This is an interesting impossibility result, but one that is irrelevant to our resolutely nonwelfarist approach.

38 B. Ackerman, *Social Justice in the Liberal State* (New Haven, CT: Yale University Press, 1980), p. 116.

39 Internal endowments must here be understood, as they have been all along, as referring to the capacities (or lack of them) people owe to their genetic inheritance or their environment over their whole lifetimes.

40 Hence, contrary to what Ackerman (ibid., p. 132) suggests, showing that "I have the ability to do some good things better than you, and vice versa" is generally not sufficient to be able to conclude that there is no dominance.

41 Genetic engineering, if not ruled out by powerful second-best arguments, should use a lottery such that

> the only embryo distributions that can be forbidden are those in which at least one member of the set genetically dominates at least one other member of the set. Thus it is perfectly possible that a blind embryo will be brought into existence in a perfectly liberal world – so long as it has other attributes that permit it to establish a relation of undominated diversity with each and every one of the fellow citizens with which it will share the planet. (ibid., p. 120).

42 Ackerman, op. cit., p. 132.

43 Even on this criterion, the boundary between a handicap and a lack of talent which does not qualify as such is to some extent technologically and culturally relative (short-sightedness or a low IQ may count as handicaps in some societies though not in others). But the underlying distinction is a more precise formulation of what Dworkin has in mind when referring to "ordinary handicaps" or to "the risks against which most people would insure in a general way" and, therefore, of the intuition behind the central distinction of his hybrid scheme ("Equality of Resources," op. cit., pp. 299, 316).

44 Ackerman, op. cit., pp. 246–7.

45 The reason for the reversal of at least one person's preferences may, but need not, be that the transfer is being used to regain the missing capacity (say, through an eye operation). The approach presented here is not capacity-focused in the narrow sense this would imply. But it is capacity-focused in the sense that the transfers are not required to compensate for a welfare deficit, but to make people able to do (in the broadest sense) at least one thing which others could not do.

46 Note that the maximum amount that can be sustainably redistributed in a differentiated way need not be the same as the highest amount that can be sustainably redistributed in a uniform way. It may be higher, because it provides stronger incentives to work to the talented (they are not given the option of remaining idle). And it may be lower because of the greater simplicity of a basic income and its contribution to a more flexible economy. See G. Akerlof, "The Economics of 'Tagging' as Applied to the Optimal Income Tax, Welfare Programs, and Manpower Planning," op. cit.; and Van Parijs (ed.), *Arguing for Basic Income*, op. cit., ch. 11, on efficiency arguments for and against targeting.

47 I do not have the option of excluding this possibility by arguing – as does Arneson for example – that it would be unfair to regard Lovely as responsible for the fact that she has a taste for her own (as it happens, expensive) leisure. In contrast with the blind person with a taste for seeing (given the assumptions made earlier in this section), there is, by assumption, at least one preference schedule genuinely available that would make Lovely better off than people in Lonely's position. It is not "her fault" that she has the talent she has, but it is "her fault" that she has no taste for using the possibilities they give her. The criterion of undominated diversity is fully consistent with people having less leisure by virtue of their talents, just as it is fully consistent with people having less income by virtue of their lack of talents. What it does exclude – indeed, what it amounts to excluding – is that one should *necessarily* (i.e., irrespective of the available preference schedule one picks) have less welfare by virtue of one's talents or lack thereof.

48   This seems to me a more direct and general way of getting to Dworkin's main practical conclusion:

> The lower the income level chosen as the covered risk, the better the argument becomes that most people, given the chance to buy insurance on equal terms would in fact buy at that level. The argument becomes compelling, I think, well above the level of income presently used to trigger transfer payments for unemployment or minimum wage levels in either Britain or the United States. There is an earning power that is so low that anyone would prefer practically any situation with a higher earning power. Under such circumstances, our scheme requires the basic income should be reduced, possibly to zero, to finance a transfer system targeted to those with low earning powers. ("Equality of Resources," op. cit., p. 321)

This approach is more general because the compensation for "ordinary handicaps" is derived in exactly the same way.

49   The approach offered here can therefore be viewed as a special case of what is being explored by Amartya Sen (in e.g., *Commodities and Capabilities*, op. cit., ch. 7).

50   This looks like a point of disagreement with Ackerman (*Social Justice in the Liberal State*, op. cit., p. 120), who is concerned to achieve "undominated diversity with each and every one of the fellow citizens with which it will share the planet," but ceases to be one if one ascribes to him the cosmopolitan assumption that we are henceforth all part of a single global community.

51   I borrow this example from Arneson ("Property Rights in Persons," *Social Philosophy and Policy*, vol. 9, 1992, § 5, pp. 201–30).

52   Jan Tinbergen, *Redelijke Inkomensverdeling* (Haarlem, Netherlands: De Gulden Pers, 1946), pp. 59–60.

53   This is why, under plausible factual assumptions, the respect of undominated diversity is consistent with a basic income that is insensitive to cost-of-living differences between different areas.

54   Hence choosing this strategy would not make the criterion of undominated diversity vacuous, contrary to what is suggested by Rakowski (*Equal Justice*, op. cit., pp. 96–7) in his (too) brief and (too) dismissive discussion of undominated diversity.

55   For example, Arneson, "A Defense of Equal Opportunity for Welfare," *Philosophical Studies*, vol. 62, 1991, pp. 187–95.

56   At least providing the preferences by reference to which equal opportunity for welfare is defined are not deemed "inaccessible" – as sometimes suggested by Arneson (see esp. ibid., § V) – if the only reason for not adopting them is that "it would be unreasonable from the point of view of [our] current values to adopt [them]." This would bring back the strong version of the expensive taste objection.

57   This argument is congruent with G. A. Cohen's shift from the one-dimensional metric of equal opportunity for welfare to the multidimensional metric of "equal access to advantage" ("On the Currency of Egalitarian Justice," op. cit., pp. 920–1).

58   This provides, it seems to me, an adequate riposte to Alexander and Schwarzschild's ("Liberalism, Neutrality, and Equality of Welfare vs. Equality of Resources," op. cit., pp. 100–2) central objection to Dworkin, that there is no "neutral" distinction between needs and wants, and hence that "for anyone who takes neutrality seriously, handicaps, cravings and expensive tastes are on a par with one another" (ibid., p. 101). It is no doubt abstractly conceivable, as they point out, that someone with particular religious beliefs *might* value blindness as a sign of divine grace (and hence not as a handicap). But using the conceptions of a good life (and of what is required for it) that are *actually* (and genuinely) held in the society considered in order to assess dominance, seems to me a sensible thing to do, as the aim is to consider the full range of preferences for the choice of which people can plausibly be held responsible.

59   This indicates how our criterion can accommodate Amartya Sen's insistence that applying the principle of "equality of basic capabilities" is bound to be culture-dependent (e.g., Sen, "Equality of What?," op. cit., p. 368), and his dissatisfaction with the goods metric on the ground that it is insensitive not just to differences in abilities but also to differences in the "social demands of particular customs" (e.g., Sen, *Commodities and Capabilities*, op. cit., p. 28).

60   The universe of preference schedules that is being taken into account need not in principle coincide with the scale on which redistribution is being considered. But I doubt that the question of distribu-

tive justice has ever been, and can ever be, seriously raised in a society that is not either culturally homogeneous, or knit together by sufficiently sizeable flows of information and people across its component cultural traditions.

61 A related but distinct – and, for my present purposes irrelevant – objection is that the implied level of compensation is politically unrealistic. See e.g., Dworkin ("Equality of Resources," op. cit., pp. 300–1) on Sen's "Equality of What?," op. cit.

62 If the level of the unconditional income has already been driven down to zero when this point is reached, this potential universal gain may simply be due to the adverse incentives generated by increased taxation. If it has not, this may be due to the fact that transfers distributed in an unconditional way (i.e., as a basic income) are simpler to administer, do not generate incentives to hide one's capacities (e.g., to pretend to be involuntarily unemployed or unfit for work), and arguably increase economic efficiency by fostering labor flexibility and spreading an entrepreneurial spirit. (As previously mentioned, however, there may also be more to sustainably redistribute in a differentiated than in an undifferentiated way.) I am here taking for granted that undominated diversity can be pursued through income taxation as well as through lump-sum taxation (of less than the level of basic income), since I depict this pursuit as consisting in diverting resources from the funding of a basic income at the highest sustainable level, without any principled restriction on the tax base.

63 Sen, "Welfare, Freedom and Social Choice: A Reply," *Recherches Economiques de Louvain*, vol. 56, pp. 462–3.

64 Do these two qualifications concede too much, at the expense of the handicapped? Let us bear in mind that for the latter, receiving resources in the form of a basic income rather than as targeted transfers has advantages too. Transfers one owes to the inadequacy of one's internal endowment tend to involve a stigma, a blow to one's self-respect, and often also, owing to the imperfect detection of talents and handicaps, a "disability trap," that is partly removed as a higher unconditional income makes some conditional transfers dispensable.

65 It is only under those circumstances that the implications here drawn from a concern with undominated diversity would coincide with those drawn by Ackerman, who argues against universal systems, such as a negative income tax, on the ground that they are too favorable to "healthy proletarians": "it would be best to design a more complex strategy that, despite heavy administrative costs, tries to identify severely handicapped citizens entitled to aid levels that are far more generous than those prevailing under the typical negative income tax proposal" (*Social Justice in the Liberal State*, op. cit., p. 268 n. 2). Outside those circumstances, I argue, justice requires that both types of system be combined.

66 Because the maximization of basic income needs to operate under the constraint of undominated diversity, special attention will have to be given to various policies that may make the constraint significantly easier to meet. Universal provision in kind (such as preventive medicine), specific provision in kind to the handicapped (say, access to public transport), or to those who would otherwise become handicapped (e.g., special educational aid to the slow learners), and the promotion of a spirit of tactful and effective help to those with special needs, are just a few examples.

67 This conception of social justice that combines undominated diversity with the maximin distribution of external endowments is further defended in P. Van Parijs, "Real Freedom, the Market and the Family. A Reply," *Analyse & Kritik*, vol. 23(1), 2001, pp. 106–31; and in P. Van Parijs, "Hybrid Justice, Patriotism and Democracy. A Selective Reply," in A. Reeve and A. Williams (eds.), *Real-Libertarianism Assessed. Political Theory after Van Parijs* (Basingstoke, UK: Palgrave Macmillan, 2003), pp. 201–16. See also P. Vallentyne, "Self-Ownership and Equality: Brute Luck, Gifts, Universal Dominance and Leximin," ibid. pp. 29–52; and A. Williams, "Resource Egalitarianism and the Limits to Basic Income," ibid. pp. 111–35, for insightful critical discussions of undominated diversity.

Liberty, Equality, Envy, and Abstraction

Michael Otsuka

The "sovereign virtue of political community" according to Ronald Dworkin, is an "equal concern for the fate of all those citizens over whom [a government] claims dominion."[1] Such equal concern requires that governments aim to realize, so far as possible, an ideal egalitarian distribution of resources as specified by his theory of "equality of resources" (p. 3). In particular, governments should aim to bring about a distribution that is egalitarian insofar as it passes an "envy test" which stipulates that nobody prefer anyone else's bundle of resources to his or her own.[2] Passing the envy test is a necessary condition of an ideal egalitarian distribution, but it is not a sufficient condition (p. 146). A set of sufficient conditions also includes a "principle of abstraction" that states that bundles of resources should be maximally sensitive to the plans and preferences of individuals (pp. 146–52). Dworkin appeals to the principle of abstraction to argue for the striking conclusion that "liberty must figure in the very definition of an ideal [egalitarian] distribution, so that, for that reason, there can be no problem of reconciling liberty and equality" (p. 135).

I hope to demonstrate the following in this chapter. Dworkin's reconciliation of liberty and equality in chapter 3 of *Sovereign Virtue* presupposes the compossibility of the satisfaction of the envy test and the realization of the principle of abstraction. It is, however, impossible to realize a distribution that is both envy-free and maximally sensitive to plans and preferences. When this conflict between the envy test and the principle of abstraction is brought to light, it will become apparent that Dworkin falls short of a complete reconciliation of liberty and equality. After briefly describing the nature and scope of the envy test in section I, I turn in sections II and III to a discussion of the presupposed compossibility of, and an explanation of the actual conflict between, the envy test and the principle of abstraction. In section IV, I show how this conflict renders Dworkin's reconciliation of liberty and equality incomplete.

I

Dworkin writes that "a fully equal distribution of resources is one in which no one 'envies' the resources others have," where "envy" is to be understood as a preference for those resources over one's own when proper account has been taken of the choices that gave rise to the resources that people possess.[3] Dworkin draws a distinction between two types of resource: "personal" and "impersonal." An individual's personal resources are "his physical and mental health and ability – his general fitness and capacities, including his wealth-talent, that is, his innate capacity to produce goods or services that others will pay to have" (pp. 322–3). Impersonal resources are "those resources that can be reassigned from one person to another – his wealth and the other property he commands, and the opportunities provided him, under the reigning legal system, to use that property" (p. 323). He illustrates the ideal of an envy-free distribution by means of his famous desert island in which people are given equal amounts of money to bid on the island's resources.[4] Such an auction will give rise to an envy-free distribution of resources if the personal resources of the islanders are equal. But if their personal resources are unequal, the auction will not satisfy the envy test, since that test is met just in case nobody envies anybody else's total set of personal and impersonal resources:

> The auction I just imagined is an auction of impersonal resources, and if personal resources are and remain unequal, the envy test will not be satisfied, either during or after the auction. Even if my impersonal resources are the same as yours, I will envy your total set of resources, which includes your talent and health as well. Once the auction has stopped, moreover, and people begin to produce and trade, your advantages in talent and health will soon destroy our initial equality in impersonal resources as well.[5]

When personal resources are unequal, it will prove notoriously difficult to conceive necessary and sufficient conditions of an envy-free distribution of total sets of personal and impersonal resources, let alone an envy-free distribution that can plausibly be described as an ideal of egalitarian justice. Problems arise in accounting both for inequalities in personal resources themselves and for differences in impersonal resources such as income and wealth to which inequalities in personal resources give rise.[6] I shall set these difficulties to one side, since the challenge I would like to pose in this chapter does not presuppose any inequalities in personal resources. I shall assume throughout the remainder of this chapter that personal resources are equal.

Given this assumption, it is relatively straightforward to conceive realizable conditions under which the envy test will be satisfied. When personal resources are equal, an envy-free distribution is realized just in case nobody would prefer anybody else's impersonal resources over a lifetime plus the choices regarding work, investment, and consumption that gave rise to these resources.[7] To illustrate: we are not entitled to infer that the envy test has been violated simply by virtue of the fact that Adrian's bank account is much larger than Bruce's, so that now Adrian but not Bruce is able to enjoy a retirement in luxury. For these differences might have arisen only because of the differing choices that Adrian and Bruce have made over the course of their working lives. They might have arisen only because Adrian chose a life of work and investment rather than of leisure and consumption, whereas Bruce chose the reverse. Suppose that Bruce would have ended up with just as large a bank account as Adrian's at the age of retirement if he had chosen as Adrian did. In this case the envy test would be met even though Bruce is now much poorer than Adrian (pp. 83–5).[8]

II

With this explanation of the envy test in place, we are now in a position to turn to a consideration of the relation of this test to the principle of abstraction.[9] This latter principle calls for a distribution of, and a system of rights regarding, resources that permit "the greatest possible flexibility in fine-tuning bids to plans and preferences" (p. 151).[10] For reasons that I shall spell out below, Dworkin's discussion in chapter 3 of the relation between the envy test and the principle of abstraction presupposes that these are compossible, not competing, ideals.

In order to describe the relation between these two principles, I shall begin by noting that resource shares are equal, according to Dworkin, only if the "opportunity cost" of each person's share is equal (p. 149).[11] Opportunity cost is equal when a distribution of resources satisfies his envy test (ibid., see also p. 70). He illustrates these claims by means of the desert island auction.[12] Dworkin argues that a "baseline liberty/constraint system" must be in place before such an auction can properly begin: that is, it must be stipulated in advance of the bidding "what one can and cannot do with or about" each resource after it has been purchased (p. 143). The envy test, however, does not itself provide a basis for determining which of these liberty/constraint systems should be guaranteed in advance:

> If the background [liberty/constraint system] stipulates that no one may use any of the resources he acquires, except in a few enumerated ways, the envy test will be met: people will make choices with those serious constraints on liberty in mind, and by hypothesis will not prefer any bundle of resources anyone else chooses given the same constraints. If the background stipulates a much larger scope of freedom of choice, the bundle each chooses will be a different bundle, but once again the auction, if successful, will produce an envy-free distribution. . . . [T]he envy test is in that way indiscriminate among systems of liberty and constraint . . . (pp. 145–6)

For this reason, the envy test "cannot provide the entire definition of an ideal distribution. Since that test is compatible with an indefinite number of different distributions . . . it can provide only a necessary condition for an ideal distribution. A liberty/constraint system is part of what is needed to complete a set of sufficient conditions" (p. 146).[13]

In order to select the appropriate baseline system of liberty and constraint, Dworkin believes that we must appeal to an "abstract egalitarian principle":

> We hold two ideas in place: the abstract egalitarian principle, which demands equal concern, on the one hand, and equality of resources, which proposes that an auction under certain conditions [namely, those that will satisfy the envy test] realizes equal concern, on the other. We select the baseline system . . . that builds the best bridge between those two ideas. We select the baseline system that gives most plausibility to the claim that an auction from that baseline treats people with equal concern. (pp. 147–8)[14]

"This bridge strategy," Dworkin argues, "endorses one powerful and general principle, the principle of abstraction" (p. 148). It endorses this principle for the following reason. The best bridge is a baseline system that reflects the "true opportunity costs" of resources: "If we can give sense to the idea of true opportunity costs, then we can select baseline provisions about liberty, as providing the best bridge between the abstract egalitarian principle [of equal concern] and the envy test, by asking which such provisions are best calculated to identify and reflect true opportunity costs" (p. 149). Dworkin maintains that "an auction is fairer – that it provides a more genuinely equal distribution – when it offers more discriminating choices and is thus more sensitive to the discrete plans and preferences people in fact have" (pp. 150–1). True opportunity cost, he argues, is reflected in a distribution that is maximally sensitive to these diverse plans and preferences – that is, a distribution that is called for by the principle of abstraction: "The principle [of abstraction] recognizes that the true opportunity cost of any transferable resource is the price others would pay for it in an auction whose resources were offered in as abstract a form as possible, that is, in the form that permits the greatest possible flexibility in fine-tuning bids to plans and preferences" (p. 151).

Dworkin's claim that the principle of abstraction provides the best bridge to the envy test presupposes a distribution that is both envy free and maximally sensitive to plans and preferences.

For if the maximally sensitive distribution, which the principle of abstraction mandates, were a nonenvy-free distribution, then the principle of abstraction would fail to construct the best bridge between the principle of equal concern and the envy test. Rather, it would construct no bridge at all because it would not even connect the former to the latter.

III

Contrary to Dworkin's presupposition of compossibility, it can be shown that the maximally sensitive liberty/constraint system, which he derives from the principle of abstraction, will give rise to a distribution that frustrates the envy test. Dworkin maintains that the principle of abstraction "establishes a strong presumption in favor of freedom of choice" (p. 148). He maintains that

> legal constraints beyond those necessary for security obviously compromise abstraction. . . . So the principle of abstraction insists that people should in principle be left free, under the baseline system, to use the resources they acquire, including the leisure they provide and protect through their bidding program, in whatever way they wish, compatibly with the principle of security [which prohibits physical assault, theft, deliberate damage to property, and trespass]. (p. 152)[15]

It follows that the principle of abstraction would condemn all laws that constrain gift giving by means of the selective imposition of a tax on it. This principle would condemn such laws for giving rise to a distribution that did not fairly reflect the preferences of those who want to acquire resources for the purpose of giving to others rather than for their own consumption.[16] Those who would like to give to others would, if selectively taxed for doing so, be unable "to tailor their resources to their plans as effectively with that constraint as they could without it" (p. 152).[17] Such a gift-friendly liberty/constraint system, which Dworkin derives from the principle of abstraction, would make it inevitable that the distribution of resources will fall short of satisfying the envy test. It will fall short for the simple reason that the envy test will be frustrated if some are allowed to become wealthier than others simply because they, and not these others, have the brute good fortune to have been chosen as the beneficiaries of gifts.

Dworkin acknowledges that the untaxed, nonmarket transfers of wealth in the form of gifts would frustrate the ideal of an envy-free distribution of impersonal resources over a lifetime. He writes:

> Suppose I consume all my resources but you economize and leave most of yours to your children. Or that you have invested skillfully and have more to leave for that reason. Or that I have more children than you, and so must divide their inheritance into smaller shares. Then, although neither of us has invaded resources properly belonging to another, our children will not have equal resources: some will envy what others have. (p. 488 n. 12)[18]

In the light of these observations, Dworkin maintains that gifts should be regulated by a tax modeled as follows on a hypothetical insurance scheme. An average member of society is deprived of specific information concerning the wealth and generosity of potential benefactors and is asked how much insurance, if any, he or she would purchase against receiving little by way of gifts. Members of society would be required to pay a tax on wealth that they transfer by way of gifts. This tax would be equal to the cost of the premium of the insurance policy that this average member of society would have purchased. Dworkin maintains that the average person would not find it rational to purchase a policy that results in the imposition of a confiscatory 100 percent tax on all gifts (pp. 347–9).[19] Hence, the tax will have the consequence that some members of society will begin and lead their lives with different amounts of wealth, not because of any difference in the choices they have made (nor because of differences in their option luck), but simply because of the unequal wealth and nonfully-taxed generosity of their parents and other benefactors.

It follows from this consequence that the envy test will be frustrated even after these taxes have been collected. Given that he describes the envy test as a necessary condition of an ideal egalitarian distribution, why does Dworkin opt for a tax modeled on hypothetical insurance which will frustrate that test? He cannot be moved here, as he was in the case of his defense of a redistributive income tax modeled on hypothetical underemployment insurance to compensate for inequalities in talent, by the infeasibility of realizing an envy-free distribution.[20] For in this case there is a simple method of realizing an envy-free distribution: a confiscatory 100 percent tax on all gifts. Why doesn't Dworkin endorse such a 100 percent tax?

The answer to this question is that Dworkin has recently made clear that he believes that there are two *competing* egalitarian demands relevant to the issue of gifts and bequests. The first is provided by the envy test. The second is provided by the principle of abstraction. While the first demands a 100 percent tax on gifts, the second demands completely untaxed freedom of choice regarding the giving of gifts.[21] Dworkin claims that a gift tax modeled on hypothetical insurance which falls between these two extremes of zero and 100 percent taxation is justifiable as a reconciliation of these "competing demands within equality itself."[22] In the light of this claim, chapter 3 should be amended to make clear that the principle of abstraction and the envy test are conflicting rather than compossible. They are to be weighed against each other and a balance struck between the two.

IV

This striking of a balance between conflicting principles makes Dworkin's theory of equality of resources safe, within the limits set by hypothetical insurance, for beneficence in the form of the giving of gifts. Since Dworkin regards the giving of gifts within such limits as among the liberties worth protecting, this balancing thereby facilitates his ambition to reconcile liberty with equality as he conceives these two values. But, as I shall demonstrate below, the conflict between the envy test and the principle of abstraction stands in the way of a complete reconciliation of these values.

Dworkin's claim in chapter 3 to have reconciled liberty and equality can be summarized as the conjunction of the following two propositions:

   (a) Liberty is justified by a principle of abstraction that itself gains justification from within distributive equality by means of an appeal to considerations having to do with the fairness of the auction. In this respect, liberty is not an independent value outside of distributive equality.
   (b) Liberty complements (another aspect of) distributive equality because the liberty implying principle of abstraction complements the envy test by determining the best among the indefinitely many possible envy-free distributions.

But it is now clear that Dworkin affirms the following proposition as well:

(c) Liberty also conflicts with and outweighs (an aspect of) distributive equality, since the principle of abstraction justifies liberties that are incompatible with and outweigh the requirement of an envy-free distribution.[23]

In the light of Dworkin's affirmation of (c), his reconciliation of liberty and equality turns out to be less than meets the eye in at least three respects. First, assertions of the following sort in chapter 3 turn out to be misleading: "If that argument [i.e., the argument summarized in the first sentence of (a)] is successful, then an attractive conception of liberty flows from the very definition of an egalitarian distribution, and so liberty and equality cannot conflict" (p. 146). This passage is misleading because (a) does not imply a denial of the conflict described in (c), whereas the passage says that it does.[24] Second, Dworkin presents a one-sided description in chapter 3 of the relation between liberty and equality by highlighting the manner, as captured by (b), in which liberty complements another aspect of distributive equality without also drawing attention to the fact that there is an important respect, captured by (c), in which liberty conflicts with that very aspect of distributive equality. My third point is that Dworkin must withdraw his claim that distributive equality "cannot be improved, even in the real world, by policies that compromise the value of liberty" (p. 182). For he now makes clear that a gift tax modeled on hypothetical insurance does precisely that: it brings us closer to the ideal of an egalitarian distribution by curtailing the liberty to give, which the principle of abstraction demands in order to strike the proper balance with the competing demand of an envy-free distribution.

Given Dworkin's normative commitments, he must acknowledge that there is a morally regrettable trade-off to be made in striking this balance. On the one hand, an envy-free distribution is, *ceteris paribus*, preferable to a nonenvy-free distribution since the former, but not the latter, eliminates the unfairness of differences in those circumstances that are the result of the vicissitudes of brute bad luck.[25] On the other hand, a distribution in accord with laws that permit complete freedom to give gifts is, *ceteris paribus*, preferable to one that is not because such freedom eliminates the unfairness of incomplete sensitivity to the plans and preferences of individuals.[26] Dworkin has written that the "proposition that some of our political ideals conflict with others is significant and threatening, because, if it is true, a community must have cause for moral regret in some circumstances no matter what it does."[27] The conflict between the envy test and the principle of abstraction gives rise to just that: cause for moral regret that, whatever a community does, it will not realize the ideal of an egalitarian distribution that is fully fair because both maximally sensitive to the plans and preferences of individuals and envy free.

We now see that Dworkin's reconciliation of liberty and equality falls short of a demonstration that principles of distributive equality do not come into conflict with liberty. The reconciliation turns out to be a demonstration that the conflict between liberty and equality is a competition intermixed with cooperation, which takes place wholly within the boundaries of distributive equality, rather than a conflict between equality and an external demand of liberty. Equality may not be at war with anything apart from itself. But a genuine conflict between liberty and equality remains in the form of a civil war.

Acknowledgement

I thank G. A. Cohen and Andrew Williams for their comments.

Notes

1 Ronald Dworkin, *Sovereign Virtue: The Theory and Practice of Equality* (Cambridge, MA: Harvard University Press, 2000), p. 1. All page references in text are to this work.
2 Ibid., ch. 2 generally and ch. 3, pp. 139–43.
3 Ronald Dworkin, "Do Liberty and Equality Conflict?" in Paul Barker (ed.), *Living As Equals* (Oxford: Oxford University Press, 1996), pp. 39–57, 45–6.
4 Dworkin asks us to suppose that "a number of [propertyless] shipwreck survivors are washed up on a desert island which has abundant resources and no native population." We are to imagine that one of the survivors is elected to distribute to each an equal and large amount of clamshells that serve as money and to list each distinct item on the island (including parcels of land) as a lot to be sold. "The auctioneer then proposes a set of prices for each lot and discovers whether that set of prices clears all markets, that is, whether there is only one purchaser at that price and all lots are sold. If not, then the auctioneer adjusts his prices until he reaches a set that does clear the markets." At the conclusion of the auction, according to Dworkin, "no one will envy another's set of purchases because, by hypothesis, he could have purchased that bundle with his clamshells instead of his own bundle" (*Sovereign Virtue*, op. cit., pp. 66–8).
5 "Do Liberty and Equality Conflict?" op. cit., pp. 46–7. This passage provides an elegant and accurate summary of points made by Dworkin in his discussion of the envy test in *Sovereign Virtue*, op. cit., pp. 81–7. See, however, Dworkin's "*Sovereign Virtue* Revisited," *Ethics*, vol. 113, 2002, pp. 106–43, 123, where he advances a different account of the envy test insofar as its application to inequalities in personal resources is concerned.
6 For a discussion of these difficulties, see *Sovereign Virtue*, op. cit., pp. 73–109, 341, and my "Luck, Insurance, and Equality," *Ethics*, vol. 113, 2002, pp. 40–54.
7 Dworkin writes: "Someone envies the resources of another when he would prefer those resources, and the pattern of work and consumption that produces them, to his own resources and choices" ("Do Liberty and Equality Conflict?" op. cit., p. 46). He also stresses that the envy test should be applied to "resources over an entire life." On this "synoptic" approach, "our final aim is that an equal share of resources be devoted to the lives of each person" (*Sovereign Virtue*, op. cit., p. 84).
8 One complication with the envy test, as formulated, is that two equally talented individuals might make the same choices regarding work, investment, and consumption, yet end up with differences in wealth that are purely traceable to "option luck," where "option luck" is "a matter of how deliberate and calculated gambles turn out" (ibid., p. 73). Dworkin believes that such differences in wealth would be consistent with equality of resources:

> We may (if we wish) adjust our envy test to record that conclusion. We may say that in computing the extent of someone's resources over his life, for the purpose of asking whether anyone else envies those resources, any resources gained through a successful gamble should be represented by the opportunity to take the gamble at the odds in force, and comparable adjustments made to the resources of those who have lost through gambles. (ibid., p. 76).

I have elsewhere considered the place of option luck in Dworkin's theory of equality of resources and will not do so here (see Otsuka, "Luck, Insurance, and Equality," op. cit.).

9   Recall that I am now assuming that personal resources are equal. From this point onward, any reference to resources should be read as a reference to impersonal resources only.

10 I shall say more regarding what this involves below.

11 This cost is measured in terms of how much others would be prepared to bid for these resources.

12 See note 4 above which describes Dworkin's auction.

13 He maintains, moreover, that equality of resources "would then be an empty, because hopelessly indeterminate, conception of equality" if it failed to provide a criterion that would allow us to select an ideal distribution from within the set of envy-free distributions (*Sovereign Virtue*, op. cit., p. 150).

14 Note that the "abstract egalitarian principle" is a different principle from the "principle of abstraction." The "abstract egalitarian principle" is in fact simply another name for the "sovereign virtue" of equal concern.

15 Elsewhere, Dworkin qualifies this claim when he says that legal constraints "to correct certain imperfections in markets" are also compatible with the principle of abstraction. See ibid., pp. 148, 156–8. I shall ignore this qualification, as it is irrelevant to the topic of this chapter.

16 Dworkin writes that he "argue[s] in chapter 3 [that] it is inegalitarian for government to tax differentially the different choices that people make about how to spend what is rightfully theirs"; he draws the conclusion that it is "therefore inegalitarian separately to tax gifts and bequests" ("*Sovereign Virtue* Revisited," op. cit., p. 125). I shall assume throughout this chapter that bequests are included within the category of gifts.

17 Dworkin is objecting in the quoted remarks to a constraint on freedom of artistic expression, but the objection generalizes to the case of a constraint on the giving of gifts.

18 See also ibid., pp. 346–9, and Dworkin's "*Sovereign Virtue* Revisited," op. cit., p. 125. It is relevant, I think, that all three of these passages about inheritance were originally published subsequent to the original publication of chapter 3. There is no acknowledgement in chapter 3 of the problem that gift giving poses for the envy test. Had there been one, I doubt that Dworkin would have claimed in that chapter that the principle of abstraction builds the best bridge to the envy test.

19 Dworkin speculates that it would be rational for the average person to purchase insurance in which the "premium rate rises steeply from zero in the case of modest gifts or a modest estate to a very high marginal proportion of very great wealth" (ibid., p. 348).

20 Dworkin acknowledges the force of the claim that redistributive taxation modeled on underemployment will not fully realize the ideal of an envy-free distribution of impersonal resources among unequally talented people. But he says he cannot conceive of means of coming closer to the realization of this ideal (see ibid., pp. 89–92, 102–9).

21 See Dworkin's "*Sovereign Virtue* Revisited," op. cit., p. 125. The argument "in chapter 3" to which he there refers is the one we have considered above which appeals to the principle of abstraction.

22 See ibid.

23 Propositions (b) and (c) are consistent because the principle of abstraction might serve both to determine the best envy-free distribution and to justify the claim that a nonenvy-free distribution is, all things considered, better than the best envy-free distribution.

24 Similarly, Dworkin writes: "if we accept equality of resources as the best conception of distributional equality, liberty becomes an aspect of equality rather than, as it is often thought to be, an independent political ideal potentially in conflict with it" (ibid., p. 121). This passage is strictly speaking true, but it suggests the following falsehood: since liberty is an aspect of distributive equality, it is not in conflict with (any other aspect of) distributive equality.

25 Dworkin writes:

> It is a ruling principle of equality . . . that it is unjust when some people lead their lives with less wealth available to them, or in otherwise less favorable circumstances, than others, not through some choice or gamble

of their own but through brute bad luck. It is bad luck to be born into a relatively poor family or a family that is selfish or spendthrift.   (ibid., ch. 9, p. 347).

26   See the penultimate paragraph of section II above, especially the passage cited from pp. 150–1 of *Sovereign Virtue* regarding the fairness of the auction.
27   Dworkin, "Do Liberty and Equality Conflict?" op. cit., pp. 40–1.

5

Cracked Foundations of Liberal Equality

Richard J. Arneson

Liberal egalitarianism is a variant of liberal political philosophy that emphasizes the obligation of society to enable its most poor and disadvantaged members to lead decent lives. Liberal egalitarianism fuses the traditional liberal theme of individual freedom and autonomy and a more radical theme of equal life prospects for all. Today the two foremost proponents of liberal egalitarianism are the philosophers John Rawls and Ronald Dworkin. The writings of both men have given liberal egalitarianism a pronounced antiutilitarian cast, epitomized in Rawls' slogan that the correct theory of justice must uphold "the priority of the right over the good."[1] Perhaps surprisingly, in his essay "Foundations of Liberal Equality," Dworkin partially reverses this priority, while making no concessions to utilitarianism, by undertaking to show that individuals who seek a good life for themselves and who conceive of the good life in terms of what Dworkin calls the "challenge model" would thereby have strong reasons to accept liberal egalitarian principles of justice.[2] In this way, according to Dworkin, ethics and political morality mutually reinforce one another – "ethics" being the theory of how to make one's life turn out best.

This way of justifying principles of justice stands in marked contrast to the procedure of the "original position" that Rawls has made famous. Dworkin himself calls attention to this comparison. The idea of the original position is to model the choice of principles of justice as a choice of terms of social cooperation made by parties who are stipulated to be ignorant of all particular facts about themselves, including facts about their conceptions of the good, and who are asked to advance their interests as best they can by choice of principles that are to regulate their common life. In other words, one is asked to put aside all one's beliefs about what is choice-worthy and worthwhile in human life when thinking about fair terms of social cooperation with other people who may differ with each other fundamentally about the good but are thought to share an interest in cooperating with others on fair terms. This strategy of isolating controversy about the good from agreement on what is fair invites the objection that if one assumes reasonable people will be utterly in conflict about the good life, it is just as reasonable to suppose that they will also be utterly in conflict about what is fair or just. For one's convictions about what is fair or just are likely to be influenced at every turn by one's convictions about what is good, and so the proposal to ignore one's conceptions of good in trying to reach a common ground of agreement on justice looks like a proposal to ignore many of one's convictions that are crucially relevant to one's thinking about justice. Any agreement produced by this blinkered procedure would not and should not carry over to commitment once the blindfolds are removed. So, at any rate, goes the objection. But then the theorist of justice appears to be in a bind: given the evident fact of widespread disagreement on the good among members of a diverse modern society, to allow convictions about the good to influence choice of principles of justice threatens to defeat the search for broad and reasoned agreement on such principles.

Dworkin has an ingenious strategy for unraveling this knot. Granted that people disagree about what is valuable in life, what gods, so to speak, merit worship, it might still be the case that at a more abstract level reasonable people will agree about the nature of the good. Moreover, there is the possibility that these abstract convictions about the good, which are generally shared, suffice to generate reasons that support one conception of justice. Dworkin's essay "Foundations of Liberal Equality" elegantly explores these possibilities. He aims to develop what he calls a "challenge" model of ethics and to argue that it better captures our convictions about the good life than other views. In this effort he develops a foil for challenge that he calls the "impact" model. Dworkin further argues that if you accept the challenge model of ethics you thereby have strong reasons to accept the theory of distributive justice that he calls "liberal equality" and which he has defended in a series of essays. Dworkin's discussion of these matters clarifies and deepens this account of distributive justice and opens up a way of justifying a conception of the right as a means to promoting the good that is neither utilitarian nor contractarian.

I find the challenge model implausible and the argument from challenge to liberal equality unconvincing for many reasons. This essay states my objections. The moral of the story is that the theory of distributive justice must split the difference between utilitarian and Kantian accounts of morality in a different way than Dworkin or Rawls supposes.

I   The Challenge Model

The challenge model, as Dworkin notes, is formal. According to the challenge model, a good life is a skillful performance, a skillful response by an individual to the challenge that is posed for all individuals by the simple fact that each one has a life to live. There are many substantively different views on the further issue of what should qualify as skillful performance in response to the challenge of life. The challenge model does not assess these views; it is a way of thinking about how we should live, not a standard for assessing how we should live.

The idea that a good life is a successful response to the basic human condition of having a life to live seems on the face of it to be mistaken. Dworkin's model is better suited to capture the idea of an admirable or praiseworthy life than the quite different idea of a desirable or choice-worthy life. An admirable life may be a disaster for the one who lives it. A poor peasant who finds himself in abject poverty might devote his life to the survival of his family, and act admirably to achieve this reasonable goal. The man's life is as skillful a performance, let's say, as one could wish. This does not suffice to show the man led a good life. Bad fortune might conspire to thwart his aims; poverty and disease destroy his family despite his best efforts. Even if the man should succeed in satisfying his ultramodest life goal, we would not say he led a good life, because we regret the grim circumstances in which he had to set such tragically limited aims. It would seem that unlucky circumstances make individuals' lives go badly on the challenge view only if they inhibit or destroy their capacity to respond skillfully to the situation in which they find themselves.

As stated, this objection is not fair to Dworkin. Dworkin's elaboration of the challenge model has it that a good life is a successful response to favorable circumstances. He gives a moral twist to this qualification regarding favorable circumstances: the circumstances of one's life must be normatively appropriate if one's life can be judged a good one on the challenge model. A good life is then a good, that is, skillful, response to a good challenge, namely, a challenge constituted by a normatively appropriate set of life circumstances.

This carefully qualified challenge model is also inadequate. Consider a woman who is blessed with favorable life circumstances, makes admirable, bold but risky, life choices, and carries out these choices with consummate skill. She clearly leads a good life as understood by the challenge model. Yet for all that has been said, this individual might be cursed with unremitting bad fortune, so that all the risks she takes turn out badly, and her life becomes a shambles. To the end she responds with skill, grace, and dignity as her life crashes down about her head. The point here is simply that the concept of an admirable life, a life that is a successful response to challenge, is different from the concept of a life that is good for the person who lives it.

A possible line of reply to this objection would hold that a good life according to the challenge model is an admirable response to favorable and normatively appropriate circumstances, and in this formula "favorable circumstances" must be understood timelessly, so that if uninsurable bad fortune regarding sufficiently important matters strikes individuals at any time in their life, then it will turn out that their lives were not lived in favorable circumstances, so were to that extent not good lives according to the challenge model. My response is a question: once this epicycle is added, what is left of the initial meaning of the concept of challenge?

A life that is a successful response to challenge, one would think, can be had even in unenviable circumstances. In a card game, whatever cards have been dealt, one can play admirably in the sense of doing the best one can with the hand at one's disposal. The challenge model most naturally interpreted would have it that the good or admirable life is a life that skillfully deploys whatever hand one has been dealt by fate. But this is not the good life in the sense in which parents would wish a good life for their children.

Even as heavily qualified by Dworkin, his challenge model does not match our intuitive pretheoretical idea of a good life. In a nutshell, the challenge model holds that a good life consists in both facing good circumstances and responding well to those circumstances.

Consider a woman who is blessed with fortunate circumstances but does not respond well to the challenge of her circumstances. Yet by good luck she satisfies her most important aims. She does a poor job of interpreting her life situation and of settling on convictions, values, and aims, but by sheer good luck she manages to settle on convictions, values, and aims that would withstand thorough rational scrutiny with full information. With respect to central issues of her life that matter crucially for her, she makes bad decisions (that is, decisions with low expected utility compared to feasible alternatives), but things generally turn out very well for her. In the crucial areas of life where she might perform well or badly, she performs badly, but again good luck prevents bad performance from giving rise to bad outcomes.

This person unequivocally fails to lead a good life according to the challenge conception. She does not respond skillfully to the favorable and normatively appropriate challenge posed by her life circumstances. But by good luck she gets what she most wants from her life, and again by good luck, her wants are sensible and choice-worthy. The challenge model must judge the woman's life a failure, and in a way it is. Her performance in response to the challenge of life is very far from admirable. But luck can be an effective substitute for prudence and other self-regarding virtues, and luck plays this role to the hilt in the nonadmirable but prosperous life we have imagined. In response to the question, is it better to be virtuous (skillful in response to life's challenge) or lucky, the answer is that it depends on how lucky and how virtuous one is.[3] In principle, at least, very good luck can compensate for any deficit of prudential virtue. The conclusion to draw is that Dworkin's challenge model of the good life subtly conflates the notion of a choice-worthy or valuable life with the quite different idea of an admirable life that emerges from favorable circumstances.

The criticism against the challenge model developed above might seem to rely on a rational preference satisfaction account of the good.[4] If so, that would weaken the criticism, because rational preference satisfaction accounts of the good are problematic.[5] But the criticism can instead lean on the less problematic family of "objective list" accounts of the good – accounts that identify the good life for people with the attainment of conditions that are valuable for those people independently of their own convictions and desires even as they might be after ideal deliberation.[6] People who failed to perform well in response to the challenge of their life circumstances could nonetheless by good luck lead good lives according to any of these objective list theories of the good (provided that the list did not specify that skillful performance in response to life's challenge is a necessary condition of a good life).

II Challenge Versus Impact

Dworkin's challenge model of ethics is presented as superior to an alternative "impact" model of a good life. The impact model "holds that the value of a good life consists in its product, that is, its consequences for the rest of the world." In contrast, the challenge model holds "that the value of a good life lies in its inherent value as a performance."[7]

Dworkin does not say whether or not he thinks that the challenge and impact models are exhaustive of the possibilities. But he does not stop to consider whether there are plausible alternatives, so to that extent the significance of showing that challenge is better than impact is unclear. In my judgment the impact model is a nonstarter, but inasmuch as there are better alternatives, the manifest inadequacy of the impact model does little to render the challenge view attractive.

According to Dworkin's conception, the impact of my life is the difference it makes to the objective value of the world. So if we add to the impact view (for example) the thesis that what is objectively valuable is pleasure and only pleasure, this augmented impact model would then hold that the value of my life can be identified with the amount of pleasure that it produced for myself and for others. The implausibility of this conception emerges into view if we imagine a life that is thoroughly miserable for the man who lives it. He experiences minimal pleasure throughout his life, and generates no pleasure for others, but by chance one day he finds himself placed to prevent a worldwide nuclear war or comparable human catastrophe by a thoroughly humdrum action, say picking some chewing gum off the floor when leaving the gum on the floor would give a signal to terrorists to unleash nuclear carnage. Let us add that this unheroic world-saving action gives no pleasurable satisfaction to the individual, so his life remains as devoid of pleasure as it had been up to this point. This life is extremely valuable according to the impact conception, because the individual's impact on the world's hedonic level turns out to be immense, but we would balk at saying the individual led a good life. This is after all not the sort of life one would wish for someone one cared about. A good life, we suppose, must be good for the person who lives it. This "good for the agent" requirement might be satisfied by a person whose life is altruistically dedicated to the good of others, if the pattern of altruistic action satisfies a plausible perfectionist standard. But the mere fact that the impact of your life happens to be good for others does not entail that the good for the agent requirement is satisfied.

The implausibility of impact does not ensure the plausibility of challenge by default. There are other well-known contenders not mentioned by Dworkin. For one example, consider a rational preference satisfaction view, as characterized in endnote 4 in this essay. If you get what you want from life, and your wants are not based on ignorance or cognitive error, then you have achieved a good life, according to this model of the good life. The rational preference satisfaction view is opposed to the impact model, because one might lead a life that has a good impact on the world without wanting to have any such impact. The rational preference satisfaction view is opposed also to the challenge model, because the fact that one leads a life that is a successful response to life's challenge does not guarantee that one succeeds in satisfying one's important self-interested preferences to a reasonable extent (and that these preferences would withstand rational scrutiny). Nor for that matter does satisfying one's major rational preferences guarantee that one's life is a success as judged by the challenge model of ethics.

For another example of an account of human good that does not fall into Dworkin's categories of challenge or impact, consider an objective list view, with these items on the list: friendship and love; pleasure and the avoidance of pain; athletic attainments; meaningful work; systematic understanding of the natural world; ethical and moral wisdom; and creative artistic, cultural, and scientific accomplishments. Again, one might score high by attaining the items on this objective list without leading a good life according to either the challenge or the impact model. The conclusion one should reach is that neither of Dworkin's models is capturing the notion of a life that is truly good for the one who lives it.

III   Parameters and Limitations

Dworkin develops a further distinction which he takes to be critical for the task of forging links between liberal ethics and liberal equality, the liberal theory of justice. This is the distinction between parameters and limitations.

Among the circumstances that individuals face, some are limits on the extent to which they can respond successfully to the challenge to live well. If a circumstance that is a limit is altered for the better, individuals are enabled to lead a better life. Other circumstances are not like this; they are partly constitutive of the challenge that individuals face, successful response to which qualifies as leading a good life. The latter type of circumstance Dworkin calls a *parameter*. A further complication in this picture is that the distinction between limits and parameters is not completely fixed independently of individual interpretation and decision. According to Dworkin, individuals in considering the circumstances they face can to some extent define their identity by deciding that some circumstances will count as parameters, whereas they might have decided differently. To borrow Dworkin's own example, a woman might decide that being Jewish and being American are facts that partially define her life challenge, or she might define her identity and hence her life challenge in another way. Depending on what she decides, being Jewish and being American could be either parameters or limits for her. Moreover, the act of self-definition that partly determines the line dividing limits and parameters in one's own life can itself be more or less successful. Part of living well on the challenge view is recognizing the challenge one faces and interpreting the challenge intelligently to the extent that it admits of variable construal. Finally, Dworkin adds that some parameters of our lives are normative. There are some circumstances that ought to be part of the set of circumstances we face. If we do not face these circumstances, our life is to that extent worse. Having the opportunity to live through a normal lifespan is a normative parameter in this sense.

In effect, Dworkin has two nonequivalent ways of drawing the distinction between parameters and limitations. One way is to define a *parameter* as a circumstance, a part of an agent's situation, that could not be altered in such a way that the change improves the quality of the agent's life.

Circumstances that could be altered in this way are limits. The other way of drawing the distinction is to define a *parameter* as a circumstance that partially constitutes the challenge to which a good response qualifies as living a good life. These alternative characterizations of the distinction are not equivalent. Living in Europe during the Nazi years might be a circumstance that partially constitutes my life challenge, so that living well is for me responding appropriately as a European to the Nazi experience. Yet it might unequivocally be the case that I would have been better off if my circumstances had been different in this regard and my life challenge had been differently constituted. It should also be noted that what individuals regard as parameters of their lives may not be that. I may identify wholeheartedly with my conviction that responding to fearful situations with brutality is noble and that my life would be to that extent worse if I lost this conviction, but in fact my conviction is profoundly mistaken and it would improve my life if I corrected this mistaken belief.

The distinction between parameters and limitations does not sharpen the challenge model so that it either constitutes a viable alternative to a suitable objective list conception of the good or poses a serious difficulty for this conception. From the objective list standpoint, some features of the world are not limits on people's prospects of valuable accomplishment but are instead conditions for certain types of accomplishment. Gravity is not a limit of a rock climber's achievement; the force of gravity must be present as an obstacle or the climber's success in getting to the top is not meaningful. But not every objectively valuable human good can be shoehorned into the category of a successful performance. By sheer good luck one can gain such goods as a long satisfying life and the pleasure of a hot bath, and these goods are not construable as aspects of a successful response to the challenge posed by basic defining features of one's life.

Dworkin holds the view that justice is a parameter of the good life. He means by this that living a good life is responding in the appropriate way to the right challenge, hence one's life is automatically worse if the wrong challenge is faced, and life circumstances that include injustice constitute one sort of wrong challenge. Dworkin's idea is not only that one who is disadvantaged by unjust conditions is thereby made worse off but also that one who is privileged by unjust conditions is thereby made worse off. According to Dworkin, living under a regime that does not conform to the requirements of justice is *ipso facto* a misfortune.

Dworkin characterizes his position as a moderate revision of a Platonic doctrine: Plato is said by Dworkin to have held that *all things considered*, living under injustice always makes one's life go worse, whereas Dworkin holds that *other things being equal*, living under injustice always makes one's life go worse. In Dworkin's terms, he takes justice to be a soft parameter and Plato takes it to be a hard parameter of the good life. To this account Dworkin adds a claim that narrows the gap between his view and Plato's. Dworkin holds that living in unjust circumstances is always a grave misfortune, one which for most people in most circumstances will outweigh any good that accrues to them by way of unjust advantages. Dworkin writes, "Plato was nearly right"[8] to think that advantages that are consequent upon serious injustice cannot improve anyone's life on the whole. Let us call Dworkin's position on this point "quasi-Platonism" to signal its affinity to Plato's stringent view.

I find Dworkin's quasi-Platonism counterintuitive, but I do not wish to press this point, because none of my criticisms of Dworkin's account of the relationship between the challenge view of ethics and liberal equality turns on it. Notice that what is most problematic about quasi-Platonism is its least defended aspect. Even if it is assumed that justice is a soft parameter, it would still be the case that one can improve people's lives by providing them benefits in excess of what justice permits, if the benefits add more to the goodness of their lives than the injustice subtracts.

Dworkin does not propose, and *a fortiori* does not defend, any procedure for determining how to weight the contribution of just circumstances as against the contribution of other factors when the task is to measure the goodness of a person's life. His claim that injustice nearly always outweighs any combination of countervailing factors is just a claim without backing by argument.

There are many possible contingent connections between enjoying unjust privileges and failing to lead a choice-worthy life. Injustice can give rise to an ideological perspective that is especially tempting to those who benefit from injustice but that thoroughly distorts the understanding of the world of those who adopt the perspective. Unjust privileges can generate snobbery and the wasted pursuit of false values, as well as envy and resentment among those who might otherwise live in harmony. But these are all contingent links that might or might not materialize. What I find unpersuasive is the claim that living under circumstances of injustice is always *per se* a grave misfortune for any person, regardless of such contingencies and quite independently of that person's own evaluative convictions on these matters. Rationality might require the admission that one's situation is unjust, without forcing the further belief that one's situation *qua* unjust is inconducive to one's welfare.

There is a tension between Dworkin's moralistic view that any injustice in the circumstances of people's lives considerably lessens the goodness of their lives quite independently of their own convictions on this matter and his assertion of the priority of ethical integrity. This assertion is discussed in section IV below. Roughly, the priority of ethical integrity holds that it cannot be better for one to lead a life other than the life one thinks best even if one is mistaken. The question arises why one's conviction about the value of one's own plan of life and course of action matters so much in the determination of the goodness of one's life whereas one's conviction about the morality of one's circumstances matters so little. If class relations in my society are unjust, according to Dworkin that makes my life substantially worse whether or not I know or care about this, but if I think surfing is the best life for me, then surfing really is the best life for me, given my conviction, even if the conviction is wrong.

IV   Tolerance, Neutrality, and Antipaternalism

Liberal equality as conceived by Dworkin significantly includes an ideal of tolerance which he defines as follows: The government "must not forbid or reward any private activity on the ground that one set of substantive ethical values, one set of opinions about the best way to lead a life, is superior or inferior to others."[9] Tolerance or neutrality so defined has controversial implications regarding the issue of paternalism, the restriction of individuals' liberty against their will for their own good. Tolerance takes no stand for or against *weak paternalism*, restriction of people's liberty against their will for their own good where that involves promoting their attainment of a goal that they endorse and are seeking to fulfill. Weak paternalism overrides individuals' judgment about the best means to fulfill a goal that they are themselves seeking to fulfill in the belief that fulfillment will be in their interest. In contrast, *strong paternalism* is restriction of people's liberty against their will for their own good where that involves promoting their attainment of a goal that they neither endorse nor are seeking to fulfill. Strong paternalism overrides people's judgment about what goals are worthy of pursuit in order to improve the quality of their life. Strong paternalistic policies for the most part violate tolerance and in this way conflict with liberal equality.

A suspicion of paternalism is part of the ethos of liberalism. Liberals ranging from Immanuel Kant to John Stuart Mill have condemned paternalism. But common-sense liberal conviction includes reason to favor as well as reason to oppose paternalism. On the one side, paternalism appears to involve meddlesome interference in what ought to be an area of individual freedom protected from social control. On the other side, if we are not skeptics, we will sometimes believe that strangers and personal acquaintances are ruining their lives by acting on blatantly unreasonable conceptions of their good, and if we accept some obligations of benevolence, we will believe that at least when the ratio of the cost to us to the benefit to the beneficiary is sufficiently favorable, we are obligated to act to prevent the lives of these men and women from falling to ruin.

These autonomy and Good Samaritan intuitions are at odds. Welfarist liberalism resolves this tension in liberalism by renouncing a principled commitment to autonomy.[10] Welfarist liberalism accommodates our inclination to respect autonomy by treating it as a rough and ready rule justified in many circumstances by expediency. Often when we are tempted to paternalism, our conviction of our own rightness is excessively confident, and in fact the people we would impose on paternalistically know their own good better than we do. In other circumstances our belief that we know other people's good better than they themselves is correct, but our belief that we can intervene effectively to improve the situation is false. In still other circumstances our beliefs that we know better than other people what is good for them and that we know how to intervene effectively on their behalf are both correct, but we incorrectly judge the motivations of those who would be called on to act paternalistically under our scheme of intervention, so that trying to put our scheme in action would make matters worse from the standpoint of those we are trying to help. In all of these cases paternalism would be wrong according to a welfarist liberal position.

Dworkin supposes that the challenge model requires that the liberal should take a stronger stand against most strong paternalism. This requirement takes shape through a series of interpretations of challenge. First, Dworkin believes that if the good life is constituted by a skillful performance, then it is impossible to improve people's lives by coercing them to do what they think valueless, because the intention of the agent qualifies the performance, so a performance cannot acquire value for agents against their conviction. For example, even if the life of prayer is superior to the life of surfing, coerced mimicry of prayer has to be inferior to freely chosen surfing. Second, Dworkin asserts that on the challenge view rightly understood, ethical integrity conditions the value of any person's life. *Ethical integrity* is achieved by someone who believes "that his life, in its central features, is an appropriate one for him, that no other life he might live would be a plainly better response to the parameters of his ethical situation rightly judged."[11] Dworkin further asserts that in judging the value of someone's life, the achievement of integrity takes lexical priority, so that no life an individual leads that lacks integrity could be better overall than any life the individual might lead that would include achievement of integrity.

The third step of the interpretation is the application of the priority of integrity to the issue of the justifiability of strong paternalism. Dworkin acknowledges that strong paternalism that results eventually in a genuine endorsement by individuals of the life that, initially, they had been coerced into performing, would not be ruled out by the priority of integrity. Dworkin also acknowledges that there are several possible causes other than paternalism of failure of integrity in a person's life. For example, individuals might suffer from weakness of will or fecklessness, and fail to live the life they regard as most worthy for them. If the individual in the absence of paternalism would fail to achieve integrity, then the priority of integrity does not rule out even strong paternalism that does not lead to a life of integrity, provided that there is no alternative paternalist policy that would enable the individual to achieve integrity. But despite these qualifications, Dworkin believes that by supporting the priority of integrity, the challenge model provides a nuanced and strengthened understanding of the grounds and limits of liberalism's principled hostility to paternalism. According to Dworkin, forbidding individuals to engage in a way of life they regard as best for themselves cannot improve their lives even if they then follow a second-best choice of life that the paternalist agency correctly views as objectively more worthwhile than the preferred forbidden way of life. In the same vein, consider a subtle paternalism that holds "that people should be protected from choosing wasteful or bad lives not by flat prohibitions of the criminal law but by educational decisions and devices that remove bad options from people's view and imagination."[12] Dworkin is of the opinion that bowdlerizing people's choices of how to live in this way cannot improve their lives because the good life is an appropriate response to non-bowdlerized circumstances. In other words, the priority of integrity includes a priority of choice making and value selection consistent with integrity. Manipulating people's choices so as to undermine the rationality of the choice destroys integrity just as much as does blocking people coercively from acting on their considered choices and values.

In response: welfarism is in principle propaternalist, and is opposed by versions of liberalism that elevate autonomy to independent status. I have no argument against versions of liberalism that give priority to autonomy over benevolence.[13] But Dworkin's challenge model does not afford a perspective that gives any special insight into this familiar conflict within the soul of liberalism. Moreover, the priority of integrity that Dworkin asserts does not plausibly organize our intuitions about the pros and cons of paternalism. Nor does the challenge model support the priority of integrity, an extreme and implausible doctrine.

Integrity as Dworkin defines it is clearly good for a person to achieve, other things being equal. What is objectionable in Dworkin's account of ethical integrity is the strict lexical priority over all other values that he assigns it. Why believe that the slightest loss of integrity should outweigh any threatened loss of any size in any other value and even any threatened combination of losses in other values? So far as I can see Dworkin gives no reason to support this extreme priority weighting, so his assertion of it is dogmatic. There are some goods that either are unachievable without a conviction of their value or even if achievable, lose all value in the absence of the conviction that they are valuable. In the case of goods of this sort, paternalistic forcing cannot improve the life of the intended beneficiaries unless it somehow causes those being coerced to value the activity they are being induced to perform. But other goods are not plausibly viewed this way. If cultural achievement is a great good, it is doubtful that a person who writes a great novel nonetheless fails to achieve a great good just because that person has eccentric philosophical beliefs that rank cultural achievement as of no value.[14]

I have urged that Dworkin's priority of integrity doctrine yields implausible verdicts about cases in which strong paternalism could improve a person's life dramatically, perhaps along many dimensions of assessment, but at the cost of a small loss of integrity. Dworkin's posited priority of ethical integrity yields implausible implications for paternalism in another range of cases. Consider lives in which ethical integrity is lacking, and will not be achieved in the absence of paternalistic intervention. Here the priority of ethical integrity endorses paternalism, and moreover endorses paternalistic intervention at any cost to the agent's values just so long as ethical integrity is thereby achieved. Once again, the priority relation that Dworkin asserts is too extreme.

Elaborating the challenge model he favors, Dworkin asserts, "my life cannot be better for me in virtue of some feature or component I think has no value."[15] But why should we hold that a central component of my life would have no value just because I hold a silly opinion that it is valueless?[16] Dworkin's claim that no aspect of people's lives can have intrinsic value for them unless they believe it has intrinsic value is implausibly extreme.

Imagine that a government imposes a strongly paternalistic policy on its citizens and that this policy eventually causes some citizens to reject those views of the good life that the government coercively disapproves. It might be held that the priority of integrity doctrine would condemn this sort of paternalism and would be right to do so. After all, giving priority to people's living their lives according to their convictions must include giving priority to maintaining conditions in which people can decide freely on their convictions. Changes in conviction brought about through coercion or manipulation of the agent violate integrity, one might suppose.

This line of thought does not support the claim that ethical integrity generates reasons to reject all strong paternalism. Coercion that is paternalistically motivated can affect the processes by which people's convictions are formed in many ways, not all of which vitiate or lessen the rationality and authenticity of these processes. Being forced to eat chocolate ice cream may lead me to appreciate hitherto unnoticed aspects of this dessert and to revise my evaluation of chocolate ice cream. Being based on experience, this postcoercion assessment may well be more reasonable than my earlier ignorant negative view of chocolate ice cream. The connections between being the object of paternalism and holding convictions in a way that is worse from the standpoint of deliberative rationality are too complex to allow any simple inference to the conclusion that paternalism must always lessen the autonomy of the agent's convictions that are affected by paternalism.

Dworkin has one further argument linking the challenge model of ethics to a thoroughgoing rejection of strong paternalism that I have not yet examined. Dworkin imagines an interlocutor who asserts that paternalism that improves the chances that an individual will choose a good life thereby improves the value of the life challenge the individual faces. Dworkin then offers a rebuttal: "This reply misunderstands the challenge model profoundly, because it confuses parameters and limitations."[17] According to Dworkin, we have no grip on the idea of what is a good life for someone apart from specifying the challenge-constituting circumstances that individuals ought to face, and then reflecting on what it would be to respond well to that challenge.

Here as elsewhere the distinction between parameters and limitations is able to do less work than Dworkin assigns it. Let us grant straightaway that other things being equal, it is better that individuals should choose their life goals from a wider rather than from an artificially narrowed set of options. A challenge that is more complex and interesting by virtue of including more options is to that extent a better challenge. But nothing in the challenge model as Dworkin conceives it blocks us from considering what would be better and worse responses by individuals to given challenges. Other things being equal, people lead better lives when they choose a better rather than worse option when faced with a given challenge. But now we have two different values, both internal to the challenge model, and the possibility of trade-offs between them. Other things being equal, it is better to choose from a wider rather than narrower range of options, and other things being equal, it is better for an individual to choose better rather than worse options when faced with a given range of them. But then if an individual would choose the worse option if presented with a wider range, and would choose a better option if presented with a narrower range, the worsening of the individual's challenge by culling alternatives paternalistically might be outweighed by the greater value of the individual's response to the smaller challenge, and if such cases exist, then nothing in the challenge model gives any reason to deny that strong paternalism can improve the life that a person leads who faces a paternalistic imposition. This discussion has presupposed that the lives that individuals lead can be graded better or worse and that in principle an observer might know better than an individual contemplating a choice which option is better for that individual. One might reject this sort of objectivism with respect to the valuation of types of lives, but Dworkin does not reject it, and instead defends an absolutist stand against a type of paternalism without any appeal to skepticism about the possibility of objective valuation in this domain. This defense does not succeed and in my view cannot.

V   Equality

There are at least two controversial elements in Dworkin's assertion of equality of resources: the claim that the currency of distributive justice should be resources and the claim that distribution of resources should be rendered equal. I discuss the latter claim in this section and the former claim in the next section.

I believe that the essence of Dworkin's egalitarianism is that unchosen good and bad fortune call for redress.[18] The case for egalitarian redistribution does not require a background of reciprocal social cooperation, so we can imagine that persons are living entirely isolated lives on separate islands. In view of the fact that no individuals can take personal credit for their good or bad fortune in finding themselves blessed with much or little talent and inhabiting an island with rich or poor resources, no individuals are morally entitled to the talents of their bodies or the resources of their island. Redistribution of resources to compensate for disparities in individuals' resource and talent holdings is morally required. How far should redistribution proceed? Dworkin's answer is that resources should be redistributed to the point at which everyone's wide resource holdings are the same (as judged by the hypothetical auction and insurance markets).[19] Taken literally, this implies that if some of the resources of the better-off islanders cannot be transferred, so that full initial equality of resources across island inhabitants cannot be achieved by transfer, then some nontransferable resources should be destroyed until equality by transfer becomes feasible. This implication of equality, that it requires wastage of resources in some circumstances, remains even if equality of resources is amended so that it calls for equality of resources at the highest feasible level for all.

Suppose instead that transfers of any and all resources are feasible but costly. When well-endowed Smith puts resources in a boat that is to deposit the resources on poorly endowed Jones's island, some of the resources will be washed overboard or spoil while the boat is drifting with the ocean currents. The cost to Smith in resources of making a transfer is then less than the gain in resources that the transfer makes possible for Jones. If we suppose that the resources available for transfer differ in their susceptibility to loss during transportation, and that less susceptible resources are transferred first, then the ratio of the cost to the giver to the benefit to the recipient increases as equality of resources is more closely approximated. Many of us would say that as this cost-to-benefit ratio becomes more unfavorable, at some point the obligation to give ceases, because the moral disvalue of the lost resources outweighs the moral value of increasing the resource share of the worse-off person. Dworkin's equality of resources principle is committed to making no allowance for this cost consideration.

The objection then to equality of resources is that it undervalues the moral significance of having more resources in people's hands. If we are concerned with equality of resources, this must surely be because resources are good for people, and more resources are better for an individual (in general) than fewer. If this were not accepted, why care about the distribution of resources at all? Equality of resources embodies an extreme priority weighting that assigns no moral value at all to any above-average holdings of resources by persons.

More can be said that challenges the moral significance of equality by interpreting in other terms the common moral intuition that it is morally a more urgent matter to get more resources to those who have less than to those who already have more. Consider again the generic situation in which some individuals have more resources than others and transfers to the worse off are feasible. If the moral flaw in the situation is absence of equality, it would seem that as increments of resources are transferred to those below average until equality is achieved, the transfer of the last increment that establishes equality is no less morally valuable than the transfer of the first same-sized increment. But some of us who have the generic egalitarian intuition that resources should be transferred think that if everyone is at very nearly the same level, it matters hardly at all that one further incremental transfer divided among all those below average takes place, so exact equality is achieved. On the other hand, it matters far more, when some are much worse off than others, that the first incremental transfer should take place, which, divided among all those who are worst off, raises them a bit from their great distance from the average. On this way of regarding the situation, what matters morally is not equality *per se* but giving priority to helping the worst off. Moreover, a further slight refinement of the example shows that it is not being the worst off *per se* that matters. What matters is not one's ordinal position, the comparison to others, but rather the absolute level of one's resource allotment.[20] After all, in a thousand-person variant of the generic situation, the person who is worst off might be hardly at all worse off in absolute terms than the best off. It is not whether one is second-worst off or thousandth-worst off that matters, but rather the amount of the absolute gap separating one's resource level and the resource level of the best off.

The preceding discussion has suggested an explanation of the intuition that when some individuals have more resources and others less through no fault or voluntary choice of their own, resources should be transferred from better off to worse off. This explanation appeals to a noncomparative principle of distributive justice. What fundamentally matters morally on this view is not what one person has compared to what other persons have. The imperative of redistribution is to help the person who in absolute terms is badly off, by the relevant standard of judgment, not to bring about some preferred relation between what one person has and what others have.

On this noncomparative conception of distributive justice, comparisons take on derivative and instrumental importance.[21] If the absolute level of resources you command dictates the moral value of increasing your level of resources, then it will turn out to be morally more valuable to achieve a gain in resources for Smith, whose resource holding measured on an absolute scale is low, than to achieve a same-sized gain for Jones, whose resource holding is not so low.

I have raised two criticisms of Dworkin's liberal equality ideal. One is that distributive equality has nothing to do with justice, because no essentially comparative principle has anything to do with justice, not at least at the level of fundamental moral reasons for picking one rather than another justice conception.

A second criticism concedes for the sake of the argument that comparisons matter, but charges that in Dworkin's ideal comparisons enter in the wrong way and with the wrong force. They enter with the wrong force in that Dworkin's equality of resources principle, like Rawls's difference principle, is too absolutist. Rawls's principle permits no trade-offs between resource gains and losses to better off and worse off. According to the difference principle, if we can achieve a gain of a penny for the worst off we should do so, no matter what the cost to the better off. Similarly, Dworkin's equality of resources implies that if we can transfer resources to create equality, we should do so, whatever the cost to the better off. The charge that Dworkin's comparisons enter in the wrong way is as follows: there is a further aspect of this second criticism that applies to Dworkin and not to Rawls. Dworkin's equality of resources principle would have it that the relationship between one person's resource shares and the resource shares of others is intrinsically morally important. The relationship matters even if the alteration that produces the improved relationship is not better for any person. Equality is morally desirable even if no person's life is improved by equality. Rawls's difference principle does not have this unattractive feature. Any transfer of resources recommended by the difference principle will improve the resource holding of some person who is worse off than the person who suffers by the transfer. Changing the relationship between one person's resource share and another's when no one is helped by the change is not recommended or even permitted by Rawls's principle. In other words, Dworkin's principle but not Rawls's conflicts with the Pareto norm when that norm is understood in terms of resources. Let us call this version of Pareto the Pareto-resource principle: if a change can be made that renders someone better off in resources and no one worse off, either that change should be made or some other such that after that alternative change no one can be given more resources without taking resources from someone else. The Pareto family of principles embodies a minimal but important aspect of fairness, one that Rawls honors and Dworkin's principle of distributive justice does not.

In a footnote, Dworkin expresses himself in a confused way on just this point, so some explanation is in order. Dworkin writes that "equality of resources, grounded in an opportunity-cost test and based on a sharp distinction between personality and circumstance, may not be inefficient and is not open to the charge that it allows the lazy to profit."[22] Liberal equality proposes that it is morally desirable to equalize everyone's circumstances, but not to compensate individuals for differences in their ambitions or for differences in their resource holdings that are brought about by people's different ambitions as they give rise to actions the expectable consequences of which are these resource inequalities. We can imagine implementing equality of resources according to this distinction by pretending that all members of a generation are the same age. When the cohort comes of age, an initial distribution is established that compensates each member of the cohort for all differences in their circumstances, but once this equal distribution is set, individuals are then free to live out their lives as they choose. Circumstances having been adjusted to establish equality, the stage is set for ambitions to express themselves without triggering further redistribution.

The easiest way to see that equality of resources so understood would fall foul of a resource efficiency norm is to consider a simple two-generation example. Equality of resources constrains transfers across generations, which would upset equality among the members of a generation. Suppose there are two classes in society, each class containing identical members. We name the classes "rich" and "poor." Rich individuals would work hard at lucrative jobs if they could pass their gains on to their children. But such bequests would produce unequal inheritance, which would frustrate equality of resources, so they are forbidden. Unable to pass along advantages to their children in the next generation in the form of bequest, the rich save less, and the resources available for initial equal distribution to the next generation are less than they would otherwise be. If this effect is sufficiently strong, there are inheritance tax policies that would result in more resources going to each member of the second generation and no fewer resources going to each member of the first generation, compared to the amount of resources each would get under a regime of equality of resources. In other words, policies that deviate from equality of resources can yield more resources for some and fewer resources for none compared to what each would get under equality of resources.

Dworkin advances the interesting suggestion that the challenge model of ethics supports the insistence on equality of resources by the liberal equality ideal of justice. The aspect of challenge to which Dworkin appeals to support equality is the idea I have called "quasi-Platonism."

According to this idea, people lead good lives insofar as they respond in the best way to the challenge of life that is posed by ideal conditions. Conditions can be nonideal by failing to pose an interesting and complex challenge. Conditions can also be nonideal because they are normatively inappropriate. In particular, Dworkin asserts that if the resources at one's disposal are different from what justice would assign, one's challenge is ill posed and to that extent one's life must be worse according to the challenge model. This means that I cannot tell whether more resources would be better or worse for me independently of determining what resource share would be just. If more resources would involve injustice, the largesse that bestows these resources on me is a hindrance, not a help, to leading a good life.

I cannot see how the line of thought that Dworkin advances is supposed to help his case for equality of resources. Let us concede for the sake of the argument that Dworkin's quasi-Platonism is correct, and that if justice requires equal shares, then individuals cannot correctly claim that if they were given more resources above their just share, then they would be better off. This claim has no impact at all on the quite different issue, whether equal shares really are just. The line of thought I have urged understands the right as a fair distribution of the good. On this view, the Pareto norm (or more exactly, the Pareto family of norms) is an element of fair distribution. The root idea here is that we should deny someone a claim to a benefit only if granting the claim imposes a cost on someone else, where a "cost" is interpreted very broadly, so that giving the benefit to you imposes costs on me if the benefit could have been given to me instead. But if a sausage is available to you, but would spoil if we try to give it to anyone else, you should get the sausage. You don't have to be specially deserving to be entitled to get a benefit that only you can enjoy. This line of thought might be found persuasive or unpersuasive. A hard-headed egalitarian might opt for equality over Pareto when they conflict. What I do not see is how it could be relevant at this point in the discussion to claim, as Dworkin does, that you cannot appeal to considerations such as the wastage of good involved in letting someone suffer to no one's benefit because whether an extra resource is really a benefit depends on what is just, and only equality is just. This would beg the question if the issue before us is precisely to decide what is just.

Dworkin is arguing (*inter alia*) against the welfarist view that the right is a fair distribution of good across persons on the ground that if one accepts quasi-Platonism, one cannot define the right independently of the good. Moreover, since the challenge model of ethics includes quasi-Platonism, the challenge model blocks any criticism of equality of resources that assumes that the right can be defined independently of the good. But the flaw in this argument is that quasi-Platonism does not have the implications Dworkin claims for it.

Let us then accept quasi-Platonism for the sake of the argument. We are then committed to accepting the idea that other things being equal, getting an unjust share of resources is bad for an individual whether the unjust share is larger or smaller than the just share. A good life is a life that responds to just circumstances.

In order to develop a welfarist view of justice compatible with this quasi-Platonism, we adopt a multistage procedure. First, we decide what constitutes people's nonmoral good. Setting moral obligation aside, what is good for a person, what will make that person's life go best? Moral rules including rules of justice are then designed so that their operation will promote the achievement of a maximal fair distribution of what is good for people. That is, moral rules are set so as to maximize a function that includes a specification of what is good for each person and a norm of fairness in the distribution of good across persons. This concludes the first stage. The second stage introduces quasi-Platonism. We correct the computation of people's welfare by taking at a discount the fulfillment of their interests that conflict with the moral rules developed in stage one.

We then recalculate what moral rules are best. Now we try to design moral rules that maximize an appropriate function of people's welfare interests corrected by the stage one moral rules. The process then is iterated until it comes to a halt in that the adjustments called for by recalculation are too small to be worth bothering about. The multistage procedure that I have sketched satisfies quasi-Platonism but allows the broadly welfarist critique of Dworkin's insistence on straight equality of resources as the norm of distributive justice. If this makes sense, then Dworkin is incorrect to dismiss these criticisms of equality of resources by appealing to quasi-Platonism. Quasi-Platonism has no power to insulate equality of resources from this line of criticism.

VI   Resources Versus Welfare

Resourcist theories of distributive justice hold that the aim of the enterprise is to gain for each individual a fair share of resources and opportunities, rather than to attempt to bring about any pattern of outcomes that results from people's uses of resources. This view involves holding individuals responsible for their ends in the sense that individuals who have received fair shares of resources are not entitled to further compensation on the ground that their chosen way of life turns out to be expensive so that they cannot achieve much satisfaction of their ends without aid from society. What counts as a fair resource share is determined independently of the aims and ambitions an individual happens to affirm. In contrast, welfarist principles of distributive justice in principle hold that individual resource shares should be adjusted to enable each to achieve a fair extent of well-being or welfare.

Dworkin is the prince of resourcists, and perhaps the theorist who has reflected most deeply on what is at stake in the choice of an interpersonal standard of comparison of people's condition for the purposes of a theory of justice.[23]

Despite the arguments Dworkin marshals, the idea that what justice fundamentally requires is providing each individual a fair share of resources or opportunities is implausible. If what morally mattered fundamentally were securing fair shares of resources, then it would be morally right and required by justice to provide these resources, if we can do so, even in a hypothetical scenario in which it is known for certain that the resources will do nobody any good. Suppose we can supply Smith his fair share of resources, but we happen to know that he will let them rot, make no use of them to benefit himself or anybody else. Still, even in this case, justice as fair resource provision insists that one ought to get these resources in Smith's hands. The welfarist by contrast holds that what matters morally at the fundamental level is enhancing the quality of people's lives and doing so in a way that distributes the good of welfare most fairly. If resource provision would do nobody any good, the welfarist holds that we should not waste the resources but should deploy them elsewhere.

We can give up the idea that justice fundamentally requires provision to all individuals of fair shares of resources or opportunities while still holding individual responsibility to be intrinsically morally important and to be a partial determinant of what we morally owe to each other. Welfarist justice can be responsibility-catering. I have discussed this issue in prior writings and will not rehearse those arguments here.[24]

Dworkin contends that the challenge model of the human good supports the position that "the justice of an economic distribution depends on its allocation of resources rather than of welfare or well-being."[25] If government were to try to arrange circumstances so that everyone attains some set level of welfare according to some particular conception of what welfare genuinely is, the government would be usurping individuals' nondelegable responsibility to interpret their own life circumstances, to define the challenge of their lives, and to identify for themselves what constitutes their good.

I have argued against Dworkin's challenge model, but even if one were to accept the core of this idea, one would then identify individual welfare with successful response to life's challenge. One would have an argument for construing welfarist justice in a particular way and not for rejecting welfarism and instead embracing resourcism.

Suppose the good life is responding well to the challenge given by the fact that one has a life to live. One's good then requires a good performance. But many features of one's environment can affect whether one performs well or badly, and the just society might (for all that has been said so far) be one that arranges the environment to maximize the chances that one performs well consistent with provision of a boost to other people's similar prospects. Here is a simple analogy. Suppose that living well is playing football well.[26] No one can live well without performing well, and individuals bear an ineliminable responsibility for the quality of their own performances. Still, society might be able to do many things – providing coaching, training, adequate football playing fields and high-quality equipment, and so on – that enhance people's prospects of playing football well, and on a welfarist view of distributive justice, would be morally required to do so (if excellent football playing constituted the human good). The welfarist conception of justice is fully compatible with a challenge model of ethics.

Dworkin offers an additional argument from challenge to resourcism. He supposes that welfarist justice must hold the good to be prior to the right in the sense that it identifies what is good independently of the right and then takes justice to consist in maximizing some function of the good. But according to Dworkin, the welfarist here is making a mistake. Ethical liberals, those who accept the challenge model of the good, "cannot separate ethics from justice," because they "must rely on assumptions or instincts of justice – about whether what we have or do is fair given its impact on our neighbors' and fellow citizens' lives – in order to decide which ways of living are ways of living well."[27]

These words recall Dworkin's master argument against the ideal of equality of welfare, which in fact generalizes to an argument against any welfarist ideal of justice.[28] Dworkin had argued that, in order to fix how well my life has gone, I need some notion of reasonable regret to anchor my assessment. I cannot reasonably regret that my life has not lasted for a thousand years or that I have not achieved what I would have achieved if I had had all the world's material resources at my disposal. According to Dworkin, what I can reasonably regret is my failure to achieve welfare I might have achieved if a fair share of society's resources had been made available to me. But the idea of "fair shares" here presupposes that one has some idea of what resource distribution is fair independently of what distribution of welfare it generates. So there is a dilemma: without a notion of reasonable regret, we cannot develop a welfarist measure of what people are owed in justice, but any attempt to articulate such a conception of reasonable regret presupposes an independent idea of fair distribution of resources, which renders otiose the welfarist measure we were trying to construct.

This clever argument fails. I submit that an objective list account of the good is, for all that Dworkin asserts, a viable approach to the measurement of welfare, and one that avoids the dilemma he poses. A full specification of the entries on the list indicates what weight any level of achievement on any dimension of achievement of any entry should get (this specification may allow for partial commensurability). But now we have a measure of what welfare or well-being level individuals attain, that allows us to compare different individuals' welfare condition without appeal to any notion of reasonable regret. Against this assertion, one might make the skeptical claim that in fact interpersonal comparisons of welfare or well-being of this sort are not meaningful, and cannot be well-defined, but Dworkin himself does not rely on such skepticism, and rightly so, because if applied even-handedly and consistently it would sweep aside theories of the right along with theories of the good.[29] As we have seen, Dworkin's project in "Foundations of Liberal Equality" is to show how (1) the reasoned conviction that some ways of life and some putative goods are intrinsically superior to others and (2) resourcist egalitarianism can be mutually supportive. So Dworkin needs his master argument against welfarism, and his doctrine is punctured by its failure.

As for Dworkin's claim about the good not being independent of the right, as welfarism requires, two responses strike me as cogent. One would simply resist the claim of quasi-Platonism entirely. I think that if a Mafia chieftain or a fierce warrior in an unjust war achieves the items on the objective list to a high degree – friendship, love, meaningful and satisfying work, cultural and scientific achievement, systematic knowledge, ethical wisdom, and the like – that person leads a good, though very immoral, life. What is the problem here? An alternative and equally cogent response would be to accept Dworkin's quasi-Platonism and determine what is good and what is fair for people via the multistage procedure described in the previous section. Either way, welfarism still looks viable.

VII Conclusion

The upshot of this critical discussion can be summarized as follows:

1   The challenge conception of ethics confounds the notions of an admirable life and a choice-worthy or desirable life. Therefore, even if the challenge view did support Dworkin's view of justice as liberal equality, the support of the challenge model would be worthless because the challenge view is unsatisfactory.

2   Dworkin contrasts the challenge model of ethics with the model of "impact," and argues that the former is superior. But the impact model is so implausible that it is hardly a recommendation of the challenge model to claim it is better than the impact model.

3   One aspect of Dworkinian liberal equality is tolerance or neutrality. Dworkin associates liberal tolerance with a principled rejection of strong paternalism and argues that the challenge conception of ethics dictates the priority of integrity, and integrity in turn requires rejection of strong paternalism. But the priority of integrity doctrine is wrongheaded, and should not be accepted even by someone who otherwise is favorably disposed to the challenge model. Liberal tolerance, interpreted by Dworkin to include a rigid antipaternalism, is an extreme and illiberal position, which should be rejected for the same reason that the priority of integrity should be rejected.

4   Liberal equality holds the norm of equality of resources to be the core principle of distributive justice. Equal distribution of resources is a coherent but implausible norm. It conflicts with the Pareto norm which holds that it is wrong to deny someone a benefit when conferring the benefit would impose no costs on anyone else. More broadly, the norm of equality of resources conflicts with the insight that the moral value of achieving a benefit for someone or preventing someone from suffering a loss depends on the losses and gains that such achievement or prevention would impose on others. The

intuitive implausibility of equality of resources is not outweighed by the reasons for equality of resources that are generated by the challenge model of ethics, for the challenge model generates no such reasons.

5   Liberal equality upholds the distributive justice norm of equality of resources. Liberal equality is then committed to the view that principles of distributive justice should be concerned at the fundamental moral level with the distribution of resources, not of welfare. Dworkin argues that the challenge model of ethics with its distinction between parameters and limitations supports the idea that principles of distributive justice should be resource-oriented, not welfare-oriented. But (a) resourcism is implausible and (b) the choice for or against the challenge model when properly conceived is in fact completely irrelevant to the resources versus welfare issue.

Acknowledgement

This essay was written for this volume in 1993 and revised in 2002.

Notes

1   John Rawls, *A Theory of Justice* (Cambridge, MA: Harvard University Press, rev. edn., 1999), pp. 27–8. Rawls's most recent statements of his version of liberal egalitarianism are his *Political Liberalism* (New York: Columbia University Press, 1996) and *Justice as Fairness: A Restatement*, ed. Erin Kelly (Cambridge, MA: Harvard University Press, 2001).

2   Ronald Dworkin, "Foundations of Liberal Equality" in Grethe B. Peterson (ed.), *The Tanner Lectures on Human Values*, vol. XI (Salt Lake City: University of Utah Press, 1990), pp. 1–119; reprinted for the most part in Ronald Dworkin, *Sovereign Virtue: The Theory and Practice of Equality* (Cambridge, MA: Harvard University Press, 2000), ch. 6.

3   The question and my answer to it are modeled on Brian Barry's question, "Is it Better to be Powerful or Lucky?" in his essay with that title, published in two parts, *Political Studies*, vol. 28, 1980, pp. 183–94 and 338–52.

4   According to a rational preference satisfaction view of the good, agents' lives intrinsically go better for them the greater the extent to which they satisfy preferences or life aims that they regard as important and that would withstand ideally extended rational scrutiny with full information.

5   For criticism of rational preference satisfaction accounts of the good, see Richard Arneson, "Human Flourishing versus Desire Satisfaction," *Social Philosophy and Policy*, vol. 16(1), 1999, pp. 113–42, along with the references cited therein.

6   On the characterization of "objective list" accounts of the good, see Derek Parfit, *Reasons and Persons* (Oxford: Oxford University Press, 1984), pp. 493–502. See also Thomas Hurka, *Perfectionism* (Oxford: Oxford University Press, 1993).

7   Dworkin, *Sovereign Virtue*, op. cit., p. 251.

8   Ibid., p. 267.

9   Dworkin, "Foundations of Liberal Equality," op. cit., p. 41. This phrase does not occur in the version of this essay reprinted in *Sovereign Virtue*.

10   I use "welfarist liberalism" as a name for liberal theories of justice that suppose that the goods whose distribution among persons are regulated by a theory of justice are to be measured by their contribution to individual welfare (or by the welfare level they make it possible for an individual to reach).

Welfarist liberalism competes with resourcist liberalism, which supposes that the proper measure of individuals' conditions for purposes of the theory of justice is not their welfare but rather their holding of goods, liberties, and opportunities. See Dworkin, *Sovereign Virtue*, chs. 1 and 2.

11 Dworkin, *Sovereign Virtue*, op. cit., p. 270.

12 Ibid., p. 272.

13 A clear discussion of this issue is in Allen E. Buchanan and Dan W. Brock, *Deciding for Others: The Ethics of Surrogate Decision Making* (Cambridge, UK: Cambridge University Press, 1989), pp. 29–47.

14 See Thomas Hurka, "Indirect Perfectionism: Kymlicka on Liberal Neutrality," *The Journal of Political Philosophy*, vol. 3, 1995, pp. 36–57. The views of Kymlicka that Hurka criticizes in this essay are for the most part the same as the views of Dworkin I criticize in this section.

15 Dworkin, *Sovereign Virtue*, op. cit., p. 268.

16 Notice the tension between what Dworkin asserts here and his discussion of the Jack and Jill example in ch. 1 of *Sovereign Virtue*, op. cit. He illustrates the implausibility of identifying the extent to which people lead lives good for them with the extent to which overall they satisfy their life aims that they regard as important. Jack and Jill lead lives that to an impartial observer look just the same, but idiosyncratic differences in their beliefs about the importance of their life aims bring it about that their lives are significantly unequal in their welfare construed as overall success (on several possible interpretations of this notion). Dworkin comments that "the differences between Jack and Jill we have noticed are still differences in their beliefs but not differences in their lives" (p. 38). To avoid this difficulty one needs a measure of individual welfare that measures individuals' genuine quality of life rather than their subjective opinions or attitudes about their quality of life.

17 Dworkin, *Sovereign Virtue*, op. cit., p. 273.

18 The statement in the text bowdlerizes Dworkin's position to some extent. Dworkin holds that the egalitarian obligation to treat all individuals impartially, with equal concern and respect, applies only to governments, since any government claims legitimately to coerce all who inhabit its territory and claims to act in the name of all those under its jurisdiction. The equality of resources ideal would not then be binding in individuals living on separate islands and not joined under a common government.

19 For elucidation of these important details of the account, see *Sovereign Virtue*, ch. 2.

20 The view counterposed to Dworkinian equality in the text is the priority view. For clear explication of this notion, see Derek Parfit, *Equality or Priority?* (Lawrence, KS: University of Kansas, 1995).

21 I believe the view sketched in the text concedes what is most plausible in the criticisms of the norm of equality of resources in Harry Frankfurt, "Equality as a Moral Ideal," *Ethics*, vol. 98 (1), 1987, pp. 21–43. For further discussion see my "Egalitarianism and Responsibility," *The Journal of Ethics*, vol. 3, 1999, pp. 225–47.

22 Dworkin, "Foundations of Liberal Equality," op. cit., p. 41, fn. 32. This statement is not included in the version of the essay reprinted in *Sovereign Virtue*.

23 See Dworkin, *Sovereign Virtue*, op. cit., chs. 1 and 2.

24 See Richard Arneson, "Equal Opportunity for Welfare Defended and Recanted," *The Journal of Political Philosophy*, vol. 7, 1997, pp. 488–97; "Egalitarianism and Responsibility," *Journal of Ethics*, vol. 3, 1999, pp. 225–324; "Luck Egalitarianism and Prioritarianism," *Ethics*, vol. 110, 2000, pp. 339–49; "Welfare Should be the Currency of Justice," *Canadian Journal of Philosophy*, vol. 30, 2000, pp. 497–524; and "Luck and Equality," *Aristotelian Society Proceedings*, supp. vol., 2001, pp. 73–90.

25 Dworkin, *Sovereign Virtue*, op. cit., p. 279.

26 The analogy might be thought inadvertently to illustrate the incompatibility of welfarism and a serious account of individual responsibility. If the good is postulated by society, and institutions are arranged to secure it, this inevitably displaces individual responsibility for choosing one's conception of value and constructing a valuable and fulfilling life. So the objection goes. In reply: individual responsibility and social responsibility can coexist. My boss's responsibility to prevent me from stealing from the company does not eliminate my own personal responsibility to avoid stealing. My own responsibility to choose and seek my good does not preclude a back-up responsibility (obligation) on the part of society

to help save me from the bad consequences for my life my choices engender. In addition, nothing in welfarist justice doctrine privileges any particular society's collective judgments concerning the nature of good and the valuable ways of living.

27   Dworkin, *Sovereign Virtue*, op. cit., p. 279.
28   Ibid., pp. 38–41 and 46.
29   But see economic "fairness theory," e.g., Hal Varian, "Equity, Envy, and Efficiency," *Journal of Economic Theory*, vol. 9, September 1974, pp. 63–91.

6

A Puzzle about Ethics, Justice, and the Sacred

Matthew Clayton

We disagree about what makes one's life go well, what makes a society just, and how we ought to acknowledge the sacredness, or inherent value, of human life. A response to such controversies offered by many prominent liberals involves siding with a particular view of justice while seeking to defend political principles, such as freedom of conscience and expression, that remain neutral with respect to the ethical and religious questions that divide us.

A leading criticism of liberalism challenges its central distinction between ideals of justice, which liberals believe can legitimately be enforced coercively, and conceptions of the good life or of the sacred, which, they believe, each individual should be free to pursue according to his or her conscience. If liberals think it appropriate, even in the face of disagreement, for the coercive apparatus of the state to be used to realize justice, then why not also permit its use to prevent people from serving false gods or lifestyles that are unworthy of pursuit? Perfectionists press that question. Denying the distinction in the opposite way, proceduralists insist that we should seek to devise a set of political procedures that can be accepted by those adhering to different conceptions of justice – egalitarians and libertarians alike – as well as those who disagree about the good. The challenge for liberals, then, is to cite a relevant distinction between issues of justice and those of ethics and the sacred on the basis of which the liberal concern with the enforcement of justice and its critique of perfectionism can jointly be defended.

No one has written more engagingly in defense of a liberal conception of these matters than Ronald Dworkin. In this paper, I seek to clarify Dworkin's conception of liberal neutrality, and to raise some questions about the plausibility of Dworkin's defense of toleration in matters of religious conviction.

I In What Sense is Dworkin's Liberalism Neutral?

Neutralist liberals generally qualify their commitment to political neutrality in three key respects. First, as we have seen, liberal neutrality is not neutral with respect to all moral choices. Instead, it claims that the state should be neutral on the question of the good, which concerns, for example, the merits of different religions and conceptions of sexuality. Thus there are numerous questions concerning distributive justice, and civil and political liberties, with respect to which liberals offer specific and partisan moral answers.

Second, liberals do not standardly advocate neutrality of effect, which seeks to ensure that different conceptions of the good are equally easy to pursue.[1] Rather, they endorse neutrality of

grounds, which holds that the state should not be guided by the inferiority or superiority of particular conceptions of the good when deciding how to act. It is plain to see how the two kinds of
neutrality can come apart. For example, a policy that refused to subsidize the pursuit of particular religious activities might lead to their decline and, thereby, render the lifestyles they support
more costly to pursue: that would be a violation of neutrality of effect that would not necessarily trouble adherents of neutrality of grounds.[2]

A third respect in which liberal neutrality is restricted is in its scope. Political neutrality reg-
ulates the operation of the state. It is not regarded as an appropriate principle to guide the decisions of individuals in their nonpolitical choices.[3] Indeed, liberals have a high priority concern to
protect the familiar set of civil liberties, such as the freedoms of conscience, speech, and
association, which facilitate individuals' engagement in particular kinds of lifestyle and belief in
specific religious doctrines. Thus liberals prescribe neutrality as a restraint only on the state.

Dworkin's conception and defense of neutrality have undergone significant revision. This is
evident in his most comprehensive treatment of these issues in his Tanner Lecture, "Foundations
of Liberal Equality,"[4] where he introduces the distinction between two ways of regarding
neutrality. Whereas previously he regarded political neutrality as an *axiom* of political morality,
Dworkin now conceives it as a *theorem* to be defended by argument from the more fundamental
principle of equal concern.[5] He believes that the state should promote the well-being of its citizens. That fundamental duty seems to be incompatible with the neutralist claim that the state
should not enforce ethical values. Much of Dworkin's Tanner Lecture is devoted to showing how
the apparent inconsistency between grounding liberalism on a conception of the good life and the
principle of political neutrality is illusory. His claim is that a sound understanding of the good
supports neutralist liberal political institutions.

The view that neutrality is a theorem to be defended through the articulation of a particular
conception of the good is strikingly different from Rawls's view. Dworkin claims that political liberals, such as Rawls, view neutrality as an axiom. We should, however, be careful in describing the
difference. A principle might be understood to be axiomatic in virtue of being a self-evident truth
in need of no defense. Interpreted in that way, it would be incorrect to view Rawls, and other
political liberals, as affirming neutrality as axiomatic. Rather, they defend the principle as a necessary condition of the attainment of an important political value: the value of stable publicly justifiable political institutions, given the inevitable persistence of a plurality of conceptions of the
good in a free society.[6] Nevertheless, in the present context we might agree with Dworkin that
neutrality is axiomatic within political liberalism in a different sense, that is, in its relationship to
the good life. In defense of neutrality, political liberals cite a feature of legitimacy – that political
principles should be publicly justifiable – and argue that claims about the good life should be dis-
regarded to serve this end. They must be excluded because they cannot generate the right kind
of consensus on political principles. Moreover, this is the case even if some particular view of the
good might itself support political neutrality. Thus the real contrast is that whereas Dworkin
claims that neutrality is a theorem in virtue of being defended by appeal to the correct understanding of ethics, political liberals support neutrality on moral grounds that indicate the extent
to which ethics should enter political philosophy.[7]

The difference between Dworkin and Rawls can be illustrated with a distinction between three
kinds of argument for neutrality: jeopardy, futility, and perversity.[8] We can distinguish between
two broad reasons for denying the appropriateness of political perfectionism, which is the view
that sometimes the state can legitimately promote particular conceptions of the good on the
grounds that their pursuit is intrinsically valuable.[9] First, if the state were permitted to promote
superior conceptions of the good this would diminish the achievement of other values. This

jeopardy argument is, I think, characteristic of political liberalism: given the fact of pluralism, the value jeopardized is the public acceptability of political institutions. Secondly, political perfectionism might be inappropriate because the state is unsuited effectively to promote valuable conceptions of the good. Were it to try to enforce the correct conceptions, it would fail or, at best, make no positive difference to the well-being of citizens. Attempts by the state coercively to promote the good life would be either self-defeating and, therefore, perverse, or would be futile. Thus the state should refrain from engaging in such well-intentioned activity. We can call these the perversity and futility arguments against perfectionism.

An initial problem for Dworkin is how to rebut the charge of inconsistency, because he aspires to defend two apparently contradictory claims: first, that the state should not attempt to use its powers to promote any particular view of the good life; and second, that political morality rests on the correct understanding of the good life. While the first claim suggests that the state should put issues about the good to one side, the second implores it to give them full consideration. Dworkin's resolution of this apparent inconsistency rests on a distinction between the *abstract* and *concrete* aspects of the good life.[10] Concrete ethical issues concern, for example, the soundness of particular religious beliefs or the value of particular kinds of sexuality. Typical disputes surrounding these issues concern the identification of which goals, projects, and relationships are worthy of pursuit. Dworkin advocates political neutrality with respect to such disputes.

In contrast, the abstract aspects of the good life involve issues such as the relationship between justice and the good life, the importance of choice or affirmation of one's concrete ethical activity, and whether the good life is in some way relative to social and economic conditions. The resolution of these issues is designed to generate a set of philosophical claims about ethics that are common to all concrete conceptions of the good and to which they should conform. Dworkin's belief is that the correct account of ethics provides a view of certain abstract aspects of the good life that justifies political neutrality on concrete ethical matters. In particular, political neutrality follows from an acknowledgement that well-being consists in the successful pursuit of an appropriate challenge, which requires, among other things, a particular relationship between agents and their substantive ethical life. Thus, once we have a firm grasp of the abstract structure of the good life, we will appreciate that political concern for citizens' well-being must be neutral concern.

Given the kind of argument Dworkin presents, it is unsurprising that the character of his conception of liberal neutrality differs from that of Rawls and others. Indeed, his conception is more permissive of government engagement with ethics than other liberal views in two key respects. First, while Dworkin offers his conception of ethics, the challenge model, as making sense of many of our central convictions about what makes our lives successful, he acknowledges that the account remains controversial. As he puts it, his ideal government would be neutral in its *operation*, but not neutral in terms of avoiding an *appeal* to controversial, albeit abstract, claims about the good.[11] Given Dworkin's appeal to what Rawls would call a comprehensive doctrine, many will be reluctant to embrace the challenge model. Dworkin himself suggests a reason for such reluctance. Consider his defense of liberal equality, which allows individuals to voice their demands for compensation according to their own ethical convictions, even if those convictions go against the challenge model of ethics. One source of support for that conception is the ideal of partnership democracy, in which individuals "see themselves as joint authors of collective decisions."[12] If individuals are to regard themselves in that way then it would appear that the case for legislation must be one that is capable of being accepted by citizens who affirm quite different views of ethics.[13] It is unlikely that the challenge model can serve as such a foundation for liberal justice.[14]

Second, Dworkin's view supports neutrality with respect to the reasons for denying liberty or for the exercise of coercion through the criminal law. He accepts that there are a number of other powers at the disposal of the government – such as short-term educational paternalism – that it may use to encourage individuals to pursue superior concrete conceptions of the good. Joseph Raz writes: "In a sense anti-perfectionism is merely a more radical restriction of the employment of means through which one may pursue conceptions of the good. It denies the appropriateness of using any political means to pursue such ends."[15] If we define a neutralist in Razian terms – as ruling out the use of *any* means to promote valuable conceptions of the good – then Dworkin must be seen as having abandoned the ideal of neutrality in favor of a noncoercive liberal perfectionism.

Nevertheless, labels are cheap. What counts is whether Dworkin's account of liberal political morality and, in particular, his defense of the cut between justice on the one hand and ethics and the sacred on the other is plausible. It is to that issue that I now turn.

II   Two Parameters

Dworkin's challenge model of ethics is a wide-ranging, rich, and subtle account that merits critical attention in its own right as a conception of the good life.[16] Here I focus on only those features of the model that bear on the issue that concerns us. Of particular relevance is his distinction between limitations and parameters in evaluating the success of a person's life.

Dworkin contrasts the challenge model of well-being with the impact model. The latter is largely an extension of consequentialist morality to the sphere of ethics. Crudely stated, it asserts that the quality of someone's life is a function of the overall consequences of that person's life for the world. In this model, ethics is viewed as derived from a theory of value, whether value is defined in utilitarian or other terms. In contrast, the challenge model asserts that well-being consists in successfully responding to an appropriate challenge. Dworkin believes that the challenge model is more plausible for a number of reasons, not least because it can explain how people's lives can go well even if they fail to contribute much of value to the world.[17]

The distinction between limitations and parameters is central to the challenge model. The circumstances in which we live, or items at our disposal, can often be regarded as limiting or enhancing our opportunity to lead successful lives. For example, my inability to speak better than rudimentary French operates as a limitation on my engagement with French culture which, were that an important goal of mine, would diminish my well-being. Similarly, my lack of scientific understanding limits the extent to which I can appreciate the nature of our world. However, there are other aspects of our circumstances that operate as parameters rather than as limitations. In the case of limitations, possession of the relevant item constitutes an aid, while lack of possession constitutes an obstacle, to what we have reason to pursue, where the latter is defined without reference to those items. If an item is a parameter of the good life, however, then that item figures in the description of the kind of life I ought to be leading. In the challenge model, parameters "help define what a good performance of living would be" for a person.[18] Examples of parameters might include "a reasonable lifespan" or "being a member of the American political community," though the location of the cut between parameters and limitations, Dworkin claims, will differ from person to person.[19]

Two parameters that shape Dworkin's liberalism are those of justice and ethical integrity. If living well involves a successful response to an appropriate challenge, then the parameter of justice can be regarded as a specification of what an appropriate challenge involves or as part of what a successful response would be to such a challenge. Living under injustice, he insists, condemns people to face the wrong kind of challenge and, to that extent, makes their lives go worse, and that is the case irrespective of whether they have more or less than justice requires.[20] Justice is also relevant in judging people's responses to the challenge they face. Individuals who enjoy a fair share of resources but who nevertheless seek to increase their share through theft or fraud would plainly be failing in their response to the challenge of living well.

Because justice is a parameter of the good life in these ways, the liberal view that justice should be enforced by the government has a clear justification. Not only is justice an important ideal in its own right that warrants enforcement, its presence is also a requirement of people pursuing successful lives. So, to the extent that government has a duty to act with concern for its citizens, it must enforce justice as a necessary part of enabling people to face appropriate challenges in their lives.

The parameter of ethical integrity is the requirement that there should be a match between the lives that individuals lead and their settled convictions about the kind of lives they ought to lead. Dworkin asks how two components of people's lives affect their well-being. The first component concerns the substantive content of individuals' ethical lives: the events in their lives, their experiences, achievements, and relationships. The second component concerns the attitude they take towards those features of their lives. Such attitudes may include regret, acceptance, or endorsement. These feelings can be regarded as describing whether people believe that their lifestyle enhances their well-being, or serves their critical interests.

Dworkin distinguishes two ways in which these components can be related. The contrast between them concerns whether people's lifestyle can enhance their well-being if they do not endorse that lifestyle. The *additive view* is that valuable experiences and achievements contribute to their well-being even if they regret the fact that their lives have these features. If they endorse them as contributing to the value of their lives, this may add still further to their well-being. Nevertheless, since valuable experiences and endorsement contribute independently to the value of people's lives, their lives can go well even if they regret the lives they are leading.[21] In contrast, the *constitutive view* holds that individuals' experiences and achievements enhance their well-being only if they endorse them, that is, only if they regard them as valuable achievements. The constitutive view is central to Dworkin's ideal of ethical integrity: "Someone has achieved ethical integrity, we may say, when he lives out of the conviction that his life, in its central features, is an appropriate one, that no other life he might live would be a plainly better response to the parameters of his ethical situation rightly judged."[22]

The choice between the constitutive view and the additive view affects our judgment of the legitimacy of state paternalism. On the additive view, paternalism seems to be justified in at least some cases, since the content of one's life and one's endorsement of it contribute independently to one's well-being. If people pursue goals that lack value, the state may be justified in interfering coercively in their lives if it can ensure that they pursue more worthwhile projects, whether or not they value them. In one way, this would enhance those people's well-being, as they would then be engaged in more valuable activities.

Dworkin believes that if we adopt the constitutive view, as we should, then restricting individuals' liberty for their own sake becomes self-defeating. Since a change in activity would improve an individual's life only if the person endorsed the change, the state is unable to improve the lives of its citizens merely by forcing them to pursue activities that are intrinsically more valuable than their previous pursuits. Even if a religious life lacks value, we cannot improve unswerving believers' lives by prohibiting religious worship: the lives they would then live would lack the endorsement required to contribute to their well-being.[23] On this view, paternalistically inspired perfectionism is futile or perverse.[24]

Ethical integrity can fail in a number of ways. One such way is "when people believe, rightly or wrongly, that the correct normative parameters have not been met for them, when they have fewer resources than justice permits, for example."[25] Note, however, that, unlike the case of convictions about the good life, if people fail to regard their situation as just, when in fact it is, the mismatch between life and conviction does not generate an objection to the government's promotion of justice. Indeed, because justice is itself a parameter of the good life, if the government were to refrain from pursuing the cause of equality it would, to that extent, be failing to promote its citizens' well-being. Well-being is a fragile good, then, which requires living under justice and recognizing that fact. It is, therefore, diminished if either justice or ethical integrity is absent; both are necessary, so the question of trade-offs does not arise. To illustrate, consider Dworkin's remarks about Hitler: "Of course it would have been better for everyone else if Hitler had died in his cradle. But on the challenge view it makes no sense to say that his own life would have been better, *as distinct from no worse*, if that had happened."[26] Hitler's life would not have gone worse had he been prevented from pursuing evil. True, lacking ethical integrity would mean that his life would not have gone well. But, because justice is a parameter of well-being, his life would not have gone any better were he permitted to pursue evil.[27]

None of this means that achieving ethical integrity on issues of justice has no bearing on institutional design. Indeed, Dworkin appeals to the ideal of integrity in defense of his conception of democracy. The good of integrity supports the protection of freedom of expression, even for those who hold views contrary to the demands of justice. Even if their views are rightly overridden in legislation or a constitution, individuals must be free to voice their convictions concerning justice. That is necessary if they are to view their participation within democratic institutions as integrated with the rest of their moral lives.[28] Still, that kind of merger of conviction and conduct justifies less restraint on the government compared to that envisaged when we think about beliefs about concrete conceptions of the good. In the case of the good, the self-defeatingness of seeking to improve people's lives by forcing them to live against their convictions condemns the use of such force. In the case of justice, the use of such force is permitted.

III   Liberal Neutrality and the Sacred

Dworkin's defense of political neutrality invites a number of questions. Some of these concern the issue of whether his ideal of ethical integrity and, more generally, the challenge model are, after all, compatible with a perfectionist political morality that permits the government to use its powers of taxation and subsidy to encourage individuals to abandon less rewarding goals in favor of more worthy pursuits. I have raised questions of that kind elsewhere.[29] Here, I raise the rather different issue of whether Dworkin's rejection of state paternalism can plausibly be extended to support a liberal position with respect to the realm of impersonal value or the sacred.

One of the most entrenched sources of disagreement within contemporary society concerns how we should interpret and respect various impersonal values. The issues of abortion, euthanasia, and capital punishment are complex, because they raise questions about whether and how human life's inherent value ought to be honored, as well as questions about justice and well-being. Liberals defend freedom of conscience as extending to impersonal values. They insist that individuals should be legally free to respond to such values in the manner that is most appropriate given their convictions; it is not the business of the state to enforce any particular understanding of life's inherent value, for example. To fix ideas, let us focus on Dworkin's treatment of abortion.[30]

Dworkin distinguishes between two kinds of reason for protecting human life: the reason against killing is *derivative* if the concern to protect human life is grounded in the rights or interests that persons are thought to have; the reason is *detached* if it does not depend upon such rights or interests. Of particular interest to Dworkin are detached reasons concerning abortion that rest upon conceptions of the inherent value, or sacredness, of human life. He argues persuasively that, on the best reading of their views, most people approach the abortion debate with the view that human life as such has value, independently of its contribution to human interests or the protection of people's rights, and he offers a critique of objections to abortion that rest upon derivative reasons to protect the life of fetuses.[31] In particular, he argues that certain objections to abortion, which rest on the attribution to fetuses of rights or interests, fail, because that attribution is implausible, at least in the early stages of pregnancy. The most interesting part of Dworkin's argument concerns the moral, political, and legal issues surrounding abortion if we understand the problem as involving the detached concern for the intrinsic value of human life rather than a concern derived from our duty to protect people's interests.

Within the context of abortion, Dworkin defends political neutrality through the principle of procreative autonomy, which recognizes, at the very least, that women have, and should have, a constitutional right to abortion. Dworkin derives this, in part, from the following principle:

A state may not curtail liberty, in order to protect an intrinsic value, when the effect on one group would be special and grave, when the community is seriously divided about what respect for that value requires, and when people's opinions about the nature of that value reflect essentially religious convictions that are fundamental to moral personality.[32]

While the state has a right to take steps to ensure that people's decisions whether or not to abort are taken responsibly, with a sense of the moral importance of the issues, "not out of immediate convenience but out of examined conviction,"[33] the state must not coerce women into conforming with particular conceptions of how the intrinsic value of human life should be protected.[34] Dworkin's main aim is to defend the principle of procreative autonomy as grounded in various parts of the US Constitution. Nevertheless, he also affirms it as a principle of political morality.[35] What is the justification of religious toleration in this area as a matter of political morality?

Dworkin says little in answer to this question, but his brief remarks indicate a similarity with his general justification of liberal neutrality:

Tolerance is a cost we must pay for our adventure in liberty. We are committed, by our love of liberty and dignity, to live in communities in which no group is thought clever or spiritual or numerous enough to decide essentially religious matters for everyone else. If we have genuine concern for the lives others lead, we will also accept that no life is a good one lived against the grain of conviction, that it does not help someone else's life but spoils it to force values upon him he cannot accept but can only bow before out of fear or prudence.[36]

The last part of the quoted remarks appeals to the ideal of ethical integrity and its associated critique of paternalism. However, the argument is unsuccessful. Let us grant, for argument's sake, the soundness of Dworkin's constitutive view of endorsement with respect to living well. It might follow that to the extent that we are duty-bound to promote people's well-being, the enforcement of a particular view of abortion would be wrong, because nobody's life goes better by being forced to serve an impersonal good that person does not affirm.[37] Nevertheless, Dworkin acknowledges the existence of other reasons for actions that apply to the state, namely, the detached duty to protect the sacredness of human life, which need not depend upon claims about the good of its citizens. Thus the ideal of ethical integrity defeats only certain reasons to be intolerant in this area. It remains to be seen whether there is a conclusive reason not to enforce some particular view of the permissibility of abortion.

An objector to abortion on detached grounds might argue in the following way: the enforcement of the correct conception of the sanctity of human life, which condemns abortion, might diminish the well-being of those who wish to abort, since they are forced to act in ways that they do not affirm. Nevertheless, the state has a duty to protect the sacredness of human life which, in this case, overrides its duty to promote the well-being of its citizens.

Indeed, another critic might resist the alleged trade-off between derivative and detached reasons that is implicit in the view just stated. In doing so, that critic might trade on Dworkin's conception of parameters discussed in the previous section to make the stronger claim that respect for the sanctity of human life, like respect for justice, is a parameter of living well. Recall that in the case of individuals who hold mistaken convictions about justice, we are not obliged, out of concern for their well-being, to allow them to act on their beliefs, except to allow them to articulate them in political discussion. Living well involves living justly, so we fail to help those mistaken about justice if we enable them to enact their views. Enforcing justice is a duty of government, and in fulfilling that duty it realizes the circumstances in which individuals can lead successful lives. Many would insist that a similar relationship holds between well-being and respect for the sanctity of human life.

In fact, Dworkin thinks that, in certain cases, the government may act to protect detached values. He cites the saving of species from extinction and the preservation of culture as examples. What makes abortion different, however, and places it as an issue on which individuals must be left free to act on their own convictions, is, first, that enforcing a particular moral conception would have special and grave effects for women and, second, that our convictions about the detached value of human life are fundamental to our moral personalities.[38] Let us consider these in reverse order. Dworkin regards our convictions about life's detached value as essentially religious, central to our self-conceptions and our conceptions of how to live. These remarks serve to distinguish the detached value of human life from the detached values of culture or the biosphere in such a way, Dworkin believes, that supports the view that living well requires the freedom to live by one's convictions about the sacredness of human life but not necessarily those concerning the preservation of biodiversity. Nevertheless, it is unclear how these remarks serve to distinguish the detached value of human life from the reasons we have to preserve justice. To be sure, our justice-based reasons connect to what we owe to each other, while detached reasons do not connect in the same way to our duties to others. Nevertheless, our justice-based reasons are, arguably, similarly fundamental to our self-conceptions and to our conceptions of how to live well, as Dworkin himself has eloquently shown. We may share a conception of ourselves as free and equal and a conception of living well as one in which an acknowledgement of that freedom and equality determines the distribution of resources in society. Nevertheless, while our conceptions of justice are fundamental in these ways, we disagree about what is the best interpretation of justice for a society of free and equal persons. If that is the case, then it is mysterious why considerations of justice may be enforced politically, while the sacredness of human life may not.

Perhaps the answer lies in the "special and grave" effects that laws prohibiting or requiring abortion would have on women: Dworkin rightly stresses that "making abortion criminal may destroy a woman's life."[39] However, the critic might reply that there are many techniques short of the use of the criminal law which the state might employ to safeguard the inherent value of life. It might, for example, use its educational institutions to encourage a belief in the correct conception of the sacredness of human life. It may also use its powers relating to tax and benefit to lessen the financial costs of pregnancy and child rearing in an attempt to protect human life's detached value. These political options aim to encourage conformity while avoiding grave consequences for women. To be sure, such measures fall short of many of the demands of antiabortionists. Significantly, however, they are also more permissive of government intervention compared to Dworkin's proposal for government to promote responsible decision making without prescribing any particular answers to questions addressing the sacredness of human life. They aim to promote conformity without coercion, rather than merely an attitude that such decisions should be made in light of an awareness of their moral importance.

One response to Dworkin's argument from special and grave effects, then, is to lessen the burden on women of an antiabortion policy without abandoning the stance against abortion. A more combative response, which gains strength as the burden on women is lessened, is to challenge the view that the concern to avoid burdens falling on a particular section of the community is a decisive or weighty consideration in determining policy. After all, certain burdens fall on individuals holding particular tastes or beliefs in Dworkin's own conception of liberal equality. Under equality of resources, people who hold expensive tastes suffer a lower level of welfare compared to others.[40] However, that is acceptable, because, according to Dworkin, equality of resources is the most attractive conception of economic justice, and is a parameter for us in living successful lives. Antiabortionists might employ a similar argument. True, women are burdened more than men by a policy that discourages abortion. Nevertheless, such a policy, they may insist, is the most attractive means of protecting life's detached value, which is also a parameter of living well.

Plainly, neither of these replies to Dworkin's defense of procreative autonomy is conclusive. No doubt the special burdens faced by individuals and the fundamental importance of religious convictions in people's lives should affect the shape of abortion law. It is not obvious, however, that they require a government to abstain from addressing the concrete question of which conceptions of life's inherent value are more or less plausible. That question may or may not be independent of the government's responsibility to act with concern for its citizens, depending on whether respect for life's impersonal value is a parameter of well-being. Either way, the demand for ethical integrity on questions of the sacredness of human life is not sufficient to settle the issue of abortion. We need to know why the ideal of ethical integrity with respect to such detached values trumps our reasons to protect those values.

Acknowledgement

For helpful discussion of the issues addressed in this paper, I thank Justine Burley, Mark Philp, and Andrew Williams.

Notes

1   See Ronald Dworkin, *Sovereign Virtue: The Theory and Practice of Equality* (Cambridge, MA: Harvard University Press, 2000), pp. 153–5, 282–3; John Rawls, *Political Liberalism* (New York, Columbia University Press, 1993), pp. 192–3. There are numerous alternative conceptions of neutrality of effect. See Joseph Raz, *The Morality of Freedom* (Oxford: Clarendon Press, 1986), pp. 110–24.

2   Neutrality of grounds has been described variously as justificatory neutrality (Will Kymlicka, "Liberal Individualism and Liberal Neutrality," *Ethics*, vol. 99, 1989, pp. 883–6), the exclusion of ideals (Raz, *The Morality of Freedom*, op. cit., ch. 6), and neutrality of intention (Jeremy Waldron, "Legislation and Moral Neutrality," in R. Goodin and A. Reeve (eds.), *Liberal Neutrality* (London: Routledge, 1989), pp. 61–83).

Peter DeMarneffe argues that neutrality of grounds is consistent with countenancing a democratic procedure that permits individuals to act on their nonneutral assessment of particular conceptions of the good to affect certain policy outcomes. Thus he claims that neutral principles do not necessarily support neutral legislation. See "Liberalism, Liberty and Neutrality," *Philosophy and Public Affairs*, vol. 19, 1990, pp. 253–74. Liberal neutralists must, therefore, buttress the argument with further considerations. Much of the remaining support can be elaborated from Dworkin's instructive remarks on majoritarianism and equality of resources. See Dworkin, *Sovereign Virtue*, op. cit., pp. 212–16.

3   There is a question about how nonpolitical choices are to be characterized. For example, in *Political Liberalism*, Rawls distinguishes between constitutional essentials and matters of basic justice, which should be decided with guidance by public (neutral) reason, and other legislative matters, such as the finance of parks, public roads, or museums, about which he is less sure that public reason applies. See Rawls's *Political Liberalism*, op. cit., pp. 212–16.

4   In Grethe Peterson (ed.), *The Tanner Lectures on Human Values*, vol. XI (Salt Lake City: University of Utah Press, 1990), pp. 3–119. An abridged and revised version of that lecture appears as ch. 6 of *Sovereign Virtue*.

5   Dworkin notes that his change of mind is evident if we read "Liberalism" and "Why Liberals Should Care about Equality," both of which are reprinted in his *A Matter of Principle* (Oxford: Clarendon Press, 1985). See Dworkin, "Foundations of Liberal Equality," op. cit., p. 7.

6   Rawls, *Political Liberalism*, op. cit., pp. 47–71, and "The Domain of the Political and Overlapping Consensus," *New York University Law Review*, vol. 64, 1989, pp. 234–45.

7   Here I understand ethics as dealing with issues of well-being. Morality deals with issues about how people ought to treat other persons and, more broadly, beings with interests. This does not prejudge the issue of whether, and the manner in which, morality enters ethics. See "Foundations of Liberal Equality," op. cit., pp. 8–9, for Dworkin's remarks on ethics and morality.

8   These terms are taken from Hirschman who uses them in a rather different context. See A. Hirschman, *The Rhetoric of Reaction* (Cambridge, MA: Harvard University Press, 1991).

9   For discussion of the varieties of perfectionism, some of which are overlooked by antiperfectionists, see Joseph Chan, "Legitimacy, Unanimity, and Perfectionism," *Philosophy and Public Affairs*, vol. 29, 2000, pp. 10–20.

10   Dworkin, *Sovereign Virtue*, op. cit., pp. 239–40, 281–4.

11   Ibid., pp. 281–4.

12   Ibid., p. 295.

13   Dworkin offers similar remarks in "Why Liberals Should Care about Equality," in *A Matter of Principle*, op. cit., pp. 205–6.

14   Note that Dworkin now claims that his liberalism does not depend on the truth of the challenge model of ethics. See Dworkin, *Sovereign Virtue*, op. cit., p. 241. Given his defense of partnership democracy that fact, if sound, is fortunate.

15   Raz, *The Morality of Freedom*, op. cit., p. 111.

16 It has received some. See, for example, Martin Wilkinson, "Dworkin on Paternalism and Well-Being," *Oxford Journal of Legal Studies*, vol. 16, 1996, pp. 433–44; Richard Arneson, "Human Flourishing versus Desire Satisfaction," *Social Philosophy and Policy*, vol. 16, 1999, pp. 135–42.

17 Dworkin, *Sovereign Virtue*, op. cit., pp. 250–60.

18 Ibid., p. 260.

19 Ibid., pp. 260–3.

20 Note, however, that Dworkin regards justice as a soft, rather than a hard, parameter of well-being. That is, while a life is always blighted by injustice, there may be other features of that life that make it a worthwhile one. Nevertheless, he thinks that there are few cases in which it is plausible to claim that the life in question went worse for being constrained by justice. See Dworkin, *Sovereign Virtue*, op. cit., pp. 263–7.

21 For defense of the additive view, see Michael Otsuka's 1989 Oxford University D.Phil. thesis, *Equality, Neutrality, and Prejudice: A Critique of Dworkin's Liberalism*, p. 82; R. Crisp, "Sidgwick and Self-Interest," *Utilitas*, vol. 2, 1990, pp. 274–6; T. Hurka, "Indirect Perfectionism: Kymlicka on Liberal Neutrality," *The Journal of Political Philosophy*, vol. 3, 1995, pp. 41–4.

22 Dworkin, *Sovereign Virtue*, op. cit., p. 270.

23 Dworkin notes that certain kinds of paternalism appear to raise few ethical problems. The state might prohibit the availability of particular unregulated foodstuffs, for example, on the ground that people do not wish to risk the consumption of infected food. Such paternalism prevents people from making choices, but does not inhibit them in the pursuit of their considered convictions or goals.

24 The futility argument claims that such a course of action would fail to improve the believer's life, because it wouldn't carry the required endorsement. The perversity argument represents a stronger claim, that ethical integrity is more important from the point of view of well-being than pursuing worthwhile projects. On this argument, the course of action as described would diminish the believer's well-being.

25 Dworkin, *Sovereign Virtue*, op. cit., p. 271.

26 Ibid., p. 268 (emphasis added).

27 In a different view, we might go further and say that Hitler's life went badly, not merely because he acted unjustly. A life of injustice, we might say, necessarily lacks ethical integrity. In this view ethical integrity involves leading a life according to convictions that are, at once, one's own and consistent with justice.

28 Dworkin, *Sovereign Virtue*, op. cit., pp. 201–2.

29 See Matthew Clayton, "Liberal Equality and Ethics," *Ethics*, vol. 113, 2002, pp. 8–22 and Dworkin's "Response" in the same issue, pp. 14–3.

30 Dworkin, "Unenumerated Rights: Whether and How *Roe* Should be Overruled," *The Chicago Law Review*, vol. 59, 1992, pp. 381–432; *Life's Dominion: An Argument about Abortion and Euthanasia* (London: Harper Collins, 1993), chs. 1–6.

31 Dworkin, *Life's Dominion*, op. cit., pp. 11–24; "Unenumerated Rights," op. cit, p. 396f.

32 *Life's Dominion*, op. cit., p. 157; see also pp. 166–8.

33 Ibid., p. 150.

34 In discussing toleration, Dworkin focuses on what he takes to be politically the most significant argument, which is the alleged right of the majority to the ethical environment that matches its view. Nevertheless, I take it that Dworkin would extend his arguments in support of procreative autonomy in rejection of perfectionist inspired enforcement as well.

35 Dworkin, "Unenumerated Rights," op. cit., p. 426.

36 Dworkin, *Life's Dominion*, op. cit., pp. 167–8.

37 For further instructive discussion of the many connections between our detached and derivative reasons for action, see T. M. Scanlon, *What We Owe to Each Other* (Cambridge, MA: The Belknap Press of Harvard University Press, 1998), pp. 218–23.

38 Dworkin, *Life's Dominion*, op. cit., p. 154ff.

39 Ibid., p. 154. Note that one powerful argument Dworkin presents against the right of a majority to forbid abortion is that consistency requires that a majority should also be permitted to require

abortion, which would be intolerable. However, for many antiabortionists, as for Dworkin, the issue of whether abortion should be legal or not is choice-insensitive, in the sense that it does not turn on the shape and distribution of people's preferences. The consistency argument does not work against those who see the issue in choice-insensitive terms. See Dworkin, *Sovereign Virtue*, op. cit., pp. 204–9 for the distinction between choice-sensitive and choice-insensitive issues.

40   Ibid., pp. 48–59.

Part II

Justice Applied

7

Dworkin on Freedom and Culture

Will Kymlicka

Throughout his writings, Ronald Dworkin has argued that individuals must be free to decide for themselves how to lead their lives (within the boundaries of justice). This commitment to freedom of choice plays a central role in Dworkin's defense of liberal political institutions, particularly the protection of civil and political liberties.

This commitment has come under attack from communitarians in two ways: some communitarians criticize liberals for overstating the value of freedom of choice; others accept the importance of freedom of choice, but criticize liberals for neglecting the social preconditions that make it possible.

Dworkin has attempted to answer both of these objections. In this chapter, I want to consider his response to the second objection. In various places Dworkin has spelled out the kind of social and cultural environment that enables individual choice. In particular, he has made some interesting suggestions about the way that choice is dependent on "cultural structures," and hence about the need for a liberal state to protect such structures.

I want to examine this idea of cultural structures more closely – how we identify such structures, how individual choice is connected to them, what measures are needed to protect them, and, more generally, what status they should have within liberal theory. I will argue that Dworkin's idea of cultural structures is legitimate and important, but that it has implications for liberal theory and practice that Dworkin has not addressed, and that raise serious challenges to liberal constitutionalism as traditionally conceived.

I Freedom of Choice and Rational Revisability

Why should we value individual choice? Some liberals seem to think that the value of choice is so obvious that it needs no defense. What could respecting people mean other than respecting their status as rational agents capable of choice? But this is too quick. We know that some people will not deal well with the decisions life requires. They will make mistakes about their lives, choosing to do trivial, degrading, even harmful things. Allowing such people freedom of choice seems an act not of respect, but of indifference, abandoning them to a predictably unhappy fate. Why shouldn't we intervene and prevent people from making such mistakes?

Since the argument for paternalistic intervention depends on the assumption that people can make mistakes about the value of their activities, one option is to deny that people can be mistaken in this way. This is the subjectivist response: judgments of value are not right or wrong, but are simply expressions of our arbitrary preferences, incapable of rational justification or criticism.

Since no way of life is better than any other, there is no basis for state intervention in individuals' choices.

This is not Dworkin's argument in defense of personal liberty. Indeed, his argument is really the opposite. According to Dworkin, we need freedom of choice precisely because we can be wrong, and liberty can help us get it right. He develops an intriguing and sophisticated defense of liberty, based on a "rational revisability" model of choice.

According to Dworkin, we want to have a good life, to have those things that a good life contains. But leading a good life is different from leading the life we *currently believe* to be good – that is, we may be mistaken about the worth or value of what we are currently doing.[1] We may come to see that we've been wasting our lives, pursuing trivial goals that we had mistakenly considered of great importance. Since we can be wrong in this way, and since no one wants to lead a life based on false beliefs about its worth, it is of fundamental importance that we be able to rationally assess our conceptions of the good in the light of new information or experiences, and to revise them if they are not worthy of our continued allegiance.[2] Allen Buchanan calls this the "rational revisability" model of individual choice.[3]

In his earlier work, Rawls also endorsed this model. He says that members of a liberal society have the capacity "to form, to revise, and rationally to pursue" a conception of the good. It is important to note that Rawls explicitly mentions the capacity to *revise* one's conception of the good, alongside the capacity to pursue one's *existing* conception. Indeed, he suggests that the latter "is in essential respects subordinate" to the former. Exercising our capacity to form and revise a conception of the good is a "highest-order interest," in the sense of being "supremely regulative and effective." People's interest in advancing their existing conception of the good, on the other hand, is simply a "higher-order interest." While it is of course important to be able to pursue one's existing conception of the good, the capacity to evaluate and revise that conception is needed to ensure that it is worthy of one's continued allegiance.[4]

Hence people have a highest-order interest in standing back from their current ends, and assessing their worthiness:

> As free persons, citizens recognize one another as having the moral power to have a conception of the good. This means that they do not view themselves as inevitably tied to the pursuit of the particular conception of the good and its final ends which they espouse at any given time. Instead, as citizens, they are regarded as, in general, capable of revising and changing this conception on reasonable and rational grounds. Thus it is held to be permissible for citizens to stand apart from conceptions of the good and to survey and assess their various final ends.[5]

We can "stand apart" from our current ends, and question their value to us. The concern with which we make these judgments, at certain points in our lives, only makes sense on the assumption that we can be mistaken. We do not just make such judgments; we worry, sometimes agonize over them. It is important to us that we do not lead our lives on the basis of false beliefs about the value of our activities. The idea that some things are really worth doing, and others not, goes very deep in our self-understanding. We take seriously the distinction between worthwhile and trivial activities, even if we are not always sure which things are which.[6]

But if we can be mistaken, why shouldn't the government intervene to protect us from making mistakes, and to compel us to lead the truly good life? There are a variety of practical reasons why this may not be a good idea. Governments may not be trustworthy, and some individuals may have idiosyncratic needs that are difficult for even a well-intentioned government to take into account.

But Dworkin has a more general objection to state intervention – namely, that lives do not go better by being led from the outside, in accordance with values the person does not endorse. As he puts it, "no component contributes to the value of a life without endorsement . . . it is implausible to think that someone can lead a better life against the grain of his profound ethical convictions than at peace with them."[7]

Consider someone who wants to lead a homosexual life, but who instead adopts a heterosexual lifestyle from fear of punishment in a society that has criminalized homosexual acts. According to Dworkin, "If he never endorses the life he leads as superior to the life he would otherwise have led, then life has not been improved, even in the critical sense, by paternalistic constraints he hates."[8] Paternalism "is therefore self-defeating."[9] It may succeed in getting people to pursue valuable activities, but it does so under conditions in which the activities cease to have value for the individuals involved.

So we have two preconditions for the fulfillment of our essential interest in leading a good life. The first is that we lead our life from the inside, in accordance with our beliefs about what gives value to life. Individuals must therefore have the resources and liberties needed to lead their lives in accordance with their beliefs about value, without fear of discrimination or punishment. Hence the traditional liberal concern with individual privacy, and opposition to "the enforcement of morals." The second precondition is that we be free to question those beliefs, to examine them in light of whatever information, examples, and arguments our culture can provide. Individuals must therefore have the cultural conditions necessary to acquire an awareness of different views about the good life, and an ability to examine these views intelligently. Hence the equally traditional liberal concern for education and freedom of expression and association. These liberties enable us to judge what is valuable in the only way we can judge such things, by exploring different aspects of our cultural heritage.

It is important to stress that a liberal society is concerned with both of these preconditions, the second as much as the first. It is all too easy to reduce individual liberty to the freedom to pursue one's conception of the good. But in fact much of what is distinctive to a liberal state concerns the forming and revising of people's conceptions of the good, rather than the pursuit of those conceptions once chosen.

Consider the case of religion. A liberal society not only allows individuals the freedom to pursue their existing faith, but it also allows them to seek new adherents for their faith (proselytization is allowed), to question the doctrine or leaders of one's church (heresy is allowed), or to renounce one's faith entirely and convert to another faith or to atheism (apostasy is allowed). It is quite conceivable to have the freedom to pursue one's current faith without having any of these latter freedoms. Indeed, there are many examples of this, particularly within the Islamic world. Islam has a long tradition of tolerating other religions, so that Christians and Jews have been able to worship in peace. But proselytization, heresy, and apostasy are generally strictly prohibited. Indeed, some Islamic states have said the freedom of conscience guaranteed in the Universal Declaration of Human Rights should not include the freedom to change religion. Similarly, the clause in the Egyptian constitution guaranteeing freedom of conscience has been interpreted so as to exclude freedom of apostasy.[10]

A liberal society, by contrast, not only allows people to pursue their current way of life, but also gives them access to information about other ways of life (through freedom of expression, including freedom to proselytize), and indeed requires children to learn about other ways of life (through mandatory education), and makes it possible for people to engage in radical revision of their ends (including apostasy) without legal penalty.

These aspects of a liberal society only make sense on the assumption that revising our ends is possible, and sometimes desirable, because they may not be worthy of our allegiance. For this reason, the "rational revisability" model provides, I believe, the most compelling defense of liberalism.[11]

Of course, this model can be questioned. Many communitarians deny that we can "stand apart" from (some of) our final ends. According to Michael Sandel, some of our final ends are "constitutive" ends, in the sense that they define our sense of personal identity.[12] It makes no sense, on his view, to say that my final ends might not be worthy of my allegiance, for these ends define who I am. Dworkin responds (rightly, I think) that "the phenomenology on which this argument rests seems wrong, or at least overstated." It is true that "no one can put everything about himself in question all at once. But it hardly follows that for each person there is some one connection or association so fundamental that it cannot be detached for inspection while holding others in place."[13]

Even if we accept the rational revisability model, it does not provide a knockdown argument for liberal institutions. Many perfectionists argue that Dworkin has exaggerated the extent to which the endorsement constraint rules out all forms of paternalism. They argue that the endorsement constraint does not preclude noncoercive and educative forms of paternalism (e.g., encouraging people to try better ways of life by providing financial inducements). A perfectionist state that employed these noncoercive means would still firmly protect individual civil and political rights, but it would be more active in promoting ways of life it sees as most worthwhile.

I will not evaluate this objection here, or Dworkin's response to it. The connection between rational revisability, the endorsement constraint, and liberal "neutrality" is in fact quite complicated.[14] My own view is that the rational revisability model supports a neutral state in some circumstances, but it may justify a (limited) perfectionist state in other circumstances.[15] My concern here, however, is with a different issue: assuming that the rational revisability model does defend the value of freedom of choice, we still need a theory of the context of choice.

II Cultural Structures as Context of Choice

Let us accept, for the purposes of argument, that people have an essential interest not only in pursuing their existing conception of the good, but also in being able to stand back and assess its worthiness, and to consider alternative ways of life. What are the social and cultural conditions that enable people to fulfill this interest?

We have already mentioned some of them, such as freedom of speech and association, which are traditionally at the heart of liberal theory. Liberals also note the need for a liberal education that gives people both information about other ways of life and the psychological capacities to evaluate them.[16]

But I want to raise a deeper question – when we make our choices, what are our options, and where do they come from? Critics sometimes say that liberals view options for choice as simply conjured out of thin air. But in fact Dworkin, like Rawls, recognizes that choices do not arise *de novo*. Rather, we examine "definite ideals and forms of life that have been developed and tested by innumerable individuals, sometimes for generations."[17] The decision about how to lead our lives must ultimately be ours alone, but this decision is always a matter of selecting what we believe to be most valuable from the range of options around us, selecting from a context of choice that provides us with different ways of life.

What defines this "context of choice" for any particular individual? What makes a particular option "available" to someone? While Dworkin has not addressed this question in depth, he has made some suggestive remarks about it in his article "Can a Liberal State Support Art?" His remarks are very concise, and he does not present them as constituting a full-blown theory of "the context of choice." In what follows, therefore, I have tried to elaborate on these brief comments, to see where they lead. While the following account is inspired by Dworkin's comments, I don't want to imply that he himself would accept all of it.

In one sense, the range of options available to us depend on the social practices around us. But, according to Dworkin (as I read him), these practices only become matters of value, or choice-worthy objects, because they are part of our *culture*. It is the fact that these practices fit into what Dworkin calls our "cultural structure" that enables us to see them as having worthwhile objectives and standards of excellence.

According to Dworkin, our cultural structure "provides the spectacles through which we identify experiences as valuable."[18] In the case of art, for example, culture "provides for us the particular paintings, performances, and novels, designs, sports, and thrillers that we value and take delight in; but it also provides the structural frame that makes aesthetic values of that sort possible, that makes them valuable for us."[19] And a "rich cultural structure" is one "that multiplies distinct possibilities or opportunities of value."[20]

Let me try to develop this suggestive comment about the connection between valuable options and the cultural structure. There are a number of steps that need to be filled in here, connecting social practices to beliefs about value to cultural meanings and language.

People make choices about the social practices around them. But if we want to understand the nature of this choice, we can't understand social practices behavioralistically, simply as patterns of physical movement. Rather, they are purposive, value-laden activities, with built-in standards of potential excellence. This is what makes them potentially worthy objects for individual choice. To have a conception of the good is not to have an instinctive reflex to do some action, but a belief about its value (a belief which, we've seen, may be wrong).

But to have a belief about the value of a practice is, in the first instance, a matter of understanding the meanings attached to it by our culture. The physical movements only have meaning to us because they are identified as having significance by our culture, because they fit into some pattern of activities that is culturally recognized as a way of leading one's life. We learn about these patterns of activity through their presence in narratives that we've heard about the lives, real or imaginary, of others. They become potential models, and define potential roles, that we can adopt as our own. We decide how to lead our lives by situating ourselves in these cultural narratives, by adopting roles that have struck us as worthwhile ones, as ones worth living. We can and should critically reflect on these cultural meanings, but they form the unavoidable starting point for our deliberations about the good life.[21]

How does a culture attach meanings to practices? According to Dworkin, it is through "a shared vocabulary of tradition and convention."[22] Language, then, is central to this picture of the cultural structure:

> Now let me concentrate on the structure of culture, the possibilities it allows . . . The center of a community's cultural structure is its shared language. A language is neither a private nor a public good as these are technically defined; it is inherently social, as these are not, and as a whole it generates our ways of valuing.[23]

Again, let me expand on Dworkin's comment. The processes by which options and choices become culturally significant to us are linguistic and historical processes. Whether or not a course of action has any cultural significance for us depends on whether, and how, our language renders vivid to us the point of that activity. And the way in which language renders vivid these activities is a matter of our cultural heritage, our "traditions and conventions." Our language is the medium through which we come to an awareness of the options available to us, and their significance; and this is a precondition of making intelligent judgments about how to lead our lives. In order to make such judgments, we do not explore a number of different patterns of physical movement, which might in principle be judged in abstraction from any language or cultural structure. Rather, we make these judgments precisely by examining the cultural structure, by coming to an awareness of its possibilities, of the different activities it identifies as significant.

What follows from this? According to Dworkin, we must protect our cultural structure from "structural debasement or decay."[24] The survival of a rich cultural structure is not guaranteed: "We are all beneficiaries or victims of what is done to the language we share. A language can diminish; some are richer and better than others."[25] Where the cultural structure is threatened with debasement or decay, we must act to protect it:

> We should identify the structural aspects of our general culture as themselves worthy of attention. We should try to define a rich cultural structure, one that multiplies distinct possibilities or opportunities of value, and count ourselves trustees for protecting the richness of our culture for those who will live their lives in it after us . . . the postulate and the program I have described [is] that people are better off when the opportunities their culture provides are more complex and diverse, and that we should act as trustees for the future of the complexity of our own culture.[26]

In short, cultural structures are valuable, not in and of themselves, but because it is only through having a rich cultural structure that people can become aware, in a vivid way, of the options available to them. Dworkin concludes his discussion by saying "We inherited a cultural structure, and we have some duty, out of simple justice, to leave that structure at least as rich as we found it."[27]

I will argue in the next section that this argument, while attractive, has consequences for liberalism that Dworkin has not noted. I should emphasize again that I am reading quite a bit into a few passages of a single article by Dworkin. He might well not agree with the interpretation I have placed on his comments. But similar claims appear elsewhere in Dworkin's corpus. For example, in "Liberal Community," when discussing the ways in which people are dependent on community, Dworkin says:

> They need a common culture and particularly a common language even to have personalities, and culture and language are social phenomena. We can only have the thoughts, and ambitions, and convictions that are possible within the vocabulary that language and culture provide, so we are all, in a patent and deep way, the creatures of the community as a whole.[28]

Similarly, in "Three Concepts of Liberalism," he says that the most urgent task facing liberal theorists is to develop a "theory of education and a theory of culture-support" to explain how a liberal society ensures that adequate options are available to people to choose from.[29]

It seems clear that Dworkin is committed to providing some theory of "cultural structures," and that this must be added to the list of the preconditions of meaningful individual choice. For such choice to be possible, individuals need not only access to information, the capacity to reflectively evaluate it, and freedom of expression and association. They also need a rich cultural structure. In Rawlsian language, we can say that access to such a cultural structure is a "primary good."

III   The Status of Cultural Membership in Liberal Theory

I think there is something true and important in Dworkin's claim about the relationship between individual choice and cultural structures. But it immediately raises three obvious questions: (1) how do we individuate cultural structures; (2) is individual choice tied to membership in one's *own* culture, or is it sufficient for people to have access to some or other culture; and (3) what if a culture is structured so as to preclude individual choice, for example, if it assigns people a specific role or way of life, and prohibits any questioning or revising of that role? I will look at these questions in turn.

First, how do we individuate cultural structures? How do we know whether there is one such structure within each country, or two, or ten? Dworkin himself invariably talks as if there is only one cultural structure in the United States. This is evident in his claim that "we inherited a cultural structure," based on a "shared language," since the "we" in this sentence is the American political community.[30]

But many countries, including the United States, contain linguistic minorities. Indeed in countries with high immigration rates, like Australia, Canada, and the United States, there are hundreds of languages spoken. If the center of a cultural structure is a shared language, do each of these linguistic minorities have their own cultural structure? And if so, does a liberal state have a duty of justice to ensure that they are all protected from "structural debasement or decay"?

The idea that a liberal state should sustain hundreds of cultural structures sounds like a recipe for chaos. Given this, we might be tempted to abandon the connection between a cultural structure and a particular language. But I think we should retain that claim, in a modified form. I believe that cultural structures are based on a common language, but that not every language spoken in a country grounds a cultural structure, in Dworkin's sense of that term.[31]

In particular, we need to distinguish two kinds of groups in the United States whose mother tongue is not English: immigrant groups and national minorities. We will first discuss the case of immigrants. When immigrants come to the United States, they bring their language with them. But they do not bring the cultural structure that their mother tongue originally supported, that is, the set of cultural practices from which they are now uprooted. They might hope to recreate that structure in their new country. But that is effectively impossible without significant government support, which is rarely if ever provided.

On the contrary, immigration policy in the United States is clearly intended to integrate immigrants within the larger cultural structure. Immigrants come as individuals or families, rather than entire communities, and settle in a dispersed way throughout the country, rather than forming "homelands." They are expected to integrate into the public institutions of the Anglophone culture. Indeed, learning English is required for citizenship in the United States (just as learning the dominant language is a requirement for naturalization in most Western democracies).[32]

Of course, immigrants are no longer expected to assimilate entirely to the dominant culture (as was the norm under the "Anglo-conformity" model, which was widely accepted before the 1960s). They are expected and enabled to maintain some aspects of their ethnic particularity. But this is primarily a private matter – at home, and in voluntary associations. Immigrants are expected to speak English in public life – for example, at school, work, and when interacting with governments and other public agencies.

Under these conditions, the immigrants' mother tongue may be spoken at home, and passed on to the children, but by the third generation, English has become the mother tongue, and there is "an almost complete breakdown in the transmission of non-English languages" to the third generation.[33] This process is sped up, of course, by the fact that public schooling is only provided in English. In fact, it is very difficult for languages to survive in modern industrialized societies unless they are used in public life. Given the spread of standardized education, the high demands for literacy in work, and widespread interaction with government agencies, any language that is not a public language becomes so marginalized that it is likely to survive only among a small elite, or in a ritualized form, not as a living and developing language underlying a flourishing cultural structure. Countries with large-scale immigration of this sort will have many ethnic groups as loosely aggregated subcultures within the dominant cultural structure, and so can be considered "polyethnic."

Some people view this refusal to support immigrants to recreate their own societal cultures as a form of prejudice or oppression. There is no doubt that feelings of prejudice and ethnocentrism have affected the treatment of immigrants. However, expectations that immigrants will integrate into the preexisting cultural structure can also be seen as a legitimate response to the distinctive features of immigration. For one thing, immigrants often lack the numbers or territorial concentration needed to recreate a viable cultural structure in their new country. Also, most immigrants chose to leave their own culture. They have uprooted themselves from their cultural structure. They know when they come that their success, and that of their children, depends on integrating into the institutions of English-speaking society. And while there are many aspects of their culture they will maintain, this will not take the form of recreating a separate cultural structure based on their mother tongue, but rather contributing new options and perspectives to the larger Anglophone culture, making it richer and more diverse. For the third generation, if not sooner, learning the original mother tongue is not unlike learning a foreign language in one's spare time – however rewarding it may be as a hobby or business skill, learning the old language is not "the spectacles through which we identify experiences as valuable," not "the structural frame" that makes different ways of life possible objects of choice.[34] For the children of immigrants, it is the Anglophone culture that defines their options.[35]

Not all of the linguistic diversity in the United States comes from immigrant groups. There are also national minorities, that is, communities whose homeland has been incorporated into the larger state, through conquest, colonization, or federation. I call these groups "national" minorities because they typically see themselves as "nations" in the sociological sense of being historical communities, previously self-governing and more or less institutionally complete, occupying a given territory or homeland, and sharing a distinct language and history. A "nation" in this sense is closely related to the idea of a "people" or a "culture"; indeed, these terms are often defined in terms of each other.

In North America, the indigenous peoples (Indians, Inuit, and native Hawaiians), Puerto Ricans, and the Québécois form national minorities.[36] Since both the United States and Canada contain more than one nation, they are not nation-states but "multination" states.[37]

The original incorporation of these national minorities was largely involuntary. In Canada, for example, Indian homelands were overrun by French settlers, who were then conquered by the English. If a different balance of power had existed, it is possible that aboriginals and French

Canadians would have retained their earlier self-government, rather than being incorporated into the larger Canadian federation.

Similarly in the United States, the original incorporation of national minorities was largely involuntary. As Stephen Thernstrom puts it, "there are sizeable numbers of people whose ancestors did not come to the United States either voluntarily or involuntarily. Instead, the United States came to them in the course of its relentless expansion across the continent and into the Caribbean and Pacific."[38] This includes the American Indians, Hispanics in the Southwest who were annexed when the United States stripped Mexico of its northern provinces from Texas to California after the Mexican War of 1846–8, Puerto Ricans, Hawaiians, and various other Pacific islanders. Few of these peoples had any choice about becoming Americans.

The situation of national minorities is clearly different from that of immigrant groups. There can be no question that these national minorities had, at the time of their incorporation into the larger state, their own cultural structures based on their distinct languages. And most have retained their distinct cultures, although this has often been in the face of enormous pressures to assimilate. In the case of many indigenous peoples, for example, there have been prohibitions on the use of their mother tongue, and attempts to break open their lands for settlement so that they have become minorities in their historical homelands.[39] The determination they have shown in maintaining their existence as distinct communities, despite these enormous economic and political pressures, shows the value they attach to retaining their cultural membership.

So the situation of immigrant groups and national minorities is different, factually and normatively, with respect to the relationship between language and cultural structure. Immigrants have a distinct mother tongue, but they do not have a cultural structure in their new country. Moreover, insofar as they voluntarily left their original culture, they can be seen as having consented to integration. National minorities, by contrast, clearly do have a distinct cultural structure. And far from having voluntarily left their culture, they have fought tenaciously against the pressures for integration that resulted from their involuntary incorporation into the larger polity.

Obviously this is an oversimplified contrast between immigrants and national minorities.[40] The extent to which immigrants chose to come, and the extent to which they have been allowed or encouraged to integrate, varies considerably, as does the extent to which national minorities have been able to maintain a distinct cultural structure.[41]

However, this is the beginning of an answer as to how to individuate cultural structures. Cultural structures are typically distinguished on the basis of language, but the language must be societal, not merely private or familial.[42] To ground a cultural structure, the language must be tied to the existence of a viable society of the sort characteristic of "nations" or "peoples" (i.e., a culturally distinct, geographically concentrated, and institutionally complete society). By this criterion, national minorities typically have their own cultural structures, immigrants typically do not.

This distinction between immigrants and national minorities is just the first step towards answering the individuation question. It raises as many questions as it answers, and it would take another paper to consider the many complexities and gray areas.[43] However, it is worth considering one important objection to the whole idea of individuating cultural structures.

According to Jeremy Waldron, the project of individuating cultural structures presupposes that cultures are somehow isolated and impervious to external influences. But in reality, he notes, there is an enormous amount of interchange between cultures. Cultures have influenced each other so much, he says, that there is no meaningful way to say where one culture ends and another begins. Indeed, there are no such things as cultures, just innumerable cultural fragments from innumerable cultural sources, without any "structure" connecting them or underlying them.

Waldron accepts that the meaningfulness of options depends on the fact that they have cultural meanings. But he rejects the assumption that the options available to a particular individual must come from a *particular* cultural structure. This assumption, he says,

> is guilty of something like the fallacy of composition. From the fact that each option must have a cultural meaning, it does not follow that there must be one cultural framework in which each available option is assigned a meaning. Meaningful options may come to us as items or fragments from a variety of cultural sources. Kymlicka is moving too quickly when he says that each item is given its significance by some entity called "our culture," and he is not entitled to infer from that there are things called "cultural structures" whose integrity must be guaranteed in order for people to have meaningful choice. His argument shows that people need cultural materials; it does not show that what people need is "a rich and secure cultural structure." It shows the importance of access to a variety of stories and roles; but it does not, as he claims, show the importance of something called *membership* in a culture.[44]

For example, Waldron notes the influence of the Bible, Roman mythology, and *Grimm's Fairy Tales* on our culture, and says that these cannot plausibly be seen as part of a single "cultural structure":

> it is important to see that these are heterogeneous characters drawn from a variety of disparate cultural sources: from first-century Palestine, from the heritage of Germanic folklore, and from the mythology of the Roman Republic. They do not come from some *thing* called "the structure of our culture." They are familiar to us because of the immense variety of cultural materials, various in their provenance as well as their character, that are in fact available to us. But neither their familiarity nor their availability constitute them as part of a single cultural matrix. Indeed, if we were to insist that they are all part of the same matrix because they are all available to us, we would trivialize the individuation of cultures beyond any sociological interest.[45]

Waldron raises an interesting point. On any liberal view, it is a good thing that cultures learn from each other. Liberals cannot endorse a notion of culture that sees the process of interacting with and learning from other cultures as a threat to "purity" or "integrity," rather than as an opportunity for enrichment. As Dworkin says, liberals want a cultural structure that is as rich and diverse as possible, and much of the richness of a culture comes from the way it has appropriated the fruits of other cultures.[46]

According to Waldron, however, it is self-defeating to tie the promotion of cultural diversity to a theory of "cultural structures." This emphasis on cultural structures thwarts the process of diversification, Waldron claims, since the only nontrivial way of individuating such cultures is to define them in terms of a common ethnic source that precludes learning from other cultures. So if we want to increase the range of valuable options available to people, we would be better off abandoning the idea of cultural structures, and instead promoting a mélange of cultural meanings from different sources.

However, Waldron's conclusion is faulty, because he ignores the most plausible basis of cultural structures – namely, a common language (used within common institutions).[47] It is clearly right that the options available to the members of any modern society come from a variety of ethnic and historical sources. But the question is, what makes these options *available* to us? This is the question Dworkin's account of "cultural structures" is trying to answer, and he suggests that options are available to us if they are part of our common language. Waldron may disagree with this, but he offers no argument against it. Indeed, I think Waldron's examples actually support Dworkin's account. For surely one of the reasons why *Grimm's Fairy Tales* are so much a part of our culture is precisely that they have been translated and widely distributed in English. Were *Grimm's Fairy Tales* only available in the original language, as is the case with the folklore of many other world cultures, they would not be available to us.

So the unavoidable, and desirable, fact of cultural interchange does not necessarily undermine the claim that there are distinct cultural structures, once we recognize that they are based on a common language. But if cultural structures are based on language, then we must also recognize that in multination countries, there will be more than one cultural structure. It seems to follow that a liberal state has an obligation to sustain the cultural structures of national minorities as well as the majority culture.

In fact, many liberal democracies already accept such an obligation, and provide public schooling and government services in the language of national minorities. Many have also adopted some form of federalism, so that national minorities will form a majority in one of the federal units (states, provinces, or cantons). These measures help ensure that minority languages survive as societal languages (not just in private or familial contexts) capable of supporting a living and developing cultural structure. Countries that follow this model include Spain (re the Basque and Catalan minorities), Switzerland (re the French and Italian-speaking minorities), Finland (re the Swedish minority), Belgium (re the Flemish and Walloons), Canada (re the Québécois); Italy (re the German-speaking minority in South Tyrol), and indeed the United States (re Puerto Rico).[48] As Jay Sigler puts it, providing a liberal defense of minority rights "does not create a mandate for vast change. It merely ratifies and explains changes that have taken place in the absence of theory."[49]

Many liberals in multination states will welcome this argument for the consistency of liberalism and special rights for national minority cultures, since they have not wanted to choose between their liberal principles and deeply rooted components of their constitutional arrangements. Other liberals, however, will view such "group rights" with suspicion. Indeed, most postwar liberals, particularly in America,[50] have opposed the idea of giving official recognition to national minorities, or to distributing government services (such as schooling) on the basis of group membership.[51]

I do not know whether Dworkin himself would welcome the implications I have drawn from his theory of cultural structures. If not, I can see two possible ways he could try to avoid them. One response would be to say that cultures don't need state assistance to survive. If the cultural structure is worth saving, one could argue, the members of the culture will sustain it through their own choices. If the culture is decaying, if a language is dying out, it must be because some people no longer find it worthy of their allegiance. The state, on this view, should not interfere with the "cultural marketplace" – it should neither promote nor inhibit the maintenance of any particular cultural structure.[52]

This response is not available to Dworkin, since the whole point of his original article was precisely to say that the "cultural marketplace" cannot be relied on to protect cultural structures even in the case of the majority culture.[53] The market failures he identifies are even greater for minority cultures.

In any event, the idea that the government could be neutral with respect to the cultural marketplace is patently false. As I noted earlier, one of the most important determinants of whether a culture survives is whether its language is the language of government, that is, the language of public schooling, courts, welfare agencies, health services, and so forth. When the government decides the language of public schooling, it is providing what is probably the most important form of support needed by cultural structures, since it guarantees the passing on of the language and its associated traditions and conventions to the next generation. Refusing to provide public schooling in a minority language, by contrast, almost inevitably condemns that language to "structural debasement and decay." Since the government provides public schooling and services in the majority language, it seems that fairness requires it do the same for minority languages.

My argument started from the premise that people's meaningful choices depend on access to a cultural structure. But do people need access to their *own* culture? Why not let minority cultures disintegrate, so long we ensure its members have access to the majority culture (e.g., by teaching them the majority language)?

Again, this second response may not be open to Dworkin, since he insists that we have a duty to protect the richness of "our own cultural structure," not just to ensure that there is some or other cultural structure that is sufficiently rich.[54]

But do people need access to their own societal culture? It would be implausible to say that people are never able to switch cultures. After all, many immigrants function well in their new country (although others flounder, and eventually return home). Waldron thinks that these examples of successful "cosmopolitan" people who move between cultures disprove the claim that people are connected to own culture in any deep way. Suppose, he says, that

> a freewheeling cosmopolitan life, lived in a kaleidoscope of cultures, is both possible and fulfilling. . . . Immediately, one argument for the protection of minority cultures is undercut. It can no longer be said that all people need their rootedness in the particular culture in which they and their ancestors were reared in the way that they need food, clothing, and shelter. . . . Such immersion may be something that particular people like and enjoy. But they no longer can claim that it is something that they need. . . . The collapse of the Herderian argument based on distinctively human *need* seriously undercuts any claim that minority cultures might have to special support or assistance or to extraordinary provision or forbearance. At best, it leaves the right to culture roughly on the same footing as the right to religious freedom.[55]

Because people do not need their own culture, national minorities can ("at best") claim the same negative rights as religious groups, that is, the right to noninterference, but not to state support.

I think Waldron is seriously overstating the case here. For one thing, he vastly overestimates the extent to which people do in fact move between cultures, because (as we've seen) he assumes that cultural structures are based on ethnic descent, not language. On his view, WASP Americans who eat Chinese food and read their children *Grimm's Fairy Tales* are thereby "living in a kaleidoscope of cultures."[56] But this is not moving between cultural structures as Dworkin uses that term. Rather it is enjoying the opportunities provided by the diverse cultural structure that characterizes English-speaking America.

Of course, people do genuinely move between cultures. But this is both rarer, and more difficult. In some cases, where the differences in social organization and technological development are vast, successful integration may be almost impossible for some members of a minority community. (This seems to have been true of the initial period of contact between European settlers and indigenous peoples in some parts of the world.)

But even where integration is possible, it is rarely easy. It is a costly process, and there is a legitimate question whether people should be required to pay those costs unless they voluntarily choose to do so. In this sense, the choice to leave one's culture is, in some ways, like the choice to take a vow of perpetual poverty and enter a religious order. It is not impossible to live in poverty.

But it doesn't follow that a liberal theory of justice should therefore view the desire for a level of material resources above bare subsistence simply as "something that particular people like and enjoy" but which "they no longer can claim is something that they need."[57] Liberals rightly assume that the desire for nonsubsistence resources is so normal – and the costs of forgoing them so high for most people's way of life – that people cannot reasonably be *expected* to go without such resources, even if a few people voluntarily choose to do so. If not a "need" in the narrowest sense of that term, nonsubsistence resources are nonetheless a "primary good" in Rawls's sense. For the purposes of determining people's claims of justice and entitlement, material resources are something that people can be assumed to want, whatever their particular conception of the good. Although a small number of people may choose to forego nonsubsistence resources, this is seen as forgoing something to which they are entitled.

Similarly, I believe that we should, in developing a theory of justice, treat access to one's cultural structure as something that people can be expected to want, whatever their more particular conception of the good. If so, then leaving one's culture (e.g., through emigration), while possible, is best seen as renouncing something to which they are reasonably entitled. This is a claim, not about the limits of human possibility, but about reasonable expectations.

I think most liberals have implicitly accepted this claim about people's legitimate expectation to remain in their culture. Consider Rawls's argument about why the right to emigrate does not make political authority voluntary:

> [N]ormally leaving one's country is a grave step: it involves leaving the society and culture in which we have been raised, the society and culture whose language we use in speech and thought to express and understand ourselves, our aims, goals, and values; the society and culture whose history, customs, and conventions we depend on to find our place in the social world. In large part, we affirm our society and culture, and have an intimate and inexpressible knowledge of it, even though much of it we may question, if not reject. The government's authority cannot, then, be freely accepted in the sense that the bonds of society and culture, of history and social place of origin, begin so early to shape our life and are normally so strong that the right of emigration (suitably qualified) does not suffice to make accepting its authority free, politically speaking, in the way that liberty of conscience suffices to make accepting ecclesiastical authority free, politically speaking.[58]

Because of these bonds to the "language we use in speech and thought to express and understand ourselves," cultural ties "are normally too strong to be given up, and this fact is not to be deplored." Hence for the purposes of developing a theory of justice, we should assume that "people are born and are expected to lead a complete life" within the same "society and culture."[59]

I think Rawls is right here. But his argument has implications beyond those that he himself draws. Rawls presents this as an argument about the difficulty of leaving one's political community. But his argument does not rest on the value of specifically political ties (e.g., the bonds to one's government and fellow citizens). Rather it rests on the value of cultural ties (e.g., bonds to one's language and culture). And of course cultural boundaries may not coincide with political boundaries. For example, people leaving East Germany for West Germany in 1950 would not be breaking the ties of language and culture that Rawls emphasizes, even though they would be crossing state borders. But a francophone leaving Montréal for Toronto would be breaking those ties, despite remaining within the same Canadian state.

According to Rawls, the ties to one's language are normally too strong to give up, and this is not to be regretted. We can't be expected or required to make such a sacrifice, even if some people voluntarily do so. But without certain rights, such as language rights and various forms of land claims and territorial autonomy, this sacrifice will be required of many minority cultures.[60]

Rawls's claim that the bonds to one's culture are "normally too strong to be given up" may seem paradoxical to some readers. What has happened to the much-vaunted liberal freedom of choice? But Rawls's view is in fact quite common within the liberal tradition. The freedom that liberals demand for individuals is not primarily the freedom to go beyond one's language and culture, but rather the freedom to move around within one's culture, to distance oneself from particular cultural roles, to autonomously choose which features of the cultural structure are most worth developing, and which are without value.[61] This view of the way we are both dependent on, and independent of, cultural practices is, I think, quite attractive.

It is an interesting question why the bonds of language and culture are so strong for most people. I suspect the answer would involve aspects of psychology, sociology, and the philosophy of mind.[62] But it does seem to be a fact, and, like Rawls, I see no reason why this fact is to be regretted.

But what about those cultures or nations that are not liberalized? Some cultures, far from enabling autonomy, simply assign particular roles and duties to people, and prevent people from questioning or revising them. Other cultures allow this autonomy to some, while denying it to others, such as women, lower castes, or visible minorities. Clearly, these sorts of cultural structures do not promote liberal values.

If the liberal commitment to protecting societal cultures flows from their role in enabling autonomy, should we not at least encourage or compel the members of illiberal cultures to assimilate to more liberal cultures?[63] But again this ignores the way people are bound to their own cultures. The aim of liberals should not be to dissolve nonliberal nations, but rather to seek to liberalize them. Of course, this may not always be possible. But it is worth remembering that all existing liberal nations had illiberal pasts, and their liberalization required a prolonged process of institutional reform. To assume that any culture is inherently illiberal, and incapable of reform, is ethnocentric and ahistorical. Moreover, the liberality of a culture is a matter of degree. All cultures have illiberal strands, just as few cultures are entirely repressive of individual liberty. Indeed, it is quite misleading to talk of "liberal" and "illiberal" cultures, as if the world was divided into completely liberal societies on the one hand, and completely illiberal ones on the other. The task of liberal reform remains incomplete in every society, and it would be absurd to say that only purely liberal nations should be respected, while others should be assimilated.[64]

IV   Conclusion

Liberals are often accused of emphasizing the value of freedom of choice, but of neglecting the social conditions of freedom.[65] This criticism cannot be made of Dworkin. He has made a number of intriguing suggestions about the way choice is dependent on social practices, cultural meanings, and a shared language.

I have tried to show that Dworkin's suggestions are attractive, and worth developing, though by no means uncontroversial. For example, one could deny his claim that cultural meanings are dependent on a cultural structure; or the claim that a cultural structure is based on a common language; or the claim that individuals are closely tied to their own particular cultural structure. Yet I think these claims are plausible. Anyone who disputes them would be required to provide some alternative account of the context of choice, of what makes meaningful choices available to people.

I have also tried to show that Dworkin's account leads naturally towards a liberal justification for the rights of minority cultures.[66] Why has Dworkin missed this implication of his theory? After all, if choice requires culture, and culture requires language, then developing a just language policy would seem to be one of the very first tasks of any liberal theory. Why then has Dworkin never discussed language rights?

The explanation, I think, is that Dworkin works with a model of the nation-state. He accepts that the state may be culturally diverse. But he assumes that this diversity is the sort that comes from "polyethnicity," that is, ethnic diversity within a single cultural structure based on a shared language.[67] He does not consider the possibility that the political community is multinational, with a diversity of cultural structures.

He is hardly alone in this.[68] Virtually all American political theorists treat the United States as a polyethnic nation-state, rather than a truly multination state.[69] Perhaps this is because national minorities in the United States are relatively small and isolated (e.g., Puerto Ricans, American Indians, native Hawaiians, Alaskan Eskimos). These groups are virtually invisible in American political theory. If they are mentioned at all, it is usually as an afterthought.[70]

But in many countries of the world – including the emerging democracies in Eastern Europe, Africa, and Asia – the status of national minorities is one of the most pressing issues. People in these countries often look to the works of Rawls and Dworkin for lessons regarding the principles of liberal constitutionalism. But if liberalism is to take hold in these countries, liberal theorists will have to address the role of cultural structures, and hence the political status of national minorities, more explicitly.

Acknowledgement

For helpful comments on earlier drafts, I would like to thank Sue Donaldson, Colin Macleod, Wayne Norman, Maurice Rickard, and the members of the legal theory workshops at Columbia University and University of California, Berkeley.

Notes

1   Ronald Dworkin, "In Defense of Equality," *Social Philosophy and Policy*, vol. 1, 1983, p. 26.
2   I won't discuss the way Dworkin has further elaborated this view in "Foundations of Liberal Equality" in Grethe Peterson (ed.), *The Tanner Lectures on Human Values*, vol. XI (Salt Lake City: University of Utah Press, 1990). In those lectures, he suggests that when forming and revising our conceptions of the good, we can employ either a "challenge" or "performance" model to measure the worth of various activities. He further argues that liberalism depends on adopting the challenge model. I do not believe that the rational revisability view presupposes either the challenge or performance model, and indeed I think that both are implausible, for reasons discussed in Arneson's chapter in this volume. Hence I will focus on the more general principle of rational revisability, which I think is consistent with many different views about how more exactly to conceive the value of different ways of life.
3   Allen Buchanan, "Revisability and Rational Choice," *Canadian Journal of Philosophy*, vol. 5, 1975, pp. 395–408.

4   John Rawls, "Kantian Constructivism in Moral Theory," *Journal of Philosophy*, vol. 77, 1980, pp. 525–8.

5   Ibid., p. 544.

6   Not all of our aims are fallible in this way. Dworkin distinguishes "volitional" interests, which are good just because we want them, and "critical" interests, which rest on fallible beliefs about what is truly good. (See his "Liberal Community," *California Law Review*, vol. 77, 1989, pp. 484–5; "Foundations of Liberal Equality," op. cit.) Many of our most important projects will be the latter.

7   Dworkin, "Liberal Community," op. cit., p. 486.

8   Ibid.

9   Ibid., p. 487. This has come to be called the "endorsement constraint." According to Dworkin, we should also be able to endorse the social conditions under which our endorsement of particular ways of life takes place, and that this will rule out even indirect forms of perfectionism. See note 14 below.

10 R. Peters and G. de Vries, "Apostasy in Islam," *Die Welt des Islams*, vol. 17, 1976, p. 23.

11 In particular, it is more plausible than the "overlapping consensus" model developed by Rawls since 1980. In his recent work, Rawls argues that some people do not see their ends as potentially revisable, and that to defend liberal institutions on this basis is therefore "sectarian" ("The Idea of Overlapping Consensus," *Oxford Journal of Legal Studies*, vol. 7, 1987, p. 24). This objection is echoed by other "political liberals" (e.g., Charles Larmore, *Patterns of Moral Complexity* (Cambridge, UK: Cambridge University Press, 1987); William Galston, *Liberal Purposes: Goods, Virtues, and Duties in the Liberal State* (Cambridge, UK: Cambridge University Press, 1991)). They want to defend liberal institutions in a way that will appeal even to those who reject the idea that people can stand back and assess their ends. Rawls's alternative is to defend individual liberty, not on grounds of individual revisability, but of social plu-ralism. That is, even if we take people's ends as fixed and beyond revision – as some communitarians have proposed – the fact that citizens in a modern democracy do not all share the same religion or con-ceptions of the good generally means that it would be wrong for the state to impose one way of life on everyone. That is true, but it doesn't explain the second half of liberalism – that is, the freedom, not only to pursue one's existing conception of the good, but also to question and revise one's way of life. Rawls's new theory provides no grounds for objecting to the sort of arrangement found in many Islamic states that tolerate diverse religions but prohibit proselytization and apostasy. I discuss this in my *Multicultural Citizenship: A Liberal Theory of Minority Rights* (Oxford: Oxford University Press, 1995), ch. 8.

12 Michael Sandel, *Liberalism and the Limits of Justice* (Cambridge, UK: Cambridge University Press, 1982), pp. 150–65; cf. Alistair MacIntyre, *After Virtue: A Study in Moral Theory* (London: Duckworth, 1981), ch. 15; Daniel Bell, *Communitarianism and its Critics* (Oxford: Oxford University Press, 1993), pp. 24–54.

13 Dworkin, "Liberal Community," op. cit., p. 489.

14 For Dworkin's account of the relationship between rational revisability, the endorsement constraint, and liberal "neutrality," see his "Liberalism," in Stuart Hampshire (ed.), *Public and Private Morality* (Cambridge, UK: Cambridge University Press, 1978), p. 27; "Can a Liberal State Support Art?" in *A Matter of Principle* (London: Harvard University Press, 1985), p. 222; "Liberal Community," op. cit., pp. 486–7; "Foundations of Liberal Equality," op. cit. See also my "Liberal Individualism and Liberal Neutrality," *Ethics*, vol. 99, 1989, pp. 883–6. For critical discussions, see Simon Caney, "Consequentialist Defenses of Neutrality," *Philosophical Quarterly*, vol. 41, 1991, pp. 457–75; Andrew Mason, "Autonomy, Liberalism and State Neutrality," *Philosophical Quarterly*, vol. 40, 1990, pp. 433–52; Thomas Hurka, "Indirect Perfectionism: Kymlicka on Liberal Neutrality," *Journal of Political Philosophy*, vol. 3, 1994, pp. 36–57; Daniel Weinstock, "Neutralizing Perfection: Hurka on Liberal Neutrality," *Dialogue*, vol. 38, 1998, pp. 45–62; Colin Macleod, *Liberalism, Justice and Markets: A Critique of Liberal Equality* (Oxford: Oxford University Press, 1998), ch. 7. This issue also arises for Joseph Raz's defense of liberalism, which relies on the endorsement constraint (see his *The Morality of Freedom* (Oxford: Oxford University Press, 1986)); and the critiques in Jeremy Waldron's "Autonomy, and Perfectionism in Raz's *Morality of Freedom*," *Southern California Law Review*, vol. 62, 1989, pp. 751–93; Margaret Moore, *Foundations of Liberalism* (Oxford: Oxford University Press, 1993), ch. 6.

15 Kymlicka, "Liberal Individualism and Liberal Neutrality," op. cit., pp. 899–904.
16 See Amy Gutmann, *Democratic Education*, 2nd edn. (Princeton, NJ: Princeton University Press, 1999); Eamonn Callan, *Creating Citizens: Political Education and Liberal Democracy* (Oxford: Oxford University Press, 1997); Stephen Macedo, *Diversity and Distrust: Civic Education in a Multicultural Democracy* (Cambridge, MA: Harvard University Press, 2000); Meira Levinson, *The Demands of Liberal Education* (Oxford: Oxford University Press, 1999).
17 John Rawls, *A Theory of Justice* (London: Oxford University Press, 1971), 563–4; see also David Spitz (ed.), *John Stuart Mill's On Liberty* (New York: Norton, 1975), p. 122.
18 Dworkin, "Can a Liberal State Support Art?" op cit., p. 228.
19 Ibid., p. 229.
20 Ibid.
21 Of course, the models and standards of excellence we learn about in our culture are often closely related to the roles and models in other cultures. For example, models and roles derived from the Bible will be part of the structure of many cultures with a Christian influence. And there are international bodies, like the Catholic Church, which actively seek to ensure this commonality among roles and models in different cultures. So in saying that we learn about conceptions of the good life through our culture, I don't mean to imply that the goods are therefore culture-specific, although some are.
22 Dworkin, "Can a Liberal State Support Art?" op. cit., p. 231.
23 Ibid., p. 229.
24 Ibid., p. 230.
25 Ibid. Dworkin's point here, as I understand it, is not that some languages are *inherently* richer than others. All human languages have an equal capacity for evolution and adaptation to meet the needs of its speakers, just as they all can decline if the cultural practices in society start to decay.
26 Dworkin, "Can a Liberal State Support Art?" pp. 229, 232.
27 Ibid., pp. 232–3.
28 Dworkin, "Liberal Community," op. cit., p. 488.
29 Dworkin, "Three Concepts of Liberalism," *New Republic*, April 14, 1979, p. 48.
30 Dworkin, "Can a Liberal State Support Art?" pp. 232–3.
31 Needless to say, there are other ways that the term "cultural structure" can be and has been used. For example, various social movements, lifestyle enclaves, and religious faiths can be said to have their own "culture." But as Dworkin uses the term, each cultural structure based on a shared language would encompass many such movements, lifestyles, and faiths. These form the options, or perhaps the "subcultures," made available by the larger cultural structure.
32 In Canada, immigrants must learn either English or French, the two official languages, to acquire citizenship. I discuss the status of French in Canada below.
33 Stephen Steinberg, *The Ethnic Myth: Race, Ethnicity and Class in America* (New York: Atheneum, 1981), p. 45.
34 Dworkin, "Can a Liberal State Support Art?" op. cit., pp. 228–9.
35 For an alternative account of the status of immigrants, see J. H. Carens (*Culture, Citizenship and Community: A Contextual Exploration of Justice as Evenhandedness* (Oxford: Oxford University Press, 2000), who argues that states have stronger obligations to enable immigrants to sustain their ancestral culture. While I believe that the integrationist policy is not unjust, neither would it be unjust to have adopted a very different immigration policy. The state could have encouraged immigrants to settle together – even set aside homelands for them – and then given them the resources, language rights, and self-government powers necessary to recreate a cultural structure based on their mother tongue. It's interesting to note that consideration was given to allowing Pennsylvania to be a German-speaking state after the American Revolution. While this would not have been inherently unjust, neither is it unjust that the American government decided not to give voluntary immigrants the status and resources needed to become national minorities. Either approach is, in principle, consistent with justice. What would be an injustice, however, is to both make it impossible for immigrants to recreate their cultural structure, and at the same time make it difficult for them to fully integrate within the mainstream cultural

structure – for example by not providing sufficient English-language training programs, and by not fighting discrimination. I think immigrants often face this injustice. Enabling integration may require some modification of the customs and institutions of the dominant culture so as to accommodate their ethnic and religious differences (e.g., regarding public holidays or uniforms). I discuss the sort of special rights immigrant groups can demand in both my *Multicultural Citizenship*, op. cit., ch. 2, and *Politics in the Vernacular: Nationalism, Multiculturalism and Citizenship* (Oxford: Oxford University Press, 1989), ch. 8. But these will typically take the form of adapting the institutions of the majority culture, not of setting up a separate cultural structure based on the mother tongue.

36   The language of nationhood is evident in these cases. For example, the provincial legislature in Quebec is called the "National Assembly"; the major organization of Status Indians is known as the "Assembly of First Nations"; American Indians are recognized in law as "domestic dependent nations."

37   Hence Canada and the United States are both multinational (as a result of colonization and conquest) and polyethnic (as a result of immigration). Those labels are less popular than the term "multicultural." But that term can be confusing, precisely because it is ambiguous between multinational and polyethnic. This ambiguity has led to unwarranted criticisms of the Canadian government's "multicultural-ism" policy, which is the term the government uses for its post-1970 policy of promoting polyethnicity rather than assimilation for immigrants. Some French Canadians have opposed the "multiculturalism" policy because they think it reduces their claims of nationhood to the level of mere immigrant ethnic-ity. Other people had the opposite fear that the policy was intended to treat immigrant groups as nations, and hence support the development of institutionally complete cultures alongside the French and English. In fact, neither fear was justified, since "multiculturalism" is a policy of supporting polyeth-nicity within the national institutions of the English- and French-speaking societies.

38   Stephen Therstrom, "Ethnic Pluralism: The US Model," in C. Fried (ed.), *Minorities, Community and Identity* (Berlin: Springer-Verlag, 1983), p. 248.

39   On the history of assimilationist pressures on the American Indians, see Lawrence Kelly, *The Assault on Assimilation: John Collier and the Origins of India Reform* (Albuquerque: University of New Mexico Press, 1983).

40   Immigration and the incorporation of national minorities are the two most common sources of ethno-cultural diversity in modern states. However, not all ethnocultural groups fall into one or other of these headings. In particular, the situation of African Americans is quite distinct. They do not fit the volun-tary immigrant pattern, not only because they were brought to America involuntarily as slaves, but also because they were prevented (rather than encouraged) from integrating into the institutions of the majority culture (e.g., racial segregation; laws against miscegenation and the teaching of literacy). Nor do they fit the national minority pattern, since they do not have a homeland in America or a common language. They came from a variety of African cultures, with different languages, and no attempt was made to keep together those with a common ethnic background. On the contrary, people from the same culture (even from the same family) were typically split up once in America. Moreover, they were legally prohibited from trying to recreate their own cultural structure (e.g., all forms of black association, except churches, were illegal). The situation of African Americans, therefore, is very unusual – virtually unique. They were not allowed to integrate into the mainstream culture; nor were they allowed to maintain their earlier languages and cultures, or to create new cultural associations and institutions. They did not have their own homeland or territory, yet they were physically segregated. Given this distinct situation, we should not expect solutions that are appropriate for African Americans to be appropriate for either vol-untary immigrants or national minorities (or vice versa). On the contrary, it would be quite surprising if the same measures were appropriate for these very different groups. Yet it is remarkable how many postwar American political theorists have assumed that black–white relations are the paradigm of ethnic relations, and that the solutions developed in that context should be applied to all ethnocultural groups, at home and abroad (see my *Politics in the Vernacular*, op. cit., ch. 9).

41   For example, refugees fleeing persecution did not choose to give up their culture. Indeed, many refugees flee their homeland precisely in order to be able to continue practicing their culture, which is being ruth-

lessly oppressed by the government (e.g., the Kurds). Hence refugees have a claim of fairness against the international community that they be allowed to recreate their cultural structure in another country. But it is not clear how this international responsibility is to be shared among or assigned to particular countries. Moreover, the line between involuntary refugees and voluntary immigrants is difficult to draw, especially in a world with massive injustices in the international distribution of resources. If a middle-class Swede chooses to emigrate to America, that is clearly voluntary, and few of us would think that she had a claim of justice that the American government provide her with free Swedish-language services (or vice versa for a middle-class American emigrating to Sweden). But if a peasant from Ethiopia emigrates to the United States, her decision may be less voluntary, even if she was not subject to persecution in her homeland, since it may have been the only way to ensure a minimally decent life for herself or her children. Indeed, her plight may have been as dire as that of some refugees. (This is reflected in the rise of the term "economic refugees"). Under these conditions, we may be more sympathetic to demands for the support needed to recreate the refugees' cultural structure. We may think that people shouldn't have to integrate into another societal culture in order to avoid dire poverty. Perhaps then we should say that in a just world, where the international distribution of resources is fair, then immigrants would have no plausible claim of justice to the sorts of resources and powers needed to recreate their cultural structure in their new country. Until that international distribution is rectified, immigrants from poor countries may have stronger claims. But clearly the only long-term solution is to remedy the unjust international distribution of resources. After all, granting language rights to Ethiopian immigrants does nothing for the far greater number of people condemned to abject poverty in Ethiopia.

42 For an interesting discussion of the idea of a "societal" or (what they call) "pervasive" culture, with its requirements for a certain level of institutional completeness and intergenerational continuity, see Avishai Margalit and Joseph Raz, "National Self-Determination," *Journal of Philosophy*, vol. 87, 1990, pp. 439–61.

43 For example, how do we individuate languages? Are Czech and Slovak two languages, or two dialects of the same language? These judgments are often arbitrary and politicized. (Linguists like to say that a language is a dialect with an army.) And what happens when a national minority is losing its language? At what point does it cease to have a distinct cultural structure and become instead a subculture within the larger culture? And who decides? I discuss these questions in my *Multicultural Citizenship*, op. cit., chs. 5–6.

44 Jeremy Waldron, "Minority Cultures and the Cosmopolitan Alternative," *University of Michigan Law Review*, vol. 62, 1992, pp. 783–4.

45 Ibid., pp. 784–5.

46 We must, therefore, distinguish the existence of a culture from its "character" at any given moment. The character of a culture can change dramatically, as the Quiet Revolution in Québec shows. In the space of a decade, French Québec changed from a religious and rural society to a secular and urban one. And of course every nation in Western society has undergone the same transition, although perhaps not as quickly. We need to distinguish these (inevitable and desirable) changes in the character of a culture from threats to the very existence of that culturally distinct society. I explore this distinction in more depth in my *Liberalism, Community and Culture* (Oxford: Oxford University Press, 1989), ch. 8.

47 Language is obviously not sufficient to individuate cultural structures, since not all Anglophones in the world belong to the same culture. As I noted earlier, a culture in our sense requires a level of institutional integration and intergenerational continuity, so as to constitute a distinct "society," not just a shared language.

48 For a more detailed discussion of these forms of "multination federalism," and the way they accommodate the linguistic and cultural rights of national minorities, see my *Politics in the Vernacular*, op. cit., ch. 5.

49 Jay Sigler, *Minority Rights: A Comparative Analysis* (Westport, CT: Greenwood, 1983), p. 196.

50   Liberals before 1940 were more amenable to minority rights. See my *Multicultural Citizenship*, op. cit., ch. 4.

51   One worry liberals have is that "group rights" inherently conflict with individual rights. This is a mistake. We need to distinguish two sorts of group rights: the rights of a group against the larger society, intended to protect the group from the economic and political decisions of the larger society ("external protections"); and the rights of a group against its own members, intended to protect the group from internal dissent and unorthodox behavior ("internal restrictions"). The rights I have been discussing – language rights, land claims, federalism – are all of the former sort. I believe that they are consistent with liberal equality, since they are intended to ensure equality between groups, not to suppress dissent within a group (see Kymlicka, ibid., ch. 3). Of course, some minority cultures demand internal restrictions as well. This raises the question of how a liberal state should treat minority cultures that are illiberal. I discuss this below.

52   This is called the "benign neglect" theory by Nathan Glazer, *Ethnic Dilemmas: 1964–1982* (Cambridge, MA: Harvard University Press, 1983), p. 124. It is explicitly endorsed by Michael Walzer, "Pluralism in Political Perspective," in M. Walzer (ed.), *The Politics of Ethnicity* (Cambridge, MA: Harvard University Press, 1982). Rawls implicitly endorses it in his "Fairness to Goodness," *Philosophical Review*, vol. 84, 1975, p. 551, and also in "The Priority of the Right Over the Good" *Philosophy and Public Affairs*, vol. 17, 1988, pp. 26–7, although he is not specifically addressing the case of ethnic and linguistic diversity.

53   Kymlicka, *Liberalism, Community and Culture*, op. cit., ch. 9. For familiar reasons relating to coordination problems, intergenerational justice, and so forth, see Dworkin, "Can a Liberal State Support Art?" op. cit.; Samuel Black, "Revisionist Liberalism and the Decline of Culture," *Ethics*, vol. 102, 1991, pp. 264–5.

54   Dworkin, "Can a Liberal State Support Art?" op. cit., p. 232.

55   Waldron, "Minority Cultures and the Cosmopolitan Alternative," op. cit., p. 762.

56   For example, ibid., p. 754.

57   Ibid., p. 762.

58   John Rawls, *Political Liberalism* (New York: Columbia University Press, 1993), p. 222.

59   Ibid., p. 277.

60   It might be thought that these measures violate Dworkin's theory of equality of resources, since they involve subsidizing some people's "chosen way of life" at the expense of others. (e.g., Dworkin's "What is Equality? Part 3: The Place of Liberty," *Iowa Law Review*, vol. 73, p. 31, and his "Liberal Community," op. cit., p. 482). But the measures I am referring to are not about promoting people's *choices*. Rather they are directed to the prior question of the social environment best for people to *make choices*. Hence they fall under Dworkin's "principle of authenticity," and the requirement to equalize circumstances. Dworkin, "The Place of Liberty," op. cit., p. 35; cf. my *Liberalism, Community and Culture*, op. cit., ch. 8.

61   For the centrality of this culture-dependent conception of freedom within the liberal tradition, see my, *Liberalism, Community and Culture*, op. cit., ch. 10; and *Multicultural Citizenship*, op. cit., ch. 4.

62   For interesting discussions of the value of cultural membership, see James Nickel, "The Value of Cultural Belonging: Expanding Kymlicka's Theory," *Dialogue*, vol. 33, 1994; Avishai Margalit and Joseph Raz, "National Self-Determination," op. cit.; Yael Tamir, *Liberal Nationalism* (Princeton, NJ: Princeton University Press, 1993); David Miller, "In Defense of Nationality," *Journal of Applied Philosophy*, vol. 10, 1993, pp. 3–16. I discuss these views in more depth in *Multicultural Citizenship*, op. cit., ch. 5.

63   This is proposed by Raz in *The Morality of Freedom*, op. cit., pp. 423–4; and by Susan Okin in *Is Multiculturalism Bad for Women?* (Princeton, NJ: Princeton University Press, 1999).

64   How liberals can promote liberalization, and more generally how liberal states should treat nonliberal minorities, is a large topic, which I pursue in more depth in *Multicultural Citizenship*, op. cit., ch. 8; *Politics in the Vernacular*, op. cit., ch. 4; cf. Michael McDonald, "Liberalism, Community and Culture,"

University of Toronto Law Review, vol. 42, 1992, pp. 113–31; Chandran Kukathas, "Are there Any Cultural Rights?," *Political Theory*, vol. 20, 1992, pp. 105–39.

65 See, for example, Charles Taylor, "Atomism," in *Philosophy and the Human Sciences: Philosophical Papers 2* (Cambridge, UK: Cambridge University Press, 1985).

66 This is not the only argument for minority rights. I noted earlier that national minorities are often pre-existing self-governing communities whose territory is incorporated into a larger state. The way in which this incorporation occurred often gives rise to certain rights. For example, if incorporation occurred through a voluntary federation, certain rights might be spelled out in the terms of federation (e.g., in treaties), and there are legal and moral arguments for respecting these agreements. If incorporation was involuntary (e.g., colonization), then the national minority might have a claim of self-determination under international law, as well as claims of compensatory justice. For some of these historical claims, see Patrick Macklem, "Distributing Sovereignty: Indian Nations and Equality of Peoples," *Stanford Law Review*, vol. 45, 1993, pp. 1311–67; John Danley, "Liberalism, Aboriginal Rights and Cultural Minorities," *Philosophy and Public Affairs*, vol. 20, 1991, pp. 168–85; and my *Multicultural Citizenship*, op. cit., ch. 6.

67 Dworkin notes that "in the modern world of immigration and boundary shifts," citizens are not identified by "racial or ethnic or linguistic type or background" ("Liberal Community," op. cit., p. 497, n. 24), and that the communal life of the political community cannot include a single "ethnic allegiance" (ibid., p. 497). But as we've seen, he does assume a common language ("Can a Liberal State Support Art?" op. cit., pp. 230, 233).

68 Rawls also equates the political community with a single "complete culture" ("The Basic Structure as Subject," in A. Goldman and J. Kim (eds.) *Values and Morals* (Dordrecht: Reidel, 1978), p. 70, n. 8; *Political Liberalism*, op. cit., p. 18).

69 The United States provide an interesting contrast here with various European countries. Countries like Belgium and Switzerland have long recognized that they contain national minorities whose language rights and self-government claims must be respected. But they have trouble admitting that they are increasingly polyethnic, and their traditional conceptions of citizenship have trouble accommodating immigrants. In the United States, by contrast, there is ample recognition that the country is polyethnic, and that immigrants must be able to become full citizens, but difficulty recognizing that the country is also multinational, and that national minorities have special claims of cultural rights and self-government.

70 I discuss some examples, taken from Walzer and Glazer, in my "Liberalism and the Politicization of Ethnicity," *Canadian Journal of Law and Jurisprudence*, vol. 4, 1991, pp. 239–56.

8

Justice in Health Care:
Can Dworkin Justify Universal Access?

Lesley A. Jacobs

The belief that a just society should pursue a policy of universal access to health care is a powerful one. Universal access to health care exists when all citizens, regardless of their socioeconomic class, race, or gender, are assured access to a certain set of basic or "medically necessary" health care services and products.[1] The strength of this ideal is evident not only in the recent health care reform initiatives in the United States, ranging from the 1997 Children's Health Insurance Program to the ongoing efforts to forge a national bill of rights for patients, but also in the existing legislation on health care in Canada and Western Europe. For political philosophers concerned with social justice, this means that it is important to understand how the policy of universal access to health care can be accommodated for in their respective visions of a just society. This chapter examines how well Ronald Dworkin's detailed vision of a liberal egalitarian society can justify universal access to health care.

Although Dworkin's work on political morality has been innovative in many different respects, there are two claims that he has advanced which are especially important and central to his vision of a just society. The first claim is that despite many deeply rooted disagreements among contemporary political philosophers, there is nonetheless a consensus around the principle foundational to all political morality in a democratic society. This principle, which Dworkin calls the *abstract egalitarian principle*, says, "government must act to make the lives of those it governs better lives, and it must show equal concern for the life of each."[2] For Dworkin, this abstract egalitarian principle reflects a platitude among philosophers and public officials, and disagreements arise principally over how to interpret it. The second claim has a central place in his particular interpretation of the abstract egalitarian principle. Specifically, Dworkin maintains that in order for a government to show equal concern for the life of each of those it governs, it must design a mechanism that distributes privately owned resources in a manner that treats each individual as an equal and to do so it must be sensitive to the different ambitions, goals, and choices of each individual. This requirement, which I will explain in more depth below, Dworkin terms "ambition sensitivity." I will argue in this chapter that Dworkin's interpretation of the abstract egalitarian principle, and especially the requirement of ambition sensitivity, is incompatible with a policy of universal access to health care.

I Equality of Resources

For Dworkin, the primacy of the abstract egalitarian principle is significant because it narrows in an important respect the scope of competing theories of distributive justice. For it suggests that the central feature of a mechanism for distributing privately held resources in a just society is that it treat all individuals as equals. Individuals have command over an equal share of the advantages of social life precisely when a distributional scheme treats them as equal. Equality of resources is Dworkin's particular theory about when a distributional scheme treats an individual as an equal. The issue I am raising in this paper is how well Dworkin's theory of equality of resources can accommodate a policy of universal access to health care. Before turning to that issue, however, it is necessary first to explain briefly the main ideas of his theory of equality of resources including especially the requirement of ambition sensitivity.[3]

At the core of Dworkin's theory of distributive justice is the distinction between an individual's personality and circumstances. Among an individual's personality, Dworkin includes features such as convictions, ambitions, tastes, and preferences. An individual's circumstances include his or her resources, talents and skills, and physical and mental capacities.[4] The peculiarity of including talents, skills, and capacities among individuals' circumstances rather than as features of their personality will be discussed below. According to Dworkin, a distributional scheme treats individuals as equals when no further economic transfer would leave them with circumstances more equal to the circumstances of any other individual. Equality of resources says, in others words, that shares are equal when people's circumstances are equal.

But this raises in turn the question of when people's circumstances are equal. A basic axiom of Dworkin's position is this: equality of resources is concerned fundamentally with the share of resources devoted to the whole life of an individual.[5] People are treated as equals when their share of resources across their lives as a whole are equal. The guiding principle for determining what constitutes equal circumstances builds on this basic axiom. It requires that any distributive scheme be sensitive to the cost of each person's life to other people. That cost is to be measured by how valuable the resources and other elements of circumstances consumed – interpreted broadly to suggest also use, and so forth – by that person are to those other people. Dworkin terms this cost the *opportunity cost* of one's life. Clearly, though, people will choose to do different things with their initial circumstances. These differences will reflect their personalities. One person might prefer to use his or her resources to produce something, someone else might prefer only to consume. The first person will over time come to have more resources than the second. But this does not mean that he or she would have been treated as less than an equal. Provided that each is equal in the circumstances devoted to the whole of their lives, the differences resulting from differences in personality do not undermine them having equal shares. It is in this sense that we might say that equality of resources is "personality-sensitive" or, to use Dworkin's preferred expression, "ambition-sensitive."[6]

If we accept, as Dworkin suggests, that distributional equality be ambition-sensitive, what then is the best way to distribute resources? What is the best way to measure opportunity costs? This role is assigned, in the first instance, to the economic market for goods. An illustration of how it determines opportunity costs is provided by Dworkin. Imagine the situation of a group of shipwrecked survivors washed up on a desert island with an abundance of resources. The issue is how to distribute equally those resources that are to be privately owned. Some form of auction or market is proposed. One basic requirement is that all of the shipwrecked immigrants enter the market on equal terms.[7] This requirement is met if everyone has the same number of counters to be used for bidding in the auction. Clamshells are suggested as counters, provided that no one values them apart from their role as counters and therefore no one wants to buy them in the auction. To ensure that the auction works properly, it is also necessary that each person receive a large number of clamshells. The most difficult task is proposing a set of prices for the resources to be sold. The person who has this task must post a set of prices that "clear the markets." Technically, this requires that only one person among the bidders is willing to pay the price for each resource and that all resources are sold. The importance of price setting in this way is that it determines how valuable each resource is to other people. We have then a way of measuring opportunity costs. Of course, if you are the buyer of a resource at the price of x clamshells, this means that you have fewer clamshells to buy other resources.

Suppose that after the prices have been set to clear the markets, the auction is run. Each person has a bundle of resources based on their bids during the auction. Unfortunately, someone is unhappy because someone else has a bundle of resources they would have preferred. In that case, the distribution would have failed what Dworkin calls the "envy test": "No division of resources is an equal division if, once the division is complete, any immigrant would prefer someone else's bundle of resources to his own bundle."[8] So the auction should be run again so that the person has the opportunity to purchase the envied bundle of resources. And again and again until the envy test is passed. The consequent bundle of resources each person would have after the last successful run of the auction would constitute an equal share.[9]

After the initial auction, the markets will stay open. This presents a problem for Dworkin's ideal of distributional equality. Everyone, it was presumed, entered the auction as equals if each had the same number of clamshells. Clearly, however, people do not have the identical endowments and capacities; some will have physical or mental handicaps, others will have highly valued talents and skills. Recall now that Dworkin includes talents and capacities among the circumstances that equality of resources seeks to equalize. Wouldn't this mean that people would not be entering the market as equals? The problem is that because talents and handicaps cannot be transferred among persons, they cannot be bid for in the auction like other sorts of more contingent goods.[10]

How then can the compensation paid to those who suffer from handicaps and other forms of underendowment be "ambition-sensitive"? Dworkin's innovative solution to this problem is to have, operating alongside the economic market for transferable goods, a progressive income tax scheme modeled on a hypothetical insurance market, in which people are imagined to have insured against being handicapped or untalented. Although his sketch of this insurance market is very complex, the basic idea that informs it is simple. Imagine that people pay an insurance premium against being handicapped or untalented based on how much each disvalues suffering from a specific handicap or being untalented in some respect. If a person turns out to suffer from a disadvantage that he or she would have been insured against, then the insurance scheme will compensate that person accordingly. The actual level of compensation paid out will depend on how many other people collect. This is because, in order for an insurance market to function properly, it is necessary for the premiums paid in to the scheme to be at least equal to the compensation paid out. And since it is important to keep premiums low, compensation is unlikely to bring the amount of resources enjoyed by someone who suffers the relevant disadvantage up to the same level of those who do not suffer the relevant disadvantage.[11] The level of compensation paid out is "ambition-sensitive" because the coverage provided by the hypothetical insurance market is supposed to reflect the actual value each person places on not having a certain talent or suffering from a certain handicap in view of the opportunity costs to others.

Dworkin's theory of equality of resources can be clarified by briefly contrasting it to two other influential approaches to defining an equal share of the advantages of social life. One approach, which can be described as an *objectivist* approach, limits the measurement of equal shares only to those resources that are deemed to be important.[12] The make-up of an individual share of resources, on this approach, clearly depends for the most part on what is judged to be important.

The basic characteristic of this judgment is that it is made from an objective point of view and not from the perspective of what a person does or would if informed want.[13] Thus, on an objectivist approach, the preferences you actually have play no role in determining the share of resources you actually receive.

It is precisely on this last point that we can differentiate Dworkin's theory of equal shares from an objectivist one. For what Dworkin makes central is the idea that the bundle of resources each person receives under equality of resources is a reflection of that person's personality in the following sense: the auction allows people to acquire resources they deem valuable at a price determined by the opportunity cost to others. Dworkin's principal objection to an account of distributional equality that does not give one's personality any place in determining one's bundle of resources is that it can be said not to treat everyone as equals.[14] Under any objectivist scheme for distributing resources, some preferences are going to be favored over others because they are judged to be more important or valuable. This has the consequence, however, of not treating as equals those who have the less favored preferences. For, according to Dworkin, treating everyone as equals, "must impose no sacrifice or constraint on any citizen in virtue of an argument that the citizen could not accept without abandoning his sense of his equal worth."[15] Now, suppose that you prefer tennis to poetry but under an objectivist egalitarian scheme you are distributed poetry books but not a tennis racket on the grounds that a life of poetry is much more worthwhile than a life of tennis. How can you accept this distribution without abandoning your sense of equal worth? The virtue of the auction is that it treats everyone as equals by allowing each to play an equal role in the determination of equal shares. There is then a very important lesson here. Treating people as equals in distributive justice requires, as a matter of procedure, that people have some control over the content of their share of the resources. To determine those shares in an objectivist manner has the consequence of not treating everyone as equals.

Dworkin's equality of resources can also be contrasted to John Rawls's "difference principle." In its simplest form, the difference principle stipulates that social and economic inequalities be arranged to the benefit of the least advantaged members of society.[16] Although Rawls and Dworkin differ on a number of issues, I shall elaborate on only one here.[17] For Dworkin, the determination of an equal share involves equalizing circumstances among people, taking into account the whole of their lives. Differences in shares thus reflect choices about consumption, occupation, and so forth, but not differences in talents and capacities. One problem with Rawls's difference principle is that it seems to make little room for such considerations. It appears to allow only for differences that make the worst off better off. Dworkin thus describes the difference principle as "one-dimensional" and "flat." And since it is flat, it fails to treat people as equals. For equal shares, on the difference principle, do not reflect the costs of one person's life to others.[18]

II Justice in Health Care

Dworkin's treatment of the issues

We are now in a position to focus our attention on the question of whether or not Dworkin's theory of equality of resources can justify a policy commitment to universal access to health care. Dworkin has written a pair of articles that explicitly address problems about justice in the distribution of health care from the perspective of equality of resources.[19] Specifically, Dworkin tries to show how the main ideas of that general theory of distributive justice, and especially the idea of ambition sensitivity, shine light on two long-pressing issues about health care distribution in countries such as the United States, Canada, and Britain. How much should a society as a whole spend on health care? How in turn should the amount to be spent on health care be rationed in terms of who should receive health care and what forms of health care should be provided? The background context for discussing these issues is the ever increasing costs of health care, costs that leveled off briefly in the late 1990s but have begun to increase rapidly again in all three countries. The dominant response to the increasing demands of health care on the public purse has been to insist that health care spending should be capped and, therefore, we must decide which health care services we can afford and which we cannot. The philosophical challenge is to identify a standard that is not morally arbitrary for making these sorts of choices.

The importance of this challenge has often been overlooked. This is because frequently in the past health care spending has been regarded as something determined by some sort of standard of "need" rather than as an issue of social choice in conditions of scarcity where spending money on health care means not spending money on some other good such as, for example, housing.[20] For Dworkin, the issue is precisely what should the basis be for making this sort of social choice about health care spending. He defends what he calls the "prudent insurance" approach to health care distribution. The core of this approach is the following principle: "A just distribution [of health care] is one that well-informed people create for themselves by individual choices, provided that the economic system and the distribution of wealth in the community in which these choices are made are themselves just."[21]

What Dworkin is getting at is that how much a just society should spend on health care is simply an aggregate of what individuals in that society would spend.[22] In other words, social decisions about health care spending should be a function of what individuals would in just circumstances spend. The point is that because spending on health care means that there is less money to spend on other valuable goods, the decision about exactly how much should be spent on health care ought to reflect how important health care is to particular individuals. The main idea, then, is that health care spending is principally a matter of individual responsibility. Against a background where there is a fair initial distribution of resources, and information about the effectiveness and costs of particular health care procedures is widely known, all individuals should be responsible for deciding for themselves how much to spend on health care based on how important health care is to them in comparison to other goods that they might acquire.[23]

The prudent insurance approach to justice in the distribution to health care is entirely consistent with and, indeed, flows from Dworkin's more comprehensive theory of equality of resources. The basic theme is that the distribution of health care must be ambition-sensitive in the sense that how much we spend on health care and which medical procedures we pay for must be sensitive to the particular ambitions, preference orderings, life plans, tastes, and commitments of each person. Introducing ambition sensitivity into the distribution of health care is significant not only because it allows us to treat social choices about health care spending as an aggregate of individual choices but also because it makes individuals directly responsible for the cost of the health care they receive.

The approach Dworkin takes to justice in the distribution of health care is especially insightful when it comes to hard choices about rationing health care spending, that is to say, deciding which medical procedures should be funded and which should not. His view is that these choices are best made when individuals are required to bear the true costs of their choices in the sense that when individuals are choosing whether or not a particular medical procedure should be funded, their choice is going to affect their access to other valuable goods and opportunities such as, for example, going on a particular holiday or acquiring a new car. Let me illustrate this by considering the important issue of just how much we should spend on health care for those in their last six months of life.[24] Ideally, of course, most of us think that it would be nice to set no spending limit and we feel uneasy with the very idea of doing so. However, not to ration health care spending in those circumstances would make it impossible to limit health care costs in our society. (In the United States, health care in those circumstances account for nearly 40 percent of total health care spending, 6 percent of the GNP.) How should we decide what is the spending limit on health care in these circumstances? Dworkin urges us when responding to imagine that whatever resources we might spend on ourselves in our last six months of life be subtracted from the total amount of resources that we could devote to the rest of our lives. The point is that given quality of life considerations at different points in our lives, it seems likely that prudent individuals would choose to spend considerable less on health care in their last six months of life than at present we do.[25]

In my view, Dworkin's discussion of health care distribution has two noteworthy features. The first is that he makes a case for applying the idea of ambition sensitivity to problems having to do with just health care.[26] The second is that he has, at least thus far, failed to extend his discussion of inequalities in skills and handicaps to the realm of health care distribution.[27] This is surprising because differences between individuals in terms of ill-health would seem to pose a threat to equal circumstances in exactly the same way that differences in skills and handicaps do since they too seem to be in most cases instances of brute bad luck. And, hence, the case for redistribution to mitigate for this threat would seem to be identical. Moreover, it seems that this kind of extension of his argument is essential to explain any sort of health care program that has a redistributive character.

Recall that for Dworkin equality of resources requires that people be equal in their circumstances and that an individual's circumstances include talents and skills, and physical and mental capacities. Presumably, too, the logic of Dworkin's distinction between personality and circumstances is such that ill-health not engendered by personal choice would also be included in an individual's circumstances. In other words, the state of an individual's health should be taken seriously in the effort to make people equal in their circumstances. The practical difficulty is that, like skills and handicaps, health is a nontransferable resource – it cannot be bought and sold in a market.

How should an egalitarian respond to the unequal circumstances that arise because of ill-health? Presumably, for Dworkin, the best way to approach the problem is through his device of hypothetical insurance markets. Imagine that people pay an insurance premium against the costs of health care based on how much each disvalues suffering specific forms of ill-health where everyone is uncertain about the particular details of their health over their life time. If an individual turns out to suffer from a form of ill-health that he or she would have insured against, then the insurance scheme will in theory compensate that individual accordingly. This approach to the problem of health distribution is "ambition-sensitive" because the coverage provided by the hypothetical insurance market is supposed to reflect the actual value each person places on not suffering from a particular form of ill-health in comparison to other goods and opportunities he or she values.

How would this hypothetical insurance market approach to addressing the unequal circumstances created by ill-health translate into a concrete health care program? What would such a program look like? Certainly, such a program would necessarily be redistributive in the sense that some people would have to pay more towards the funding of such a health care program than they would require in actual health care, and others less. In other words, implementing a health care scheme modeled on Dworkin's hypothetical insurance markets requires (indirect) redistributive transfers from certain individuals to other individuals. This is not a surprising conclusion since Dworkin has shown how the use of hypothetical insurance markets in skills and handicaps can be translated into a progressive income tax system that is redistributive in character.

The relevant issue, for our purposes, is whether or not this health care program will guarantee universal access to health care. Would Dworkin's hypothetical insurance market in health care translate into a system where all citizens are assured access to a certain set of basic or "medically necessary" health care services and products?

Health care as an in-kind transfer

I shall now introduce a distinction which must be given careful attention in an examination of the problem of justifying universal access to health care. Redistribution is ordinarily pursued through what economists and public policy analysts call redistributive transfers. A redistributive transfer can, for our purposes, be understood as a payment to an individual or institution that does not arise out of current productive activity. Redistributive transfers can be either in-kind or in cash.[28] Benefits, as I shall use the term, denote particular in-kind or cash transfers. In-kind redistributive transfers involve the transfer of specific goods in some form or another. The central point is that a policy of universal access to health care involves the use of in-kind transfers and does not allow citizens to trade off health care benefits for cash or other goods. In-kind benefits other than health care include education, housing, and food stamps. These differ from benefits in cash. Typical cash benefits are child benefit, tax credits, social assistance, unemployment insurance, disability insurance, and social security pensions. This type of benefit leaves it up to the recipient what to spend the cash on. For the operation of cash redistributive transfers, it is obviously necessary for there to be economic markets that allow people to buy goods with their cash benefits.[29]

Sometimes the issue over whether to use cash transfers or in-kind transfers for redistribution is reduced to an ideological one dividing right and left on social policy. Cash transfers supposedly entail a capitalist market system while in-kind transfers supposedly require provision by a large bureaucratic state, sometimes pejoratively described as "socialism." But this presentation of the issue over whether to use cash transfers or in-kind transfers is misleading. In-kind transfers do not necessarily entail direct state provision. Consider the case of health care. It is, of course, possible for the government to provide health care, perhaps along the lines of the British National Health Service. Alternatively, health care could be provided by private physicians and hospitals but with the government issuing health care vouchers or credit cards for people to use as payment for these services where payment schemes are negotiated between the health care providers and the government. This is, for example, the way that state-funded health care is delivered for the most part in Canada and the United States. Likewise, food stamp schemes are generally structured to allow the poor to buy food at reduced prices from private firms.

Discussions of redistributive social policy generally distinguish between the aims or ends of a policy and the means or methods for achieving those aims or ends.[30] Thus, for any redistributive transfer policy, we first want to know the aims of the policy and then how best to achieve those aims. The aims are ethical judgments reflecting distributive justice: what, for instance, is a fair share? What then is the best means of redistributive transfer? This is the way that the choice between cash transfers and in-kind transfers is often perceived. The familiar argument for cash transfers based on efficiency has this character. The presumption generally made is that the aim of a redistributive transfer is to increase to the maximum the welfare of the recipient. Since individuals generally are the best judges of what is in their own best interests, cash benefits are preferable to in-kind ones because they allow people to buy whatever will maximize their own welfare.[31] The point is that given the aim of maximizing the recipient's welfare, cash transfers are the best means to achieve this aim. But – and this is very important – if it could be shown that in-kind transfers are a more efficient way to maximize the welfare of the recipient, then they would be the best means. On this approach, the choice between cash and in-kind redistributive transfers is a purely technical one to be decided by experts who do the necessary calculations.[32]

In my view, this approach rests on a mistaken presupposition. The presupposition in dispute is that a principle of distributive justice that justifies the basic policy for a redistributive transfer does not also sometimes require a particular means of transfer. I believe, on the contrary, the following: sometimes the normative justification for a redistributive policy entails whether to use a cash transfer or an in-kind transfer.[33] If what I believe is true, then it is a mistake to view the choice between them as always a mere technical issue. It follows from my claim that we can distinguish functionally between three sorts of justifications for redistributive transfers. First of all, there are justifications for redistribution that require cash transfers. Secondly, there are justifications for redistribution that require in-kind transfers. Thirdly, there are justifications for redistribution that treat the choice between cash and in-kind transfers as a mere technical matter.

The prima facie *case for cash transfers*

This threefold distinction is directly relevant to how successful Dworkin's vision of a just society is at accommodating a policy of universal access to health care. It is my view that most discussions of justice in the distribution of health care have paid insufficient attention to the fact that a successful justification of universal access to health care must make the case not just for a redistributive health care policy but more specifically for the use of in-kind rather than cash transfers. (I put off until section III below explaining more precisely why universal access requires in-kind benefits.) The relevant questions for our purposes are: can Dworkin's hypothetical insurance market in health care justify the use of in-kind redistributive transfers? Can his approach to justice in health care be translated into a system where everyone will be guaranteed some minimal standard of health care?

The argument in this subsection will proceed through two steps. First, I shall defend the thesis that Dworkin's theory of equality of resources, because of its insistence on the requirement of ambition sensitivity, is compatible with the use of cash transfers but generally is incompatible with the use of in-kind transfers. This is what can be described as Dworkin's *prima facie* case for the use of cash transfers. Second, I will examine three cases in which there appear to be good grounds within Dworkin's theory of distributive justice for using in-kind transfers and show why they do not have any bearing on the problem of justifying universal access to health care. The upshot of this argument, then, is that Dworkin is unable to justify the existence of a policy of universal access to health care in his detailed liberal egalitarian vision of a just society.

The main pillar of Dworkin's theory of equality of resources is this: the determination of equal shares requires that everyone be treated as equals and as such be ambition-sensitive. In other words, a person's share of resources must reflect his or her personality – preferences, goals, ambitions – and the cost to others. It is my view that this grounding idea of Dworkin's is basically on the mark. I have tried to emphasize above how for Dworkin the market is the distributional mechanism that meets these requirements. In the desert island example, everyone was provided with some clamshells with which they could bid for the various resources on offer. In actual markets, cash has very much the same function as Dworkin's clamshells. We can use it to buy goods in those markets. In effect, then, the initial allocation of clamshells on the desert island is like a cash transfer in the real world.

The *prima facie* case for cash redistributive transfers, like Dworkin's argument for the use of clamshells, rests on the claim that any other type of transfer would result in not everyone being treated as an equal. The virtue of cash is that it is able to track the relative value each person places on having command over some resources rather than others. Cash transfers are inherently ambition-sensitive. To put it another way, cash benefits conform to what Dworkin calls the principle of abstraction. The principle of abstraction holds that any distributive scheme that purports to treat individuals as equals must maximize the freedom individuals have to do what they wish.[34] The attraction of cash for Dworkin is precisely that it allows people to buy whatever they want. The relevant contrast is to in-kind benefits which do set considerable constraints on how they can be used.

The general incompatibility I am suggesting between Dworkin's requirement of ambition sensitivity and the use of in-kind transfers can be illustrated more clearly through an example. Consider the case of a man who has through bad luck contacted a serious illness. An operation can be performed that will treat this illness. Suppose that the patient is a citizen in a state that operates a health care scheme that guarantees universal access and that the operation in question will be covered under this scheme. But the ill person is peculiar because he says that he would rather have the money spent on something else, some good he values more than health care. (It is easy to imagine, at present, an AIDS patient saying precisely this sort of thing; he would prefer to have certain resources in cash so that he could use it to do things in life he had always wanted to do instead of spending it on expensive medical equipment designed to prolong his life.) Why shouldn't the health care scheme compensate him in this form rather than by paying for the operation? For an egalitarian concerned with the requirement of ambition sensitivity, it seems only logical that if the normative foundations for the health care scheme rest on distributional equality, then it does make sense to compensate the patient with whatever he values the most, whether that is health care or some other good of the equivalent cash value. In that case, however, the health care scheme should cease to operate through an in-kind transfer. Instead, it should compensate with cash transfers that would allow recipients to make their own choices about the value of health care relative to other goods. But then we would no longer have a health care scheme that guarantees universal access.[35]

This general case against in-kind transfers is reinforced by our earlier discussion of the intricacies of Dworkin's equality of resources. The general argument for giving the immigrants clamshells and having the auction rather than having some individual simply divide up the resources into bundles is that this second approach would not treat everyone as equals in the sense that the relative value each person places on the resources would not have been taken into account in the division of the resources. Presumably this also counts as a general objection against an in-kind transfer justified by a consideration of distributional equality. An in-kind transfer that aims to equalize people in terms of particular goods has been described as "specific egalitarianism."[36] This, however, clearly depends on what I have termed an objectivist approach to defining an equal share of society's resources, because some resources are deemed to be important – those to be equalized – without consideration of the recipient's own relative ordering of resources. It would, therefore, seem consistent to apply Dworkin's criticism of the objectivist approach to specific egalitarianism, namely, that it fails to treat people as equals.

Dworkin's critique of Rawls is also telling. Although Rawls may not be able to accept all arguments in favor of in-kind transfers, nevertheless, because the difference principle is flat and not ambition-sensitive, there may not be an inherent objection to all in-kind transfers. The fact, however, that Dworkin's equality of resources does have this added complexity is what makes it a better interpretation of that abstract distributional theory. So we seem to reach the conclusion that a health care scheme grounded on equality of resources generally requires the use of cash redistributive transfers, not in-kind transfers.

My analysis so far has been designed to establish, on the one hand, that a *prima facie* commitment to cash transfers flows from the requirement of ambition sensitivity and, on the other hand, that there is a general incompatibility between the requirement of ambition sensitivity and the use of in-kind transfers. Now, while Dworkin might concede that this analysis of his theory of distributional equality reveals a *prima facie* commitment to cash transfers, he might nevertheless resist the conclusion that equality of resources never allows for the use of in-kind transfers. It seems that equality of resources can make room for at least three possible egalitarian grounds for in-kind transfers: (1) efficiency, (2) externalities, and (3) superficial paternalism. While considering these grounds in turn, the issue I want to keep in clear sight is whether any of these are capable of justifying the sort of in-kind redistribution involved in the provision of universal access to health care.

Unlike many of those who are committed to equality,[37] Dworkin denies that this commitment requires a trade-off between equality and efficiency. His argument can be briefly summarized.[38] The basic metric for measuring when individuals each have an equal share of resources is, as we saw above, what Dworkin terms opportunity costs. Opportunity costs reflect how much others value a resource that someone else has. Efficiency is principally a matter of maximizing social wealth or the total resources available in a society. It follows, then, that the value of efficiency can be measured in terms of opportunity costs. Greater efficiency may have a detrimental effect on some people by, for example, denying to them certain resources that would otherwise have been available. But improved efficiency would increase the total resources available in society and, as a result, make bigger the resource shares of others. The point is that deciding whether or not to promote efficiency in a particular instance requires the balancing of these opportunity costs. Although in some cases this balancing might work against efficiency, it is likely that in most cases the opportunity costs of those who benefit from efficiency will outweigh those who lose from it and, therefore, equality of resources will favor improved efficiency in those cases. There is not, then, an inevitable trade-off between distributional equality and efficiency.

The fact that Dworkin is able to defend improved efficiency on egalitarian grounds may seem directly relevant to the provision of health care. After all, many of the debates over the provision of health care revolve around issues of efficiency. There is at present, for example, some powerful evidence to suggest that the Canadian system of health care provision is much more efficient than the existing American model.[39] But, for our purposes, it is important to note that these efficiency arguments generally only establish a case for why the state should coordinate the delivery of health care; they do not *directly* establish the efficiency of universal access. The basic argument noted above for cash benefits is that they are the only sort of transfer that treats people as equals. The idea is that a health care benefit, for example, does not treat as an equal someone who would prefer something else over health care. Logically, then, it would make sense under equality of resources to provide everyone with a cash benefit which they could then at their own discretion use to buy health care insurance coverage, perhaps from a Health Maintenance Organization or the state.

Efficiency considerations would enter into the debate when determining how much cash would be involved in such a transfer. If, for example, the state was able to provide coverage at a premium of $1200 in comparison to $2000 by private firms, the appropriate level of cash benefit would seem to be $1200. Indeed, assuming that the preference structure of individuals such as our AIDS patient is an exception, it might even make sense to provide everyone, in the first instance, with health care benefits under a state-administered scheme with an opting out clause which allows individuals to withdraw from the scheme and receive instead the cash equivalent of that benefit. Of course, given the effects their opting out may have on the economy of scales benefits that derive from a state-administered health care scheme, it might even be the case that the cash benefit ends up being slightly less than the market exchange value of the health care coverage from which they opt out. The important point is that an argument for providing universal health care benefits cannot be based on weighing up the opportunity costs of this sort of benefit in comparison to cash benefits since the level of cash benefits can be set so as to offset any costs of providing them rather than in-kind benefits.

Another way Dworkin might try to defend universal access to health care is on the grounds that when it comes to the provision of health care, market pricing mechanisms are inadequate because of the externalities that occur because of imperfect information or knowledge. And Dworkin maintains that the freedom of choice required by the principle of abstraction can be limited in such a case.[40] The point is that given the existence of externalities in the case of health care, it might be appropriate to make distributive transfers less ambition-sensitive and provide individuals with in-kind health benefits instead of cash. The classical argument against having markets in health care has been made by Kenneth Arrow.[41] As Arrow points out, prospective patients do not have sufficient knowledge to make decisions about treatment, referral, or hospitalization and, thus, to judge *between* competing sellers of health care services. This means, then, that the market pricing mechanism ceases to be an accurate way to track how people would prefer to have health care resources allocated. Arrow's concern is with people who want health care but lack the knowledge required to make informed choices about the type of health care they want. None the less, while it might make sense to have experts making decisions about the sort of health care a patient should receive, it goes against the very core of Dworkin's egalitarianism to say that individuals are not their own best judges of whether or not they value health care over other non-medical goods. My point is that while individuals may lack the knowledge to make an informed choice between competing health care providers, there is not a parallel information problem when we are considering whether individuals value health care more or less than other (nonmedical) goods which they could buy with the same amount of cash.[42] Yet it is precisely this sort of information problem that warrants on egalitarian grounds an in-kind health care benefit rather than a cash one.

The final way in which Dworkin might try to defend in-kind health care benefits and, therefore, universal access to health care is on the grounds of what he calls "superficial" paternalism – "forcing people to take precautions that are reasonable within their own structure of preferences."[43] It might be argued that many of the people who will choose to spend their cash on something other than health care are experiencing some form of *akrasia* or weakness of will. And in these cases the superficial paternalism involved in providing an in-kind health care benefit instead of simply cash is warranted since, quite clearly, such transfers would treat people as equals since by definition they are "ambition-sensitive." The problem is that in the case of the AIDS patient who would prefer some resource other than health care, we cannot justify providing him with health care on the grounds of superficial paternalism since the provision of health care does not reflect his own structure of preferences – he is not suffering from *akrasia*. In other words, while superficial paternalism might warrant providing health care benefits in some instances, it is unable to justify the use of in-kind health care benefits in all instances, which is what is presupposed by universal access to health care.

III   Why Universal Access Requires In-kind Transfers

The argument that Dworkin's abstract egalitarian principle is inconsistent with a policy of universal access to health care turns on my insistence that such a policy requires in-kind transfers. This requirement has generally been overlooked in normative examinations of universal access to health care and many legal and political philosophers maintain that universal access to health care exists when individuals have at some point in their lives enough money to buy sufficient insurance coverage for "medically necessary" health care services and products if they want it.[44] I have yet to ground my claim that universal access to health care requires in-kind transfers. Let me briefly try to do so.

At the normative core of the policy of universal access to health care is the principle that competition is an inappropriate device for the allocation of "medically necessary" health care services and products.[45] In other words, individuals should not be treated as competitors for health care. Health care should not be regarded as a prize. Although tragic choices about health care resources are inevitable, those who are the beneficiaries of modes of health care allocation and those who are not should not be viewed as winners and losers, respectively. What universal access to health care does is deny that health care is a prize for winners. Since everybody has access, nobody can be said to be a loser. By relying on the use of in-kind health care benefits that cannot be traded for cash or other goods, a scheme of universal access does not allow individual citizens to compete against each other for health care services and products. Reliance on cash instead of in-kind transfers to guarantee access would entail an allocation mechanism such as a market or auction where individuals would compete against each other for scarce health care resources. The upshot of such a competition would, of course, be a situation where there are winners and losers in the allocation of health care.

The principle that health care should not be subject to competition provides a succinct explanation for why ability to pay is an inappropriate standard for the allocation of health care. What is morally problematic about ability to pay is not the implied commodification of health care but rather the standard context in which ability to pay operates, for example, where prices are set so that buyers bid competitively against each other until the markets clear. Seen in this light, it shouldn't be a surprise that Dworkin's egalitarian vision stumbles in the realm of health care policy. For his theory of equality of resources, as we saw above, strives to be "ambition-sensitive," and this condition is met when the opportunity costs to others of a scarce resource are determined by imagining individuals bidding in competition with each other in an auction for that resource.

IV   Conclusion

This paper establishes, then, that Dworkin is unable to justify universal access to health care under his theory of equality of resources. This is a significant conclusion because it provides us with a clear case where Dworkin's detailed vision of a just society differs from what many of us intuitively imagine to be a just society. That is to say, for many of us, in a just society each citizen will be guaranteed access to a minimal standard of health care. Now it seems that Dworkin could respond by putting pressure on the intuitive idea that universal access to health care should be guaranteed in a just society. In our existing social circumstances, universal access to health care is such a powerful ideal (it might be said) because of the background condition of vast inequalities in wealth. When someone does not have access to health care, this is commonly a consequence of their being poor. But in Dworkin's vision of a just society, if people did not have access to health care, this would be because they had decided to forego that access to health care for something else; it is not, then, because they are poor. Health care distribution does not operate in a situation where the background condition is vast inequalities in wealth. Instead, every instance where people do not enjoy access to health care can be traced to the choices they have made. In this sense, each individual is responsible for the size and shape of the share of health care he or she receives. The upshot, then, is that perhaps we should on reflection revise our intuitions about the place of universal access to health care in a just society.

I have two comments on this sort of response. The first concedes that this line of reasoning may be right. Perhaps we really should give up on the ideal of universal access to health care in a just society. But I suspect that this concession is more significant than it first appears. In my view, the underlying judgment that gives the ideal of universal access to health care such power is the belief that in some sense access to health care is special, it is different from many other goods in this respect. This does not mean that the provision of health care should not be weighed against the provision of other goods in the context of a social choice. (Health care should not be provided at any cost.) It just means that access to health care should be treated as a special case in a theory of distributive justice. And Dworkin's treatment of health care distribution does not capture this.

My second comment is to note that even if Dworkin is right that our intuitions about universal access to health care in a just society are wrong, the main argument of this paper is still significant because it suggests a serious problem with Dworkin's recent attempt to use the idea of hypothetical insurance markets and prudent insurers to illuminate contemporary debates about health care distribution in existing societies. In those contemporary debates, there is a very widespread commitment to the importance of universal access to health care. Dworkin's approach to justice in the distribution of health care is unable to provide public officials with normative grounds for this commitment. This is especially striking in Dworkin's discussion of the recent health care reform proposals in the United States. At the very core of those proposals is a commitment to universal access to health care. Yet Dworkin does not attempt to ground that commitment, nor, as I have shown, is he able to.

Acknowledgement

I am grateful to G. A. Cohen, David Donaldson, Eric Rakowski, and Andrew Williams for especially helpful written comments on earlier drafts of this paper. I would also like to acknowledge here the support of a major research grant from the Social Sciences and Humanities Research Council of Canada.

Notes

1   Universal access to health care differs from equal access to health care. "A principle of equal access to health care," explains Amy Gutmann, "demands that every person who shares the same type and degree of health need must be given an equally effective chance of receiving appropriate treatment of equal quality so long as that treatment is available to anyone." See "For and Against Equal Access to Health Care," in S. Gorovitz, R. Macklin, A. Jameton, J. O'Connor, and S. Sherwin (eds.), *Moral Problems in Medicine*, 2nd edn. (Englewood Cliffs, NJ: Prentice-Hall, 1983), p. 558. The belief that the nation's health care system should achieve equal access is, I think, less widely held than the belief that there should be universal access. The possibility of ever achieving equal access in an industrial society seems doubtful, given obstacles posed by residents of rural areas.

2   Ronald Dworkin, "What is Equality? Part 3: The Place of Liberty," *Iowa Law Review*, vol. 72, 1987, p. 7. This paper has been reprinted in Ronald Dworkin, *Sovereign Virtue: The Theory and Practice of Equality* (Cambridge, MA: Harvard University Press, 2000). Page references are to the original.

3   A much more detailed general examination of Dworkin's theory of distributional justice can be found in my book, *Rights and Deprivation* (Oxford: Oxford University Press, 1993), ch. 5.

4   Dworkin, "The Place of Liberty," op. cit., pp. 18–19; "What is Equality? Part 2: Equality of Resources," *Philosophy and Public Affairs*, vol. 10, 1981, p. 302 (this paper has also been reprinted in *Sovereign Virtue*, op. cit.). Note that Dworkin sometimes expresses this distinction in terms of the contrast between a person and his or her circumstances. G. A. Cohen in "On the Currency of Egalitarian Justice," *Ethics*, vol. 99, 1989, esp. pp. 916–44, argues that Dworkin has misdescribed this crucial cut and that the correct one should be between choices and brute bad luck. This relocation does not have any serious implications for my argument below. For Dworkin's response to this criticism, see *Sovereign Virtue*, op. cit., pp. 287–99.

5   Dworkin, "Equality of Resources," op. cit., p. 310.

6   Ibid., pp. 333, 338.

7   Ibid., p. 289.

8   Ibid., p. 285.

9   Ibid.

10 "The Place of Liberty," op. cit., p. 18, n. 19.

11 This is what Dworkin calls "co-insurance" on p. 325 of "Equality of Resources," op. cit.

12 The classification of the objectivist approach as a theory of what constitutes for an individual an equal share of resources may be overlooked because Dworkin includes it in his treatment of equality of welfare. He points out, however, that this view is "a statement of equality of resources in the (misleading) language of welfare." See Dworkin's "What is Equality? Part 1: Equality of Welfare," *Philosophy and Public Affairs*, vol. 10, 1981, p. 226 (this article is also reprinted in *Sovereign Virtue*, op. cit.).

13 The objectivist theory of equality of resources has two attractive features. First of all, it avoids the difficulty of having to distribute extra resources to people with expensive tastes. Expensive tastes make this demand only if nonobjectivist standards for distribution are used. Others do not therefore have to carry the burden of those people's costly lives. Secondly, it secures the individual from interference by the government and other individuals. This is because no one has a stake in the preferences you actually have because those preferences do not determine your share of society's resources. See T. M. Scanlon, "The Significance of Choice," *The Tanner Lectures on Human Values* (Salt Lake City: University of Utah Press, 1988), vol. VIII, pp. 200–1.

14 "Equality of Resources," op. cit., pp. 285–7. I have in mind especially his arguments against (1) transforming all available resources into a stock of plover's eggs and claret, and (2) the divider creating bundles that will favor some tastes over others.

15   Ronald Dworkin, "Why Liberals Should Care About Equality," in *A Matter of Principle* (Cambridge, MA: Harvard University Press, 1985), p. 205.

16   John Rawls, *A Theory of Justice* (Cambridge, MA: Harvard University Press, 1971), p. 302.

17   Two others are the role of the original position and the emphasis on group rather than individual comparisons. See "Equality of Resources," op. cit., pp. 339–45.

18   Ibid., p. 343.

19   Ronald Dworkin, "Justice in the Distribution of Health Care," *McGill Law Journal*, vol. 38, 1993, pp. 883–98, and "Will Clinton's Plan be Fair?" *New York Review of Books*, January 13, 1994, pp. 20–5. The latter has been reprinted with slight revisions in *Sovereign Virtue*, op. cit., ch. 8.

20   See especially Charles Fried, "Rights and Health Care – Beyond Equity and Efficiency," *New England Journal of Medicine*, vol. 293, July 31, 1975, and *Right and Wrong* (Cambridge, MA: Harvard University Press, 1978).

21   Dworkin, "Will Clinton's Plan be Fair?" op. cit., p. 23. Note, however, that Dworkin qualifies this principle in what he regards as two minor respects: (1) some measures may be necessary to protect people from making imprudent choices, especially when they are young, (2) measures may be necessary to protect future generations. See ibid., p. 23 n. 12, and "Justice in the Distribution of Health Care," op. cit., pp. 889–90, n. 3.

22   See especially Dworkin, "Justice in the Distribution of Health Care," op. cit., p. 889.

23   Ibid., p. 893.

24   Ibid., pp. 891–2 and "Will Clinton's Plan be Fair?" op. cit., p. 23.

25   Dworkin has discussed at length decisions of this sort based on quality of life considerations in his *Life's Dominion* (New York: Alfred A. Knopf, 1993), chs. 3, 7–8.

26   Dworkin in an earlier paper applied the idea of ambition sensitivity to the issue of whether or not in a just society it is permissible to allow "private" medical insurance based on ability and willingness to pay that complements the health insurance coverage everyone enjoys. See "The Place of Liberty," op. cit., pp. 43–51.

27   He indicates sympathy with this idea, however, on p. 43, ibid.

28   This distinction can also be expressed in terms of restricted and unrestricted transfers. Unrestricted transfers are in cash while restricted transfers might involve either in-kind state provision or a voucher scheme. See Lester C. Thurrow, "Government Expenditure: Cash or In-kind Aid?" *Philosophy and Public Affairs*, vol. 5, 1976, p. 364.

29   To sustain the distinction between cash and in-kind transfers, it is absolutely essential that in-kind benefits not be exchangeable. See R. A. Musgrave and P. B. Musgrave, *Public Finance in Theory and Practice*, 3rd edn. (New York: McGraw-Hill, 1980), p. 103, n. 19.

30   Nicholas Barr, *The Economy of the Welfare State* (London: Weidenfeld and Nicolson, 1987), p. 97.

31   Thomas Schelling, "Economic Reasoning and the Ethics of Policy," *The Public Interest*, vol. 63, 1981, p. 60.

32   Barr, *The Economy of the Welfare State*, op. cit., p. 98.

33   See, for a similar claim, Steven Kelman, "A Case for In-kind Transfers," *Philosophy and Economics*, vol. 2, 1986, pp. 57–9.

34   Dworkin, "The Place of Liberty," op. cit., pp. 25, 28.

35   Of course, someone may say at this point in my argument that although everyone is not guaranteed access to a minimal standard of health care, everyone has the money to buy that standard of health care, *if they want it*. But this overlooks the fact that a policy of universal access to health care guarantees people that standard of health care, whether they want it or not. See also the discussion in section III.

36   J. Tobin, "On Limiting the Domain of Inequality," in E. S. Phelps (ed.), *Economic Justice* (London: Penguin, 1973), and Albert Weale, *Political Theory and Social Policy* (London: MacMillan, 1983), ch. 6.

37   The classic statement is Arthur Okun, *Equality and Efficiency: The Big Trade-off* (Washington, DC: The Brookings Institution, 1975).

38 Dworkin, "Why Efficiency?" in *A Matter of Principle*, op. cit., pp. 267–73.

39 See, for example, Pat and Hugh Armstrong with Claudia Fegan, *Universal Health Care: What the United States Can Learn From the Canadian Experience* (New York: The New Press, 1998).

40 Dworkin, "The Place of Liberty," op. cit., pp. 32–3. Note too that an important part of Dworkin's intro-duction of the idea of prudent insurers into the health care distribution debate is conditional on indi-vidual insurers not suffering from imperfect information or knowledge (see subsection "Dworkin's treatment of the issues" above).

41 Kenneth Arrow, "Uncertainty and the Welfare Economics of Medical Care," *American Economic Review*, vol. 53, 1963, pp. 946, 951, and esp. 965–6.

42 Cultural resources are, in my view, the sorts of resources that do give rise to this sort of information problem. The reason is that cultural resources tend to generate our ways of valuing and, therefore, it is difficult to understand how they themselves can be pure objects of valuation. The relevant contrast is to health care resources which do not generally generate our ways of valuing. Dworkin argues that cultural resources pose a problem for market pricing mechanisms for this reason in "Can a Liberal State Support Art?" in *A Matter of Principle*, op. cit., esp. pp. 228–30.

43 Dworkin, "Foundations of Liberal Equality," in Grethe Peterson (ed.), *The Tanner Lectures on Human Values*, vol. XI (Salt Lake City: University of Utah Press, 1990), p. 85.

44 See e.g., John Harris, "What is the Good of Health Care?" *Bioethics*, vol. 10, 1996, pp. 269–91, and "Justice and Equal Opportunities in Health Care," *Bioethics*, vol. 13, 1999, pp. 392–413; Thomas Pogge, *Realizing Rawls* (Ithaca, NY: Cornell University Press, 1989), pp. 181–96; and Robert Veatch, "Single Payers and Multiple Lists: Must Everyone Get the Same Coverage on a Universal Health Plan?" *Kennedy Institute of Ethics Journal*, vol. 17, 1997, pp. 153–69. I have scrutinized the views of these three in some depth in my book, *Pursuing Equal Opportunities: The Theory and Practice of Egalitarian Justice* (New York: Cambridge University Press/Cambridge Studies in Philosophy and Public Policy, 2003), ch. 7.

45 I have defended at length this claim in §7.2 of *Pursuing Equal Opportunities*.

9

Equality of Resources and Procreative Justice

Paula Casal and Andrew Williams

Procreation poses many important questions for moral and political philosophy. Ronald Dworkin's work on the ethical and legal status of abortion has explored some of those questions in characteristically creative style.[1] However, procreation raises further questions, which remain under-explored both by Dworkin and his contemporaries. In this chapter we address various issues that arise because procreative decisions can have beneficial or detrimental effects on nonconsenting third parties. Our aim is to understand how a resource egalitarian conception of distributive justice should evaluate those effects.

Though now relatively neglected, the detrimental effects of procreative decisions were once the subject of considerable debate among those interested in egalitarian conceptions of justice. Most famously, Thomas Malthus criticized collectivist egalitarians, like William Godwin, by claiming that their proposals were vulnerable to a fatal demographic counterargument.[2] According to that criticism, systems of equality, involving common ownership of resources and provision of welfare, face the following trilemma. Such schemes will either fail to check the standing tendency for population to grow more rapidly than the supply of resources, so leading to a continual decline in individual living standards. Or instead they will succeed in doing so, but only by either jeopardizing procreative liberty to an intolerable degree or by abandoning their own fundamental principles. Thus, on the basis of certain assumptions about fertility and scarcity, Malthus argued that prosperity, liberty, and equality could not be achieved jointly. Faced with the need to choose, he claimed his contemporaries should reject equality.

Because of the flawed empirical assumptions Malthus relied upon, a frequent response to his work is dismissive. We believe, however, that his concern with the relationship between fertility and egalitarianism remains of interest. To establish its importance, we shall explore not collectivist egalitarianism, but Dworkin's very different conception of *equality of resources*, in which private ownership plays a central role. We shall assume that individuals should be accorded a legal right to determine the size of their families free of penalties by the criminal law, and ask how the exercise of that right bears upon equality of resources. Having outlined the most salient aspects of that conception of equality, we proceed as follows.

First, we distinguish two types of effect which the production of children might generate, namely a positive and a negative externality, and then explain their relevance to one particular resourcist treatment of procreative justice. Second, considering the former effect, we examine the suggestion that, for reasons of fairness, the costs of reproduction should be borne not only by parents but also by nonparents who benefit from the public good of additional children. While accepting some distinct incentive arguments for socializing the costs of production of public goods that otherwise would be undersupplied, we cast doubt on the suggestion. Third, discussing the more morally urgent case of negative externalities, we argue that, when overpopulation threatens, resource egalitarianism ideally demands that individual parents bear the costs of their actions. Thus we suggest that procreative justice is asymmetric: very roughly, even if parents produce a public good, justice (as fairness), need not require their activity be subsidized, yet when their actions threaten a public bad, justice (as equality of resources) may require that they be taxed.

I Welfarist and Resourcist Egalitarianism

In a series of important articles, building upon attempts within economics to define a criterion of equity nonreliant on interpersonal comparisons of welfare, Dworkin has developed one of the leading liberal egalitarian conceptions of distributive justice.[3] We begin with the briefest sketch of that conception, a central aspect of which we then emphasize.

In developing his view, Dworkin criticizes *welfare equality* as a plausible ideal for justice in the distribution of privately owned *impersonal resources*, or "parts of the environment which can be owned and transferred," such as raw materials or manufactured goods.[4] On that view, justice requires that each set of resources devoted to individuals' lives is equal in value, in the following respect: with their set of resources, each owner either does, or could, achieve a similar level of personal success, estimated according to their own judgment of what renders their life valuable to them.[5] In opposition to welfare equality, Dworkin instead defends *liberal equality*, or *equality of resources*. According to that ideal, a just distribution of resources is one that could have emerged from a specific hypothetical process, involving individuals aware of their actual values and preferences. He then argues that three features of the process confer moral appeal upon its outcomes.

First, the process involves an auction over private ownership rights in impersonal resources for which individuals have equal purchasing power. And second, within that auction lots are divided in a way that is maximally sensitive to the preferences of the participants. Because of these two features, Dworkin suggests, the distribution resulting from the auction will, in important respects, escape both *unfairness* and *arbitrariness*. Thus, since symmetrically situated in the bidding process, on completion of the auction no individual will prefer any other individual's share of resources. Furthermore, envy will have been eliminated through a process in which each individual plays an equal role, and no individuals are able to rig the outcome to suit their particular values.

Despite these merits, Dworkin recognizes that the resulting distribution might still suffer from a further form of injustice if some individuals suffer from brute bad luck in their *personal resources*, or "qualities of mind and body that affect people's success in achieving their plans and projects," such as "physical and mental health, strength and talent."[6] For example, the congenitally disabled might still prefer the capabilities of the able-bodied, or, once production and trade are possible, the less talented might prefer the greater access to impersonal resources enjoyed by the more talented. To remedy this distinct defect, the hypothetical process involves a third important feature, a fair insurance market. Within it, individuals – aware of their ambitions and the distribution of good and bad luck but ignorant of their personal fortune or vulnerability – are able to purchase cover against inequalities in their circumstances arising from brute bad luck. Thus, even if the hypothetical process does not fully eliminate envy, it will involve a mechanism for redistribution between fortune's victims and beneficiaries, the extent of which will depend on the aggregate operation of the insurance market.

To appreciate more fully the dissimilarity between the two ideals previously sketched, note the different ways in which welfare and resource egalitarians relate the two fundamental aspects of an individual's life that Dworkin refers to as *personality* and *circumstance*. The former term desig-nates individuals' reflective convictions about, and preferences for, their own good, while the latter encompasses those conditions that they conceive to advance or to limit their own good, either instrumentally or intrinsically.[7] Personality, then, is manifest in individuals' conative states – provided they do not prefer their absence – such as taste, ambition, attachment, and preference, while circumstance, in contrast, encompasses at least individuals' impersonal and personal resources. Hence a diver's passion for exploring submarine landscapes, for example, is an aspect of his or her personality, which renders that individual's diving gear and fitness, respectively, important impersonal and personal resources.

In calculating the value of the circumstance an individual occupies, welfare equality focuses upon the relation between that circumstance and the individual's own personality. Thus, in deter-mining when distinct individuals' circumstances are equal in value, welfarists ask how much welfare they actually, or could, derive from those circumstances, given their specific personalities. For them, whether circumstances are equal depends only on whether individuals do, or could, enjoy equal welfare. The costs in terms of foregone resources to others of them doing so is con-sidered irrelevant to the requirements of equality, since those individuals are not regarded as enti-tled to resources as such, but only insofar as they contribute to their welfare.

Such a thought, however, is alien to resource egalitarianism. As Dworkin continually empha-sizes, it requires that the value of resources devoted to each life be equalized in a manner that depends on their value not only to their owners but to nonowners. Its ideal achievement demands, among other things, that nobody attaches a higher value to another's resources than to their own, but is quite consistent with some failing to attain similar levels of personal success to others. Thus, in calculating the value of the economic circumstances an individual occupies, liberal equality focuses on the relation between those circumstances and others' personalities. The extent of that value depends not on the welfare prospect of its occupant, but rather on the *opportunity costs* borne by nonoccupants, measured in terms of how much they would bid for those circumstances in the hypothetical auction. Their value is no greater that of other individuals' circumstances only if they would pay no more for them than for their own.

Dworkin has frequently stressed that the relation between one's circumstance and others' per-sonalities plays a more central role in his view than in its welfare egalitarian rival. For example, he writes,

> Under equality of welfare, people are meant to decide what sorts of life they want independently of information relevant to determining how much their choices will reduce or enhance the ability of others to have what they want . . . Under equality of resources, however, *people decide what sorts of life to pursue against a background of information about the actual cost their choices impose upon other people and hence on the total stock of resources that may fairly be used by them.*[8]

Thus, the achievement of distributive justice requires that each individual can become, as Dworkin puts it, ". . . someone who forms his ambitions with a sense of their cost to others against some presumed initial equality of economic power."[9] In the following sections we attempt to estab-lish what implications, if any, this aspect of liberal equality has for the ambition to procreate.

II   Resource Egalitarianism and Procreation

To do so, we return to the desert island scenario that Dworkin usefully employs to illustrate the market process favored by liberal equality. Describing it, he asks us to

[s]uppose a number of shipwreck survivors are washed up on a desert island which has abundant resources and no native population, and any rescue is many years away. These immigrants accept the principle that no one is antecedently entitled to any of these resources, but that they shall instead be divided equally among them.[10]

In applying that principle Dworkin suggests the immigrants would be concerned to eliminate envy, to combat arbitrariness and to compensate for brute bad luck, and so would attempt to implement, or mimic, the auction-insurance scheme sketched above.

Now let us complicate the initial scenario by imagining not merely the production and exchange of manufactured goods, but human reproduction. Suppose that, having implemented the auction-insurance scheme, different groups of immigrants then produce children at varying rates and that their doing so reflects differences in their personalities rather than their circumstances.[11] For example, none are driven by a parental or sexual craving they repudiate, and there is no variation in individual couples' capability to conceive, or vulnerability to unwanted pregnancy, which gives rise to any preference for others' personal resources. Thus, parenthood is not a condition that calls for compensation at some level to be calculated according to the hypothetical insurance market.

Instead the variation in fertility has its origins within individual personality and option luck. It arises because of diversity in individuals' desire to procreate, or willingness to risk procreation as an unintended consequence of sexual activity. Some immigrants decide upon a life with many children because of, for instance, their religious beliefs or their enjoyment of the delights and challenges of parenthood. Others aim for fewer or no children, because of their convictions about the grave and daunting moral responsibilities of parenthood or their valuing alternative forms of human creativity to a greater degree. Given a resource egalitarian concern that "people decide what sorts of life to pursue against a background of information about the actual cost their choices impose upon other people," we might now wish to ask how they should conceive those costs and attempt to ensure their just distribution.

In addressing those questions we shall also assume that the immigrants would aim to ensure that the impersonal resources devoted to the lives of newly born islanders be of no less value than those enjoyed by the previous generation, with whom they will interact and form a political community.[12] Had those newcomers arrived by accident rather than by design at different times then there would be weighty egalitarian reasons against giving latecomers fewer initial resources when a more egalitarian distribution is attainable. We presume then that the newly born might object to anything less than equality on similar grounds. Such a presumption is debatable, but without powerful opposing reasons, seems warranted.[13] The immigrants' aim, therefore, is a natural application of their commitment to equality of resources.

If this assumption is granted, then acting on a desire for children may produce effects on third parties that are strikingly different from those associated with many other ambitions. For example, if after the auction one group of entrepreneurial immigrants decides to invest their own resources in a risky commercial venture then, even if it fails, their undertaking it will not require a reduction in the share of resources legitimately available to others. However, provided the total stock of resources available for distribution does not increase with the addition of further children, the same need not be true if the group decides instead to reproduce. To consider the matter starkly, suppose that couples within the former group each produce four children, while the remaining immigrants forego parenthood. If so, and total resources remain constant, then, even if each couple divides their resources among their offspring on reaching maturity, those children may still prefer the resources enjoyed by members of the former group. Thus an equal share of resources can be secured for them only if the share of those who remained childless is diminished. If we grant the previous assumption, then those childless islanders are required to relinquish some of their resources, not because of their own choices but those of others.

The previous example possesses an important further feature. Recall that the addition of extra children did not increase the stock of resources available for distribution to an extent that maintained its size per capita.[14] That feature is important, since if the contrary were the case, and procreation always did so, then it would be less pressing to ask about the extent to which some individuals can be required to bear the economic costs of others' children. However, unfortunately for both the immigrants and humanity, that feature is not unrealistic. Population growth under some realistic conditions will lead not only to diminished per capita resource availability in the short term, but also greater pollution and depletion of nonrenewable resources in the long run.[15] Nevertheless it is important to remember that under other conditions procreation will possess the benign consequence it elsewhere lacks. For children, as many have observed, need not be simply a form of consumption for their parents. They may also be a form of investment, which, via the creation of human capital, enhances the stock of resources available for distribution in a way preferable not only to their parents but to others. For example, on maturity they may ensure that the initial generation of immigrants enjoys a level of goods and services that otherwise would have been unavailable. Moreover, population growth might also stimulate technological changes, or facilitate economies of scale, which enable the immigrants to use the finite natural resources available to them more efficiently.

Thus, depending on initial conditions, the arrival of further children may have very different aggregative implications on the total stock of resources available for egalitarian distribution. We shall, therefore, assume that procreative acts, like other forms of production or consumption, may possess both *negative* and *positive externalities*. They may confer either costs or benefits upon nonproducers that arrive without their consent and are not intended by the agent(s) producing them.[16] Before elucidating the present relevance of this distinction, we turn to the question of how the immigrants might ensure that newly born islanders enjoy an equal share of resources. We begin with a suggestion made by Eric Rakowski in his attempt to develop a theory of distributive justice, termed *equality of fortune*, broadly inspired by equality of resources.[17]

III   Equality of Fortune

Rakowski's suggestion contrasts two methods whereby the immigrants might attempt to ensure that each newly born islander receives an equal share.[18] According to the first method, *universal provision*, each islander contributes, while on the latter, *parental provision*, the requirement to do so is confined to those responsible for the new individual's existence.

Rakowski forcefully argues that the first proposal is vulnerable to a decisive objection. He writes:

> If new people just appeared in the world from time to time, like fresh boatloads of unwitting settlers, and did not owe their birth to the actions of present members of society, then the foregoing principles [i.e. of universal provision] would come into play. But babies are not brought by storks whose whims are beyond our control. Specific individuals are responsible for their existence. It is therefore unjust to declare . . . that because two people decide to have a child, or through carelessness find themselves with one, *everyone* is required to share their resources with the new arrival, and to the same extent as its parents.[19]

Posing the following challenge he immediately adds,

> With what right can two people force all the rest, through deliberate behavior rather than brute bad luck, to settle for less than their fair shares after resources have been divided justly? If the cultivation of expensive tastes, or silly gambles, or any other intentional action cannot give rise to redistributive claims, how can procreation?

Rakowski's remarks may persuade some proponents of universal provision to pause, but they are not as decisive as they first appear.[20] His objection rests, we shall argue, on a minor premise that his opponent need not accept.[21]

According to that premise, as Rakowski himself states it, if universal provision is instituted then each immigrant "is required to share their resources with the new arrival" in a way that forces them to "settle for less than their fair shares after resources have been divided justly." Our previous remarks about the positive external effects of procreation, however, suggest that universal provision need not involve such a requirement. For an expansion in the island's population could, through the various mechanisms mentioned, increase the total resources available for redistribution. Furthermore, it could do so to such an extent that each individual would prefer the set of resources associated with the expansion compared with the set that they would otherwise have held.[22] If that were in fact the case, then even if the childless were required through compulsory taxation to contribute to the production of human capital, in the form of others' children, then their being made to do so would not jeopardize their initial share of resources. In such fortunate circumstances those children's parents could credibly claim that they, as Locke's original appropriators might remark in their defense, do "not lessen but increase the common stock of mankind."[23]

Thus, even if the advocates of universal provision were to grant Rakowski's major premise – that no individuals be forced to accept less than they would have enjoyed in an equal initial division – they need not concede his objection without considering the extent to which procreation exhibits a positive externality. To appreciate such a possibility, consider the following analogy. If one islander burns vegetation on her property, and the ash deposited on her neighbors' land makes it more productive, then they cannot automatically reject her request to supply resources to clean her property, or condemn her seizing such resources, *on the ground that doing so would diminish their initial share of resources.* Whether they can in fact do so will depend upon possibly complex counterfactuals about the resources they would have enjoyed without her activity, and their preferences regarding them.

Before proceeding to express agreement with other aspects of Rakowski's position, we first attempt to explain why he does not anticipate the previous reply to his objection, despite the fact that he recognizes population growth might be claimed to produce positive externalities. Such is the case, we conjecture, because he envisages the advocates of universal provision appealing to those externalities as a defense of their position rather than as merely a rebuttal of his objection. Believing that such an appeal is ill-equipped to serve the former purpose, Rakowski implicitly infers that it cannot play the latter more modest role. That inference, however, is invalid. The mere fact that population growth is universally advantageous does not, as we shall later argue, establish an enforceable requirement for all its beneficiaries to contribute something to its production. Nevertheless, it may suffice, as we have already shown, to establish that the requirement is not as costly to others as Rakowski supposes, and therefore perhaps unobjectionable on resource egalitarian grounds.

To confirm this conjecture, consider how Rakowski treats the appeal to positive externalities, which he states as follows: "One might try to argue that because additional persons will in time benefit people other than their parents, *everyone ought to contribute to the stock of resources to which those additional persons are entitled*; it would be unjust to allow them to profit without paying the price."[24] Clearly then, as the italicized phrase suggests, he envisages the appeal constituting what we have termed a defense rather than a rebuttal. Insofar as he undermines it only in the former guise, our reply to his objection retains force.

To assess whether that is the case, note how Rakowski dismisses the relevance of positive externalities to his position. He does so by arguing that,

> ... externalities of this sort rarely seem significant, and in any event parents and siblings are apt to be by far the major beneficiaries. It is highly questionable, furthermore, whether one person may compel another to pay for a benefit the latter did not request. If A landscapes B's yard while B is away on holiday and then demands that B pay him for his trouble, even though B never agreed to pay, then A has no legal right to payment. Nor does he appear to have a moral claim.[25]

The bulk of this statement leaves our objection untouched. In his initial remark about the probability and distribution of procreative externalities, however, Rakowski does challenge not only one defense of universal provision but also our rebuttal of his objection. The challenge, however, lacks force for at least two reasons. First, it does not question the occurrence on some occasions of significant externalities, but only their frequency. Yet this is inadequate to warrant the constant opposition to universal provision that Rakowski's statements express. Second, his doubts about the frequency of positive externalities require some empirical support but receive none, and for that reason are unpersuasive. Our suggestion that an advocate of universal provision might reject the minor premise of Rakowski's argument, therefore, remains intact.

IV   Procreation and the Appeal to Fairness

From the previous discussion of one treatment of procreative justice we may conclude that whether the production of children is accompanied by positive or negative external effects upon a community's stock of resources has moral relevance to the demands of justice. The presence of the former may suffice to establish that procreators are not akin to polluters, who can justly be required to compensate those whose resources diminish in value because of their activity. Some, though as we saw not Rakowski, argue for a more ambitious conclusion.[26] According to them justice demands that, where procreation generates a sufficiently large nonexcludable positive externality, the economic burden of producing children should be shared. It should, for reasons of fairness, be borne by all those who willingly benefit from those children's existence, rather than solely by those responsible for it.

In this section we turn to criticize that suggestion, which is commonly voiced by, among others, those who fear the long-term effects of population decline on current adults within the developed industrial economies.[27] Before describing the suggestion in greater detail, it is important to note that it need not be animated by any such fear, for it appeals to a principle of justice rather than merely efficiency.[28] Thus it does not possess the following form, familiar from economic arguments for the collective provision of public goods. According to that type of argument, if at least some of the benefits of additional children are nonexcludable, while their financial costs are considerable, then there is a danger of the good being undersupplied. Intervention is then warranted if it changes the structure of incentives facing potential procreators in a way that improves everyone's prospects. We shall not discuss such arguments further, but suppose that they could be accommodated within liberal equality since their form has been endorsed by Dworkin in dealing with the provision of other public goods, and some transaction cost problems.[29]

Instead, the argument we are about to consider applies even if there is no risk of undersupply. It might be voiced by immigrants who are confident that sufficient individuals will choose to become parents, but nevertheless are unsure whether those parents should be left to bear the full costs of feeding, clothing, and educating their children out of their fair share of resources, or should instead be the beneficiaries of subsidies or tax allowances. Furthermore, it is also important to emphasize that the argument is not animated by a concern for the interests of children themselves. It is consistent with such a concern, which quite appropriately should possess great weight in actual societies, where economic inequality abounds, and no perfect mechanism exists to ensure that the just level of transfer between parents and their children takes place. But the argument still applies even if there is no risk that children will receive an unjust initial share of resources when individuals other than their parents are not required to contribute to it.

As we initially mentioned, a principle of fairness, rather than attention to either inefficiency or vulnerability, grounds the present argument for universal provision. To understand its source consider Rawls's widely discussed statement of one such principle, according to which,

> a person is required to do his part as defined by the rules of an institution when two conditions are met: first, the institution is just (or fair), that is, it satisfies the two principles of justice; and second, one has voluntarily accepted the benefits of the arrangement or taken advantage of the opportunities it offers to further one's interests.

Explaining its intuitive rationale, Rawls adds,

> The main idea is that when a number of persons engage in a mutually advantageous cooperative venture according to rules, and thus restrict their liberty in ways necessary to yield advantages to all, those who have submitted to these restrictions have a right to similar acquiescence on the part of those who have benefited from their submission. We are not to gain from the cooperative labors of others without doing our fair share.[30]

What then are the implications of fairness, thus conceived, for the choice between universal and parental provision facing Dworkin's immigrants?

An advocate of the former proposal, inspired by Rawls's principle of fairness, might advance the following argument for child allowances or parental tax exemptions. The initial distribution of resources is *ex hypothesi* fair. Furthermore, additional children create a positive externality that those with few or no children willingly enjoy, and would be prepared to pay for if, as is in fact not the case, they would otherwise be excluded from it. Yet the production of those children, let alone guaranteeing them a fair initial share of resources, has financial costs for their parents, who, since they cannot acquire ownership rights in their children, receive no return for bearing those costs. Thus, other things being equal, they will enjoy a lesser share of resources than those who have fewer children. Under such circumstances, it is unfair for the latter to contribute nothing to the production costs of children from whom they benefit. They should, therefore, be required to share those costs through universal provision via child allowances or tax exemptions.

The previous argument, we suggest, has some force. Furthermore, it actually is invoked, in a rough form, by many who argue that the costs of producing further children should be socialized because their benefits cannot be internalized. For example, Rolf George condemns what he describes as the *imbalance* between parental burdens and nonparental benefits by appealing, among other considerations, to a principle of fairness.[31] Stressing the nonexcludable positive externalities they generate, he writes:

> Children grow up and become, among other things, providers of pensions. They are, or should be, free agents, but they are also production goods, capital investments. They cost a substantial sum to produce. Now since they are free agents, escaping thus the control of their investors, they become *res omnia*, benefit everyone. Who should reap the benefits they have to dispense?[32]

George then proceeds to draw a comparison, clearly intended to be forceful, in which appeal to a principle of fairness is implicit. He asks us to

> [i]magine a group of people who get together to build a dam, or some other public project. Now suppose that the benefits of the dam are turned over, without compensation, to those who did *not* help build it. Not only that, they are given those benefits precisely *because* they did not help. Would this not be unjust? In what does this injustice differ from the imbalance? I suggest there is no relevant difference. The imbalance is unjust . . .[33]

We now turn to ask how much force such an appeal actually possesses. Should liberal equality endorse Rawls's principle of fairness, and if so, does it secure George's conclusion?

The former question is the subject of considerable debate, since the principle has been subject to frequent criticism.[34] Referring to it under a different name, and echoing one of Robert Nozick's notorious objections, Dworkin himself has written that,

> the fair play argument assumes that *people can incur obligations simply by receiving what they do not seek and would reject if they had the chance.* This seems unreasonable. Suppose a philosopher broadcasts a stunning and valuable lecture from a sound truck. Do all those who hear it – even all those who enjoy and profit from it – owe him a lecture fee?[35]

The appeal to fairness stated above, however, need not possess the italicized feature which Nozick and Dworkin – arguably incorrectly – find present in Rawls's view. Thus, even if their objection is acceptable, it is inapplicable, since the above argument assumed that individuals would prefer population growth even if they were required partly to finance it.

Suppose then that the appeal to fairness survives the Nozickian challenge rehearsed by Dworkin. Its critics might rather pursue another libertarian route, mentioned by Rakowski, which asserts that an actual request is necessary in order to generate an enforceable obligation toward one's beneficiaries. But since the price of such pursuit is, among other things, the rejection of the principle of fairness in any form, we shall adopt a more economical strategy. It suggests that, even if the principle, modified to escape Dworkin's remarks, is plausible, it will not sustain universal provision as its conclusion.

To understand why the inference from principle to conclusion is invalid, note that the principle concerns a very specific class of positive externalities. It does *not* claim that individuals are required to contribute to the costs of producing *any* spillovers from which they benefit, even if they would be willing to pay the requisite price. Such a claim, which renders all such externalities the source of corresponding enforceable obligations, would be highly implausible. Instead the principle concerns nonexcludable goods that are produced by *cooperative activity* in which individuals *bear some cost*, which they would not otherwise bear, *in order to produce the good*. Thus both the intentions of, and the costs borne by, producers of public goods are central to the appeal of the principle of fairness. It condemns those who take advantage of such individuals rather than simply those who freely enjoy goods for which they would be prepared to pay.

If the previous diagnosis of the attraction of the principle of fairness is plausible, then merely enjoying the beneficial consequences of others' procreative activities need not violate the principle. Such is the case for at least two reasons. First, the production of those externalities is consistent with a wide range of parental motivation. For example, in having children, parents might not aim to produce those effects either by themselves or as part of a cooperative venture. Instead they might have those children regardless of others' cooperation, or whether a positive or even negative externality resulted from their decision.[36] Second, in describing the immigrants we assumed that those who chose to procreate did so because it advanced their own well-being, or that of their loved ones. Furthermore, that assumption was not an extravagant one to make about either fictional parents or most actual parents. In such circumstances, we conclude, the principle of fairness is unsuitable as a defense of universal provision.[37]

Admittedly, however, the moral significance of procreation might differ in other circumstances. Suppose, for example, the immigrants resemble members of an endangered tribe who feel morally bound to reproduce, perhaps at considerable costs to themselves as individuals, to ensure continuity of their community. Although an appeal to the principle of fairness might have more force in such circumstances, they are nevertheless very different from the imaginary or actual conditions we address. For, as George himself stresses, developments in advanced economies "have left for most people only one motivation for having children (when children are intentionally conceived), namely, the expected gratifications of parenthood. These may range from the enjoyment of infant cuteness to pride in the children's achievements to such things as the perpetuation of a name or keeping wealth or a business in the family, etc."[38] But, he goes on, "it is absurd to suppose, that people have children in order to give those who have none a more comfortable retirement."

In thus characterizing parenthood, George himself supplies a morally relevant difference that damages the comparison to which he appeals. Presumably the labor performed by the workers in his dam-building example, unlike that of parents on his own admission, was both arduous and undergone as a means to produce certain beneficial consequences. Had those consequences been a pleasant surprise, which followed an enjoyable physical activity, one would regard an appeal to some principle of fairness on their behalf very differently. So, even if we grant that such workers suffer an injustice when they receive fewer benefits from their toil than nonworkers, little follows in the quite dissimilar procreative case.

George's example, however, does suggest a convenient means of introducing the issue to which we now turn. Modifying it, let us suppose that instead of some public good, the builders' labor threatens to produce some negative externality, such as flooding or loss of productivity in adjacent land, the price of which consequently diminishes. Should those landowners be compensated by the builders for such a loss? Or should they instead be expected to bear it, and even pay the builders for their unsolicited and harmful construction? In the following section we ask analogous questions about procreation.

V   Internalizing the Effects of Procreation

Those questions arise since, as we have already mentioned, under some circumstances the addition of new members to a society may, on balance, diminish rather than improve the circumstances of some previously existing members. Such burdens might involve the following: a reduction in the per capita share of both privately and publicly owned natural resources (mineral reserves, energy sources, fisheries, forests, etc.); an increase in pollution, crowding, noise, and environmental problems; an excess supply of labor and thus increased unemployment; and greater demand for public health and education.[39] Our remaining remarks address the implications of resource egalitarianism in such circumstances.

Clearly the presence, extent, and distribution of many such burdens will depend greatly on the institutional background adopted by a society. Laissez-faire institutions, for example, might leave the funding of children's education to the discretion of parents or charities, in which case reproduction would lead to a lesser diminution in others' resources than might otherwise be the case. More interventionist institutions, however, would confer upon children an enforceable entitlement to education, thereby producing such a burden. Nevertheless such institutions could exhibit important variations in how they distributed such burdens. Some, like many existing welfare states, might require each taxpayer to share the child's educational expenses, thus subsidizing the ambitions of parents at the expense of those with no or fewer children. Others might adopt J. S. Mill's position and, insofar as circumstances allow, legally require the cost to be borne by parents, providing educational subsidies only to the poor.[40]

As this case illustrates, the character of specific background institutions will affect whether procreation has negative externalities or whether instead its costs are internalized. Thus children will generate an externality in a welfare state. However, provided no parents are too poor to finance the required transfers to their children, they need not do so in a Millian society. We assume that in a resource egalitarian society no parents would, through brute bad luck, suffer such impoverished circumstances. The question then is whether the background institutions of such an egalitarian society should, in addition, ensure that the effects of procreation are internalized or whether they would rather permit parents to produce negative externalities.

Suppose, for example, that one immigrant couple have a single child, while their neighbors produce six. Should the former subsidize the education and health care for the larger family, bear the greater environmental costs they generate, and, moreover, perhaps relinquish a portion of their wealth to ensure that each new inhabitant eventually enjoys an equal share of resources across his or her life?

Some of Dworkin's remarks, quoted earlier, suggest that resource egalitarians should resist such a proposal for the following reason. They, unlike welfare egalitarians, believe that a just society's institutions, and in particular its price system, should ensure that "people decide what sorts of life to pursue against a background of information about the actual cost their choices impose upon other people and hence on the total stock of resources that may fairly be used by them."[41] Institutions that are not designed to internalize, to any degree, the negative effects of procreation will not ensure that potential parents are aware of the costs to others of them enlarging their society. Thus, just as in actual societies the environmental costs of many products are not reflected in the market prices paid by their consumers, the true opportunity costs to others' resources of reproduction may be masked to parents. As already mentioned, discrepancies such as these may be morally significant if they result in inefficient outcomes.[42] But they are not of concern to resource egalitarians *only* if they do so. For equality of resources itself may be jeopardized if individual shares are not protected from diminution as a result of others' expensive ambitions. Given such a possibility, we provisionally conclude that resource egalitarians have at least a defeasible reason to ensure that the costs generated by additional children are not completely socialized but, at least to some degree, internalized. Only by doing so can individuals form their parental ambitions in the manner considered appropriate by Dworkin, namely "with a sense of their cost to others against some presumed initial equality of economic power."[43] Such a conclusion, however, might meet with a number of critical responses, two of which we address in our remaining remarks.

The first such response denies that institutions that socialize the costs of children jeopardize equality even if they diminish individuals' per capita share of impersonal resources. It claims that equality of resources is preserved, provided that such institutions allocate the burdens equally and the distribution of resources remains envy-free. Thus it is perfectly consistent with ideal justice, construed as equality of resources, that some bear the economic costs of others' procreative ambitions. Although some resource egalitarians might welcome this suggestion, there are good reasons to doubt that it is available to them. The suggestion supposes that the maintenance of envy-freedom is sufficient to preserve equality of resources. But, as we have already seen, the elimination of envy is only one aspect of that ideal. Some other components, we now argue, render negative procreative externalities more problematic.

Suppose, for a counterexample to the first response, that some immigrants, inspired by the Easter Islanders, propose a compulsory head tax in order to create a fund that subsidizes sculpture, making viewing and production available to all in public places and studios. With some provisos soon to be discussed, we assume that Dworkin's view opposes such a proposal, on the grounds that it would unjustly deprive other immigrants of resources that are rightfully theirs. In this respect it resembles the welfare egalitarian's view that more privately owned resources should be awarded to finance the ambitions of those with expensive tastes. It differs merely because in depriving some of their privately owned resources it does not transfer those same ownership rights to other individuals. Rather it converts them into publicly owned resources earmarked for a specific purpose, thereby preserving envy-freedom while still favoring the ambitions of sculptors over nonsculptors.

As noted earlier, Dworkin objects to the egalitarian welfarist view by, among other things, describing the case of Louis, who contemplates acquiring certain expensive tastes, for instance, for fine food, opera, or skiing. Here, Dworkin claims, egalitarian justice demands only that,

> Louis has a choice. He may choose to keep the presently equal resources I said he had, and settle for a life with the enjoyment he now has but without the tastes and ambitions he proposes to cultivate. Or he may keep his present resources and settle for a life that *he* deems more successful overall than his present life, but one that contains less enjoyment.[44]

Nevertheless, he immediately insists,

> It is quite unfair that he should have a third choice, that he should be able, at the expense of others, to lead a life that is more expensive than theirs at no sacrifice in enjoyment to himself just because he would, quite naturally, consider *that* life a more successful life overall than either of the other two.

In respect of the latter type of choice, we suggest resource egalitarians have reason to treat individuals contemplating having children similarly. Thus, though potential parents should be allowed to decide whether or not to increase family size, some injustice exists if resources are redistributed from others to their offspring as a result of their reproductive decision. Transfers to the latter, in the case without positive procreative externalities presently under consideration, should ideally take place at the expense of only their parents' share of resources and should not impinge upon others.[45]

We noted earlier, however, the provisional nature of the above resource egalitarian objection to the public provision of a good such as sculpture. We now briefly explain why such an objection is provisional, namely because Dworkin acknowledges that there are at least two legitimate reasons for intervention even in egalitarian market processes. The former arises from a *derivative* concern with persons' interests, while the latter stems from a *detached* concern with the achievement of certain impersonal goods, which Dworkin terms *intrinsically* valuable. Even if each reason has force in relation to some other activities, we shall suggest that in neither case do such considerations support subsidies to procreation.

Consider first the derivative argument. In addressing the question "Can a Liberal State Support Art?" Dworkin has replied affirmatively, at least where doing so is necessary in order to preserve individuals' awareness of the complex and diverse forms of life open to them.[46] Thus, under appropriate circumstances, public funding of sculpture would not unjustly deprive some people of resources they legitimately hold. Suppose that conclusion is granted. It is surely implausible to think that the concern to sustain a diverse cultural environment could support a similar conclusion about procreation. Though it might become still more expensive, such an entrenched and familiar form of life as parenthood is unlikely, in the foreseeable future, to slip from public awareness in the same way as the endangered cultural structures Dworkin has in mind. Does the detached argument fare any better than the derivative argument as a means to exempt procreators from the presumption that individuals should bear the costs of their own ambitions?[47]

More recently, in *Life's Dominion*, Dworkin suggests that it can be legitimate for the state to protect certain objects of cultural or environmental value not (merely) because of their contribution to the well-being of particular individuals but due to their intrinsic worth.[48] Perhaps there are circumstances under which such an argument might be extended to procreation. Imagine, to take extreme instances, that the continued flourishing of either humanity itself or of some specific human community is intrinsically valuable, and can be secured only by reproductive subsidies funded by compulsory taxation. If subsidization of art or nature does not compromise equality of resources, as Dworkin's suggestion implies, then why does that of human reproduction do so, even where it diminishes the size of per capita resources?

A full treatment of this important question must await another day. It would address whether resource egalitarianism can coherently leave sufficient moral space for the collective pursuit of cultural and environmental goods on grounds other than the correction of market failure or the achievement of informed choice against a background of diversity. Even without such a treatment, however, there is a more immediate reason to be skeptical, namely the fact that, under foreseeable conditions, the quantity of impersonal goods produced by procreators is not about to fall below any morally significant threshold. Here apparently we concur with Dworkin's previously noted observation that "it is a general assumption throughout the world that overpopulation is a more serious threat than underpopulation."[49] Since the detached argument fares no better, we conclude the provisos on our earlier assumption do not undermine its significance.

VI   Tolerating Externalities

It remains necessary to describe and evaluate a second response to the conclusion that institutions that externalize the costs of children jeopardize equality. It claims that to internalize those costs risks jeopardizing equality to an even greater degree. Requiring high procreators to shoulder such burdens would produce unacceptable inequalities in the circumstances of children from small and large families, since it would be beyond the means of many parents with numerous offspring to ensure that they did not prefer some other children's circumstances. For example, parental income and wealth might be insufficiently large to eliminate envy.[50] Moreover, even if parents could obtain sufficient impersonal resources by choosing to work for longer hours, or in less desirable positions, that might itself disadvantage their offspring in some other no less morally relevant respect. Therefore, the second response concludes, governments with a genuine concern for equality should tolerate the existence of procreative externalities.

It is noteworthy that the second response does not reject our central claim that the achievement of *ideal* justice requires the absence of negative procreative externalities. The response merely warns that even greater evils will arise if steps are taken to eliminate such an imperfection. Such a view is quite consistent, for there is no logical difficulty in claiming that a society that socializes the costs of children is *in one way* unjust, while conceding that one that refused to do so might display an even greater injustice.

For illustration, compare G. A. Cohen's treatment of Rawls's difference principle, which forcefully argues that Rawlsians should recognize the injustice of certain types of incentive-generating inequality.[51] It does so on roughly the ground that such inequalities would not be required if the ethos characteristic of a truly just society was widespread. Individuals would then be animated by nonenforceable egalitarian norms in their occupational choices, as well as their political decisions, and so large incentive payments would not be necessary to improve the expectations of the least advantaged. In this respect, Cohen suggests, many actual incentives resemble ransom payments, for they reward actions the performance of which is required rather than optional, and would be forthcoming if each individual fully complied with the demands of justice.

Nevertheless, Cohen acknowledges, the judgment that an incentive-generating inequality is unjust is quite consistent with conceding that, all things considered, such an inequality should not be eliminated. Indeed, as he explains, overall justice itself may mandate its preservation. Thus,

> One might say, to a child's guardian: the kidnapper is unjustly threatening the safety of the child, and justice to the child therefore demands that you pay him. And one might say, to legislators in a structurally unequal society: the talented are unjustly indifferent to the plight of the poor, and justice to the poor therefore demands that you do not impose very high taxation.[52]

Since we have not so far suggested how, all things considered, resource egalitarian institutions should respond to individuals whose reproductive decisions threaten others' resources, we could address the second response to our argument similarly.

So, echoing Cohen, we might say to legislators in a society where some parents are unjustly indifferent to the effects on others of their procreative decisions, that justice to their children demands that they not be taxed more highly. To do so, however, need not exempt those parents from criticism at the bar of egalitarian justice. The fact that requiring others to share the costs of their procreative ambitions is the lesser of two evils does not render their conduct just, any more than capitulating with a ransom demand concedes the legitimacy of kidnapping. Nor need it preclude attempts to create an ethos inhospitable to their indifference, which might diminish its incidence in the long term.

Indeed, J. S. Mill himself recognized the latter possibility. Responding to Malthusian fears about a collectivist egalitarian regime's tendency to overpopulation, he writes:

> There would certainly be much ground for this apprehension if Communism provided no motives to restraint, equivalent to those which it would take away. But Communism is precisely the state of things in which opinion might be expected to declare itself with greatest intensity against this kind of selfish intemperance. Any augmentation of numbers which diminished the comfort or increased the toil of the mass, would then cause (which now it does not) immediate and unmistakable inconvenience to every individual in the association . . . In such altered circumstances opinion could not fail to reprobate, and if reprobation did not suffice, to repress by penalties of some description, this or any other culpable self-indulgence at the expense of the community.[53]

While he does not recommend the "penalties" this passage appears to condone, it is worth noting that a concern with aspects of the moral environment is present in Dworkin's work as well as that of Mill.

Thus, examining the famous Supreme Court decision in *Roe v. Wade*, he concludes:

> States do have a legitimate interest in regulating decisions its citizens make about abortion. It was mysterious, in *Roe* and other judicial decisions, what that interest was, but we have identified it as the legitimate interest in maintaining a moral environment in which decisions about life and death are taken seriously and treated as matters of moral gravity.[54]

Although here Dworkin aims to ensure only that individuals make decisions in a spirit sensitive to their gravity, rather than to encourage specific choices, it is clear he recognizes that a society may be deficient in its mores as well as its legislation and governmental policies. It appears that he would not reject attempts to secure an ethos inhospitable to indifference on the ground that public institutions, rather than individual sentiments, are the appropriate objects of political concern.

We conclude then that, even if the second response is correct in suggesting that the enforced elimination of negative externalities will produce even greater injustices, our previous observations still possess philosophical importance, and may be relevant to practice.[55] For the response does not even engage with the central theoretical claim that such externalities jeopardize ideal justice, understood as equality of resources. Furthermore, the response does not undermine attempts to create an ethos fostering responsibility in the exercise of procreative liberty. If resource egalitarians now take such proposals more seriously than they otherwise would, then our task for the moment is complete.

Acknowledgement

For helpful discussion of this paper we thank Arthur Applbaum, Hilda Bojer, Vittorio Bufacchi, Justine Burley, Matthew Clayton, G. A. Cohen, David Estlund, Erin Kelly, Paul Kelly, Lionel MacPherson, Lukas Meyer, Peter Nicholson, Eric Rakowski, Debra Satz, Hillel Steiner, Peter Vallentyne, and Katherine Watson, as well as participants in seminars at London School of Economics, Nuffield College, Oxford, Stanford University, and University College, Cork.

Notes

1   See Ronald Dworkin, "Unenumerated Rights: Whether and How *Roe v Wade* Should be Overruled," *University of Chicago Law Review*, vol. 59, 1992, pp. 381–432; *Life's Dominion* (New York: Alfred A. Knopf, 1993).
2   The argument is developed in the chapters "Of Systems of Equality. Godwin" and "Of Systems of Equality (continued)," T. R. Malthus, *An Essay on the Principle of Population*, ed. D. Winch (Cambridge, UK: Cambridge University Press, 1992), but see especially pp. 78–80. There Malthus asks, "What . . . is to prevent the division of the produce of the soil to each individual from becoming every year less and less, till the whole society and every individual member of it are pressed down by want and misery?" He then considers two solutions. The *illiberal egalitarian solution* holds that "in a state of equality, the necessary restraint could only be effected by some general law," but fails to satisfy Malthus, who proceeds to ask:

> how is this law to be supported, and how are the violations of it to be punished? Is the man who marries early to be pointed at with the finger of scorn? is he to be whipped at the cart's tail? is he to be confined for years in a prison? is he to have his children exposed? Are not all direct punishments for an offence of this kind shocking and unnatural to the last degree?

In sharp contrast, Malthus claims the *liberal inegalitarian solution* is "so natural, so just, [and] so consonant to the laws of God and to the best laws framed by the most enlightened men." It requires that "each individual should be responsible for the maintenance of his own children," but demands a departure from collectivist principles since "the operation of this natural check depends exclusively upon the existence of laws of property, and succession; and in a state of equality and community of property could only be replaced by some artificial regulation of a very different stamp, and a much more unnatural character."
3   Most importantly, see Ronald Dworkin, "What is Equality? Part 1: Equality of Welfare," *Philosophy and Public Affairs*, vol. 10, 1981, pp. 185–246; "What is Equality? Part 2: Equality of Resources," *Philosophy and Public Affairs*, vol. 10, 1981, pp. 283–345; "What is Equality? Part 3: The Place of Liberty," *Iowa Law Review*, vol. 73, 1987, pp. 1–54; "Foundations of Liberal Equality," in Grethe B. Petersen (ed.), *The Tanner Lectures on Human Values*, vol. XI (Salt Lake City: Utah University Press, 1990) and reprinted in S. Darwall (ed.), *Equal Freedom* (Ann Arbor: Michigan University Press, 1995); *Sovereign Virtue* (Cambridge, MA: Harvard University Press, 2000). See also H. Varian, "Distributive Justice, Welfare Economics and the Theory of Fairness," *Philosophy and Public Affairs*, vol. 4, 1974, pp. 223–47.
4   See Dworkin, "Foundations of Liberal Equality," op. cit., p. 37.
5   The distinction between actual and potential welfare levels is necessary to accommodate views such as Richard Arneson's principle of equal opportunity for welfare within welfare equality. That view employs a modified welfarist standard of interpersonal comparison, sensitive to the extent to which all individuals are responsible for their welfare level, for example, because of their deliberate cultivation of preferences that are more expensive to satisfy than those of others. It may escape counterexamples to welfare equality such as Dworkin's case of Louis, but, Dworkin argues, remains vulnerable to the case of Jude. For Arneson's view see his "Equality and Equal Opportunity for Welfare," *Philosophical Studies*, vol. 56, 1989, pp. 77–93. For the two cases see Dworkin, *Sovereign Virtue*, op. cit., pp. 49, 58. Since our concern is to assess the implications of liberal equality, rather than oppose welfarism, we shall assume that Dworkin is correct, but for further discussion see G. A. Cohen, "On the Currency of Egalitarian Justice," *Ethics*, vol. 99, 1989, p. 925; A. Williams, "Equality for the Ambitious," *Philosophical Quarterly*, vol. 52, 2002, pp. 377–89.
6   Dworkin, "Foundations of Liberal Equality," op. cit., p. 37.
7   See ibid., pp. 106–110.

8   Ibid., p. 69, emphasis added. See also ibid., p. 149, where he writes "Equality of resources uses the special metric of opportunity costs: it fixes the value of any transferable resource one person has as the value others forgo by his having it."

9   Dworkin, *Sovereign Virtue*, op. cit., p. 81. Dworkin also argues that the achievement of personal well-being itself requires such circumstances, since it is best understood as a response to a challenge in which the possession of a just share of resources is a parameter against which success is to be judged. See his "Foundations of Liberal Equality," op. cit., pp. 71–5, 93–8.

10 Dworkin, *Sovereign Virtue*, op. cit., p. 66.

11 To preempt misconstrual of later suggestions, note that they are meant to apply in societies that have achieved the other demands of liberal equality, and not necessarily in societies, like the United States, which, as Dworkin recognizes, fall severely short of that standard.

12 As applied to the first two generations of immigrants, the assumption is consistent with Dworkin's remarks about inheritance, or "the troublesome issue whether those who have amassed wealth through sacrifices in their own lives should be allowed to pass this on as extra wealth for their children," and his suggestion that "[e]quality of resources must find some way to recognize and at least reduce inequality generated in this way, perhaps . . . by regarding one's situation as a beneficiary as an in principle insurable hazard" (see, respectively, Dworkin's *Sovereign Virtue*, op. cit., p. 109 and fn. 12). The assumption is also consistent with Dworkin's view that "our concern for future generations is not a matter of justice" since that view concerns distant individuals whose identity is not yet fixed (Dworkin, *Life's Dominion* (New York: Alfred A. Knopf, 1993), pp. 77–8). For further discussion of the general issue, or "Non-Identity Problem," see Derek Parfit, *Reasons and Persons* (Oxford: Clarendon Press, 1984), ch. 16.

13 Similarly Rakowski claims that "everyone born into a society is entitled, at a minimum, to the same quantity of resources that all who participated in the original division of the community's goods and land received" (Eric Rakowski, *Equal Justice* (Oxford: Clarendon Press: 1991), p. 150, and, for a plausible qualification, fn. 2).

14 Note that Dworkin himself recognizes that treating justice as a parameter of personal well-being does not preclude regarding aggregate as well as distributive matters as appropriate objects of ethical concern. For example, in Dworkin's "Foundations of Liberal Equality," op., cit., pp. 73, 94, fn. 49, he suggests that, provided distributive justice is secured, individuals have reason to be concerned with the magnitude of resources available for distribution. Thus, denying that he is concerned exclusively with distribution, he writes:

> I do not mean, of course, that the absolute value or quality of the resources a person commands makes no difference to the life he can lead, so long as he has a just share of whatever there is. Someone who lives in a richer community or age, with a just share of its wealth, faces a more interesting and valuable challenge, and can lead a more exciting, diverse, complex and creative life just for that reason . . . I could have a better life, I assume, if circumstances changed so that justice allowed me more resources.

He subsequently notes that "the challenge a person faces is more interesting and valuable as his and his community's prosperity increases; so we prefer to have a greater to a lesser stock of resources, provided that in each case our stock is just."

15 Indeed many think such conditions hold in the world today, and that rapid population growth – along with other factors such as domestic and international injustice, and corrupt and inefficient political and economic institutions – is one fundamental source of human misery. Dworkin (*Life's Dominion*, op. cit., p. 115) may have such a view in mind when he writes that "no American state could plausibly claim an interest in increasing its population: it is a general assumption throughout the world that overpopulation is a more serious threat than underpopulation." For further discussion of this complex issue see, for example, K. Lindahl-Kiessling and H. Landberg, *Population, Economic Development, and the Environment* (Oxford: Oxford University Press, 1994); A. Sen, "Population: Delusion and Reality," *New York Review of Books*, vol. XLI, September 1994, pp. 62–71; D. Pearce, *World Without End* (Oxford:

Oxford University Press, 1993), ch. 6; R. D. Lee and T. Miller, "Population Growth, Externalities to Childbearing, and Fertility Policy in Developing Countries," in *Proceedings of the World Bank Annual Conference on Development Economics, 1990* (supplement to the *World Bank Economic Review* and the *World Bank Research Observer*), pp. 275–304.

16 For an illuminating discussion of various competing definitions of externality see D. M. Hausman, "When Jack and Jill Make a Deal," *Social Philosophy and Policy*, vol. 9, 1992, pp. 95–8, 110–13.

17 How other resourcist conceptions address problems of procreative justice is an interesting question, worth further study. For example, Hillel Steiner's left-libertarian conception does not balk at taxing parents, but justifies it as the payment of rent for a natural resource (*germ-line genetic information*) that they have unilaterally appropriated, but to which a common entitlement exists. See his *An Essay on Rights* (Oxford: Blackwell, 1994), pp. 273–80.

18 See Eric Rakowski, *Equal Justice*, op. cit., pp. 150–5. The first method involves a number of variations depending on whether population size is constant, falling, or growing.

19 Ibid., p. 153. Displaying similar exasperation, John Stuart Mill complains:

> when persons are once married, the idea, in this country, never seems to enter any one's mind that having or not having a family, or the number of which it shall consist, is amenable to their own control. One would imagine that children were rained down upon married people, direct from heaven, without their being art or part in the matter; that it was really, as the common phrases have it, God's will, and not their own, which decided the numbers of their offspring. (J. S. Mill, *Principles of Political Economy, Books I–II*, J. M. Robson (ed.), *Collected Works of John Stuart Mill*, vol. II (Toronto: Toronto University Press, 1965), p. 369)

20 Hillel Steiner describes the passages quoted above, with the exception of Rakowski's first sentence, as "surely correct." See Steiner, *An Essay on Rights*, op. cit., p. 278.

21 Others might object more fundamentally by challenging, as follows, Rakowski's conviction that provision should be organized differently in the two scenarios he describes, involving unwitting settlers and children: surely in the former instance the resources which the original immigrants share with the new arrivals are not morally speaking "theirs," since the extent of each immigrant's entitlement was conditional upon population size not expanding. Why then in the latter instance should the immigrants' entitlements not be treated as conditional in exactly the same way, in which case universal provision should not be described as requiring the immigrants to share "their" resources?

The resourcist view that our initially equal share of resources should not diminish due to changes in other individuals' postauction preferences suggests an immediate answer to such a challenge. It supplies a reason for entitlements not to be conditional upon population changes produced by choice even if they are conditional on changes wrought by fate.

22 Because such changes would be preferred they could be considered improvements even if Dworkin is correct to claim that "Once social wealth is divorced form utility . . . it loses all plausibility as a component of value . . . It is false that . . . an individual is necessarily better off if he has more wealth, once having more wealth is taken to be independent of utility information" (*A Matter of Principle*, op. cit., p. 245).

23 J. Locke, *Two Treatises of Government*, ed. P. Laslett (Cambridge, UK: Cambridge University Press, 1960), ch. 5, § 37, p. 294.

24 Rakowski, *Equal Justice*, op. cit., p. 153 (emphasis added).

25 Ibid., pp. 153–4.

26 For provocative and original discussion see R. George, "Who Should Bear the Cost of Children?" *Public Affairs Quarterly*, vol. 1, 1987, pp. 1–42, and "On the External Benefits of Children," in D. T. Meyers, K. Kipnis and C. F. Murphy, Jr. (eds.), *Kindred Matters: Rethinking the Philosophy of the Family* (Ithaca, NY: Cornell University Press, 1994), pp. 209–17. For a response see Paula Casal, "Environmentalism, Procreation, and the Principle of Fairness," *Public Affairs Quarterly*, vol. 13, 1999, pp. 363–76.

27 For a popular expression of the view see J. Rauch, "Kids as Capital," *The Atlantic Monthly*, August 1989, pp. 56–61.

28 For the latter type of argument for subsidized procreation see, for example, N. Folbre, "Children as Public Goods," *American Economic Review*, vol. 84, *AEA Papers and Proceedings*, 1984, pp. 86–90; S. P. Burggraf, "How Should the Costs of Child Rearing be Distributed?" *Challenge*, September–October 1993, pp. 48–55.

29 See, for example, Dworkin, "Can a Liberal State Support Art?" in *A Matter of Principle*, p. 223, and his discussion of the "Principle of Correction," in *Sovereign Virtue*, op. cit., pp. 155–8.

30 See John Rawls, *A Theory of Justice*, rev. edn. (Cambridge, MA: The Belknap Press of Harvard University Press, 1999), p. 96.

31 See George, "Who Should Bear the Cost of Children?" op. cit., pp. 28–31.

32 Ibid., p. 31.

33 George stipulates that those who eventually benefit from the dam do so *because* they did not create it, in order to maintain an analogy with an earlier example in which parents, having spent more on their children, are less able in later life to purchase their labor than nonparents, who chose instead to save. For the example see ibid., pp. 1–3.

34 See, for example, R. Nozick, *Anarchy, State, and Utopia* (New York: Basic Books, 1974), pp. 90–5; A. J. Simmons, *Moral Principles and Political Obligations* (Princeton, NJ: Princeton University Press, 1979), pp. 101–42. For a more favorable account see R. J. Arneson, "The Principle of Fairness and Free-Rider Problems," *Ethics*, vol. 91, 1982, pp. 616–33.

35 Dworkin, *Law's Empire* (Cambridge, MA: Harvard University Press, 1986), p. 194 (emphasis added).

36 Indeed, to claim that the production of children generates positive *externalities* implies, on Hausman's aforementioned account, that their effects on third parties were not intended.

37 Those who doubt this conclusion should ask themselves whether fairness requires a subsidy for those who, in circumstances where population reduction is a public good, unintentionally and costlessly produce positive externalities by choosing not to become parents.

38 See George, "On the External Benefits of Children," op. cit., pp. 209–10.

39 For further discussion of the positive as well as negative economic consequences of procreation, and an attempt to quantify their combined value in different countries, see R. D. Lee and T. Miller's "Population Policy and Externalities to Childbearing," *Annals of the American Academy of Political and Social Science*, vol. 510, 1990, pp. 17–22; "Population Growth, Externalities to Childbearing, and Fertility Policy in Developing Countries," op. cit. Other effects, such as an unwelcome reduction in our moral options induced by the needs of yet more human beings or distress at their suffering, although important to many, are less amenable to economic analysis.

40 See J. S. Mill, *On Liberty* in J. N. Gray (ed.), *On Liberty and Other Essays* (Oxford: Oxford University Press, 1991), ch. 5, p. 117, where he writes:

> It still remains unrecognized, that to bring a child into existence without a fair prospect of being able, not only to provide food for its body, but instruction and training for its mind, is a moral crime, both against the unfortunate offspring and against society; and that if the parent does not fulfil this obligation, then the state ought to see it fulfilled, at the charge, as far as possible, of the parent.

Cf., J. S. Mill, *Principles of Political Economy and Chapters on Socialism*, ed. J. Riley (Oxford: Oxford University Press), 1994, Bk. V, § 8, pp. 339–41.

41 Dworkin, *Sovereign Virtue*, op. cit., p. 69.

42 For discussion see F. Miller and R. Sartorius, "Population Policy and Public Goods," *Philosophy and Public Affairs*, vol. 8, 1979, pp. 148–74.

43 Dworkin, *Sovereign Virtue*, op. cit., p. 81.

44 Ibid., p. 56.

45 In this respect the analogy with Louis is only imperfect, since he keeps his initial share of resources even if he adopts an expensive ambition.

46 For further discussion see Dworkin, "Can a Liberal State Support Art?" op. cit., p. 233, where he claims, "We inherited a cultural structure, and we have some duty, out of simple justice, to leave that structure at least as rich as we found it." Endorsing that claim, see also Dworkin's "Foundations of Liberal Equality," op. cit., p. 85, fn. 44, where he insists "citizens should choose against a background that includes opportunities and examples that have been thought to be a part of living well by reflective people in the past and that are part of a cultural heritage."

47 The question is complicated by the fact that Dworkin subsequently entertains, but does not explicitly endorse, a further derivative argument for collective provision. It involves substantive considerations about what personal goals are worthy of desire rather than simply procedural considerations about the importance of choices being informed by an inheritance and made in conditions of diversity. Thus, in the footnote previously cited in note 46 above, he proceeds to emphasize that "nothing in my argument here denies that a state that has fulfilled the requirements of justice can properly use public funds to support what the market will allow to perish, on the substantive ground that art improves the value of lives available in the community." It is debatable whether Dworkin could endorse such an argument consistently with employing the view that justice is a so-called parameter of well-being in order to render ineffective certain attempts to advance substantive conceptions of the good. Doing the latter, in Dworkin's "Foundations of Liberal Equality," p. 116, he insists that individuals "cannot make their own lives better by ignoring the limits justice sets to their power to have a cultural or social environment more congenial to them, because justice is a parameter of the life good for them." Whatever force this type of claim has as a strategic limit on political perfectionism depends on the extent to which resources, if at all, can be set aside from the process of equally dividing privately owned resources and employed to advance some other legitimate political aspiration than justice. If one argues that it is considerable, and such resources may be employed to subsidize procreation because so doing improves the value of lives available, one jeopardizes an important element of liberal equality. We shall not, therefore, pursue the suggestion further here, since our aim is to address procreation from within liberal equality.

48 See Dworkin, *Life's Dominion*, op. cit., p. 154, where he writes, "government sometimes acts properly when it coerces people in order to protect certain intrinsic values: when it collects taxes to finance national museums or when it imposes conservation measures to protect endangered animal species. . . ."

49 Ibid., p. 115.

50 In *Sovereign Virtue*, op. cit., p. 488, fn. 12, Dworkin, touches upon this possibility. There he writes:

> Suppose . . . I have more children than you and so must divide their inheritance in smaller shares. Then, although neither of us has invaded resources properly belonging to another, our children will not have equal resources: some will envy what others have. Equality of resources must find some way to recognize and at least reduce inequality generated in this way, perhaps . . . by regarding one's situation as a beneficiary as an in principle insurable hazard.

It is unclear why he does not consider whether differential reproduction could involve invasion.

51 See G. A. Cohen "Incentives, Inequality and Community," in Stephen Darwall (ed.), *Equal Freedom* (Ann Arbor: University of Michigan Press, 1995), pp. 331–97.

52 Ibid., p. 326.

53 J. S. Mill, *Principles of Political Economy, Books I–II*, op. cit., p. 206.

54 Dworkin, *Life's Dominion*, op. cit., p. 168, and cf. pp. 148–54.

55 Moreover, the suggestion may not hold in certain circumstances. Much will depend on the range of policies available to the state to achieve redistribution within the family. For example, as Rakowski (*Equal Justice*, op. cit., p. 166) notes, it might be possible to allow parents to pay the cost of their children after the latter have reached maturity. If it were feasible to prevent them saving at an earlier date to cover such payment, then such a scheme would be more likely to internalize costs without jeopardizing the upbringing of children from large families.

10

Morality and the "New Genetics"

Justine Burley

Our knowledge of natural phenomena has increased exponentially over the past 50 odd years. A portion of this knowledge is so obscure that puzzles surrounding it are the preoccupation of only a select few, for example, making sense of quantum mechanics in terms of what we experience in everyday life and have an intuitive feel for. Other knowledge gains have been discernible to most of us, their impact on human welfare celebrated and feared in roughly equal measure. The discoveries of atomic fission and the chemical nature of gene structure are cases in point; respectively they led to profound understanding of physical and biological processes, which altered our worldview and has been accompanied by moral disquietude. Somewhat ironically, the destructive power granted by nuclear physics poses far less sophisticated challenges to our morality than do life-enhancing developments in genetics. Ronald Dworkin's assessment of these latter challenges is that the "new genetics" pitches us into "moral free-fall."[1] This chapter focuses on the moral sea change that Dworkin argues is threatened by certain advances in genetics and related fields of scientific inquiry.

When, in 1953, James Watson and Francis Crick unveiled the molecular structure of deoxyribonucleic acid (DNA) in the journal *Nature*, they concluded with the pithy sentence: "It has not escaped our notice that the specific pairing we have postulated immediately suggests a possible copying mechanism for the genetic material."[2] Five decades on, these elegant words have been retrospectively imbued with meaning in the way history typically reserves for the remarks of political or military leaders lauded for prescience. This is because Watson and Crick's observation did not simply provide a molecular explanation for how all biological life propagates itself from one generation to the next, it also presaged "the age of biological control,"[3] an era in which we can choose what kind of people are produced, in what kind of way.

On a loose construal of the term, biological control is neither new nor requires hard science. In ignorance of genetic mechanisms, selective breeding of certain plants and animals was nonetheless possible and had dramatic consequences for the gene pool (think of the Pekinese). Prior, however, to the unraveling of gene structure and a series of breakthroughs triggered by it, the instruments of control exercised over *human* procreative outcomes were relatively blunt ones – laws proscribing incest, cultural prohibitions on interracial marriage, the crude "scientific" methods employed by Social Darwinism in the nineteenth century and by various eugenic movements in the twentieth century, choice of mate.[4] It is now apparent that one day we may wield the power to dictate the genetic make-up of human individuals with some precision.[5] We are poised to enter the age of biological control, squarely, with the application of cloning by nuclear transfer[6] to humans.[7] Even if this likelihood is not realized, research on gene modification, embryo screening, prenatal testing, and various assisted conception techniques have taken us one step across the threshold.

In chapter 13 of *Sovereign Virtue*,[8] Ronald Dworkin tackles a set of normative questions posed by recent advances in bioscience: should genetic testing be allowed? Who should have access to genetic information? What approach to health insurance would avoid victimization of the genetically unlucky and also prevent adverse selection? May embryos/fetuses be terminated if they possess identifiable genetic defects? Are genetic engineering and human cloning morally permissible? Dworkin replies to all of these questions with characteristic acuity: an issue is distilled from a messy debate, and then given shape and clarity in the context of his liberal egalitarian framework. To help elucidate and provide answers to them, Dworkin first summons into action his distinction between derivative and detached values, elaborated in *Life's Dominion*[9] (and which is discussed critically in chapters 11, 12, and 13 of this volume).

On Dworkin's view, derivative values pertain to the interests of particular individuals. They often invite interpersonal comparisons along some dimension – raw cost–benefit analyses or more refined desiderata, such as conceptions of justice or fairness.[10] Dworkin classes debates over whether and how far genetic testing should be allowed, who may know about the genetic information ascertained from tests, and those about insurance practices, as disputes about derivative values:[11] they necessarily involve personal interests, and cannot be arbitrated persuasively without reference to whether and how serving these interests may affect the lives of others. Genetic testing, for example, may be desirable even for diseases with no available treatment because it may be in the interests of an afflicted individual to plan for a foreshortened life. But that benefit to the individual cannot be viewed in isolation of the interests of others; provision of testing for individual benefit needs to be weighed against its consequences for, say, the provision of basic health care. I do not propose to object to the mainly permissive (albeit indeterminate) policy stances Dworkin endorses regarding any specific genetic development that he classes as a matter of derivative value. Most of these are eminently sensible and there is little room left, at least as I see it, for constructive disagreement. Nor shall I tackle Dworkin on whether he is right to marshal the derivative value side of his distinction in relation to these issues (even though there is space for disagreement here). This is because the aforementioned set of questions embodies, as Dworkin rightly says, merely new cases of familiar problems and therefore entails no fundamental readjustments to our thinking about morality.[12]

What I do propose to approach critically is an arresting claim made in the context of Dworkin's discussion of genetic engineering and reproductive cloning: "[W]e are entitled to think [in the light of these developments] that our most settled convictions will, in large numbers, be undermined, that we will be in a kind of moral free-fall, that we will have to think again against a new background and with uncertain results."[13] The most weighty objections to genetic engineering and cloning speak to what Dworkin calls *detached* values.[14] Detached values differ from derivative values in the chief respect that they neither depend on nor presuppose the rights or interests of any particular person. Rather, they are intrinsic to an event or object in some other way.[15] Dworkin suggests that, when people level the objection at human cloning that it is wrong to "play God," they are formulating, however clumsily, an objection of a detached kind. That is, even if the consequences of cloning are bad for no one, it is maintained that cloning should be banned because it involves something that is always wrong, namely offending some view of the "sacred."[16] And this is where Dworkin's discussion becomes really engaging. What exercises critics of cloning and genetic engineering (factual misassumptions aside) Dworkin tells us, is some ill-defined sense of *radical moral dislocation*.

The insight that our morality may not, in the face of the "new genetics," quite be up to the job, is not unique to Dworkin.[17] However, the way in which he understands this to be the case, and what this perceived inadequacy implies, is both novel and fascinating. And, as I shall argue, it is exaggerated on one count and plain wrong on another. Dworkin argues that the mere possibility that we might control the genetic make-up of our offspring strikes at the very "spine of our ethics and our morality" because it undermines "the crucial boundary between chance and choice" that has shaped our entire moral experience.[18] Dworkin writes:

> My hypothesis is that genetic science has suddenly made us aware of the possibility of a similar though far greater pending moral dislocation [than did changes in deathbed medicine]. We dread the prospect of people designing other people because that possibility in itself shifts – much more dramatically than in those other examples – the chance/choice boundary that structures our values as a whole, and such a shift threatens, *not to offend any of our present values, detached or derivative, but, on the contrary, to make a great part of these suddenly obsolete.* Our physical being – the brain and body which furnishes each person's material substrate – has long been the absolute paradigm of what is both devastatingly important to us, and in its initial condition, beyond our power to alter and therefore beyond the scope of our responsibility, either individual or collective.[19]

For the remainder of this chapter I shall be probing Dworkin's "hypothesis" from a number of different angles. I shall be pressing three general questions: which areas of our ethics and morality are under threat? Is Dworkin correct that we face a state of moral free-fall? If not, what might speak for this strong claim? In section I, I tackle the first of these questions. I go on in section II to evaluate the force of Dworkin's hypothesis.

I shall not be opposing Dworkin on grounds of moral skepticism. It is not the credence of morality I shall be doubting. Rather, I want to deny that the possibility of controlling the genetic fate of children portends any great moral crisis *per se*. What motivates Dworkin's hypothesis, I shall argue, is that developments in genetics present a crisis *for his own liberal egalitarian approach* (which is a rather different thing to the rest of us being in the grips of moral free-fall). First, *in practice*, his theory of distributive justice, which accords a pivotal role to genetic chance in delimiting moral responsibility, is only a pale approximation of modern liberalism in the age of biological control. The mechanism he has built in to the theory to redress inequalities traceable to differences in individuals' mental and physical capacities cannot be of service in a world in which controlling genetic fate is possible. But this is not to say that alternative conceptions of political morality, ones that are less selectively focused on genetic chance than Dworkin's, are unavailable. Not only are they available, they are also better equipped to deal with genetic advances in keeping with one of the guiding aims of Dworkin's own conception of political morality – mitigation of inequalities that are the product of bad luck. This is the subject of discussion in the final subsection of this chapter. Second, the most obvious area of conventional ethics that Dworkin's hypothesis relates to is the area of reproduction: the subject of the subsection headed "Liberty and procreation." Procreative liberty will see change as clinical applications of genetic science develop. Dworkin suggests that the flat principle of bodily integrity may become an artifact of conventional morality, and also that the right to reproductive freedom (which encompasses bodily integrity), may lack the force required of it for us to continue in the conviction that it is a fundamental human right. On my view, changes there will be, but these in no way are tantamount to moral free-fall in this area of ethics. Third, and relatedly, Dworkin's current justification of reproductive freedoms proves defective when considered against the backdrop of a world in which genetic control is possible. But this merely provides a clear demonstration that certain issues may not appropriately be defended by appeal chiefly to the argument from "religion," however much that kind of defense might facilitate real-world political compromise. Fourth, neither component of Dworkin's account of ethical individualism provides *adequate* guidance on the question of what can be reasonably expected of procreators in a world where controlling genetic fate is possible. Revisions of these principles, or additional principles, are required. However, in this regard, Dworkin is constrained. But, other arguments are on hand to furnish an adequate account, and they are familiar ones. In his chapter "Playing God," Dworkin is sounding the death knell of his own theory. It is striking that this has gone largely unnoticed by his critics.

I   The Hypothesis of Moral Free-fall

Moral free-fall and moral truth

Before I elaborate Dworkin's hypothesis in detail, it is important to obviate the merest hint that Dworkin's claim about impending moral free-fall is a claim about abstract morality. Dworkin is emphatic that he is not suggesting science has succeeded in undermining the idea that there is such a thing as moral truth.

> The terror that many of us feel at the thought of genetic engineering is not a fear of what is wrong; rather it is a fear of losing our grip on what is wrong. *We are not entitled – it would be a serious confusion – to think that even the most dramatic shifts in the chance/choice boundary somehow challenge morality itself: that there will one day be no more wrong.*[20]

To make sense of this last phrase we can helpfully appeal to Dworkin's discussion of moral objectivity in his article "Objectivity and Truth: You'd Better Believe It."[21] There, Dworkin's project is to establish that evaluations of the status of moral values *necessarily* take place within the domain of moral judgment itself. This is the point to which his rebuttal of different brands of moral skepticism returns time and again. Dworkin's self-professed stance on the issue of moral truth is that he is a "realist."[22] His own realist position accommodates both moral error and a high degree of moral indeterminacy. He allows that we may be mistaken about what is right, and also that we may never know for *certain* what the right answer is, but denies that abstract morality is defeated as a consequence. It does not matter whether the source of error is morality itself, for example, unrefined moral sensibility, or nonmoral, that is, factual.

The problem for morality that Dworkin's moral free-fall hypothesis identifies emanates from a nonmoral domain. In the course of Dworkin's attack on moral skepticism he makes it plain that facts of any ilk (including revelations about hard psychological determinism), do not undermine the idea of moral truth.

> Morality is a distinct, independent dimension of our experience, and it exercises its own sovereignty ... *We may well discover that what we now think about virtue or vice or duty or right is inconsistent with other things we also think, about cosmology or psychology or history. If so, we must try to re-establish harmony, but that is a process whose results must make moral sense as well as every other kind of sense. Even in the most extreme case, when we are offered grounds for scorching doubt, we still need moral judgment at some deep level to decide whether that doubt is justified and what its consequences for virtue and vice, duty and right, really are. No matter what we learn about the physical or mental world, including ourselves, it must remain an open question, and one that calls for a moral rather than any other kind of judgment, how we ought to respond.*[23]

Some will doubtless be tempted to interpret the above passage as amounting to no more than the claim that there will always be moral questions, and will counter that it offers no proof of a realist stance on the questions themselves. Extensive treatment of Dworkin's arguments against skepticism, however, is not within the purview of this inquiry. For present purposes the quoted passage suffices to underscore that, for Dworkin, no factual increments in science, genetic or otherwise, *could ever* compromise the objective status of moral values. His moral free-fall thesis relates to our standard ethical opinions and the moral background informing these views. New factual information indicates that these views may be wrong, and although Dworkin thinks it is far from evident what they should be replaced by, none of this touches moral truth: "non-moral discoveries cannot undermine or structurally change morality without morality's help. They furnish information that engages with deep substantive moral judgements, and their impact depends on what those deep judgements declare or assume."[24]

Having clarified what Dworkin's thesis is not a thesis about, we need now to supply a positive account of it. The task in the remainder of this section is to spell out which aspects of morality Dworkin claims are threatened by the "new genetics," and in what ways.

The hypothesis elaborated

Nowhere has Dworkin expressed as forcefully the crucial role that genetic chance plays in shaping our morality as he has done in "Playing God." It is no small irony that he does so to make the point that, if science continues to move in a certain direction, a substantial portion of our ethics and our morality may need to be discarded.

Three dimensions can be adduced from Dworkin's various formulations of the moral free-fall thesis. Taken together, they are jointly sufficient for (his understanding of) moral free-fall. These are:

1   A descriptive factual claim about genetic chance no longer obtaining to the same degree, to the human condition;
2   A descriptive psychological claim about the level of importance we have attached to genetic chance, and cannot avoid thinking about differently in the light of certain developments in genetics;
3   A normative claim about it being soon inappropriate for genetic chance to circumscribe the boundary of personal and collective responsibility.

These three dimensions of the moral free-fall thesis are run together in parts of Dworkin's discussion but it is worth pausing to consider each individually.

The factual claim
In "Playing God," Dworkin entertains several factual scenarios regarding the extent of control that genetics will afford over the outcomes of reproduction:

* absolute control – the *fantasy* of parents choosing *any* phenotype for their children;[25]
* extreme control – the likely possibility that parents will be able to select an entire genotype for their child from a huge array of cell donors/sellers (e.g., using human reproductive cloning);[26] and,

- moderate control – the likely possibility of improvements in gene identification (through preconception and postconception testing) and successful gene manipulation (e.g., by gene additions/deletions/modifications, and gene-targeted pharmaceuticals) for a *modest* number of traits or disorders.[27]

We should note that there is some ambiguity on Dworkin's part as to how reliant the moral free-fall thesis is on the *actualization* of *any* of the above scenarios. Dworkin suggests that the "bare possibility" of them is sufficient to engender in us a sense of moral dislocation.[28] He also states that their bare possibility is sufficient warrant for a re-evaluation of our existing views.[29] And in places he also argues as if moral free-fall will only occur if cloning and/or genetic engineering become more than a theoretical possibility. This ambiguity is not unimportant. For one thing, it begs the question of what form(s) of control are *necessary* for moral free-fall. For another, it prompts reasonable doubt about the desirability of a good chunk of any moral theory resting heavily on *contingent* scientific facts.

Dworkin is not unaware that forms of control over the genetic fate of children were exerted in the absence of complex science (think of what motivates laws proscribing incest).[30] Nor is he unaware that a whole host of developments in the biosciences (e.g., in vitro fertilization (IVF), and preimplantation genetic diagnosis (PIGD) progressively have afforded such control. Clearly, Dworkin seizes on the examples of cloning and genetic engineering because they offer means of precise control over procreative outcomes. But do recent facts about genetics justifiably command so much of his attention when, for example, facts about the beneficial effects of taking folic acid (i.e., reducing the incidence of spina bifida) before conceiving a child and in the early stages of pregnancy, have invited none? It seems to me that cloning and genetic engineering are not necessary conditions of Dworkin's moral free-fall thesis, whatever his own ambiguity on this point. A modicum of control over reproductive outcomes, which has for some time been within the realm of the possible, should have been sufficient to raise identical worries about existing moral practices and convictions in Dworkin's mind. This conclusion suggests that Dworkin may rather have been hedging his bets in clinging to the chance/choice distinction in the way that he has done.

Whatever direction genetic science moves in, we can confidently claim here that luck with respect to the outcomes of procreation will always obtain. Genetically directed reproduction will likely *never* be *wholly* controllable. A sizeable gulf between genotype and phenotype will remain, even in the fantasy scenario of "absolute" control. Although genotype and phenotype are inextricably linked, it is impossible that any genetic or any cellular technique (e.g., cloning by nuclear transfer) could ever enable the *full* design of phenotype. Never could they control *fully* even traits like appearance (phenotype),[31] and certainly they could not allow anything approximating full control of human behavior (also phenotype). This is because of the influence of a variety of epigenetic factors, for example, environmental effects, on the expression of genes. These nongenetic factors are ill defined, unpredictable in their effect, and uncontrollable, and so they do not differ conceptually, for Dworkin's purposes, from what he refers to in "Playing God" as genetic chance, and elsewhere as "brute bad luck." The important point remains, however, that (part of) what I have described above as moderate control is already possible, and this, to restate my previous point somewhat differently, underscores that we are neither strangers to the idea of controlling genetic fate, nor have we been destabilized long term by the notion.[32]

The psychological claim

Dworkin makes a number of statements describing our psychological attitude to genetic luck, including: "The popularity of the term 'genetic lottery' itself shows the centrality of our conviction that what we most basically *are* is a matter of chance not choice," and "It is a striking phenomenon, now, that people take pride in physical attributes or skills they did not choose or create, like physical appearance or strength. . . ."[33]

What people do think and have thought is fundamentally an empirical matter. Although it would be spurious to disagree wholly with what Dworkin says, we can note the partiality of his account; a crucially relevant feature of our psychology has been omitted. It seems to me the following propositions are more or less equally true to those of Dworkin:

- The popularity of the term "social lottery" shows the centrality of our conviction that what we most basically *are* is a matter of chance not choice.
- It is a striking phenomenon, now, that people take pride in family background and in other sources of social and economic opportunities they did not choose or create.

I am insisting here that people regard who and how they are as having much to do with others' choices surrounding the circumstances of their birth and life, and not just with genetic luck. Of course we do not choose our genes, nor, however, do we choose our parents, to be born, or the society into which we are born, and we recognize that the former is tied to parental choice and the latter to innumerable choices of others. (By no one is this point made better than Laurence Sterne in his *Tristam Shandy*.) The impact of this choice-related backdrop to our lives is of great and enduring significance for preference formation, talents, health, and character more generally. Dworkin himself would have no hesitation in agreeing with this last statement.[34] So why does he insist that the immutability of genetic make-up has held *special* psychological importance?

In "Playing God" (and elsewhere[35]) this special importance is virtually impossible to disentangle from what Dworkin says our normative response to it has been. His descriptions of the manner in which we have thought of the fixed nature of genetic fate unfailingly embraces the maxim: cannot = not-ought; if genetic fate is uncontrollable, no one has any responsibility for it. But even with the normative trained onto the descriptive claim in this way, it is difficult, I think, to make a strong case for the special psychological importance of genetic over social luck. For example, as gestured at above, it is difficult in terms of how these two forms of luck relate to the circumstances into which we are born. That one's parents chose to bring one into existence at a certain time, in a certain setting (geographical, historical, socioeconomic), is just as much a matter of chance, and just as fixed, and just as important to us as our genetic complement.[36] Dworkin by and large has always underplayed the psychological impact of these nongenetic features on the person. He thinks that if control over the genetic fate of offspring is granted by genetic science, our psychological world will be rocked. Since we are long accustomed to the idea of the uncontrollable role of others' choices in relation to our own lives, I don't see why this should be so. That parents may replace God or (to an extent) the "Blind Watchmaker" is no small event, but those of us who attribute greater moral significance to social luck than Dworkin need make no *major* conceptual adjustment to how we think about the relation between chance and choice, and who we most basically *are*.

The normative claim

As mentioned above, Dworkin's selective focus on our attitude to genetic chance is inextricably linked to the view that this sort of chance is appropriately central to our moral thinking. Indeed, Dworkin argues that the *overall structure* of our morality and ethics *depends* "crucially on a fundamental distinction between what we are responsible for doing or deciding, individually or collectively, and what is given to us, as a background against which we act or decide, but which are powerless to change."[37] Whose ethics, whose morality? The short answer is: Dworkin's. On the assumption that genetic make-up *can* be chosen, Dworkin may no longer rely on genetic chance, in the way he has done, in delimiting responsibility. A new parameter of personal and collective responsibility must be defined.[38] This is the nub of the moral free-fall thesis.

On my view the raw *fact* that one day new members of society may be more the products of others' *detailed* procreative choices *does not warrant the forecast of free-fall*. And I have registered strong doubts that the raw *psychological realization* of this possibility amounts to much. As for the claim that there will be a seismic boundary shift to our values such that a great part of them, derivative and detached, will become obsolete, this we can only really assess by examining how conventional ethics and morality in the relevant areas will look in a world of genetic control.

The normative claim applied

I infer that Dworkin predicts his ethical and moral values "quake" on the basis of concerns about: (1) procreative liberties such as the right to reproductive choice, and the liberal precept of bodily integrity; (2) the deeper moral framework with which Dworkin justifies these; and (3) his theory of distributive justice, which seeks to reconcile the demands of equality with responsibility, by attributing vastly greater moral significance to the vagaries of genetic over social luck. I now want to say something further about each of these areas.

1 *Procreative liberties.* I read Dworkin to be forecasting changes in status of the current liberal precept of bodily integrity and the right to reproductive freedom which are so dramatic that neither will be recognizable. Hence I read his forecast as part of the moral free-fall thesis. In an age of biological control, if we fail to ensure possible good genetic outcomes from reproduction by screening prospective parents, prenatal testing and therapy, embryo manipulation, cloning, and the like, our offspring have no blind genetic mechanism or the gods to curse. Instead, they have us to condemn, morally and legally. The fact that genes might be selected implies that the realm of personal responsibility has expanded to include the personal responsibility of procreators for the detailed outcomes of their reproductive choices.[39] This same fact also implies that we, as a collective, have a *strong* reason to take interest in whether or not technical options either to prevent wholly or to minimize harm to offspring are pursued by members of society. If we take seriously the idea that preconception or postconception actions/inactions of parents can blight a child's life, then the conclusion may be drawn that prospective parents can permissibly be forced to undergo certain procedures. Dworkin on the whole decries coercion of this kind. That policy makers might be tempted by it, I believe, informs, in part, his dramatic claim about genetic control threatening to rumble many of our current ethical views. In the first subsection of section II, I shall argue that while Dworkin's worry about the fate of both bodily integrity and the right to reproductive freedom is substantial and important, moral free-fall is not entailed (or even likely) by a change in the application of either.

2   *Ethical individualism compromised.* Accepted ethical practice regarding procreation is informed in Dworkin's theoretical framework by a more critical moral background, what Dworkin calls "ethical individualism." This he characterizes in "Playing God" as comprising two components. First is regard for the sanctity of human life, according to which, "it is objectively important that any human life, once begun, succeed rather than fail – that the potential of that life be realized rather than wasted."[40] (Regard for the sanctity of life should not be confused with the view that fetuses have interests that must be protected no matter what. On Dworkin's account, in the absence of sentience, fetuses can have no interests at all.[41]) The second component of ethical individualism, the principle of special responsibility, while it acknowledges that life is sacred, stipulates that "each individual – the individual whose life it is – has a special responsibility for each life, and in virtue of that special responsibility he or she has the right to make the fundamental decisions that define, for him, what a successful life would be."[42] Thus Dworkin's moral free-fall hypothesis, when further unpacked, would appear to bear not just on ethical practices and convictions, but also on the more critical features of Dworkin's self-described "humanist" morality. It seems to me that Dworkin's claim about detached and derivative values risking obsolescence is also motivated by the fact that the "new genetics" poses a twofold problem for ethical individualism. If we possess the power to choose the genetic make-up of our children, then some account of the responsibilities of would-be parents is needed, and so is some account of adequate powers for a person. Dworkin's sanctity of human life principle does go some way towards specifying such an account, but it is too effete – it stresses respect for life *once that life has begun*. This principle has nothing much helpful to say about the goodness or badness of procreative decisions prior to the creation of lives, which nonetheless directly affect the quality of those lives. Another principle may be required, or further responsibilities may need to be added to the existing principle.

In addition, Dworkin's principle of special personal responsibility would seem to speak against government insisting to prospective parents that there are morally preferable standards in mental and physical capacities for new lives. It would also seem to speak against all but the most modest measures to ensure that those intent on having children endeavor to bring these about.

Neither of these lacks in Dworkin's approach, however, are tantamount to instances of moral free-fall as regards the wider domain of morality they concern.

3   *Concerns about equality.* Dworkin himself does not discuss the implications of recent genetic science for his theory of equality at any length, but he makes it clear that he is aware of them. Dworkin has long argued in favor of a liberal egalitarian approach that insists that government must treat the lives of those it governs as having "great and equal importance" by ensuring that economic and other policies reflect that importance (equal concern). And also that government must leave people free to live their lives according to their own respective conceptions of what makes a life go well (equal respect), so long as these conceptions are consonant with the idea that living well is living justly (a feature of Dworkin's notion of the "good"). Dworkin's conception of equal concern gives primacy to the (genetic) chance/choice distinction by championing an economic structure that is sensitive to differences in lifestyle choices with which people identify, but insensitive to unchosen differences in people's mental and physical capacities. To ensure that the second aim is achieved fairly and efficiently Dworkin advocates state-run compensatory mechanisms, modeled on his hypothetical insurance scheme[43] (see subsection "Genetic luck cum social luck" below). The prudent insurance approach aims to situate people equally with respect to their *ex ante* risk of developing health-related deficiencies. A society governed by Dworkin's

conception of equality denies compensation to individuals for resource shortfalls that are traceable to "option luck" (the outcome of lifestyle choices with which the agent identifies), and mandates compensation for individuals who are the victims of "brute bad luck."[44] In the context under
consideration, brute bad luck pans out as bad genetic luck. Herein lies the problem posed by
genetic developments for Dworkin's approach to distributive justice.

On the assumption of genetic control, hitherto compensatable resource shortfalls, that is, those
traceable to deficits in people's mental and physical capacities, no longer count as such on
Dworkin's view, at least as I shall argue. Instead they are more properly regarded as instances of
noncompensatable brute bad social luck because they can be traced to parental choice. Dworkin ges-
tures at the problem when he writes: "We once accepted the condition in which we were born as
a parameter of responsibility . . . not as itself a potential arena of blame."[45] Even if these deficits
are regarded as compensatable by Dworkin, such compensation would not actually be feasible
because, as I shall argue, no hypothetical insurance market could be modeled that would have any
instructive value for real-world practice.

I suspect that it is the implications of the "new genetics" for the centerpiece of Dworkin's conception of political morality (which I spell out in detail in the chapter's final subsection) that motivate, in large measure, the free-fall hypothesis. Dworkin recognizes that his theory is less attractive
in the age of biological control and he states that revisions will be required, although what these
are he does not make explicit. My own view is that if Dworkin is to remain faithful to one of the
central tenets of his own theory of egalitarian justice, namely choice sensitivity, it is difficult to
see how he can resist embracing a libertarian approach *in practice* (not justification) in the sort of
cases subject to review here. Of course he could abandon the pivotal role he has accorded the
chance/choice distinction in his political philosophical writings, but then his theory will be unrec-
ognizable. Regardless, I shall argue, the part of morality that Dworkin's theory of equality is *one*
expression of, is not imperiled by the "new genetics."

In sum, thus far, Dworkin's hypothesis is not a comment on abstract moral values, rather it relates
to current ethical practices and the moral framework that justifies them. The nub of the thesis
just is the chance/choice boundary *as it has been drawn and deployed by Dworkin*. This distinction,
he argues, structures our values as a whole, and the change to that structure demanded by advances
in genetics "threatens, not to offend any of our present values, detached or derivative, but, on the
contrary, to make a great part of these suddenly obsolete." Whether the thesis stands or falls,
however, really can only be assessed by looking at specific implications of it for ethics and morality. Does the "new genetics" really lead *us* into moral free-fall?

II   The Moral free-fall Hypothesis Evaluated

In this section I aim to assess the *overall* force of Dworkin's hypothesis. I contend that if his thesis
is to mean anything much at all, the following propositions must be supported in our analysis of
it: (1) If the genetic facts we possessed until recently obtained, then our standard ethical opinions
are correct. (2) The antecedent to that conditional is now false so there is no guarantee that our
current moral views are tight. (3) Furthermore, if the new genetic facts obtain, then our previous
opinions are wrong.[46] It will be seen in the two subsections below that Dworkin's moral free-fall

hypothesis, when applied to the three areas outlined above, accepts (1), endorses (2) selectively, and agrees with (3) primarily because he perceives several key components of his own theory to be in jeopardy. Dworkin's moral free-fall hypothesis will be found wanting because it is limited in this last way, and because a plausible and palatable alternative account of *our ethics and morality* exists in the relevant areas. An accurate assessment of ethics and morality in relation to the "new genetics" should have led Dworkin to renounce his own approach, not to forecast moral free-fall.

Liberty and procreation

I shall now scrutinize the implications of Dworkin's moral free-fall thesis for human reproduction. Current freedoms connected to procreation is the most obvious area of ethics and morality that would be affected were we one day to possess the ability to dictate the genetic make-up of our offspring. If we cannot demonstrate that moral values will be in crisis in this domain, then the free-fall thesis starts to look suspect.

Dworkin has formulated the right to reproductive freedom as the right of individuals "to control their own role in procreation unless the state has a *compelling* reason for denying them that control."[47] While his justification of this right is complex,[48] it will suffice for the moment to state it as follows. In any genuinely democratic culture, "people have the moral right – and the moral responsibility – to confront the most fundamental questions about the meaning and values of their own lives for themselves, answering to their own consciences and convictions. . . ."[49] Dworkin's discussion of the fate of this right in the light of genetic science underscores two main problems. The first is connected to the increased range of procreative options that genetic and related areas of science may make possible.

Many of us regard reproductive freedom as a fundamental human right, for example. Can we continue in that conviction once we acknowledge even the bare possibility that such a right, once granted, would extend to the freedom to clone oneself or to design a child according to some supposed standard of perfection?[50]

I read the worry Dworkin tables in the quoted passage as less of a problem for the right (the application of rights does change over time, the right to reproductive freedom being no exception) and more of one for how he has *grounded* it. The weakness I have in mind is with Dworkin's liberal stance on matters of deep-seated moral conviction about detached values. When individuals maintain that it is desirable to engineer a child according to some standard of perfection, they are, according to Dworkin, asserting a particular view about the *detached* value of human life, a view integral to their moral outlook, which is, as Dworkin puts it, "essentially religious." Dworkin has argued that the state must remain neutral on *most* matters of detached value; it may not interfere with choices made on the basis of them, by imposing constraints, and generally it may not seek to foster a particular view of the "sacred" on the part of its citizens.

Tolerance is a cost we must pay for our adventure in liberty. We are committed, by our love of liberty and dignity, to live in communities in which no group is thought clever or spiritual or numerous enough to decide essentially religious matters for everyone else.[51]

As Dworkin argues for the right to reproductive freedom, it might very well permit too much in the age of biological control. However, there are many reasons that should command the attention of policy makers when they are devising legislation about reproduction; the notion that *most* detached views of the sacred can be lumped into one "hands-off" category is unpersuasive, and consideration of the "new genetics" helps us to see why.[52] The point, as I have just put it, rightly invites the objection that I have failed to make any case here at all. Dworkin has never believed that other reasons cannot be brought to bear in policy making over procreation, or that all detached views may be acted on with impunity, or that government may not legislate on some detached views. However, as I argue under the subsection "Procreative freedom and Dworkin's ethical individualism," the problem for Dworkin is that a plausible account of what morally can be expected of potential parents is demanded in the age of biological control, yet he is sorely constrained in recommending such an account. As already noted, it is anathema to his general approach to political morality for *government* to impose views on citizens about what gives life value. Moreover, from what he says in "Playing God" I doubt he would be prepared to endorse the measures that might be required to ensure that, whenever possible, whoever comes to exist surpasses a certain level of well-being. I shall aim to make this case in the context of discussion over preconception procreative decision making.

Shelving that issue for the time being, I want to insist that we *can* continue in the conviction that the right to reproductive freedom is fundamental regardless of what genetics offers. To help make the point broadly, let us consider a second problem presented for conventional morality which Dworkin identifies: if we do ever control the outcomes of procreation with precision, people may take the view, not unreasonably, that coercion of parents might be one way to avoid bad ones. Thus Dworkin writes:

> [The] flat principle of bodily integrity [i.e., the prohibition on forcing people to submit to a medical procedure they object to, like embryo testing] may, however, be one of those artifacts of conventional morality that seemed well justified before the possibilities suggested by modern genetic medicine were plausibly imagined, but not after. If we are to accept a more fundamental principle of concern for the lives of everyone, that principle of bodily integrity may one day have to be modified.[53]

One can only agree with Dworkin that it is not considered ethical today to force people to undergo medical procedures of any kind. What Dworkin intends by his usage of "flat" bodily integrity, may, as he says, become an "artifact," but much else that is currently of value to us about the principle would obtain. One can also agree with Dworkin that present-day democratic states typically do recognize wide scope for individual choice in the area of reproduction, and also that it is likely that we may have strong reasons not to allow people as free a reign with procreative choices in the future as we do currently. In spite of this agreement, we can comfortably maintain that the right to reproductive freedom would still be weighty. This is for the simple reason that this right as well as the precept of bodily integrity respectively cover many cases. The former guarantees freedom from state interference in choice of partner, of whether and when to conceive, of the means of conception and contraception, and of whether to continue with or terminate a pregnancy. The liberal principle of bodily integrity is intended to apply to a huge range of medical interventions, not just those connected to procreation. The force of the right and the precept we are discussing will therefore persist. The scope of both may be diminished in the age of biological control, on one or another dimension, but both would continue to play many important and familiar roles. Many of these we now take for granted, but there is every reason to suppose that in our future world they will be foremost in our thinking about what is essential to protect.

My point, then, is simply that: although Dworkin obviously has good reason to raise concerns about the future status of reproductive freedom and bodily integrity, it is proving difficult to make a convincing case for radical moral dislocation in respect of these features of our ethics and morality. This point is made clearer below when we ask whether the commonsense liberal justification for coercing people to ensure good genetic outcomes from procreation in a future world really differs from the one underpinning accepted coercive norms bearing on the treatment of children in today's world.

Procreative freedom and Dworkin's ethical individualism

A question that we have ignored so far, but which the previous discussion begs, is how we should respond to the interests of people not yet in existence. As we will see, Dworkin has no *satisfactory* answer to the question. To help us think more clearly about this I shall posit three cases, all involving preconception harms:

1 Failure of an adult to test himself or herself for a profound (i.e., personhood-affecting) disorder that could be treated so as to avoid its transmission to any fetus conceived;
2 Failure to eliminate a gene or set of genes in gametes that would cause serious health problems;
3 Failure to select a gene or set of genes in gametes that would afford "normal" powers.

Typical in discussions of 1–3 is the claim: X course of action/inaction wrongs the interests *of the resulting child*.

Claims like this one give rise to what Derek Parfit has termed the nonidentity problem.[54] That is, they cannot explain what it is that might be thought problematic about a 1–3-style decision, which results in a child being damaged. To show why let us consider the following two cases. The first is Parfit's and involves a 14-year-old prospective mother:

> This girl chooses to have a child. Because she is so young, she gives her child a bad start in life. Though this will have bad effects throughout the child's life, his life will, predictably, be worth living. If this girl had waited for several years, she would have had a different child, to whom she would have given a better start in life.[55]

My analogue to this case is: a woman chooses to have a child and pursues 1, 2, or 3. The opposite course of action in each case would have prevented harm to any fetus conceived. Because she chooses to conceive in ways 1, 2, or 3 she gives the child a bad start in life. Though her choice will have bad effects on and throughout the child's life, the child's life will, predictably, be worth living. If this woman had not chosen to procreate by the means 1–3, she would have had a different child, to whom she would have given a better start in life.

In both cases, two courses of action are open to the prospective mother. If the 14 year old waits to conceive, a completely different child will be born. Likewise, if the woman chooses the converse of 1, 2, or 3, the child born will be a completely different one. In criticizing these women's pursuit of the first option available (i.e., conception at 14, and 1–3, respectively) people are apt to claim that each mother's decisions will probably be worse for her child. However, as Parfit notes, while people can make this claim about the decisions taken it does not explain what they believe is objectionable about them. It fails to explain this because neither decision can be worse for the particular children born; the alternative for any of them was never to have existed at all. The badness claim about pursuing the first option in the above cases cannot therefore be a claim about why these children have been harmed: it is better for these children that they live than not live at all.

With this problem in mind let us recall the critical ideal directing ethical practice in procreation in Dworkin's theory – ethical individualism. The first component – the sanctity of human life principle – does not govern lives that have not yet begun. This part of Dworkin's view appears therefore to offer no firm guidance with 1–3, and like cases. We should not ignore, however, that the principle is an expression of a general regard for the instrinsic value and importance of all human lives. But this is not only vague, when we seek to fill it in to devise specific responses to our cases, it also looks as though Dworkin might be hamstrung. It is, I think, difficult cogently to reject the idea that decision making about people who have not yet been brought into existence, but who will be, should include not only consideration of the welfare levels that they will enjoy, but stipulation and enforcement by government of what it takes to achieve these levels.

There are plenty of examples from conventional morality relating directly to parental responsibilities to existing children from which we can draw to structure a response to the question of what, morally, can be exacted from people who wish to procreate. If reasonable measures are not taken by parents to ensure the health and safety of actual offspring, parents are obligated by officers of the state to correct these problems, or children are removed from the guardian's home. Coercion is permissible, in other words, when the vital interests of children are endangered.

Consistent with this would be the notion that if we are are able to dictate the genetic fate of children, thereby enabling better lives for them, then we ought not to shirk the responsibility of doing so. But we shall want a way to explain what we find problematic about certain procreative decisions that does not come up against the nonidentity problem, and that contributes to an account of what our responsibilities as parents in the age of biological control might include.

Parfit posits claim "Q," as one solution to the nonidentity problem. "Q" says that: "If in either of two possible outcomes the same number of people would ever live, it would be worse if those who live are worse off, or have a lower quality of life, than those who would have lived."[56] This claim, unlike the claim discussed above about the badness of 1–3, can explain the goodness and badness of the procreative decisions that might be taken by the two women in the above cases – it avoids the problem of nonidentity. The difficulty with this solution in the cases under review (and with consequentialism applied to the "new genetics" more generally), is that it is overly morally demanding. For example, given certain assumptions about the effectiveness and safety of cloning, "Q" would *require*, in the age of biological control, that people employed cloning as *the* method of creating a child; it would be the surest way of avoiding genetic-based disease because the technique grants the possibility of knowing what the genetic outcome of procreation will be in a very detailed (though not perfect) fashion.

Parfit does, however, argue that "Q" might be plausibly qualified; some things, he concedes, may matter more than suboptimal outcomes.[57] His own example is that a society might believe that the pursuit of equality is more valuable than promoting economic growth. Parfit, then, is a pluralist (albeit a tentative one): he argues that "Q" is a helpful principle with which to evaluate moral judgments, but he does not think that this principle should necessarily be used to the exclusion of all others. The endorsement of a "Q"-qualified principle offers one plausible nonnovel solution to the problem under consideration.

I suggest that an appropriate qualifier to "Q" might be an account of equality of opportunity that insists that, whenever it is technically possible, parents be required to ensure for their offspring what Daniels has called "species-typical normal functioning."[58] Constitutive of the account we are sketching here is the notion that the liberty of parental choice matters more than the *best* procreative outcomes that could be achieved, but not more than adequate outcomes, as these have just been defined. One concedes this may be stretching Parfit. But a view like this would avoid being too demanding in the way that "Q" unqualified is; it would enable decent lives on one dimension, whenever that is possible, and it would minimize somewhat the number of cases in which coercion might be thought warranted to prevent harm to offspring.

Our distaste for coercion of prospective parents does not convincingly outweigh the moral importance of securing for our offspring some "normal" range of powers. I claim this in reference to the commonsense liberal view that parents cannot do whatever they like to their offspring just because they, for example, are irresponsible or because they hold certain religious beliefs. Thus John Stuart Mill insisted that liberty is rightfully constrained when the vital interests of a drunkard's dependents are at stake;[59] thus the legal decisions rendered that deny to Jehovah's Witnesses the right to refuse a blood transfusion on behalf of their children. At the same time, under existing sociolegal arrangements, although parents frequently detract from their children's future in a plethora of other ways, the state does not intervene in these cases presumably because no egregious harm to their offspring can be demonstrated. The measures that are currently taken to protect the interests of children are examples of the liberal principle of security of the person in operation. Are we really dealing with anything qualitatively morally different in the cases of preconception harms under discussion? True, no one exists yet in cases 1–3, but we have substantiated, with Parfit's help, the idea that nonexistence does not negate consideration of the rightness and wrongness of procreative decisions that would affect the quality of the lives of those who come to exist.

Dworkin would doubtless reject this proposed solution, not solely because it is pluralist but also because it smacks of welfarism. I wish to stress that it is highly doubtful as to whether some of the issues raised by the "new genetics" can be accommodated without moral pluralism. Moreover, I do not think that any account of political morality that denies the legitimacy of an objective standard of what counts as adequate powers for a person can survive in the age of biological control. Could Dworkin offer one? It would seem both that he cannot, and also that he probably would not desire to. Dworkin's discussions of welfarist conceptions of justice, and his own liberal egalitarian approach (about which we shall shortly say more), deny the legitimacy of positing any objective measure of welfare for individuals. Specifically, he is opposed to objective list-drawing regarding normal powers. Generally, his entire moral project is opposed to consequentialist reasoning at the level of what he would call "principle" (as distinct from "policy").

The second component of ethical individualism, the principle of special responsibility would appear to be weighted in favor of parental free choice in cases 1–3. Dworkin, unlike Parfit, cannot link the choices involved to the interests of whomever comes to exist as a consequence of them. Of course he may wish to call up his sanctity of life principle, but that principle, as I have said, is incapable of performing the work required here. If it were, we would have seen Dworkin arguing rather differently over current preconception reproductive choices about which it can be reasonably predicted deleterious outcomes will result. What is needed for the age of biological control is a principle that stipulates not just concern for lives once begun, but a certain kind of concern for future lives, one that can be promoted and enforced by government on the grounds that, regardless of parental preferences, it is objectively in the interests of the resulting person, whoever that may be.

The facts that Dworkin's theory is not equipped to explain what might be wrong with *some* procreative decisions that affect the interests of offspring, and one robust type of solution to this problem requires we depart from his theoretical framework, help us to see part of what may have motivated the free-fall hypothesis Even if I am wrong about this last claim, we can note in closing this subsection that we are not strangers to the moral and political philosophical territory in the preceding discussion. As we have applied it to conventional ethics and morality regarding reproduction, therefore, Dworkin's moral free-fall thesis is not persuasive.

Genetic luck cum social luck

I demonstrated immediately above that the moral free-fall thesis is not supported by our examination of its application to the area of human reproduction. When we considered moral free-fall in this area of conventional ethics and morality we saw both exaggeration, and that Dworkin's own views require revision. Familiar moral philosophical territory has been traversed with no sense that we are ill-equipped morally for the future. In this final subsection of my chapter, I want to show that it is not accurate to claim moral free-fall in the domain of distributive justice, unless, that is, one is wedded to Dworkin's conception of it.

The chance/choice distinction, absolutely fundamental to Dworkin's theory of liberal egalitarian justice, has come under attack from thinkers residing in several different camps in mainstream political philosophy[60] (and is discussed critically and in depth in Part I of this volume). I do not want to rehearse this plenitude of objections here for they would distract us from our current examination of Dworkin's shaken confidence in parts of contemporary ethics and morality. Later on I will draw selectively from the critical literature to demonstrate that alternatives to Dworkin's theory exist that can better (morally) accommodate *developments in genetics*. First, however, we need to bring out the seriousness of the problems posed for Dworkin's theory by the "new genetics."

I have noted already that Dworkin's theory of equality promotes hypothetical insurance to redress inequalities in resource holdings traceable to unchosen differences in individuals' natural capacities.

> Someone who is born with a serious handicap faces his life with what we concede to be fewer resources, just on that account, than others do. This circumstance justifies compensation, under a scheme devoted to equality of resources, and though the hypothetical insurance market does not right the balance – nothing can – it seeks to remedy one aspect of the resulting unfairness.[61]

Hypothetical insurance requires us to imagine how much insurance protection against risk we would have purchased, if we had had the opportunity to do so on equal terms, and in view of what insurers would have charged for premiums in a competitive market.[62] Individuals who suffer deficiencies in their mental and physical capacities are to be compensated according to the results of the scheme.

I contend that Dworkin's insurance approach cannot cope with inequalities that are traceable to relative differences in natural capacities in the age of biological control, assuming these differences are the product of parental choice. I emphasized above that if we can control the genetic fate of our offspring, then the idea that genetic make-up is a matter of brute genetic luck is no longer persuasive. The genetic make-up of all children in the world we are considering relates directly to choice and not chance. Even if offspring suffer from the negligence of their parents, their bad luck, being social luck, seems to merit no compensation according to the terms of the hypothetical insurance market.[63]

Dworkin has written that:

[t]he mix of personal ambitions, attitudes and preferences that I find in my community, or in the overall state of the world's resources, is not in itself fair or unfair to me; on the contrary, that mix is among the facts that fix what it is fair or unfair for me to do or to have.[64]

On the basis of the quoted passage it would not appear that it is open to Dworkin, as his conception of justice stands, to compensate individuals for bad genetic outcomes traceable to choices made by their parents. It is timely to ask: assuming that the technologies are widely and freely available, what might move people to deny a good genetic hand to their offspring? Based on the current complexion of society we can reasonably infer that in the age of biological control, two classes of parent would not take recourse to technologies designed to ensure what the majority regards as being "good" genetic and other health for any child they plan to have. These are: the "feckless," and those members of society who hold views about what makes a life worthwhile which do not make room for the intervention of medical genetics. By definition, feckless individuals do not intentionally harm their fetuses. From empirical evidence relating to women who currently fail to safeguard the interests of late-term fetuses, we know that typically they have fallen prey to one or more of the following: poor education, deprived socioeconomic backgrounds, poverty in adult life, drug addiction or use, sexual and other forms of violent abuse. These women have disjointed thought processes and behave irresponsibly and recklessly (and, according to some states' laws, criminally).

Falling into the latter, much more numerous, group are: members of certain religions for whom technology is anathema to prescribed beliefs (e.g., devout members of the Amish community); individuals who do not consider certain powers, like the ability to hear, or "average" mental/physical capacities, as either desirable or essential components of a fulfilling life; people who prefer to have a genetically related child over having a healthy child who is not biologically related, and those who would find preferable methods (that is, artificial methods that offer superior genetic outcomes to natural procreation) rebarbative. I think it highly probable that many parents would refuse to avail themselves of technologies that could produce better outcomes than natural procreation (cloning, assuming the safety of that technique, for example, would *always* be preferable to natural procreation because the genetic outcomes of cloning, i.e., healthy genes, could be predicted with far greater accuracy than any instance of natural procreation, a method fraught with risk). The reason behind these decisions might be religious in the conventional sense of that term, or they might be "essentially religious" ones, in Dworkin's sense of that term. Regardless, according to Dworkin, the background against which we enter the world counts as "a parameter of justice": "Other people's needs and opinions are not resources that can be justly or injustly distributed among us: they are, to repeat, part of what we must take into account in judging what injustice is or what justice requires."[65]

It might be objected here that I am missing the obvious, that is, that Dworkin could still use his hypothetical insurance scheme to overcome the problem I have identified. He could argue that individuals might insure against the possibility of genetic defects or a *relatively* inferior set of healthy genes even when both are related to parental choice. He could press us to supply some morally meaningful difference between ill health suffered by an adult that was caused by, for example, physical assault, and shortfalls in genetic powers that were caused by a parent's bad procreative choices. I don't, however, see quite how Dworkin can let in this kind of insurance.

Recall that Dworkin's theory of equality seeks to situate people equally *ex ante* with respect to the risk of developing various "handicaps"; it does not aim to make people equal in resources after those risks have materialized differently for different individuals.[66] The problem is that *ex ante* insurance decisions rely on what people, hence prospective parents, accord importance to in respect of health. If the suggestion above is right, to wit that a community would consider it of greater value to have, for example, a genetically related child than one of average health who was not biologically related, then we are back to square one.

The second problem, as I see it, is that, in the age of biological control, insurers would not be prepared to offer premiums that protected people against the risk of genetic handicaps. This is because the premiums they would have to devise would not be based on the incidence of genetic disease in a community. Instead they would have to be based on the *dispositions of parents* regarding all of those technologies that they might or might not *choose* to access. I have been supposing that two classes of people would not access technologies with a view to preventing harm to their offspring: the feckless, and what I suggested would be a numerous group of people, a group comprised of people with certain conceptions of the good, for example, devout individuals for whom technology is anathema, people who think it important to have genetically related children even if that is at the cost of having children who possess some genetic defect or weakness, and those for whom the thought of relatively safer methods of procreation, say, cloning, is repugnant for nonreligious reasons. Of course, many other examples might be given. This kind of information would be extremely difficult to ascertain in a market setting, so much so that insurance companies would be acutely uncomfortable about offering any insurance for genetic-related disease. The insurance industry turns a profit precisely because it relies, in large part, on accurately predictive information about risk. (Indeed, that is why the industry currently does not seek to use much of genetic information that is available about individuals when setting their premiums – too little is known about the mere possession of many genes for that information to be used for tidy profit.) They could not derive this kind of information in any scenario when the risk of genetic disease was defined by the vagaries of parental choice. If no insurance is possible, it follows that no compensation will be forthcoming.

Dworkin may not object in reply that the limitations of actual insurance practices are irrelevant. He himself appeals to actual insurance practices to help defend himself against critics who charge his theory, for example, with meting out too little or too much compensation.[67] Moreover, he structures his own hypothetical insurance scheme in line with actual policies. Provisionally, we can conclude that Dworkin is committed to accepting that individuals who are born with avoidable suboptimal endowments in the age of biological control are not personally responsible for their genetic endowment are still responsible for the life they make against the background of that endowment, and receive no state monetary assistance.

Dworkin may nevertheless believe that justice requires compensation for the children of parents who failed to ensure an adequate genetic hand for them, and embrace another strategy. It may be that this explains Dworkin's comment in "Playing God":

> [My] analysis of fair insurance might have to be revised, of course, along with almost every other relatively concrete judgment of fairness, if the most extravagant promises of genetic engineering were realized. *We would then have to consider, in our moral free-fall state, how far children should be held accountable for choices their parents made.*[68]

The most obvious reading of this passage "how far children should be held accountable for choices their parents made" is that, the day detailed genetic control proves possible, Dworkin's theory of liberal egalitarian justice overnight becomes the uncomfortable bedfellow of libertarianism, at least in practice. Up to now, libertarians have set themselves apart from Dworkin (and equal opportunity theorists) by insisting that the sources of the range of conditions that beset us divide into *three* relevant categories – our choices, others' choices, and chance.[69] In the area of procreation, Dworkin has tended to regard others' choices and chance as one undifferentiated category.[70] As Dworkin's theory currently stands, and on this first reading of the passage, Dworkin looks set to join hands with left-libertarians, like Hillel Steiner, who would leave the business of seeking compensation for avoidable bad genes to the people afflicted by them.[71] For the purposes of my argument, one can remain agnostic about the desirability of both wrongful life suits and criminal actions by the state.[72] Holding a negligent parent legally liable may well be justified, but the possibility of this should not deter a state monetary response to the offspring of negligent parents. Why? As a practical matter, it is doubtful children would ever succeed in exacting any compensation from parents who failed to access technologies if they fit the profile of those feckless pregnant women who currently behave in negligent ways. Second, and importantly, it is my view (one shared by others) that an adequate political morality should seek to mitigate brute bad luck, even if that luck is "social" luck, and especially when that social luck entails poor health.

Furthermore, the lead in to Dworkin's ambiguous statement about responsibility and children is the phrase: "if the most extravagant promises of genetic engineering were realized." I do not see why Dworkin thinks he has to wait for the most extravagant promises to be realized, when it should be clear to him that his deployal of the chance/choice distinction is problematic *now*. Do we really rest something as important as our political morality on contingencies such as "what ifs" about genetics? Dworkin has been unmoved philosophically by other developments in science that have enabled us to influence the genetic make-up and the health more generally of our offspring, and that have occurred during the time he was constructing his conception of justice. Now it seems that we have to wait for extreme genetic control to be possible before he reconsiders his theory. This strikes me as dubious, to say the very least.

I wish now to consider a possible alternative to Dworkin's theory that I think can accommodate advances in genetics much more palatably than equality of resources. G. A. Cohen, in "On the Currency of Egalitarian Justice," argues against Dworkin's theory of equality of resources and in favor of what he calls "equal access to advantage."[73] On Cohen's view, the state may not hold people responsible for inequalities that result from tastes, preferences, and so forth, that were not *deliberately* cultivated by the agent. (I would say the preference for genetically related children might very well be one of these.) It also compensates people for instances of bad luck that stem from unchosen background societal conditions. For the first reason, Cohen's approach would award compensation to the offspring of the feckless, and for the second it would compensate damaged children of the devout, and of those otherwise motivated, such as those who would eschew artificial means of procreation in favor of more traditional methods. For all of Cohen's own examples as to why Dworkin has placed his "cut" in the wrong place, I believe that the one under consideration here makes the strongest case for his approach. It is misguided to deny state compensation to children who are born with some or other defect on the grounds that it is traceable to the choices and behaviors of their parents. There are other theories that we might have drawn from to make our case: Arneson's, Sen's, and Roemer's approaches also furnish the means to deal with the problem I have highlighted for Dworkin's theory. It is no accident that all of these views are welfarist (in type) conceptions of justice.

In respect of equality, Dworkin's moral free-fall hypothesis is therefore found wanting. Although Dworkin does not *focus* on the implications of genetic control for his theory of distributive equality, he is well aware of the problems that I have been discussing. I have argued that there are already palatable approaches that can cope with the new knowledge from imminent applications of genetic science. These theories demarcate the boundary of personal and collective responsibility differently to Dworkin. They are more akin to conventional morality than the relevant redistributive component of his own theory. Some of these theories afford compensation if certain sorts of suffering is involved (e.g., Sen's); others, like Cohen's, are more discriminating and award compensation for brute bad luck, construed generously. The reason that they are superior is because they do a better job than Dworkin's theory of capturing the intuition that it is unfair for people to suffer through no fault of their own, whether that suffering is traceable to genetic or social circumstances. State concern for citizens requires, I believe, this more full-blooded response. Therefore *we* are not in moral free-fall in this area of morality – Dworkin's theory is.

Dworkin is absolutely right that "[t]he questions raised by the specter of cloning and dramatic genetic engineering are morally instructive even if these techniques are not possibilities. . . ."[74] In my own examination of these questions above I have argued that Dworkin's moral free-fall hypothesis is not persuasive. But it draws attention to the fact that Dworkin's own theory is deficient in several important respects. These deficiencies are not new, they have been troubling all along – no complex science, that is, was necessary to see this. Alternative approaches to ethical practice regarding procreation and to political morality are on offer which Dworkin had good reason to take seriously long prior to cloning and genetic engineering becoming likely possibilities. The "new genetics" may supply grounds to reject his theory in part or whole, but it does not pitch us into moral free-fall. There is no moral void to fill.

Acknowledgement

This chapter has benefited from much helpful discussion with Alan Colman, and from written comments by Ranjit Banerji, Paul Snowdon, and Hillel Steiner. Thanks are also due to Richard Dawkins (evolutionary matters), Richard Nickerson (quantum mechanics), and to Matthew Clayton, enduring critic.

Notes

1 Ronald Dworkin, "Playing God: Genes, Clones, and Luck," in *Sovereign Virtue* (Cambridge, MA: Harvard University Press, 2000), ch. 13, see p. 446. "Playing God" was originally written as a summary paper of the 21st Century Trust Conference on genetics at Merton College, Oxford in March 1998, which Ronald Dworkin chaired, and at which I was a participant. It was first published in *Prospect* in May 1999.

2 J. Watson and F. Crick, "Molecular Structure of Nucleic Acids: A Structure for Deoxyribose Nucleic Acid," *Nature*, vol. 171, 1953, pp. 737–8. The discovery of DNA is documented in J. Watson's *The Double Helix*, Introduction by S. Jones (Harmondsworth, UK: Penguin, 1999). For an interesting and somewhat divergent account to the one Watson provides of Rosalind Franklin's role in unmasking gene structure, see Anne Sayre, *Rosalind Franklin & DNA* (New York: Norton, 1978).

3 Ian Wilmut, one of the pioneers of cloning research, has made the term fashionable. "The Age of Biological Control," in Justine Burley (ed.), *The Genetic Revolution and Human Rights* (Oxford: Oxford University Press, 1999), ch. 2.

4   For detailed treatment of the rise of and rationale for eugenics programs in twentieth-century Germany
    see Paul Weindling, *Health, Race and German Politics Between National Unification and Nazism
    1870–1945* (Cambridge, UK: Cambridge University Press, 1989); Benno Müller-Hill, *Murderous
    Science. Elimination by Scientific Selection of Jews, Gypsies and Others: Germany 1933–1945*, trans. G.
    Fraser (Oxford: Oxford University Press, 1988).

5   Note that I do not write "control the genetic-make up of human *populations*." While this is a scientific
    possibility, it is not likely to be a favored political policy by any liberal democratic government. There
    has been debate over whether intended applications of the "new genetics" – the alleviation or avoid-
    ance of disease for the benefit of the individual concerned – are best described as "eugenic," given that
    the term is typically associated with state-run attempts to influence the genetics of groups of people
    for ideological reasons. On this point see Jonathan Glover, "Eugenics and Human Rights," in Justine
    Burley (ed.), *The Genetic Revolution and Human Rights* (Cambridge, UK: Cambridge University Press,
    2000), ch. 5. See also A. Buchanan, D. Brock et al., *From Chance to Choice: Genetics and Justice*, op. cit.,
    ch. 4, for insight into the usage of the term, past and present.

6   I. Wilmut, A. E. Schnieke, J. McWhir, A. Kind, and K. H. Campbell, "Viable Offspring Derived from
    Fetal and Adult Mammalian Cells," *Nature*, vol. 385, 1997, pp. 810–13. The discovery of DNA was not
    required for the success of cloning experiments. Cloning has now been carried out in seven mammalian
    species. Notwithstanding the differences in reproductive systems between humans and these species,
    the prediction that human cloning is possible is a reasonable one. However, experiments in animal
    models have demonstrated that efficiency rates are low and prenatal and postnatal abnormalities high.
    See for further factual discussion, Alan Colman, "Somatic Cell Nuclear Transfer in Mammals: Progress
    and Applications," *Cloning*, vol. 1, 2000, pp. 185–200.
        For a rebuttal of the view that safety concerns are a knock-down objection to human reproductive
    cloning see Justine Burley, "The Ethics of Therapeutic and Reproductive Human Cloning," *Seminars
    in Cell and Developmental Biology*, vol. 10, 1999, pp. 287–294, esp. pp. 290–1. For argument against the
    claim that human cloning should be banned because it would produce deficits in child welfare see Justine
    Burley and John Harris, "Human Cloning and Child Welfare," *Journal of Medical Ethics*, vol. 25, 1999,
    pp. 108–13; cf. S. Holm, "A Life in Shadows: One Reason Why We Should Not Clone Humans,"
    Cambridge Quarterly of Healthcare Ethics, vol. 7(2), Spring 1998, pp. 160–162; Ruth Deech,
    "Human Cloning and Public Policy," in Justine Burley (ed.), *The Genetic Revolution and Human Rights*,
    op. cit., ch. 8; Matthew Clayton, "Procreative Autonomy and Genetics," in Justine Burley and John
    Harris (eds.), *A Companion to Genethics* (Oxford: Blackwell, 2000), ch. 14. Eva Hoffman provides a fic-
    tional account of the psychological torments of a cloned child in *The Secret* (London: Secker and
    Warburg, 2001), reviewed by Justine Burley, "Exactly the same but different," *Nature*, vol. 417, May 16,
    2002, pp. 224–5.

7   Despite much recent hype about human cloning being imminent, it is clear that modified
    procedures will have to be developed if primate cloning is to be successful. At the time of revising
    this chapter, new data was published showing that numerous attempts using established methods
    of nuclear transfer in the rhesus monkey failed to produce a single pregnancy, and also that
    early embryos, where examined, showed abnormal chromosome numbers in their cells (C. Simerly
    et al., "Molecular Correlates of Primate Nuclear Transfer Failures," *Science*, vol. 300, 2003,
    p. 297).

8   Dworkin, "Playing God," op. cit.

9   Ronald Dworkin, *Life's Dominion: An Argument about Abortion and Euthanasia* (London: Harper Collins,
    1993), see especially, pp. 11–4, 19–20, 60–5, 108–9, 115–7, 121–6.

10 Dworkin, "Playing God," op. cit., p. 428.

11 Ibid., pp. 429–37.

12 Ibid., p. 437.

13 Ibid., p. 446.

14 Ibid., p 438.

15 Ibid., p. 428.

16   Ibid., p. 443.
17   John Roberston, *Children of Choice: Freedom and the New Reproductive Technologies* (Princeton, NJ: Princeton University Press, 1994); Ronald Green, *The Human Embryo Research Debates* (Oxford: Oxford University Press, 2002), e.g., pp. 125– 31; A. Buchanan, D. Brock et al., *From Chance to Choice*, op. cit.
18   Dworkin, "Playing God," op. cit., p. 444.
19   Ibid., pp. 444–5 (my emphasis).
20   Ibid. (my emphasis).
21   Ronald Dworkin, "Objectivity and Truth: You'd Better Believe It," *Philosophy and Public Affairs*, vol. 25(2), Spring 1996, pp. 87–139.
22   Ibid., p. 127. Dworkin says the term is an apt description of his position in that he embraces the "face-value view."
23   Ibid. pp. 127–8 (my emphasis).
24   Ibid., p. 127.
25   For example, "If we were to take seriously the possibility . . . that scientists really have gained the capacity to create a human being having any phenotype that they or their prospective parents choose – then we could chart the destruction of our moral and ethical attitudes starting at almost any point" (Dworkin, "Playing God," op. cit., p. 445).
26   See Dworkin's discussion in ibid., pp. 440–2.
27   Ibid., p. 442.
28   For example, "My analysis of fair insurance might have to be revised, of course, along with almost every other relatively concrete judgment of fairness, *if the most extravagant promises of genetic engineering were realized*" (Dworkin, "Playing God," op. cit., p. 451, my emphasis).
29   See, for example, Dworkin's claim about the right to reproductive freedom on p. 447 of "Playing God."
30   This was a particular problem for King Henry VIII, in the 16th century, who was obliged on several occasions to seek a papal dispensation to marry a genetically related family member. See Antonia Fraser, *The Six Wives of King Henry VIII* (London: Phoenix Press, 2002).
31   If a parent were to select, for example, an eye-color gene for a child, whether it gave the desired result (e.g., a hazel-eyed child) would often depend on nongenetic factors such as biological events in the intrauterine environment.
32   When Patrick Steptoe and Robert Edwards produced the first so-called test tube baby, Louise Brown, in 1978, there were public cries of "abomination." IVF is now widely practiced and the origins of children born of the technique go unnoticed by all except a minority of critics preoccupied with embryo wastage.
33   Dworkin, "Playing God," op. cit., p. 445.
34   There are several such statements, for example: "[T]he conventional distinction we all make between circumstances [i.e., genetic make-up] and personality does not assume that we have chosen our personality, and so would not be undermined by any argument, general or metaphysical, that we could not have chosen it." (Dworkin, "Equality and Capability," in *Sovereign Virtue*, op. cit., p. 294).
35   For example, and esp., Dworkin, "Equality of Resources," *Sovereign Virtue*, op. cit., ch. 2.
36   Note that it is also deeply relevant to our genetic complement.
37   Dworkin, "Playing God," op. cit., p. 443.
38   Ibid., p. 445.
39   S. Shiffrin, "Wrongful Life, Parental Responsibility, and the Significance of Harm," *Legal Theory*, vol. 5, July 1999, pp. 117–48.
40   Dworkin, "Playing God," op. cit., p. 448.
41   Dworkin, *Life's Dominion*, op cit., p. 18.
42   Ibid.
43   Dworkin, "What is Equality?: Part 2: Equality of Resources," in *Sovereign Virtue*, op. cit., ch. 2. For a full discussion of luck and insurance see pp. 73–83.
44   Dworkin, "Equality of Resources," in *Sovereign Virtue*, op. cit., ch. 2.
45   Dworkin, "Playing God," op. cit., p. 445.

46   Paul Snowdon suggested that I structure the challenge this way.

47   Dworkin, *Life's Dominion*, op. cit., p. 148.

48   See chs. 12 and 13 of this volume for detailed exposition and critical discussion.

49   *Life's Dominion*, op. cit., pp. 167–8. See also Ronald Dworkin, *Freedom's Law* (Oxford: Oxford University Press, 1996), pp. 104–5; Ronald Dworkin, Thomas Nagel, Robert Nozick, John Rawls, Thomas Scanlon, and Judith Thomson, "The Philosophers' Brief on Assisted Suicide," *New York Review of Books*, 44, March 27, 1997.

50   Dworkin, "Playing God," op. cit., p. 447. This is one of the few examples in "Playing God" where Dworkin incorporates proposition (2) into his moral free-fall thesis, to wit some of our moral views may not be tight now.

51   Dworkin, *Life's Dominion*, op. cit., pp. 167–8.

52   For further in-depth discussion of this point, see the chapters by Kamm and Rakowski in this volume.

53   Dworkin, "Playing God," op. cit., p. 450.

54   D. Parfit *Reasons and Persons* (Oxford: Clarendon Press, 1984), ch. 16. The following discussion of non-identity follows what John Harris and I argued in our "Human Cloning and Child Welfare," op. cit.

55   Parfit, *Reasons and Persons*, p. 358.

56   Ibid., p. 360.

57   See Parfit's discussion of Jane's Choice (ibid., pp. 375–7).

58   Norman Daniels, *Just Health Care* (Cambridge, UK: Cambridge University Press, 1985).

59   John Stuart Mill, *On Liberty* (London: Everyman, 1972).

60   G. A. Cohen, "On the Currency of Egalitarian Justice," *Ethics*, vol. 99, 1989, pp. 906–44; R. Arneson, "Equality and Equality of Opportunity for Welfare," in L. Pojman and L. Westmoreland (eds.), *Equality: Selected Readings* (Oxford: Oxford University Press, 1997), pp. 229–41, and "Liberalism, Distributive Subjectivism and Equal Opportunity for Welfare," *Philosophy and Public Affairs*, vol. 19(2), Spring, 1990, pp. 159–94; C. Macleod, *Liberalism, Justice and Markets* (Oxford: Clarendon Press, 1998); J. Roemer, *Egalitarian Perspectives* (Cambridge, UK: Cambridge University Press, 1994), and *Theories of Distributive Justice* (Cambridge, MA: Harvard University Press, 1996), ch. 7; A. Sen, *Inequality Re-examined* (Oxford: Clarendon Press, 1992), chs. 1–5, esp. pp. 12–13, 33–4, 37–8, 42, 74, 77, 80.

61   Dworkin, "Equality of Resources," op. cit., p. 81.

62   See Dworkin's reply to Van der Veen in *Symposium on Ronald Dworkin's Sovereign Virtue*, *Ethics*, vol. 113, 2002, pp. 120–2.

63   See ch. 2 of *Sovereign Virtue*, op. cit.

64   Dworkin, "Equality and Capability," op. cit., p. 298.

65   Ibid, pp. 298–9.

66   This Dworkin clarifies in his reply to Van der Veen, *Symposium on Ronald Dworkin's Sovereign Virtue*, op. cit., p. 121.

67   See, e.g., Dworkin's reply to Elizabeth Anderson in ibid, pp. 113–18.

68   Dworkin, "Playing God," op. cit., p. 451. My emphasis.

69   See for example, Hillel Steiner, "Silver Spoons and Golden Genes," in Justine Burley (ed.), *The Genetic Revolution and Human Rights*, op. cit., ch. 6; "Choice and Circumstance," *Ratio*, vol. X, 1997, pp. 296–312.

70   This is made apparent by Casal's and Williams' discussion in ch. 9 of this volume.

71   See Steiner, "Silver Spoons and Golden Genes," op. cit.

72   The number of states in the USA that now treat behaviors that jeopardize the health or life of the fetus as criminal increased by 32 percent from 1992 to 1995. Women are jailed to prevent them from taking drugs that might damage their fetuses, and have been charged with homicide for drug-related fetal deaths.

73   G. A. Cohen, "On the Currency of Egalitarian Justice," op. cit.

74   Dworkin, "Playing God," op. cit., p. 447 (my emphasis).

Part III

Abortion, Euthanasia, and Assisted Suicide

11

Autonomy, Beneficence, and the Permanently Demented

Seana Valentine Shiffrin

Ronald Dworkin's *Life's Dominion*[1] addresses the debates about abortion and euthanasia that have exercised comptemporary American politics. His book and earlier articles[2] urge us to discard portraits of these issues that paint irresoluble conflicts of rights. Instead, he suggests that we should reconceptualize these debates to reflect a recognition that what propels them is an essentially religious disagreement about the intrinsic value of human life.

A human life, Dworkin thinks, has a subjective value that is a function of the interests its bearer takes in that life. Dworkin also contends that we all share the conviction that, independent of its subjective value, human life is intrinsically valuable, that is, it is valuable in itself. It may be valuable even when its bearer does not take an interest in his or her life. Independent of the bearer's attitudes, the life is miraculous and we regard it as in some way "sacred" or "inviolable." Dworkin regards the consensus that life has intrinsic value as a shared, but essentially religious, idea. Thus he sees the social disagreement over our *characterization* of this intrinsic value as a religious dispute.[3] For some the intrinsic value of each life resides in its being the product of divine creation or, alternatively, the product of natural evolutionary processes. For others, it has intrinsic value because it is a complex, vibrant product of a cultural, social, or individual human achievement (pp. 68–101).[4]

Those who regard the natural or divine contribution to life as paramount may regard abortion and euthanasia as manifesting deep disrespect for life's sanctity. These acts end lives that are the outcomes of these processes. By contrast, those who regard the human investment as the critical locus of value believe that abortion and euthanasia may not threaten or disregard the intrinsic value of human life. There is a relatively minor investment represented in the fetus, whereas the comatose, those in constant pain, or those no longer in command of their mental faculties, can make only a negligible contemporary contribution to this process.

In Dworkin's view, reconceptualizing these debates as religious disputes justifies liberal approaches that vest individuals with the ultimate decision-making authority over these matters. Principles of freedom of conscience and religious neutrality make it inappropriate for the state to take positions about why human life has intrinsic value, how much value it has, and how best to respect that value. Likewise, it would be inappropriate for the state to restrict personal liberty to protect that value. Its role must simply be to protect the rights and interests people have in their lives and in living out their convictions. Consequently, Dworkin believes that while it is legitimate for the government to encourage serious thought about the sanctity of life, the government may not force any single view about spirituality on citizens (pp. 150, 157, 168). For instance, Dworkin contends that the government may encourage reflection about the value of human life by educating its citizens (read women) about abortion (pp. 169–70).[5] But it may not enforce any particular view about how the sanctity of life may best be respected, for example, by banning the option of abortion outright.[6]

Dworkin's philosophical and legal views about the connection between the abortion issue and the sanctity of life are rich and thought-provoking. It is no surprise that they have sparked a significant amount of critical attention and commentary.[7] His views about the connection between respect for autonomy and control over the end of life, while ground-breaking and arguably more provocative, have received less attention.[8] In this chapter I examine these views. I focus on his argument for implementing advance directives that specify what treatment should be given to people who have become permanently demented. In section I, I provide an overview of Dworkin's analysis of the problem of the permanently demented. In section II, I argue that the reasons to respect the autonomy of the fully competent fail to justify extending the range of autonomous control over self-regarding life-and-death decisions enjoyed by competent people to include prospective control over what should happen to themselves if they become permanently demented. I also argue that Dworkin's conception of autonomy is flawed. It leads him to disregard the autonomy that demented people may be capable of exerting. In the third section, I argue that Dworkin's complementary analysis of our duties of beneficence to demented people does not and cannot emerge from a neutral stance toward the sanctity of life. If I am right about the relevant considerations of either autonomy or beneficence, then there may be reason to question seriously whether we should abide by advance directives concerning conditions of dementia. At the very least, I aim to show that Dworkin's argument as it stands is incomplete. More needs to be shown if we are to implement these directives with any degree of moral confidence.

I

Dworkin argues that decisions concerning the prolongation of life and euthanasia properly rest with individuals. The government may not adopt or enforce any particular view as to how to pay tribute to the sanctity of life. It may not dictate that respect for life entails prolonging it as long as possible or, alternatively, that respect for life is best shown by preventing its degeneration into a dependent state of horrific pain, dementia, or permanent vegetation. Instead, people should be encouraged to write their own advance directives that direct what should be done should they become terminally ill, fall into a persistent vegetative state, or become demented. In Dworkin's view, it is appropriate for the state to act on reasons of beneficence and respect for individual autonomy. These considerations dictate respect for individuals' judgments about the value of their lives. Thus these directives should be implemented, whether they direct us to continue or to curtail the lives at stake.

With respect to permanently demented people in particular, Dworkin argues that their rights of autonomy and to beneficence entail that we should respect the decisions of their *past* competent selves about what should be done should they become demented. He claims that we would be mistaken to conceive of demented people as persons with rights of autonomy and interests of their own, distinct and separable from those of their previous competent selves. Rather, in Dworkin's assessment, *qua* demented people (that is, abstracting entirely from their connection to their past competent stages of life), such people have no rights of autonomy at all. They lack the requisite capacities for the attribution of such a right to make any sense.

As to what is in the best interests of permanently demented people, the argument becomes more complicated. Dworkin distinguishes between what he calls one's *experiential* and one's *critical* interests. Something is in one's experiential interest if one enjoys the experience of doing it, like listening to jazz, and runs counter to one's experiential interest if it provides an unpleasant experience such as discomfort, boredom, pain, or nausea. Dworkin believes that although we have a great yen to satisfy our experiential interests, generally, the fulfillment and frustration of these interests, considered by themselves, do not make a life better or worse. We do not, he observes, think a person's life has been a worse life if that person has undergone a great deal of painful dental work (p. 201). Critical interests are interests the satisfaction of which make a life genuinely better and the frustration of which makes a life worse. What lies in one's critical interests are things that will contribute to a good life and that one *should* want, such as interests in accomplishment, in having close relationships with one's family, and in living a morally decent life. Importantly, these interests are the kinds of interests about which people may be mistaken. Such mistakes themselves can make a life go worse.

Dworkin maintains that a demented person *qua* demented person lacks a critical interest in continuing to live. Demented people may have experiential interests in their lives. They may have good or bad experiences within them; they can, for instance, enjoy comfort and reassurance or feel pain and fear (p. 227). They cannot, however, take a view of their lives as a whole, and hence they cannot form opinions about their critical interests. That is, they cannot assess what renders their lives a success or a failure and what, within a life, pays proper heed to the sanctity of life (pp. 201, 230). Moreover, Dworkin thinks that not only are demented people incapable of understanding what is in their critical interests, they cannot do anything to further their critical interests. He claims they are incapable of the acts and attachments that give life value. Value, he notes, "cannot be poured into a life from the outside; it must be generated by the person whose life it is, and this is no longer possible for [the demented person]" (p. 230).

But, for Dworkin, we take an improper view of demented people if we regard them solely *qua* demented people. They must be understood as people whose history is composed mostly of stages of clarity and competence, but who have become demented. The autonomy rights and interests of these whole persons should be understood in the light of their life histories that encompass far more than their period of dementia. These people can be affected by what happens to them in their demented state. A competent, but terminally ill, person may regard the final painful stage of a terminal disease as not worth living and perhaps as a stage that tarnishes the image of a vital life. Likewise, Dworkin imagines that people prior to their decline into dementia may have considered carefully the effect of a demented stage at the end of their lives upon the value of their lives as a whole. They may have decided that "a life ending like that is seriously marred," because it would degrade the previous accomplishments and deliberative direction that previously characterized their lives (p. 231). Consequently, they may exercise their autonomous judgment and sign a living will directing that they be denied medical care and nutrition should they become demented. Others differ and have alternative conceptions of the proper value of life and its sanctity. They may think their appreciation of life is best paid tribute by persevering through life to the end, even with diminished capacities. They may direct that they be permitted to live on during dementia (assuming there are available funds for maintenance and care).[9] Dworkin holds that these sorts of previously issued judgments by those who have become demented reflect their assessments of their critical interests. These judgments must be honored if we aim to respect these people and to protect their interests.[10] In his view, both considerations of autonomy and beneficence counsel us to respect and implement advance directives – whether to terminate or to prolong the lives of permanently demented people – even when we profoundly disagree with the content of these directives and even when the demented people's expressed contemporary wishes contradict these directives.

These are striking views with heady implications for the lives and deaths of demented people. In what follows, I will not examine or challenge Dworkin's views about the rights of conscious and competent individuals to continue treatment, to refuse treatment, or to end their lives through more active means. I agree that we should take seriously the idea that conscious and competent individuals have a right to die (as well as a right to live, no matter how wretched the existence). I am troubled, however, by approaches that treat the situation of permanently demented people as of a piece with these cases – that is, analyses that extend the right of competent individuals to choose their course while competent to include a right to dictate what should happen to them if they become demented. I do not intend to offer a knock-down argument against such approaches, but to present some concerns about the legitimacy of implementing advance directives about dementia, concerns that emerge from doubts about Dworkin's analysis of autonomy and beneficence.

II

This section focuses on assessing what reasons are provided by respect for autonomy to follow advance directives concerning the cessation or the continuation of the life of a demented person, especially when the demented person now expresses some will to the contrary.[11] My primary aim is to scrutinize Dworkin's analysis of autonomy and to suggest that it is overly narrow. A fuller understanding of autonomy jeopardizes Dworkin's conclusions about the binding force of advance directives in the case of dementia. Contrary to Dworkin's contention, the demented's (*qua* demented) exercise of the will may well engage some autonomy values. At the same time, Dworkin's own analysis of autonomy's value fails to provide the requisite justification for demonstrating the legitimacy of advance directives in cases involving permanent, involuntary, and significantly degenerative personality change.

There are three important questions to press concerning Dworkin's argument for honoring advance directives about dementia:

1　Does respect for autonomy provide us with a reason to implement these advance directives?
2　Does respect for autonomy provide us with *no* reason to respect the contemporary wishes of the demented?
3　Is Dworkin's analysis of our duties of beneficence to permanently demented people persuasive?

I address the first two questions in this section and the third in the following section. I will argue that with respect to the moderately demented and the severely demented, the answer to the first question is no. With respect to the second question, I will argue that the wishes of some permanently demented people concerning the continuation of their lives have some autonomy value worthy of our respect, even if these wishes do not express a reflective unified character. The severely demented who are almost vegetable-like or who have radically self-contradictory wishes may not be able to convey any clear wishes at all, in which case it may be true that they may not exercise autonomy. Still, even in the case of the severely demented, if my first argument is correct, the advance directive issued by their prior selves may not exert much moral pull *qua* its autonomy value. In such a case, we should not be guided by the advance directive. Rather, we are left with the difficult task of divining what is in such patients' best contemporary interests. I will argue in the following section that Dworkin's rendering of beneficence does not offer plausible guidance for this task. In fact, his account is in tension with the major theme of the book.

Before proceeding to discuss autonomy in greater depth, it is worth becoming clearer about the subjects of our concern. Dworkin limits his discussion to considering those who have become *permanently* demented, that is those people who suffer from an acquired,[12] persistent, and irreversible impairment of intellectual function, characterized by compromised language skills, memory skills, visual and spatial skills, emotional reactions, personality expression, or cognition.[13] Different stages of dementia correspond to different levels of functioning. The mildly demented suffer a moderate level of memory loss, some spatiotemporal disorientation, and have enhanced difficulties handling problems. Still, they exert generally good judgment, may still perform many tasks inside and outside of the home, and generally retain the capacity for independent living with some assistance and prompting.[14] For the moderately demented, independent living may be hazardous and assistance may be required for personal care. Though they have severe memory loss, they retain some highly learned material, and often clearly recognize close friends and family members. They can be taken outside the home, but their social judgment is impaired and their interests are restricted. Many moderately demented people are in denial about their condition, although some indicate awareness that they are behaving abnormally and are undergoing a progressive intellectual decline.[15] Moderately demented patients, even in the moderately severe stage, can engage sporadically in effective communication and may still enjoy living.[16] The severely demented possess only memory fragments, require continuous supervision, cannot maintain personal hygiene, are largely incoherent or mute, and are incapable of making judgments or solving problems.

Unfortunately, it is unclear to which of these stages Dworkin intends his conclusions to apply. Dworkin declares early in his discussion that his attention is restricted to those in the late stage of dementia who have lost all memory and sense of self-continuity; cannot attend to their own needs and functions; are incapable of sustaining projects, plans, or desires of even a very simple structure; but who may harbor a desire to live (pp. 218–19). Later, however, he elaborates, arguing that:

> When a mildly demented person's choices are reasonably stable, reasonably continuous with the general character of his prior life and inconsistent only to the rough degree that the choices of fully competent people are, he can be seen as still in charge of his life and he has a right of autonomy for that reason . . . But if his choices and demands, no matter how firmly expressed, systematically or randomly contradict one another, reflecting no coherent sense of self and no discernable even short-term aims, then he has presumably lost the capacity that it is the point of autonomy to protect. (p. 225)

I will discuss Dworkin's views about autonomy later. At present, I am interested in this passage for what it reveals and fails to reveal about the subjects of Dworkin's conclusions. The passage suggests at one point that the test to determine whether advance directives should trump the patient's contemporary wishes turns upon whether the demented's judgment is discontinuous with the judgment of the patient's past selves. Only a few sentences later, the test becomes whether the contemporary judgments are themselves radically self-contradictory, a rather different criterion. Dworkin's articulated standards leave it unclear whether he intends to extend his conclusions to those moderately demented people who may express occasional firm preferences that are not themselves radically self-contradictory, but are not continuous with their past character, are less consistent than the choices of the fully competent, and do not flow from a clearly defined, reflective character. Further, despite Dworkin's pronouncement that he will limit himself to the severely demented, the cases he discusses involve people who appear moderately demented. One patient, Margo, maintains persistent, though simple, desires and projects. She pretends to read, attends art classes, and loves sandwiches. Her medical student attendant declared that she was "undeniably one of the happiest people I have ever known" (p. 221).[17] Such examples appear to indicate a willingness on Dworkin's part to extend his conclusions to a broader category than those in late-stage dementia. In any case, whether this interpretation correctly gauges Dworkin's intention, as I will argue, his accounts of autonomy and beneficence seem subject to such extension.

To simplify syntax, I will refer to the subjects of my concern in the following way. I will refer to a person when in a stage of competence as P_1. I will refer to the person occupying the same body as P_1, but when in a stage of dementia, as P_2. I will assume, with Dworkin, that P_1 and P_2 are not different people but rather pick out different selves or different stages within the same person's life.[18]

In Dworkin's view, if prior to the onset of dementia I sign a living will that declares that my life should be terminated if I mentally deteriorate to a particular stage, then no matter how much I enjoy my life, and insist upon its continuation at the time, others will show fundamental respect for me by "allowing" my death (or by killing me, depending on the contents of the directive). In this example, P_1 issues the directive that P_2 is to be killed and P_2 pleads against this directive's implementation. Alternatively, if, when competent, I direct that I must continue living during my demented stage no matter what – even if I am in utter pain and begging for relief – then others will show me respect by refusing to allow my death; they would disrespect me by providing lethal relief.

Dworkin's justification for these conclusions runs as follows. When deliberating about what action to take concerning the continuation of the lives of demented people, we must consider their rights of autonomy as well as their rights to our beneficence. Considerations about respect for autonomy, he thinks, come down in favor of adhering to advance directives, as an analysis of two main justifications for respecting autonomy reveals. The first, the *evidentiary account*, stresses that we should respect the decisions of others and refrain from interfering with others' lives without invitation, because individuals generally make the best judgments about what is in their own best self-regarding interests (pp. 222–3). Respecting other people's autonomy is, as a rule, the best way to promote their welfare, and not simply because among their various desires is the desire for control. But these grounds give us little reason to respect the expressed wishes of demented people, because it is less plausible to think that they generally make the best judgments about what is in their best interests.

Dworkin finds the evidentiary account inadequate, however, or at least incomplete, for two reasons (pp. 223–4). First, the evidentiary view cannot explain why respect for autonomy would direct us, as he thinks it does, to permit people to behave in ways that they themselves acknowledge as contrary to their best interests. Second, it neglects those cases in which one justifiably and understandably uses one's autonomy to further the interests of others, even at one's own overall expense. These considerations lead Dworkin to posit that some other justificatory ground must support respect for autonomy. He contends that an appeal to "integrity" may supply this missing ground. On this account, autonomy commands respect because it protects the capacity to express one's character through one's actions, to create and fashion a distinctive personality that propels one's life, and thereby to structure a life around one's own values. Dworkin argues that this view does not assume that every action a person performs will reflect consistency or structure, but that autonomy "encourages and protects people's general capacity to lead their lives out of a distinctive sense of their own character, a sense of what is important to and for them" (p. 224).[19]

Appeal to the *integrity account* clearly addresses the second shortcoming of the evidentiary account. I may wish to lead a life structured not only around furthering my own self-regarding interests, but also devoted to fulfilling interests of others. I may also reasonably commit myself to other forms of value, even if such pursuits are ultimately to my detriment or only indirectly serve my self-regarding interests. Less clear, though, is how an appeal to the integrity-based view could justify protection for acknowledged akratic behavior. One might, of course, be in some peculiar and precious way dedicated to living a rakish, imprudent life driven by a misguided but beguiling romanticism. But for those for whom akratic action is entirely out of character or unintentional, it is unclear how the integrity-based account lends support for respecting those actions. Dworkin might argue that the freedom to perform actions that are out of character is necessary for developing the ability to perform actions within character, but then, if this instrumental move works to support the integrity account, why couldn't similar arguments be made to support the evidentiary account? Perhaps the appropriate argument here is that without the freedom to deviate from one's values, the significance of one's accomplishment in creating and sustaining a life guided by certain values is lessened. Perhaps also all self-propelled actions contribute to a self-fashioned character and life, although the sum of these actions may produce a different product than what one hopes or intends to create.

In any case, Dworkin argues that neither account would compel us to respect a permanently demented patient's requests, expressed preferences, or decisions. Demented people lack the capacities of character structuring presupposed by the integrity account and the capacities for savvy deliberation presupposed by the evidentiary account. Both accounts point us toward following the directives issued by those people while they were in full command of their capacities. Suppose, however, that although P_1 directed that she be killed were she to become demented, that P_2 is happy and expresses desires to continue living while exhibiting terror at the prospect of her death. Shouldn't her contemporary wishes supersede her past decision? Doesn't respect for autonomy dictate that we should refrain from acting contrary to P_2's expressed wishes?

Quite the contrary, says Dworkin. Keeping the demented person alive where her precedent self has asked that she be killed in such a state "violates rather than respects her autonomy" (p. 229). He justifies this fairly chilling conclusion by asking us to reflect upon the case of a temporarily deranged Jehovah's Witness. He regards the case as analogous to the situation of the demented. Dworkin persuasively observes that it would be wrong to provide a transfusion to a demanding, yet temporarily deranged, Jehovah's Witness. It is not that agents cannot reverse or retract their previous decisions. Agents may change their minds, but only under the proper conditions. The deranged Jehovah's Witness, Dworkin observes, lacks the necessary capacity for a fresh exercise of autonomy. Her demands, therefore, cannot overturn her previous resolve. Her former decision remains in force because no new decision by a person capable of autonomous deliberation has annulled it. On the integrity-based value of autonomy, we respect the autonomy of the Jehovah's Witness by respecting her decisions about the character of her life made when she was in full control of her deliberative capacities. Likewise, Dworkin believes that the integrity-based view supports the idea that we should not indulge the deranged since they lack the necessary capacities to make decisions that contribute to the aim of building and expressing a coherent and distinctive character. Given his analysis of the Jehovah's Witness case, Dworkin thinks that it follows that we respect the autonomy of the demented person best by allowing her to die as per her previous directive, despite any contemporary protestations or signs of happiness.

I am skeptical about the analogy between the Jehovah's Witness case and the demented patient. My unease about this case can be traced to a suspicion that Dworkin neglects an important aspect of the grounds for valuing autonomy. This aspect may be uncovered by examining the force of the Jehovah's Witness example and identifying some disanalogies with the case of the demented.

Although Dworkin does not emphasize this feature, it seems important to his example that the derangement of the Jehovah's Witness is temporary and further, that if the life is saved, the Jehovah's Witness with full capacities will reemerge. She will regard our decision to deliver a transfusion with horror and revulsion. Dworkin rightly insists that the prospect of the Witness's regret cannot be what motivates us to respect the Jehovah's Witness's prior decisions against treatment. We should accede to a lucid Jehovah's Witness's request for treatment even if we know that person will later regret the decision. Anticipated regret, then, cannot be the salient feature restraining us from providing treatment (p. 228). There is an important asymmetry, however, between the Jehovah's Witness case and the cases of dementia. In the Jehovah's Witness case, the Witness's capacity for full-blown autonomy (a capacity to render decisions which is characterized by a stable, developed character and a fully rational intellect capable of assessing options and of engaging in self-reflection) has not been permanently lost but rather lies in abeyance. We may regret that we cannot accede to the deranged Witness's request for treatment, but we refrain from doing so because we have evidence of the Jehovah's Witness's true autonomous decision. We know that she will reemerge with this full capacity and our action will have frustrated its aim. In the case of permanent dementia, though, the capacity for full-blown autonomy is lost and will not be recovered.

This places the decisions and requests of the permanently demented person in a different light. It is one thing to refuse to listen to those who have temporarily lost their senses and act extremely out of character, but who will, or can, in time, return to their senses and will have to live with our action. We might think metaphorically about their deranged behavior in terms of an alien self who has temporarily commandeered their bodies. We decline to obey them because a very different personality with a different form of judgment will have to live with the effects of their temporary yet powerful reign. It is both that they will regret the decision *and* that the decision was made under conditions that were not true to themselves. In the case of the permanently demented, however, the "real" self will not return and be forced to live with the consequences of a temporary period of insanity. This makes a difference. In the Jehovah's Witness case, P_1 will return, is the more capable decision maker, and will have to live with the decisions for a long period of time. Where more permanent dementia sets in, the two factors come apart. P_1 may be the more capable decision maker, but P_2 will have to live with the consequences of the decisions, not P_1. Given that the fully capacitated self has been permanently effaced, our reason for overriding the expressed will of the deranged self diminishes. Since she is now operating with all of her possible decision-making capacities characteristically in force, limited though this set may be, there may be a reason to treat her expression of her will as a retraction of her previous decision.

Dworkin contends that there is nothing about P_2's judgment that commands any respect. Her decisions do not promise to teach us much about what is in her best interests. Further, she cannot reflect upon her critical interests at all, and hence she is not capable of making the kinds of decisions that the integrity-based view recognizes as exercises of autonomy. Keeping in mind the Jehovah's Witness case, however, it may be apparent that Dworkin glosses over an important dimension of autonomy's importance: the basic value of being in control of one's experience and in not having experiences forced or imposed upon one when one's will is to the contrary. The value of basic control over, and self-direction of, one's experiences, even momentary and slight ones, is an important ground for respect for autonomy distinct from the two foundations Dworkin discusses. Certainly, the evidentiary and integrity accounts identify strong central reasons for respecting autonomy, but the value of self-determination is not fully captured by the values pegged by these accounts. Understanding that one's choices generally best promote one's welfare or express one's character may isolate what is noble and most prized about the achievement of leading an autonomous life. Yet these values do not exhaust why we think people have some strong rights of control over their lives. There are many cases in which people do not choose what is in their best interests, and in which their choices will not contribute substantially to the conscious creation or expression of a distinctive character structured around a set of values, yet in which there is still *some* (much!) reason to respect those people's choices and to refrain from forcing a contrary decision upon them. We value and respect autonomy in part because we recognize that one's life is solely one's own and that one must bear and endure singly one's own conscious experience. Given this, the right and ability to select for oneself the contents of this experience is fitting and appropriate. To a certain extent, one is wronged if one's self-regarding experience is dictated or imposed by another. Respecting other people's decisions is not simply a way to promote their welfare or to facilitate the valuable process of their creating and expressing a distinctive character. In a more basic way, I believe it serves as an acknowledgement of the moral importance of the uniqueness and separateness of persons and the deep, irreducible fact that one's life is the only life one has. These facts do not just amount to the fact that one's *character* is distinct from that of others. There is more to one's mental life than is properly regarded as part of one's character (take, for instance, pain). Moreover, even when misdirected or confused, a life determined from within (driven by that person's will) is more valuable and distinctively human than one manipulated and steered by others.

Notably, the dispute that I am pursuing here with Dworkin is not the familiar dispute about whether autonomy has intrinsic or extrinsic value.[20] My challenge is not to the type of evaluation Dworkin assigns to autonomy (its intrinsic value) but to his identification of what it is in virtue of which autonomy has value. Dworkin has identified its intrinsically valuable features too narrowly. It is not just in virtue of autonomy's expressive nature that it is intrinsically valuable but also in virtue of its being a manifestation of individual control.

I do not dispute the integrity-based account or its relative importance. I simply wish to stress that this broader dimension of control merits recognition and exerts some moral force that makes a difference to our understanding of the conditions under which one's autonomous control extends into the future. It is difficult to elaborate fluently upon what exactly this other dimension of control consists in or why it is important. I can only gesture at what I take to be basic facts carrying moral significance: one's life and one's conscious experience are one's own, distinct from others; the simple exercise of control over one's experience reinforces the special relation one has to one's experience and has some value independent of what it accomplishes. Rather than repeating these invocations of the ineffable significance of separateness and self-determination, I will attempt to render the thought more appealing by way of two routes: first, by investigating the motivations behind the integrity account and second, by considering some overlooked aspects of the case of children, to whom demented patients are often compared.

Dworkin's integrity-based account of autonomy locates the justificatory ground for respect for one's chosen action in the capacity to have a distinctive character and to act from it. Only where this capacity exists over an extended and continuous period of time does one have the requisite abilities to participate under the banner of integrity, and only then can one claim rights to autonomy. But suppose we probe deeper and ask why it is important to be able to *act* out of a distinctive personality once it is formed. Why exactly is the integrity-based account compelling? The suggestion that seems correct to me, at least in part, is that autonomous action attempts to synchronize one's inner and outer life. Autonomous action permits one to try to fashion a life or even just momentary happenings and feelings that accord with one's subjective aims, desires, and visions of oneself and one's experience. Autonomy, then, facilitates a sort of unity between one's will and self-consciousness and one's endured experience, and life, more broadly conceived. When autonomy's exercise proceeds at its best, the unity one achieves will result in a distinctive, self-fashioned personality that coordinates with the life lived. This is a valuable and important accomplishment in itself, but it is hard to believe that it is a prerequisite for autonomy's having any intrinsic value, or that its value is substantially different in kind from the value of exercises of self-control that are not closely connected to the expression or creation of a distinctive character. If I am right about its elaboration, then the deeper layer of rationalization supporting the integrity account would point us beyond this account and toward the broader, "control" account of which the integrity account is a prominent, but only partial, component.

This further elaboration of the justification of the integrity account raises some difficulties, though, for the defense of advance directives about dementia. On the one hand, if autonomy's value derives from the importance of unifying one's experience with one's projected vision of oneself and one's personality, then why would we think that autonomy rights should extend control to include stages of one's life in which one's personality has abruptly ended? For in such a case, the unity cannot be achieved and the personality expression is mostly illusory and insufficiently genuine.

On the other hand, if my suggestion is right about the underlying motivations behind the appeal to integrity, then the value of autonomy may be reduced in cases in which one's capacity to form and express a personality has diminished, but it will not be extinguished. Even if people lack a coherent character structured around an ordered scheme of values, they may well have desires, aims, and preferences that could be synchronized with the content of those of their experiences that they and others can control.

There are two components of the value of autonomy on this account. First, there is the value of forming one's subjective desires and one's will, and their being unified with one's lived experience. Second, there is the value of effecting this unity through one's own action. Those with normal capacities may be capable of both and may actively contribute to the achievement of a rich and complex personal unity. This activity is usually part of the process of forging a distinctive character. Demented people may lack the abilities to effect this unity (and hence some forms of intervention may be justified to help them bring about what it is they will or want). Further, that which can be unified may be more paltry and dilute. Still, to the extent that they can express their will, some of what is of value about autonomy is at stake here. They surely can attempt to control the nature of their lived experience and to experience (although perhaps not effectuate it on their own) a unity between their subjective aims regarding their life and experience, and its reality.

Even where people are incapable of carrying out or expressing their will but we can discern its content, acknowledging the importance of this kind of unity distinguishes a type of substituted judgment from a "best interests" approach. The typical form of substituted judgment discussed in the medical ethics literature, what I will call SJ_1, refers to an attempt to assess what people would want in some circumstance were they able to assess the situation competently. This corresponds quite closely to Dworkin's understanding of what lies in an agent's best interests.[21] A distinct sort of substituted judgment, SJ_2, attempts to glean what people, as they are currently capacitated, actually do want, though they may be incapable of expressing and implementing their desires. The former type of substitute judgment, though a popular conception, is given no support by the analysis of autonomy's value where competence will not be restored. To the contrary, where there has been significant and permanent personality change, the moral significance of the results of SJ_1 should be called into question. There may be a large gap between what people do and will continue to want, given their extant personality and abilities, and what they would want were they competent. What the competent self may want of and for the incompetent self may differ dramatically from what the incompetent self actually wants. Given that the competent self will not have to live with his or her directions and the incompetent self may not welcome them or recognize them as his or her will, it is unclear what autonomy values are furthered by SJ_1 in the case of permanent personality change.

There are, however, autonomy-based reasons to attend to the results of SJ_2. The fact that one cannot *express* or *implement* one's will does not eviscerate the value of there being some unity between one's will and one's experience. SJ_2 is simply a means of discovering what it would take to achieve this unity.

Both forms of substituted judgment are not fully "substitutable" for the first person exercise of autonomy. Absent from both forms is the control over one's life that is achieved through self-implementation.[22] On both the integrity and the control accounts of autonomy, there is a special significance to one's engaging in processes of *self*-creation and *self*-direction. These accounts may recognize autonomy value in some types of substituted judgment, but they may still exhibit a principled preference for actual or first personal judgments and implementation.

The point I am trying to make may be approached from a different direction. As I remarked earlier, demented people are often analogized with children to make obvious the permissibility of paternalism toward the demented. But this analogy should set off some alarms. If we were to accept the evidentiary and integrity accounts as the sole underpinnings of the value of autonomy, then shouldn't we begin to wonder why we respect children's decisions as often and in the ways we do? Much attention is paid to the permissibility of paternalistic interference for children. It is routinely emphasized that children lack proper deliberative capacities for autonomous decision making. Strangely, there is little attention to the fact that paternalistic interference is not continuously exercised over many aspects of children's lives. Further, many paternalistic actions are often exercised with a measure of reluctance and regret (albeit outweighed by the good we are accomplishing), as though we are both impeding and overcoming something of value.

Why do we respect so many of children's decisions and preferences about their own lives? Often, the evidentiary or the integrity accounts will not supply a persuasive answer. Children do not always or consistently know what is in their best interests. Moreover, few of them conceive of or have the capacity to conceive of their actions as expressing a sense of self or a character constructed to reflect a chosen structure of values. As in Dworkin's description of the demented, many of their decisions may not flow from a coherent character or form part of a reflective project to construct such a character around a system of values. Nonetheless, absent substantial risk or miscalculation of possible benefit, children's decisions and preferences exert substantial moral weight and command our respect (though how much weight is recognized varies from parent to parent), even though their deliberative and reflective capacities are diminished and insufficiently developed to be convincingly assimilated into the evidentiary or integrity models of valuable autonomous behavior. Even where we override their preferences, we feel the residual need to justify our control and interferences. Our justifications are not always simply educatory but often apologetic and justificatory in tone and content.

Surely, some of why we respect children's decisions can be explained by the thought that decision making helps them to develop the proper skills and capacities required for "true" autonomous action later. This, however, cannot be the full explanation, and it certainly is not the simplest and most straightforward explanation in all cases. Not all of the everyday, trivial decisions children make are necessary for this learning process nor pertinent to the development of their characters. Further, it would not explain the residual justificatory obligation in cases in which justified paternalism takes place. Most pertinent to my claim, though, is the reaction we have to terminally ill children who we know will not grow into adulthood and will never have the fully developed intellectual and intentional capacities and the moral sensibilities associated with "full autonomy" and its richest realization. This case provides a more germane analogy to the case of dementia than that supplied by an analysis of our general treatment of children with full futures. In this case, I do not think that our conviction that we should accede to many of the terminally ill children's plans and demands would wane, even in cases where we thought the plans were seriously (though not dangerously) flawed. Respect for the fact that the children's lives is theirs would exert force over us even where their capacities were not fully developed and could not become fully developed through practice. Our reactions to this case show, I think, that we recognize that there is some value simply to expressing one's will and thereby determining the nature of one's experience, even where such control does not reliably maximize one's interests or contribute to the conditions necessary for a life with full Dworkinian integrity and unity.

Dworkin argues that showing respect for autonomy of people who have become demented requires respecting their *precedent autonomy* by respecting the decisions they forged before the decline into dementia. He also argues that precedent autonomy surmounts any interests to the contrary these people might now have. I contest both of these claims. As I have been arguing, the decision that is the product of precedent autonomy may conflict with the preferences that the demented person currently exhibits or expresses. The precedent decision may direct that people be killed or allowed to die should they become demented, although while demented they resist this decision and affirm a willingness to live. Alternatively, prior to dementia, they may direct that no assistance be given to them to enable them to die, although during their dementia, while in pain and distress, they repeatedly articulate a will to die. Dworkin insists that respect for autonomy entails following these precedent decisions because the person cannot retract this decision through a fresh exercise of the will. I am less sure of this conclusion. There is some value to the will that demented people express. These expressions may command our respect as exercises of autonomy, albeit etiolated ones, and they may suffice to nullify previously made decisions. Exercise of this type of autonomy might not command respect where fuller capacities for autonomy were present but suppressed (as in the case of the temporarily deranged). But if this control autonomy is the only type available, given the person's capacities, there may be better reasons to take heed of it. Unlike the Jehovah's Witness case, a self with an altogether different will is not going to have to live with the results of the action undertaken. That a person's full capacities have been permanently stripped from him or her provides reason to challenge the continuing force of a past decision. It may also lend greater weight to the exercise of whatever capacities remain.

One might speculate that what really motivates the suggestion that there is reason to honor the demented person's preferences is a rather different objection: that the demented person is a different person from the issuer of the advance directive. If the person has changed this considerably, perhaps it is questionable whether the demented person is indeed the same person as the person who wrote the advance directive. Not only have there been significant physical and psychological changes in the person, but these changes did not occur under conditions in which it was possible for the person undergoing change to subject it to conscious direction or control.[23] If the demented person is not the same person who wrote the advance directive, then there is no autonomy-centered reason to respect the advance directive. The power of autonomous decision does not extend this far.

Dworkin acknowledges that his conclusions depend upon the assumption that personal identity survives dementia. He frequently reiterates that demented people are not new, distinct persons from the persons with heightened intellectual powers who once occupied their bodies. Rather, their dementia represents a stage of an entire life of those who have become demented. Instead of examining Dworkin's defense of this position, I am more interested in disputing a potential objection that the autonomy considerations I have forwarded disguise and depend upon psychological reductionist views about personal identity. To dispel this suspicion, let us take it as a given that, for Dworkin's reasons or for others, personal identity is preserved where a person declines into dementia, even if there is a radical, abrupt change in character.

I resist the claim that if personal identity is maintained, then it follows that respect for autonomy entails that P_1's decisions about P_2 rightly govern P_2. There is something puzzling about Dworkin's conjunction of claims that P_2 is a person, that P_2's decisions do not manifest autonomy values, and that P_1's decisions should legitimately control P_2. Dworkin's justification for ignoring P_2's decisions derives from the fact that P_2's capacities are diminished and her personality is shifting and unstable. But if shifts in personality are sufficient to disqualify one from exercising respectable autonomy, then it is unclear why the major shift in personality and in capacities undergone by P would not pose a barrier to justifying the extension of P_1's power over P_2. If the value of P_1's autonomy is explained in virtue of the expression of P_1's *continuing* character, then dementia cases should trouble us, for they are marked by a sharp, uncontrollable, and unmeditated disruptive change in character. Given this disruption, it is puzzling why Dworkin would think it was obvious that P_2's life was properly governed by P_1's decisions. For what happens to P_2 and what P_2 does cannot seriously be taken as a *direct* expression of P_1's character. That P_1 could indirectly express her character by manipulating P_2 does not justify such actions, any more than it would justify coercing a third party on the grounds that such coercion might express something about oneself. The directness of expression is a vital condition for underwriting protections for autonomy under the integrity account.

Strangely, it is often assumed that if nonreductionism about personal identity were true, we could confidently explain such things as binding promises over our future selves no matter what their features and differences. It may not be so simple if the justification for respecting autonomy does not coincide with the account of what explains continuity of personal identity.[24] Suppose, for instance, the justification for respecting autonomy emanates from considerations relating to the expression of personality or character, and the correct account of personal identity appeals to bodily continuity, or continuity of the brain. Then there is a further question beyond whether and how autonomy has value: namely, we must confront the issue as to what the proper temporal boundaries governing autonomous decisions are. Depending on the account of autonomy, it may not be obvious that the temporal range of one's control should extend to encompass the entire span of one's existence as the same person over time. Even if psychological reductionists like Parfit are mistaken about what personal identity consists in, they may still be right about the conditions necessary for assessing responsibility.[25]

Thus far I have argued that precedent autonomy may lack the range necessary to justify the application of advance directives to demented people. Second, I have argued that, contrary to Dworkin's claims, there is no warrant to conclude that the expression of the demented person's will has *no* autonomy value whatsoever. We have some reason to implement their will, even when it conflicts with the directions of their past competent selves. I have not attempted to show that the will of demented people should command anywhere near the respect we owe to the competent. As with children, the will of demented people may have some autonomy value, but that may not tell the whole story. The autonomy of demented people may command some of our respect, but they need greater guidance about what sorts of things will achieve their ends and greater help to implement them. Further, given their diminished capacities for deliberation, their autonomy could, in appropriate circumstances, be trumped by our concern for their interests. If either of the critical tasks I have been pursuing is successful, then we must investigate what is in the interest of the demented person.[26] In the next section, I argue that Dworkin's account of beneficence cannot salvage his defense of advance directives and that the account is in some tension with his stance of religious neutrality.

III

Dworkin recognizes that apart from any respect we owe to the demented person's autonomy, whether previously or contemporaneously exerted, we must also explore what duties of beneficence we have toward the demented. Not surprisingly, Dworkin believes that considerations of autonomy and beneficence both support honoring the advance directive. Even if precedent autonomy as valued by the integrity account cannot extend its reign over P_2, the directive may be the best available evidence of P's interests.

Dworkin argues persuasively that P_1 may feel that P has strong "critical" interests concerning what happens to P_2. Some may feel that a life of unity and integrity may be spoiled if a prolonged stage of dementia is tagged on to the end of it. As Dworkin puts it, "as we judge a literary work, . . . [a] bad ending mars what went before" (p. 27). Even so, it remains to be shown that P_1's interests concerning P_2 are relevant to our beneficent concern for P_2.

Dworkin's effort to meet this burden may be reconstructed in the following way. He acknowledges that demented people experience pleasure and pain and therefore have contemporary experiential interests. Demented people also have critical interests, although they are incapable of sound reflection about them. These critical interests, however, attach only to P_2 *qua* P, that is, through her connection to P_1; she has none *qua* P_2 alone. These critical interests of P_2 arise in virtue of P_1's more complex character; P_1's vision of the unity, integrity, and character of her life; and her previously entertained views about how her life expresses and respects the sanctity of life. Dworkin argues that P_2 has no critical interests in any forward-looking way. That is, P_2 *qua* P_2 has no positive critical interest in the continuation of her life since P_2 is incapable of forming and pursuing the acts and attachments that give life value. The value of a life, Dworkin insists, must be generated from the inside, and this is no longer possible for P_2 to do, given her diminished capacities (p. 230). Her continued existence can only serve her critical interests insofar as her existence would be a symbol of P_1's persistence or tenacity, qualities that P_1 more resolutely and deliberately manifested.

Prima facie, this position seems like a strange one for Dworkin to occupy. Given his professed aim to avoid partisanship about the sanctity of life, it seems odd for him to say that the life of the demented cannot be made valuable enough for it to be in the demented person's critical interest *qua* demented person for it to continue. I will return to this difficulty later on, but I will here articulate a possible line of reply to continue the exposition of Dworkin's view of beneficence.

Perhaps Dworkin would attempt to evade this difficulty by arguing that the reason why continued life cannot lie within the critical interests of demented people is not that their life itself is not valuable, but due to some fact about the *nature* of a critical interest. Dworkin's thought may be that for a person to have a critical interest, it must be possible at least for it to be grasped, recognized, and adopted by that person. Since demented people cannot have a perspective on what it is that makes their lives go well, they cannot, therefore, *qua* demented people, have critical interests.[27]

If demented people *qua* demented are unable to have critical interests, then conflicts may arise between P_2's contemporary experiential interests and P_1's critical interests (as well as with P_1's precedent autonomy). But no conflict can arise between the *critical* interests of P_1 and P_2. This latter claim, that P_2 cannot generate critical interests that diverge from P_1's, permits Dworkin to advance a reconciliatory strategy that eliminates the possibility of conflict between autonomy values and beneficence. Dworkin argues that since precedent autonomy will likely be guided by P_1's assessment of her interests and since such decisions will reflect P_1's weighing (or otherwise taking account of) of her critical interests against P_2's experiential interests, there is no conflict between respecting precedent autonomy and discharging our duties of beneficence toward P_2. "Once we accept that we must judge [the demented person's] interests as she did when competent to do so – then the conflict between autonomy and beneficence seems to disappear" (p. 231). Beneficence, in Dworkin's view, provides us with a separate positive ground for respecting advance directives, because their implementation will further the critical interests of P.

There are a number of difficult issues over which this argument too hastily glides. First, there is the question as to whether – if beneficence is our aim – we should place priority on the critical interests of P_1 over the experiential interests of P_2. Dworkin does not provide a strong justification for sharply discounting P_2's experiential interests. He merely notes that these interests would have been taken into account by P_1 when contemplating the advance directive. If P_1 has legitimate authority over P_2, because of P_1's autonomy, that might give us reason to act as though P_1's decision was well-considered and took all relevant factors into account. Surely, though, it does not settle that the *beneficent* thing to do, therefore, is to satisfy the critical interest of P_1. There are reasons to doubt the evidentiary strength of the advance directive. Although people may generally assess their own interests well, imagining what it would be like to be demented and to endure experiences not entirely accessible to mental and emotional processing is not an easy task. There are reasons to doubt how perceptive P_1's judgment would be about the importance and nature of these experiential interests. Dworkin's claim cannot be that P_1's assessment just makes it the case that the denial or frustration of the assessed critical interests is *perforce* counter to P's best interests. Such a move would represent backsliding on his previous acknowledgement that one can get it wrong as to what is in one's critical interests (see, e.g., p. 202), and would be inconsistent with his critique of the purely evidentiary account of autonomy.

Dworkin needs to argue that critical interests just matter more than experiential interests do, full stop. This may often be true, but the case of demented people challenges this generality. For reasons similar to those already discussed, we should worry about whether the critical interests of P_1 should exert much moral force, given P's abrupt change in personality. Even if on the best account of personal identity, P_1 and P_2 are the same person, given the dramatic personality change P has undergone, it is unclear whether we should think of P_1's interest in how P_2 is treated as highly morally salient. P_1's interest may be entirely understandable. P_1 and P_2 share a body, a history, and some psychological features and habits; they are the same person, and this alone could surely make it understandable that P_1 takes an interest in P_2's condition. Further, P's circle of friends and family may transfer their attachment to P_1 to include concern for P_2 as well, despite P's lack of a continuous character. That does not mean, though, that we should afford much weight to the interests of P_1 in our treatment decisions of P_2. By analogy, we would not be compelled to give much weight to an understandable interest P_1 might take in her doppelganger, given the inevitable connections others might make between them, if our aim were to act beneficently toward the doppelganger. Because P_2's psychological composition differs so radically from P_1's and because P_2 cannot self-consciously contribute to the life project envisioned by P_1, it is not obvious that the beneficent concern for P we evince during P_2's life should naturally focus upon P_1's interests. That is, where there has been substantial involuntary psychological change, maintenance of metaphysical personal identity may not be what is relevant from the normative, beneficent viewpoint.

The persuasiveness of this point about interests may well depend upon the plausibility of the earlier discussion about the temporally restricted range of P_1's autonomy rights and interests. Dworkin's account of beneficence is vulnerable in independent ways, though. Suppose Dworkin is right that P_1's critical interests should exert some legitimate moral force over and above the weight that the interests of others in P_2 exert. Another issue stands in the way of affirming the propriety of implementing advance directives, namely whether P_1's critical interests displace or outweigh P_2's experiential interests.

We might be inclined, with Dworkin, to think critical interests have greater weight. They reflect a more sweeping, deliberate, and deep vision of a life. They concern what makes a life go well, not simply what makes it enjoyable. In the life of a person with a multifaceted personality and an ability to be self-reflective, whether one's whole life goes well seems obviously of greater moment than whether fleeting pleasures are enjoyed or pains endured. Further, reflective people's ability to understand their critical interests and their importance may allow them to cope with and rationalize the frustration of experiential interests. Demented people, however, do not have a personality as fitted to coping with the frustration of experiential interest in this way. They cannot appreciate the significance of their critical interests as P_1 conceives them, nor can they grasp their connection to themselves. It seems cruel in such cases to force such people to live through agony so that they will fulfill a critical interest of living a life marked by fortitude and perseverance, an interest they no longer recognize, accept, or even understand. Likewise, it seems barbaric to ignore the experiential interests of people whose lives are filled with simple joys and delights and to cut these lives off short – to kill them – so that the entire life of P is unsullied by a lingering period of intellectual deterioration and decline. If all that people are capable of is awareness of their experiential desires, there are good reasons for such interests to play a more prominent role in one's analysis of beneficence than they do against the backdrop of deeper critical interests.[28] Whether or not it is appallingly cruel to implement a directive that runs counter to the only remaining interests a person has, surely it stretches the notion of beneficence to a breaking point to disregard these experiential interests in the name of kindness.

Dworkin considers the objection that experiential interests may take on greater significance in circumstances of dementia, but his replies sidestep the point. He acknowledges that demented people lack a sense of their own critical interests, but he analogizes to the case of the permanently vegetative and argues that their obliviousness to their critical interests does not provide us with "a good reason for ignoring their fate" (p. 232). Of course, I do not advocate disregard for demented people's fate. Quite the contrary. What is at issue is what proper regard for their fate consists in and whether it requires placing very strong weight on their contemporary desires and interests. Analogizing to the case of the persistently vegetative is inapt. The persistently vegetative person has no consciousness whatsoever and hence no experiential interests. We may be convinced that advance directives should govern our actions toward persistently vegetative patients but nothing would follow about demented patients, because the complexity of their case involves their having ongoing, conscious lives.

In any case, I suspect that the situation of demented people is even more difficult. So far, I have argued that Dworkin fails to give a persuasive interpretation of beneficence that would support implementing advanced directives as such. The experiential interests of demented people may conflict with the directive's dictates. These interests plausibly exert more moral force than Dworkin admits.

There is yet a further problem with Dworkin's analysis of beneficence. Dworkin is overcasual in his dismissal of possibility that P_2 may have critical interests of her own that are independent of P_1's assessed critical interests.

Dworkin's denial that P_2 may have critical interests of her own is unconvincing. He only directly addresses the case in which the advance directive instructs the termination of P's life pursuant to P_1's critical interests. Here, he takes pains to stress that the demented person cannot have a positive critical interest in continuing her life since the life itself cannot manifest any internally generated value.

But the plausibility of such a maneuver, I suspect, derives from the narrow range of examples Dworkin attends to at this point. While advancing this claim about critical interests, Dworkin addresses only the question of whether it could be in one's positive critical interest to continue living. This, however, leaves open a significant hole. Even if positive value cannot be "poured into a life" from outside it, because active agency, identification, and reflection are necessary to grasp and realize the positive value of the life, surely it must still be possible for a life to go badly due to externally originating forces that have an effect on the person: that is, it surely is still possible for negative value to be brought into a life from the outside. Indeed, Dworkin must concede the possibility of external forces affecting the value of a life if he is to make any sense of the practice of writing and respecting advance directives to protect one's critical interests. As Dworkin argues, how one dies and whether one's body persists past the point of one's mental lucidity can be a matter within one's critical interests, even if one's death or one's continued existence is not self-inflicted or self-generated; he makes this point even about persistent vegetative patients who are not aware of their existence, much less able to contribute to it. If so, then it seems surely plausible to say that if a demented person's life is full of pain and misery and empty of the compensation of pleasure, that sort of existence – taken in itself – is not simply a hedonic disaster but is not a worthwhile life at all. It is in the critical interest of that person not to continue it.[29] If the contents of a life can run counter to one's critical interests, independent of one's awareness or ability to conceive of them, then it is not only possible for demented people to have critical interests, but it is possible for the critical interests of the demented person, along with that person's experiential interests, to conflict with the critical interests of P_1.

We cannot easily conclude that the beneficent thing to do is to further the critical interests of the demented person as that person conceived them prior to the onset of dementia, for they may have changed dramatically along with the person's capacity to conceive of them. Before affirming that implementation of the advance directive is permissible, much less required, we would have to consider whether there are any reasons to hold the previously conceived of critical interests as exerting force, and then we would have to explain why they would trump the person's contemporary critical interests. I do not know how any general argument, abstracting from the particulars of a specific case, would go and I doubt one could be easily constructed.

Further, if Dworkin concedes the possibility that externally originating events can run counter to one's critical interests, then soon we will be led to ask why it could not be possible for externally originating events to further one's critical interests – to make one's life go better – although one made no positive, reflective contribution to their furtherance. As Dworkin explains it, whether something is in one's critical interest depends upon whether it makes one's life as a human being go well. So the question we should ask initially is not what demented people are capable of constructing out of their lives, but whether the life of a demented person *qua* demented person can go well or badly at all. I have tried to suggest some ways in which demented people can have terrible lives, such as when they are kept in constant pain out of which they can make no sense in order to serve purposes they cannot understand, much less identify with. Surely it is also possible that the life of demented people can go well in ways not orchestrated or even understood by those people. They may thrive to the best of the abilities they have. This could render their lives good ones – certainly better than lives characterized by frustration and despair.[30] Moreover, their continued livelihood may provide solace and joy to their loved ones. They may receive care and concern from other human beings. Participating in these relationships can make one's life go well and may make persistence part of one's critical interests even if this life is not directed by any self-conscious vision or plan. It seems possible, then, that continuing or ending life could impact the critical interest of a demented person *qua* demented person. Contrary to Dworkin's suggestion, there is no easy assurance available to us that the path of beneficence is drawn by people's conception of their critical interests when they were lucid. And if that path is not clearly drawn, then the claim that precedent autonomy and beneficience coincide is in trouble. The critical as well as the experiential interests of demented people can diverge from the interests of those people as they conceived them prior to dementia. These freshly generated interests must command some of our concern. If that concern is directed at the demented patient, our beneficent impulses may well conflict with precedent autonomy.

These intuitive worries may be grounded in a more explicit account of the difficulty that Dworkin's claims about the demented's critical interests place him in. Dworkin has explicitly ruled out taking a position on the sanctity of life. He has also persuasively argued that part of what makes a life go well may depend upon whether it reflects and respects the sanctity of life. If Dworkin consistently refrains from taking a position on the conditions under which life has intrinsic value, how intrinsic value is properly respected, and specifically, whether it has value only when enjoyed or affirmed by reflective beings, then he will not be able to rule out the claim that the demented person has a critical interest in living in such a way that reflects and respects the sanctity of life. Thus to remain consistent with his stance of neutrality, Dworkin cannot, for instance, eliminate the possibility that demented people have a critical interest in continuing their lives even if those lives lack much intentional reflection, direction, or internal drive. This is not to say that Dworkin's implicit substantive (in his view, religious) position about critical interests is thereby proven to be wrong. There is much to be said for his underlying view that what makes a life positively valuable depends on internal generative activity and self-awareness. This view may indeed reflect the proper understanding of what is intrinsically valuable about human life. The problem, though, is that this view cannot underwrite his arguments for advance directives if these arguments are supposed to fit into a framework that maintains its religious agnosticism.

If Dworkin's conclusions about advance directives are to be defended, a different line of justification needs to be presented. Dworkin seeks to defend advance directives without taking a controversial stand on the value or sanctity of life. He thinks this can be accomplished by embarking on a neutral analysis of autonomy and the nature of interests, critical and experiential. But if I am right that an analysis of the nature of critical interests will not assure us of the coincidence of considerations of beneficence and autonomy, then Dworkin will have to make arguments about the substantive content of these interests. He will have to argue more directly that the life led by a demented person cannot matter and cannot have value. He must argue that the life that is led will not contain experiences of a type that are worthy, but not because the nature of critical interests and valuable lives are such that it is impossible for external events to impact them. Dworkin will have to argue, rather, that the capacities of a demented person are simply too impoverished to befit a human being, and that such a life is not worthwhile. This argument will surely engage him directly in the debate about the nature of the sanctity of life.

Perhaps one could defend this somewhat exalted standard of what it takes to make a life worthwhile. On that issue, I will not comment. I will instead make some concluding remarks about the theoretical position Dworkin is placed in. Dworkin could depart from neutrality. To defend the implementation of advance directives calling for termination of the demented life, he could take the view that the critical interests a demented person may have in continuing life are insufficiently important to make the life worthwhile. This would expose that his defense of advance directives does not sit comfortably with a position of religious neutrality (as Dworkin conceives of it), but rather flows from a substantive view about which kinds of lives have objective value. Further, such a defense of directives would be importantly partial. If Dworkin adopts the substantive defense, then he will be harder pressed to defend, as a matter of beneficence, implementing any particular advance directives that require that the demented life be prolonged, despite the critical and experiential interests of the demented patient. If Dworkin abjures taking the substantive line on the sanctity of life, then the argument for implementing advance directives falls importantly short. For, if my arguments have merit, then it is possible for the demented person to have interests that deeply conflict with the interests and decisions the person rendered when lucid. It is then a much more difficult task than Dworkin allows to reach the conclusion that the beneficent way to treat demented people is to disregard their contemporary interests and to further their prior interests and decisions. Fulfillment of past relinquished desires may play some role in one's contemporary interests, but we tend to believe that their importance diminishes significantly if they are replaced by disparate contemporary interests.

At their strongest, the arguments I have presented show that Dworkin is mistaken to hold that we treat demented people with most respect by implementing advance directives. Far from being morally required to do so, we may not even be morally permitted to do so. The contemporary interests and the will of demented people may clash with their exercise of precedent autonomy and the critical interests they had before they became demented. We show respect for the demented by allowing their contemporary interests and their voiced will to exert substantial influence on our deliberations.[31] At their weakest, the arguments show that Dworkin's neutral defense of advance directives is importantly incomplete. For it to be convincing, we either need some account about how we may resolve the clash between the contemporary interests and the past interests of the person that favors the latter, or we require a revamped account of autonomy that can more convincingly explain why prior decisions merit respect and should be implemented even when they conflict with beneficence properly understood. This, as I have suggested, is a particularly difficult claim to sustain on the integrity account of autonomy as well as upon the alternative control account I have forwarded. In any case, Dworkin's reconciliatory approach leads him to avoid tackling these difficult balancing questions. If I am correct, we will have to face them.

214 SEANA VALENTINE SHIFFRIN

Acknowledgement

I am grateful to Torin Alter, Justine Burley, Ruth Chang, Laura Cherry, Sean Foran, Marc Lange, Herbert Morris, Michael Otsuka, Eric Rakowski, Steven Shiffrin, and the members of the UCLA Law and Philosophy Discussion Group for helpful conversations and written comments about this material. Enid Colson provided valuable research and bibliographic assistance.

Notes

1 Ronald Dworkin, *Life's Dominion* (New York: Knopf, 1993). Page references in the text and notes are to this book unless otherwise specified.
2 See e.g., "Autonomy and the Demented Self," *The Milbank Quarterly*, vol. 64, 1987, pp. 4–16; "Philosophical Issues Concerning the Rights of Patients Suffering Serious Permanent Dementia," in *Philosophical, Legal and Social Aspects of Surrogate Decisionmaking for Elderly Individuals: Contractor Documents for the Office of Technology Assessment* (PB87-234126) (Washington, DC: Office of Technology, May 1986); "The Right to Death," *New York Review of Books*, January 1991, pp. 14–17; "Unenumerated Rights: Whether and How *Roe v. Wade* Should Be Overruled," *University of Chicago Law Review*, vol. 59, Winter 1992, pp. 381–432; "The Center Holds!" *New York Review of Books*, August 1992, pp. 112–15. Relevant chapters also appear in *Freedom's Law* (Cambridge, MA: Harvard University Press, 1996), and in *Sovereign Virtue* (Cambridge, MA: Harvard University Press, 2000).
3 For criticisms of this conception of the religious and of his interpretation of the First Amendment see Student Note, "Inside Out, Within and Beyond, or Backwards?" *Harvard Law Review*, vol. 107, 1994, pp. 943–7, and Eric Rakowski, "The Sanctity of Human Life," *Yale Law Review*, vol. 103, 1994, p. 2049.
4 Dworkin characterizes the dispute about the sanctity of life as one regarding the "relative moral importance of natural and human contributions to the inviolability of human lives" (p. 91). Presumably, though, another aspect of the dispute concerns the relative weight that should be given to the intrinsic, impersonal value of life when it conflicts with the subjective value of a life. This is at least some of what is at issue in debates about the right to die.
5 This "encouragement" may include the demand that they come to a definite decision about their pregnancies by a particular date. Dworkin's view that late-term abortions may be prohibited, because it is reasonable to expect women who seriously reflect to come to a decision earlier, is based on his dubious presupposition that women who elect late abortions do not take the sanctity of life seriously. But information relevant to one's decision may not be available until late into the pregnancy and relevant factors may change within a pregnancy. Elsewhere, Dworkin acknowledges that acting on reasons relating to the future health of one's child or one's familial or financial situation can reflect a serious view about the sanctity of life; why should the emergence of these reasons late into pregnancy make acting upon them frivolous? Finally, consider a person who, from the onset of pregnancy, struggled hard to consider the relevant issues and to make a commitment to the future child. As the pregnancy progressed and she experienced its mounting burdens, she realized that she could not make the kind of full-fledged good-faith commitment to the life it merited, so she aborted out of respect for the importance of a life's going well. As Dworkin recognizes, philosophers who devote their lives to understanding the significance of life frequently change their minds and have not been able to reach a stable consensus within four to five months. If those who study the subject believe the problem to be extremely difficult and perhaps intractable, why is it reasonable to expect faster deliberation on the part of pregnant women in particular? Why is lengthy deliberation ending in late-term abortion a sign that the woman was "indifferent to the moral and social meaning of her act" (p. 170)?

6   Laurence Tribe originally made an argument along these lines in "Foreword: Toward A Model of Roles in the Due Process of Life and Law," *Harvard Law Review*, vol. 87, 1973, pp. 1–53, although he retreated from the position in *American Constitutional Law*, 2nd edn. (New York: Foundation Press, 1988), p. 1350.

7   See e.g., T. M. Scanlon, "Ronald Dworkin and the 'Sanctity of Life'," *New York Review of Books*, vol. 40, July 1993, pp. 45–51; Galen Strawson, "The Termination of Wrongs and Rights," *The Independent*, June 1993; Student Note, "Inside Out, Within and Beyond, or Backwards?," op. cit.; and Laurence Tribe, "On the Edges of Life and Death," *New York Times Book Review*, May 16, 1993, Section 7, pp. 1, 41. Since the present essay was first written more has been written on these subjects and Dworkin's positions.

8   Since I wrote this, two prominent and excellent exceptions have come to my attention: see Sanford H. Kadish, "Letting Patients Die: Legal and Moral Reflections," *California Law Review*, vol. 80, July 1992, pp. 857–88; Agnieszka Jaworska, "Respecting the Margins of Agency: Alzheimer's Patients and the Capacity to Value," *Philosophy and Public Affairs*, vol. 28, 1999, pp. 105–38. I regret there is inadequate space here to discuss my substantial agreement with them as well as my few reservations.

9   Dworkin discusses financing care in "Philosophical Issues Concerning the Rights of Patients Suffering Serious Permanent Dementia," op. cit.

10 This argument assumes that there is a higher order critical interest (or a condition on critical interests) that people have in living their lives according to their own assessments of their critical interests, even when these assessments are mistaken. Dworkin does not argue directly for this premise in the book, although he hints at it at p. 106. A more extended argument for "the constitutive view of value," the view that nothing may contribute to the value of a person's life without that person's endorsement, appears in his "Foundations of Liberal Equality," in Grethe Peterson (ed.), *The Tanner Lectures on Human Values*, vol. XI (Salt Lake City: University of Utah Press, 1990), pp. 75–86.

11 There may be some question about whether the seriously demented have a will or can exhibit preferences about the continuation of their lives. Some in the advanced stages of dementia may not be capable of the resistance I imagine. Only some of my conclusions will apply to their cases. Dworkin, however, does not limit his conclusions to those people and insists that out of respect for their autonomy, we may best respect people by implementing these directives even when they do express "choices and demands" (p. 225) and "wishes" (p. 228) to the contrary in their demented state. Later, I discuss his characterization of the demented. I will not take on the more challenging task of ascertaining how other decisions regarding the content of the lives of the demented should be made, should they continue to live, and who should make them.

12 This rules out those people who are born mentally impaired. My focus is on those who once functioned normally and who undergo mental decline.

13 See Jeffrey Cummings et al., *Dementia: A Clinical Approach*, 2nd edn. (Boston: Butterworth-Heineman, 1992), pp. 1–2.

14 See A. F. Jorm, *The Epidemiology of Alzheimer's Disease and Related Disorders* (London: Chapman and Hall, 1990), pp. 26–7.

15 See Joseph Foley, "The Experience of Being Demented," in Robert Binstock et al. (eds.), *Dementia and Aging* (Baltimore: Johns Hopkins Press, 1992), chapter 2, pp. 30–43.

16 See, e.g., Barry Reisberg et al., "The Final Stages of Alzheimer's Disease: Issues for the Patient, Family and Professional Community," in Richard Mayeux et al. (eds.), *Alzheimer's Disease and Related Disorders* (Springfield, IL: Charles Thomas, 1988), pp. 12–16.

17 Other patients Dworkin describes as subject to his conclusions could not run a tub but recognized family members and were enheartened to see them. They could engage in simple activities with pleasure.

18 Dworkin, "Philosophical Issues Concerning the Rights of Patients Suffering Serious Permanent Dementia," op. cit. Other commentators have challenged advance directives on the grounds that the demented person is not identical to the author of the directive and on the grounds that the demented being is not a person at all. See e.g., Dan Brock, *Life and Death* (Cambridge, UK: Cambridge University

Press, 1993), pp. 356–87; Dan Brock and Allen Buchanan, *Deciding for Others* (Cambridge, UK: Cambridge University Press, 1990), and Eric Rakowski in this volume. I will argue that the central moral issue does not turn upon whether personal identity is maintained or disrupted, but hinges upon the abrupt involuntary change in personality.

19   For a similar account, see Gerald Dworkin, *The Theory and Practice of Autonomy* (Cambridge, UK: Cambridge University Press, 1988), pp. 17, 20, 26.

20   The evidentiary account treasures autonomy in the latter way, for its usefulness as a causal lever shunting agents toward their greatest welfare. One might read the "integrity" account as indirectly instrumental too, as prizing autonomy because it allows expression of one's character, where such robust expression over a lifetime ultimately promotes a person's welfare. Such a reading is possible, but I think mistaken. If integrity's value were instrumental, one would expect to encounter worries about whether bad decisions should be respected, even if their detrimental impact on the person's welfare were far greater than the self-expression they facilitated. The integrity account, as I understand it, does not aim to identify the goal that autonomy serves but instead identifies what it is about autonomy that makes it intrinsically valuable. It is in virtue of autonomy's exercise being a way in which one's character is created and expressed that it has intrinsic value and should be respected.

21   Not all take a "constructivist" approach to delineating what is in a person's best interests. In more objective accounts of interest, the contrast between substituted judgment and beneficence is sharper.

22   Thus I disagree with the claim that actual consent enjoys no intrinsically privileged moral status over hypothetical consent. See Eric Rakowski, "Taking and Saving Lives," *Columbia Law Review*, vol. 93, 1993, pp. 1114–15.

23   The lack of control over tremendous personality change is relevant in distinguishing between the case of dementia and more commonplace forms of character transformation and evolution.

24   Robert Adams and Jennifer Whiting both allude to related doubts about whether the truth of nonreductionism would provide justificatory reason for harboring concern for our future selves and for others' future selves. Robert Adams, "Should Ethics be More Impersonal?" *Philosophical Review*, vol. 98, 1989, pp. 439–84 at 455; Jennifer Whiting, "Friends and Future Selves," *Philosophical Review*, vol. 95, 1986, pp. 547–80 at 547.

25   Parfit and his critics frequently write as though his ethical theses about selves hold only if his theory of personal identity is true. See chapters 14 and 15 of *Reasons and Persons* (Oxford: Oxford University Press, 1984). But Parfit's arguments about personal identity often proceed by asking what is important about ourselves. On these issues, Parfit may well be right. Even if the metaphysical inferences do not follow, his normative insights about the significance of psychological change, especially severe disruptive change, might still hold.

26   This task would also present itself if there were no advance directive available. Dworkin suggests that a substituted judgment inquiry asking what the person would have chosen would both respect the person's autonomy and that the identical inquiry would ascertain the person's best interests (pp. 191–2). He does not take a stand on what to do if, contrary to his presuppositions, what is in the person's best interests differs from what that person would have chosen. Elsewhere, Dworkin criticizes substituted judgment as not promoting autonomy values at all. See "Autonomy and the Demented Self," pp. 14–15. As I argue in the text, substituted judgment as it is typically conceived, SJ_1, carries little autonomy value. SJ_2 has some autonomy value, but its results should not necessarily wholly determine our actions with respect to the permanently incompetent if there is a sufficiently serious conflict with the person's best interests.

27   This interpretation finds support in his arguments in favor of constitutive over additive models of value in his "Foundations of Liberal Equality," op. cit., pp. 77–8.

28   There is another argument for placing greater weight on the experiential interests of demented people over their critical interests. When a life has the potential to go superbly, experiential frustrations seem of paltry importance in comparison with the caliber of critical interests at stake. If due to constrained

capacities or limited circumstances, a life can go better or worse but cannot be a very good life, then the significance of experiential interests might be thought to be more closely comparable to the significance of critical interests. How excellent the life can be, it might be suggested, has a bearing upon whether critical interests automatically overwhelm experiential interests.

29 See also "Foundations of Liberal Equality," op. cit.: "Our lives may go badly . . . not just because we are unwilling or unable properly to respond to the circumstances we have, but because we have the wrong circumstances" (p. 69).

30 Such a story seems consistent with, and even reminiscent of, some of Dworkin's approving remarks about the model of challenge, the idea that living well is a matter of successfully meeting the challenges that a life presents. See "Foundations of Liberal Equality," op. cit., pp. 57, 60, 67. Dworkin's related arguments for the constitutive model of value, the view that nothing contributes to the value of a person's life unless it is endorsed by that person, do not actually rule out the possibility that various activities may lie within P_2's critical interests. Dworkin insists that it could not further one's critical interests to lead a life that one despised and actively reviled as unworthy (ibid., p. 76). Dworkin's arguments appeal to our intuition that a life cannot go well if it is actively *rejected* by a person. This intuition, however, is entirely consistent with the belief that demented people's lives may go well and may go better than they otherwise would if they contain certain features and activities, even if the people lack the capacity to recognize that their way of life furthers their critical interests.

31 I have not, however, discussed how one should balance the autonomy values against any conflicting contemporary interests. Such a task would have to be taken up to give a full account of the proper treatment of the demented.

12

Ronald Dworkin's Views on Abortion and Assisted Suicide

F. M. Kamm

Ronald Dworkin has made important contributions to the discussion of the legal and moral problems of abortion and physician-assisted suicide. In this chapter, I wish to consider his views on these matters as they are expressed in his book *Life's Dominion*,[1] and in "The Philosophers' Brief on Assisted Suicide,"[2] of which he is a coauthor. While Dworkin raises significant and useful points, I have reservations about certain distinctions and arguments that he advocates.

I   *Life's Dominion* Argument

Summary

In his book *Life's Dominion*, Ronald Dworkin makes certain claims about the nature of the intrinsic value of life, the nature of inviolability, the badness of death, and the grounds for the permissibility of abortion. I shall summarize and then examine several of these claims.

Dworkin thinks that we believe in the sacredness of individual human life (including early fetal life). Though he uses the same term, Dworkin's doctrine of the sacredness of life is very different from what has come to be known as the sanctity-of-life doctrine. (The latter implies that all human life has equal value – regardless of stage of development – and that intentionally killing innocent human life is prohibited.) Dworkin says that sacredness is a form of intrinsic value, which is value that something has independently of whether it serves anyone's interests instrumentally. The disconnection from serving interests is complete, since the sacredness of the individual life is independent even of its serving the interests of the entity whose life it is. Dworkin explains that such sacredness holds in the case of the early fetus because the fetus[3] has no interests that life can serve, as it has never had a mental life (which seems to be a prerequisite for having interests) (p. 16). Hence the value of the sacred is detached, rather than derivative, from interests. Further, Dworkin says that the intrinsic value he is describing is also objective value, which is value that exists independently of whether anyone cares about it. The sacred, he says additionally, is non-incremental value: that something sacred is valuable is not a reason to produce more of it, but it is a reason to treat properly what exists of it. Thus one need not maximize sacredness. "Sacred" suggests a religious interpretation of intrinsic, nonincremental, objective value (my acronym for this is INOV), so Dworkin identifies a secular term that he believes conveys what he means by sacred: "inviolable." Furthermore, entities besides human life can be sacred, for example, other species or works of art.

What makes something have INOV? Dworkin considers the sacred primarily in terms of the history of the entity. God, nature, and human action as creative forces give INOV to many of their products; the more investment of these creative forces in the entities, the more value they have. Also, a bad cause can deprive an entity of INOV; Dworkin believes that this is why some may think that a fetus that results from rape has less INOV than one that does not (p. 95).

Destroying an entity that has INOV always has negative weight. But when does it have more, and when less, negative weight? Dworkin presents a special thesis, which I call the investment waste thesis (IWT), in order to answer this question: roughly, a death becomes worse as the ratio between the outcome of a creative investment and the creative investment itself decreases. However, if one has invested creatively in an entity, but it has already returned completely on the investment in it, will never return on the investment in it, or will not return much on the invest-ment in it, then its death is not very bad. He writes: "We regret the waste of a creative invest-ment not just for what we do not have, but because of the special badness of great effort frustrated" (p. 79). So the death of a 60-year-old person is less bad than that of a 20-year-old person; though more has been invested in the 60 year old, more return on the investment has also been reaped by that person. But a lot has been invested in the 20 year old without the person reaping much of a return yet. In the case of an early fetus, much life is lost if it dies, but little has been invested in it, so there is not much waste. The older the fetus becomes, other things being equal, the more investment is lost without return when it dies.

A crucial problem for abortion, in Dworkin's view, is that at least two different types of cre-ative investment exist – biological/natural (or God-driven) and human – and a woman and a fetus will embody both types to greater and lesser degrees (p. 91). For some people, God's or nature's investment is of paramount importance, and the continued existence of that natural or God-given component offers a significant payoff. For other people, the human creative investment and the payoff in terms of human achievement are more important. Balancing these sources of INOV (sacredness) and their presence in the fetus, in the woman, and in anyone else affected positively or negatively by an abortion, Dworkin thinks, is not a matter of philosophical argumentation; it comes closer to a matter of religious belief (where this does not necessarily imply belief in a deity). The state should not interfere with decisions that depend on religious belief.

The fetus and the woman represent different instances of INOV, and the two can conflict, since there is more human investment in the woman, and primarily God's or nature's investment in the fetus. The IWT also has implications for deciding whether a woman's death, or other losses suf-fered without an abortion, is worse than the death of her fetus if it is aborted. Dworkin argues that at least in the view of some, *more* has been invested in the woman than in the fetus, and so it is worse if she, rather than the fetus, is not given the opportunity to return on an investment. But the woman also has interests and rights, since she is a person in a philosophical, a moral, and a constitutional sense. As already noted above, in Dworkin's view it is obvious that the fetus has no interests or rights and is not a person in a philosophical or constitutional sense. Dworkin argues that no one could believe that the early fetus has either interests or rights that protect those inter-ests, since it has never had mental states. When preserving rather than destroying an entity that has INOV would conflict with the rights and interests of a full-fledged person who has INOV, then the INOV of the less-than-full-fledged person can be overridden, at least legally.

Questions

Dworkin attempts to understand the fetus as an entity that has no interests in retaining its future life and in the development of its potential to become a human person. This means that if we were to save its life or allow its transformation into a person, we could not be doing it *for its sake* in order to benefit it. Dworkin also attempts to show that even if this is true, a fetus need not therefore lack value. (Indeed, an entity having the potential to develop into a better entity may contribute to its value.)

I agree with both parts of this analysis. Its plausibility can perhaps be seen better when applied to a nonhuman object. For example, a work of art can have great value – and it could be wrong to destroy it without good reason, but it is not for its sake (on account of its interests in surviving) that we should save it. A table that magically had the potential to turn into a person would also have greater value than an ordinary table, but it would not be for its sake that we would allow it to transform.[4] However, I have questions about some of the specifics of Dworkin's views.

Does Dworkin really have a theory of the intrinsic value of life?

Although a sacred entity is supposed to be valuable intrinsically, Dworkin says that it is sacred because of its history. He says that "the nerve of the sacred lies in the value we attach to a process or enterprise or project rather than to its results considered independently from how they were produced" (p. 78). One might argue that the value of life is not intrinsic if history is at its core, for this seems to situate the entity (life) in relation to something else (a process leading to life), the combination of which has value. This means that life would have extrinsic rather than intrinsic value, that is, value conditional on its being part of a certain whole. This is consistent, though, with its being valuable as an end, rather than as a mere instrument. (Similarly, happiness might be valuable only conditional on merit, but the happiness of those who deserve happiness can be sought for its own sake, not merely as an instrument.) Dworkin makes the mistake of thinking that intrinsic value is to be contrasted with instrumental value, and he is eager to argue that life is valuable not merely instrumentally. But as Christine Korsgaard has argued,[5] intrinsic is to be contrasted with extrinsic, not with instrumental. What is instrumental is to be contrasted with what is an end. Hence Dworkin seems to have a theory about the extrinsic, but noninstrumental, value of life.

Does the value of life respond to changes in its cause in the way that Dworkin describes?

In the case of many things (e.g., persons), it may be possible to tell whether they have value by examining their properties independently of their history. Suppose that one's value as a person depended on one's history. Then if one were deceived about one's past, and one had been created as a rational and self-conscious being one second ago by some rape of nature, perhaps one would not have the value one thought that one had. This conclusion seems incorrect, however.[6] Likewise, in some people's views, instances of life itself (e.g., fetuses, caterpillars) have intrinsic value independently of their histories because of their complexity, animation, or other characteristics. For this reason, we should doubt the claim that the fetus that results from rape has less intrinsic value because it began in the frustration of the woman's life. This does not mean that history is irrelevant to the value of all things. Arthur Danto has argued that two physically identical objects can have different value because one was made to express a certain point of view and the other is just the result of a random series of events. The first entity is a work of art and has properties the other lacks (such as being a statement) in virtue of its history.[7] Still, if Rembrandt had created "The Nightwatch" under coercion, would the painting have been any less valuable? I do not think so.[8]

Can an intrinsic value be nonincremental?

Dworkin claims that once a human life has begun, it is important that it go well, but this does not *entail* that the more lives that go well the better. That is, we do not have a reason to create more of what is undoubtedly valuable. The following leads to a crucial question in dealing with this claim: suppose that we believe that through history, the world has so far contained 40 billion happy people. Then we discover that in fact we miscalculated and there have really been 80 billion people in the same time period, each of whom lived a life no better or worse than the 40 billion. Should we think that the history of the world is better in at least one way than we previously thought just because of the increment? If yes, then the value of persons' lives would be incremental. But perhaps we should not think that the more populous world has a point in its favor in virtue of the additional people. Then, Dworkin's view about the nonincremental value of human life would be true. Note that even if we think that the value of human life gives us a reason to create more of it (when there is no danger of the species or the valuable things disappearing if we do not), this does not mean that we have an obligation to create more of it, or that there are not countervailing reasons not to create more of it.

Is Dworkin's use of "inviolability" correct?

Although he says that the secular term that expresses his idea of sacredness is "inviolability," Dworkin's notion of the sacred does not really involve inviolability as commonly understood, that is, as implying a strong impermissibility of destructive attacks on an entity. Dworkin believes that almost everyone thinks that the fetus is sacred or inviolable (pp. 13, 25). His evidence that even liberals on abortion believe this is that few people view a very early abortion as a morally neutral event, like cutting one's hair; it has negative moral significance, even if it is on the whole justified (pp. 33, 34). He says: "I shall assume that conservatives and liberals all accept that in principle human life is inviolable in the sense that I have defined, that any abortion involves a waste of human life and is therefore . . . a bad thing to happen, a shame" (p. 84). But this is hardly evidence for inviolability as ordinarily understood, since this sort of badness can rather easily be overridden for many worthy purposes. After all, it is a waste, a bad thing to happen, and a shame if a kitten must be destroyed for scientific research, but a kitten is not inviolable. Dworkin's notion of inviolability is merely that something bad happens when something dies or is destroyed, not that it is extremely hard (if not absolutely impossible) to morally override a prohibition on causing this death. But it is the latter that is the mark of inviolability as ordinarily understood.

Most importantly, Dworkin's notion of inviolability is part of the theory of value (which is about good and bad states of affairs) rather than part of the theory of the right (which deals with what acts are permissible and impermissible). But when we say someone is inviolable because there is a strong prohibition on causing that person's death, we do not mean only that something bad (even very bad) will happen if he or she is killed. For if it were just the badness of someone being killed that accounted for the prohibition on killing, it should be permissible to minimize such badness by killing one person in order to *prevent* more killing of other people. Yet, inviolability suggests this is not permissible.

It would be better if Dworkin had used other terms. For if all Dworkin thinks is entailed by something being "inviolable" is that a bad thing happens when it is destroyed, it is seriously misleading to use this term. (In public debate, just redefining a term that is commonly used in another way can mislead one's audience.) It is also misleading to call an entity "sacred" if one thinks that its destruction involves nothing more than that something bad happens, as this does not capture the great barrier to destruction that a sacred entity presents.

Is the investment waste thesis correct?

Let us test the implications of the IWT. First, are late abortions worse than earlier ones for the reasons that the IWT provides? Suppose that a fetus began from conception much more fully developed than it does now, though it still had no consciousness, and it had the potential for further normal human development. This at least seems like a very significant product from little invest-ment. On the other hand, imagine a fetus that gestates for two years at great cost to those who help it grow and is still only at the stage of a normal embryo; if it continues to gestate in its lengthy fashion, it will realize the potential of a normal human being. It seems that according to the IWT, the death of the second fetus is worse than that of the first, because there is more wasted invest-ment. But this seems incorrect.[9] The properties of the first fetus now, as well as its future poten-tial, seem to make the death of the first fetus worse than that of the second, independently of differential investment. So, contrary to what Dworkin suggests (p. 88), if a first-trimester fetus were to have the properties of a second-trimester fetus, I believe that we would not care less about it just because less had been invested in it.

This example involves variation in two variables – product and investment – simultaneously. That is, product A is *better* than product B, and investment x (to produce product A) is *less* than investment y (to produce product B). A simpler set of cases would involve the same product – let us say the better one, A – as a result of differential investment, x in one case and y in the other. I believe that as the product improves, it becomes the dominant factor in deciding how important destruction would be, so that destruction of the entity into which more was invested would not be worse. (The extra investment, we might say, becomes a morally irrelevant factor.) However, in another example of this simpler model, investment might matter more. That is, hold the product constant in the two entities but make it the less good product B – minimal development – and imagine that investment x produced B in one case and investment y produced B in the other case. Here it may indeed be worse for the entity due to the greater investment (y) to be destroyed. Finally, we could imagine a case in which the products varied but the investments were the same. In this case, it is worse if the better product is destroyed. The intuitive results in all these cases suggest that the quality of the product is a more important factor than is the investment in decid-ing which death is worse.

Dworkin has responded to the case that I described as involving less investment to produce a more complexly developed fetus and more investment to produce a less complexly developed fetus, by claiming that "nature's investment in a fetus is not just a matter of gestation times, but of com-plexity of development as well."[10] In other words, he denies that the more complex fetus can be the one with less investment in it. But this answer, I think, results in the boundaries between investment and product becoming unclear in his theory. Given any property the entity has (for example, consciousness) that one can describe without any knowledge of the entity's history, Dworkin's view (based on his response) seems to be that we can automatically say that there was investment in it of that property. We need no knowledge independent of the entities' properties to describe an investment history for it.

How could one retain the idea that waste of investment has a role independent of waste of the product? Possibly in the following way: one sees many properties that the entity has, and from this, Dworkin might say, one sees that there was investment of these properties, and hence much investment has taken place. But suppose that the properties are all bad ones. So, considered on their own, they would give no reason not to destroy the entity. However, there has been much investment of the entity with these properties that would be wasted if it died. Does that give us a reason not to destroy it? I think not. Hence, I think that it is right to conclude that most of the work in determining how bad a death of a fetus is is a function of the quality of its properties rather than the investment in it.

Second, Dworkin's IWT, independent of any concern about rights, suggests that an assessment of the relative importance of abortion to two women should turn on the degree to which the investment in them is paid off. Suppose that one is a poor, mistreated young woman, who has not invested in herself and who has not been invested in by anyone else apart from her parents in creating her. She becomes pregnant and wants an abortion because she has decided to try to make something of her life and a pregnancy would interfere with this. Suppose that the other woman is well cared for and highly educated, someone who has invested time and energy in herself and who has been invested in by parents who creatively raised her. She wants an abortion because pregnancy would interfere with her life plans. The IWT alone seems to say that, because of the differential investment, it is worse if the second woman does not get an abortion than if the first women does not. But this seems wrong.

Is Dworkin's account of conflicts between values (with and without consideration of rights) sufficient to account for the permissibility of abortion?
First, consider the outcome of conflicts between a woman and a fetus, taking into account only the creative values – natural, God-given, and human – that the woman and the fetus represent, and postponing the issue of interests and rights. I wish to suggest that, on its own, the discussion of value will not resolve as much as Dworkin suggests.

Recall that Dworkin thinks that there is something *prima facie* wrong with a human act that destroys the sacred once it exists (pp. 74, 75, 78, 84); it is an intentional frustration of creative investment. Does Dworkin likewise emphasize active preservation of the sacred? At certain points he seems to. He says, for example, that it is important that the human race survive and prosper (p. 76) and that sacred things flourish (p. 74). Nevertheless, if Dworkin were as deeply concerned with preserving the sacred as he is with not destroying it, he would have to support efforts to prevent naturally occurring miscarriages as strongly as not destroying fetuses. By contrast, what if we considered not harming entities that have INOV as more important than aiding them? Suppose that a woman wants an abortion because she would die without it. If we do not permit the abortion, she, as an entity that has INOV, will die because we do not aid her. But if we perform the abortion, we actively destroy something that has INOV (although perhaps something less valuable than the woman is). If the destruction versus not-aiding distinction were sufficiently important, it could outweigh the fact that the woman has greater INOV (in the opinion of some). Hence, abortion might not be permitted if only INOV-related factors mattered.

Further, if the abortion issue were only a matter of conflicting entities that have INOV, independently of the fact that one of the entities that have INOV imposes on the body of the other, one would probably be able to find other decisive objections to abortion. For even if one ought to aid entities that have INOV as well as not destroy them, it is not generally true that one is permitted to destroy an entity that has INOV, even one of relatively little value, in order to save an entity that has INOV of greater value. For example, if a woman's fetus were on its own in an external gestation device, not imposing on the woman, it is not clear that it could be appropriated and destroyed in order to help her. It seems, therefore, that in order to justify abortion one must take seriously the fact that the entity in question that has INOV – the fetus – is imposing on the woman.

Second, let us consider the role of rights. Dworkin seems to assume that rights protect interests, and so an entity with no interests could have no rights. But some rights at least may not protect interests (understood as some aspect of well-being), but rather express the dignity of the subject who has them. For example, subjects that have no interests to be protected could have rights to freedom of expression or worship, I think, because these behaviors are important for reasons other than that they serve the interests of those who have the rights. However, even if we deny that rights protect only interests, we could insist that an entity that is not a subject at all cannot have rights, and this is true of a fetus, at least in virtue of its never having had mental states.

Dworkin does consider that women do not merely have INOV, but are also persons with interests and rights.[11] When the preservation of an entity that has INOV would interfere in a *serious way* with rights and interests, especially when the value to be attributed to the entity that has INOV is a matter of religious dispute, Dworkin favors the dominance of rights and interests, at least as a legal matter. But, I would claim, since in abortion the *destruction* of an entity that has INOV is at issue, the question arises of *how* an entity that has INOV not being destroyed can interfere with the rights and interests of a person. Let us examine an analogy: it is one thing to say that a person may not be severely imposed upon in order to preserve a work of art, and we may even destroy it in order to stop its imposing on that person. It is another thing to say that one may destroy just any work of art because, if we do not, something else will interfere with a person's rights and interests. Again, it seems to me that the details of how the fetus imposes on the woman, and whether, if we do not destroy it, she will wind up aiding it when she is not obliged to, are important to justifying the fetus's destruction. Dworkin may not disagree, but he does not investigate these details. So it turns out that if one wishes to show that a fetus may permissibly be destroyed in order to help a woman, some of the same distinctions may have to be attended to if the fetus merely has INOV as would have to be attended to in order to justify abortion if the fetus were a person with rights.[12]

Is Dworkin correct to describe opinions on abortion as a matter of constitutionally protected religious belief?

Introducing *any* secular equivalent of the sacred (such as inviolability) seems to introduce a different kind of trouble. For Dworkin wants to argue that views about the intrinsic value of life and debates about the weighing and balancing of intrinsic value are fundamentally religious rather than philosophical (pp. 93, 156). Dworkin defines the religious as distinguishing a view that answers the questions he thinks that religion has dealt with in the past, for example, "What is the ultimate value and meaning of human life?" (p. 163). But many of these issues *have* traditionally also been discussed by secular philosophy, which is typically contrasted with religion. For example, secular philosophers have asked: "What is the meaning and point of human life?" and "Does a person's life matter independently of its use to him or her?" Dworkin places these questions under the topic of the sanctity of life, but clearly moral philosophers as well as theologians have discussed them. A clear example is Kant, who said that rational humanity was an end-in-itself, that is, a categorical end; whether people cared about their lives or not, they had a duty to make something of their lives.[13] While Dworkin seems to think that moral philosophy deals with the realm of interests rather than the realm of the sacred, as he defines it, this does not seem to be true of such moral philosophers as Kant.

When Dworkin discusses euthanasia, he seems to allow more overlap between the realm of interests (dealt with by moral philosophy, in his view) and the realm of the sacred (dealt with by religion, in his view), for he speaks of concern for the dignity of human life in discussing both realms. He says that critical interests are one's concerns that one's life has amounted to something, independently of how it merely felt as one was living it (the latter being one's experiential interest). Indeed, Dworkin says that believing in critical interests is a species of believing in the sacredness of life (p. 215). But if one's critical interests are a matter of moral philosophical reflection, why cannot the same issues of the worth of life also be a matter of philosophical reflection?

In what sense is such philosophical reflection classifiable as religious? One suggestion, made by Thomas Scanlon,[14] is that Dworkin thinks that certain types of secular philosophical thought (about the meaning and point of life) are religious in the *constitutional sense*; they are to be treated for *constitutional purposes* the way religions are treated. But why are secular philosophical views on the meaning and point of human life *constitutionally religious* while other secular philosophical views are not? After all, philosophical and scientific views that deal with other questions historically dealt with by religion, such as the origin of the universe and whether God exists, are not religious.

My sense is that Dworkin ultimately wants to use "religious" (or "constitutionally religious") to connote an area of discourse that is not subject to rational proof. This keeps it outside the area of political debate. Dworkin would take this route if the following hypothesis were true: Dworkin, unlike John Rawls, believes that (what Rawls refers to as) comprehensive philosophical doctrines (e.g., Kantianism, utilitarianism, and in general, the best philosophical arguments available) *do* have a place in public discussion of issues.[15] While Rawls brackets discussion of many issues on the grounds that they are part of particular comprehensive philosophical doctrines and not part of public reason,[16] if my hypothesis is correct, Dworkin must find some other way to bracket discussion of certain issues. Dworkin could do this by classifying views that are not subject to rational argument as part of religion, or at least part of religion for constitutional purposes.

A significant problem for this approach arises, though, if it turns out that discussion of these questions, including the weighing of natural and human creative inputs, is capable of more rigor and conclusiveness than Dworkin thinks. In that case, such discussion can enter the category of secular philosophy, which cannot be classified as religious in a constitutional (or any other) sense. Thus one objection to Dworkin's position derives from the view that a discussion of the meaning of life is philosophical rather than religious, and so any view on this issue is philosophical rather than religious. Accordingly, the legal enforcement of some view of intrinsic value could not be disallowed on the grounds that it is a religious view that the state should not impose.

But a different problem internal to Dworkin's position exists, because, after all, Dworkin does not think that the state must, or should, be totally uninvolved in regulating abortion. He thinks, for example, that the state should encourage women to make abortion decisions in a responsible way because intrinsic value is at stake.[17] But when philosophers have discussed the meaning and point of human life, some have argued for the value of characteristics or functions of personhood, whether in humans or in other animals, such as consciousness and rationality. They have concluded that mere life (the "pulse in the mud," so to speak) is worthwhile primarily as a *means* to such functions as sentience or self-consciousness.[18] This, of course, implies that they have concluded that *life itself* does not have much value, which is a position Dworkin might think is either only one possible "religious" position on this question or else a nonreligious view.

Suppose that only some *positive* answer to the question of whether life has intrinsic value is religious. Then Dworkin's view that the state has a "legitimate interest in maintaining a moral environment in which decisions about life and death are taken seriously and treated as matters of moral gravity" (p. 168) involves the state in taking sides with a religious view and against a nonreligious view (that life has no intrinsic value). But separation of church and state should mean that the government cannot side with religion against atheism. On the other hand, if taking any negative *or* positive view on the issue of whether life has intrinsic value is religious, the state, in intervening to see that women consider abortion to be a grave matter, would be siding with one religious view over another. This too is ruled out by separation of church and state. Even if the state intervened just to have people think about what might possibly be an important religious matter, it would still be in a position analogous to one in which the state encouraged people to think about the possibility that there is a God. This also is something the state may not do if there is separation of church and state.

Finally, recall that Dworkin's notion of the sacred is about value that is not derived from interest, and not value that it takes a great deal to override. He himself says that there is something sacred about even a not very good work of art (i.e., one lacking in aesthetic value) (pp. 78–9, 80–1). This suggests that even if all people agree that the fetus is sacred, Dworkin has provided no more reason for state-mandated waiting periods before destroying a fetus than for state-mandated waiting periods before destroying a not very good painting (if it were imposing on someone's body).

Is Dworkin's hard-line view correct?

Dworkin also holds that abortion would be morally impermissible if the fetus were a person. (I call this his hard-line view.) He takes this position because he thinks that parents have a special duty to support their children (pp. 111 nn. 4–5, p. 249), and it is never permissible to kill one innocent person to save even the life of another (pp. 32, 94). I disagree with the hard-line view. For example, I do not think that if someone has acquired your genetic material and, without your consent, created a person who is your genetic offspring, you are required to support it in your body to save its life. I also believe it is permissible sometimes to kill an innocent person who is imposing on someone else, especially when the person killed will lose only life that is being provided by that imposition.[19]

However, notice that even if sometimes it is true that we may abort a fetus that is a person from conception on, this does not show that we may abort a fetus that has *developed into* a person, having started as a nonperson.[20] This is because if the fetus were a person from conception, there would be no time when it would be possible to abort a nonperson. Therefore, it matters less whether one has an early or late abortion, for one will be aborting a person whenever one aborts. But if the fetus develops into a person, then abortion would be possible at a time when we would not then be killing a person. If killing a nonperson is a far less serious issue than killing a person is, in failing to abort early we will have lost the opportunity to perform a morally less serious act. Suppose that we want to have an abortion and the fetus has already developed into a person. We cannot simply argue for the permissibility of killing a person in the manner that we would if the fetus was a person from conception on. Rather, we must argue for the permissibility of killing a person given that we failed to take advantage of the opportunity to end the pregnancy without killing a person. This may be harder to do than simply arguing for the permissibility of killing what was always a person. For it may be correct to penalize someone for failing to perform the morally less serious act by restricting permission to perform the more serious act. Likewise, suppose that the fetus develops in morally significant stages and that it is morally worse to kill it at a later stage rather than at an earlier one, even if it is never a person. Then arguments for the permissibility of killing a creature that had always had the properties of a later-stage creature need not necessarily justify killing it if we could have killed it when it had different properties.

Hence it is a mistake to argue as follows: (1) either the fetus is a person or it is not a person; (2) it would be permissible to abort it if it is a person; (3) it would be permissible to abort it if it is not a person; (4) hence, it is permissible to abort it. For even if premise (2) is true of a fetus that was always a person, it may not be true of a fetus that develops into a person.[21]

Conclusion

Dworkin believes that newborn infants should be treated as persons from a moral and legal point of view, even though they are not self-conscious and the latter characteristic may be a requirement for being a person from the philosophical point of view. If we add this and his hard-line view to our previous discussion, we can describe an alternative to Dworkin's views that captures some of what his position commits him to, but revise other components in light of the previous discussion. The alternative involves both *philosophical* (vs. religious) disagreement on the value of the early fetus and agreement that it is not a person.

The alternative is as follows: the state should not interfere with a person's own decision on abortion when (1) there is still philosophical disagreement (that might eventually be resolved) on the value of a fetus that has never been conscious, and (2) the state's taking one side would impose significantly on the rights and interests of a person. One can afford to enforce a philosophically contested position on some people (taxation, for example) only when there is no comparable physical impact on any given person and when other people's rights and interests may be at stake, as they are not in killing an early fetus. When the fetus reaches the point when, like infants, we should declare them persons for moral and legal purposes, no abortion is permitted. Just as one cannot kill an infant in order to help its parent, nor kill any person merely in order to help another person, so one may not kill a late fetus in order to help a pregnant woman.

No doubt Dworkin would find this alternative unappealing. First, it does not focus on religion or make use of the constitutional principle of separation of church and state to limit governmental interference with abortion. Second, he believes in allowing some exceptions for abortion late in pregnancy despite his hard-line view. But, given his views on infants and the fact that late fetuses have the same characteristics as many slightly premature infants, he may not be allowed to make these exceptions unless he rejects the hard-line view.

II   "The Philosophers' Brief" Arguments

Summary

In "The Philosophers' Brief on Assisted Suicide," Dworkin et al. argue that if it is permissible to omit or terminate medical treatment with the intention that the patient die, it is permissible to assist in killing with the intention that the patient die, at least when the patient consents. One reason they give for this is that there is no intrinsic moral difference between killing and letting die. Another reason is that they think that people have a right to make important personal choices about their own lives, and whether to be killed or let die could equally be a means to facilitating these choices.

One part of their argument builds on the U.S. Supreme Court's 1990 decision in *Cruzan v. Missouri*, in which the Court majority assumed (if only for the sake of argument) that patients have a constitutional right to refuse life-preserving treatment. Dworkin et al. say that the existence of a right to refuse treatment also implies a right to assistance in suicide. If, as *Cruzan* indicates, it is permissible for doctors to let a patient die even when the patient and the doctor intend the patient's death, then, Dworkin et al. think, it is permissible for doctors to assist in killing. In the preface to "The Philosophers' Brief on Assisted Suicide," written after the U.S. Supreme Court heard oral arguments on the case, Dworkin notes that several justices rejected this link between *Cruzan* and the assisted-suicide cases. These justices sought to distinguish them by reference to a "common-sense distinction" between the moral significance of acts and omissions: assisting suicide is an act and thus requires a compelling moral justification; in contrast, not providing treatment is an omission, a matter of "letting nature take its course," and can be justified more easily.

Dworkin says in the Preface that "the brief insists that such suggestions wholly misunderstand the 'common-sense' distinction, which is not between acts and omissions, but between acts or omissions that are designed to cause death and those that are not." This means that Dworkin et al. believe that common sense denies that there is ever a moral difference between action and omission *per se*, and only a moral difference between intending and not intending (even while foreseeing) death. Presumably, the latter *moral* distinction will only matter sometimes, since, he thinks, intending death is sometimes justified.

Counterarguments

Action/omission versus killing/letting die

The first thing to notice is that Dworkin et al. construct their argument on the assumption that when a doctor assists patients in committing suicide by giving them potentially lethal pills, the doctor intends the patients' deaths. They try to show that this is permissible. But it need not be true that the doctor has this intention; in giving the patients potentially lethal pills, the doctor may only *intend* to give them a choice of whether to live or die. Hence, even if it were wrong to intend patients' deaths in combination with acting to help them attain this end, this need not be what is involved in assisting a suicide. However, since Dworkin et al. try to defend assisted suicide on the assumption that the doctor does intend the patent's death, I will continue to make the same assumption.

I agree that the *act/omission* distinction will not bear much moral weight in this setting, but this does not mean that if intending versus foreseeing death matters, it alone matters. For killing versus letting die, which is not the same as act versus omission, may matter. When doctors remove life-sustaining treatment by pulling a plug at time t, they act (though do not necessarily kill) and their act could be as permissible as not starting treatment at time t (an omission). As I have argued elsewhere, if doctors are terminating aid at time t that they (or the organization whose agent they are) have been providing, then in certain cases they *let die* rather than kill, and their act is as permissible (or as impermissible) as not starting treatment at time t would be.[22] The doctors let die, even though they act, because (1) the patient dies of some underlying cause whose effects the life support was counteracting[23] and (2) the patient loses out only on life he or she would have had with the support the doctors (or organization whose agent they are) are providing. Consider the following analogy: I am saving a man from drowning and I decide to stop. Even if I must actively push a button on my side to make myself stop, I still let the person die rather than kill him, and my act is as permissible (or impermissible) as not beginning to provide aid. By contrast, suppose that (1) were true but (2) were not, because some stranger, who was neither providing the life support nor owned the machine that was providing it, pulled the plug. This would be a killing (whether it was permissible or not).

Is there always a moral difference between letting die (by act or omission) and killing? I do not think so. Some terminations of aid could be killings that would be no more difficult to justify than cases of letting die (that involve omissions or acts). Hence, if killing versus letting die sometimes matters morally, this does not mean it must always matter. For example, suppose that one particular hospital in a community has faulty electrical wiring. If the doctors at that hospital accede to a patient's request to discontinue treatment by pulling the plug on the life-support machine, she will get an electric shock and die (Faulty Wiring Case I). In another hospital, if the same patient stopped getting treatment, she would die immediately of her underlying condition. I think that in these cases it is no harder to justify discontinuing treatment when this kills than to justify discontinuing treatment that just lets the patient die; it is not true that if the patient is in one hospital, she may not have aid terminated, but if she is in the other hospital, she may. In Faulty Wiring Case I, the patient is killed because condition (1) is not satisfied; but the fact that condition (2), which is always present in letting die cases, is present in this particular killing case, helps render the particular killing on a moral par with letting die.

Indeed, we might go even further: suppose that a patient requests termination of treatment, but we are physically unable to end his connection to a machine by just pulling the plug or turning off the machine. Instead, we would have to first give the patient an electric shock (which would kill him) in order to be able to disconnect the machine from him (Faulty Wiring Case II). In Faulty Wiring Case I, the shocking that leads to death is foreseen, not intended. In Faulty Wiring Case II, the shocking is intended as a means to remove a patient from the machine. I do not believe that the patient must continue to get unwanted treatment just because we would have to kill him as an intended means in order to stop his getting life-saving treatment, at least if he would die in any case if he did not get the treatment.

There are also other commonly accepted instances in which doctors kill their patients, and there is a no legal prohibition on doing this. When a doctor gives morphine to ease pain, foreseeing that it will also cause death, the doctor also acts, and kills (though without intending to kill). Yet it is permissible to do this.

Killing/letting die versus intending/foreseeing death

However, I part company with Dworkin et al. when they argue that, once patients have consented, we can *always* move from the permissibility of letting the patients die while intending their death to the permissibility of assisted suicide that involves patients killing themselves. Killing and assisted killing are not always on a moral par with letting die. Let me explain by reference to some cases.

In all the first type of cases, doctors act *against* their patients' wishes to live. Dworkin et al. agree that doctors may permissibly deny a lifesaving organ to a patient who wants it, in order to give it to another, but *not* kill a nonconsenting patient in order to get that patient's organ for another. They say that this is not because of a moral difference between letting patients die and killing them, but because the doctors merely foresee death in the first case, whereas they intend it in the second. Intending patients' deaths against their wishes makes the behavior impermissible, according to the authors of "The Philosophers' Brief on Assisted Suicide." I shall now try to show, first, that intending patients'death against their wishes does not make not-aiding impermissible, and, second, that in the absence of intending patients'deaths against their wishes, killing can be wrong while letting die is not wrong.

Suppose that a doctor who denied an organ to a patient and gave it to another person who needs it more did this because the person denied was his enemy whose death he intended; giving the organ to the needier person was only a pretext. Though we can conclude that the doctor has a bad character, I do not think that we should conclude that he acted impermissibly in giving the organ to the needier patient.[24] This shows that intending patients' deaths when it is against their wishes does not necessarily make not-aiding impermissible.[25] Here is another case: a doctor is on her way home. All she can still do on her required time on duty is save a patient who, if he dies, will provide organs to save five others. Just then, two patients are admitted who will die unless she takes care of them. As this will take her over her shift, she would not be required to do so, and she would not do so except for the fact that helping them means that she cannot help the one patient whose organs would be helpful. She stays to help the two only in order that the one will die and his organs can be used to help the five. I believe that she acts permissibly (and supererogatorily) in saving two rather than one, yet she had a wrong intention.

Now, I shall defend the claim that killing versus letting die can make a moral difference in the absence of intending death against a patient's wishes. If it were intending death and not killing that makes a moral difference in the case where doctors kill patients in order to get their organs for others, it should be as permissible to kill patients when their death is *not intended* as it is to let them die when their death is not intended. Suppose that a doctor, in order to transplant an organ (innocently gotten) into the neediest patient, uses a chemical that he *foresees* will seep into the next room where another patient lies, killing that patient. In this case, the doctor does not intend the death of the patient in the other room, but only foresees that patient's death as a side effect of the chemical. Presumably, though, transplanting when this effect will occur is wrong, even if it cannot be done otherwise, because it is a killing. Yet letting the patient next door die simply because one is busy transplanting into the neediest patient is permissible. So in cases in which we merely foresee death, killing may be wrong, even if letting die is not. This shows that there is a *per se* moral difference between killing and letting die that can lead to differential moral judgments in at least some cases.

Another way to show that the difference between killing and letting die can matter is to show that when a patient does not want to die, letting die with the intention that death occur might be permissible, though killing with such an intention is not. I have already said that sometimes the letting die would not be wrong (as in the case discussed above) when the doctor chooses to aid two people instead of one, only because she intends the death of the one. Compare this with a killing in which the doctor would use the only way of saving two people merely because that way of saving the two will kill another person as a side effect. This killing is impermissible.

Dworkin *et al.* claim that a doctor who lets patients die of asphyxiation against the patients' wills, intending that they die so that their organs are available for use in others, has done something wrong, as has a doctor who kills the same sort of patients, intending them to die. When the letting die and the killing are both wrong, as in these cases, I would say that this is because both doctors aim against the welfare of their patients and violate their rights. The first doctor violates the positive right to treatment without doing anything important instead (such as saving two other people); the second doctor violates the negative right against being killed. But this does not always imply, as Dworkin et al. think, that a "doctor violates his patient's rights whether the doctor acts or refrains from acting *against the patient's wishes* in a way that is designed to cause death."[26] This was already shown by the case where the doctor aids two people merely because this will lead her to let die one other person who does not wish to die. But there are other types of cases that show this as well. For example, suppose that patients do not want to die, but it would be in their interest to die. If a treatment is experimental, or in general something to which the patients have no positive right, it may be permissible to deny it to them because death would be in their own best interest.[27] I do not believe that the patient acquires a right to have the experimental therapy merely because the doctors' reason for refusing it is that they aim at a death which is in the patient's interests but which the patient does not want. But it would violate patients' rights and be morally wrong to kill those patients if they did not want to die, even if it were in their best interests to die and the doctors acted for their best interests. Once again, we see a case where a moral difference between killing and letting die surfaces.[28]

Next, consider the type of cases in which the patient consents to death. These are the cases that bear directly on whether the killing/letting die distinction is morally relevant in assisted-suicide contexts. Does the distinction between killing and letting die make a moral difference when deciding on the *scope* of permissible refusal of treatment versus the scope of permissible assistance to killing? Dworkin et al. seem to suggest that the scope should be the same, saying that if doctors can turn off a respirator, they can prescribe pills. Prescribing pills is a way to assist patients to kill themselves, even when they are not currently receiving life support, and it is this sort of assisted killing that Dworkin et al. think is permissible. In addition, by turning off a respirator, they have in mind, I believe, cases where the patient is then left to die. It is these sorts of cases of killing and letting die that I shall compare first.

Mentally competent patients may legally refuse treatment, intending to die, even when it is *against their best interest* to do so and, on many occasions, even when they could be cured. Presumably, in many of these cases, they could also insist on the doctor terminating treatment, even if their intention is to die. Furthermore, even if the doctors in these cases improperly intend that the patients die, the treatment must be terminated. *This is because the alternative to letting the patients die is forcing treatment on them.* We think that the right of mentally competent patients not to be physically invaded against their will is typically stronger than our interest in the patients' well-being (even if the right could be overridden for considerations of public safety). But if such patients ask for assistance in killing themselves when it is against their medical interest to die, it might well be morally *im*permissible to assist in killing them. This is, at least in part, because the alternative is not forcing treatment on them. Certainly, if someone's reason for wanting to die is to sacrifice himself as a martyr in a political protest, it would be ludicrous to go to a doctor for assistance, though he could have a doctor terminate treatment. Even if his own nonmedical best interests were at stake – for example, he must die in order to ensure his glorious postmortem reputation – it would be inappropriate for a physician to assist in his killing. So, contrary to what Dworkin et al. say, doctors might in some cases be permitted and even required to turn off a respirator, even when they intend death, but not be permitted to give pills that will cause death.[29]

Why is judgment about the best interests of the patient only determinative in the case where we give something to patients that will cause their death but not when we allow them to die by nontreatment or by terminating treatment? Philippa Foot argues that when we actively interfere with people, we must be concerned not only with whether they will our interference with them but also whether we harm them.[30] Both their right to autonomy and our duty not to harm apply. If we give patients a death-producing drug, even when they take it themselves, and even if we just foresee their deaths, I think that this dual condition on active interference applies.[31] When we let patients die by disconnecting life support, not interfering with autonomy is shown to be the dominant consideration, overriding concern with welfare. For if we do *not* let the patients die, we will be interfering with them against their wishes, violating their right to autonomy. Not doing this dominates acting in their interests. By contrast, if we do not help patients carry out suicides they will for themselves when we think that it is not good for them, we do not interfere with them against their will. We respect their right to autonomy, which is essentially a negative right not to be interfered with. It is true that we will not be promoting their autonomy as a value (i.e., we will not be seeing to it that their own values determine their lives). But it is a mistake to assimilate autonomy as a value to autonomy as a right for promoting others' autonomy may interfere with our own autonomous choice not to do them harm or otherwise involve ourselves with their lives. In sum, we can insist on acting for competent patients' good even against their will only when doing so does not involve our violating their right to noninterference.

So the alternative to letting die has such a morally objectionable feature – forcing treatment, which a patient has a right we not do – that even if we think that the competent patient's and the doctor's intentions are wrong, we must permit termination of aid. In contrast, the alternative to assisted suicide may simply be leaving patients alone; this often does not violate any of their rights against us, and so we can, and sometimes we should be required to, refuse to help them because we disapprove of their goals. Many people – including Supreme Court justices whom Dworkin cites – might, then, reasonably distinguish terminating treatment from assisting in a suicide. The move from *Cruzan*'s right to refuse treatment to the permissibility of assisted suicide is, therefore, not generally available.[32]

The argument against the general moral equivalence of assisting suicide and terminating aid, even when the patient consents to these, also helps us see that sometimes killing or assisting in killing will have the same moral standing as terminating aid. For example, in Faulty Wiring Case I, we will kill a patient or assist in killing her if we help the patient disconnect herself – if we are involved in terminating treatment. This is because she dies of the electric shock from disconnection. But since the patient will continue to be interfered with against her will if we do not do this, we should disconnect her from life support.

In sum, I have argued that the approach of "The Philosophers' Brief on Assisted Suicide" – which claims that when terminating treatment while intending death is permissible, assisting suicide while intending death is also permissible – does not succeed. In particular, I argued that it is not always permissible to assist killing while intending death when it is permissible to let die or terminate support while intending death. Even if it is sometimes permissible to assist killing while intending death when it is permissible to let die intending death, this would not be because there is no intrinsic moral difference between killing and letting die (including terminating life support), because, I argue, an intrinsic difference shows up in several cases.

A theoretical argument

I have examined the case-based arguments in "The Philosophers' Brief on Assisted Suicide" for Dworkin et al.'s conclusion that the distinction between killing and letting die does not matter *per se*. These arguments contrast with the second, more theoretical, argument that Dworkin et al. make in favor of physician-assisted suicide. They adopt the theory proposed in *Planned Parenthood v. Casey* – that people have a right to self-determination in the most intimate and important matters in their lives – and from that theory deduce a right to determine the time and manner of death, and by implication, whether by a letting die or a killing. But does this theory then endorse the conclusion that people have a right to assisted suicide from a willing physician, if they decide that their medical treatment is consuming too much of their families' finances or if they wish to give up their life for some noble cause, given that they would have a right to refuse treatment for these reasons? I suggest that this theoretical argument is too broad if it yields these conclusions.

Alternatives

First alternative

There is a type of argument that might be constructed to show that if we may let people die while intending their death, it is also permissible to assist in a killing while intending the death. When *death is (at least) a lesser evil*,[33] the greater good is a medically appropriate aim (e.g., having no pain rather than gaining postmortem glory), and the patient consents, then assisting in the killing with the intention to bring about death will be permissible if letting die while intending death is permissible. This is (I believe) a different argument from those presented in the brief. It does not imply that, if patients consent, we may always assist in their suicide, even when it is against their interest to die (because death is not then a lesser evil by comparison with continuing on in their lives). Notice that when we add the qualifier "when death is (at least) a lesser evil" (as well as patient consent), we get a certain moral equivalence of assisting in a killing and letting die. We can get the first premise in "The Philosophers' Brief on Assisted Suicide" argument (i.e., terminating treatment while intending death is permissible) without assuming that death is (at least) the lesser evil, for it is permissible to terminate treatment at the wishes of a competent patient even when death is a greater evil than living on and so not in a patient's interest. Because the first premise can be true without "the lesser evil" clause, we *cannot* move easily from the first premise to the conclusion that assisting in a killing, too, is permissible, for the plausibility of the conclusion is often dependent on the truth of the clause. It may be true that in those circumstances (i.e., when death is a lesser evil, the greater good is a medically appropriate aim and the patient consents), it will also be true that killing or assisting in a killing is as acceptable a means to death as letting die. I have not denied this.

Second alternative

A second alternative to the argument in "The Philosophers' Brief on Assisted Suicide" focuses on the goal of patient autonomy. This goal goes beyond seeing that we do not interfere with a competent patient's negative rights not to be given unwanted treatment. On one model of doctoring, a doctor should fundamentally be an agent of a patient's wishes in health-related matters, so long as this is not clearly harmful to the patient. This model has a different emphasis from a second one that says that a doctor should fundamentally aim to promote a patient's welfare, at least so long as this does not interfere with a patient's negative rights against unwanted interference.[34] According to the first model, a doctor may assist suicide when the patient thereby seeks to avoid a health problem, so long as the death is not clearly against the patient's interest. The doctor may, but need not, aim at the death, as it need not be clear that the death is in the patient's best interest.

Third alternative

Dworkin et al. try to argue that if we may let die (including terminating treatment) while intending death, then we may assist killing while intending death. By contrast, we can argue that if we may treat patients when they consent, though we *foresee* that this treatment will rapidly kill them, then we may kill or assist in killing patients when they consent while *intending* their death. Consider the four-step argument below. Assuming patient consent:

1   Doctors may permissibly relieve pain in a patient (e.g., by giving morphine), even if they know with certainty that this will cause the death of the patient as a foreseen side effect,

when death is a lesser evil and pain relief is a greater good and only the morphine can stop the pain.[35] Call this the morphine for pain relief (MPR) case.

2   Doctors may permissibly intentionally cause other lesser evils to patients when these are the means to their medically relevant greater good (e.g., a doctor might permissibly intentionally cause patients pain temporarily, if only this would keep them from falling into a permanent coma).[36]

3   When death is a lesser evil for a person, it is not morally different from other lesser evils.[37]

4   Therefore, when death is a lesser evil and pain relief is a greater good for the same person (just as it is in step 1), it is also permissible to intentionally cause death, or assist in its being intentionally caused, when it alone can stop pain. (For example, we could give morphine, which itself no longer relieves pain, in order to induce death.)

Here is an alternative four-step argument. Assuming patient consent:

1a   Doctors may permissibly relieve pain (e.g., by giving morphine), even if they know with certainty that *this causes death as a foreseen side effect in the same patient* (and even if death is a greater evil than pain), when death is unavoidably imminent in any case (e.g., in a terminal patient) and the morphine alone can stop pain.

2a   Doctors may permissibly intentionally cause other (greater) evils that are unavoidably imminent anyway when these are the means to producing (lesser) goods in the same patient. (For example, suppose that it is worse to be blind than *to be deaf*. If a patient will shortly be blind anyway, it would be permissible to intentionally cause the blindness, if only this would prevent the patient from also going deaf.)

3a   When death is an imminent evil for a person, it is not morally different from other imminent evils.

4a   Therefore, doctors may permissibly intentionally cause death, or assist in its being intentionally caused, when death is imminent anyway and it alone can stop pain in the same patient (even if death is a greater evil and relief of pain is a lesser good).

In the alternative four-step argument, we need not assume that a shorter life with less suffering can be better for someone than a much longer one with more suffering, only that it is in one's interest to die somewhat sooner when death would come soon anyway and only dying sooner can reduce suffering.

The general structure of the two four-step arguments is to show that in some carefully circumscribed cases, if we may permissibly kill people or assist in causing their death where we foresee the death as a side effect, we may also kill them, intending the death, or assist them in intentionally causing their own death, when the death is the means to a greater good. Note that the arguments do not *merely* say that the doctors in the first step of each argument may give the morphine for pain relief, even if they also intend their patients' deaths, though this is true. In such a case, the morphine they give would relieve the patients' pain, even if that is not the doctors' reason for giving them the morphine. Rather, the arguments are concerned in their conclusion with more than this; they are concerned with a doctor who (it is reasonable to think) could have no other reason for giving morphine besides killing, since the morphine itself no longer relieves pain but it does cause the death that is the means to pain relief.

The four-step arguments are directed against the common use of the doctrine of double effect (DDE) to rule out suicide. The DDE says that it is impermissible to intend lesser evil, even as a means to a greater good, but it is permissible to pursue greater good by innocent means, even foreseeing that lesser evil will certainly occur as a side effect. One need not agree with the more radical claim that the distinction between intending and foreseeing evil never makes a moral difference, in order to hold that sometimes the distinction makes no moral difference. It makes no difference, for example, when the lesser evil is A's pain, when we have A's consent and the greater good is A's life: we may act merely foreseeing the pain or intending it, as premise (2) in the first four-step argument claims.[38]

I noted above that we may go directly from letting die while intending death to killing while intending death, *if death is a lesser evil*. This qualifier is not necessary in a four-step argument. This is because letting die may be permissible even when death is not a lesser evil (or imminent), but giving a medicine with merely foreseen fatal effects will not be permissible unless death is a lesser evil (or imminent). Because, in a four-step argument, we *cannot get the first step* without death being at least the lesser evil (or imminent), we can move more easily from it to the conclusion that killing is permissible.

Still, as I claimed above, it is true that in those circumstances (i.e., when death is a lesser evil, the greater good is a medically appropriate aim, and there is patient consent), it will also be true that killing or assisting in a killing is as acceptable a means to death as letting die. I have not denied this. Why, then, focus on the four-step argument rather than the (assisting) killing-equals-letting-die-when-death-is-a-lesser-evil argument? My sense is that it is helpful to show that it is permissible to intend (i.e., someone of good character could intend) the patient's death, when the only reason that could reasonably justify doing what kills or assists killing is that it kills or assists killing. I am here trying to distinguish (1) cases in which someone intends a death, but the properties and effects of the act are such that another agent could reasonably justify doing the act without intending the death (because, for example, the morphine stops pain directly), from (2) cases in which someone intends a death and the properties of the act are such that another agent could not reasonably justify doing the act without intending the death (because only death stops the pain).

We have considered cases where doing an act is permissible, even though the intention of the agent for the death of the patient was bad. This was true when we imagined a malicious doctor terminating treatment at a patient's request, though doing this is against a patient's interest, only because he intends the patient's death. In such a case, another agent who did not intend the death would have good reason to act in the same way, that is, so as not to force treatment on someone. Similarly, when a doctor gives morphine that will relieve pain because he intends its other, death-causing properties, another doctor would have reason to do the same act intending only the morphine-caused pain relief while merely foreseeing the death. But if morphine no longer relieves pain, yet can still induce death, it is reasonable to think that only a doctor who intends death would have a reason to give the morphine.[39]

When we allow that it is permissible to *let die* while intending death, we can do so without inquiring into the morality of intending deaths as such, since (as argued above) the alternative to allowing termination of treatment is forcing treatment on someone, and not doing this could provide a justifying reason for termination. Hence even someone who incorrectly intends the death of patients might permissibly unplug them at their request. But when we want to kill or assist in killing someone, forcing treatment is not the alternative, so then what we must do is show *why*, when death is a lesser evil or imminent, doing what could only be explained because we intend death is morally acceptable. This is what we are forced to do by the four-step arguments. By contrast, "The Philosophers' Brief on Assisted Suicide" argument, even modified (as above) threatens to conceal the importance of doing this by leading us to think that we have already argued for the permissibility of doing what could only be explained by intending death when we conclude that letting die while intending death is permissible.

However, notice that the fact that the four-step arguments show that there is a morally acceptable intention to cause death is compatible with any particular doctor having a morally unacceptable intention to cause death while still acting permissibly in intentionally causing death. For example, suppose that the doctor knows that the only means to stop the patient's pain (the greater good) is to cause the patient's death (the lesser evil). However, this doctor does not intend that the patient not be in pain; she only wants to have the experience of intentionally killing someone as her end in itself. She differs from another doctor who has the morally acceptable intention to produce death as a means to stopping pain. Yet she may proceed. This is because the objective features of the act – regardless of anyone's intention – remain the same: the death is a lesser evil to a person that causes greater good to that same person, and the person consents to the lesser evil. It is these constant objective features that make it true that the intention that focuses on them *is* morally acceptable (rather than vice versa).

This point is the basis for the more radical critique of the doctrine of double effect, namely, that intention *per se* never makes a difference to the moral permissibility of an act.[40] If this radical claim is true, then Dworkin et al. will be wrong in holding that intending a harm rather than merely foreseeing it can account for the impermissibility of an act.

A doctor's duty?

Finally, Dworkin et al. claim that patients have a right to assisted suicide only from a willing physician. They do not claim that a doctor has a duty to assist suicide. I believe that yet another four-step argument for such a duty may be available, as puzzling as the existence of such a duty seems. Assuming patient consent:

1b   Doctors have a *duty* to treat pain (e.g., with morphine), even if they foresee with certainty that it will make them cause the patient's death soon, because death is a lesser evil and pain relief is a greater good, or because death is unavoidably imminent (even if it is a greater evil) and only morphine can stop the pain.

2b   Doctors would have a *duty* to intentionally cause evils (e.g., pain, blindness) for a patient's own medical good, when the evils are lesser and the goods to be achieved by them greater, or when the evils are unavoidably imminent anyway (even if greater) and they are the only way to achieve a medically relevant good.

3b   When death is a lesser or imminent evil for a person, it is not morally different from other lesser evils.

4b   Therefore, doctors have a *duty* to intentionally cause the patient's death or assist in its being intentionally caused, when death is a lesser evil (or imminent anyway) and pain relief is a greater good (or just as good) for the patient and only death can bring it about.

Call this last four-step argument the duty argument. It is important because some have claimed that doctors' *professional ethic* in particular implies that they may not engage in physician-assisted suicide. By contrast, this argument suggests that doctors' professional ethic calls for them to perform assisted suicide. It is also important because it shows that a doctor's conscientious objection to killing a fetus in abortion could be permissible while such an objection to assisted suicide is not. This is because a doctor could also conscientiously refuse to intentionally cause such evils as blindness in a fetus for the sake of helping a woman in whose body the fetus lies. Harming people for their own greater good is morally different from harming some being for the sake of the good of another being. If one continues to believe that doctors may conscientiously refuse to assist in suicide, one will have to show what is wrong with the duty argument for the opposite conclusion.

Acknowledgement

This article is a revised version of my "Ronald Dworkin on Abortion and Assisted Suicide," *Journal of Ethics*, vol. 5, 2001, pp. 200, 221–40. I thank Ronald Dworkin for his response to that article, in his "Replies to Endicott, Kamm, and Altman," in the same issue, pp. 265–6. I hope that this revision is improved over the earlier version.

Notes

1 Ronald Dworkin, *Life's Dominion: An Argument about Abortion, Euthanasia, and Individual Freedom* (New York: Alfred A. Knopf, 1993). Page references in the text and notes are to this book unless otherwise specified.

2 Ronald Dworkin, Thomas Nagel, Robert Nozick, John Rawls, Thomas Scanlon, and Judith Thomson, "The Philosophers' Brief on Assisted Suicide," *New York Review of Books*, 44, March 27, 1997, pp. 41–7.

3 Like Dworkin, for simplicity, I shall use "fetus" to describe all stages of a conceptus, including the embryo stage.

4 I discuss this point in connection with stem cell cloning in "Embryonic Stem Cell Research," *Boston Review*, vol. 27(5), October 2002, pp. 29–32.

5 Christine Korsgaard, "Two Distinctions in Goodness," *Philosophical Review*, vol. 92, 1983, pp. 169–95.

6 A similar issue, I argue, arises where one considers the moral significance of cloning. If cloning a person is morally wrong, it is not because the value of the person who results will be less because of his or her origin. For discussion of this, see my "Cloning and Harm to Offspring," *N.Y.U. Journal of Legislation and Public Policy*, vol. 4(1), 2000–1, pp. 65–76.

7 Arthur C. Danto, *The Transfiguration of the Commonplace* (Cambridge, MA: Harvard University Press, 1981), pp. 1–5.

8 In his response to my "Ronald Dworkin on Abortion and Assisted Suicide," Dworkin agrees with this, but argues that a mechanical copy of "The Nightwatch" would not have the value of the original painted by Rembrandt. I agree with this. (Indeed, I think that it is another example of Danto's point cited in note 7 above.) But notice that a mechanical copy of an embryo or a human person, which is how we might characterize a clone that is not the result of sexual reproduction, does *not* have less value than the original of which it is a clone.

9 The use of a hypothetical case that alters biology as we know it is not meant to deny that, in biology as we know it, the death of a late fetus is worse than the death of an early fetus. The hypothetical case just helps us zero in on why exactly we think that the late fetus's death is worse.

10 Dworkin, "Replies to Endicott, Kamm, and Altman," op. cit., p. 266.

11 It is worth noting that in allowing that women do have a high degree of INOV or have significant futures in which the investment might be repaid, as well as rights and interests, Dworkin is taking a position

on an issue that, some argue, is at the heart of the abortion debate, namely, the proper role for women. That is, many think that antiabortion forces really take the view that women have little value relative to fetuses, or at least that their nonmaternal futures have little value relative to fetuses. Dworkin here disagrees.

12 On the latter sort of arguments, see Judith Jarvis Thomson, "A Defense of Abortion," *Philosophy and Public Affairs*, vol. 1, 1971, pp. 47–66; F. M. Kamm, *Creation and Abortion* (New York: Oxford University Press, 1992).

13 See Immanuel Kant, *Fundamental Principles of the Metaphysics of Morals*, trans. Thomas K. Abbot (New York: Macmillan, 1985).

14 Letter from Thomas Scanlon, Professor of Philosophy, Harvard University, to Frances M. Kamm (April 1994).

15 See John Rawls, *Political Liberalism* (New York: Columbia University Press, 1996), which discusses limits on the use of comprehensive doctrines. Dworkin defends judges' use of moral arguments to determine what the general constitutional principles, such as liberty and equality, amount to (pp. 118–27).

16 See Elizabeth Wolgast, "The Demands of Public Reason," *Michigan Law Review*, vol. 94, 1994, pp. 1936–50.

17 See pp. 168, 170. If someone does not have an abortion, a person will result (a locus of rights and interests as well as INOV). Given this should Dworkin not also favor the state encouraging women to think responsibly about having an abortion if the child will not be properly cared for?

18 See, e.g., Aristotle, *The Nicomachean Ethics*, ed. David Ross (Oxford and New York: Oxford University Press, 1980); Jonathan Glover, *Causing Death and Saving Lives: The Moral Problems of Abortion, Infanticide, Suicide, Euthanasia, Capital Punishment and Other Life-or-Death Choices* (Harmondsworth, UK and New York: Penguin, 1977); and Michael Tooley, "Abortion and Infanticide," *Philosophy and Public Affairs*, vol. 2, 1972, p. 44 (who imposes a "self-consciousness requirement" for an organism to possess a "serious right to life").

19 Judith Jarvis Thomson first defended the permissibility of some abortions, even if the fetus is a person, in "A Defense of Abortion," *Philosophy and Public Affairs*, vol. 1, 1971, pp. 47–66. My argument against the hard-line view can be found in my "Abortion and the Value of Life: A Discussion of *Life's Dominion*," *Columbia Law Review*, vol. 95, 1995, pp. 160–221, esp. pp. 185–221, as well as in my *Creation and Abortion*, op. cit.

20 I first made this point in *Creation and Abortion*, op. cit., pp. 174–5. I do not think Thomson considered this gap in her defense of abortion.

21 For more on this issue, see ibid., pp. 174–5.

22 See F. M. Kamm, *Morality, Mortality*, vol. II (New York: Oxford University Press, 1996).

23 Note that this underlying cause need not be the original illness from which the patient suffered. It could be some dependence on life support for oxygen that the patient did not originally have but has acquired.

24 If we care about the doctor (for example, he is our child), we may, however, wish that he had been prevented from acting permissibly in accord with his bad character. For example, we may wish he had overslept and never had the opportunity to act out his bad intention.

25 Judith Jarvis Thomson, one of the coauthors of the brief, argues similarly in "Physician-Assisted Suicide: Two Moral Arguments," *Ethics*, vol. 109, 1999, pp. 497–518.

26 Dworkin et al., "The Philosophers' Brief on Assisted Suicide," op. cit., p. 45.

27 It would not *violate their rights* even if death were not in their interest, since the treatment (by hypothesis) is not one to which they have a right. Still, refusing this treatment when it is in the patients' interest to live, could be impermissible for reasons other than that it violates a right.

28 However, it is worth noting that possibly it is sometimes permissible to kill patients when it is against their interests to die, they do not want to die, and the doctor intends their death. Recall the "Faulty Wiring" cases. There, it was as permissible (or impermissible) to detach a patient from a life-support machine when this killed him (by shocking him) as when it let him die. Suppose that a patient who is on life support in the hospital with faulty wiring does not want to die and it is not in his interest to die. But 10 other patients come into the hospital and they can be saved if and only if they, instead of the

single patient, are hooked up to this one life support system. Perhaps it is permissible to detach him for this purpose, though we will be killing him against his wishes when it is not in his interest. Furthermore, if the only person who can detach him and attach the 10 is someone who does so only because he or she intends the single person's death, I do not think that this alone would make detaching him impermissible ("Faulty Wiring Case III"). Killing, in this case, may be permissible because it involves terminating life support by those who have jurisdiction over providing the life support. This does not show that killings or assisting in killings that do not involve terminating life support would be permissible when patients do not want to die and it is not in their interest to die. Again, showing that killing sometimes makes a moral difference does not show that it always does, and showing that it sometimes does not make a moral difference does not show that it never does.

29 In *Compassion in Dying v. Washington*, the majority of the U.S. Supreme Court suggested that they could not distinguish morally or legally between what is already permitted – both terminating treatment intending death and giving morphine foreseeing death – and assisting in a killing intending death (see 79 F.3d 790, 823 [9th Cir. 1996], *rev'd nom. Washington v. Glucksberg*, 117 S.Ct. 2258 [1997]). Yet the *Compassion in Dying* Court was concerned to limit the doctor's right to assist in killing patients to cases where the patients' lives are going to end shortly anyway and death is not against their interests. Suppose, however, that the distinction between giving pills to a person who is not on life support *and* terminating life support when this allows the patient to die makes no moral or legal difference (as claimed by the justices). Then, terminating treatment should be permitted *no more broadly* than assisting killing. For example, treatment should be required for a competent nonterminal patient who will die without it. But it is not required. The justices may have mistakenly thought that if intending death does not rule out terminating life-saving treatment and killing does not rule out giving morphine for pain relief that will also kill, the combination of intentionally killing must be permitted, even when what kills serves no other purposes (such as pain relief). But the premises do not imply the conclusion, I think.

In his response to the original version of this article (which did not differ in substance from this chapter on the issue of assisted suicide), Dworkin said: "Kamm agrees that the distinction between act and omission is not morally relevant in the context of the assisted suicide cases and I agree with her the distinction is sometimes morally important in other, very different, cases" (Dworkin, "Replies to Endicott, Kamm, and Altman," op. cit., pp. 263–7). But we can now see that while I argued above that the distinction between acts and omissions is inadequate, I have also now argued that the different *distinction between killing and letting die can be morally relevant in the context of the assisted-suicide cases*, not just in "very different" cases. For the case in which a doctor may terminate life-saving aid for competent patients when it is against their interest to die, but not give pills to assist competent patients to die when it is against their interest to die, is meant to show this. (I did not say that the distinction between acts and omissions "is morally important in other, very different, cases.") In his response, Dworkin seems not to distinguish the acts/omissions distinction from the killing/letting die distinction, yet I argued that it was important to do so.

30 Philippa Foot, "Euthanasia," *Philosophy and Public Affairs*, vol. 6, 1977, pp. 85–112.

31 However, I also think that under one model of doctoring, if patients will interference, the doctor may help them if it is merely not clear that this will be harmful. For more on this, see below.

32 This is especially true because the *Cruzan* Court did not base its view that patients have a right to direct termination of treatment on the view that sometimes death is not against the patient's interest.

33 I add "at least" since some may think that death can be a positive good. I also assume that death is not only at least a lesser evil, but the least evil of the alternatives to living on. (I owe the latter point to Seana Shiffrin.)

34 I introduced these two models in my "Physician-Assisted Suicide, Euthanasia, and Intending Death," in M. Battin, R. Rhodes, and A. Silvers (eds.), *Physician-Assisted Suicide: Expanding the Debate* (New York: Routledge, 1998), pp. 28–62.

35 Again, I assume that death is not only a lesser evil, but the least evil of the alternatives to pain in the circumstances. Saying that death is the lesser evil suggests that it must not deprive the person of so many future goods that the loss of them is a greater evil than the pain would be. However, it may be

that some near-future event will be so bad that, even if it would eventually be followed by an outweighing degree of good, one should not have to go through it. There is a deontological quality to this reasoning – for just as the deontologist says that there are some things one need not do to promote the best consequences in general, this reasoning claims that there are some things people might reasonably not go through even to promote the best consequences for themselves. When I say that death could be the lesser evil, and so overall in a person's best interests, I should be understood to include the possibility that it instead prevents an event that one could reasonably wish to avoid regardless of an outweighing future good.

36 Here we might also imagine a case in which a doctor only assists the patient by giving him or her the means of causing the lesser evil of pain, and the patient intentionally causes it.

37 I thank Michael Otsuka for suggesting that I bring out this suppressed premise in the three-step argument presented in F. M. Kamm, "A Right to Choose Death," *Boston Review*, vol. 22, 1997, pp. 21–3.

38 The first four-step argument speaks of death as a lesser evil. Is death an evil at all, and is it being a lesser evil necessary for the first four-step argument? If death were no evil at all but actually good for the patient, the DDE could not be used to raise an objection to assisted suicide. Judith Thomson (in "Physician-Assisted Suicide: Two Moral Arguments," op. cit.) argues that death (1) is no evil at all if one's future will contain only bad things in it, and (2) is, on balance, no evil if a few goods in one's life will be outweighed by great bads. By contrast, I am willing to say that death is an evil in (1) and (2). This is because I think that the elimination of the person is something bad in itself, even if it has as a part the elimination of the person's pain (whether or not it also eliminates some goods the person would have had had he or she lived on). And it is the elimination of the person that is being intended; it is not just a side effect, by hypothesis. (Note also that in the MPR Case where the morphine relieves the pain, the death is most clearly an evil, since the elimination of the person does not involve as a part of itself elimination of pain, the pain already having been eliminated by morphine.)

39 When Thomson criticizes the DDE (in "Physician-Assisted Suicide: Two Moral Arguments," op. cit.), she focuses on cases of kind (1), claiming that the DDE is shown to be wrong because acts done by an agent who intends an evil are not therefore impermissible. This strategy is, I believe, effective against the DDE as usually presented. This is what I would call its "token version." That is, it declares an act wrong on the basis of the intention of the particular agent who does it. But one might try to offer a "type version" of the DDE, which declares an act wrong on the basis of the intentions it is reasonable to attribute to *any* agent who would do that type of act. These examples are not, I think, effective against the type version of the DDE. By contrast, the four-step arguments are intended to be effective even against the type version of the DDE, since it claims that even if no agent could reasonably justify doing the act without intending death, it is permissible to do the act.

40 For which Thomson argues in her "Physician-Assisted Suicide: Two Moral Arguments," op. cit.

13

Reverence for Life and the Limits of State Power

Eric Rakowski

Life's Dominion is Ronald Dworkin's elegant attempt to persuade thoughtful opponents of abortion and euthanasia to cease advocating their legal prohibition. If the morality of abortion, assisted suicide, and the killing of permanently comatose patients depends not on the comparative forcefulness of different persons' competing interests but rather, as Dworkin maintains, on how life's sacredness or inherent worth is best respected, then disagreements about their moral propriety are in his view profoundly religious in character. Because we all agree "that it is a terrible form of tyranny, destructive of moral responsibility, for the community to impose tenets of spiritual faith or conviction on individuals," Dworkin claims that even the most vociferous critics of abortion and mercy killing must on reflection acknowledge "that it is no part of the proper business of government to try to stamp them out with the jackboots of the criminal law" (p. 15).[1]

At the same time, Dworkin contends, governments need not stand by idly as citizens profane what is inviolable. Contrary to what some liberals believe, the state's mandate goes beyond securing people's rights and advancing their other interests. Governments may rescue endangered species, save architectural jewels from the wrecking ball, and keep forests pristine, not only because existing or future people will benefit but because these natural or human creations are believed to be inherently valuable. Likewise, Dworkin argues, the state may restrict the availability of abortion and euthanasia out of respect for life's sanctity, so long as it does not smother individuals' freedom to choose life or death for their unborn progeny or for themselves.

Nevertheless, a government does not lose its legitimacy, Dworkin appears to say, if it fails to foster or defend whatever has intrinsic value (in addition to people's welfare), as it would if it neglected to safeguard the personal rights of its citizens. That political leaders *may* protect intrinsic values by fencing individual liberties does not mean that they are obliged to put intrinsic values first.

The three sections of this essay test in succession these three sets of claims. Section I asks why respect for life's sanctity must yield to a broadly accessible right to end a pregnancy or to speed one's own death *if* the aim of protecting intrinsic values may in other circumstances justify abridging personal freedoms. Section II then shifts ground to question a crucial assumption underlying the argument of section I: Dworkin's supposition that governments may pursue ends other than shielding rights and improving the material prospects of sentient beings, such as elevating private moral deliberation. Finally, section III tries to determine whether Dworkin in fact believes that life is intrinsically valuable, what he thinks respect for that value entails in the face of people's contrary desires, and whether there is anything unique about the political problem posed by this apparent collision between personal interests and life's inherent worth.

I   Why is Freedom to Choose Death
More Important Than Protecting Life's Inherent Worth?

In *Life's Dominion*, Dworkin offers two distinct, though at times confusingly interwoven, moral arguments for the claim that women should be free to abort their pregnancies and that people should be legally entitled to assistance or, at a minimum, acquiescence in ending their lives when they lose all awareness or their will to live.[2] The first argument appeals to a commitment to religious tolerance which he assumes that citizens of liberal democracies share; the second, which receives far less emphasis (perhaps because it lacks the first argument's novelty), rests on the alleged impermissibility of severely curtailing the liberty of rational adults to fashion their lives as they see fit, in order to affirm some value that cannot be traced to the welfare of other conscious beings. In my view, Dworkin's unusual first argument has little force, but his second, conventional argument is correct in outline and conclusion. Given Dworkin's assumptions, the conclusion of his second argument cannot be sustained in the categorical form in which he states it, however. Equally important, justifying a strong right to abort an unwanted pregnancy or to obtain help in dying is not possible without discussing much more thoroughly than Dworkin does in his book both the morality of abortion and infanticide and justifications for paternalistic coercion.

Abortion, suicide, and religious tolerance

Whether a belief is religious, Dworkin says, depends on its content. Although he does not supply a list of necessary or sufficient conditions for a belief to count as religious, Dworkin avers that "convictions about why and how human life has intrinsic objective importance" deserve that label. Even when these convictions make no reference to divine command or supernatural values, they "speak to the same issues – about the place of an individual human life in an impersonal and infinite universe – as orthodox religious beliefs do for those who hold them" (p. 163). Whether they are "shadows of religious beliefs," as they are for people who are devout in traditional ways, or whether they are more "general, instinctive" beliefs about life's inherent worth, as they are for almost everyone else, these convictions "are decisive in forming our opinions about *all* life-and-death matters – abortion, suicide, euthanasia, the death penalty, and conscientious objection to war" (p. 155). To be sure, "not every woman who decides to have an abortion broods first about why and how human life is sacred" (p. 165). Yet "[m]any who do not nevertheless act out of convictions that . . . presuppose views about that essentially religious issue" (p. 165). Likewise, Dworkin declares, people's opinions about whether it is better to be kept alive in a permanent vegetative state than to be killed or left to die, or about whether they should accelerate their death to spare themselves and others the last stages of a painful or infantilizing disease, necessarily implicate their convictions about life's point and value, even if those convictions do not explicitly channel their reasoning.

Once we realize that disagreements about these matters are "at bottom *spiritual*" (p. 101) because they result in major part from "*essentially* religious beliefs" (p. 155), Dworkin contends, we should tolerate actions flowing from beliefs about the morality of abortion and euthanasia even if we consider them misguided, as we refrain from persecuting people whose religious convictions we reject. Opponents of abortion and euthanasia therefore should not seek to stop their performance except by means of persuasion, for the same reason that they would not force a church or a mosque to shut its doors.

Although this argument constitutes the main thrust of *Life's Dominion*, it undergirds only a weak case against outlawing abortion, assisted suicide, or euthanasia. Two reasons typically have been given for why we should be especially reluctant to interfere with religiously motivated conduct. First, insofar as our aim is to bring other people genuinely to share true *beliefs*, we will not succeed by forcing them to observe certain rituals or by forbidding forms of dress, diet, family life, or worship. Faith itself cannot be compelled, and making martyrs rarely wins sincere converts. Second, to the extent that we object to the faithful's *actions*, the criminal law may prove an ineffective tool for halting unwanted conduct. If believers fear that obeying the law will earn them eternal damnation or some dreadful spiritual loss, threatening them with fines or imprisonment might not frighten them into complying but instead inflame dangerous opposition. Physical restraints could prevent members of unpopular sects from acting as we believe they ought not to act, of course, but incarceration is costly and divisive. Hence, the argument concludes, all but the most offensive of religiously inspired actions should be allowed.

Neither of these familiar arguments applies to abortion or euthanasia. Their foes' main wish is not to ensure correct belief; it is the perceived immorality of the actions that prompts their opposition. The first reason therefore gains no foothold. Moreover, legal penalties might well deter people from having or assisting with abortions or euthanasia, in a way that legal sanctions cannot stop somebody running from a more terrible fate than dungeons or death. Few, if any, who seek abortions or who want help in ending their lives believe that they have a religious duty to kill their fetuses or themselves. Their faith might allow abortion or suicide under certain conditions, but it is unlikely to decree either. Secular incentives ranging from threatened punishments to free medical care to child support and adoption services therefore might alter people's decisions. To be sure, these incentives may not dissuade the most desperate of pregnant women or agonized patients, but that is true of virtually all criminal sanctions. Finally, abortion, physician-assisted suicide, and euthanasia usually require the aid of medical personnel or other professionals whose actions generally are witnessed or recorded and who could lose their livelihoods if they disregard the law. Legal threats would discourage most of them from helping.

The tradition of *religious* toleration to which Dworkin appeals fails to encompass most abortions, suicides, and killings at the deceased's prior request for two main reasons. First, when we exempt from legal rules those whose religious beliefs impel them to disobey, we insist that they act from a religious motive. But virtually none of the women seeking abortions or patients requesting lethal injections or the cessation of life support invoke religious imperatives in justifying their decisions. They maintain instead that there is no religious impediment to their heeding self-interest or following some nonreligious ethical command. This is not the same as offering a religious reason for their choice. Nor does the fact that most people who condemn abortion and euthanasia cite religious principles make the motives of those who reject those principles religious. A Hindu's belief that cows should not be killed for food hardly converts their slaughter by non-Hindus into a religiously inspired – and protected – action, just as a Cherokee's belief that a copse is sacred does not immunize a rancher's decision to raze it. To borrow an example from American constitutional law, we might agree that the state should be required to pay unemployment benefits to people who are fired because their faith forbids them to work on their Sabbath. But we would not be equally inclined to help people who had no religious objection to working on Saturday or Sunday if they were discharged because they insisted on watching movies instead.

The main failing of Dworkin's argument from religious toleration is that it defines religiously motivated action more broadly than our tradition of toleration approves. Convictions about how best to lead one's life or the relative importance of one's personal ambitions are not necessarily religious in character. Consider one of Dworkin's chief examples. Deciding whether to comply with military conscription when one's country is at war requires that one assess the wrongness of killing in certain situations and the value of one's own survival. These are, unquestionably, normative judgments about matters of life and death. But that does not make all refusals to fight *religious* acts. Some refusals may stem from simple cowardice. Others may be corollaries to moral convictions that do not merit the appellation "religious." The American Supreme Court decisions Dworkin discusses allowed men who conscientiously opposed participating in *all* wars to avoid military service on religious grounds. But those cases did not suggest that conscripts who opposed only wars they considered unjust could qualify for a religious exemption. The legislative and judicial policies on which Dworkin's argument draws treat people who regard intentional killing as *sometimes* permissible as making an ordinary moral judgment, not espousing a religious belief. The same can be said, however, of the views of women who think abortion at least sometimes permissible, or of doctors who would help some but not all desirous people gain an early death – the overwhelming majority of those who favor either practice. Dworkin might think that this established approach to granting religious exemptions draws a false line, even though he invokes it. But he cannot recommend a new distinction without weakening an argument that is overtly premised on *conventional* notions of religious toleration.

Dworkin's argument encounters a second limitation. Dworkin contends that prior to the moment at which a fetus acquires a primitive form of sentience – during the sixth month of gestation, at the earliest – it cannot have an interest in continued life and therefore has no right to live. Thus, he says, disagreements about the morality of abortion before that date are disagreements about the fetus's sacred or intrinsic value, and those disputes necessarily are religious in character. It is hard to see, though, what is distinctively religious about these disputes. If disagreements about the relative value of people's lives once they are conscious – disagreements, say, about whether a child or a middle-aged adult should be helped if doctors can save only one life – are moral rather than religious, as Dworkin believes they are, why do the adjectives swap places when the value of preconscious life lands in the balance? Deciding how morally important is an eight-month-old fetus's or a newborn's claim to life entails assessing the significance of that being's potential to become an intelligent, self-conscious person with complex desires and interests; deciding whether a preconscious fetus's claim is weaker requires the same type of judgment about the significance of the future somebody would have enjoyed to the wrongness of killing that person and the appropriate conception of personal identity on which to rely. Why should a decision to kill based on the second determination be a religious choice that governments must respect, whereas a decision to put one life ahead of another based on the first determination is not, given that both turn on judgments about how personal identity is best measured and on the importance of lost futures? So long as opinions about the morality of abortion depend on beliefs about the nature and significance of personal continuity over time and the harm that death causes, rather than on spiritual insight, those who act on those opinions enjoy no immunity from governmental regulation, given well-established notions of the justifiable reach of state authority.

As for euthanasia and suicide, there is no reason why a preference to die that is not rooted in the spiritual necessity of leaving this life should be regarded as religious and, for that reason, be better protected from social intrusion than preferences regarding important matters *within* a person's life, such as a desire to marry, to cohabit, or to engage in dangerous pursuits. Whether early abortion or euthanasia should be permitted depends not on how often each raises in pregnant women's or patients' minds questions about life's significance that religions sometimes attempt to answer. It depends instead on the value of personal liberty relative to the value of ensuring that people reach the right decision and relative to the significance of possible harms to others from permitting, or not permitting, either practice.

Dworkin's distinction between individual rights or interests and intrinsic values

Dworkin's argument that the state may not outlaw early abortion and euthanasia entirely even if they are morally wrong pivots on a distinction between two justifications for legal prohibitions. First, laws may seek to protect the rights or further the interests of beings that are conscious or that were conscious (if, in this second case, legislators believe that dead or permanently comatose persons have interests that survive their loss of awareness). Criminal statutes barring people from harming others intentionally and subsidies for farmers are illustrations. Second, laws may aim to honor, secure, or bring into being whatever has intrinsic value. Conserving great art, expanding human knowledge, saving endangered species, preserving natural beauty, and making life better for future generations are Dworkin's examples. These two sets of aims appear to exhaust the universe of justifications for governmental action, in Dworkin's view, although a single law or policy may serve ends of both sorts simultaneously.

Dworkin's division of aims is puzzling because of the truncated meaning he assigns the concept of intrinsic value. For example, safeguarding a sentient being's interests (whether or not those interests are sufficiently important to be shielded by moral claims that have the status of rights) seems itself to be intrinsically valuable or to protect something that is intrinsically valuable. Apparently to the contrary, Dworkin asserts that it is a life's "personal" or "subjective" value, which depends on "how much *he* wants to be alive or how much being alive is good for him" (pp. 72–3), "that a government aims to protect, as fundamentally important, when it recognizes and enforces people's right to life" (p. 73). But what does "fundamentally important" mean here if not that guarding the right or that which the right shelters is itself noninstrumentally valuable? Dworkin's definitions shrink the class of intrinsically valuable objects and events to an unusual degree, excluding many things that are ultimately valuable.

Nevertheless, it would be a mistake to make much of this terminological peculiarity. It merely facilitates reference to what Dworkin considers a crucial distinction in vindicating governmental action. His central claim is that these two types of justification – protecting personal interests and advancing everything else that is inherently valuable – do not have equal authority to license official actions that constrict the rights or impede the interests of sentient beings. The first is far more powerful. This difference in their authority, Dworkin further contends, has decisive ramifications for regulating early abortion and euthanasia.

Dworkin formulates the major premise of his argument as follows:

> A state may not curtail liberty, in order to protect an intrinsic value, when the effect on one group of citizens would be special and grave, when the community is seriously divided about what respect for that value requires, and when people's opinions about the nature of that value reflect essentially religious convictions that are fundamental to moral personality.   (p. 157)

Dworkin notes that in his view people have a "stronger" right to personal autonomy than this premise describes (p. 157 n. 15). I will assume in the discussion that follows that the stronger right he has in mind but did not specify is this: all citizens have a right that the state not curtail their liberty in order to protect an intrinsic value (other than people's interests, if they count as intrinsically valuable) when the effect on them, perhaps together with its effects on others, would be grave.[3] Dworkin's second condition – requiring serious community division – seems an unnecessary requirement, for surely a person's moral right to autonomy cannot be hostage (at least I assume that Dworkin would not consider it hostage) to the size of the majority wishing to choke that person's liberty. If only a few women in a religiously conservative community felt burdened by a complete prohibition of abortion because the community was united rather than seriously divided in its view of what respecting incipient life requires, their moral right to abort their pregnancies would not evaporate. The third condition's limitation on state action when disagreements about intrinsic values originate in essentially religious convictions also seems superfluous. Though it may reinforce claims to liberty for religiously *motivated* conduct, it does not significantly strengthen the argument for a right to abortion and euthanasia for reasons already given.

The minor premise of Dworkin's argument is that bans on abortion, assisted suicide, and euthanasia stem predominantly from convictions about intrinsic value, rather than from the belief that abortion or a voluntary death before life has ebbed away would harm people's rights or interests.

In the case of abortion, Dworkin realizes that popular rhetoric belies this claim, because opponents frequently denounce abortion as an assault on an unborn child's right to live. But that rhetoric, he asserts, poorly reflects their actual opinions, for two reasons. First, "[i]t makes no sense to suppose that something has interests of *its own* – as distinct from its being important what happens to it – unless it has, or has had, some form of consciousness: some mental as well as physical life" (p. 16). After all, we do not credit inanimate objects with morally significant interests. Mount Kilimanjaro has no interest in keeping climbers from littering its slopes, even if people and other living creatures do. Nor is life, or the mere potential to acquire consciousness, sufficient for ascribing interests. We would not say that baby carrots have an interest in not being eaten, or that Dr. Frankenstein's monster had an interest in being brought to life when it was just an assemblage of parts awaiting an electrical charge (p. 16). Because a fetus cannot experience even primitive sensations before its cortical and thalamic neurons form synapses around the end of its sixth month, it cannot have interests before that time; *a fortiori* it has no rights during the first two-thirds of a normal pregnancy, because rights presuppose interests that they secure. Dworkin concludes that people who claim that a fetus has a right to live from some point early in pregnancy must be misstating their position.

Dworkin's second reason for saying that people who oppose early abortion must in fact be offering an argument based on the fetus's intrinsic value is that they typically espouse views that he regards as inconsistent with a fetus's having a right to live. If a fetus really had such a right from the moment it was formed, the state would have no choice but to proscribe abortion in all circumstances, because "[p]rotecting people from murderous assault – particularly people too weak to protect themselves – is one of government's most central and inescapable duties" (p. 31). Yet even resolute opponents of abortion generally except pregnancies that resulted from rape or that imperil a woman's life. They could not do so, Dworkin maintains, if they genuinely regarded abortion as akin to murder. "It would be contradictory," he says, "to insist that a fetus has a right to live that is strong enough to justify prohibiting abortion even when childbirth would ruin a mother's or a family's life but that ceases to exist when the pregnancy is the result of a sexual crime of which the fetus is, of course, wholly innocent" (p. 32). Similarly, even if a woman may defend herself against a fetus threatening her life, someone who considered abortion a violation of a fetus's right to live could not condone helping her, because "very few people believe that it is morally justifiable for a third party, even a doctor, to kill one innocent person to save another" (p. 32). Nor could former Vice President Quayle, who opposed abortion, support hypothetically his daughter's decision to have an abortion (as he said he would should she ever decide to have one) if he really thought that abortion would mean the murder of his grandchildren (p. 20).

Hence, people who object to early abortion must do so, Dworkin concludes, not because they think a fetus has interests that killing it offends, but because they regard human life as intrinsically valuable even before consciousness dawns. Dworkin attempts to elucidate the idea that abortion "is intrinsically a bad thing, a kind of cosmic shame" (p. 13) – which he thinks that people on both sides of the abortion debate share – by tracing its similarities to popular attitudes towards natural species, art, and future generations. All are widely thought to be intrinsically valuable, he says, because of the creative investment that God, nature, or humanity has poured into them. In like fashion, people deem a fetus intrinsically valuable because of the divine or natural investment in its life. This investment increases as the fetus grows, amplifying its value. Similarly, the investment a couple makes in planning a pregnancy (if a pregnancy is planned), procreating, and carrying a fetus add to the fetus's value and make a pregnancy's termination a sad loss. Furthermore, a fetus's intrinsic value, like that of a naturally occurring species but unlike that of our knowledge of the cosmos (the more, the better), does not generate a duty to bring it into being. It has "sacred" rather than "incremental" value. It is unimportant that there are not more people, just as it does not matter that the earth lacks one more species of bird; but once a fetus or a species exists, it would be a shame, a cause for regret, were it to die because of what we deliberately did or did not do (pp. 73–5).

The intrinsic value of fetal life furnishes a reason for the state to protect that life, as it does endangered species or magnificent paintings. But Dworkin's major premise is that the state may not impose a grave burden on a group of persons, throttling their liberty, to protect intrinsic values. It follows that governments may burden pregnant women in small ways out of respect for life's inherent worth. They may encourage women to reflect on the morality of abortion early in pregnancy (pp. 150–1), or ban abortions after four or five months for women who earlier passed up an opportunity to end their pregnancy (pp. 170–1). But governments may not make *all* abortions illegal, because it is a grave burden involuntarily to bear a child, give birth, and either raise the child or allow its adoption.[4]

Dworkin offers a parallel argument with respect to euthanasia and suicide. Some people believe, he reports, that even after a body has lost consciousness forever, its life retains intrinsic value, so that it would be an affront to the divine or natural investment in that life to extinguish it. Or they think that a cancer patient ought to fight to the last, even if in great pain, because life's value is dishonored by a willful death. But keeping people alive after they earlier expressed a desire to die should they become permanently comatose, or preventing them from finding oblivion when they choose, collides with their right to determine how their lives should go, including how it should end. Thus, to the extent that justifications for prohibiting euthanasia or assisted suicide turn on the alleged value of life itself (rather than on the interests of people who might be killed against their settled wishes were either practice legal), those justifications must bow, according to the major premise of Dworkin's argument, to individuals' right to select their fate. Although Dworkin acknowledges that regulations based on people's interests are essential to protect against hasty decisions or unwanted killing, he contends that the law may not wholly eclipse a competent patient's right to choose death: "Making someone die in a way that others approve, but he believes a horrifying contradiction of his life, is a devastating, odious form of tyranny" (p. 217).

Dworkin's minor premise

Dworkin's conclusions depend in part on his claim that the principal justification for criminalizing early abortion, euthanasia, and the facilitation of suicide draws on the perceived disrespect these actions betray for life's inherent value. In a long review of *Life's Dominion*, I have questioned this claim and several of the reasons that Dworkin offers in its defense.[5] I shall summarize some of those doubts here, but my account will be brief, because I wish to focus on the solidity of Dworkin's major premise.

Begin with Dworkin's second reason for saying that the debate over the moral permissibility of early abortion is actually about how weighty life's intrinsic value is. Could former Vice President Quayle support his daughter's decision to have an abortion if he thought that a fetus had a right to live? Are exceptions to a law banning abortion for pregnancies endangering a woman's life or resulting from sexual crimes consistent with a fetus's having such a right? The answer to both questions is "Yes."

If one believes that a fetus has a right to live, but that its right is much weaker than a normal adult's right to live, one can support a daughter's decision to have an abortion even if one thinks it wrong, particularly if one believes the decision to be personally difficult or one considers the arguments on behalf of abortion to be strong though not decisive. Vegetarians can respect omnivorous friends. Moreover, even somebody who thinks that abortion should be illegal in almost all cases can make an exception for women whose lives are in danger or whose pregnancies resulted from rape. If a fetus's right to live pales beside a pregnant woman's right to survive, there is no inconsistency in allowing her to abort to save her life. Even if the fetus's right were equally powerful, one could favor the person one knew. If a toddler pointed a loaded gun at one's friend and the only way to save the friend was to shoot the toddler first, one permissibly could do so.[6] In addition, an exception for pregnancies resulting from rape could be justified by the weakness of a fetus's right to live when set against the pain of bearing and raising a child conceived in that way – a horror for many women that dwarfs the burden of caring for a child conceived intentionally or even accidentally.[7]

Dworkin's arguments do not prove that abortion's opponents believe a fetus has no rights; they show only that some exceptions to a ban on abortion could be challenged (though perhaps not decisively) *if* a fetus's right to live were as strong as an adult's. But few people would make that claim. Indeed, by Dworkin's reasoning, one could argue that most people believe that a viable fetus late in pregnancy has no right to live, though it probably can experience some sensations and thus may be a subject with interests, because they would not punish a late abortion as they would murder. But that argument would be as invalid as Dworkin's reverse inference. Many people who condemn late abortions would say that a fetus then does have a right to live, but that its right does not always prevail over a woman's right not to carry it to term, as when caring for the child would be burdensome because of the child's seriously debilitating physical or mental abnormalities.

Now turn to Dworkin's first reason for insisting that people who deplore early abortion must ground their condemnation in a conviction about intrinsic value rather than rights. Is it true, as Dworkin contends, that a being cannot have interests before it is conscious, because interests presuppose the existence of someone whose interests they are, someone from whose perspective life can go better or worse? The answer depends on how "interest" is defined. If one maintains that the term cannot be predicated of beings that never were conscious, as Dworkin does, then it follows logically that the debate over the morality of abortion prior to the sixth month cannot be over whether a fetus has interests. Hence, it must be about something else, and since Dworkin assigns every other possible reason for valuing a fetus's continued existence (apart from its effects on other people) to the realm of intrinsic value, the debate must, by definition, be about intrinsic value.

Nonetheless, this seems an odd way to characterize the debate over the morality of early abortion, because the question of whether the state may curtail abortion to protect a preconscious fetus's putative claim to live, in virtue of the interests it would acquire if it became conscious, overlaps more with debates over which rights or interests the state must protect than it does with debates over whether the state should protect certain allegedly valuable entities that will never have interests they can recognize as their own. I defer further discussion of this issue to the next subsection, however, because one can assume that Dworkin did not intend to limit the state's authority to regulate early abortion purely by means of definition, but wished only to locate the defense of his view about state authority within a broader justification of his major premise.

Before assessing the merits of that premise, it is worth noting that Dworkin's argument runs less smoothly with respect to euthanasia and assisted suicide. People who are conscious plainly have interests that a young fetus cannot, and it is easy to see why many also would say that previously conscious people who now are comatose have interests in virtue of their former consciousness that a preconscious fetus does not. Moreover, their interests are not confined to what would satisfy their preferences. As Dworkin remarks, people have an interest in leading the best life they can, even if that is not the life they most want. How they die can affect how good their life is. The justification for prohibiting assisted suicide or euthanasia, insofar as it does not rest on the danger of abuse or mistake, is that taking one's life intentionally is not in one's interests. This claim appears straightforwardly to raise a question of paternalism: may the state force people to act, or force others to act with respect to them, in what the majority deems their best interest when they judge differently? It is divorced from intrinsic value as Dworkin defines the term – a value that is independent of what people "need or what is good for them" (p. 71; also p. 73).

Dworkin's tacit response to this objection is to distinguish between everything that objectively is in a person's interests, apart from honoring whatever intrinsic value bare life has, and the intrinsic value of bare life. This allows him to generate a conflict between a person's interests and rights, on one side, and government efforts to respect bare life's inherent worth, on the other side. But the conflict seems contrived. Dworkin himself appears to realize this when he says that someone's convictions about what objectively would improve his or her life can "best be understood as a special application of his general commitment to the sanctity of life" (p. 215). Perhaps the obverse puts the matter more accurately: people's beliefs about whether living on painfully or unconsciously respects what is intrinsically valuable can best be understood as an aspect of their beliefs about what constitutes a good life. In any case, the two are inseparable. It is hard to see how it could be in somebody's best interests to die in a way that *on balance* insults life's inherent value (if indeed it has any).

For this reason, Dworkin's assertion that restrictions on euthanasia and assisted suicide parallel abortion regulations is strained, indeed unconvincing.[8] Euthanasia and assisted suicide prompt the question of whether a majority may compel other people to live or die in a way the majority considers best, notwithstanding those people's contrary convictions or preferences and any personal cost to them (at least while they are conscious), where what principally is at stake is the objective quality of their own lives.[9] By contrast, abortion raises the question of whether a majority may compel a woman to act contrary to her own beliefs or preferences, at some cost to her, where what principally is at stake is the value of something *independent* of her life. That difference is crucial in determining whether the state may intervene. Notice, however, that even if the parallel Dworkin suggests is unpersuasive, his argument for individuals' liberty to decide how they will die nonetheless may be valid. The personal and social costs of compulsion might well outweigh the considerations favoring prohibition. This simple argument just cannot be presented as a mirror image of Dworkin's argument for procreative autonomy.

Dworkin's leading premise: The moral preeminence of personal autonomy

Dworkin's major premise – that the state may not gravely burden an individual (or, in his formulation, a group of persons) to protect an intrinsic value – invites two challenges *if* one assumes that the state legitimately may protect such values. The first questions the foundation of this categorical claim, whereas the second disputes Dworkin's defense of it with respect to early abortion and euthanasia when it is conjoined with his claim that lawmakers need not consider the morality of either action in recognizing that outright prohibition would be a mistake.

How can we know that intrinsic values must yield?
The first challenge asks how Dworkin can claim that the state may never impose substantial restrictions on personal liberty in the service of an intrinsic value (other than the value of furthering the interests of conscious beings), without assessing, one by one, the relative moral importance of every intrinsic value that the state might champion. After all, Dworkin assumes that the state sometimes may put intrinsic values ahead of people's interests. It may tax them and limit their movements to fund museums or keep a species from perishing (p. 154). How can one know *a priori* that no intrinsic value can ever justify seriously hampering a sentient being's interests or preferences?

Given Dworkin's assumptions, I see no way to justify his major premise without looking at specific conflicts between interests and intrinsically valuable entities or events. Declaring that important interests universally trump intrinsic values would be unwarranted on anything other than an inductive basis. Moreover, the broad declaration embodied in Dworkin's major premise seems false. In Dworkin's view, intrinsic values at times *can* take precedence over very substantial interests, including an interest in life itself. If the only sure way to save one species were to kill off within its habitat certain predators (which elsewhere are abundant), Dworkin would consider that measure within the state's authority, though it would sacrifice the lives of conscious beings to protect an intrinsic value (while, to be sure, also protecting the subjective interests of individual prey). Perhaps he would even condone taking human lives to protect inherently valuable objects in rare cases, though this is much less certain. Suppose, for example, that stopping a terrorist from dynamiting the Uffizi inevitably would slay an innocent captive the terrorist was using as a shield.

To be sure, imaginary cases like this often fail to elicit firm intuitions and they are muddied by a concern for the interests of other people (who might enjoy the art or be hurt by the terrorist in the future) and by the possible applicability of other moral principles (such as the principle of double effect or justification by appeal to the victim's hypothetical consent).[10] Other potential illustrations, such as funding arts projects when public health care is needed, at a predictable cost measured in suffering or death, raise different problems. These cases at least suggest, however, that if the state may protect intrinsic values, there is no way to demonstrate that these values must bow to people's or animals' salient interests without adjudicating particular conflicts.

If, however, that conclusion is right, then the distinction between intrinsic values and personal interests as justifications for state action, which in Dworkin's view revolutionizes our understanding of how abortion may be restricted, has at best modest significance. We need to look case by case, and there is no way to say in advance that early abortion, assisted suicide or euthanasia may not be outlawed simply because the government is seeking to compel respect for life's sanctity (if Dworkin accurately characterizes the state's aim). That a woman's liberty or a patient's freedom has priority might well be the right result; indeed, I agree with Dworkin that it is. But if there is no way to show that important personal interests *necessarily* have priority over intrinsic values, the argument for individual autonomy does not profit from the distinction Dworkin introduced. Moral generalizations might well parallel that division, but one would like to know much more about *why* they do than Dworkin offers.

The morality of early abortion and state paternalism
The second challenge to Dworkin's argument follows on the first. Given that we cannot know whether the state may impose grave burdens on people to promote some intrinsic value before measuring the importance of that value against the burden's magnitude, why should we conclude that a woman's right to end her pregnancy cannot be abridged out of respect for the inherent worth of fetal life? Why is the state forbidden from criminalizing assisted suicide and euthanasia on that ground?

Dworkin's answer seems to run as follows. Whether abortion should be permitted prior to a fetus's first sensation (which in Dworkin's view antedates its acquiring a *right* to live),[11] or whether suicide or euthanasia should be allowed, is a debate over the intrinsic value of life and the processes that create, infuse, and direct it. This debate resembles disagreements over the value of art, natural species, cultural evolution, or other entities or processes that embody human, natural, or divine creativity. Because we know that protecting these other entities and processes cannot justify substantial impositions on people's freedom, we can infer that protecting the inherent worth of human life cannot justify such impositions. It would, moreover, be particularly inappropriate for the state seriously to curtail individual liberty to protect the inherent value of human life, because beliefs about that value are religious in nature and a liberal state ought not to act from religious reasons.

This argument – which I *think* is Dworkin's – has several weaknesses. I have elsewhere aired my misgivings about Dworkin's attempt to explicate the alleged intrinsic value of fetal and post-conscious life by analogy to the value that natural species or art possesses and in terms of various types of "investment" in that evolving life.[12] If those objections have force, Dworkin's inference from what the state may do to preserve art or natural wonders is shaky. But even if the value that paintings or organic groups possess is in some important way similar to the value of fetuses and irreversibly comatose bodies, it would not follow necessarily that the value of personal autonomy guarantees pregnant women the chance to choose abortion or patients the opportunity to end their lives voluntarily. These issues must be settled on their merits – that is the conclusion of the first challenge I put – and that means assessing the morality of early abortion and suicide and determining the state's role as an enforcer of morality, both where the alleged interests of a helpless being are at stake and where an agent's own welfare and the well-being of others who might be affected adversely hangs in the balance. Dworkin strives to show that lawmakers need not delve into these moral issues, but in fact there is no alternative. We can infer nothing about how the state may regulate abortion from what it may do to protect rare birds or Old Master paintings, and these issues are no more religious than other questions about people's moral claims that legislators must address.

Consider the question of when a human being acquires an interest in continued life sufficient to generate a right to live. Dworkin claims that the state must protect that right once it comes into being, in the absence of an overriding contrary public interest deriving from the similar interests of other persons (p. 151). But on what basis are politicians to determine the inception of that right? Surprisingly, Dworkin does not say, just as he never says at what point in a person's development that right actually does come into being. I find this omission perplexing, because in Dworkin's scheme this is not merely a question of private morality but of the state's duty. Dworkin seems not to think that the state must begin protecting human life during pregnancy, because he accepts that women may obtain abortions during the third trimester to save their lives, even though he says (I think mistakenly) that it would be wrong to perform those abortions if a fetus then had a right to live, and because he believes that women who did not realize that they were pregnant before the third trimester should still be given a chance to abort (p. 171). But how late after birth the state must in his view punish anyone who kills a child, as a moral matter rather than as a matter of US constitutional law, *Life's Dominion* does not tell.

Nevertheless, despite Dworkin's silence on this point there can be no doubt that deciding when the state must begin defending human life because people then have a *right* to continue living raises the same *type* of issue as the debate over the moral permissibility of abortion. If politicians may – in fact, must – address the first matter, there seems no reason why they may not address the second. Both determinations entail asking when a human being has the right sort of physical, psychological, spiritual, or social connection to the self-conscious person it could become – a person aware of itself as existing over time, able to project itself imaginatively into the future and to prefer some achievements or experiences to others, and thus possessing a right not to be killed – to make taking its life wrong.

There are three main classes of answers to this question, each with a myriad of variations. The first is that no connection works: only *after* a conscious being has the developed self-awareness that *contemporaneously* affords it a right to live (which may be no more complex than the consciousness of a young child) does it have that right. A being has no right to live prior to experiencing the kind of self-awareness essential to ground that right. The second is that weak psychological connections work, even if the later stages of a person are not linked directly to the earliest stages by memory but only by a series of partly overlapping psychological dispositions, desires, and short-term remembrances. Thus, even if a seven-month-old fetus lacks the mental life essential to *then* give it a right to live – if its development were arrested, so that its mental life never became more complex than that of a mollusk, it would not be seriously wrong to kill it – its tenuous mental connections via intermediate levels of consciousness to the self-aware person it will become if not killed confer that right upon it, even though its right to live might be weaker than that of a person with more robust psychological links to a self-conscious person. In virtue of those connections, the argument runs, it can be said to lose all or some of the valuable future that would make killing its later self wrong.[13] The third answer is that nonpsychological links also suffice, so that an entity that will develop into a self-conscious person can at some point prior to the beginning of consciousness already acquire a right to live, though perhaps not one as strong as the right of an adult human being.[14]

Dworkin apparently holds that arguments of the third class cannot be used by a legislature to justify curtailing a woman's procreative autonomy, but that a legislature may rely on arguments of the second class to ban abortion because they apply only after a fetus is conscious. But why? Either this is because of the type of arguments offered, or it is because arguments of the third class are all false. The first fork cannot be correct, because these arguments are not only secular but of precisely the same sort as other arguments that concededly might be offered to outlaw killing a fetus or a child. If, however, Dworkin chooses the second fork, then he cannot plausibly claim to be advancing an argument that can stand above the fray and bring abortion's detractors and proponents into agreement on a more abstract principle limiting government authority. Dworkin must then be asserting a controversial position of his own about the morality of early abortion – one that he defends only cursorily in his book, without exploring the implications of his reasoning for the morality and legality of late abortion or infanticide. I see no reason for Dworkin to be dismayed at finding himself in the thick of this debate, and in my view he would not be wrong to argue against the third group of answers. His predicament explains, though, why *Life's Dominion* is unlikely to have the reconciling impact he may have hoped it would.

As to suicide and euthanasia, Dworkin makes no attempt to distance himself from controversies over the value of unconscious life in a persistent vegetative state or possible justifications for government paternalism. He takes positions in both debates. This is as it should be, for disagreements over whether the law should permit these killings have little in common with disagreements over whether we should invest for future generations or save the rain forests. But for just that reason Dworkin cannot pretend to offer a loftier principle around which divided opinions can rally. What is novel in *Life's Dominion* – its attempt to reconceive disputes over abortion and euthanasia more abstractly as religious quarrels – is also what is least convincing in Dworkin's argument.

II What Justifies the State's Safeguarding Intrinsic Values?

One of Dworkin's principal assumptions, by which he believes that some restrictions on abortion may be justified, is that the state may lessen people's liberty out of respect for intrinsically valuable entities. Dworkin evidently regards this proposition as self-evident: "I can think of no reason why government should not aim that its citizens treat decisions about human life and death as matters of serious moral importance" (p. 151). If pressed for a reason why governments *may* adopt this aim, presumably he would point to accepted practice, for he lists plentiful examples of government regulations apparently serving that purpose, without probing their propriety. Laws protecting endangered species, promoting artistic creation, and making life better for people who will be born in the next century are uncontroversial, he assumes, and since Dworkin believes that their purpose is to uphold intrinsic values, the state must be justified in reducing freedom for these ends.

Dworkin's reasoning invites two objections. First, it is highly contestable whether the ambition of these laws is to protect intrinsic values, rather than to satisfy people's desires or advance their objective interests. For example, many reject (while Dworkin accepts – see p. 77) Derek Parfit's claim that so-called duties to future generations are not really duties to other people at all, but expressions of what it would be intrinsically valuable to cause to exist.[15] Likewise, many believe that the sole reason to save some species (we certainly do not wish to save all) and to help the arts flourish is that they may enrich the lives of present and future people, as sources of medicine or food, reflection or delight. In any case, people's prereflective explanations of why certain protections are important must yield to their thoughtful conclusions, and these might not mention intrinsic values at all, beyond those relating to personal well-being and social justice.

The second objection is that even if Dworkin's explanation of these laws is correct, it is not obvious why the promotion of intrinsic values should be seen as within the state's authority. Are we to imagine (to use the image of an ideal social contract) that people have joined together not only to secure their interests within the boundaries that justice imposes, but also to safeguard

something other than their interests? Why would they do that? Or are we to think of the protection of intrinsic values as advancing their *moral* interests? Given that emigration is rarely possible without great personal cost, it is certainly questionable whether advancing people's moral
interests by means of coercion or the expenditure of public funds is an acceptable aim of a liberal
state. Stretching, we might view this as a continuation of the state's tutelary role in educating
minors. But would adults really trust (and pay taxes for) the government to tell them what would
make them better people?

Merely posing these questions does not show, of course, that the state has no business
promoting intrinsic values. Nor do they indicate all the ways in which one might justify the
collective protection of intrinsic values. My aim in asking them is to point out several of the
difficult issues that Dworkin's thesis raises but that his book neither mentions nor addresses.
Defending the thesis requires a much longer argument than Dworkin supplies. His claim that
the state may protect intrinsic values also prompts three, more limited, sets of questions.
Dworkin may have convincing answers, but *Life's Dominion* offers few clues as to what they might
be.

First, how far does the principle that governments may encourage responsible personal choice
extend? Dworkin maintains that "[a] state might aim that its citizens treat decisions about abortion as matters of moral importance; that they recognize that fundamental intrinsic values are at
stake in such decisions and decide reflectively, not out of immediate convenience but out of examined conviction" (p. 150). Presumably, he endorses a parallel position with respect to suicide and
euthanasia. But does the state's authority to promote responsible choice end there? (And even if
it does end there, would not the government also be bound to press women who are *not* planning
to abort to consider the moral arguments *for* abortion, given the effects of childbearing and rearing
on their own lives and that of their children?[16] Would it equally be obliged to remind the ailing
elderly that they can choose death, perhaps noting some philosophers' claims that they have a duty
to die?) If governments may constrain all decisions that potentially turn on intrinsic values that
people might not fully appreciate, Dworkin's position would sanction measures that many people
– including Dworkin – think intolerable. On this rationale, for example, governments apparently
could fund compulsory religious instruction or public announcements reminding people of the
importance of their religious choices.[17] Or perhaps the state could mandate counseling before
allowing people to cohabit or marry, or permit them to watch pornographic videos only after
attending a class on moral virtue. Dworkin does not explain why his view would not allow governments to enact these policies. I am unaware of a convincing way to distinguish policies designed
to induce reflection about intrinsically valuable entities or processes from policies aimed at making
people think about the objective importance of how they lead their lives – certainly none that puts
decisions about euthanasia or suicide on what Dworkin regards as the right side of that line. Of
course, Dworkin could admit that his view would permit all these policies without agreeing that
any or all of them are desirable. I suspect, however, that he would resist doing so, though *Life's
Dominion* does not say on what basis.

Notice that one could approve of waiting periods or informational requirements for women
seeking abortions or people completing advance medical directives by adopting a narrower principle than the one Dworkin announces. One could say that governments may protect against
ill-informed or rash decisions out of a paternalistic concern for citizens' *nonmoral* welfare, in particular the regret people might later feel or the burdens they might then resent if they decide in
ignorance or under pressure from friends or relatives. That narrower principle would harbor fewer
dangers for those who prize liberty of thought and action. It might not, on balance and in light

of other goals, justify much restriction on abortion or assisted suicide, but the type of reason it affords would not imperil other values as greatly as Dworkin's broad-gauged principle does.

Second, why does the state's alleged authority to protect intrinsic values allow it to try to compel women contemplating abortions early in their pregnancy, or patients thinking of shortening their lives, to "recognize that fundamental intrinsic values are at stake in such decisions and [to] decide reflectively" (p. 150), but *not* to induce them to honor that value in what the community deems the proper way? When the government strives to protect an endangered species, on account of what Dworkin regards as a judgment about its intrinsic value, the government tries to protect *that species*, not individual reflection on how valuable it is. The law does not require property owners to wait a month and read four essays on environmental ethics before draining their marshland if that would cause the demise of a rare turtle; instead, it prohibits them from removing the water, in order to ensure the turtle's survival. Nor does the law ask people to stop and think about the intrinsic value of a Victorian facade before flattening one building to erect something more useful; it simply prevents the building's demolition. The parallels Dworkin enlists involve attempts to conserve what the majority considers valuable, at some acceptable (because moderate) cost to individuals' liberty. They do not treat thoughtfulness itself as the value worth supporting.

A complete prohibition of abortion or euthanasia, Dworkin argues, would impose excessive burdens on women or patients nearing death. But that cannot explain why the state may do no more than facilitate moral reflection. The state could permit abortion and euthanasia while working to discourage them, in ways that might be burdensome but not unduly so.[18] That is the parallel to legislative efforts to protect art and natural species (or to reduce smoking), consistent with respecting a pregnant woman's or a patient's ultimate freedom to decide between life and death.

The German federal constitutional court's 1993 abortion decision exemplifies this approach.[19] The court held that women may obtain abortions during the first 12 weeks of pregnancy, but only if lawmakers determine that this is the most effective way to protect the lives of unborn persons and of pregnant women. Legislators might reasonably believe that permitting early abortions will save the lives of some fetuses, the court said, because criminalizing all abortions might only force women to obtain them in other countries or cause them to end their pregnancies in dangerous ways. Lawmakers might conclude that fetal life would be better protected if women could abort safely, but only after they underwent counseling aimed at *dissuading* them from aborting by emphasizing the fetus's right to live and describing the forms of state assistance available to women and children. If the legislature tries to change women's minds in this way, the court held, it must make them wait at least three days after receiving counseling before they may terminate their pregnancies. Nevertheless, the choice remains theirs, and they are constitutionally entitled to anonymity when receiving mandated advice. If one assumes, as Dworkin does, that the state may protect intrinsic values as long as it does not impose grave burdens on only some individuals and it allows them to make their own decisions about abortion and their own deaths, why may the state not attempt in this way to discourage (while permitting) abortion, assisted suicide, and euthanasia? Or why may it not require or encourage pregnant women to listen to the heartbeats of the children they are carrying or view ultrasound images of their fetuses before choosing abortion?

There is, as Dworkin notes, much controversy over the value of fetal life or the bare animation of a comatose person (p. 151). The existence of controversy cannot, however, be the reason why a majority must refrain from doing what it believes right. There is controversy over the value of preserving old houses and obscure fish, too, yet Dworkin does not contend that disagreement precludes a legislature from prohibiting their destruction. In fact, some of these disagreements revolve around issues that could be characterized as religious (using Dworkin's definition), such as the propriety of preserving species when natural processes seem pointed to their destruction, or conflicts between saving a species and safeguarding the lives or happiness of all of its current members when culling would be good for the larger group over time.[20] Given Dworkin's premise about the legitimacy of the government's protecting the majority's conception of intrinsic values, it is not obvious why the same reasoning cannot apply to abortion and euthanasia.

Of course, if it can, many would regard that as a powerful indictment of the premise. Because environmental and aesthetic regulation can be defended adequately (in my judgment) exclusively by reference to people's interests, the price of rejecting Dworkin's assumption about the state's authority to protect intrinsic values would not be high. Rejecting it also would allow one to side-step this potential threat to the permissibility of abortion and euthanasia, as Dworkin apparently cannot.

Third, why may the state's aim *change* from promoting reflection to protecting fetal life at some point in pregnancy *prior* to the fetus's becoming sentient and thus acquiring interests of its own? Dworkin contends that the state may prohibit nontherapeutic abortions exclusively out of respect for life's inherent value after a woman has had "ample opportunity" to decide whether to continue her pregnancy (p. 169). Many people are convinced, he says (though Dworkin remains silent as to his own view), that the longer a woman waits before ultimately aborting, the more she insults life's value. On this basis, the state may ban nontherapeutic abortions once "a somewhat earlier point in pregnancy" than viability is reached (p. 171), on the assumption that women who wait until this point to solicit an abortion are "indifferent to the moral and social meaning" of their actions or "contemptuous" of life's value (p. 170). But before this point, the state may not even try to dissuade women from aborting, let alone outlaw abortion; all it may do is encourage women to think before acting, without tilting their reflections in the slightest way.

What triggers this radical shift in the government's authority? Dworkin never says. If the government could actively deter abortions all along out of regard for the value of a developing life while initially leaving women free to decide, then it would make sense that at some point during pregnancy the growing value of that life could justify the government in closing off further choice. But Dworkin denies that the state may play that deterring role until the critical point has been passed. Similarly, if the critical point coincided with a person's acquiring a right to live, the government could – it may even be required to – stop nontherapeutic abortions unconditionally. But that, too, is not Dworkin's position, because the critical point at which the state's role permissibly may shift is for him much sooner, at a time prior to sentience and viability. Plainly, there is a larger majority in North America and Western Europe for outlawing abortions at four months than at two months. I surmise, however, that Dworkin would not rely on a supposed increase in consensus to defend governmental coercion after the fourth or fifth month, for that response apparently would license even earlier bans if enough people thought they were morally justified, so long as pregnant women still had a fair opportunity to choose abortion. Dworkin could, I suppose, defend his assertion that what the government may do in the name of life's inherent value changes dramatically between the third and the sixth month of pregnancy by claiming that life really *does* have sufficient inherent value at that point to warrant a ban on abortion. But this is not his argument in *Life's Dominion*, because he explicitly declines to state how much (if any) inherent value fetuses or paintings or species have (pp. 81, 207). I am therefore at a loss to say how Dworkin would explain this surge in the state's authority to regulate abortion.

To be sure, it is unclear exactly which abortions Dworkin thinks the government may proscribe after the fourth or fifth month. He demands an exception not only for pregnancies that endanger a woman's life, but also for pregnancies that went unnoticed by the pregnant woman (p. 171). As for other women who desire nontherapeutic abortions after the fourth or fifth month, Dworkin says that the community "has a right . . . to protect its culture" from the "indifference" of women to "the moral and social meaning" of their actions (p. 170). But what if a woman sincerely claims that she was not indifferent – that she wrestled with the decision and decided only late in pregnancy that in her view it would be better to abort, after giving due deference to the value of fetal life (which might in her view be nil)? She would not have acted out of indifference. Again, suppose that a woman's situation has changed. Imagine that the man whose potential child she is carrying has just left her or died and that she now believes she cannot raise it without great sacrifice. May she abort out of conviction rather than indifference? Or can the state stop her to ensure that other people do not misinterpret her behavior, thinking it overly disrespectful even though she acts reflectively? If she may abort, could *any* abortions be banned in practice, given that nearly every woman who wanted a late abortion would mouth the required conviction? Would some decision maker be charged with assessing a woman's credibility? Dworkin needs to describe more precisely how we should go about answering these questions, for on his theory they bear crucially on the reach of the state's legitimate authority.

One final point in regard to reflection and indifference. Dworkin insists that the motives of those whose actions might fail to respect intrinsic values typically have no bearing on whether governments may prohibit those actions to protect those values. The community's decision that the value should in some way be given its due becomes law, and the fact that a timber company executive thinks the spotted owl a blight rather than a natural wonder is irrelevant. Why, then, should motive matter in the case of abortion or euthanasia, as Dworkin seems to suggest it does? If the argument I outlined in section I is correct, the answer cannot be that these decisions are inherently religious, whereas every other decision based on intrinsic values is not (apart from those driven by patently religious convictions, such as forms of worship or dress). I am not sure, however, what Dworkin might offer in its place.

All of the difficulties confronting Dworkin's view I have sketched can be avoided if the state may not protect intrinsic values at all, but may act only to further the nonmoral interests either of all sentient beings or of full-fledged members of the political community.[21] Accepting this view need not mean abandoning environmental protection legislation or arts sponsorship, because both plausibly can be regarded as serving people's nonmoral interests, although counterarguments might in either case prevail. Working through the vexing issues Dworkin's position raises makes this alternative view of the state's legitimate purposes all the more inviting.

III   How Ought the State to Honor Life's Sanctity?

Life's Dominion tries to sketch the boundaries of state authority, to say how far the state *may* go in protecting life that is not yet conscious or that will never regain consciousness. It is silent about what the state *should* do in recognition of the value of that life. This question demands an answer not only in deciding whether, or where, to draw a line tied to fetal sentience or to the developing person's acquisition of a right to live, beyond which nontherapeutic abortions will be penalized. Governments need to decide whether to allow clinics to furnish couples with information about the sex of a fetus, knowing that the information might lead them to end a pregnancy; or to let doctors remove eggs from aborted fetuses and implant them in nonfertile women who want to bear children; or to empower people to choose, in advance and irrevocably, how they will be nursed

– or killed – if they become profoundly demented; or to deny publicly funded medical care to patients in persistent vegetative states. How should we reason about the government's responsibilities when people's rights do not dictate legislation?

One of *Life's Dominion*'s disappointing omissions is its refusal to provide even a hint of what Dworkin believes the state ought to do to protect life's intrinsic value in any of these instances, or to suggest how we should evaluate collisions between this value and people's desires. In the case of fetal life, one possibility, of course, is that he thinks the state ought to do nothing at all, perhaps because he himself holds the view (though he never pronounces this or any other opinion) that fetal life is devoid of value. After all, Dworkin advocates no limitations on the availability of abortion at any time during pregnancy, and the many possible constraints he discusses, from mandatory waiting periods to the provision of free health care for women who give birth instead of aborting to official efforts to persuade women to carry pregnancies to term, he rejects without exception as overly burdensome or as proceeding from improper motives. Although Dworkin admits that a state may ban abortions one or two months prior to fetal sentience (with narrow exceptions) out of regard for what most people consider the intrinsic value of fetal life, he nevertheless contends that fetal viability is "the most appropriate point at which a state could properly assert its derivative interests in protecting a fetus's interests, and its own detached interest in responsibility" (p. 170), because at that point a fetus might be thought to have interests of its own. Of course, it is *only* at that point that a fetus acquires interests of its own, so it is only then that a state could possibly assert an interest in protecting them that derives from the fetus's interests. If fetal life has any intrinsic value independent of a fetus's interests, it seems in Dworkin's view to be puny, for that value is unable to advance the appropriate date for state protection from the moment the state secures a "derivative" interest in the well-being of the possibly sentient fetus capable of surviving outside the mother. The alleged intrinsic value of fetal life seems for Dworkin to be an idle wheel, incapable of rolling forward the morally optimal time for state intervention. One wonders whether Dworkin believes any of the claims about the intrinsic value of fetal life he reports as commonplace. Dworkin pointedly declines to endorse those claims, just as he refuses "to recommend or defend any of these widespread convictions about art and nature" he describes, noting without denying that "[p]erhaps they are all, as some skeptics insist, inconsistent superstitions" (p. 81).

Fortifying the suspicion that Dworkin himself attributes no significant intrinsic value to previable fetal life is the absence of any discussion in *Life's Dominion* or elsewhere of whether or how this possible value ought to influence a pregnant woman's own decision making when the choice is hers. Dworkin's consideration of the plant-like existence of people who permanently have lost their capacity for rational consciousness strengthens this inference. In a report published prior to *Life's Dominion*, Dworkin concludes that "it is against the evaluative interests of a permanently demented patient to prolong his life."[22] A life of dependency without "a sense of personality and agency" and thus without achievements cannot genuinely be rewarding, Dworkin declares: "Though . . . some people think a life better just because it is longer, no matter what the value of the additional life considered on its own, that view seems to demean rather than celebrate life, and most people would reject it."[23] It seems to follow that life without any experiences at all or only the most rudimentary experiences, of the sort lived by those who are permanently comatose, is in Dworkin's view bad for the person kept alive. Its intrinsic value is negative. One then wonders, however, whether the same logic holds in part for fetal life that is cut short before the fetus becomes sentient or self-aware. If bare life, without any structure imposed by consciously chosen purposes, is without value in the case of formerly conscious persons, should that not be equally true of entities that have never been conscious? And if it is not true – if blank existence at both ends of life is equally valueless – then it is hard to see how the abortion of a preconscious fetus could in any way insult whatever intrinsic value life has. It is worth repeating that Dworkin does not identify this view as his own. But he also does not argue that it is misplaced.

Dworkin is only slightly more forthcoming on the subjects of assisted suicide and euthanasia. He believes that mentally competent patients ought to be able to enlist help in ending their lives, at least if their desire to do so survives a waiting period of unspecified duration designed to insure that their wishes are firm following reflection (p. 173). Indeed, in an amicus brief to the U.S. Supreme Court that he coauthored, Dworkin argued that patients suffering from terminal illnesses have a right under the U.S. Constitution to end their lives with the aid of willing physicians.[24] In *Life's Dominion*, he nevertheless says nothing precise about how that right ought to be implemented, given the possibly deleterious effects of assisted suicide on the rights of already existing people who might be harmed by abuses or mistakes that legalization makes more likely. Although many of his remarks suggest that he would favor honoring people's requests, when they were competent, to withhold life-sustaining medicine or nutrition or perhaps even to kill them should they become seriously demented,[25] he does not declare his position. Nor does he indicate whether the state should provide medical care at public expense to patients who are in persistent vegetative states or who have lost all or most of their rational faculty, or whether it should allow private individuals to purchase care for themselves if they end up this way or should permit their friends or relatives to keep them alive at their own expense. What emerges plainly is that Dworkin's notion of what makes a life valuable counsels against prolonging the life of people who have lost their rational self-control irretrievably. Although he starts by reporting a conflict between partisans of personal autonomy and an allegedly widely shared belief that life's inherent value is best respected by prolonging it, he ends with a different conflict. The tough question for Dworkin is not whether to bring about the death of seriously demented or unconscious people who earlier expressed a desire to die if they ever were in that state, but whether to keep alive people in those states who earlier indicated a wish to have their existence extended or whose relatives now express that desire. He does not say what the ideal government policies would be.

Regardless of Dworkin's own view as to the intrinsic value of preconscious, unconscious, and unreasoning conscious life, his argument raises the further question of how public officials should decide which measures to adopt to shelter or advance what some, but not all, citizens believe to be intrinsic values, within the regulatory domain bounded by personal rights upon which the state may not trespass except to vindicate other rights. If officials have no obligation to the values themselves but only to the people whom they serve, then ought their decisions to reflect their constituents' opinions, or what they believe would be their opinions after informed deliberation? Should they decide instead by their own best lights? Dworkin offers no guidance to political actors, but perhaps there is little to be said. The choice that political representatives face of whether to act as conduits, or as independent judges whose decisions are subject to later ratification or rejection at the polls, or to navigate a middle course, is not unique to balancing intrinsic values against personal interests. It is endemic to representative democracy.

IV   Conclusion

Life's Dominion challenges a common understanding of what the debates over criminalizing abortion, assisted suicide, and euthanasia are fundamentally about and it defends, with originality and conviction, an unpopular solution. I have questioned several of Dworkin's main theses, because the orthodox account of the issues underlying these debates seems to me largely correct. Aborting a fetus and demanding help in ending one's life rarely are spiritually motivated actions that are entitled to the legal protection afforded by our tradition of religious toleration. Typically, they deny certain religious views by implication, but that does not make them religious conduct.

Opposition to abortion or euthanasia may stem from spiritual revelation or instinctive revulsion, but it frequently has a moral philosophical origin. In the case of abortion, it commonly grows out of a conception of personal identity and of the significance of physical or mental continuity that makes killing an animate being wrong in virtue of the future it might have had; in the case of suicide and euthanasia, it rests on notions of what makes a life valuable and, with respect to the force of advance directives governing the treatment of badly demented individuals, on whether personal identity continues despite radical psychological changes. Opposition may, of course, also be grounded in concern about the possibly unfavorable impact of abortion, assisted suicide, or euthanasia on health care workers, innocent victims, or, over time and more subtly, virtually all citizens.

Laws properly may be based on reasons of all these kinds. Dworkin's distinction between intrinsic values and personal interests does not persuasively define two spheres of legislation of necessarily varying breadth. Whether laws prohibiting or permitting abortion or euthanasia are correct hinges primarily on whether a fetus has a moral claim to protection from the woman carrying it or whether unconscious or badly demented people have a similar claim against their former competent selves that a state may enforce. Their correctness depends as well on whether the government justifiably may force people to act in what others deem their own moral good. The question lawmakers must answer is how forceful a fetus's or psychologically altered person's claims (whatever they may be) are and how compelling the arguments for paternalistic restraints are, together with perils to third-party interests, relative to the loss of personal autonomy and experienced hardships to mothers or the ailing elderly if their freedom to shape their future were limited in some way.

Disagreements about these issues may be intractable, yet I see no way to escape them in crafting a political solution. *Life's Dominion* does not offer us, I think, a persuasive reason to set aside as irrelevant the morality of abortion or euthanasia in determining how the state may regulate them. Responsible lawmakers cannot shun the moral issues they raise. What Dworkin has done, eloquently and partly despite himself, is help us see the necessity and the difficulty of social compromise.

Acknowledgement

Thanks to Samuel Scheffler and Jeremy Waldron for helpful comments. A nearly identical version of this essay appeared in *Utilitas*, vol. 13, no. 1, March 2001, pp. 33–64, copyright Edinburgh University Press.

Notes

1   All page references in the text are to Ronald Dworkin, *Life's Dominion: An Argument about Abortion and Euthanasia* (New York: Knopf, 1993).

2 Dworkin also sketches an argument of American constitutional law to the same effect. Because his interpretation of constitutional provisions depends heavily on which principles of political morality he believes are correct, Dworkin's legal analysis closely tracks the arguments considered in this essay and it founders if they do. But Dworkin's legal analysis also turns on the proper reading of a number of American judicial decisions, for no interpretation of the Constitution's text is likely to persuade if it strays far from precedent. Even if his moral argument is persuasive, his constitutional argument might not be. I shall not assess Dworkin's legal argument separately, although it is worth noting that his argument is not unprecedented and that its forbears have convinced very few American legal scholars.

3 I cannot think what "special" might add to "grave," unless it is meant to reinforce what is implicit in the phrase "one group," namely, that the same heavy burden would not be borne by everybody equally. Presumably, this constraint on legislation is not the sole limit on policies designed to advance intrinsic values. Some laws would not *gravely* hamper people yet lie beyond a liberal state's legitimate power to promulgate. Imagine a dress code for adults purporting to serve the intrinsic value of beauty, with an exception for religiously mandated attire. Its burden could be made moderate, but that hardly suffices. How tightly a law pinches in its attempt to promote an intrinsic value thus cannot be the only test of its legitimacy. It seems impossible to describe what more is needed, however, without assessing the weights of the competing values in particular instances, which is exactly the type of moral evaluation that Dworkin seeks to avoid in his book.

4 Dworkin's argument that the state may not effectively abridge a woman's right to decide whether to bear a child but may forbid abortion once a fetus has some mental life tracks the analysis in Jed Rubenfeld, "On the Legal Status of the Proposition that 'Life Begins at Conception'," *Stanford Law Review*, vol. 43, 1991, pp. 599–635.

5 Eric Rakowski, "The Sanctity of Human Life," *Yale Law Journal*, vol. 103, 1994, pp. 2049–118.

6 Not everybody accepts this claim, of course, and not all who do would offer the same reason for accepting it. For one argument in its favor, see Judith Jarvis Thomson, "Self-Defense," *Philosophy and Public Affairs*, vol. 20, 1991, pp. 283–310, esp. pp. 305–10.

7 For careful analysis of numerous arguments for the permissibility of abortion that assume a fetus is a moral person with a right to live, see Frances M. Kamm, "Abortion and the Value of Life: A Discussion of *Life's Dominion*," *Columbia Law Review*, vol. 95, 1995, pp. 160–221, esp. pp. 185–220.

8 The parallel is stronger though hardly perfect in the case of advance directives governing the care people receive after they become profoundly demented, to the extent that one believes the demented patients are in important ways different people from their earlier selves. I shall not discuss the problem of advance directives for severe dementia here. A powerful defense of precedent autonomy that largely agrees with Dworkin's is Norman L. Cantor, "Prospective Autonomy: On the Limits of Shaping One's Postcompetence Medical Fate," *Journal of Contemporary Health Law and Policy*, vol. 8, 1992, pp. 13–48. For trenchant criticism of Dworkin's view, see Rebecca Dresser, "Missing Persons: Legal Perceptions of Incompetent Patients," *Rutgers Law Review*, vol. 46, 1994, pp. 609–719.

9 The legalization of euthanasia or assisted suicide also raises important worries about possible harms to those who do not choose either. The most common fears are that the medical care offered to terminally ill patients might explicitly or tacitly be reduced, that incentives to develop better palliative treatments might diminish, that some people might mistakenly be left to die or be killed, that patients might inappropriately be pressured to choose death, and that some might intentionally be killed against their wishes if illegal killings can more easily be hidden. Apart from possible pressures to end a pregnancy, these concerns do not exist or are not prominent with respect to the legalization of abortion.

10 I develop a notion of hypothetical consent that may justify killing some people to benefit others in Eric Rakowski, "Taking and Saving Lives," *Columbia Law Review*, vol. 93, 1993, pp. 1063–156, esp. pp. 1104–50.

11 Between the onset of sentience and the point at which a human being acquires a right to live, claims of intrinsic value presumably can be combined with claims based on the fetus's interests in opposing abor-

tion. Dworkin seems to rely on this conjunction when he says that the beginning of fetal sentience is the most appropriate point for the state to choose for banning abortions *if* it does decide to impose a ban (p. 170).

12   Briefly, I think that Dworkin exaggerates the similarities between the way people value preconscious fetuses and the way they value natural species or art. It is hardly accidental that nobody attributes rights to abstract entities (like species) or to painted canvas, as many people do to fetuses. Dworkin's assertion that some people tie the *prima facie* wrongness of abortion to the increasing *natural* investment in the developing fetus, moreover, seems to me to explain little, given that people do not attribute positive normative significance to *everything* that occurs naturally. Indeed, often they are loath to interfere with natural processes, not out of an approving respect for nature's creative energy but out of an instinctive dread of awakening its terrifying power. See Bernard Williams, "Must a Concern for the Environment be Centered on Human Beings?" in Lori Gruen and Dale Jamieson (eds.), *Reflecting on Nature* (New York: Oxford University Press, 1994), p. 51. Tying the *prima facie* wrongness of abortion to the increasing divine or human investment in the fetus fares no better, because we do not conceive of a creator-God as an investor with finite time and resources, more of which will be squandered if an investment is canceled later rather than earlier; nor do we think that the morality of abortion turns on whether a woman planned her pregnancy or spent a great deal of money or heartache undergoing some form of assisted conception, but rather on what her reasons are for ending her pregnancy when she does. Finally, grouping the diverse sources of many people's revulsion at abortion under the vague label of "investment" seems not only to overgeneralize but also to overintellectualize reactions that often are visceral and incapable of coherent expression. I spell out these and other misgivings at length in Rakowski, "The Sanctity of Human Life," op. cit., pp. 2066–81. For other doubts about Dworkin's account of investment and the difficulties his theory encounters in distinguishing "sacred" from "incremental" intrinsic values, see Ken O'Day, "Intrinsic Value and Investment," *Utilitas*, vol. 11, 1999, pp. 194–214; Linda Barclay, "Rights, Intrinsic Values and the Politics of Abortion," *Utilitas*, vol. 11, 1999, pp. 215–29.

13   For an example of this view, see Bonnie Steinbock, *Life Before Birth* (New York: Oxford University Press, 1992), pp. 60–2, 68–71.

14   As illustrations, see Don Marquis, "Why Abortion is Immoral," *Journal of Philosophy*, vol. 86, 1989, pp. 183–202, and Warren Quinn, "Abortion: Identity and Loss," *Philosophy and Public Affairs*, vol. 13, 1984, pp. 24–54. For criticism, see Peter K. McInerney, "Does a Fetus Already Have a Future-Like-Ours?," *Journal of Philosophy*, vol. 87, 1990, pp. 264–8.

15   Derek Parfit, *Reasons and Persons* (Oxford: Clarendon Press, 1984), pp. 351–79. Critiques of Parfit's view include: John O'Neill, "Future Generations: Present Harms," *Philosophy*, vol. 68, 1993, pp. 35–51; Matthew Hanser, "Harming Future People," *Philosophy and Public Affairs*, vol. 19, 1990, pp. 47–70; James Woodward, "The Non-Identity Problem," *Ethics*, vol. 96, 1986, pp. 804–31. This claim might suggest that human life is incrementally valuable rather than sacred, though Dworkin would deny it. I assume that he would say that the human race as an entity already exists, hence that humanity can be seen as intrinsically valuable, with an important story that it would be a shame to end prematurely.

16   See Sarah Stroud, "Dworkin and *Casey* on Abortion," *Philosophy and Public Affairs*, vol. 25, 1996, pp. 140–70, esp. pp. 161–6.

17   Rakowski, "The Sanctity of Human Life," op. cit., pp. 2081–4; T. M. Scanlon, "Partisan for Life," *New York Review of Books*, July 15, 1993, pp. 45–50, esp. p. 48. Sarah Stroud argues that, if Dworkin's claim that choosing abortion typically entails making a religious decision is correct, virtually no regulation of abortion could be justified, at least consonant with the U.S. Constitution, including laws aimed at fostering responsible decision making: "Imagine, for example, that rabbis were forced by state law to provide all those who wished to join a temple with material prepared by the state outlining the majority's objections to the Jewish religion . . . [o]r were told they needed to consider their decision further for another twenty-four hours and then come back." (Stroud, "Dworkin and *Casey* on Abortion," op. cit., p. 152).

18   What counts as encouragement or discouragement depends, of course, on where the baseline is set. For example, Dworkin evidently does not regard public subsidies for women who elect to give birth either

as discouraging abortion or as inducing childbirth (at least not impermissibly), for he condones them. His reason is that child-rearing subsidies "encourage women to reflect about abortion and understand its moral gravity" without feeling the pressure of "financial necessity" (p. 174). Others might easily see these subsidies as a departure from the morally required neutrality on which Dworkin insists.

19 The court's judgment was expressly premised on the *right* of a fetus to live after implantation (at the latest), however, not on the intrinsic value of human life in general. *Urteil des Zweiten Senats* vom 28, Mai 1993, 1993 EuGRZ 229, 242 (BVerfG 1993) ("Die Schutzpflicht für das ungeborene Leben ist bezogen auf das einzelne Leben, nicht nur auf menschliches Leben allgemein.").

20 See Richard Stith, "On Death and Dworkin: A Critique of his Theory of Inviolability," *Maryland Law Review*, vol. 56, 1997, pp. 289–383, esp. p. 312 n.127.

21 A lucid, detailed statement of that view is contained in Joel Feinberg's four-volume work, *The Moral Limits of the Criminal Law* (New York: Oxford University Press, 1984, 1985, 1986, 1988).

22 Ronald Dworkin, "U.S. Congress, Office of Technology Assessment, Philosophical Issues Concerning the Rights of Patients Suffering Serious Permanent Dementia" in *Philosophical, Legal, and Social Aspects of Surrogate Decisionmaking for Elderly Individuals* (PB87–234126) (Washington, DC: Office of Technology Assessment, 1987), p. 47.

23 Ibid.

24 Ronald Dworkin, Thomas Nagel, Robert Nozick, John Rawls, Thomas Scanlon, and Judith Thomson, "The Philosophers' Brief on Assisted Suicide," *New York Review of Books*, March 27, 1997, pp. 41–7.

25 For references, see Rakowski, "The Sanctity of Human Life," op. cit., p. 2107.

Part IV

The Reach of Law

14

Associative Obligations and the State

Leslie Green

Some of our moral obligations hold irrespective of local conditions and arrangements. It is not as members of a particular community that we ought to tell the truth or refrain from harming others. These duties bind us as members of the human community or, to put it another way, of no community at all. In contrast, our obligations as Canadians, or Catholics, or chiropractors are more particular in their force. People associated in these smaller groups have special duties which come, as F. H. Bradley said, with their stations. Legal and political theorists have again become more interested in such associative obligations. Membership in ethnic, religious, or occupational groups is rarely a matter of free choice and, even when it is, the duties it brings are not themselves freely chosen. Associative obligation thus seems a potentially attractive model for the relationship between citizens and their states.

Ronald Dworkin challenges skeptics about political obligation to "either deny all associative obligations or show why political obligation cannot be associative."[1] There may be reasons to hesitate over the idea of associative obligations in general, but here I pursue the second alternative. More exactly, I argue that his account of these matters fails, and that a version of consent theory is better able to accommodate the social dimension of political life, although it cannot show that every citizen has an obligation to obey the law, even in a just community.

I Legitimacy and Consent

The law is a realm of obligation and duty; it acts not as our advisor but as an authority that must be obeyed. Whether we are justified in accepting law's self-image is the problem of political obligation. The democratic tradition has long favored consent as the best answer to that problem. But it has been uncertain just what consent theory amounts to. In particular, it often equivocates perilously between two different claims:

(1) Only if someone consents to obey the law does he or she have an obligation to obey it.

(2) Everyone has an obligation to obey the law because everyone has consented to obey it.

These differ in ground and force. The first is a critical moral thesis, the second an explanatory, partly factual, one. However, the second is so obviously false that, as David Hume said, it would take a philosopher to believe in it. Many people do nothing that amounts to consent; the fiction that by just living peacefully within the territory of a state we "tacitly" consent to obey its laws is one of the great embarrassments of the democratic tradition.

By "consent theory" I intend only (1). This is stronger than (2) and not supported by it: the latter is consistent with there being any number of grounds of political obligation so long as everyone has happened to invoke one of them. The former requires consent but leaves it open whether anyone has given it. Notice three further points. First, (1) is a claim about moral obligations only; it does not deny that there are other reasons for obeying the law, including self-interest, courtesy, and fear. Second, its content is an obligation to obey the law, where this is understood to be the law of one's own state. This may be a *prima facie* obligation in that it may have to be weighed against other urgent considerations and may, in the end, yield to them. But before yielding it makes a special claim. It asks us to take the law itself as a reason for acting as it requires and for not acting on some otherwise valid reasons for disobeying. The law may, of course, be vague or controversial, leaving room for argument about what, if anything, it does require. But when that argument is resolved in a certain way, it is meant to carry a *prima facie* duty of obedience, not only to good laws, or laws that promote social cooperation, or laws that guarantee rights, but to all laws that claim our obedience. Finally, (1) does not say that consent is sufficient for legitimacy. For one thing, other necessary conditions have to be fulfilled: consent must be free and informed. And the consent must also meet substantive conditions on its validity. No one could get an obligation to obey the Nazi government by making a free and informed promise to do so. Consent binds only if there are reasons for holding that those actions that are signs of consent create duties because they are performed in the belief that performing them does create duties. The power to create duties for ourselves is one worth having, but only in certain circumstances. The power to bind oneself to obey a tyranny, like the power to promise to commit murder, is morally valueless.

If we were to defend (1) how would we go about it? A partial answer is reserved for section IV below, but I want to motivate the discussion by showing how hard the task is and thus giving encouragement to the kind of position that Dworkin defends.

We might interpret (1) as a specification of a more general claim:

(3)   For any action V, one has an obligation to V only if one consents to V.

If that is right, then the obligation to obey the law must be voluntary because all obligations must. This thesis might appeal to those with a highly individualistic outlook, but it is, I think, intuitively implausible. Most people find it offensive to suppose that parents have no duty to see that their children are cared for unless they agree to it, or that we have no duty not to discriminate against minorities unless we promise not to. But this is not simply a surd collision of worldviews. There is something deeply problematic about (3) on its own terms. Like (1), it only states a necessary condition for obligation. It does not explain why any consent binds. Here, Hume did teach us something useful. Suppose agreement creates obligations. Why is that? Because there is an obligation to keep our agreements. Now this obligation cannot without circularity itself be grounded in agreement; it must be a nonvoluntary obligation. And if there is one, why not others?

In reply to this objection, some theorists set up a conceptual picket-line around obligations. "There are many kinds of moral reasons," they concede, "including reasons for keeping agreements, but these are not 'obligations' properly so called. They are urgent moral considerations, or perhaps 'natural duties.' Thus, promises give rise to obligations but one only has a natural duty to care for one's children." This view can certainly be made consistent, though ordinary language chafes in the straightjacket. The problem, however, is not that the distinction it proposes is incoherent but that it is unimportant. It matters only if the different sources of obligations and duties correlate with other morally significant differences between them. What might these be? Not urgency. The natural duty to keep promises is no less urgent than the obligation to keep a particular promise, nor is the duty not to harm others less urgent than the obligation to return what one borrows. Does the difference correlate with directionality? No, because not all obligations are personal and not all duties are general. The obligation not to assault others binds us to refrain from assaulting anyone, while the natural duty to care for one's children is normally thought to bind parents only to their own children. Because the distinction between natural duties and obligations is substantively idle no one is going to be very disappointed to discover that while there is no obligation "strictly speaking" to obey the law there is nonetheless a natural duty to do so that binds with just the sort of force that we attribute to obligations.[2]

The third defense of (3) argues the other way round. It attempts to assimilate apparently non-consensual obligations to consensual ones by arguing that they are grounded in *hypothetical* consent. Whether this can work depends on the success of some version of moral contractualism and I cannot discuss that here. But we can investigate its significance if successful. Suppose, as Rawls argues, that if we had been among the rational but uninformed parties in the "original position" we would have agreed to bear a nonconsensual duty to obey the law. (Rawls holds that if they made it depend on consent they would have endless doubts about whether others were bound to obey, which would undermine confidence in public institutions.) That argument snatches defeat from the jaws of victory. To justify the obligation to obey the law or to keep promises on the ground that it would be rational to have such practices does not show that those are after all voluntary obligations. It shows that, although not voluntary, they are nonetheless rational. In contrast, a consent-based theory must take *actual* agreement as having moral significance. It may even allow one to incur some binding obligations that it was not rational to agree to. A consent theorist must show that there is special value in empowering people to create duties for themselves by agreement, not just that it would be valuable to be bound by such duties.

Thus, (3) is wrong and the quick defense of (1) therefore fails. If consent is necessary for the obligation to obey the law, it is not because of the nature of obligation in general, but because of the content of this particular obligation. This is the point at which the theory of associative obligation begins to look damaging to the consent thesis. Political association is in many ways similar to other nonvoluntary relationships in which we do not feel the need for consent. Common moral thought holds that friends, for example, owe each other special duties of loyalty, respect, support, and so forth, which partly constitute their relationship but which do not, or need not, arise as a matter of contract or agreement. As Aristotle saw, there are different kinds or levels of human community, and friendship, unlike a business deal, is marked by deep and intrinsically valuable relations among people. Similar obligations are often thought to bind people to their neighborhoods, families, partnerships, professions, religions, or ethnic groups. Does the state also belong on this list?

There are certainly enough analogies to make it worth discussing: people rarely choose their states, they do not agree with all their laws, nationality structures their identities, political relationships grow organically, and membership in a state may, ideally at least, have intrinsic value. But there are also disanalogies, of which the following are the most important.

States are huge organizations, binding together millions of people who have varied backgrounds and interests. Thus the intensity and depth of social relations familiar in smaller associations are likely to be absent in the state. As Rousseau put it, "The more the social bond is stretched, the slacker it becomes."[3] Moreover, as scale increases, the ability of any individual citizen to control the association dwindles. Though structured by social convention, friendships, marriages, partnerships, and so forth are all more responsive to the will of their members than is any state. Individual citizens, even in a democracy, are *law-takers* just as individual consumers in a competitive market are price-takers. This is not to deny the possibility of genuine popular control of governments; it is to remind us that such control is essentially collective in form. To exercise it therefore requires organization and the ability to bear substantial transaction costs. The modern state is thus quite unlike the family, tribe, neighborhood, or other face-to-face communities. The state claims obedience from individuals who can only control the state in groups. Apart from physical size, the state is imposing in its normative dimensions. In all modern states, the law claims supreme authority over our most vital interests. Even the most minimal constitutional regime claims power to regulate personal relationships, property, and the terms of membership in any other association. It is not that the law requires absolute obedience; on the contrary, it usually recognizes a variety of exemptions from its rule. But even a state that takes rights very seriously, and promises in good faith that there are some things it will never require of its citizens, rests on its own word. The scope and supremacy of the state's claim to authority mean that the stakes in the political community are the highest. Together, these features of the state are sufficiently important to shift the argumentative burden back again. We are now entitled to expect a positive account of the ways in which the state can be understood as a community.

II Obligations of True Community

Dworkin says that we have "a duty to honor our responsibilities under social practices that define groups and attach special responsibilities to membership . . ." (p. 198). These duties are not consent-based; their content and liability is said to depend on group practices rather than on individual agreement. This dependence, however, is normative. It is vital to distinguish between the claim that group membership *identifies* our obligations and the claim that group membership *justifies* or validates them. A lawyer, for example, has professional duties that come with the role, but this does not show that those duties are also morally binding. A profession may make demands which no one should concede. Note that this does not rest on any sharp distinction between facts and values, as if the character of the group's practice were a matter for the sociologist and its binding force a matter for the moral philosopher. But any theory for identifying associative obligations must allow that they may be unjustified, even *prima facie*.

How then can associative obligations ever be validated? What, for example, turns one's duty as neighbor into a moral duty? That will depend on the character and point of neighborly relations, on the way the duties in question serve that point, and on whether there are good reasons for regarding the fact that people live in the neighborhood as a ground for thinking them bound by the duties. If the point of neighborhood is to facilitate social contact and local cooperation, then one might be able to defend an associative duty to welcome new neighbors as instrumental to its point. Other duties may be noninstrumentally justified. Courtesy does not merely facilitate neighborly relations but partly constitutes or expresses them. But neither sort of argument can validate everything a neighborhood might require. A new neighbor who votes differently in local elections has no obligation to switch allegiance in order to fit in with the community, nor can a neighborhood impose duties on its members to shun minority ethnic groups.

Suppose, however, that we seek "not just an interpretation of a single associative practice, like family or friendship or neighborhood, but a more abstract interpretation of the yet more general practice of associative obligation itself" (p. 197). How will we validate these obligations? Immediately we face a serious problem. What is the point of association in the abstract or in general? What duties does it impose and how do they serve or express its point? This is indeterminate. There is no point of association *as such* and no generic responsibilities attach to it. One cannot produce moral reasons for the general act-type "doing what is required" any more than one can explain the point of "being associated." We can only justify associative obligations locally, in reference to the points of actual associations. This is not the relativistic claim that each association defines obligations that are morally binding for it. On the contrary, each must satisfy sound general principles, but these principles must operate on the points and characters of real associations. Any general truths about associative obligations will follow only as generalizations about particular cases, not as deductions from a general theory of association as such.

Fortunately, Dworkin is better than his word, for his claims about association in general are in fact defended in the only way they could be, by considering moral relationships in groups like families, friendships, and partnerships and implicitly generalizing from them. On that basis, he distinguishes between a "bare" community that satisfies the minimal conditions for group life, and a "true" community that imposes moral obligations.

To begin, every true community must first be a bare community as defined by social practice (pp. 207–8).[4] Next, members must think that their obligations are *special*, holding in a distinctive way among the group's members and not holding in that way among everyone in the world. Their responsibilities must also be *personal* in that they are owed to members of the group as individuals rather than to the group as a whole. And they must also derive from a more general duty of *concern* for the well-being of its members, which concern is *equal* in the sense that the group's role distinctions and distribution of benefits are held to be in the interests of all and are compatible with the assumption that the well-being of each member is of intrinsically equal value. When held in the correct spirit, these mark a sort of reciprocity so that people "share a general and diffuse sense of members' special rights and responsibilities from or toward one another, a sense of what sort and level of sacrifice one may be expected to make for another" (p. 199). "Collectively these conditions are said to justify associative obligations as such: If the conditions are met, people in the bare community have the obligations of a true community whether or not they want them . . ." (p. 201).[5]

Now, although Dworkin incautiously says these conditions reflect beliefs or "attitudes" of the members, his considered view is that they are "interpretive properties" of the group: "practices that people with the right level of concern would adopt – not a psychological property of some fixed number of the actual members" (p. 201).[6] That is to say, a bare community becomes a true community if a certain complex argument holds about it, irrespective of its members' beliefs and attitudes. Thus, "Political obligation is then not just a matter of obeying the discrete political decisions of the community one by one, as political philosophers usually represent it. It becomes a more protestant idea: fidelity to a scheme of principle which citizens have a responsibility to identify, ultimately for themselves, as their community's scheme" (p. 190).

This certainly helps turn Rousseau's objection. If group life is independent of affective ties, then any set of people might be involved in it, even when related by nothing more than the anonymous and bureaucratic machinery of a large modern state. There is therefore nothing in Dworkin's conditions for true community that limit associative obligations to small, close-knit communities.

Does this account also accommodate the state's claim to authority? Surprisingly, Dworkin does not explicitly address the point and his central example counts against it. He notes that the paradigm for associative obligations is the nonvoluntary association of siblings. It is significant, he says, that the virtue of fraternity is the one taken as a model for this realm (p. 437 n. 20). But what is the content of fraternal or sororal obligations? Mutual aid and respect, perhaps, but scarcely *obedience*. That is why the associative model most often deployed by earlier political theorists was not in fact horizontal associations among siblings, but the vertical hierarchy in which children were thought to owe a duty of obedience to their parents. This was not chosen because parents and children were somehow believed to be more truly associated than siblings, but because two common justifications for authority relations were held to apply here.

First, there is the instrumental argument based on the need for obedience in child rearing. Children need parental authority to guide their development because they are not yet fully competent judges of their own or others' interests.[7] Suspending their own judgment about certain matters and acting instead on their parents' directives will better promote the proper ends of family life. On the other hand, according to John Locke, parents need a right to obedience because they are charged with a duty of caring for their children and thus require the normative powers necessary for the exercise of that duty. Together, these were thought to justify a nonvoluntary obligation of children to obey their parents.

There is one obvious hurdle in extending such arguments beyond the family context, however. Political theory must apply to adults of mature judgment. Is the authority of the state justified because we all need to be treated like children? A familiar reply to this objection runs as follows. Even in the state, there are nonetheless some areas in which adults do need authoritative guidance. For example, certain questions of social policy turn on knowledge that only state officials have, or on which only they can be relied to act in good faith. The state can also take a broader view and ensure that the public interest is served through the coordinated activity of many individuals and groups. This will, of course, apply only in some circumstances and only to some people, so the state's claim to bind everyone will have to be qualified. But there is a deeper problem. Even if there are some things that only the state can do, it has not been shown that the state can do them only if its citizens have or recognize an obligation to obey it. The state can rely on a wide variety of techniques to secure their compliance, including persuasion, exhortation, reward, and coercion. The above arguments do not establish that it also needs a duty of obedience.[8]

Not all traditional arguments for familial obligations were instrumental. Both Locke and Rousseau held that, after children reach the age of reason, parental authority may continue with their consent or because it is psychologically salient among other reasonable authority structures.[9] Others attempted to justify obligation as an appropriate expression of attitudes such as gratitude, trust, or honor.

Why is an obligation of obedience ever an appropriate expression of some attitude?[10] Can we answer: it is just a matter of social convention that it is expressed in this way? We normally take evaluative attitudes towards these conventions, however, and interpret "appropriate" to mean a "desirable" or "fitting" expression and not just a "usual" one. What Locke says about the biblical injunction to honor one's parents is instructive here:

> A Man may owe *honour* and respect to an ancient, or wise Man; defence to his Child or Friend; relief and support to the Distressed; and gratitude to a Benefactor, to such a degree, that all he has, all he can do, cannot sufficiently pay it: But all these give no Authority, no right to any one of making Laws over him from whom they are owing.[11]

Locke thus distinguishes obligations imposed by the legal system from the other kinds of duties we typically owe. Social relationships may bring very stringent obligations without amounting to an obligation to obey their commands. Yet they are all appropriate to the relationships in question. One *thanks* a benefactor, *respects* the wise, *defends* a friend. But one does not *obey* them as an expression of the relationship. For Locke, obedience is out of place in all these contexts whereas it would be fitting in the relationship of Creator and created, or of parent and child. But that is because there are other, primary, grounds sufficient to validate authority in these contexts.

Dworkin offers an example with which we can test this point. Suppose some community has a practice of arranged marriages according to which daughters have an obligation to defer to their fathers' choice of spouse for them while sons do not. Suppose further that this is a true community; that its practices can sustain a good-faith interpretation as being grounded in respect and equality between the sexes. If so, he argues, daughters owe their fathers a genuine associative obligation. The obligation is just a *prima facie* one which may ultimately be overridden "by appeal to freedom or some other ground of rights," but although defeasible it cannot simply be ignored:

> The difference is important: a daughter who marries against her father's wishes, in this version of the story, has something to regret. She owes him at least an accounting, and perhaps an apology, and should in other ways strive to continue her standing as a member of the community she otherwise has a duty to honor. (p. 205)

This liberal-minded account is, unfortunately, inconsistent with the story as told. For what the community requires of daughters is *deference* to their fathers' will, not respectful audience followed by free judgment and, if necessary, apology. *Prima facie* deference is not the same as respectful audience. The fact that it is *prima facie* only means that it is not conclusive, that other values like freedom or autonomy may still weigh against it. We cannot argue this way: "Because there is a residue or trace of duty shown by the obligation to apologize, there must be a *prima facie* obligation to defer." That does not follow at all, because the defeated obligation might only have been a duty to consider their fathers' wishes, or give some weight to their advice. The fact that the community requires deference, and that there are moral reasons for daughters to apologize, does not give *prima facie* validity to the community's requirements.

We must take care not to be misled by the fact that associative obligations may only claim *prima facie* force. The normative character of an obligation is not identified by whether it is *prima facie* or conclusive, but by the function it is meant to play in the practical reason of those whom it binds. A duty to defer requires that daughters be willing to act on their fathers' wishes rather than their own in at least some cases where they conflict. Thus the question is not whether, once the fathers' wishes are in the balance, they will win out against other considerations. The question is how and in what form they get onto the balance in the first place. The father in Dworkin's example is not offering his daughter advice in the spirit in which her stockbroker informs her about the market. He is not inviting her to estimate its reliability and value and then act on it as she sees fit. He is asking her to suspend her own judgment with respect to marriage and defer to his. The fact that a true community's practices require this of daughters does nothing to justify it.

We have thus found no positive argument to show that associative obligations are entitled to the binding force they claim. At most, Dworkin has shown that two objections may be answered: that the state is too large for intense social relations, and that some associations treat their members iniquitously. The depsychologized view of community meets the former point, and the normative conditions for true community rule out some kinds of iniquity. Nonetheless, these are merely among the necessary conditions for legitimacy. A community must not only be well ordered internally; it must also have appropriate relations with other communities. (A caste system creates no obligations because it treats its members badly; but neither does the Ku Klux Klan, however it treats its own.)

III   Integrity and Obedience

I have not yet mentioned the centerpiece of Dworkin's argument. He holds that "the community has its own principles it can itself honor or dishonor, that it can act in good or bad faith, with integrity or hypocritically, just as people can" (p. 168). A community with integrity is a community of principle, and it satisfies the conditions of true community as well as can be expected in the real world. "A community of principle . . . can claim the authority of a genuine associative community and can therefore claim moral legitimacy – that its collective decisions are matters of obligation and not bare power – in the name of fraternity" (p. 214)[12]

Dworkin's theory of integrity is complex and merits discussion in its own right (see chapters 15, 16, and 17 of this volume.) Here I will only examine its relevance to the problem of legitimacy. If integrity is important only because it shows that the conditions of true community are satisfied, then it adds nothing to the argument already considered and rejected, for true community is not sufficient for obligation. That, however, leaves open the possibility that a state with integrity is both a true community and, on independent grounds, a legitimate one.

Integrity is, for Dworkin, a kind of consistency, but not just the bare formality of treating like cases alike; it is a principled coherence that also provides criteria for the likeness of cases. A community of principle is one whose directives can be interpreted as a coherent and defensible (though not necessarily ideal) scheme. Integrity explains why we would prefer either a regime prohibiting all abortions or one allowing free choice to one in which women born on even days are allowed them while those born on odd days are not. Such checkerboard regimes incorporate arbitrary, unprincipled distinctions among people and cannot be interpreted as schemes of principle at all, even when they give each citizen an equal say over the outcome and when that outcome minimizes injustice.

Does a scheme satisfying integrity have any *prima facie* claim to the obedience of those under it? Dworkin's personification of the community gives it ideals with which it can keep or break faith. We can therefore learn about the force of integrity by considering the way it operates in our evaluation of other agents.

All but the most crude rigorists discriminate among judges whose political principles they reject. On the other side of the barricades there are hacks, hypocrites, and bumblers; but there are also committed, sincere, and principled people. It is interesting that we admire the latter even though they are, from the perspective of justice, more dangerous precisely because they are immune from *ad hominem* attack. While rejecting their principles, and even fearing their influence, we respect them nonetheless.

Our regard for a person with integrity, however, is based on what unites us, not on what divides us. We are both people, whose aims, projects, and values are subject to the distortions of self-interest, backsliding, dissembling, and all the other ordinary vices of human life. Those who apply the values they hold in a steady and fair-minded fashion thus deserve respect at least for having mastered what anyone must master. But these are virtues of the person, not of the principles. It may be true that to identify the aims as a scheme of principle at all we must first be able to see it under the aspect of some good, to conceive of it as connected, if only remotely, with intelligible values. We could not, to take Foot's famous example,[13] regard a man as acting on principle or pursuing a conception of the good who was devoted to clasping and unclasping his hands, unless he also thought that was a kind of exercise, or prayer, or music, or something else whose general type we could recognize as valuable. But vast canyons of incomprehension can divide this plateau of understanding. (Consider, for example, the worldviews of prochoice and right-to-life activists.) To establish a bridgehead of intelligibility with someone's principles does not show that they are admirable, but only that they are capable of being admired.

Secondly, and this is the main point, integrity creates no duty to obey those who display the virtue. The virtues of agents do not give reasons for taking their directives as binding, for integrity does not even ensure that the directives are desirable ones. Notice again that this is not correctly described as saying that they have *prima facie* authority over us, which is then outweighed by the fact that the principles are wrong. It might be said that to obey people of integrity would be a fitting display of trust in their judgment and good faith. But we have already seen the error in that argument. People of integrity may be entitled to admiration or respect (though it even sounds a bit forced to say that we have a *duty* to admire them); but they are not, just on that account, entitled to our obedience. The mere fact that someone is trying in good faith to rule you is no reason whatever to obey.

None of this changes when integrity is an attribute of the community personified rather than an individual. We may impute personality to the community, says Dworkin, because it is morally desirable to do so. In principle, this is a perfectly reputable way of arguing, though some of Dworkin's reasons for thinking it desirable are, I think, strange ones. If we personify the community, then we can think of it as having integrity, and "a political society that accepts integrity as a political virtue thereby becomes a special form of community, special in a way that promotes its moral authority to assume and deploy a monopoly of coercive force. This is not the only argument for integrity, or the only consequence of recognizing it that citizens might value" (p. 188).

I shall come to those other arguments and consequences shortly, but let us first pause over the above claim. Why is talking about the community in a way that makes its coercive power liable to justification a "consequence . . . that *citizens* might value"? Are we to understand that they value their community being the kind that has justified coercive power? Would the argument be that if they are going to be coerced anyway, it is best that their coercer be justified, and therefore best that they think about it in ways that promote its justification? Surely all this is desirable only if the state's coercive power *is* justified. Dworkin may be confusing integrity's value to the citizens with a different one: the value to the *theorist* of being able to explain the legitimacy of the state. I return to this possibility in section V.

Consider now the other advantages of integrity. Dworkin says that if we impute personality to the community and see it as capable of having integrity, then we will have the instrumental benefits of a more open and efficient legal system, as well as the noninstrumental value of being self-legislators, willing a scheme of principle and united in a continuing effort to keep faith with it. Imputing personality to the community is thus good because it makes possible the sense of integrity, which is also good. As stated, however, the argument is crucially indecisive. Personifying the community may make it possible to see it as having the new virtues Dworkin mentions, but it also makes it possible to see it as having a new set of vices, such as hypocrisy and bad faith. Like the hypothesis of free will, integrity opens some doors only by closing others. In any case, none of these virtues suggests any new ground of obligation. Openness, efficiency, and moral autonomy do not require that citizens take the law as binding nor do they give reasons for doing so. A legal system may promote these ends provided that it enjoys sufficient compliance to work well; it does not require universal compliance nor does it require that those who comply take the existence of law as among their reasons for doing so. These virtues may contribute to our sense that our community is an attractive one, but not to the different and more ambitious thesis that it has legitimate authority over us.

Does Dworkinian integrity capture the social dimension of political life in a way that other theories cannot? This is doubtful. Dworkin holds that obligations may be controversial, because it is a matter for interpretation what the law really requires. More exactly, he holds that all social obligations are to be interpreted in light of "a protestant attitude that makes each citizen responsible for imagining what his society's public commitments to principle are, and what these commitments require in new circumstances" (p. 413). Interpreting the law, or any other social practice, is thus not a matter of trying to understand what it communicates to us; rather it is a matter of imposing or projecting our purposes onto it: "Each citizen, we might say, is trying to discover his own intention in maintaining and participating in that practice"; he is engaged in "a conversation with himself" (p. 58).

This has profound consequences for a social theory of obligation. For one thing, it turns principled civil disobedience into obedience to true law, since the disobedient are merely trying to keep faith with their own intentions in maintaining the practice of law.[14] Moreover, since not only the requirements of the community but also its boundaries are matters of interpretation, it turns my question of whether another person is a member of my community into a matter of trying to discover my own purposes in regarding that person as a member. I ignore the issue of whether this is a sound theory of interpretation.[15] But if it is, then the sort of admiration due to personal integrity is entirely without analogue, not because the state is a collectivity rather than an individual, but because its *bona fides* and single-mindedness are *our* contributions to it. They are our own attempts to see it in its best light. If we succeed at this, what deserves admiration – the law or our own ingenuity in interpretation? There is no difference here, because the law's requirements are, for each individual, simply his or her own best interpretation. In collapsing the distinction between a social practice and an individual view of it we can no longer make sense of admiring an agent with whom we disagree. What seemed like a tempering of individualism now returns, through the protestant character of interpretation, as individualism with a vengeance. The communal-sounding notion that an association of integrity must keep faith with its own principles turns out to mean that each must create a monadic view of its aims and see it as keeping faith with him or her. The sense in which this is an associative theory of obligation seems vestigial.

IV   Individuality and Community

It is difficult not to feel the urge for a social account of legitimacy, but important to yield to it in the right way. There are two main options. Some, like Dworkin, attempt to make community part of the *normative* conditions for legitimacy, by which I mean the way duties are acquired. But one might instead incorporate community into the *evaluative* conditions that justify a particular mode of acquiring duties. One attractive combination of these positions makes political obligation bind only through consent, while maintaining the evaluative thesis that consent rests on social rather than individual considerations.

It is time to get clearer about the notion of "social" values. Although there is no agreement about what ethical individualism amounts to, three theses are commonly associated with it. The first is *egoism*, the view that everyone does or should act only to promote their own interests, such as increasing their own wealth, status, or power. The second is *instrumentalism*, which holds that all social relations and institutions are of value only to the extent that they promote the ends of individual persons. Finally, there is the weak thesis that I shall call *humanism*, according to which morality must have some connection (not necessarily instrumental) with the interests of persons.

When political theorists talk about the need for community or decry individualism, any or all of the above theses may be in play. A surprising amount of ink is wasted criticizing egoism which, Hobbes and a few economists aside, no serious theorist has ever defended. More interesting are the other two theses. Humanism is accepted by nearly all moralists (with the possible exception of Nietzsche and some divine command theorists). Whatever its merits in general moral philosophy, however, humanism seems fundamental to any acceptable theory of political morality. Although there may be other ends in life, the political realm is mainly concerned with the fates of people. The real battleground is thus over instrumentalism.

Classical liberals often justified consent by instrumental considerations arguing, for example, that it gives agents the power to protect themselves from duties they do not want, or that it allows them to enter mutually beneficial arrangements with others. But it clearly has other roles too. Consider its place in marriage as practiced in our culture. No one can get married except by their own consent, though marriage brings with it duties not all of which are results of consent. Some people object to this. Why should consent not structure the whole relation, such that each duty constitutive of the role is subject to a separate agreement to bear it? Some people find the contractualization of personal relationships appealing, others find it appalling. It is clear, however, that to defend our institution of marriage we would need to show that there is value in a common social role that cannot be characterized in that way.

Role duties have a relative objectivity, by which I mean not that they are self-justifying or uncontroversial, but that they are recognized as being partly beyond the control of their subjects. Roles are social and not individual creations. One can choose not to be an undertaker, but not to be an undertaker with no duty to be decorous. Not all roles impose valid duties, however. The traditional gender roles in our societies are among those that do not. When are they valid? Here, we need a two-part explanation. First, one needs to justify the clustering of duties into a role at all. Why not instead have complete flexibility in these matters and allow people to construct their own roles as they go and according to their circumstances? Radical individualists would no doubt favor this as giving fullest expression to the sovereignty of will. They might of course concede some minor instrumental benefits to having standard patterns of social interaction, and they might permit roles as default options. Ideal human relations, however, they would see as polymorphous and contractual. Against such a view, considerations like those which Joseph Raz elaborates with great power in his discussion of the social nature of value,[16] seem to me persuasive. Common roles may be valued because they are common and embody social relations that are valuable for their own sake and not merely as means to individual ends. They are valuable *to* individuals, so humanism is not denied, but they are valued *as* social relationships in a way that egoists and instrumentalists would reject. Beginning with the ancient world, part of the value of citizenship was recognized to lie in its character as a shared status purporting to transcend other divisions among people. The individualist ideal of a multiplicity of different social contracts does not adequately capture this.

Nonetheless, to defend common social roles does not show why they bind their incumbents. Thus we come to the second problem. Why should socially constituted roles create valid duties? There is no single answer here, rather there is a variety of different considerations. Some role duties do bind nonvoluntarily, most plausibly when others are nonvoluntarily dependent[17] on their performance (such as infants on their parents) or when the duties benefit others but are modest in their demands (e.g., the duty of teachers to be punctual). Others bind only when assumed by agents with a degree of awareness about the duties the role brings. Now we reach the point where the consent thesis may be defended directly. Is the role of citizenship one that can bind nonvoluntarily?

It might seem initially plausible that others are nonvoluntarily dependent on our performing our duties as citizens. If one breaks the law, it will often harm others, or fail to promote our mutual interests, or impose unfair burdens on them. But these are all good reasons on their own for doing as the law requires, and we need to show how the fact that law requires a certain action is itself a further reason for acting. Consider, therefore, a case where the law requires some action and the above considerations are absent. Two things seem evident: in this case the law claims to obligate, but other citizens are not dependent on one's doing as it requires. It is therefore false to think that they are nonvoluntarily dependent on our accepting the state's claim to authority. At most, they are dependent on our complying with the law in those cases in which it would be harmful not to do so. There is no plausible argument that establishes that every act of disobedience always harms someone. Nor can it be said that what citizenship requires of us is only modest, for every state makes extensive claims to our allegiance. The social role of citizenship is not, then, liable to the same justifications as the familiar sorts of nonvoluntary roles.

Roles can, however, also come to bind with our consent. Because not every kind of consent will be valid, the necessary conditions must still be satisfied. Suppose that Dworkin has correctly identified these in his account of true community, and suppose that consent to obey such a community would be valid because it partly constitutes the valued common status of citizenship. Consent therefore binds, not because it protects citizens or permits them to bargain with each other, but because it is part of a valuable social relation. On this view, the obligations *of* members will be defined socially, through the practice of membership in their society, while the obligation *to be* a member remains an individual one. This only scratches the surface of a role-based theory of consent, and before it could even be developed several objections would have to be met. Dworkin has put some of the more important ones and it is convenient simply to take them in turn.

1   Consent to the role of citizenship, even if given, would not be valid. Here, Dworkin joins sides with Hume in maintaining that there can be no real choice about membership in the state. "[E]ven if the consent were genuine, the argument would fail as an argument for legitimacy, because a person leaves one sovereign only to join another; he has no choice to be free from sovereigns altogether" (p. 193). But Dworkin has picked a bad partner, for Hume vastly overplays his hand. It is true that a free choice depends not only on the mere existence of alternatives, but also on their character. But the implied description of the available alternatives is wrong and perpetuates a persistent fallacy. It supposes that one must either accept the authority of the state or else emigrate. The dilemma is obviously a false one for there are many other alternatives recognized and practiced in our own political culture. One may, for example, remain in the country, participate in its affairs, obey the law when conscience so counsels, but reject the moral authority of the state. Those who comply in such a peaceful and principled fashion will, in a reasonably just state, support the government and avoid sanction, but the law will create no obligations for them. We might say they are *in* though not *of* the political community. But it would be wrong to think of them as deeply alienated. On the contrary, they may continue to identify with many of the traditions and values of the community; their allegiance will just not extend to its state.

2   Role duties are "not formed in one act of deliberate contractual commitment, the way one joins a club" (p. 197).[18] Even supposing the duties in question to be valid, this objection is misleading. Consent theory does not require duties be assumed by "one act," whatever that means. Nor are all consent-based duties contractual, in the sense that they define the terms of a bargain. (Is joining a club always contractual?) On the contrary, they may be assumed by actions, by omissions, and by series of actions and omissions that collectively amount to the deliberate assumption of a role. (Consider the commitments involved in choosing to become a lawyer.)

3   Role duties extend beyond explicit agreement to include the spirit or purposes of the relationship in question (pp. 200, 210). Again, consent theory is not committed to the contrary view. An act of consent may create duties both explicitly and implicitly. (Consent to an end, for example, may include consent to its necessary means.) Indeed, if Dworkin's general theory of interpretation were correct then it would apply here too, and acts of consent would bind agents to many duties required by implication and coherence.

4   Role duties are often not thought to be voluntary. "[W]e are rarely even aware that we are entering upon any special status as the story unfolds" (p. 197). "[P]eople in the bare community have the obligations of a true community whether or not they want them . . ." (p. 201). This is the crux of the matter, but it begs the question. First, we must not confuse wanting to assume an obligation with wanting an obligation or wanting to perform it. I may assume an obligation that I do not want in order to get something else that I do. And it is characteristic of all valid obligations, whatever their source, that they must be performed irrespective of the agent's wishes. So Dworkin's observation that we become most conscious of our obligations at the point of performance is irrelevant. He is correct, however, to hold that choice is absent if a role or status was blundered into, or happened upon, without even the awareness that anything significant was happening. If political roles bind in these circumstances then consent theory is wrong. But do they? The arguments from true community and from integrity did not establish it.

I do not think it can be denied that the political role is weakly voluntary, in the sense that one has no obligation to assume it and it can be terminated at will. But if it is only weakly voluntary then it is not binding. A high degree of awareness is necessary on the part of citizens in order to validate their duties to obey. First, any state is liable to change. It is not enough to trust the present rulers, because political obligations are not held to bind only to a particular administration or government. Weakly voluntary duties are not sufficiently sensitive, since they emerge and disappear slowly and possibly without any awareness of what is happening. Second, recall again that in the political community the stakes are the highest. Drifting in and out of an association claiming supreme authority, dimly aware of what is happening, is much more serious here than in the normal ebb and flow of relationships like friendship. These are powerful positive reasons for thinking that the validity of the civic role must rest on consent and they complement the reasons for rejecting competing theories.

All this is intelligible, however, only if we can think of people as giving or withholding their consent. Some communitarians (though not Dworkin) hold that this is inconsistent with a sound view of personal identity. They say that people cannot be distanced from their social roles, for these *constitute* their identity. The thought that there is some essential, noumenal Self, capable of giving or withholding its consent, is in their view a foolish and politically dangerous abstraction. That is the argument. It fails because it is sufficient for consent theory that people can distance themselves from their *political* role. Consent is intelligible provided only that fully constituted agents – complete with genders, religions, values, and all the rest – can put, understand, and answer one question: should I concede the authority of the state? Might someone deny even this much distance, and insist that citizenship itself must be constitutive of our personalities, so that the question cannot even be asked? Put that way, it is clear which view is the foolish and danger-ous abstraction.

Consent theorists insist on the importance of a lively awareness of role duties, but may, and I think should, reject instrumental or egoistic views that equate consent with a bargain. And their political sociology may learn from Hegel, Burke, or Durkheim in as much as it places community and custom at center stage in explanations of why people obey their rulers. But they will give them only bit parts, and certainly no speaking roles, in the theory of legitimacy.

V   The Universality of Obligation

Let us take stock. I defended the thesis that consent is necessary for the obligation to obey, and rejected Dworkin's account of associative obligation. But I have not shown that everyone consents to obey the law and, indeed, any theory purporting to show that would be suspect. It therefore follows that some people may have no obligation to obey, even when the state is reasonably just and the conditions of true community are satisfied. Is the scent of *reductio* in the air? Doesn't a theory of law *have to* explain how law obligates? Dworkin thinks so: "A conception of law must explain how what it takes to be law provides a general justification for the exercise of coercive power by the state, a justification that holds except in special cases when some competing argu-ment is specially powerful" (p. 190, cf. p. 110). I conclude by sketching some doubts about that alleged constraint on a theory of law.[19]

Certainly there is something intuitively odd about the assumption. Would we begin a theory of criminal justice by first assuming that our practices of punishment are justified and then seeking the theory that best shows why they are? It may be of the nature of punishments that they purport to be a form of justice rather than terror, but our theories must test the credentials of that claim. We must therefore start tentatively, and ask whether punishment is ever justified, in what forms, and under what conditions. Why is this not also the right procedure for thinking about political obligation?

For Dworkin, "law" is a deeply controversial and value-laden concept. Nonetheless, like H. L. A. Hart,[20] he thinks that we do in fact agree at an abstract level about the kind of thing that law is. He says that there is an "uncontroversial" (p. 94) consensus that ties the concept of law to that of justified coercion. "[F]or us," he writes, "legal argument takes place on a plateau of rough con-sensus that if law exists it provides a justification for the use of collective power against individ-ual citizens or groups" (pp. 108–9). This is a slightly dark formulation. The existence of a legal system obviously does not justify every sort of collective power. Governments coerce people without relying on law (e.g., by using their market power) and are sometimes justified in doing so. Moreover, the rule of law is only a necessary condition for justified coercion. Not only the forms of justice but also its substance must be in order.

In truth, however, Dworkin's concept of law does incorporate a substantive theory of justice, as can be seen in this narrower restatement of it.

> Our discussions about law by and large assume, I suggest, that the most abstract and fundamental point of legal practice is to guide and constrain the power of government in the following way. Law insists that force not be used or withheld, no matter how useful that would be to ends in view, no

matter how beneficial or noble these ends, except as licensed or required by individual rights and responsibilities flowing from past political decisions about when collective force is justified. (p. 93)

Now the plateau has eroded to become the narrow ledge of Dworkin's own "rights thesis." This is a much more substantial claim than the general one, but it is miles from any uncontroversial plateau of agreement even in "our" societies. Indeed, Dworkin's rights thesis is one of the most controversial claims of modern jurisprudence.[21]

The plateau has two interesting features. First, it exhibits a Kelsenian vein that often works to the surface of Dworkin's thought. On this view, the point of law is not to govern interpersonal relations directly, by imposing duties or setting standards of behavior, it is to govern them indirectly by instructing officials when to use and withhold force. Is this plausible or does it distort the point of, say tort or contract, to see them as primarily guiding and constraining governments in their use of force? Our discussions about these areas of law do not seem to make or require that assumption. Second, Dworkin's plateau makes it a necessary condition of all justified forcing, and even all refraining from forcing, that it be authorized by earlier political decisions. This cannot be taken literally, however, for we regard force as justified in some matters about which there have been no prior decisions at all. But "past political decisions" is for Dworkin only another metaphor for his favored coherence argument: a coercive act can be brought within its ambit if it is arguable that it is not inconsistent with past decisions and that it furthers whatever purposes it is morally desirable to impute to those decisions.

I think that both of these views are mistaken as claims in general legal theory, but neither point need be argued here. It is sufficient to see that this narrow concept of law does not in any case entail anything about the obligation to obey. One person may be justified in coercing another without first needing, or consequently acquiring, a right to obedience, even when the justification for coercion is the protection of rights. Dworkin denies this last claim, however:

These two issues – whether the state is morally legitimate, in the sense that it is justified in using force against its citizens, and whether the state's decisions impose genuine obligations on them – are not identical. No state should enforce all of a citizen's obligations. But though obligation is not a sufficient condition for coercion, it is close to a necessary one. A state may have good grounds in some special circumstances for coercing those who have no duty to obey. But no general policy of upholding the law with steel could be justified if the law were not, in general, a source of genuine obligations. (p. 191)

It is true some obligations should not be enforced, but that is irrelevant to the question of whether the state can enforce some requirement only if there is no obligation *to obey*. The above passage confounds

(4) The state may only coerce people to make them perform actions that they have an antecedent obligation to perform,

with

(5) The state may only coerce people who have an obligation to obey it.

Now (4) is probably false, but what matters here is the truth of (5), and (4) does nothing to establish that. One may have an antecedent obligation to do or refrain from some action even if there is no obligation to obey the state. An anarchist can believe that there is a moral obligation not to murder and also deny that the criminal law creates any moral obligations.

In most contexts the difference between justified coercive power and authority – the power to impose obligations on others – is clear enough.[22] I am justified in resisting unlawful arrest, but have no authority over the offender. The Allies were justified in coercing the Nazis but had no right to command German citizens. In cases of self-defense and sometimes even other-defense one may therefore be justified in coercing those over whom one has no authority at all. Most people believe that a reasonably just state can sometimes coerce outsiders, at least to protect its own citizens and probably for some other purposes too.

What then remains of Dworkin's claim that if law is to employ coercive sanctions as a "general policy" then it must "in general" be a source of moral obligation? I take the implied contrast to be between a general policy and special cases or between a rule and its exceptions. One could admit that when fighting a just war or acting in self-defense one is entitled to coerce others, but see these as exceptions to the general policy that one may only coerce those over whom one has legitimate authority. But are these in fact exceptions to some general policy? Which policy? Why are these circumstances "special" ones? If we had an independent argument to the effect that a government requires authority in order to coerce, then that would be a good start, but that is precisely what is at issue. Moreover, the government's right to enforce its will need not rest on any general policy but only on a cluster of *different* considerations which, taken together, justify its use of force. It may be justified in coercing those who murder in order to protect those at risk, in coercing those who break contracts in order to protect valued social practices, and in coercing those who negligently harm others in order to establish a public framework for reciprocity, and so on. Taken together, the set of such reasons covers much legitimate enforcement. Coercion can thus be generally justified without there being a general justification for coercion.

Finally, even if there were, over and above this heterogeneous set of "special considerations" a further general one, it would almost certainly be weaker than the special considerations themselves. Reflective opinion is divided on the theoretical question of whether, apart from the general moral obligation not to assault people, there is a separate obligation to obey the law.[23] But it is united in thinking that if there is, the first is still the more weighty. The main moral reason for not assaulting people is that it harms them, not that the law prohibits it.

The existence of a general obligation to obey is not therefore a necessary condition for the state to be generally justified in enforcing the law. It is not even a sufficient condition, for a just state has a duty to use the least harmful means effective in securing a reasonable degree of compliance. Other things being equal, exhortation and inducement are preferable to steel as means of upholding the law. There is, I conclude, no warrant for the transcendental tone of Dworkin's question – how is it possible that there is a general obligation to obey the law? – and thus no threat to consent theory from this quarter. Universal political obligation is not a fixed point of moral consciousness, crying out for explanation. It is a controversial and, I think, false political claim. Any residual unease with the notion of a reasonably just state, or a true community, which lacks authority over some of its members can be dispelled by considering that, on anyone's theory, every just state imposes no obligations of obedience on *some* people, namely, those living in other states. The only remaining question is whether anyone within its own territory is in the same position. Put that way, the denial of political obligation may begin to look less strange, and consent, as an account of this special relationship, more attractive.

Acknowledgement

A version of this chapter was first published in Allan Hutchinson and Leslie Green (eds.), *Law and the Community – The End of Individualism?* (Toronto: Carswell, 1989), pp. 93–118. It appears here with the kind permission of Carswell.

Notes

1 Ronald Dworkin, *Law's Empire* (Cambridge, MA: Harvard University Press, 1986), p. 207. Page references in the text and notes are to this book unless otherwise specified.

2 This is John Rawls's view: *A Theory of Justice* (Oxford: Clarendon Press, 1971), p. 114.

3 *The Social Contract*, trans. M. Cranston (Harmondsworth, UK: Penguin, 1968), Bk. II, ch. 9, p. 90.

4 Dworkin says disappointingly little about this part of the theory. He thinks that "political practice" adequately defines the boundaries of the United States and UK (excepting Northern Ireland). But this places too much emphasis on law and not enough on practice, especially in light of devolution in the UK. With respect to the USA, Dworkin takes the several states each to be political communities. But New York is a community in a very different way from, e.g., Utah (to say nothing of communities that are not states, like Puerto Rico). And one does not have to look far beyond Britain and America to find even more complex communities, such as in Canada. Finally, there are the further issues of resident aliens, illegal immigrants, prisoners, future generations, etc. The convenient notion that "bare" political communities coincide with constitutional divisions thus seems too simple for these purposes.

5 Here Dworkin presents them as sufficient conditions for associative obligations. At pp. 204 and 207 what he says is consistent with them being necessary or necessary and sufficient. At pp. 213–4 they seem sufficient once again. This hesitation is no accident, as we shall see.

6 In the above quotation, "fixed number" must mean "any number." It follows from Dworkin's theory of interpretation that the community believes that p provided there is some proposition q that some of its members do believe and p coheres the best theory justifying their belief that q. Thus p is an interpretive property of the *community's* belief even although no *member* of the community actually believes it.

7 This point is often neglected. The authority that parents typically claim over their children would not, I think, be justified by paternalistic considerations alone. Children can be taught to act prudently in their own self-interest through exhortation and reward. Parents need authority to command their obedience in large part because children do not give sufficient weight to the interests of others, within and without the family, and because exhortation and reward are often less effective here. Political theorists often wrongly jumped from the correct observation that parents' authority lapses when children mature, to the conclusion that it does so merely because the children have become capable of looking out for themselves. Equally important is the fact that this is when the child's moral sense should develop as well.

8 I discuss this in greater detail in my *The Authority of the State* (Oxford: Clarendon Press, 1988), chs. 4 and 5.

9 Locke writes, "Thus 'twas easie, and almost natural for Children by a tacit, and scarce avoidable consent to make way for the *Father's Authority and Government*. They had been accustomed in their Childhood to follow his Direction, and to refer their little differences to him, and when they were Men, who fitter to rule them?" *Two Treatises of Government*, ed. P. Laslett (Cambridge, UK: Cambridge University Press, 1963), II, §75, p. 360. Salience arguments, however, are only relevant to the question of who should have authority, not to the question of whether any authority is justified. That is one of Locke's mistakes in §82 where he defends the authority of husbands over wives on the ground that men are "abler and stronger." Even if the factual claim were sound, the argument fails because it does not show why either of them must have authority over the other. Disagreements about common interests can be settled in many other ways.

10   For a defence of obedience as an expression of identification with one's society see J. Raz, "Government by Consent," in J. R. Pennock and J. W. Chapman (eds.), *Authority Revisited: Nomos XXIX* (New York: New York University Press, 1987). I criticize Raz's position in my "Law, Legitimacy and Consent," *Southern California Law Review*, vol. 62, 1989, pp. 795–825.

11   Locke, *Two Treatises of Government*, op. cit., II, §70, p. 356.

12   Sometimes (e.g., p. 216) Dworkin only claims that a community with integrity has a *better* claim to legitimacy than other communities. For obvious reasons, this is too weak as a defense of political obligation. The government of the USSR may have had a better claim to legitimacy than the unreformed government of South Africa, but both fell far below any plausible threshold at which their citizens could owe a duty of obedience.

13   P. Foot, "Moral Beliefs," *Proceedings of the Aristotelian Society*, vol. 59, 1958–9, p. 83.

14   Those who are civilly disobedient "act to acquit rather than to challenge their duty as citizens" (Ronald Dworkin, *A Matter of Principle* (Cambridge, MA: Harvard University Press, 1985), p. 105). Note that they acquit their duty as citizens, not merely in the trivial sense of disobeying the law in order to obey other, more stringent, duties of citizenship, e.g., to improve the law. Dworkin's claim entails that, properly understood, they are obeying what the law really requires, i.e., what each does well to understand it as requiring.

15   For criticism see G. J. Postema, "'Protestant' Interpretation and Social Practices," *Law and Philosophy*, vol. 6, 1987, p. 283.

16   Joseph Raz, *The Morality of Freedom* (Oxford: Clarendon Press, 1986), ch. 12.

17   For a vigorous defense of dependence as a ground of obligations see R. E. Goodin, *Protecting the Vulnerable* (Chicago: University of Chicago Press, 1986).

18   Raz makes the same point in *The Authority of Law* (Oxford: Clarendon Press, 1979), p. 257.

19   I say a bit more about this issue in "Who Believes in Political Obligation?" in W. Edmundson, (ed.), *The Duty to Obey the Law* (Totowa, NJ: Rowman and Littlefield, 1999), pp. 301–17.

20   Stripped of rhetoric and certain dubious claims, the only important difference between Dworkin's methodological claims for the "plateau" and Hart's account of the concept of law is that Dworkin explicitly limits the range of his theory to Anglo-American common-law legal systems.

21   As Dworkin himself once recognized. See *Taking Rights Seriously* (Cambridge, MA: Harvard University Press, 1977) (Dworkin as critic of "the ruling theory of law").

22   See further Green, *The Authority of the State*, op. cit., pp. 71–5, 149–53, 242–3.

23   See L. Green, "Law and Obligations," in J. Coleman and S. Shapiro (eds.), *Oxford Handbook of Jurisprudence and Legal Philosophy* (Oxford: Clarendon Press, 2002), pp. 514–47.

15

Speaking with One Voice:
On Dworkinian Integrity and Coherence

Joseph Raz

In this chapter I shall examine Ronald Dworkin's attitude toward coherence as revealed by the central chapters of *Law's Empire*. The interest in doing so is not merely an interest in understanding Dworkin. In "The Relevance of Coherence," chapter 13 of my *Ethics in the Public Domain*, from which this chapter is drawn, I refuted the suggestion that there is a distinct virtue of coherence through loyalty to the past which justifies deviating from the precepts of justice and fairness.[1] I will suggest below that Dworkin's view of law as integrity is subject to the same criticism independently of whether it does favor coherence. This shows that the argument I deployed in "The Relevance of Coherence" catches theories other than coherence theories. It applies to any idealizations of the law that diminish the importance of the doctrine of authority and the role of politics in its explanation. It is an objection of principle to any doctrine that requires the courts to adjudicate disputes on the assumption that the law speaks with one voice, regardless of whether this univocality expresses itself through a doctrine of coherence or in some other way.

For Dworkin, explaining the nature of law is offering an interpretation of the law. This is not the place to assess his view of the nature and role of interpretation. I merely want to discover the way it does or does not interact with considerations of coherence. The ambivalence begins at the beginning. At the most basic level, Dworkin explains interpretation as follows: "constructive interpretation [of which the interpretation of the law is an instance] is a matter of imposing purpose on an object or practice in order to make of it the best possible example of the form or genre to which it is taken to belong."[2] Here, interpretation is defined in terms of strong monistic coherence. Coherence, as we know, means close systematic interdependence of all the parts. Seemingly, Dworkinian interpretation is conceived from the start as committed to strong monism, for it is committed to finding *one* purpose that unites and dominates all the parts of the interpreted object or practice – dominates, for in the postinterpretive stage (p. 66) what the practice requires is adjusted to suit the imposed purpose.

But is it right to attribute to Dworkin this commitment (which is never justified even by a shadow of an argument) to strong coherence? Perhaps his reference to one purpose is simply a *façon de parler*; perhaps Dworkin is willing to contemplate a plurality of unrelated purposes imposed by the interpretation, which shows whatever is interpreted as being the best of its kind. In the more detailed general description of interpretation, he writes of "some general justification" for the practice (ibid.). A general justification can be monistic, exhibiting a high degree of coherence, but it need not be. It may be of any degree of coherence down to pluralistic justifications by a plurality of unrelated elements. The evidence is ambiguous, tending on balance to support an unargued-for endorsement of monistic coherence where the interpretation of social practices is concerned.[3]

The tendency toward strong coherence seems to reappear when Dworkin introduces integrity:

> It will be useful to divide the claims of integrity into two more practical principles. The first is the principle of integrity in legislation, which asks those who create law by legislation to keep that law coherent in principle. The second is the principle of integrity in adjudication: it asks those responsible for deciding what the law is to see and enforce it as coherent in that way. (p. 167)

Dworkin's first principle is to guide legislators in making law. My concern is with the second principle, which determines both how cases are to be decided and what the law is, because, according to Dworkin, these two question are one and the same. How the courts should determine the law is far from clear from this statement. What stands out is the duty to see the law as coherent. But does the principle as stated really express an endorsement of coherence? It seems to do so because the word appears in its formulation. We know, however, that coherence is often used to indicate no more than the cogency or even the intelligibility of a principle or an idea. Which way does Dworkin mean to use it? Dworkin's earlier discussion of interpretation, which, to be any good, must be understood to lead to a strongly, monistically coherent view of interpretation, suggests that he means something similar here.

But does he? A few pages later he states (discussing integrity in legislation): "Integrity is flouted . . . whenever a community enacts and enforces different laws each of which is coherent in itself, but which cannot be defended together as expressing a coherent ranking of different principles of justice or fairness or procedural due process" (p. 184). There is no trace of one point or purpose here. The degree of coherence is much less; it is merely that of ranking a plurality of irreducibly distinct principles of justice and fairness. This is still a commitment to a greater degree of coherence than exists, given that, in fact, such principles are not rankable. My purpose is simply to point out the difficulty in attributing any definite view on coherence to Dworkin.

When Dworkin turns from integrity in legislation to his explanation of law as based on integrity, coherence simply drops, quietly and without comment, out of the picture: "According to law as integrity, propositions of law are true if they figure in or follow from the principles of justice, fairness, and procedural due process that provide the best constructive interpretation of the community's legal practice" (p. 225). It is inconceivable that Dworkin would have allowed coherence to disappear without explanation had he been genuinely committed to it. It is especially important to remember that there is nothing in *Law's Empire* to suggest that the principles of justice are not themselves irreducibly plural, and the same is true of fairness and procedural due process.

I suggest, therefore, that his is not a coherence explanation of either law or integrity. His position is as explained in the previous quotation: the law consists of those principles of justice and fairness and procedural due process that provide the best (i.e., morally best) set of sound principles capable of explaining the legal decisions taken throughout the history of the polity in question. Whether or not such principles display any degree of coherence, in the sense of interdependence, is an open question. Thus while coherence may be a by-product of the best theory of law, a preference for coherence is not part of the desiderata by which the best theory is determined. The reason for thinking that Dworkin is not at all committed to the desirability of coherence is that his text is ambivalent and that, while Dworkin argues at length that interpretations are necessarily evaluative, and that they try to show their object as the best of its kind, and that the interpretation of the law is committed to integrity, he never provides any reason whatsoever to suggest that coherence is a desideratum in correct interpretations.

Three objections may be raised to the conclusion that Dworkin's theory of law contains no commitment to any degree of coherence. First, in the quotation above, while coherence is not specifically mentioned, it is implied in the reference to "constructive interpretation," for, as we saw above, interpretation must, according to Dworkin, be not only coherent but monistic. This would be a decisive argument but for the fact that Dworkin's commitment to a monistic view of interpretation must itself be questionable, partly on textual grounds, partly because it is so unlikely that he would have committed himself to such an initially implausible view without even a shadow of an argument to support it.

Second, it may be argued that while integrity (in adjudication) itself is not committed to coherence, this does not show that either the law or adjudication need not be based on a set of principles displaying tight coherence, because integrity is only one element in law and adjudication. This is a matter of some delicacy. Clearly, integrity is not a conclusive ground for good legislation. While legislators should value integrity for its own sake, they may find that other considerations prevail and thus may compromise it (pp. 181, 217). The adjudicative principle of integrity has, however, a different status from that of the legislative principle. On the one hand, it is a principle about how courts should decide cases. On the other hand, it is a principle identifying the grounds of law (p. 218) and, as such, is the touchstone distinguishing what is the law from what is not (p. 225). As a principle about how the courts should decide cases it is merely *prima facie* (p. 218), and there may be cases in which the courts ought not to compromise justice and fairness for the sake of integrity. But in the second capacity it is definitive. Rules that do not pass the test of integrity are not part of the law.

The two aspects of the principle are consistent. It merely means that sometimes courts ought not to decide cases on the basis of the law, but that they should overturn it and lay down a different rule. Less clear, however, is whether this imperative – the requirement that judges go against the law when it calls for too great a sacrifice of justice for the sake of integrity – is a legal or a nonlegal one. That is, does *Law's Empire* recognize a legal duty on the courts to decide cases on appropriate occasions by transcending the law, or does the book hold that legally the courts ought always to apply the law, but morally they sometimes should not do so? Most theorists agree that the latter is sometimes the case. Many legal theorists believe that the former is always the case, though not normally for the reasons indicated in *Law's Empire*. When courts are legally required to apply nonlegal considerations they are commonly said to have discretion.[4] Dworkin has first distinguished himself as a legal theorist who denies that courts are ever legally required or permitted to do anything other than apply the law (to the facts). It therefore would seem that, while he holds that courts always have and sometimes should exercise moral discretion to transcend the law, they are never legally allowed to do so. This position indicates a major development in Dworkin's views. In the past he had no independent theory of law. Unlike theorists like H. L. A. Hart, Hans Kelsen, and others who distinguish between (1) "what is the law?" and (2) "what considerations should guide courts in deciding cases?" and hold that the answer to the second includes more than the law, Dworkin has always identified the two questions. His theory of adjudication was his theory of law. The answer to the question what considerations should guide courts in deciding cases answers the question of what is the law. Given that assumption,[5] courts have no discretion and must always obey the law. In *Law's Empire*, a new position emerges. We have a concept of law that is totally independent of any reference to adjudication.[6] This leaves room for the possibility of discretion. As we saw, Dworkin allows that such discretion exists. He still seems to differ from other theorists, however, in thinking that in exercising discretion courts violate the law. But that is a moot point. First, he does not explicitly say this. Second, because according to *Law's Empire* the reasons to deviate from the law are open moral reasons that guide the action of the courts in appropriate circumstances, it is not clear why the law should not be understood to sanction them. Even writers like myself and others whose understanding of the law allows room for the role of extralegal considerations in adjudication hold that the law recognizes the practice of resorting to them, a recognition that is expressed in the very fact that courts do so openly and without any legislation or directive to stop them. In the past, Dworkin has suggested that there be no resort to extralegal considerations in adjudication. There was never a strong argument to justify this, and he does not repeat this claim in *Law's Empire*. It is now moot whether and why Dworkin does not accept judicial discretion as legal practice. Be that as it may, given that the requirement to go against integrity is a requirement to go against the law, there is nothing we can learn from it about the degree of coherence in the law.

I have to admit that there are further unclarities in the position advocated in *Law's Empire*. In the course of Dworkin's extensive discussion of the *McLoughlin* case,[7] he says "but here . . . questions of fit surface again, because an interpretation is *pro tanto* more satisfactory if it shows less damage to integrity than its rival. [The judge] will therefore consider whether interpretation (5) fits the expanded legal record better than (6)" (pp. 246–7). This seems to imply that integrity is a matter of achieving the greatest possible fit with past legal records. We know from the general discussion that fit is but one of two dimensions that identify the law. The other is value. If so, then integrity is but one, and not – according to *Law's Empire* – a lexically prior consideration in determining the content of the law and what the courts may legally be required to do. Hence it may well be that Dworkin regards the law as much more coherent than his commitment to integrity would suggest, for it may be that the combination of the two dimensions will make it so. But this line of thinking gives undue weight to the one text in which Dworkin equates integrity with fit. It seems best to disregard it.

The third and final objection to my earlier conclusion that *Law's Empire* assigns no importance to coherence in the law is that my arguments turn on close textual analysis. This, according to the objection, is the wrong attitude toward the understanding of a book that does not carefully formulate the views it advocates. The general feel of the book suggests that coherence is to be striven for. Perhaps it is impossible to say in advance what degree of coherence is to be achieved. But the drift of the argument suggests that coherence is a distinctive advantage, and that therefore one should strive to end up with a view of the law that regards it as coherent as possible, provided not too much violence is done to other values.

There is something to this point. The position it assigns to *Law's Empire* is explicitly advocated by Hurley,[8] who seems to think that she is following Dworkin with regard to the law. The difficulty is that Dworkin provides no argument to support that position, unless the suggestion is made that the arguments for integrity are also meant to be arguments for coherence.[9] If so, then they have been dealt with above. My feeling that Dworkin does not regard coherence, as understood here, as a virtue at all is strengthened by his use of the term at times to convey other ideas, and by his belief in the virtue of coherence when understood in some of those other ways. He believes that the law is coherent = intelligible, he believes that the law is coherent = holistic, and, more distinctively, he believes that the law speaks with one voice (on the strength of the argument canvassed in Part V of "The Relevance of Coherence"). There I took that requirement to imply at least a preference for coherence = unity. But there is no sign that Dworkin does so, nor is there any reason to do so. Speaking with one voice may mean no more than that the law is not arbitrary nor reflects changes of mind or policy. For Dworkin, "speaking with one voice" means also that the law does not reflect compromises among people or factions. Whatever "speaking with one voice" means in Dworkin's writings, it can be represented as "coherence," and it is a way of employing "coherence" unrelated to the concerns explored here. Finally, "coherence" is sometimes used by him to indicate fitting the historical record.[10] This again has nothing to do with coherence as explored here. None of this shows that Dworkin does not regard coherence as unity as desirable. The degree to which, and the reasons for which, *Law's Empire* is committed to coherence must remain moot.

But if I am right in the main conclusion above, namely that there is nothing in the book's advocacy of what Dworkin calls interpretation and integrity to require an endorsement of, or any presumption in favor of, coherence, does this not undermine my own criticism of the value of Dworkinian integrity offered above? Not so. My criticism of integrity is valid even if integrity is not taken to support coherence. It relies on one feature of integrity only: that it advocates acting on principles that may never have been considered or approved, either explicitly or implicitly, by any legal authority, and that are inferior to some alternatives in justice and in fairness. The objections I raised were to this as groundless in morality and as deriving from a desire to see the law, and judicial activities, as based to a larger degree than they are in fact, or should be in morality, on an inner legal logic which is separate from ordinary moral and political considerations of the kind that govern normal government, in all its branches.

Acknowledgement

This chapter is an edited version of the Appendix to Joseph Raz, "The Relevance of Coherence" first published in the *Boston University Law Review*, vol. 72, March 1992, pp. 273 ff. and reprinted in Raz, *Ethics in the Public Domain: Essays in the Morality of Law and Politics* (Oxford: Clarendon Press, 1994) as chapter 13. The Appendix is at pp. 319–25. I am grateful to Brian Bix, Penelope Bulloch, Michael Harper, Robert Bone, Avishai Margalit, Sidney Morgenbesser, and Kenneth Simons for comments on earlier drafts.

Notes

1   See Part IV of "The Relevance of Coherence," in *Ethics in the Public Domain*, op cit., pp. 295–301.

2   Ronald Dworkin, *Law's Empire* (Cambridge, MA: Harvard University Press, 1986), p. 52. Page references in the text and notes are to this book unless otherwise specified.

3   For several additional references to one purpose in *Law's Empire*, see pp. 67, 87, 94, 98. Other locutions, however, are more open to pluralistic justifications.

4   The term does not mean that they can do what they like. Its meaning in the debates in legal theory is that courts are entrusted with more than applying the law. Their task – their legally appointed task – includes power to revise and develop the law, which they do with guidance from legal standards that direct them to step beyond the bounds of the law and apply moral considerations.

5   I call it an assumption as Dworkin has never argued for it. It may seem that he has not realized, at least not at the beginning, that it is this point that he disputes in the work of Hart and others; i.e., he may not have realized that once this assumption is granted the question of whether courts enjoy discretion is settled. Of course, if everything they can take into account is the law, they do not have (so-called strong) discretion to go outside the law. See Raz, Postscript to "Legal Principles and the Limits of Law,"

in M. Cohen (ed.), *Dworkin and Contemporary Jurisprudence* (Totowa, NJ: Rowman and Allanheld, 1984), pp. 81–6; chapter 8 of *Ethics in the Public Domain*, op. cit.

6   Dworkin states: "The law of a community . . . is the scheme of rights and responsibilities that meet that complex standard: they license coercion because they flow from past decisions of the right sort" (p. 93).

7   *McLoughlin v. O'Brian*, 1 App. Cas. 410 (1983).

8   Susan Hurley, *Natural Reasons* (New York and Oxford: Oxford University Press,1989), p. 262.

9   This is indeed Hurley's view. Ibid, pp. 262–3.

10   See Raz, "The Relevance of Coherence," op. cit., pp. 280–2; ibid., p. 280, n. 8.

16

Integrity: Justice in Workclothes

Gerald J. Postema

In common-law practice, precedent is said to be binding, albeit not absolutely. Extensions or restrictions of the rules of past decisions are made by appeal to the principles underlying those and related decisions. When the underlying principles recommend themselves to our reasonable moral judgment, decisions grounded in those principles also receive our approval. In that case, the fact that a particular decision is an application or extension of a precedent might seem to play no essential justifying role. We might even be inclined to say, with Fred Schauer, that precedent matters "when and only when the precedent (as perceived by the current decision-maker) is mistaken – only when past wrong decisions can provide reasons for decision despite their wrongness, and therefore precisely and only because of their pastness."[1] This may overstate the point somewhat, but it highlights an initially puzzling feature of common-law reasoning: precedent seems to claim allegiance just when it least deserves it. The puzzling phenomenon disappears immediately, of course, if we deny legal precedent any moral force whatsoever. Law, we might say, claims allegiance to precedent, but this claim is morally groundless. However, this response dissolves rather than solves its puzzle. The puzzle arises precisely because we grant that precedents, at least sometimes, have moral as well as legal force, despite the fact that the precedent decision is morally wrong.

It is tempting to express the puzzle this way: according to common-law practice, decision makers must follow *morally incorrect* principles, and, insofar as we seek to provide normative grounding for common-law practice, we are committed to the view that decision makers are *morally required to follow morally incorrect principles*. This is a paradox, if not a simple contradiction, is it not? No, it is neither; it is just an unfortunate and misleading way of putting an otherwise plausible and important point about reasoning from precedent. The point is that, morally speaking, prior decisions, especially prior official decisions, are relevant and often decisive for the proper decision of present cases, even if the prior decisions are themselves open to reasonable objection. This substantive moral point, which common-law jurisdictions institutionalize in the doctrine of *stare decisis*, needs an argument in its defense. But when the moral force of precedent is debated, the fundamental issue disputed is not whether past decisions alter the present decisional landscape, but rather how and to what extent they do so. The controversy is not about whether the best decision in the present case can be found by ignoring the past-determined context of the case, but rather about how to understand and account for the normative relevance of the past.

Broadly speaking, there are two ways to represent or attempt to account for the normative relevance of past decisions. The first we might call the "external justification" or "externalist" account.[2] On this view, the past decision is relevant because it, or the rule for which it stands, has important *causal* effects, especially effects on the beliefs and behavior of citizens and officials. For example, citizens rely on expectations encouraged by judicial decisions; hence, citizen confidence in the judiciary is enhanced by conformity and weakened by lack of conformity to precedent. Conformity to precedent also enhances predictability and the institutional efficiency of official decision making.

Although most externalist arguments are predominantly consequentialist, some may have strong deontological elements, for example, the argument that it is unfair to defeat legitimate expectations. All externalist arguments disregard entirely the merits or normative grounds of the decisions and focus instead on the "content-independent," and in that sense "external," features of precedential decisions. This content independence makes it easy to explain the apparent puzzle of the moral force of precedent mentioned above: even mistaken past decisions may have moral force by virtue of their content-independent features. If we were inclined to express ourselves paradoxically, we might say that judges are morally required to do the morally wrong thing, except that the decision would be "morally wrong" only when viewed superficially, ignoring the moral significance of the fact of the decision and its effect on the present context of decision making.

The alternative, "internal justification" or "internalist" approach may be the dominant methodology in the practice of Anglo-American law.[3] The internalist approach takes into account the fact of the past decision and its causal or external consequences, but it also looks to the reason or rationale of the decision (which need not be the rationale articulated in the court's opinion). The internalist's aim is to find a sound reason *for the rule* of the precedent case, not merely a sound reason for acting in *accord with* the rule. Justification for following the precedent is sought (in part) in the rule itself and in the rational appeal of the deeper principle that it can be seen to serve. This principle explains, in Dworkin's familiar terminology, a precedent's "gravitational force" – why the precedent binds both in its "explicit extension" and beyond it.[4]

However, the internalist must explain how precedent can bind not only when it is judged to be legally and morally correct, but also when it is questionable or even judged wrong on the merits. For if the decision is morally mistaken, then the principle on which it rests must be morally mistaken as well. But how can a mistaken principle *justify* a subsequent decision? Our original puzzle about the moral force of precedent seems to have returned. Alexander and Kress argue that the internalist sets us on the track of the morally best morally incorrect principles, which is a paradoxical, if not an unintelligible, quest.[5]

We might seek to dispel the paradox by making the quest self-consciously counterfactual.[6] The aim of common-law reasoning, it might be said, is to identify those principles "that would be correct moral principles in a world in which most of the extant legal rules and decisions, including those that are in fact morally incorrect, were morally correct."[7]

On this view, an incorrectly decided case binds courts in subsequent cases because, in a world in which the precedent case were correct, analogous decisions in subsequent cases would also be correct. However, internalists must regard this as an unfriendly suggestion, because it fails to explain the morally binding force of precedent. Just as hypothetical agreements are not agreements, so counterfactual justifications of this kind are not justifications. If the world *were* as we might counterfactually stipulate, we might *then* have reason to follow the precedent case, but this gives no one any reason to do so in the *actual* world. Furthermore, by cutting the tether to the actual world, and to actual moral principles and the judgments they inform, the counterfactual methodology makes it impossible to identify the principle of the precedent case or even a relatively small set of alternative principles. On this counterfactual understanding, the "moral appeal" dimension of Dworkin's interpretive methodology collapses into the "fit" dimension with no remainder, for an indefinite number of (counterfactually morally correct) principles can be shown to "fit" the precedent case. Thus the internalist approach is emptied of all content on this counterfactual interpretation.

Ronald Dworkin proposes an alternative resolution of the apparent paradox that Alexander and Kress charge to the internalist's account. He claims that precedent cases have binding, gravitational force because they are governed by and are in service of a political value he calls *integrity*.[8] Although integrity is closely related to justice, the two are distinct. According to Dworkin, integrity is a *bona fide*, real-world value of political morality that grounds binding obligations on moral agents, especially legal officials. However, the notion of integrity is controversial; many deny there is such a political value. Alexander and Kress are prominent among the integrity skeptics. Although I will not take the time to demonstrate this here, I believe that all the arguments that make up their case against legal principles can be reduced to, or rest essentially upon, the claim that there simply is no good reason to recognize integrity as an intelligible value of political morality.

I disagree. Integrity is an important value of political morality – perhaps the most immediately important such value governing law and its administration – although I fully agree with skeptics that a compelling case for integrity has not yet been offered. The aim of this essay is to construct a case for integrity, and in doing so provide an argument for the internalist approach to the moral force of precedent. I draw liberally on Dworkin's discussion of integrity, but my argument is not a reconstruction of Dworkin's. Indeed, at some crucial points my conception of integrity departs from Dworkin's, and my argument takes a rather different route from his. Nevertheless, both my conception of integrity and my argument for it remain akin to Dworkin's, close enough at least to count as a defense of what Alexander and Kress and their fellow skeptics deny.

I   Integrity: The Notion

Integrity and the concept of law

The value of integrity has a respected, if sometimes contested, place in interpersonal morality.[9] The question I want to address, however, is whether it should be placed alongside values like justice, fairness, liberty, equality, community, benevolence, and desert as an important constituent of *political* morality. More specifically, I am interested in whether integrity provides us with standards distinct from those provided by the other political values, standards by which we must assess our law and its interpretation and application.

To fix the notion of integrity, we must first consider some very general features of law, features of what Dworkin calls "the concept of law."[10] Broadly speaking, law is a pervasive social institution or practice which provides a framework of practical reasoning for individual citizens and for society as a whole acting through government officials. The distinctive feature of this framework is that officials and citizens alike seek to justify their actions by appeal to rules or principles drawn from past political decisions of the community, as recorded in the books and reflected in the practices of its law. So conceived, law serves at least two broad social goals: (1) to facilitate and coordinate the pursuit of both the common goals of the community and the goals of its members, and (2) especially where the exercise of coercion is involved, to constrain the community and its members to actions and policies consistent with public principles. The rules, precedents, and principles of law ground reciprocal obligations between the community and its members and define a framework by which the government is held accountable to citizens and citizens are held accountable to each other.

This concept of law defines integrity's career. Integrity gives specific content to the abstract legal notion that present official or private actions are warranted by the past through *principles* derived from past decisions. Integrity explains *how* past political decisions yield present practical directives. It also purports to provide rational support for this generative capacity by linking law's project, understood in terms supplied by integrity, to more fundamental values of political morality. That is, it purports to explain why such directives are normative for officials and citizens. So integrity claims to be more than merely a method or technique of practical reasoning specially adapted to law's distinctive tasks; it also claims to be a substantive value of political morality. Although distinct from other political values, it takes its moral focus and force from the service it renders more fundamental values, in particular justice and fidelity.

The core idea of integrity

In this context, the core idea of integrity is coherence of action and of principle. To legitimate the actions of the community and its members, the principles drawn from past decisions and actions of the community must (in the ideal case) express a unified, common, and relatively comprehensive vision of justice for the community.[11] Integrity demands that, through its officials, the community act on a coherent set of principles of justice even when its citizens disagree about what the correct principles of justice are.[12] We can identify several important components of this core idea of integrity.

First, integrity is a norm of *unification* called forth by a more fundamental social *unity*. Dworkin insists that those who are bound by integrity must view the community as if it were a single individual moral agent.[13] This personification of the community, however, is not a deep feature of the notion of integrity; it is merely a heuristic device. Yet, as such, it gives expression to the important and deep assumption of the unity of the community. The demand for integrity arises only when the decisions and actions of a community and its members, viewed both synchronically and diachronically, are internally related, that is, as potentially in harmony or in conflict, as extending or qualifying each other, and as bearing on the meaning and affecting the practical force of each other. For only when this is the case can there arise an intelligible demand for their *unification* into a scheme that relates them to a common, albeit complex, set of themes, purposes, or principles. That is to say, integrity *assumes* there is some compelling moral reason for treating the various actions and decisions as unified in this way, namely, as internally related and thus needing unification. The reason will have to be one of political morality (as opposed to a metaphysical, epistemological, or prudential practical reason). Where we do not have sufficient reason to regard these actions and decisions as internally related – where we lack reason to treat their agents as forming a single community calling for unification – integrity has no place, just as considerations of loyalty and friendship have no place between strangers.

Second, integrity also calls for *internal justification*. Integrity maintains that the obligations, responsibilities, and rights of citizens and officials go beyond the explicit extension of the community's settled rules. It also maintains that past decisions and actions not only have "external effect" or causal traces, but also generate or bring to bear norms or principles drawn from those past decisions and actions and its settled rules.

Third, the principles sought by integrity are principles of *justice*. The concept of justice gives shape and direction to integrity's quest for principled unity of the community's past and present. "Justice," as I shall use it, is meant to include all that falls under the terms "justice," "fairness," and "due process," as Dworkin defined those terms in *Law's Empire*.[14] While relatively broad, this notion of justice is limited by the fact that our focus is on the integrity of law in the context of political society. Thus justice in and of the community is integrity's guiding star.

Fourth, integrity calls on officials and citizens to view their practice as the expression of a *coherent* set of principles, but the notion of coherence I use here is a deliberately weak one. It merely signifies an intelligibility, a unity of vision, under the notion of justice. It is not meant to invoke other, more precise or technical notions of coherence. In particular, it does not require that the principles must be reducible to a single master principle (monism) or a set of formally ranked principles. Nor does coherence suggest that the principles must each entail, imply, or justify each other. This kind of coherence can obtain among distinct and irreducible principles which may even conflict in specific cases from time to time. The "unification" that integrity seeks is just the weak constraint on a set of principles requiring them to fit together into an intelligible, practically and morally meaningful whole under the concept of justice.[15] Coherence of this sort is not a logical or quasi-logical notion like consistency or mutual entailment. Rather, it is a morally substantive notion and it is always judged, and must always be defended, on substantive grounds. Most importantly, integrity does not assume that coherence is desirable in itself such that the more coherent a set of principles is (as measured along one of the previously mentioned, more or less formal scales), the greater is the integrity of the practice in question. Finally, integrity regards coherence as an *ideal*, a normative *project*. Thus, our best efforts may only achieve an approximation of coherence. This is especially true of law. Oliver Wendell Holmes pressed this point against C. C. Langdell and the formalists of his day. Law, he maintained, "is always approaching and never reaching consistency. It is forever adopting new principles for life at one end, and it always retains old ones from history at the other, which have not been absorbed or sloughed off. It will become entirely consistent only when it ceases to grow."[16]

Fifth, integrity is essentially *historical*. Integrity seeks to forge a common vision of justice from the past public decisions and actions of the community. The search for principles of justice undertaken in the name of integrity is historically situated; integrity takes past decisions and actions as its point of departure and normative compass. Our past practice bears the shape of our common life, while forcing us to address the question of what this shape is.

Sixth, integrity requires officials and citizens to seek *common*, *public* principles of justice in their common past. The exercise of practical reasoning disciplined by integrity is a common, public activity – an activity of the community as a whole and of its members regarding themselves as members.[17] In her 1997 Carus Lectures, Annette Baier spoke of the social nature of reasoning, especially practical reasoning, as "a commons of the mind."[18] Her metaphor is even more apt for the political past, as reported and recorded in the books and reflected in the practice of law. Past actions and decisions provide a kind of commons, a common resource and inheritance, available to each member, not for merely private purposes, however noble, but for the purpose of forging a common just future.

The present conception of integrity departs from Dworkin's original notion at this point. According to Dworkin, the attitude of integrity is "a protestant attitude that makes each citizen responsible for imagining what his society's public commitments to principles are, and what these commitments require in new circumstances."[19] This "protestant" attitude, while rightly highlighting individual responsibility, ignores the interactive, public character of the practical reasoning demanded by integrity.[20] Dworkin himself observes at one point that "the community as a whole and not just individual officials one by one must act in a principled way."[21] That is correct, I believe, but I would add that the community achieves integrity only when its members seek *as a community* to act from a coherent vision of justice.

Integrity and regret

Finally, integrity is hollow and fraudulent if it does not balance *respect* for past practice with a more self-critical attitude which I will call *regret*.[22] Integrity calls for responsible coherence of action and principle. This makes it a complex virtue, for it calls for coherence of principle, coherence of action with principle, *and* appropriate responses to departures from each. Integrity, or its failure, are often most evident in the manner in which we seek to restore equilibrium between action and principle. As Lynne McFall reminded us, "[a] person who admits to having succumbed to temptation has more integrity than the person who sells out, [and] then fixes the books. . . ."[23] Integrity sometimes calls for recognizing violations of principle, resisting the temptation to abandon or rearticulate the principle to accommodate the violation, and responsibly acting to restore the equilibrium. Thus, when integrity calls on us to determine what our common past practice commits us to now and in the future, we must responsibly balance respect for our past practice with appropriate regret for it. We cannot simply hold fixed our principles and self-deceptive high ideals and refuse to take responsibility for actions that fail to conform to them; nor can we simply take the actions of the past as fixed – as coherent expressions of principle – and ask only what principles these actions serve. Integrity demands that we recognize the possibility of hypocrisy at both of these levels and that we act on sound judgment in response to it.

Dworkin's notion of integrity does not rule out this complexity, although sometimes his interpretive project of "showing the practice in its best light" seems to lose sight of the dimension of regret.[24] At times, Dworkin's "interpreter" seems more like an outside observer seeking a charitable *explanation* of the community's behavior than a member of that community taking responsibility with others for their practice. Dworkin's interpreter treats elements of the practice that do not fit the interpretation merely as others, "mistakes" perhaps, but not integral features of past practice with the same moral significance for the present as duly accounted for elements. However, this is not the attitude of a responsible participant in the practice, or member of the community whose practice it is, let alone that of a responsible official speaking and acting for that community. Nietzsche warned that "as long as the past must be described as something worthy of imitation, . . . so long, at least, is the past in danger of being somewhat distorted, of being reinterpreted according to aesthetic criteria and so brought closer to fiction. . . ."[25] Without regret, interpretation of our past becomes disengaged and aesthetic at best, and celebratory revisionist history at worst.

In the context of law, regret involves two related responses to problematic decisions, rules, or actions of the past. First, it involves isolating the offending items from the body of legal materials of the polity and limiting the influence of the offending items on the principles drawn from them in the name of integrity, thereby limiting their contribution to the guidance and justification of decisions and actions in the present.[26] This limiting of the normative influence of past decisions and rules can take a variety of more or less drastic forms, ranging from localizing their influence to some specific area of the law where its influence is less pernicious, to restricting the decisions to its narrowest terms (for example, to cases "on all fours" with it), to draining it of all normative force by reversing or overruling the decision. Second, regret also involves acknowledging, and in appropriate ways correcting and compensating for, the legacy of the offending rules or decisions in the body of law itself and in the lives of those who have suffered under them. Integrity calls for sensitive judgment to determine the just balance of respect and regret regarding the past, and in determining the appropriate response of regret in its two dimensions.

Insofar as regret calls for some form of localizing short of eliminating the normative influence of offending rules or decisions of the past it compromises to some extent the law's coherence. It may not be possible to integrate completely into an intelligible vision of justice elements of our recorded political past which nevertheless exert some normative force on present decisions. Where regret is indicated, what Raz calls the "global coherence" of law is likely to be compromised.[27] Raz is highly critical of accounts of law that insist on global coherence, while he recognizes the importance of some kinds of "local coherence."[28] However, in contrast to this notion of islands of local coherence in a globally noncoherent body of law, integrity admits islands of compromised coherence in a body of law that strives still for coherence. It is important to stress that these compromises of coherence do not pose a challenge to integrity. They are the product of regret which is an essential component of integrity. So the balance of respect and regret, and regret's determination of the kind and extent of isolation of offending rules and decisions of the past, are matters determined within and in the service of integrity. Because integrity is an important moral value, this balance is a moral balance; however, it is not a balance, all moral things considered, of concern for the past with other distinct morally relevant considerations. The principles in the name of which regret is exercised are drawn not from some account of morality considered independently of the past decisions, rules, and actions of the polity, but from principles embedded in them.

Thus complex integrity forces us to make room for the kind of deeply upsetting argument that Frederick Douglass made in his *Fourth of July Oration of 1852*,[29] "What have I, or those I represent to do with your national independence?" he asked.

> The existence of slavery in this country brands your republicanism as a sham, your humanity as a base pretense, and your Christianity as a lie. . . . Are the great principles of political freedom and natural justice, embodied in the Declaration of Independence, extended to us? . . . This Fourth of July is *yours* not *mine*. You may rejoice, I must mourn.[30]

The power of this argument comes directly from the fact that it appeals to principles historically professed, but only partially practiced. Integrity, however, requires that we view and take responsibility for our *whole* past, not just the agreeable parts. It requires that we establish coherence of action with professed principle, not by accommodating the violation by adjusting the principle, but by adjusting the practice and forcing it in new directions.

Joseph Raz recently criticized coherence theories of adjudication, and integrity theories to the extent they depend on coherence, for "idealiz[ing] the law out of the concreteness of politics."[31] "The reality of politics leaves law untidy," he argues.[32] Coherence theories, however,

> attempt to prettify it and minimize the effect of politics. . . . But, in countries with decent constitutions, the untidiness of politics is morally sanctioned . . . by the morality of authoritative institutions. There is no reason to minimize its effects, nor to impose on the courts duties which lead them to be less just than they can be.[33]

However apt Raz's criticism may be of simpler coherence theories of adjudication, it should be clear that his charge of "idealizing the law out of the concreteness of politics" cannot be laid at the door of a notion of integrity that demands a proper balance of respect and regret for the past. There is nothing pretty or idealized about the kind of argument Douglass mounted, an argument that calls for integrity of the more complex kind I have urged. Indeed, I will argue the complex integrity that I have described operates in and on the untidy reality of politics.

In defense of integrity

Thus far I have only sketched a cartoon of the notion of integrity I wish to defend. Far more detail can be drawn in to make the picture complete, and in those details lie many devilish difficulties. Yet I propose to proceed boldly on the assumption that each of the devils can be met and ultimately subdued. My task is to try to defend the notion I have roughly sketched above, leaving to other hands the task of drawing in its details. Let me make clear, however, that my aim is to answer challenges to the intelligibility of integrity as a value of political morality. In the concluding section, I will argue for the relevance of this value to law, but my aim is not to defend in this essay an integrity theory of (the nature of) law, let alone Dworkin's own "law as integrity" theory. What I have to say here may be useful for that project, but it is not my project here. I will be satisfied if I can make a persuasive case for the moral importance of integrity.[34]

Integrity assumes, but does not itself demonstrate, the truth of three claims. First, integrity presupposes that the various actions and decisions of people have sufficient unity – that they are actions of a community – such that they call for the kind of normative unification that integrity sets as a project for the community's members. Second, integrity assumes that justice is public and political such that integrity's project is not individual, but communal. And third, integrity rests on the assumption that the community's past is normative for its present and future. Regarding the first assumption, the task is not to demonstrate its truth, but rather to identify those conditions that must obtain for it to be true in any particular group of people. This is a difficult and important task on which there has been very little work. However, I will not undertake this task here, as I suspect that the source of skepticism about the place of integrity in political morality lies elsewhere. Skepticism can be traced to the second and third assumptions. Thus my defense of integrity will focus on the political and historical character of integrity, and thus on its links to *justice* and *fidelity*, the two more fundamental values of political morality that integrity serves. My defense of integrity as an important value governing law will succeed if I can show (1) that justice is public and political in the way integrity assumes; (2) that, in communities meeting the conditions of unity presupposed by integrity, the past is normative for them in the complex way integrity describes; and (3) that law is governed by integrity so understood. These tasks structure the remainder of this essay.

II   Integrity and Justice

Distinct but closely related

Dworkin insists that integrity is an independent value of political morality, distinct from justice and fairness.[35] His claim does not rest on an argument that these values are rooted in fundamentally different moral concerns, as one might argue in the case of justice and benevolence.[36] Rather, he appeals to the possibility of conflict between them and the thought that in some cases it is right for integrity to prevail, but that in other cases the injustice of the decision or rule recommended by integrity may be so great that its moral claim is utterly defeated.

Many integrity skeptics argue against Dworkin that either integrity is simply parasitic on justice and so not a distinct virtue, or distinct but not a recognizable moral value at all.[37] Critics argue that although integrity requires principled consistency, the principles are either morally correct principles of justice, in which case integrity simply is justice, or they are morally objectionable and so cannot claim our allegiance. But this argument identifies integrity with a merely formal notion of justice or equality and does not apply to the richer notion of integrity described in the previous section. On the basis of this argument alone, then, it would be a mistake to conclude that there is no fundamental difference between integrity and justice.

Yet even Dworkin admits that these values are closely related on some deeper level:

> We accept integrity as a political ideal because we want to treat our political community as one of principle, and the citizens of a community of principle aim not simply at common principles, as if uniformity were all they wanted, but the best common principles politics can find. Integrity is distinct from justice and fairness, but it is bound to them in that way: integrity *makes no sense* except among people who want fairness and justice as well.[38]

According to Dworkin, the quest for integrity is linked closely to the pursuit of justice. What is the nature of this relationship?

The circumstances of integrity

Integrity, I shall argue, is justice in a certain guise: justice in political workclothes. But, if they are related in this way, how can justice override, let alone utterly defeat, demands of integrity? Taking a cue from Jeremy Waldron, I suggest that the answer can be found in what he calls "the circumstances of integrity."[39] Recall that, according to Rawls and Hume, the circumstances of *justice* are those general features of human beings and their natural and social environments in which alone justice has a point – conditions in which alone justice is both necessary and possible.[40] There is a rough analogy between the circumstances of justice and the operating conditions of a thermostat. Thermostats regulate temperatures in a building, but they work only within a certain range of temperatures. Beyond that range, they cannot function and are liable to melt or freeze.[41] Where the circumstances of justice are not found, intelligible questions of justice do not arise and demands for justice lose their point. Where they are found, there is reason to press for justice and to hope that it might be achieved. Moreover, these circumstances broadly define the task that justice must perform. In Hume's familiar formulation, the circumstances of justice fall somewhere between a utopia, in which there is no scarcity of resources or conflict of interests regarding the use of the resources, and a dystopia of radical scarcity or radically opposed and irresolvable conflicts of interest.[42]

Likewise, Waldron suggests that the "circumstances of integrity" are conditions that make possible and define the practical task of integrity.[43] These circumstances also fall between utopian and dystopian extremes. In a community where officials and citizens hold basically the same views regarding justice, and their institutions largely conform to these views, integrity has no place. This is the utopian extreme relative to the circumstances of justice. The dystopian extreme can take one of three forms: (1) there may be no community among a scattered and divided group of people or at least not enough unity to warrant a search for a common framework of justice; or (2) there may be some hope for such community, but the rules, decisions, and standards of the community are not merely "untidy," but hopelessly and irremediably chaotic; or (3) while they may not be chaotic – indeed, they may be rationally ordered to a high degree and terrifyingly efficient – they are deeply and irremediably corrupt and unjust, not in merely this or that case but pervasively.

From this artlessly presented list a writer with Hume's literary skills could fashion a tale of social life in which integrity would no longer have a rational or moral point. It is not that in such conditions life would be devoid of integrity and be the worse for it, but rather that in such conditions there would no longer be reason to seek integrity. The moral of such a tale would suggest the essential circumstances of integrity – those conditions of human beings and their social and natural environments in which there would be a point to the pursuit of integrity. Among those conditions we would find the following. First, the people bound to integrity's quest live together in some sort of community with some degree of unity. Second, in this community members correctly regard it as appropriate to expect, indeed to demand, justice of their institutions and arrangements. Third, there is disagreement (possibly deep disagreement) in the community over what justice requires of citizens and their institutions. Thus, from the perspective of at least some citizens, existing institutions fail to meet standards of justice. Not only are standards of justice contested, but so are important institutions and arrangements in the community, and the resulting contest is formulated in terms of contested principles of justice. Fourth, for most citizens, however, the injustice is not so extreme that they find no moral reason for seeking to preserve the community or for working for justice in it. Finally, while the multiplicity and diversity of convictions of justice have their disparate effects on the community's institutions, these institutions are not regarded by members as irremediably chaotic.

This is the soil into which integrity sends its roots. The tale, had we told it, would show that integrity is not only historical, but also essentially political. Integrity has an intelligible role and moral force where justice is both feasible and in dispute. When justice is no longer worth seeking, or is unfeasible, or when the claims of justice are clear to all members of the community, then integrity no longer has a mission. Integrity is a virtue in the real, untidy world of politics, but we should not confuse this world with the world of Realpolitik, for integrity disciplines politics with a conscience. It charges citizens to forge and act on a coherent, common vision of justice. They must practice politics with an eye fixed on the ideal of justice. As Waldron observes, "[Integrity] is a value whose job it is to come into play when the place properly assigned to justice in the life of a community – the role of determining a proper distribution of rights and duties, burdens and benefits, etc. – turns out to have been filled by disparate and competing conceptions of justice itself."[44]

Integrity makes sense only among people who want justice, but disagree about what justice requires. In this sense, integrity depends on and serves justice. But in this real world of politics it serves justice by displacing it. When people committed to justice in their community recognize that there is a sincere, reasonable, and principled disagreement about what justice requires, the pursuit of justice changes direction.[45] In the circumstances of integrity, justice is pursued obliquely: integrity replaces justice as the primary target. It requires members of a community to ask themselves: because as a community we aspire to justice, to what justice-approximating principles are we committed in virtue of our past collective decisions? Integrity is justice in political workclothes, with its sleeves rolled up.

Justice and integrity in conflict

Despite this close relationship between justice and integrity, we can still explain the appearance of conflict between them. First, justice can appear to defeat, even extinguish, integrity's moral force in cases in which a community's practice falls below a threshold level of justice, such that there is no moral reason to seek integrity. In less extreme situations, even in normal, untidy politics, justice can appear to conflict with integrity when we think of justice abstracted from the real world of politics, and ignore the public dimension of justice.[46] In such circumstances, integrity may require one outcome and (idealized) justice another. Alexander and Kress object that integrity demands that we "abandon our moral principles,"[47] which of course is a price we may not pay. But their objection rests on a misunderstanding about what *justice itself* requires, for, in the circumstances of integrity, justice itself demands that we seek some common understanding of the requirements of justice. In those circumstances, Waldron rightly observes that, "at the level of discretion, the game is not one 'in which each tries to plant the flag of his convictions over as large a domain of power or rules as possible.' Exercises of social power must claim legitimacy in relation to the community as a whole."[48] To pursue justice in the circumstances of integrity without regard to the rest of one's community is in effect to *abandon* justice, or at least to fail in a fundamental way to understand the nature of that pursuit. Far from recommending a form of "moral alienation," as Alexander and Kress fear,[49] integrity gives proper direction and discipline to the pursuit of justice.

My aim in this section has been to explore the relationship between justice and integrity. The key claim is that integrity comes into play as a significant moral value, as a moral imperative, when there is a point to seeking justice but there is serious disagreement about what justice requires – when there is reason to forge or at least work to approximate a common conception of justice and to work for institutions and arrangements in our community that conform to it. What reason might there be to forge such a common conception? One might maintain that it is required by a principle of treating each other as equals or according each other equal respect, or perhaps the reason is simply that we desire such a community. However, the more fundamental reason to pursue a common conception of justice is that it is required by structural features of justice itself. Or so, at least, I shall now argue.

III The Public Character of Justice

My proposal for understanding integrity depends on the assumption that integrity is deeply linked to justice and that justice is essentially political in the sense that justice can only be achieved *in common*. Justice, I maintain, is not only a public good, but it is also a common product, a product of common deliberation and common action. And, I maintain, this is true not just contingently, in view of those features of the world that pursuers of justice must accommodate, but in virtue of the very structure and point of justice itself. If my case for the moral force of integrity is to succeed I must defend this assertion. I undertake to do so in this section.

The concept of justice in view

Before I begin, let me say that I do not claim that the thesis of the public and political character of justice holds for every use of the term justice. Over the centuries the term has permitted a wide variety of uses without loss of intelligibility. A systematic Aristotelian study of these uses might seek to identify a central or focal use and relate other legitimate uses to it as extensions in many directions from this common starting point. That, however, is not my task. Recognizing that there may be some uses of the generic notion that may not comport fully with my thesis[50] does not dissuade me from advancing the thesis for the exceedingly common and arguably most important use in our discussion of integrity and law. The justice I have in mind is the same justice we hope for and demand from law. It is the target we set for our law and the rule by which we measure it. To call it "legal justice," however, would narrow the notion too far, for the notion of justice I have in mind is not justice as defined by law, but justice that stands as the judge and measure of law.

By this notion, justice is right order of, and a framework of public justification in, historical communities of rational, moral persons.[51] We can isolate three essential and closely interrelated components or dimensions of justice so understood. I shall assume as common ground the claim that justice defines right order for rational moral persons. Expressed abstractly, this idea is uncontested. More controversial is the claim that justice necessarily assumes some kind of relationship or community among rational, moral persons, and that it essentially defines a framework for public justification in such a community. These are the lemmas I need to establish if I am to offer a convincing argument for the claim that justice is essentially political.

Justice in and of communities

Consider our common starting point: justice is right order of rational, moral persons. The first thing to note is that justice is not only right or rational order *of* rational, moral persons, but right order *for* them. That is, justice is a normative order, providing agents with prescriptive guides which recognize in their content and practical force that the agents are rational, moral persons. Moral persons are rational: they can order their desires and understand their natural environment enough to determine how best to fulfill those desires; they also have the self-control and deliberative capacities necessary to act effectively on this understanding. Moral persons are also social: they are dependent on each other for both material and moral survival. They must work together to satisfy their physical needs, and they depend on each other for the development and maintenance of a sense of self, of purpose, and of direction. In *The Republic*, Plato extends this notion of justice beyond the snapping point when he argues that justice is primarily a matter of relations among parts of the soul.[52] His insight is deep and important; however, his mistake was to apply this insight to the wrong entity. The insight is that justice is not merely an order imposed from the outside on otherwise unrelated parts, but is rather the proper order for things *of a kind*, thereby *constituting* the related parts as well as the whole. That is to say, justice is *constitutive* (or more modestly, partially constitutive) of rational, moral persons. By defining their relations to each other and thereby constituting the community of which they are members, justice is fundamental to the nature of rational, moral persons. Justice is right order of a certain kind of thing: of a community of rational, moral persons. It defines proper relations among members *regarded as members*.

We can put the same point in Humean terms. Justice arises as a problem and a project for rational creatures only insofar as they are materially and morally interdependent, that is, only insofar as they are related in certain ways and have the biological and psychological characteristics that make those relations necessary for survival. To speak of justice between creatures commits one to the view that they are already related, or at least potentially related, such that certain kinds of practical problems of social interaction arise and must be dealt with collectively. Justice presupposes a common stock of goods or bads that are the products of their life together which must be allocated individually. It also defines a structure of duties, rights, and responsibilities that governs interactions of individual members of the community. These essential features of justice are neatly summarized in Hume's image of a vault.[53] Benevolence, like a wall, can be built out of individual acts, no one of which is essential to the structure as a whole; however, justice, like a vault, carefully defines the relationships among all the individual parts. On the strength of these relationships, the edifice stands secure. That kind of structure is not for every kind of social interaction or social setting among human beings, but in historical communities among rational, moral persons the vault must be constructed. Only when there is reason to rightly order a *community* of moral persons does the blueprint of justice become morally relevant.

Unfortunately, it has been easy for philosophers to ignore the fact that justice is by its nature always located in, and is a kind of ordering of, human communities. This is especially tempting for those who think that basic to all forms of injustice are inequalities that are arbitrary from a moral point of view – lacking positive moral justification.[54] This leads them to infer from differences between parties for which no moral justification can be found that the relatively disadvantaged party is the victim of injustice. This, they think, is true not only in historical communities where the differences are structured into patterns of treatment that affect access to common resources, benefits, or protections, and mark inequalities in the status of members of the community, but also between parties entirely unrelated, belonging to distant and unrelated societies – for example, people on physically and historically widely separated islands between which there is no communication. Mere differences in ability to meet basic needs or develop important human capacities (so-called "natural inequalities") are thought to be unjust inequalities, which ought to be corrected in the name of justice, if correction is possible. The relative advantages and disadvantages are said to be unjust simply because they are morally arbitrary.

Sometimes arguments of this kind are advanced in defense of an egalitarian conception of justice. But we do not have to abandon egalitarianism to see the mistakes in this kind of argument. The argument rests on two confusions. The first is a confusion of justice with other grounds or kinds of moral consideration, such as humanitarian concern or benevolence. Justice is essentially comparative: it calls for a balancing of benefits or burdens – a proper and in some sense equal distribution of advantages and disadvantages. It also lays a special obligation on those who are better off to bear the burden of rectification. In contrast, benevolence or humanitarian concern are focused on human well-being and not on balancing or equalizing resources. To the extent that human beings have legitimate, serious needs and it is possible to meet them, we have reason, in the name of humanity, to undertake to meet them if it is possible. No special obligation lies on those who are better off in this respect, except for the fact that those who are better off may be able to sustain the loss better than others. In particular, no special claim to equalize the advantages and disadvantages, in the spirit of justice, lies against the advantaged parties. We can explain the intuitive moral pressure we feel when we learn of the needs of distant and unrelated people in moral terms other than justice.

The alleged injustice of "natural inequalities" also rests on a more fundamental confusion. It confuses *differences* with *inequalities*. This is a mistake even when the differences carry with them disadvantages for which there is no apparent moral justification. Differences are inequalities only when there is some relationship between the parties such that the difference is properly regarded as at least *prima facie* illegitimate, and so in need of legitimation. It is not enough to claim that there is no moral justification for the difference; the difference must be morally unjustified. A difference is *morally unjustified* only if moral justification is called for and found lacking, but not all differences call for justification. The "morally arbitrary" differences that strike us as unjustified are those that, in virtue of features of persons and their relationships, have a distinctive moral character. They are differences that make a *moral* difference when they should not. Mere differences can be identified in nonevaluative terms, but *inequalities* presuppose an evaluative standard and a context in which comparing the advantages and disadvantages of the parties against that standard is appropriate. These conditions are met just when there is a moral relationship between parties that calls for such comparative judgments. Such judgments are called for only when the parties can plausibly be regarded as members of the same community and the disadvantages of one party are relevantly compared to the advantages of the other in relation to some common stock against which both can legitimately make claims. In other words, justice insofar as it demands a kind of equality presupposes a moral relationship of mutual interdependence, that is, a community. For it is *as members* of such a community that each can make claims against the others by making claims against a common stock that is the product of their life together.

Public justification

Justice, then, is right order of communities of rational, moral persons. It is also a framework of principles for public justification of their common institutions and social arrangements and for actions within these institutions and arrangements. For rational, moral persons who are members of the same community it is important not only that they *be* in the right kind of relationships, but also that they can *recognize* the relationships as right. This is because moral persons are concerned not only with the benefits of just arrangements, but with what those arrangements say publicly about the moral status of each member. Justice is not only normative, it is also expressive. It nourishes those who hunger for recognition as persons alongside other persons,[55] comembers of a common enterprise. Justice speaks to a critical need of moral persons, a need that exists alongside, and sometimes even outstrips in importance, the needs addressed by the specific goods that justice distributes.

Justice is not merely a result, an ordering that obtains in or among social elements; it is also a structure of principles that can be understood and applied to behavior. Even more than this, justice provides a lens through which all members sees themselves and the relations that bind them to comembers. It is no accident that this expressive and reflective device is a set of normative principles, for it is fundamentally as rational, moral persons, who can govern their actions and interactions by principles they publicly endorse, that they acknowledge each other. Their recognition of each other as rational moral persons takes the form of endorsement of a set of principles by which they justify their individual actions and common institutions. Thus this justification must be public – a matter of offering reasons *to each other*. Those who speak the language of justice are thereby committed to justifying the claims they make in the name of justice to comembers insofar as they are reasonable and willing to do the same. The mandate of justice is not only to set social arrangements in right order, but to make the rightness of that order manifest to every member of society.

Justice is also public in another way: to speak the language of justice is necessarily to speak to the community, or to individual members of it, in the name of the community. It is to speak of responsibilities and obligations, claims and commitments, of the community as a whole, and of individuals in their capacity as members. Thus one speaks not for one's own part only, expressing a private preference for the ordering of relationships or the distribution of goods, but rather for the whole community, from a point of view common to members and available to them insofar as they regard themselves as members.

Justice in progress

Thus far we have viewed justice statically, as if it were already in place, fully mature, in a more or less ideal "well-ordered society." However, as much as that perspective dominates our reflections about justice, it is not the practical reality we face as we move into the political arena, where we are as likely to struggle over what justice requires as over the best way to meet its demands. Thus we must also look at justice in its dynamic dimension, in the process of formation. I have argued that justice is public in the sense that it is a public good in the familiar economist's sense of that term, and so is enjoyed publicly, and in the sense that it provides a scheme of public justification, and so is deliberated about publicly. From these two premises we can draw the conclusion that justice is by its very nature *political*, and in that further sense public.[56] By this I mean that it is essential to justice that it be achieved only through the group efforts of members of political society working out its basic terms.

This is most evident from the fact that justice is a public good, for as such it can be achieved only through coordinated, collective action. In the world in which we live, we can secure the public good of justice only if we work in concert with others; we do so not only for the community, but also inevitably with the community. This simply follows from the fact that justice is a public good. Nothing in this, however, precludes the *imposition* of just order on a community, save the contingent fact that none of us is able to impose such order.

However, the fact that justice provides a framework for public justification, and so requires not merely right order but manifest right order, rules out the imposition of just social order even if it were empirically possible. It makes justice inseparable from politics, the product of common effort. This claim is not immediately evident, I admit. Were not the great legendary Lawgivers – individuals such as Solon, Lycurgus, Jehovah on Sinai – allegedly fashioners of just order? One might argue that Hobbes's proposal to let the Sovereign define for us the just and the unjust is not inconceivable, it is just politically unfeasible and morally risky. However, my claim is that the realities corresponding to these myths are conceivable only by ignoring that the rightness of the order must be manifest, or by implicitly assuming that justice is not reasonably in dispute, or is silent in the face of reasonable disputes. But each of these conditions is mistaken.

The myth of the Great Lawgiver imagines the apolitical creation of a just regime, but this is conceivable only if we focus exclusively on justice as right order. However, justice is *manifest* right order, a scheme of public principles by which members of the community can justify their actions and institutions to each other. Moreover, in the nonideal conditions of ordinary political life, that is, in the circumstances of integrity, what justice requires is itself reasonably in dispute. To ignore these conditions is to restrict justice to ideal conditions. But justice speaks even in the nonideal conditions of ordinary political life. Justice requires that its fundamental concerns be respected in the processes by which justice is deliberated even when the details of its substantive principles are reasonably in dispute. Justice addresses not only "well-ordered societies," but also societies in the circumstances of integrity, where justice is still in the process of formation.

Thus, in the circumstances of integrity, justice cannot be imposed. It is not enough that right order be established, it is equally important, from the point of view of justice itself, that right order be established through ordinary politics – through reasonable members of political society working together to forge a conception all can recognize as reasonable. As I noted earlier, if, in the circumstances of integrity, justice must be manifest to all reasonable persons, then we cannot regard the pursuit of justice as a game "in which each person tries to plant the flag of his convictions over as large a domain of power or rules as possible."[57] When one encounters reasonable challenges to one's principles of justice, one is forced to shift deliberative as well as practical focus, to identify a basis from which to achieve something approaching agreement about the principles of justice in question. The struggle for justice takes a more oblique form. The door is opened for integrity.

Integrity and the two faces of justice

This argument suggests that justice always has two sides or faces, one ideal and the other consensual. Between them there is always a tension. The key to understanding justice in its dynamic dimension is to keep this tension fully in mind. In "the circumstances of integrity," where there is a point to seeking justice but wide disagreement about what justice requires, integrity stands between "ideal justice" (justice *sans* politics) and mere convention or consensus (political agreement *sans* justice). Integrity keeps the essential tension clearly in focus. It tethers visions of justice to the historical circumstances of particular political societies, and equips politics in those societies for a common struggle for justice.

However, precisely because this tension is always manifest, those who seek justice may never be fully satisfied where the circumstances of integrity obtain. They seek an ideal that can be achieved only based on common agreement around principles of right social order. Yet the principles for which they fight are likely to appear either too ideal, and so unlikely to attract the requisite consensus, or too ad hoc or conventional, and so too accommodating to political demands of the moment. This explains, perhaps, why we are inclined to insist that integrity and justice can conflict, even as we admit, with some discomfort, that integrity must be preferred. The sense of conflict comes from our looking to justice sans politics, while our admission that integrity must, for the moment, be preferred gives due credit to the political side of justice.

Integrity, I have argued, simply is justice properly situated in politics, keeping the essential tension between the ideal and consensual dimensions of justice clearly in sight. The moral force of integrity lies, at least in part, in the need to approximate justice in the political circumstances in which we find ourselves. If we accept that justice issues genuine moral demands, then we must also accept that integrity does so as well, otherwise justice must remain silent in communities that fall short of well-ordered societies. Moreover, integrity is capable of issuing genuine moral demands, not because it is parasitic on justice as the notions of consistency or formal justice are said to be, but in the more complex way in which integrity focuses the pursuit of justice in the circumstances of integrity. We are bound to the complex discipline of integrity whenever we have reason to seek justice in the circumstances of integrity.

IV Fidelity

We are now in a position to consider the link between integrity and fidelity. My thesis is that fidelity takes the shape of integrity in a community bound to pursue justice in the circumstances of integrity. Integrity focuses the pursuit of justice in a specifically historical way, that is, through constructing principled accounts of the community's past decisions and actions. Integrity assumes that a community's past practice is normative for the community and its members. This assumption must be shown to be reasonable if we are to connect integrity as described and defended here to law, for it is the essentially historical character of law that integrity is said to justify.

One reason why it is reasonable to seek approximations of justice in the past political decisions of a community may be that, in the circumstances of integrity, we are more likely to achieve a degree of (at least temporary) principled agreement in this indirect way, than through some more direct approach. The focus of public debate regarding justice is more concrete and limited and so more likely to attract agreement. The past decisions, we might say, represent a form of moral capital in political society,[58] the appropriate exploitation of which over time can yield increasingly satisfying agreements of the right kind.

There may be some force in this argument – I do not dismiss it out of hand – but it appears too weak to bear the full weight of the case for the historical character of integrity. This case, I believe, rests more securely on the link between integrity and the political value of fidelity. Thus I will argue that fidelity takes the shape of integrity in a community bound to pursue justice in the circumstances of integrity.

The notion of fidelity

Fidelity is a matter of keeping faith with a common past. Hume, a political conservative but still a child of the Enlightenment, maintained that, while "every thing be produc'd *in time*, there is nothing real, that is produc'd *by time*." [59] Against this Humean sentiment Dworkin asserts, in defense of the alleged "gravitational force" of legal precedent, that "the very fact of [the] decision, as a piece of political history, provides some reason for deciding other cases in a similar way in the future."[60] Anthony Kronman even more pointedly maintains that we are bound by past decisions "in the sense of being obligated to respect [the past] for its own sake . . . just because it is the past we happen to have."[61] With this especially bold and unqualified assertion, Kronman seeks to highlight the intrinsic moral value of fidelity to the past against the overwhelmingly dominant modern view that the past at best has instrumental value. However, Kronman's thesis is implausible and fails to grasp the nature of the value of fidelity.

Kronman is right to resist the appeal of reducing the value of the past to its merely instrumental value for the future. He goes wrong when he suggests that this value is absolute, or theoretically primitive, or in some way *sui generis*. There is a clear sense in which fidelity has intrinsic value, but the value it accords to the past is not accorded to the past just considered in itself – "merely because it is the past," as Kronman puts it.[62] The moral and practical force of fidelity can be understood only insofar as it is related to other values we hold dear. Fidelity is not an instrumental value, if by this we mean that its value is a function of the value of the consequences it causally brings about, but it has its value only *in service* of other values. Fidelity is the mode in which we express our commitment to certain other values. Its value, then, is intrinsic, but not self-sufficient.

It is easy to misunderstand fidelity's evaluative valence because it is common for us to speak of fidelity to law, or to principle, or to the past. However, the moral value of fidelity is fundamentally an interpersonal (and possibly intrapersonal) value. It arises from relationships of a certain sort and is directed towards parties to those relationships. Duties of fidelity are owed to people, not to theories, principles, rules, or events. Fidelity is a matter of keeping faith with our common past as the appropriate mode of keeping faith with each other as comembers of the community to which we are committed.[63] By "keeping faith with each other" I mean interacting on terms and in ways appropriate to the moral nature of the relationship among us. This is the thesis I shall here defend, but a further clarification is required before I do so.

Fidelity is a complex value; it recognizes that the past can be normative for us in a complex way. Fidelity calls for respect for the decisions and actions of the past, but this respect is tempered by what I earlier called regret. Fidelity demands a *critical* respect for the past. This is not a normative demand imposed from the outside; it is implied by the fact that fidelity serves other values, in particular, the fact that fidelity identifies the appropriate mode of keeping faith with others. If fidelity required only a straightforward and simple imitation of the past, it would confuse its usual mode with its more fundamental end: it would confuse mere conformity with the past, and fidelity to rules or events, with keeping faith with each other as comembers of a community to which we are committed. With this in mind we are in a position to consider an argument for fidelity so understood.

Temporally extended values

My argument begins with the notion of temporally extended values, which I borrow from Thomas Hill, Jr. "Some of our values," Hill observes, "are cross-time wholes, with past, present, and future parts united in certain ways . . . [They are] 'organic unities' – i.e., wholes the value of which is not necessarily the sum of the values of the parts."[64] For goods of this kind, he continues, "[t]he value of any moment often depends on what came before and what we anticipate to follow. . . . The past is seen as more than a time of accumulated debts and assets, and the future is valued as more than an opportunity for reinvesting and cashing in assets."[65] To illustrate his point, Hill considers how one might view the situation in which one negligently wronged another person. One might see that past action not simply as generating a duty to compensate the victim, but in a quite different way that links past, present, and future together as internally related components of a valued relationship.

> One may say, for example, that the *whole* consisting of your life and your relationship with [the victim] will be a better thing if you acknowledge the wrong and make efforts to restore what you have damaged. . . . [T]he requirement [to compensate] is just what is required to bring about a valuable connected whole with past, present, and future parts – the best way to complete a chapter, so to speak, in two intersecting life-stories.[66]

While some values are temporally extended, other values are indifferent to time, or at least for them time is not fundamental. Pleasure, liberty, autonomy, and life itself do not seem to be temporally extended values. For example, autonomy is genetically temporal: it comes into being over time. It may even be epistemically temporal: it manifests its existence to others over time. Yet it does not appear to be evaluatively temporal: its value does not seem tied up with its mode of coming to be or its manifestation to others.

In contrast, some goods are evaluatively temporal; the values they embody are temporally extended. The clearest examples of temporally extended values are found in human relationships, but they are familiar in intrapersonal contexts as well. Respect for oneself, or personal integrity, is one such value. Consider the following example.[67] Throughout her life, Jean's mother was always generous to people who had fallen on hard times. She provided food and clothing to them and sometimes even let them stay in her house until they could get back on their feet. After her mother's death, Jean resolved to actively support local efforts to find shelter for the homeless, in honor of her mother. On the anniversary of her mother's death, Jean realized with shame that her resolve had weakened to the point that it had completely slipped her mind over the past six months. Not only had the needs of some homeless people not been met, but also she had failed. Her resolve had turned omission into failure. During the year, she had reason to write out a check to the homeless shelter and to volunteer from time to time, not only because the needs of the homeless were great, but also because this need had a special significance to her life in virtue of her resolve and its meaning to her. The resolve had given a certain determinate shape to her life, and to her relationship with her mother; it gave her reasons rooted in the meaningfulness of living out that life over time. Personal integrity, as well as the shape of her relationship to her mother, imposed a demand on her which was continuous over time, because the self (and this relationship) had integrity only in and over time.

Temporally extended values are found even more clearly in interpersonal relationships. Hill offers a compelling illustration.[68] John and Mary are friends; they mutually value their friendship and the trust and respect for each other that are at its core. Recently, Mary has been the victim of insulting and abusive behavior by other people, and John worries that he also has said things that unintentionally may have insulted her. But Mary has not let on that she has been hurt, and he fears that he may make matters worse by creating what he regards as groundless suspicions. In view of the value of their friendship to both of them, he asks himself what response would best affirm the relationship he has and wishes to continue with her. Hill continues:

> Given their history together, it is important to him to do his part towards restoring the relationship if it indeed has been marred by perceived insults or suspicions. To be sure, he wants *future* relations of mutual trust and respect, but not at any price and not by just any means. Their history together is not irrelevant, for what he values is not merely a future of a certain kind but that their relationship over time be of the sort he values.[69]

Hill's example clearly shows that the value of friendship is temporally extended. Friendship connects people to each other over time, giving their interactions special moral significance to them. Loyalty gives expression to this moral significance. Fidelity to the past that friends share with each other is one very important way in which they recognize and manifest their regard for each other as friends. It is, of course, the mutual value of the friendship that gives friends reasons to keep faith with each other; it is in this soil that fidelity takes root. In the absence of this relationship, the same people would not have this reason to keep faith with each other. In this respect, as we have seen, fidelity is in the service of other values and to that extent presupposes them.

It is also worth noting another feature of this example of friendship. There are complex links between past actions, interactions, and events involving friends, on the one hand, and the friendship and its value to them, on the other. The value of friendship is temporally extended, as we have seen, and so it depends on the way the friends integrate their past, present, and future. Friends are committed to each other, but it would often be a mistake to regard the moral value of the friendship as the product of their commitment, on the model, say, of a promise or contract. The commitment is an expression of their recognition of the value of the relationship. Moreover, the relationship and its moral significance for the friends may have emerged over time through their interactions and shared experiences which, as Aristotle reminded us, enrich and are enriched by their common perception and common discourse.[70]

Justice as a temporally extended value

In our personal lives and in interpersonal relationships like friendship, the past makes its presence felt practically and morally in virtue of the fact that its significance for us lies in its relationship to a whole whose value is extended over time. The past is not merely the source of causal traces that we must now take into account in our practical or moral reasoning; rather, the past has evaluative or normative significance for present deliberation and action (as does the future), because the values that demand attention in our deliberation are temporally extended values that embrace and integrate the past, the present, and the future. From the perspective of temporally extended values, time's arrow points in more than one direction. More precisely put, the evaluative relationships among the parts of temporally extended value-wholes[71] are multidimensional, characterized by mutuality rather than unilateral determination. This is evident in the examples considered thus far, but it is also clear when we consider the value of a community that makes justice a fundamental aim. Here, again, fidelity finds a home, for fidelity in a vital, complex way links past, present, and future in communities aspiring to justice.

Justice is right order of historical human communities. It is temporally extended value because it gives public, moral shape to the temporally extended value of community for us. Let us consider first the value of community and then observe the way justice gives shape to this value.

The historical character of living communities, as opposed to abstractly conceived ones, is obvious and does not need to be demonstrated. However, to say that a community is historical is to say more than merely that it has a history – that it endures over a period of time and that events in it could be recorded should anyone find it interesting to do so. For in that limited sense, "flies of a summer" and the herd grazing in the field have a history.[72] The historical character of human communities is fundamentally different. It is a function of self-conscious common memory framed and informed by a sense of significance that gives the historical events a distinctively human value. This sense of significance is borne of decisions, aims, commitments, and practices that establish and nourish human relationships and give a meaningful structure to individual human lives.

Moreover, the value of community, and the values available to us in communities, are essentially historical values. In Burke's evocative image, society is a partnership extended over time "between those who are living, those who are dead, and those who are to be born."[73] Like partners in an ongoing contractual relationship, generations are bound together in relations of mutual dependency.[74] One generation is dependent on preceding generations for the material, moral, and cultural resources that make possible human and autonomous lives. Without those resources not only would opportunities for a wide variety of meaningful pursuits be closed to us, but also we would not generally have the ability to judge our own goals as worthy of pursuit. At the same time, the previous generation is dependent on its successors for the achievement and preservation of the goals and projects that give their lives significance precisely by the fact that they transcend the limits of their biological existence. This dependency has many dimensions. Not only must the projects of the past be embraced by the present, or their accomplishments preserved, but they must be understood, interpreted, and given practical shape so that, in the new circumstances of the present, the projects of the past can be pursued intelligently. Past practice bears the stamp of our common life, but at the same time it forces us to address together the question of what this shape is and shall be. Our attempt to give it shape for the present and future depends on how we expect it to be received and followed in the future. Each generation bears this relationship of mutual dependency both to its predecessors and its successors. Each generation must look both to the past and to the future for the evaluative shape of its present actions. In this, Kronman observes, there is mutual vulnerability: we cannot force our ancestors to provide us with the material, moral, and cultural resources we need for a full and rich life; likewise, our ancestors cannot force us to embrace their projects (or their understanding of them), and we are in no better position with regard to the generations to come.[75]

Thus the values available to us and only realized in historical communities, including the value of community itself, are temporally extended values. These values are given distinctively moral shape by justice. In relatively large, nonintimate communities, justice is the structure in which partners recognize and respect each other as comembers. In virtue of its public dimension, justice is concerned with the messages we send to each other regarding our respective places in the community. The way we arrange our communal affairs, and distribute the benefits and burdens of common life, expresses our regard for each other as fellow members of the community. Justice gives a special focus to temporally extended value of community. Through it, we give expression to our regard for each other across generations and to our regard for current fellow members. In this way, the value of justice, too, is temporally extended.

Fidelity calls for keeping faith with the past as a way of keeping faith with each other. We can now see why this is important: fidelity gives explicit shape to the historical dimension of justice. We can also see why fidelity requires us to hold a complex attitude with regard to the past – a combination of respect and regret – for fidelity relates past, present, and future in the service of justice, that is, in the service of making the community over time an expression of justice. To accomplish this a certain way of understanding or interpreting the public and political actions of the community is needed. These actions must be regarded as committed to and directed towards establishing and maintaining justice. At the same time, fidelity requires that the community take full responsibility for its actions and the arrangements it enforces. The arrangements must be recognizable as expressions of just and proper regard for each member as an equal member of the community, or at least as bona fide attempts to give concrete shape to that fundamental attitude. Respect for past practice, then, must always be in the service of the aspiration for justice, and hence never uncritical.

In communities aimed at justice, where not only the reality falls short of the standard, but the standard itself is in dispute, fidelity is integrity. Integrity is the form fidelity takes in the circumstances of integrity, that is, in a community committed to justice but divided over what justice requires. Integrity is the way members of such a community keep faith with each other and with their collective commitment to justice as the fundamental mode of their relationships. In such circumstances, only integrity can give expression to that fundamental common commitment.

V Integrity and the Law

I have argued that fidelity takes the shape of integrity in a community bound to the pursuit of justice in the circumstances of integrity. It remains, finally, for me to show that law provides a natural medium in which to seek justice in the way integrity prescribes.

Integrity, as explained and defended here, need not be realized only in law. It is conceivable that other practices less formal and less formally institutionalized than law might also be bound by this important value of political morality. Yet these other practices are likely to look very much like less formal analogues of law, for law seems by its nature and its governing regulative idea to be committed to the discipline that integrity imposes on collective practical reasoning. Law is historical by its very nature. As Kronman says,

> . . . respect for past decisions is not a characteristic of certain legal systems only. It is rather a feature of law in general, and whenever there exists a set of practices and institutions that we believe are entitled to the name of law, the rule of precedent will be at work, influencing, to one degree or another, the conduct of those responsible for administering the practices and institutions in question.[76]

Law is a framework of practical reasoning that anchors the public justification of decisions and actions to past communal decisions and actions. This is not exclusively true of reasoning from precedent, but it is most clearly and immediately evident there. Reasoning from precedent by analogy is not mere imitation, nor is it a matter of prediction, nor some version of formal consistency. It is an evaluatively informed assessment of the normative significance of the past decision for the instant case, as well as of the significance it might hold for the future. Reasoning from precedent is as much "forward-looking" as "backward-looking." That is to say, the values that govern precedent are temporally embedded in just the way I described integrity to be in the previous section. I need not pursue this argument any further here, as Alexander and Kress made the case well in their discussion of the practice of common-law reasoning.[77]

There is a further, stronger connection between law and integrity. Not only does legal argument tend to take the shape integrity recommends, but it *must* do so because the legitimacy of law in circumstances of integrity depends on its being manifestly governed by the aspiration to justice. The governing regulative idea of law is not merely consistency, order, or even authority. Any of these, without the manifest project of directing all resources towards justice – towards manifest right order in the community – is not worthy of our allegiance, has no legitimacy, and so at best can only command prudent compliance. Only if law is governed by the demands and discipline of integrity can it claim legitimacy where there is deep and fundamental disagreement about justice. If it is disciplined by integrity, public reasoning that purports to bind (and is likely to affect) all members of the society can be seen to be in the service of law's regulative idea, even when the demands of that regulative idea are in dispute.

Yet, despite all that has been said, it might still seem that law is an implausible focus for the discipline of integrity. In the circumstances of justice, there may be deep disagreements about justice, and we can expect them to be reflected in assessments of the law. Many citizens may judge the past actions of the community as reflected in the practices of law to be seriously, perhaps even pervasively, unjust. Why, then, should they be inclined to treat these practices as defining commitments of the community, as integrity counsels?

This is an important challenge, but it can be met. Recall that integrity has a point only in the circumstances of integrity. These circumstances include not only disagreement about what justice requires, but also the fact that it is reasonable for members to regard their community as aspiring to justice and that social and political arrangements are not irremediably unjust. If these circumstances do not obtain, then, like a thermostat in temperatures beyond its operative range, integrity no longer functions; it no longer makes any moral claim. In such circumstances it would be unreasonable to expect citizens to look to the law as the point of departure for the pursuit of a publicly defensible vision of justice. However, where the circumstances of integrity do obtain, it is reasonable for citizens to regard their community as aspiring to justice. Moreover, it is likely that the law will be the record of this aspiration, for, by virtue of its prominent place in the life of a community, it will be the primary locus of the community's efforts to realize the aspiration to justice. Integrity is valid and binding only in its distinctive circumstances, but where those circumstances obtain it commands the allegiance of all who aspire to justice.

This suggests one further objection to my linking of integrity to law. It might be argued that in circumstances of justice historic disputes regarding justice will inevitably leave their traces in the law. Different conceptions of justice have influenced substantial portions of the law at different times in history. Thus integrity's demand that law be seen as issuing from a coherent vision of justice seems extravagant and dishonest. Is it not better to acknowledge that, due to the history of political struggles, one set of principles underlies one part of the law, a different set underlies another part, and so on? A more honest account of the society's commitments rooted in its law would seem to be a kind of patchwork quilt. Does not coherence, in the unlikely event it could be achieved, simply mask the political reality of law, encouraging an exercise in self-deception rather than integrity?[78]

This complex objection is open to several different interpretations. The first understands the aim of constructing a coherent vision of justice from the community's past actions to be a kind of historical narrative or description. On this view, the requirement of coherence invites distortion of the real political history of law. But this objection merely rests on a misunderstanding of the task of practical deliberation disciplined by integrity. The aim is not to chronicle a community's past from some neutral observer's point of view, but rather to uncover in that past principles governing its actions in the present. In view of these quite different aims, it should not be surprising if the results are different.

Second, the objector may be making a skeptical argument. On this reading the objection is that integrity's demand of coherence has no ground in moral or practical reason. There simply is no moral reason to act from principles that fit together in a coherent vision of justice, the skeptic might argue. So, if principles underlying one part of the law do not fit intelligibly with those underlying a different part, that is no matter for concern. This is a fundamental challenge to the claims of this essay, but it strikes me as utterly implausible. If we accept that law is fundamentally governed by the aspiration to justice, we cannot accept with equanimity an acknowledged and unresolvable incoherence, for incoherence undermines any attempt to do justice in a community. Of course, principles may fail to fit together intelligibly, not because they clash, but precisely because they *do not* conflict, as the principles of French and Iranian constitutional law, or the principles of mechanics and electronics, may be very different yet not in conflict. But that could be true only if the noncohering principles of law do not meet on the same logical, theoretical, or practical plane. That surely is not the case with the laws of any given political society.

Third, the objection might more plausibly take a distinctively moral form. The critic may point out that in our imperfect world where "the debris of past political struggles"[79] is preserved in the books and practices of law, we are forced to make compromises by a morality mindful of concrete circumstances and the limits of political feasibility. We only make the ideal the enemy of the good and feasible if we reject approximations to morally sound solutions because they reduce the coherence of law.[80] However, this argument does not challenge the notion of integrity that I have tried to defend. First of all, the notion of coherence I rely on is intentionally very weak.[81] Second, integrity, as I understand it, is a complex moral standard calling for a proper and defensible balance of respect and regret regarding past rules and decisions of a polity.[82] Regret, I have argued, accepts *in the name of integrity* certain compromises of coherence – pockets of incoherence in a body of law that nevertheless strives for coherence. As it stands, this objection does not undermine integrity's claim to moral force and relevance in the context of law.

But the moral objection might be pressed again, this time more pointedly. "[I]n countries with decent constitutions, the untidiness of politics is morally sanctioned . . . by the morality of authoritative institutions."[83] These institutions are authorized to give direction to human affairs and to control social interaction through their deliberate decisions. Given the vagaries of politics, we have no reason to expect the decisions and actions of these institutions over time to fit neatly into a coherent system of rules and principles.[84] The moral basis for the authority of these institutions, and thus the grounds for accepting their less than coherent results, are typically traced to two different but arguably related sources: the need for coordination of human affairs and social interaction and the place of such institutions in a robust democracy.

A satisfying reply to this objection calls for a general discussion of fundamental issues of normative political (and especially democratic) theory. It is too late in this essay to address these issues fully. In lieu of such a discussion I will merely suggest what I believe the eventual outcome of that discussion will be and leave to another occasion a proper discussion of this important objection and the issues it raises. First, coordination arguments, as important as they are in this context, are never sufficient grounds for legislative and adjudicative institutions. Taken alone, they give too much weight to considerations of social order and not enough to other important moral concerns like justice. Because we are likely to be talking about political societies in the circumstances of integrity, we must ground the legitimacy of authoritative institutions in an argument that includes both integrity and coordination. Similarly, a plausible theory of democracy will have to include integrity as a key commitment of democratic adjudicative institutions. Thus I agree that authoritative institutions can be morally justified and that this may involve morally sanctioning "untidy politics," at least up to a point. But this is not because integrity is supplanted, but because the moral case for the legitimacy of those institutions depends in part on their ability to meet the demands of integrity on the law.

Theorists who reject integrity as the governing idea of law's distinctive form of public practical reasoning – whether they be natural lawyers, positivists, or latter-day pragmatists – either reject justice as law's fundamental governing ideal, or they misunderstand what justice by its nature demands. Appeals to justice that are not given recognizable public content supplied by the law itself must either give us an account of the public resources they draw upon or stand convicted of misunderstanding the nature of their appeal, and thus failing in their appeal. For justice, as we have seen, is necessarily public. To make decisions of law in the name of justice is to make them in the name of the community as a whole. It is never sufficient for those empowered to make such decisions to do so on the basis of what they, for their own part only, regard as morally best. Authority has its important place in this approach, but always governed by and in the service of justice. Where justice is pursued in the circumstances of integrity, justice will require that officials vested with such authority be governed by the discipline of integrity. Authority freed from integrity's discipline is free to ignore politics, and the very circumstances that demand that we pursue justice indirectly, in the name of justice itself. Theories that refuse to recognize the demands and discipline of integrity deprive official decisions and actions of legitimacy at precisely the point at which it is needed most.

Acknowledgement

This chapter appears here with the kind permission of the *Iowa Law Review*. The original version was published under the same title in vol. 82, 1996/97, pp. 821–56.

Notes

1 Frederick Schauer, "Precedent and the Necessary Externality of Constitutional Norms," *Harvard Journal of Law and Public Policy*, vol. 17, 1994, p. 48.

2 For a discussion of the "externalist" approach see generally Larry Alexander, "Constrained by Precedent," *Southern California Law Review*, vol. 63, 1989, pp. 1–64 (describing three general models of precedent, including the natural, rule, and result models); Frederick Schauer, "Precedent," *Stanford Law Review*, vol. 39, 1987, pp. 571–605 (delineating the external sources of precedent and describing its flexibility in operation).

3 See Larry Alexander and Ken Kress, "Against Legal Principles," *Iowa Law Review*, vol. 82, 1996/97, p. 748.

4 See Ronald Dworkin, *Law's Empire* (Cambridge, MA: Harvard University Press, 1986), pp 123, 128–9 (explicit extension); Ronald Dworkin, *Taking Rights Seriously* (Cambridge, MA: Harvard University Press, 1997), p. 111 (gravitational force). In the "explicit extension" of a precedent are all the cases to which it applies clearly and incontestably.

5 See Alexander and Kress, "Against Legal Principles," op. cit.

6 Larry Alexander proposed this counterfactual account of the methodology of common-law reasoning in "Constrained by Precedent," op. cit., pp. 28–34, 38; see also Alexander and Kress, "Against Legal Principles," op. cit., p. 748 n. 47 (suggesting counterfactual methodology as "the best description of the dominant methodology for dealing with precedential constraint").

7 Alexander and Kress, "Against Legal Principles," op. cit., 748 n. 47.

8 See Dworkin, *Law's Empire*, op. cit., pp. 225–58, 410.

9 For a critical discussion of the philosophical literature on integrity as a personal moral virtue see Cheshire Calhoun, "Standing for Something," *Journal of Philosophy*, vol. 92, 1995, pp. 235–60.

10 Dworkin, *Law's Empire*, op. cit., p. 93.

11 Ibid., p. 134.

12 Ibid., p. 166.

13 Ibid., pp. 167–75.

14 Ibid., pp. 176–8, 404–7.

15 I agree with Joseph Raz that this weak notion of coherence is the notion at the core of Dworkin's idea of integrity in *Law's Empire* (see pp. 165–7), despite some language in that work that suggests a stronger notion. For Raz's defense of this interpretation and references to *Law's Empire*, see Joseph Raz, "The Relevance of Coherence," in *Ethics in the Public Domain* (Oxford: Clarendon Press, 1994), pp. 303–9, a part of which forms chapter 15 of this volume.

16 O. W. Holmes, *The Common Law*, ed. M. DeWolfe Howe (Boston: Little, Brown, [1881]1963), p. 32.

17 I have defended a notion of public, plural, practical deliberation in three papers: "Morality in the First Person Plural" *Law and Philosophy*, vol. 14, 1995, pp. 35–64; "Public Practical Reason: An Archeology," *Social Philosophy and Policy*, vol. 12, 1995, pp. 43–86 [hereinafter Postema, "An Archeology"]; "Public

Practical Reason: Political Practice," in Ian Shapiro and Judith Wagner DeCew (eds.), *NOMOS XXXVII: Theory and Practice* (New York: New York University Press, 1995).

18   Annette Baier, *The Commons of the Mind* (Chicago: Open Court, 1997).

19   Dworkin, *Law's Empire*, op. cit., p. 413.

20   For a more general criticism of Dworkin's theory of law and interpretation along these lines, see Gerald J. Postema, "'Protestant' Interpretation and Social Practices," *Law and Philosophy*, vol. 6, 1986, pp. 283–319.

21   Dworkin, *Law's Empire*, op. cit., p. 184.

22   I use "regret" as a term of art. I intend it to encompass the capacities to acknowledge and take responsibility for mistakes and to take appropriate steps to correct and compensate for the wrongs they cause.

23   Lynne McFall, "Integrity," *Ethics*, vol. 98, 1987, pp. 5–20, at p. 7.

24   This may be true of Dworkin, *Law's Empire*, op. cit., p. 257. See Raz, "The Relevance of Coherence," pp. 282, 298 (arguments against global coherence in law); ibid., pp. 299–303 (defense of local coherence).

25   Friedrich Nietzsche, *On the Advantages and Disadvantages of History for Life*, trans. P. Preuss (Indianapolis, IN: Hacket Publishing, [1874]1980), p. 17.

26   For purposes of illustration I assume here a mode of reasoning on the model of Dworkin's theory of interpretation. See Dworkin, *Law's Empire*, op. cit., pp. 45–86. On that model, actions of the past exert their influence over present decisions beyond their "explicit extensions," through the principles drawn from (and justifying) the past decisions, which principles, then, guide deliberations in present cases.

27   Raz, "The Relevance of Coherence," op. cit., p. 298.

28   See ibid., pp. 282–98 (arguments against global coherence in law) and pp. 299–303 (defense of local coherence).

29   F. Douglass, "Fourth of July Oration," in Herbert J. Storing (ed.), *What Country Have I? Political Writings by Black Americans* (New York: St. Martin's Press, [1852]1970), p. 28.

30   Ibid., pp. 31–2, 36.

31   Raz, "The Relevance of Coherence," op. cit., p. 298.

32   Ibid.

33   Ibid.

34   Thus the important objections that Raz raised against coherence theories of law and adjudication (see ibid., pp. 282–98), do not challenge my project here, first because the notion of coherence he has in mind is much stronger than the one I am using, and second because his most important arguments are directed against coherence theories of law and adjudication. At the conclusion of this essay, I will briefly consider possible extensions of Raz's arguments to the notion of integrity defended here.

35   See Dworkin, *Law's Empire*, op. cit., pp. 176–84.

36   For example, one might argue that benevolence is concerned with promoting the overall good or well-being of persons and lends itself easily to aggregating over persons and maximizing, while justice is concerned with the way individuals are treated, or with the right distribution of resources and opportunities in a community, or the right sort of relationships among members of a community, values that typically resist aggregation and maximizing.

37   See e.g., Alexander and Kress, "Against Legal Principles," op. cit., p. 755; Raz, "The Relevance of Coherence," op. cit., pp. 296, 298 (maintaining that "[s]peaking with one voice . . . is not an independent ideal with the moral force to lead us to endorse solutions less just than they need to be" but rather is just "a by-product of an ideal situation"); Denise Reaume, "Is Integrity a Virtue?" *University of Toronto Law Review*, vol. 39, 1989, pp. 392–3 (rejecting Dworkin's assurance that consistency has independent value and stating that fairness, justice, and procedural due process require consistency). But see Raz, "The Relevance of Coherence," op. cit., pp. 303–9 (giving reasons to doubt that integrity as Dworkin understands it requires coherence or speaking with one voice).

38   Dworkin, *Law's Empire*, op. cit., p. 263 (emphasis added).
39   See Jeremy Waldron, "The Circumstances of Integrity," *Legal Theory*, vol. 3, 1997, pp. 1–22.
40   See David Hume, *Enquiries Concerning Human Understanding and Concerning the Principles of Morals*, ed. P. H. Nidditch (Oxford: Oxford University Press, 3rd edn. [1752]1975), pp. 183–92; John Rawls, *A Theory of Justice* (Cambridge, MA: Harvard University Press, 1971), pp. 126–30.
41   This analogy is used by Robert Nozick for a different purpose. See Robert Nozick, *The Nature of Rationality* (Princeton, NJ: Princeton University Press, 1993), p. 35.
42   See Hume, *Enquiries*, op. cit., pp. 183–92.
43   See Waldron, "The Circumstances of Integrity," op. cit., pp. 5–9.
44   Ibid., p. 12.
45   "[I]ntegrity – like fairness – is a political value that approaches issues of justice from an oblique angle – an angle defined functionally by the need to deal with the fact that various decisions to which our community has already committed itself have been made on the basis of disparate and conflicting conceptions of justice" (ibid.).
46   I explain and defend the public dimension of justice in the following section.
47   Alexander and Kress, "Against Legal Principles," op. cit., p. 784.
48   Waldron, "The Circumstances of Integrity," op. cit., p. 19 (quoting Dworkin, *Law's Empire*, op. cit., p. 211).
49   See Alexander and Kress, "Against Legal Principles," op. cit., pp. 784–5.
50   For example, divine or cosmic justice, or justice between individuals in a "state of nature."
51   By "right order" I mean a rationally defensible and morally imperative structure or arrangement, a moral blueprint, regarded not only in the abstract but also as realized in some community.
52   Plato, *The Republic*, trans. Paul Shorey (Cambridge, MA: Harvard University Press, 1967), Book IV.
53   See Hume, *Enquiries*, op. cit., p. 305 (explaining that human well-being, raised by the social virtue of justice, may be compared to the building of a vault).
54   An argument of this kind can be found in Brian Barry, *Theories of Justice* (London: Harvester-Wheatsheaf, 1989), pp. 238–9. The idea that injustice can be best understood as an inequality between persons for which there is no moral justification is at the core of Rawls's "intuitive argument" for his principles of justice. See Rawls, *A Theory of Justice*, op. cit., pp. 72–5. There is a helpful discussion of this argument in Will Kymlicka, *Contemporary Political Philosophy* (Oxford: Oxford University Press, 1990), pp. 55–8.
55   For the centrality of mutual recognition to the moral enterprise, see Postema, "An Archaeology," op. cit., pp. 76–85.
56   Burke seemed to have this sense of the term "political" in mind when he said, "Political arrangements, as it is a work for social ends, is only to be wrought by social means, there mind must conspire with mind." See Edmund Burke, *Reflections on the Revolution in France*, ed. Conor Cruise O'Brien (Harmondsworth, UK: Penguin Books, [1790]1969), p. 281.
57   Dworkin, *Law's Empire*, op. cit., p. 211.
58   Govert Den Hartogh, Professor of Philosophy, University of Amsterdam, suggested this thought to me, although I do not think he is inclined to endorse the argument as a whole.
59   David Hume, *A Treatise of Human Nature*, ed. P. H. Nidditch (Oxford: Oxford University Press, 2nd edn. [1739]1979), p. 509 (emphasis added).
60   Dworkin, *Taking Rights Seriously*, op. cit., p. 113.
61   Anthony T. Kronman, "Precedent and Tradition," *Yale Law Journal*, vol. 99, 1990, pp. 1036–7.
62   Ibid., p. 1039.
63   This is the thesis I set out in "On the Moral Presence of the Past," *McGill Law Journal*, vol. 36, 1991, p. 1170. My argument below revises in several respects the defense of the thesis found in that essay. I will not identify the changes here.
64   T. Hill, Jr., *Autonomy and Self-Respect* (Cambridge, UK: Cambridge University Press, 1991), pp. 202–03.
65   Ibid., p. 202.

66 Ibid., p. 204.

67 I have used this example in "On the Moral Presence of the Past," op. cit., p. 1174. It is based on an example of Joseph Raz, *The Morality of Freedom* (Oxford: Clarendon Press, 1986), pp. 385–6.

68 See Hill, *Autonomy and Self-Respect*, op. cit., pp. 204–5.

69 Ibid., p. 205.

70 See Aristotle, *The Nicomachean Ethics*, trans. Hippocrates G. Apostle (Dordrecht: D. Reidel Publishing, 1975), Book 1, 1170b, ll. 11–2.

71 Recall that Hill suggested that we conceive of temporally extended values as organic unities. See text accompanying note 64 above.

72 "Flies of a summer" is, of course, Burke's famous phrase. See Burke, *Reflections on the Revolution in France*, op. cit., p. 193. Aristotle drew the contrast between cows sharing a pasture and human interactions that have an essential historical and common significance. See Aristotle, *The Nicomachean Ethics*, op. cit., p. 177 (Book 1, 1170b, ll. 11–4). Nietzsche gave this Aristotelian thought an ironic twist:

> Consider the herd grazing before you. These animals do not know what yesterday and today are but leap about, eat, rest, digest and leap again; and so from morning to night and from day to day, only briefly concerned with their pleasure and displeasure, enthralled by the moment and for that reason neither melancholy nor bored. It is hard for man to see this, for he is proud of being human and not an animal and yet regards its happiness with envy because he wants nothing other than to live like the animal, neither bored nor in pain, yet wants it in vain because he does not want it like the animal. . . . In this way the animal lives *unhistorically* . . . [Man] is moved, as though he remembered a lost paradise, when he sees a grazing herd, or, in more intimate proximity, sees a child, which as yet has nothing past to deny, playing between the fences of past and future in blissful blindness. And yet the child's play must be disturbed: only too soon will it be called out of its forgetfulness. (Nietzsche, *On the Advantages and Disadvantages of History for Life*, op. cit., pp. 8–9)

73 Burke, *Reflections on the Revolution in France*, op. cit., pp. 194–5.

74 I follow Kronman's discussion here, see Kronman, "Precedent and Tradition," op. cit., pp. 1067–8. However, I describe the relations among generations in terms of mutual *dependency* rather than mutual *indebtedness* as Kronman does, because the latter begs the question of the normative upshot of the mutual dependence. I believe mutual dependency establishes the special historical character of communities; the value of communities to us both as individuals and as members of these communities is, then, temporally extended in a deep sense. In virtue of the temporally extended character of the values available to us in historical communities, fidelity imposes its normative demands on us. That is why we are "indebted."

75 See ibid., p. 1067.

76 Ibid., p. 1032.

77 See Alexander and Kress, "Against Legal Principles," op. cit., pp. 745–52 (discussing legal principles in jurisprudential thought).

78 This argument was suggested to me by Raz's remarks in "The Relevance of Coherence," op. cit., pp. 280, 298, but I do not claim that the paraphrase in the text exactly captures the main thrust of Raz's argument.

79 This is Raz's phrase (ibid., p. 280).

80 Again, an argument along these lines is suggested by Raz (ibid., pp. 296–7), but I am taking the argument out of its complex context and directing it by extension to my integrity thesis. My reply is aimed at the argument above, not Raz's.

81 See pp. 293–6 in the text above.

82 See pp. 296–8 in the text above.

83 Raz, "The Relevance of Coherence," op. cit., pp. 298–9.

84 See ibid., pp. 284–5.

17

The Rule of Law as a Theater of Debate

Jeremy Waldron

The rule of law is one of a cluster of ideals that constitute the core of modern political morality: the others include democracy, human rights, and perhaps also the principle of free markets. These ideals are so tightly clustered that there is a tendency to use any one of them as surrogate for all the others: "democracy" becomes code for human rights too, or "the rule of law" becomes code for rights, democracy, and markets.[1] That's a nuisance from an analytical point of view, because it prevents us seeing the distinctive light cast in our political morality by each of the separate stars in this constellation. And it can mislead us about the history and dialectics of these ideals. In some ways, the rule of law is more fundamental than the others. Democracy cannot exist unless procedures of election and accountability are secured by law; markets presuppose the integrity of legal rules defining property and contracts; and as the Universal Declaration of Human Rights states in its preamble, it is widely thought to be "essential, if man is not to be compelled to have recourse, as a last resort, to rebellion against tyranny and oppression, that human rights should be protected by the rule of law."[2] Moreover, the rule of law is arguably the oldest and most enduring theme in Western political thought. From Aristotle to Antonin Scalia, from Sir John Fortescue to John Locke, from Dicey to Dworkin, the rule of law has provided a perennial topic for political and legal writing for more than 2,500 years, as jurists and statesmen explore and elaborate the idea that laws might rule instead of men, and that "King Nomos" might prevail over the power of tyrants, mobs, and absolute monarchs.[3]

The prominence of this theme in our thought is in part a reflection of the fact that we can never quite agree what it amounts to.[4] To some the rule of law refers to the authoritative imposition of order in a society: clear rules are laid down whose likely impact in various situations can be ascertained well in advance, and these rules – which one can find in the texts of statutes and precedents – are enforced rigorously in every situation to which they apply, without fear or favor.[5] To others, the essence of the rule of law is reasoned deliberation, particularly as it is exercised in judicial settings.[6] On this account, the rule of law is the very opposite of the imperious imposition of a posited set of rules. A society is ruled by law in this sense when power is not exercised arbitrarily, but only pursuant to intelligent and open exercises of public reason in institutions and forums set up for that purpose. The function of legal texts is to frame and facilitate those processes, not short-circuit them. Settlement and predictability matter less on this second account than they do on the rule-book conception; that is, it matters less that we know in advance what the final determination of a given issue is going to be, more that we have some assurance about the procedures and activities that will attend that determination. I shall call these two conceptions of the rule of law "the rule-book model" and "the proceduralist model."

There are, of course, other conceptions in the literature as well.[7] Ronald Dworkin introduced what might be regarded as a third conception in his essay "Political Judges and the Rule of Law,"

JEREMY WALDRON

when he contrasted what I have already referred to (following his example) as "the rule-book conception" with what he called "the rights conception."

> It assumes that citizens have moral right and duties with respect to one another, and political rights against the state as a whole. It insists that these moral and political rights be recognized in positive law, so that they may be enforced upon the demand of the individual citizens through courts or other judicial institutions of the familiar type, so far as this is practicable. The rule of law on this conception is the ideal of rule by an accurate public conception of individual rights.[8]

Now, if the rights conception referred only to *legal* rights, then there might be a case for regarding it as a subspecies of the rule-book conception. The argument has often been made that individual rights depend on clear rules of positive law, that legal predictability is key to the liberty that rights protect, and that the essence of legal rights is that law keep faith with the expectations that were established when it laid down its rules. After all, how can I be said to have a legal right unless the provision securing that right is clear, settled, and determinate in some public legal text?[9] I say a case *might* be made to that effect. But I doubt that Professor Dworkin would accept it. For him the existence of rights in law is so tightly bound up with moral argument about justice and argument about how we are required as a matter of principle to respond to antecedent legal materials, that any rule-book conception of them would make a mockery of the moral standing that these rights are supposed to have.

Anyway, the conception of the rule of law defended by Professor Dworkin in "Political Judges and the Rule of Law" is distinguished by its emphasis on *moral* rights, and by the directness of the link that it seeks to establish between that idea and the idea of legality. A society committed to the rights conception of the rule of law makes an important promise to each citizen, according to Dworkin: "It encourages each individual to suppose that his relations with other citizens and with his government are matters of justice."[10]

> The rule of law on this conception is the ideal of rule by an accurate public conception of individual rights. It does not distinguish, as the rule-book conception does, between the rule of law and substantive justice; on the contrary it requires, as part of the ideal of law, that the rules in the rule-book capture and enforce moral rights.[11]

The reference to "accuracy" seems particularly important. Moral rights are there – objectively – to be captured and enforced. There is a truth about rights and justice that our public conceptions ought to embody, but that they might or might not embody accurately. No doubt people will disagree about which propositions concerning moral rights are true and which false; consequently, on this conception, they will disagree about whether their society is in fact keeping faith with the rule of law ideal. But Dworkin makes much of the point that objectivity is not incompatible with disagreement:[12] "The rights conception must suppose that a state may fail along the dimension of accuracy even when it is controversial whether it has failed."[13] Anyway, *every* conception of the rule of law is going to require that some controversial judgments be made in the application of the ideal – judgments that may be impossible to prove to the satisfaction of everyone and that may be true or false nonetheless. The only difference in the case of this third conception – which I shall call the objectivist conception of the rule of law[14] – is the link between legality and what purport to be objective judgments about moral rights (as opposed to objective judgments about the enactment of texts or the integrity of procedures).[15]

But here's a question. If the rule of law is identified – as it is in Dworkin's conception – with law's getting it right so far as moral rights are concerned, does any importance attach to the procedures by which this happens or the means by which we as a society make the attempt to get moral rights right? Is it important for the rule of law that we try to establish the truth about rights and justice by *legalistic* means – such as procedures of litigation and deliberation and decision by judges? Does it matter that we use procedures like these – as opposed to, say, divination or appeals to tradition? I am asking in other words: is Dworkin's conception of the rule of law a purely objectivist conception, or are there also important elements in it of what we have called the proceduralist approach?

In "Political Judges and the Rule of Law," Professor Dworkin considers the possibility that "[a] government of wise and just officers will protect rights . . . on its own initiative, without procedure whereby citizens can dispute, as individuals, what these rights are."[16] That might seem to suggest that if he ever had to choose between familiar legal procedures, on the one hand, and, on the other hand, more accurate determinations of rights by entirely nonlegalistic means – for example, Solomonic judgments for particular cases by a philosopher-king – he would choose the latter. It is perhaps not entirely a silly dilemma to pose. There have been those who have urged us to turn away from procedural legalism if we ever want to reach a society ruled by enlightened values.[17] Admittedly, many who take this view also repudiate talk of moral rights as among the values they want us to be accurately ruled by, and some repudiate talk of justice as well. They suggest that law should respond to other values, like efficiency, compassion, or progress, and it is in the service of these that they propose we should deploy political methods other than legalistic procedures. But it is not hard to imagine that someone might think this about moral rights as well. For all we know, moral rights may be better served by nonlegalistic than by legalistic means; perhaps we should aim at the outcomes rights call for by discretion, command, and administration rather than through the more laborious processes of courts and litigation.[18] Or, if the critics were right that rights and justice were hopeless as moral ideals and should be replaced by other values, then presumably anyone who wholeheartedly accepted the objectivist conception would have to follow them in that.[19]

The general point is this. Some critics say we can reach better outcomes – *whatever* "better" turns out to mean – by using procedures other than those that are stressed in the proceduralist conception of the rule of law.[20] They say that when procedures and morally desirable outcomes diverge, we should follow the outcomes. And maybe they are right. So my question for Professor Dworkin is this: will he follow them in that, if he is ever put to the choice? Or, to focus the matter slightly differently: does he think a commitment to the rule of law permits one to follow outcomes rather than procedures in a dilemma like this? Or putting it yet another way, and mindful of the point we began with, that the rule of law is not supposed to epitomize the sum of all good things: does a commitment to the rule of law represent at least in part a belief that public power should be exercised in a particular way, rather than just *any* way that offers the morally best outcomes?

My hunch is that there is in fact a very substantial proceduralist element in Ronald Dworkin's conception of the rule of law, and that at times it is ascendant over the objectivist element that we have been discussing. That is what I shall argue in the rest of this chapter. Indeed, I shall try to show that, throughout Professor Dworkin's work, he has really responded to his main adversaries – the defenders of the rule-book conception (whom he regards as mainly legal positivists) – with a version of the proceduralist conception rather than with a version of the objectivist conception. He says that it is the objectivist conception that he is really working with, but I think he works comfortably with it only so long as it keeps company with the proceduralist conception.

When they threaten to part – as they did in the dilemma I posited – Dworkin is as likely to go with the conception of the rule of law that stresses commitment to certain procedures as with a conception that is open to any political procedures provided they reach the right result.

Before going on, I would like to warn readers that this chapter is almost entirely expository, which doesn't mean that it gets Dworkin right necessarily, but that its aim is mainly to understand what I think of as a very interesting conception of the rule of law emerging from his work. I think it is mainly a proceduralist conception, and I want to clear away some other strands of Dworkinian jurisprudence – like "the right answer thesis" – that, if interpreted in the wrong way, are in danger of obscuring our view of it. I have no particular objection to the position that I am attributing to Dworkin. In a tangle like this, clarification is task enough.

I

Proceduralist views inevitably face two ways. On the one hand, respecting the integrity of a given set of procedures means trusting them to determine outcomes rather than specifying an outcome in advance and pursuing it by any means necessary. On the other hand, respecting the integrity of a given set of procedures also seems to mean respecting the outcome that they yield, and once it is determined that that *is* the outcome, it may mean abiding by it in a spirit rather like that of the rule-book conception. From this point of view, the procedures are a way of defining what gets into the rule-book, and so the distinction between these first two conceptions of the rule of law may not be so clear after all.

We see this in the account of the rule of law that emerges from the classic Legal Process materials of Henry Hart and Albert Sacks.[21] Though many jurists associate this work – naturally enough, in view of its title – with a normative emphasis on procedures,[22] the leading principle of the Hart and Sacks materials is actually a principle of settlement. Hart and Sacks begin by stressing the need for processes of social decision, interpretation, and change, but the terms in which they do so refer insistently to people's need for settled understandings. And they proceed quickly to identify legality, not so much with the processes themselves as with the determinations that might emerge from them:

> Implicit in every such system of procedures is the central idea of law – an idea which can be described as *the principle of institutional settlement*. The principle builds upon the basic and inescapable facts of social living: . . . namely the fact that human societies are made up of human beings striving to satisfy their respective wants under conditions of interdependence, and the fact that this common enterprise inevitably generates questions of common concern which have to be settled, one way or another, if the enterprise is to maintain itself . . . The principle of institutional settlement expresses the judgment that decisions which are the duly arrived at result of duly established procedures of this kind ought to be accepted as binding upon the whole society unless and until they are duly changed.[23]

Admittedly the Hart and Sacks principle can be read in two ways – one emphasizing the sheer fact of settlement, the other emphasizing "duly arrived at." (On the second reading, the rule of law is perhaps not violated when citizens or officials refuse to defer to a determination that they judge has not been duly arrived at, either because of some procedural defect or because in their opinion the institution that reached the decision was not competent to do so.) And it is true that in the broader legal process school, the Hart and Sacks principle of settlement was complemented by theories of institutional competence, claiming, for example, that courts are better at settling certain kinds of issues than others.[24] As I read the materials, however, it is important not to conflate institutional settlement and institutional competence.[25] Claims of institutional competence are contributions to disputes about the allocation of institutional authority – disputes that themselves require settlement. Suppose an official believes that a certain type of issue would be better settled by a judicial than by a legislative process. If the constitution in fact entrusts such issues to the legislature, then the principle of institutional settlement requires respect for *that* determination, and it follows from this that the legislature's decision on the matter counts as "duly arrived at," irrespective of anyone's opinion about its merits or about the merits of the prior decision that allocated authority in this way.[26]

As I said, this approach can therefore quickly bridge the apparent gap between rule-book and proceduralist conceptions of legality. After all, the rule-book conception doesn't just privilege any old set of rules. At least in its positivist manifestations, it privileges the rules that have emerged from certain institutional *sources* of law,[27] which means rules that have emerged as a result of the operation of specific institutional procedures – the judgments of *this* set of courts or the deliberations and votes of *this* legislature. So if a proceduralist conception of the rule of law is to avoid degenerating into a rule-book conception, there must be elements in it that in some sense privilege the continuing operation of the procedures over the specification of the rulings that, at particular times, have emerged from their operation. Somehow the dynamics of the procedure must be kept alive. But that is a tall order because – it may be thought (and this, surely, was what Hart and Sacks meant about institutional settlement) – the point, surely, of setting up and operating procedures is to secure outcomes. We deliberate and vote in the legislature so that bills become law. We litigate in order to settle disputes and allocate liability. These are not processes we initiate for the fun of it. So what would it mean to privilege procedure over outcome? What sense could there be in it? And even if it made sense, how could it be done?

Two (rather abstract) analogies come to mind. The first is from the theory of justice, specifically the historic entitlement theory of Robert Nozick. Nozick is famous for contrasting his historical entitlement conception of justice with what he calls "current time-slice conceptions."[28] A time-slice conception focuses on the profile of individuals' holdings of wealth and resources at a given time (and judges it in terms of equality or the maximization of utility or conformity to some pattern), whereas an historical entitlement conception judges individual holdings on the basis of how they came about. Nozickian historical entitlement is mostly procedural.[29] But it is not just procedural in the sense that the procedures run and then there's an outcome, and the justice of that outcome is simply its having resulted from these procedures. It is procedural also in the sense that the procedures are ongoing, and one does violence to them by concentrating on distribution-at-a-time at all. What is wrong with the current time-slice approach, according to Nozick, is that it treats as static a situation that is inherently dynamic. The distribution of resources through markets and so forth is not like a race where there is an activity followed by a finishing line and a result, and that's that. Each result immediately becomes the basis for further activity. The goods I bought yesterday – the justice of whose being in my possession is defined by procedures of sale and purchase – are goods I may sell tomorrow. And the overall distribution of resources that results from whatever procedures run tomorrow will in turn be itself just a momentary phase in the continuous operation of the economy. Nozick's procedural principles of historic entitlement are recursive: they operate restlessly and repeatedly upon the outcomes that their operation generates.[30]

I suppose the analogue of this would be a legal system that allowed for repeated and indefinite appeals of a given outcome, or repeated litigation on the same subject. This is something we know legal systems try to avoid – precisely in the interests of what Hart and Sacks would call settle-ment. They allow for only one or two levels of appeal and they have doctrines like *res judicata*, issue–preclusion, and double jeopardy. Interestingly, though, the Hart and Sacks principle of institutional settlement takes possibility of recursion into account: "[D]ecisions which are the duly arrived at result of duly established procedures . . . ought to be accepted as binding . . . *unless and until they are duly changed*."[31] Even if a *particular* outcome cannot be litigated and relitigated indef-initely, general issues implicated in that outcome can be revisited. Supreme courts can overturn their own precedents and bills that have failed in one legislative session may be reintroduced in the sessions that follow.

Equally interesting is the way that Ronald Dworkin seizes on this possibility in elaborating his conception of the rule of law. In his early writing on civil disobedience, Dworkin considered the predicament of citizens who believe that the law allows something that most of their fellow citizens and most officials believe it prohibits.[32] One common analysis of this predicament is that these citizens may appeal the decision they disagree with, but that they are bound to accept the authoritative word of the official body empowered to render a final determination – the highest competent court, for example – and that once that court has ruled, respect for the rule of law requires the citizens to simply comply with its ruling. Dworkin rejects this, in part because it ignores aspects of our legal practice that allow the same issue – if not the same particular case – to be argued and reargued over and over again.

> [A]ny court, including the Supreme Court, may overrule itself. In 1940 the Court decided that a West Virginia law requiring students to salute the Flag was constitutional.[33] In 1943 it reversed itself, and decided that such a statute was unconstitutional after all.[34] . . . We cannot assume, in other words, that the Constitution is always what the Supreme Court says it is. Oliver Wendell Holmes, for example, did not follow such a rule in his famous dissent in the *Gitlow* case.[35] A few years before, in *Abrams*,[36] he had lost his battle to persuade the court that the First Amendment protected an anarchist who had been urging general strikes against the government. A similar issue was presented in *Gitlow* and Holmes once again dissented. "It is true," he said, "that in my opinion this criterion was departed from [in *Abrams*] but the convictions that I expressed in that case are too deep for it to be possible for me as yet to believe that it . . . settled the law." Holmes voted for acquitting Gitlow, on the ground that what Gitlow had done was no crime, even though the Supreme Court had recently held that it was.[37]

There is no departure here from the rule of law, Dworkin implies, even though the position seems unsatisfactory from the point of view of rule–books and settlements.[38]

A second analogy reinforces the point. Think of the procedures of scientific inquiry. A given hypothesis in physics or biology may be supported by the evidence; it may withstand rigorous testing; the results may be replicated in laboratories all over the world; the hypothesis may fit with the surrounding science; it may be fruitful for further discoveries; and so it may take its place in the pantheon of currently accepted scientific laws. But no law is ever so well–established by these procedures that it cannot be revisited, and subjected again to critical tests in the light of new evidence or new structures of inquiry. And this is not just because scientists enjoy running these procedures. It is because they are committed to the idea of objective truth on the matters that any given hypothesis addresses, truth that is supposed to stand independent of any attempt we might make to get at that truth. Thus the ultimate acceptability of a given hypothesis is not just a func-tion of its having survived any finite amount of testing and scientific scrutiny – and, in that sense, of being the outcome of the operation of certain procedures. Its acceptability is supposed to be a matter of objective truth and falsity, which means that there is always something beyond our procedures in the light of which it makes sense – and can sometimes be sensible – to run the procedures yet again, to see whether the hypothesis can be falsified.[39] The idea of objective truth is capable then of reproaching what our procedures have generated. But at the same time, since the procedures are all we have, the idea of objective truth underwrites any attempt to block the repeated running of the procedures in the interest of settlement or "knowing where we stand." Now it is true that the idea of objective truth also provides us with some basis for criticizing and revising the procedures we use, not merely revisiting their outcomes. But that just reinforces the point. Objectivity subverts settlement – whether it is the settlement implicit in a given outcome or the settlement implicit in the view that a given set of procedures are the ones we ought to use to determine outcomes.

Throughout his work, Dworkin has used the idea of objective right answers in just this way, to subvert conceptions of the rule of law oriented towards settlement, predictability, and determinacy.[40] I said at the start of this chapter that he believes – as most of us do – that objectivity is not incompatible with disagreement.[41] And one might go further than this. On some accounts, an assumption of objectivity is *necessary* for disagreement: otherwise what would people think they were disagreeing about?[42] If moral positions were purely subjective, there might be *opposition* between one person's attitudes and another's, but there would not be anything that one person was affirming and another denying, or anything that one person thought true and the other thought false.[43] Now it is no doubt silly to suppose as a general matter that the only point of talking about objective truth or falsity in a given field is to *facilitate* disagreement in that field – to keep the argument alive, as it were, and stop people disengaging on the grounds of *de gustibus non disputandum*. Those who insist, for example, on the objective truth of the proposition that torture is always wrong do so because they care about *torture*, not because they care to have a jolly good debate on the subject. Still, when one reads what Professor Dworkin writes about objectivity, it is striking how much of what he says is directed at those who would discredit argumentation about the matters that Dworkin thinks are objective, as opposed to those who in his view have got some issue objectively wrong. The skeptics and postmodernists who come under attack in his article "Objectivity and Truth – You'd Better Believe It," for example, are attacked for thinking that philosophical debate on moral and other objective-sounding matters is a waste of time.[44] They are not trying to discredit our convictions – some (like Richard Rorty, for example) say they share them[45] – but rather our methods and practices of defending them. Indeed the gist of Dworkin's case in this article is to treat these as "pointless, unprofitable, wearying interruptions . . ."[46] and to deny to them – as far as possible – the availability of any argument about the objective status of moral truth that could be isolated from first-order moral issues themselves. There may be a debate to be had about whether people have an absolute moral right not to be tortured, but Dworkin suggests there is no separate debate to be had about whether our judging that people have an absolute moral right not to be tortured corresponds to moral reality. There is just first-order moral debate, and the article is as strident against those realists who invite a second-order debate by talking about moral facts and moral reality as it is against those antirealists who would take up the invitation and perhaps seek to discredit our practices of (first-order) argumentation.[47]

Again, the effect of the commitment to objectivity in shaking loose the grip of settlement is evident in Professor Dworkin's early writings on civil disobedience. He acknowledges some sort of need for settlement in the law – "It is of course inevitable that some department of government have the final say on what law will be enforced. When men disagree about moral rights, there will be no way for either side to prove its case and some decision must stand if there is not to be anarchy"[48] – and he recognizes that, whatever their jurisprudence, citizens may have to come to terms with the decisions of powerful institutions as a matter of individual prudence.[49] But still, to the extent that legality depends on moral argument, there is always a basis for refusing to accept any particular determination as final: "A citizen's allegiance is to the law, not to any particular person's view of what the law is." In fact, Dworkin's insistence on the existence of objective right answers to constitutional and legal questions (not just to moral questions) has exactly this effect of undermining settlement. "[N]o judicial decision," he says, "is necessarily the right decision."[50] True, a determination by a court may make a difference to what the law is, as a matter of prece- dent.[51] But the difference it is supposed to make is itself a matter of moral argument – I shall say more about Dworkin's view of this in section II – and that too is an argument about an objective issue, an argument that any particular fallible human decision maker may get wrong. So citizens who believe a court has made a legal or moral mistake (about this or anything else) are not morally required to accept its determination as conclusive. Particularly where they conceive the matter to be one of moral importance, they must be allowed to persevere with their challenge:

> It is one thing to say that an individual must sometimes violate his conscience when he knows that the law commands him to do it. It is quite another to say that he must violate his conscience even when he reasonably believes that the law does not require it, because it would inconvenience his fellow citizens if he took the most direct, and perhaps the only, method of attempting to show that he is right and they are wrong.[52]

Indeed, Dworkin defends the practice of citizens' continuing to defy the courts when they think the courts have made a mistake precisely as a way of galvanizing the procedures that define our legal system:

> If our practice were that whenever a law is doubtful . . . one must act as if it were valid, then the chief vehicle we have for challenging the law on moral grounds would be lost. . . . [C]onsider . . . what society gains when people follow their own judgment in cases like this. When the law is uncertain . . . the reason usually is that different legal principles and policies have collided, and it is unclear how best to accommodate these conflicting principles and policies. Our practice, in which different parties are encouraged to pursue their own understanding, provides a means of testing relevant hypotheses. . . . The record a citizen makes in following his own judgment, together with the arguments he makes supporting that judgment when he has the opportunity, are helpful in creating the best judicial deci- sion possible. This remains true even when, at the time the citizen acts, the odds are against his success in court.[53]

One comes away from reading these early articles with the impression that what matters, in Dworkin's view of the rule of law, is that the avenues of argument and challenge remain open. Any principle of settlement is subordinated to the importance of the procedures that allow citi- zens as much as judges to pursue the possibility that the law is not what it says on the rule-books and that society has not kept faith – as its authoritative determinations claim to have kept faith – with principles of right and justice.

I have said that this emphasis in Professor Dworkin's work is underwritten by his commitment to the principle of objective right answers to moral and legal questions. But in the papers we have been discussing, he is at pains to distance himself from any reification of the objectivity criterion. He rejects as "nonsense" the view that "there is always a 'right answer' to a legal problem to be found . . . locked up in some transcendental strongbox."[54] Moreover – and quite strikingly, from our point of view in this chapter – he insists that his own talk of right answers is meant "only to summarize as accurately as I can many of the practices that are part of our legal process."[55]

> Lawyers and judges make statements of legal right and duty, even when they know these are not demonstrable, and support them with arguments even when they know that these arguments will not appeal to everyone. They make these arguments to one another, in the professional journals, in the classrooms, and in the courts.[56]

Skeptics may criticize those practices as fatuous, and as we have seen, Dworkin uses the idea of objective right answers as a vehicle for responding to such skepticism. But the point is not to get any particular legal position accepted as objectively true. The point is to understand the purposes that are served by legal argumentation.

> I understand those purposes to be . . . the development and testing of law through experimentation by citizens and through the adversary process. Our legal system pursues these goals by inviting citizens to decide the strengths and weaknesses of legal arguments for themselves, or through their own counsel, and to act on these judgments, although that permission is qualified by the limited threat that they may suffer if the courts do not agree.[57]

Right answers as such do very little work in this picture; but they frame and underwrite Dworkin's sense of the argumentative practices, procedures, and activities whose ascendancy in a society is, he thinks, definitive of the rule of law.

II

Turning now from Dworkin's discussion of civil disobedience to his main work in legal theory, we find something very similar. The "right answer thesis," when it was introduced into his jurisprudence, was not there to vindicate the claims of any particular legal proposition. It was there, and Professor Dworkin argued for it, in order to counter the suggestion explicit in H. L. A. Hart's legal positivism that in hard cases the sources of law may run out, leaving the decision maker – usually a judge – to come up with a determination on some basis other than legal argument.[58] On Hart's positivist account, there may have to be an end to the process of *legal* argumentation, and if a decision is reached it may have to be reached on some other basis. But the case that Dworkin makes – a case that we will not examine here – is supposed to show that the possibilities for the methods and processes of legal argumentation are much deeper and more extensive than that.[59] This position is expressed using the idea of "the right answer" and associating it with the thesis that even in a hard case one of the parties has a right to win.[60] But since Dworkin denies – here as much as in the writings on civil disobedience – that any alleged right answer is self-certifying as such, what we have is actually an account of how and why we should persist in arguing about the answer to hard cases, underwritten by the notion of an objectively true outcome. We have, in short, a technique for lawyers and judges – a technique that is supposed to be made compelling by Dworkin's account of how his ideal judge proceeds rather than by his account of where his ideal judge ends up.[61]

In interpreting his position this way, I have no particular investment in showing that Professor Dworkin really does or really does not believe in right answers to hard legal questions. As we have seen, he says he doesn't believe in one particular version of the right answer thesis – the transcendental strongbox account.[62] In other places, the thesis that there are right answers seems to be something that he does want to defend. But what he mainly wants to defend it from, I think, are denials that would have the consequence of crippling or blocking the procedures of legal argumentation. So Dworkin's repeated insistence that there can be right answers even though there is protracted disagreement among members of the community as to what these right answers are, is not, as it seems to be, an attempt to protect the right answer thesis from a particularly troubling objection. It is, rather, very close to the heart of the matter: if claims of objectivity and the persistence of argument were not associated in this way, the right answer thesis would not be doing the work that he wants it to do in his jurisprudence.

In *Law's Empire*, the right answer thesis is notable by its absence. I am not saying it is explicitly denied. But the book is mainly given over to an account of how lawyers and judges proceed and what justifies requiring them to proceed in that way. Again, how they proceed, Dworkin says, is by *arguing*, and the book "tries to grasp the argumentative character of our legal practice. . . ."[63]

> Legal practice, unlike many other social phenomena, is *argumentative*. . . . People who have law make and debate claims about what law permits and forbids that would be impossible – because senseless – without law and a good part of what their law reveals about them cannot be discovered except by noticing how they ground and defend these claims.[64]

Having said that, I should add that Professor Dworkin does not treat legal argumentation simply as an aesthetic. Another way he characterizes legal practice is in terms of its "propositional" character,[65] which reminds us that the argument is *about* something and about something that matters.[66] But there is less emphasis on objectivity in *Law's Empire* than there is in some of Dworkin's other writings. His tactic, in an interesting section on "external skepticism" is to defuse the debate about objectivity, rather than take one side in that debate and defend it.[67] Metaphysical issues, he says, should not be allowed to distract us from the practice of argumentation about law and justice, and it must not be allowed to infect our explication of the issues at stake in such argumentation.

The conception of law defended in *Law's Empire* is a particular account of the connection between the way we justify present exercises of power and the relation between past decisions that have been made in the community. The general idea of the rule of law, Dworkin says, is this: "Law insists that force not be used or withheld, no matter how useful that would be to ends in view, no matter how beneficial or noble those ends, except as licensed or required by individual rights and responsibilities flowing from past political decisions about when collective force is justified."[68] Now, it would not be hard to put a gloss on that which accorded with the rule-book conception – under the rule of law, force may not be used unless licensed in advance by antecedently posited rules (laid down in statutes or precedents, for example) – and that conception would justify the doctrine in terms of the importance of notice and predictability for those upon whom force is likely to be used. But Dworkin's gloss on the idea of law again emphasizes the *argumentative* character of the relation between present force and antecedent decisions. It isn't just a matter of pointing to a justification in the existing materials; it's a matter of arguing from those materials, arguing about their interpretation and arguing about the general principles that they (arguably) presuppose. He notes as a matter of fact that lawyers and judges tend to worry away at statutes and precedents long after they have exhausted any possible significance these could have as bases of predictability: "[O]ur judges actually pay more attention to so-called conventional sources of law

like statutes and precedents than conventionalism allows them to do."[69] And he believes that it is
the task of jurisprudence to explain this persistence in argumentation.

The explanation he offers – law as integrity – is not something whose details we will examine
here. Briefly: it is the idea of a certain sort of community, where people accept that they are bound
together by reciprocal obligations that run deep and pervasively through their existing practices
of mutual concern and respect. They treat particular obligations that they may have been found
to have to one another in particular cases not as limited to those circumstances but "as derivative
from and expressing a more general responsibility active throughout [their] association in different ways."[70] To honor this commitment, when any particular issue comes up for present decision,
they are bound to delve relentlessly into the established terms of their association to ascertain how
the present issue would best be decided in view of the deep commitments they think of themselves as having already taken on. That is what Professor Dworkin means by the rule of law –
decision making in the context of that sort of practice. He believes it gives a distinctive flavor to
a community's political culture:

> Politics has a different character for such a people. It is *a theater of debate* about which principles the
> community should adopt as a system, which view it should take of justice, fairness, and due process.
> . . . Members of a community of principle accept that their political rights and duties are not
> exhausted by the particular decisions their political institutions have reached, but depend, more gen-
> erally, on the scheme of principles those decisions presuppose and endorse.[71]

Of course, this "theater of debate" is likely to be characterized by disagreement. People will disagree about what principles our existing decisions presuppose, and they will disagree too about
what would be attractive or eligible principles to consider for this role. And Professor Dworkin as
always wants to resist any skeptical claim that such disagreement makes the argument futile or
inconsequential. Once again, if there is a role for the idea of "right answers" in *Law's Empire*, it
is to block this move – that is, as before, to underwrite, with the idea of objectivity, the point of
persisting with argument in the absence of consensus. Mostly, though, "law as integrity consists
in an approach, in questions rather than answers."[72] Whatever its role in the book, the idea of
objective right answers is not supposed to condemn as violations of the rule of law political arguments that in an objective sense *fail to get it right* about the principled relation between present
issues and antecedent decisions. Instead it seems as though the demands of integrity are satisfied,
on Dworkin's view, in the *attempt* to ascertain and work from deeper principles implicit in
existing decisions.

> We want our officials to treat us as tied together in an association of principle, and we want this for
> reasons that do not depend on any identity of conviction among these officials, either about fit or about
> the more substantive principles an interpretation engages. Our reasons endure when judges disagree,
> at least in detail, about the best interpretation of the community's political order, because each judge
> still confirms and reinforces the principled character of our association by *striving* in spite of the
> disagreement, to reach his own opinion instead of turning to the usually simpler task of fresh
> legislation.[73]

The expressive value of integrity is confirmed, he says, "when people in good faith *try* to treat
one another in a way appropriate to common membership in a community . . . and to see each
other as making *this attempt*, even when they disagree about exactly what integrity requires in particular circumstances."[74]

All of this argues, in my view, for a conception of the rule of law that is, in the last analysis, proceduralist rather than objectivist. A society ruled by law, according to Dworkin, is a society committed to a certain method of arguing about the exercise of public power. A society shows its allegiance to the rule of law by dint of its commitment to asking certain questions and approaching them in the right way. And it is distinguished, ultimately, from societies that lack such a commitment not by the substance of what it does – substantively respecting moral rights, for example – but by the procedures that it unflinchingly follows. "Law is not exhausted by any catalogue of rules or principles [or] . . . by any roster of officials. . . . Law's empire is defined by attitude, not territory or power or process."[75]

III

My characterization of Dworkin's account of the rule of law as a proceduralist conception may be misunderstood. In modern constitutional theory, terms like "proceduralism" and "legal process" are associated with views that confine constitutional review to procedural or quasi-procedural issues. According to John Hart Ely, for example, judges may review legislation for defects in the procedures involved in its enactment or in order to maintain the integrity of the democratic process; but they should not address issues of substance in exercising what is in fact quite a problematic power, from a democratic point of view.[76] Now Professor Dworkin is a critic of this view: he does not believe that procedural issues can be separated from substantive issues in the way that Ely implies, nor does he accept that there is a serious issue about the democratic status of judicial review that needs to be addressed in this way.[77] On Dworkin's theory, judges have no choice but to follow the instruction of the Constitution and address substantive issues of moral right. And a regime in which they are empowered to do this may well be a better democracy precisely because of their ability to address substantive as well as procedural issues in this way.[78] But none of this detracts from what I have referred to as the proceduralist aspect of Dworkin's own jurisprudence. In constitutional law, Dworkin's position is that important issues of rights must be dealt with through a set of procedures appropriate to their character as issues of principle, and this applies whether the issues themselves are issues about political procedures or not.

Reference to constitutional theory, however, does give us the opportunity to consider more closely the kind of procedures that Professor Dworkin has in mind in his conception of the rule of law. I have used the words "argument" and "argumentation" over and over again to refer to these procedures. But we need to pin things down a little. The complaint is often heard that Dworkin's proceduralism does not necessarily imply any commitment to participatory values. Allan Hutchinson is one of the severest critics on this score: "Despite paying lip-service to 'a theater of debate,' *Law's Empire* is about accepting and assuming political obligations and not about participating in the making of them. . . . In *Law's Empire*, judges have been elevated to the rank of moral prophets and philosopher monarchs. For citizens, politics has become a spectator sport."[79] And Silas Wasserstrom says something similar about Dworkin's legalistic "theater of debate":

> Nor am I at all sure what the "theater of debate about which principles the community should adopt as a system" is supposed to be like, but I suspect it would not be very moving or dramatic, even for the community's few moral philosophers who attend or participate. . . . I have no clear idea what the politics of the community of principle would be like, but I suspect its politics would be rather rarified and effete, and would involve very few ordinary citizens as active participants.[80]

I have my own doubts about Dworkin's commitment to democratic politics,[81] but I think this is a little unfair. Several times in *Law's Empire*, Dworkin indicates that it is the responsibility of each citizen, not just each judge, to try to figure out what integrity requires: in a community governed by the rule of law "each citizen has a responsibility to identify, ultimately, [a scheme of principle] for himself, as his community's scheme," and to organize his dealings with other citizens on that basis.[82] Indeed Professor Dworkin appears to think that one of the advantages of an American-style system of judicial review is that it actually improves the quality of debate among members of the public:

> When an issue is seen as constitutional, . . . and as one that will ultimately be resolved by courts apply-
> ing general constitutional principles, the quality of public argument is often improved, because the
> argument concentrates from the start on questions of political morality. . . . When a constitutional
> issue has been decided by the Supreme Court, and is important enough so that it can be expected to
> be elaborated, expanded, contracted, or even reversed by future decisions, a sustained national debate
> begins, in newspapers and other media, in law schools and classrooms, in public meetings and around
> dinner tables. That debate better matches [the] conception of republican government, in its empha-
> sis on matters of principle, than almost anything the legislative process on its own is likely to produce.[83]

He may or may not be right about this.[84] But so far as the characterization of his conception of the rule of law is concerned, it is evident that Dworkin does not think citizens are required to submit to oligarchic nonparticipatory determinations of what law, rights, and principles add up to. The discussion of civil disobedience that we studied in section II of this chapter makes that quite clear, and it indicates that the proceduralism of Dworkin's may not be regarded as a purely spectator sport.

We have seen that throughout Dworkin's writings, the idea that there are objective right answers to the conundrums that legality poses for us helps invigorate and keep open the legal and politi-cal processes that he favors. It is true that this gives a particular objectivist spin to Dworkin's theory of institutional competence, and sometimes he says things like this: "The best institutional structure is the one best calculated to produce the best answers to the essentially moral question of what the democratic conditions actually are, and to secure stable compliance with those con-ditions."[85] He uses this also as a basis for some skepticism about legislative procedures, which he says may not be "the safest vehicle for protecting the rights of politically unpopular groups."[86] But he is also sometimes willing to say that "[l]egislatures are guardians of principle too,"[87] and that if lawmakers ask themselves the right questions and proceed in the right, responsive to con-cerns about integrity and principle in their deliberations, then their procedures too are constitu-tive of the rule of law.[88]

I have mostly shied away from asserting that Dworkin's conception of the rule of law is unequivocally proceduralist. We have seen throughout that there are elements of the objectivist and the rule-book conception, and no doubt other conceptions too. It is a delicate exercise in tri-angulation, as it were, to see how a given conception responds to the interlocking concerns about settlement, process, and objectivity that are implicated in the rule of law ideal. All of them in various ways pay tribute to the needs and concerns of ordinary people and what they expect from their law.[89] What I have tried to do, however, is to emphasize those parts of Professor Dworkin's conception of legality that find respect for individuals and their rights in the manner in which we proceed in our legal system, not just in the notion of objective principles or in the reality of estab-lished settlements. The rule of law prevails in a community, according to Dworkin, when its "col-lective decisions [are] made by political institutions whose structure, composition, and practices treat all members of the community, as individuals with equal concern and respect."[90] A society committed to the rule of law in this sense may well use courts more than a society without such a commitment. But that is not merely because – and I think not mainly because – courts are more likely to get things right. It is rather that courts are supposed to exhibit in their forms, structures, and procedures a determination to take seriously the issues of right that they are addressing. A society committed to the rule of law

> encourages each individual to suppose that his relations with other citizens and with his government are matters of justice, and it encourages him and his fellow citizens to discuss as a community what justice requires those relations to be. It promises a forum in which his claims about what he is entitled to have will be steadily and seriously considered at his demand.[91]

For these purposes, taking rights seriously is not so much a matter of getting rights right; it is a matter of conveying in the *way* in which we make our decisions that we understand that rights are involved. Personally, I believe that the same argument can be made, on certain favorable assumptions, for legislatures too: they too have their own way of respecting in their structures and procedures the equality of respect due to the opinions of ordinary men and women.[92] But I shall not try to persuade Professor Dworkin of that now. This chapter, as I said at the beginning, is supposed to be an exposition of his account of the rule of law, and it is intended to bring out proceduralist themes in that account that are in danger of being downplayed in a jurisprudential environment that continues to be obsessed with the right answer thesis.

Notes

1   For this observation, see Joseph Raz, "The Rule of Law and its Virtue," in his collection *The Authority of Law: Essays on Law and Morality* (Oxford: Clarendon Press, 1979), p. 210.
2   Universal Declaration of Human Rights (1948), Preamble, para. 3.
3   For these references: see Aristotle, *Politics*, Bk. III, chs. 10–11,15–16; Antonin Scalia, "The Rule of Law as a Law of Rules," *University of Chicago Law Review*, vol. 56, 1989, p. 1175; Sir John Fortescue, *In Praise of the Laws of England* (1468) from Fortescue, *On the Laws and Governance of England* (Cambridge, UK: Cambridge University Press, 1997), p. 17; John Locke, *Second Treatise*, ch. 11; A. V. Dicey, *Introduction to the Study of the Law of the Constitution Eighth Edition of 1915* (Indianapolis, IN: Liberty Press, 1982), pp. 110–22; Ronald Dworkin, "Political Judges and the Rule of Law," in *A Matter of Principle* (Cambridge, MA: Harvard University Press, 1985), ch. 1. For "King Nomos," see Donald Kelley, *The Human Measure: Social Thought in the Western Legal Tradition* (Cambridge, MA: Harvard University Press, 1990), p. 283.
4   See the discussion in Jeremy Waldron, "Is the Rule of Law an Essentially Contested Concept (in Florida)?" *Law and Philosophy*, vol. 21, 2002, p. 137, and Richard Fallon "The Rule of Law as a Concept in Constitutional Discourse," *Columbia Law Review*, vol. 97, 1997, p. 1.
5   See Scalia, "The Rule of Law as a Law of Rules," op. cit., and also F. A. Hayek, *The Constitution of Liberty* (London: Macmillan, 1960), chs. 9–10, for versions of the "rule-book" view.
6   See Fallon, "The Rule of Law as a Concept in Constitutional Discourse," op. cit., pp. 18–21, for a fine account of this proceduralist view.
7   One that is very important, but that I shall not spend much time discussing in this paper, links the rule of law to equality before the law. For example, see Dicey, *Law of the Constitution*, op. cit, p. 114:

We mean . . . when we speak of the "rule of law" as a characteristic of our country, not only that with us no man is above the law, but (what is a different thing) that here every man, whatever be his rank or condition, is subject to the ordinary law of the realm and amenable to the jurisdiction of the ordinary tribunals.

 8 Dworkin, "Political Judges and the Rule of Law," op. cit., pp. 11–12. (This essay was first published as a Maccabaean Lecture in the *Proceedings of the British Academy*, vol. 64, 1978, p. 259.)
 9 For a powerful version of this argument, see Jeremy Bentham, *Principles of the Civil Code*, in C. B. Macpherson (ed.), *Property: Mainstream and Critical Positions* (Oxford: Blackwell, 1977), p. 41.
10 Dworkin, "Political Judges and the Rule of Law," op. cit., p. 32.
11 Ibid., p. 12.
12 Compare J. L. Mackie, *Ethics: Inventing Right and Wrong* (Harmondsworth, UK: Penguin, 1977), p. 21 with Michael Moore, "Moral Reality," *Wisconsin Law Review*, 1982, at pp. 1089–90.
13 Dworkin, "Political Judges and the Rule of Law," op. cit., p. 13.
14 Here I differ slightly from Fallon, who calls this sort of conception "a substantive conception" of the rule of law: see Fallon, "The Rule of Law as a Concept in Constitutional Discourse," op. cit., pp. 21–4. That term can be misleading for it is also used to refer to noninstrumental conceptions: see Margaret Jane Radin, "Reconsidering the Rule of Law," *Boston University Law Review*, vol. 69, 1989, pp. 781–819, at pp. 787–8.
15 See Fallon, "The Rule of Law as a Concept in Constitutional Discourse," op. cit., pp. 23–4.
16 Dworkin, "Political Judges and the Rule of Law," op. cit., p. 12.
17 For a long time, this was a theme of Marxist jurisprudence: see, e.g., Evgenii Pashukanis, *Law and Marxism: A General Theory* (London: Ink Links, 1978). See also Mark Tushnet, "An Essay on Rights," *Texas Law Review*, vol. 62, 1984, p. 1363.
18 For the possibility of this disjunction between moral rights and legalistic means, see Jeremy Waldron, "A Right-Based Critique of Constitutional Rights," *Oxford Journal of Legal Studies*, vol. 13, 1993, pp. 18–51, at p. 30; see further Jeremy Waldron, *Law and Disagreement* (Oxford: Clarendon Press, 1999), pp. 217–21.
19 After all, morality is not rights-based just because we think it is. That too is an objective question, and anyone defending what I have called the objectivist conception of the rule of law surely believes that we should be ruled by an accurate conception of moral rights only on condition that the idea of moral rights is a good idea. Otherwise we should seek to capture in our public policy and public decisions whatever other moral ideas are objectively better.
20 See, e.g., Edward L. Rubin, "Law and Legislation in the Administrative State," *Columbia Law Review*, vol. 89, 1989, p. 369.
21 Henry M. Hart and Albert M. Sacks, *The Legal Process: Basic Problems in the Making and Application of Law*, ed. William N. Eskridge and Philip P. Frickey (Westbury, NY: Foundation Press, 1994).
22 See e.g., Fallon, "The Rule of Law as a Concept in Constitutional Discourse," op. cit., pp. 18–19.
23 Hart and Sacks, *The Legal Process*, op. cit., p. 4.
24 See, e.g., Lon Fuller, "Forms and Limits of Adjudication," *Harvard Law Review*, vol. 92, 1978, p. 353.
25 I discuss this also in Jeremy Waldron, "Authority for Officials," in Lukas Meyer, Stanley Paulson, and Thomas W. Pogge (eds.), *Rights, Culture, and the Law – Essays After Joseph Raz* (Oxford: Oxord University Press, 2003), pp. 45–70.
26 Thus Hart and Sacks say, for example, that the principle of institutional settlement "forbids a court to substitute its own ideas for what the legislature has duly enacted" (Hart and Sacks, *The Legal Process*, op. cit., p. 1194). And they say it also commands respect for precedent: "Respect for the principle of institutional settlement demands . . . [that what] a legislature has duly determined ought not to be set at naught by any other agency or person. What earlier judicial decisions have duly settled ought not to come unsettled" (ibid., p. 147).
27 For the sources thesis, see Raz, *The Authority of Law*, op. cit., pp. 47 ff.

28   Robert Nozick, *Anarchy, State and Utopia* (Oxford: Basil Blackwell, 1974), pp. 153–60.

29   For the distinction between pure-procedural and other approaches to justice, see John Rawls, *A Theory of Justice* (Oxford: Oxford University Press, 1971), pp. 73–7.

30   For this feature of Nozick's theory, see Lawrence Davis, "Comments on Nozick's Entitlement Theory," *Journal of Philosophy*, vol. 73, 1976, pp. 836–44, at pp. 838–9.

31   Hart and Sacks, *The Legal Process*, op. cit., p. 4.

32   Ronald Dworkin, "Civil Disobedience," in *Taking Rights Seriously*, rev. edn. (London: Duckworth, 1977), p. 210.

33   [*Minersville School District* v. *Gobitis*, 310 U.S. 586 (1940).]

34   [*West Virginia State Board of Education* v. *Barnette*, 319 U.S. 624 (1943).]

35   [*Gitlow* v. *New York* 268 U.S. 652, 672 (1925).]

36   [*Abrams* v. *United States* 250 U.S. 616, 624 (1919).]

37   Dworkin, "Civil Disobedience," op. cit., pp. 213 and 211; I have reversed the order of these two excerpts, but it does not affect the gist of Professor Dworkin's argument.

38   But compare the statement in Ronald Dworkin, *Freedom's Law: The Moral Reading of the American Constitution* (Cambridge, MA: Harvard University Press, 1996), pp. 124–5, supporting *stare decisis* on the issue of abortion.

39   It will be evident that this paragraph is heavily influenced by a Popperian view of scientific method. See, e.g., Karl Popper, *Conjectures and Refutations: The Growth of Scientific Knowledge* (New York: Basic Books, 1962). But I do not think that any of the issues between Popper and his critics are relevant here, except for those critics who deny the existence of objective truth and perhaps also those inductivists who believe that certain methods are capable of establishing general propositions finally and conclusively. I don't think there are very many people in that latter group; but there are of course thousands in the former category.

40   There is also an element of substantive justice in the Hart and Sacks conception, as when they say (Hart and Sacks, *The Legal Process*, op. cit., p. 6):

> [T]he principle of institutional settlement operates not merely as a principle of necessity but as a principle of justice. This means attention to the constant improvement of all the procedures which depend upon the principle in the effort to assure that they yield decisions which are not merely preferable to the chaos of no decision but are calculated as well as may be affirmatively to advance the larger purposes of society.

But it does not appear to do the same work as it does in Dworkin's writing.

41   See note 12 above.

42   The classic version of this argument is found in G. E. Moore, "The Nature of Moral Philosophy," in his book *Philosophical Studies* (London: Routledge and Kegan Paul, 1922), pp. 333–4. See also Oliver A. Johnson, "On Moral Disagreements," *Mind*, vol. 68, 1959, p. 482.

43   Arguably, this does not apply to projectivist or quasi-realist positions like that of Simon Blackburn, which – though rejecting objectivity – do not present moral judgments as mere reports of attitudes; see Simon Blackburn, *Essays in Quasi-Realism* (New York: Oxford University Press, 1983).

44   Ronald Dworkin, "Objectivity and Truth – You'd Better Believe It," *Philosophy and Public Affairs*, vol. 25 (1996), p. 87.

45   See, e.g., Richard Rorty, "Human Rights, Rationality and Sentimentality," in S. Shute and S. Hurley (ed.), *On Human Rights: The 1993 Oxford Amnesty Lectures* (New York: Basic Books, 1993), pp. 115–16; "Solidarity or Objectivity?" in his collection, *Objectivity, Relativism and Truth: Philosophical Papers Volume I* (Cambridge, UK: Cambridge University Press, 1991), p. 33.

46   Dworkin, "Objectivity and Truth," op. cit., p. 139.

47   Ibid., pp. 104–5.

48   Dworkin, "Taking Rights Seriously," in *Taking Rights Seriously*, op. cit., p. 186.

49   Dworkin, "Civil Disobedience," op. cit., p. 213: "[A] man must consider what the courts will do when

he decides whether it would be prudent to follow his own judgment. He may have to face jail, bankruptcy, or opprobrium if he does."

50 Dworkin, "Taking Rights Seriously," op. cit., p. 185. The view that what the courts finally determine is law by definition, Dworkin regards as "wrong, and in the end deeply corrupting of the idea and rule of law" – see Ronald Dworkin, "Civil Disobedience and Nuclear Protest" in *A Matter of Principle*, op. cit., pp. 115–16.

51 Dworkin, "Civil Disobedience," in *Taking Rights Seriously*, op. cit., pp. 211 and 214.

52 Ibid., p. 214.

53 Ibid., pp. 212–13. Again, I have altered the order of some of the passages in the excerpt without, I think, altering their sense.

54 Ibid., p. 216.

55 Ibid.

56 Ibid.

57 Ibid., pp. 216–17.

58 H. L. A. Hart, *The Concept of Law*, 2nd edn. (Oxford: Clarendon Press, 1994).

59 See especially "The Model of Rules I and 'Hard Cases'," in *Taking Rights Seriously*, op. cit.

60 Ibid., p. 82.

61 For Hercules' "technique" see ibid., pp. 129–30.

62 See text accompanying note 54 above; see also Dworkin, *Taking Rights Seriously*, op. cit., p. 337.

63 Ronald Dworkin, *Law's Empire* (Cambridge, MA: Harvard University Press, 1986), p. 14.

64 Ibid., p. 13.

65 Ibid., p. 14.

66 *Law's Empire* opens with the words "It matters how judges decide cases" (ibid., p. 1).

67 Ibid., pp. 76–86.

68 Ibid., p. 93.

69 Ibid., p. 130.

70 Ibid., p. 200.

71 Ibid., p. 211.

72 Ibid., p. 239. See also ibid., p. 412: "I have not devised an algorithm for the courtroom. No electronic magician could design from my arguments a computer program that would supply a verdict everyone would accept once the facts of the case and the text of all past statutes and judicial decisions were put at the computer's disposal."

73 Ibid., p. 264 (my emphasis).

74 Ibid., p. 190 (my emphasis).

75 Ibid., p. 413.

76 John Hart Ely, *Democracy and Distrust: A Theory of Judicial Review* (Cambridge, MA: Harvard University Press, 1981).

77 Dworkin, "The Forum of Principle," in *A Matter of Principle*, op. cit., pp. 33–71, pp. 57–69.

78 See Dworkin, *Freedom's Law*, op. cit., ch. 1. For a critique of this position, see Jeremy Waldron, "Judicial Review and the Conditions of Democracy," *Journal of Political Philosophy*, vol. 6, 1998, p. 335, and *Law and Disagreement*, op. cit., ch. 13.

79 Allan C. Hutchinson, "Indiana Dworkin and *Law's Empire*," *Yale Law Journal*, vol. 96, 1987, pp. 637–55, at p. 654. For "theater of debate," see Dworkin, *Law's Empire*, op. cit., p. 211 and the passage cited at text accompanying note 71 above.

80 Silas Wasserstrom, "The Empire's New Clothes," *Georgetown Law Journal*, vol. 75, 1986, pp. 199–314 at p. 265.

81 See Waldron, *Law and Disagreement*, op. cit., ch. 13.

82 Dworkin, *Law's Empire*, op. cit., pp. 190, 213.

83 Dworkin, *Freedom's Law*, op. cit., p. 345.

84 For a critique, see Waldron, *Law and Disagreement*, op. cit., pp. 289–91.

85 Dworkin, *Freedom's Law*, op. cit., p. 34.

86 Ibid.

87 Ibid., p. 31.

88 See Dworkin, *Law's Empire*, op. cit., pp. 167, 176, and 217–19.

89 For an interesting discussion of the values associated with legality, see also Ronald Dworkin, "Hart's Postscript and the Character of Political Philosophy," pp. 24–8, available at ⟨http://www.law.nyu.edu/clppt/program2001/readings/readingshart/rdhartcolloquium2.pdf⟩.

90 Dworkin, *Freedom's Law*, op. cit., p. 17.

91 Dworkin, "Political Judges and the Rule of Law," op. cit., p. 32.

92 See Waldron, *Law and Disagreement*, op. cit., chs. 3–5 and 10–11. See also Jeremy Waldron, *The Dignity of Legislation* (Cambridge, UK: Cambridge University Press, 1999).

Part V

Replies to Critics

18

Ronald Dworkin Replies

Ronald Dworkin

Critics are a writer's best allies, and a lucky writer has powerful critics. I am very grateful to those who have contributed to this fine collection, and particularly grateful to Justine Burley for her ambition, skill, and thoroughness in designing and editing the book. My responses to the various essays are of strikingly different lengths, and I must emphasize that the length of my response to an essay in no way reflects a judgment on its importance or quality. I have thought it most helpful to reply to detailed criticism of my own work. Some of the essays offer extensive criticism and therefore call for fuller replies; the topics covered in some of these are more diverse and wide-ranging than others, and call for even longer comment. Other essays are mainly original explorations of topics that I have also discussed. These are distinct contributions that have given me, as they will give others, important new insights, but I can say less in response to them on this occasion. All the essays are complex, and raise a number of issues. I have not been able to reply to all of these: I have had to be selective but I should now say (chagrined by past experience) that my failure to comment on a particular criticism or interpretation of my work does not signal agreement. None of the essays lacks robustness, and some of them, including Burley's own essay about genetics, G. A. Cohen's essay about expensive tastes, and Leslie Green's essay on political obligation announce refutations of positions they rightly take to be fundamental to large parts of my work. These essays, in particular remind us that drama is philosophy's spice.

Part I

G. A. Cohen

Professor Cohen's long and wide-ranging essay is full of drama. He defends his view that many people with "champagne" tastes should be given extra resources with which to satisfy those tastes. Indeed, he now thinks that many more such people qualify for extra funds than he formerly thought. He also insists that I have significantly but covertly changed my own mind about distributive justice in recent years, and that the shift is a "large concession" to rival views. He also declares that a state of affairs may be unjust even though no one was responsible for or could remedy the supposed injustice, and that compensating people with expensive tastes is actually a "radically egalitarian" step because it subverts markets. I do not agree with any of these claims. I continue to think that he is wrong about expensive tastes. My supposed concession is only his invention. Justice is relational, and the demands of justice are limited to what people can do. The market is not the enemy of equality but, properly disciplined, indispensable to it. However, Cohen has explored in greater depth than anyone else the case that justice requires giving people with expensive tastes more resources, and his arguments are particularly revealing and helpful. I must respond to them in detail.

We need a brief background. In 1981, in an article that is now chapter 1 of my book *Sovereign Virtue*, I argued that the concept of welfare (or well-being or utility) is unsuited to one prominent role that many philosophers and economists have assigned it: welfare cannot serve, as they claim it can, as the metric of a just distribution of a community's wealth, opportunities, and other resources. Utilitarians think that a distribution of wealth and opportunity is just if it raises the average level of welfare in the pertinent community to the highest attainable level. Welfare egalitarians think a distribution just if it leaves people in that community as nearly equal in welfare as is possible. It has been an embarrassment to all such welfarist theories that they appear to recommend transfers that would strike most people as unjust. Utilitarianism seems to require extra resources for happy and fortunate people who are particularly adept at generating welfare from resources, taken from miserable, unfortunate people who are not. Equality of welfare seems to recommend extra resources for people with expensive tastes, taken from people with simpler requirements, because the former need more money to achieve equal welfare. Utilitarians and welfare egalitarians have struggled to avoid these counterintuitive consequences.

I did call attention to these traditional objections, but my own argument against welfare-based theories of justice was more general. I said that "welfare" is so ambiguous (or abstract) that neither utilitarianism nor welfare egalitarianism can be assessed until its proponent specifies some more concrete conception of welfare – some more specific account of what he takes a person's welfare or well-being to consist in. I then suggested that once a more concrete conception is specified, any welfarist theory loses whatever appeal it might have had. Suppose, for example, that welfare is defined (as many philosophers including Cohen on some occasions have defined it) as buzzes of pleasure, so that the more buzzes a person has the greater his overall well-being is said to be. It is implausible that justice requires either maximizing the total number of buzzes or equalizing the number of buzzes each person has because (among other reasons) people disagree markedly about how important pleasure buzzes actually are to what they take to be their overall well-being or success. Very few people think that pleasure is all that matters in an overall worthwhile or successful life, and even those who think pleasure matters to some important degree disagree about that degree. I offered parallel objections (which Cohen summarizes in his new essay – see p. 5[1]) to the claim that justice consists in maximizing or equalizing welfare on any of the other discrete conceptions of welfare that I distinguished: preference satisfaction, relative success in realizing one's own ambitions in life, and overall success in realizing some objective standard of success in life. I discussed the possibility that justice consists in either maximizing or equalizing welfare, not on one of these distinct conceptions, but in some amalgam or compound of them. I argued that none of the distinct conceptions I had identified could plausibly figure even as components in a more ecumenical or pluralistic conception.[2]

In chapter 2 of *Sovereign Virtue* I tried to develop an alternative, nonwelfarist account of distributive justice that aims at making people equal in the various resources with which they confront their lives rather than in any measure of the success they achieve. In that and later essays, also now consolidated in that book, I pointed out what I took to be important theoretical differences between the two conceptions of equality and of justice.[3] Two are pertinent to this response. First, welfare-based theories must suppose either that some conception of well-being that permits at least rough interpersonal comparisons is shared by everyone, or that, so far as people disagree about where their well-being lies, the state or community should decide the matter for everyone. Resource-based theories, on the contrary, assume that people differ, sometimes radically, in their opinions about what makes their lives go overall better or worse. They insist that people should govern their lives according to their own convictions on that matter. Second, a welfare-based theory assumes that people develop their tastes and form their ambitions independently of any assumptions either about the resources that will or should be available to them. Resource-based theories assume, on the contrary, that people develop their tastes and form their ambitions taking probable resource allocation into account as a factor, not just a discovery they must confront after that reflection is complete. They also insist that people should reflect on their lives and ambitions in that way, and, in particular, that they should develop tastes, form ambitions, and make choices with an eye to the opportunity costs to others of those choices. In these and other ways, I argued, resource-based theories of justice are more sensitive to people's ethical psychology and more consistent with an attractive view of people's responsibilities to other people.

If these general arguments against welfarist measures of justice are successful, then of course it follows that justice does not require compensating people with champagne tastes just because they need more money to secure equal welfare. People are responsible for their own tastes in the sense that they must make their choices about which of these to cultivate and satisfy given a fair share of collective resources, a share that is not increased if they decide to pursue some particularly expensive goal.

In a 1989 article Cohen endorsed a form of equality of welfare, and he accepted the counterintuitive result that appears to follow from this: he said that people who are either born with expensive tastes for rare food or drink or beautiful objects or who acquire such tastes as a result of their upbringing (though not people who have deliberately cultivated such tastes) should indeed receive extra resources.[4] He said that my refusal to recognize this is inconsistent with the more general thrust of my argument. Since I believe that people should be compensated for their bad luck in disease, accidents, and handicaps, and since, in his view, people's uncultivated expensive tastes are just their bad luck as well, I am inconsistent in not endorsing compensation for that form of bad luck. In his new essay in this collection, he repeats his general view but abandons the parenthetical exemption. He now thinks that justice requires extra resources for people with expensive tastes even if, at least for the most part, they have deliberately cultivated those tastes.

Cohen on welfare

A community that measures justice either wholly or partly in terms of the sum or distribution of welfare must specify some particular conception of welfare. Cohen believes that he can defend equality of welfare without specifying any such conception, however: he thinks that the question of what welfare is and of whether it should be made equal are distinct issues, and that the latter can be addressed while taking no position on the former.[5] This is implausible. How can we understand why welfare should be made equal without first understanding what welfare is? Cohen says he aims merely to "refute" my argument that equality of welfare is a false goal. But my argument is that welfare egalitarianism cannot be defended once a particular conception of welfare is specified. How can he hope to refute my argument without showing that equality of welfare is defensible on at least some specific conception of welfare?

In any case, we must glean what we can from Cohen's scattered remarks about what welfare is. In his earlier article he said that welfare, at least for purposes of justice, is either a buzz of pleasure or a tick of desire satisfaction.[6] He sometimes suggests, in his present essay, that he has changed his mind about that. But elsewhere in this essay he says that he has not. "A person's tastes are expensive in the required sense," he now says, "if and only if . . . they are such that it costs more to provide that person than to provide others with given levels of satisfaction or fulfillment."

Elsewhere he says that "In the present acceptation, people have expensive tastes if, for example, ordinary cigars and cheap wine that give pleasure to most people leave them cold, and they can get something like that pleasure (and, *ex hypothesi*, *not* a greater one) only with Havana cigars and Margaux" (pp. 6).

In some places he says that welfare might be a complex matter so that, for example, someone with nobler tastes and ambitions might have higher welfare in one dimension just for that reason, and someone with tastes that are easier to satisfy and therefore more often satisfied might have higher welfare in a different dimension for that reason (see Appendix, p. 25). But equality of welfare (or any other welfarist theory of justice) needs an overall metric that combines whatever different dimensions of welfare it sets out, so that it can finally compare two people's overall welfare. Cohen offers no overall metric; indeed he does not even specify dimensions. In other places he declares that what counts as welfare for purposes of egalitarian justice might differ from occasion to occasion (p. 21). But he provides no explanation of which conception of welfare is important in which context, or why any of them is decisive on any occasion.

Still elsewhere he says that his ultimate standard of distributional equality is not equality of welfare but "equality of opportunity for advantage," which he describes as "equality of opportunity not for welfare alone but for a vector which includes that, *and* resources, *and* need satisfaction, and, perhaps, other advantages" (p. 19). But he does not tell us what conception of welfare figures in the larger phenomenon of advantage, or why "need satisfaction" is not either all of welfare or an element in welfare rather than something nonwelfare; or what "other advantages" he has in mind. It is unclear, moreover, what larger concept he imagines "resources" and "welfare" to be components of. If one person has more welfare than another (on any specified conception or on some compound of conceptions) of welfare but fewer impersonal and personal resources, what metric determines whether they are nevertheless equal in "advantage"? It cannot be welfare, because welfare is concededly unequal. It cannot be resources however measured. Nor is the ordinary meaning of "advantage" helpful: we say that some people have the advantage of a good character, but Cohen cannot mean that resources should be transferred from them to others to make overall advantage more equal. It remains unclear how the appeal to advantage either clarifies or changes his position.

Markets and morals

We should note a question Cohen puts to himself: why is the issue of expensive tastes sufficiently important to justify the trouble he has taken with it over many years? He accepts that, in practice, no government could go very far toward making people equal in their enjoyment or satisfaction or welfare on any other conception; he agrees that government could at most make what he calls "general" subsidies to groups of people with particularly expensive tastes: those who love opera, for example, or expensive art books. He also accepts that it might seem "peculiar that a person, that is, me, whom most people would account more radically egalitarian than Dworkin, should be tender" toward people with expensive tastes. "The answer," he reports, "is that it is not a tiny issue at all: the correct assessment of the justice of the market is at stake here" (p. 17).

On my view a market in goods and service is indispensable to justice because only a market can measure what one person has taken for himself by identifying the opportunity cost to others of his having it, so only a market can allow people who enjoy a fair distribution of resources to preserve that fairness through their later decisions of occupation, investment, and consumption. Of course an actual market can serve justice only if its results are adjusted to compensate not only for inevitable market imperfections of different kinds, but also for the fact that people do not face actual markets with a fair division of resources. I have attempted to describe techniques, some of them based on hypothetical insurance calculations, for improving the market's fairness in those dimensions.[7] Cohen, however, thinks that a market is in principle unjust for just the reasons that I think it is indispensable. His antimarket argument depends largely on a single example, however: he says that we would think it wrong for a lending library to charge more money to those borrowing its expensive books than its cheap ones.

It is an odd example because, as he concedes, market efficiency would argue against rather than for most libraries charging for books at differential rates. Lending and other libraries do have budgets, however, and they make cost/benefit decisions in other ways, chiefly in their acquisitions policy. These decisions are of course influenced by what they think most people want to read: general libraries do not buy, for example, technical journals or books with a limited professional audience. Libraries are ordinarily subsidized, however, because they supply public goods (an enlightened and cultured citizenry, we think, makes for better democracy) and they therefore should and do also buy reference books, including some art books, even if relatively few readers use these. But subsidized libraries certainly should not aim to cater for every taste, no matter how expensive: we know from the market that some people find great satisfaction in reading their novels expensively bound in finely tooled leather or in paging through lavish large-format art books. No doubt some people who buy such books derive less satisfaction from buckram and ordinary art books than others do, but it would be scandalous for a public library to spend even a minor part of its budget to satisfy them.

So Cohen's lead example seems to undermine rather than support his suspicion of markets. He offers another antimarket argument, however, that we must also consider. Centralized political decisions about resource distribution are fairer than market decisions, he insists, because the former can be finely tuned to satisfy each taste in a community to a degree proportionate to the overall demand for that taste, while a market might give a taste minority nothing at all. A command-economy state can decide, for example, to build one opera house and nine sports stadiums in a large territory in which the great majority prefers sports to opera, while market forces might mean no opera house and 20 stadiums in such a community.[8] But though particularly altruistic majorities may try to allocate resources proportionately in that way, markets will do that much more efficiently, because politics cannot effectively produce the full range of demand and cost information that markets are designed to generate, and because markets do not depend on altruism to produce proportionality. True, in practice in a market economy, scattered opera lovers might face high transaction costs in securing an opera house through market transactions, and might encounter "lumpy" goods problems as well, so that political action may be needed to correct or mimic a market: in that case, however, politics has not rejected a market as unjust but on the contrary tried to imitate its justice.[9] Cohen's discussion illustrates the flaw in the common assumption of self-styled "radical egalitarians" that market efficiency is inherently an enemy of equality. Markets can indeed exacerbate injustice when resources and bargaining power are unfairly distributed. But a fair market from a fair distribution, in addition to its undeniably greater efficiency, protects minority interests better than a command economy directed by majoritarian politics is likely to do.

Justice and feasibility

Cohen's view is counterintuitive not just in his conclusion that people with ordinary tastes should be taxed more heavily to give extra funds to those with champagne tastes, but in the more general idea that government can sensibly aim to make its citizens equal in their well-being or their success in living. How could government discover how many buzzes of pleasure each citizen has had in the last tax year (for example)? Or decide what concrete policy programs would make buzzes more equally distributed even in the short term, let alone in a longer run in which tastes would change in myriad and unpredictable ways in response to those programs? Cohen replies that such epistemic, technical, and administrative problems are irrelevant when considering what justice requires because "a demand of justice is not something that the state, or, indeed, any other agent, is in a position to deliver" (p. 18).

Separating justice from feasibility in that way frees Cohen from any need to support his theoretical claims by showing that they could be put into practice, and how. But the separation seems even more counterintuitive than his position itself. (He says that I am myself committed to that odd view of justice, but I have explicitly repudiated it (p. 18).[10]) To be sure, justice does not depend on what is politically feasible, or even on what is reasonable to do. A distribution may be unjust even if no politician could persuade the nation to pay taxes to correct it; treatment of suspected terrorists might be unjust even if it is reasonable given security threats.[11] But it is theoretically misleading, as well as pointless, to say that justice demands what even people with the best and most selfless will cannot do: that it is unjust that people who are born horribly crippled are not cured, for example, when there is no cure. Justice is relational: it is a matter of how people should treat one another, not of how the world should otherwise be. That seems particularly true of the distinct virtue of equality:[12] a community realizes the political virtue of equality when it treats each of its members with equal concern on the right conception of what equal concern requires. That relational view of justice encourages even those political philosophers who write at the most abstract level to focus their attention on what can actually be done, and political philosophy is most interesting as well as most valuable when that focus is secure. If we limit the demands of equality to what a community of good will and dedication can actually achieve from time to time, we show how justice is feasible and therefore why it is all but imperative.

What bad luck?

We may now move to Cohen's general argument for compensating people with expensive tastes. He thinks they have had bad luck and deserve compensation for that reason. But what has their bad luck been? In my response to his earlier critique I distinguished (though not in these terms) two forms of bad luck that people might claim because their tastes are expensive: bad *preference* luck, which is their bad luck in having the preferences they do because these preferences are expensive, and bad *price* luck, which is bad luck in the high cost of the preferences they have.[13] The difference appears when we ask whether the claimant would rid himself of the preference if he could; whether he would take a costless pill with no side effects to do that. Suppose wealth is distributed equally in his community but B finds that his taste for opera is more expensive to satisfy, night by night, than his friend A's taste for rock, and he therefore has fewer pleasure buzzes (say) than A does. B might think it his bad luck, given the distribution of resources and preferences in his community, that he has been saddled with a taste for opera, and he would happily take the pill I described. In that case he thinks that he has bad preference luck. Or he might refuse the pill because he doesn't wish to cease loving opera, but he would certainly wave a magic wand to make opera cheaper. He thinks he has bad price luck.

I thought that Cohen had made two arguments in his 1989 essay, one based on each of these two versions of bad luck. I said that the bad-preference-luck version assumes that people treat their own tastes as they treat features of their physical constitution, like the state of their liver, that either contribute to or detract from what they really want, which is welfare conceived as some distinct psychological state like a buzz of pleasure or as a tick on a list of assignments. I considered the bad-price-luck argument more briefly: I said that justice cannot treat the tastes and preferences of others, which determine prices, as compensable bad luck.[14] Cohen now says, however, that he never meant to offer a bad-preference-luck claim, even though several statements in his earlier article, including what he now calls his "flagship" formulation, did suggest that version of the claim.[15] He now insists that the bad-price-luck version of the claim is the only version he meant to offer, and he has reformulated the "flagship" statement to reflect this. (Though even in the new essay, when the argumentative chips are down, he slips back into the vocabulary, at least, of the bad-preference-luck claim[16].)

I emphasized what I took to be Cohen's bad-preference-luck argument because many other critics of my views about equality have pursued a similar argument, and because I thought that version of the bad-luck argument, for all its faults, much stronger than his bad-price-luck version, which is not even yet an argument. Suppose A, the rock-lover, and B, the opera-lover, have the same resources. B does not regret his expensive taste for opera though of course he wishes that opera were cheaper. He does not think his life goes overall worse with a taste for opera than without it, even at his present level of resource, and he would not take the pill I described. Does justice then require transferring resources from A to B to allow B to hear more opera? That would make A's well-being less and B's well-being greater than each now is. So the transfer could seem justified, even to someone who aims at equality of well-being, only if B were now worse off than A now is. But B doesn't believe that he is worse off than A, and could not honestly claim to be. Of course, if he thought that his overall well-being was just a matter of buzzes of pleasure, and that he got fewer buzzes than A because opera is so expensive, then he would think he was worse off than A, and would take the proffered pill. But he is not a buzz addict, and he does not think himself worse off. Indeed, no one, including A, might think that B is worse off than A. So no reason has yet been offered, even to welfare egalitarians, to explain why the transfer would be just.

We must take care to make an obvious distinction here. Of course B is worse off than he would be if opera cost less. That is true of almost everyone. Whatever we want – sugar or spice or castles in Spain, fast cars, or tiny Titians – we would be better off if it were cheaper. We all have bad price luck in the sense that our price luck might be considerably better. But the pertinent question, as Cohen says, is whether someone with expensive tastes who thinks he is better off for having those tastes is worse off, under some appropriate assumption about distribution, than someone else whose cheaper tastes he would not wish to have.

So Cohen can formulate a bad-price-luck argument for compensation only if he can meet a further challenge that we might state in two parts. First, he must identify a conception or dimension of welfare such that when wealth is equally distributed B is indeed worse off than A on that conception or in that dimension. Second, he must provide some reason to think that justice requires that A and B be equal in welfare defined in *that* way, in spite of the fact that B himself rejects that way of defining his overall welfare; in spite of the fact, that is, that B does not think himself worse off than A all things considered. Cohen recognizes the need for such an argument, but he does not provide one. He makes an inappropriate *ad hominem* point. He says in his Appendix (p. 25) that I cannot insist that B is entitled to compensation from A only if B considers himself "all things considered" worse off than A, because on my own view someone who has fewer resources can claim compensation from someone who has more even if the former thinks himself better off than the latter all things considered. But it is the core of my position that justice does not depend on any comparison of welfare, either all-things-considered or in any distinct conception or dimension, and so of course I think that justice may require transfers from rich people whose welfare is lower on some or any conception to poor people whose welfare is higher. Cohen claims, however, that justice does depend on welfare comparisons, and he must therefore explain why welfare-all-things-considered is not the appropriate standard. He says that even if B is no worse off than A all things considered, B may be worse off "in his shoes" than A is in his shoes: he means that B may be worse off in the distinct sense that he can satisfy fewer of his preferences or ambitions than A can. Some philosophers think that people's welfare, all things considered, is indeed defined by their "relative success," so that B is worse off all things considered if he is less able to satisfy his desires than A is able to satisfy his. But Cohen apparently agrees with me that relative success does not constitute overall welfare (p. 5), and that is, in any case, the premise of his bad-price-luck argument. He therefore needs some argument why relative success is nevertheless the right metric of distributive justice; why justice demands transfers in the name of welfare equality when those who gain think they are already overall better off than those who lose.[17] His difficulty underscores the danger in his initial assumption that he can defend equality of welfare without confronting the question of what welfare is.

The psychology of taste

Cohen discusses the generation of taste in his new essay, but some further background is necessary to put his remarks into context. In what is now chapters 1 and 2 of *Sovereign Virtue* I distinguished between two sorts of properties people have: their physical state and other capacities or handicaps, on the one hand, and their personality, including their tastes and ambitions, on the other. I said that a proper conception of equality would seek to compensate someone for a physical or other handicap, but not for aspects of his personality, except so far as he treated the latter as actually handicaps like cravings he would want not to have. In his 1989 article Cohen said that I was right to propose a "cut" of some kind, for these purposes, between different kinds of properties, but he insisted that I had put the cut "in the wrong place": I should allow compensation, he said, for someone's handicaps *and* for her tastes that are particularly expensive to satisfy provided that she did not cultivate those expensive tastes deliberately. Since he would not compensate for deliberately cultivated expensive tastes, he said, his view was different from a straightforward equality of welfare that would compensate for all expensive tastes no matter what their genesis.

In *Sovereign Virtue* I said that Cohen's suggested distinction was insufficiently deep and was therefore illusory.[18] People who cultivate expensive tastes deliberately do so not irrationally or perversely but because, like Jay Gatsby, they have "second-order" tastes that they did not deliberately cultivate and that recommend cultivating "first-order" expensive tastes. They want to be the kind of person who has distinctive and refined first-order tastes, and they cultivate those tastes for that reason. The upshot, I said, was that Cohen's view, clarified in this way, would require compensation for all expensive tastes and so was just equality of welfare "under another name." In the present essay he changes his view to bring it closer to explicit equality of welfare. He now believes that justice demands extra resources for most people with champagne tastes even if they have deliberately cultivated those tastes provided that they "identify" with their tastes; if they do, he says, it is unreasonable to expect them to ignore or try to eliminate them. Even so, he says, his view is not coextensive with full equality of welfare because he would not compensate for certain expensive tastes that are deliberately acquired for unsatisfactory reasons: those, for example, that someone cultivates knowing that she might not have enough wealth to satisfy them but gambling that she will,[19] or that someone cultivates for snobbish reasons.[20]

He thinks that my criticism of his original distinction depends on an assumption that "responsibility for the consequences of a choice requires responsibility for the (always more or less constraining) situation in which it is made," and he rightly adds that "we normally suppose no such thing" (p. 21). That comment is puzzling for at least three reasons. First, it should be evident that I reject that assumption: my entire argument that people should bear the consequences of their choices, even when these choices are made out of tastes they have in no way chosen or cultivated, depends on rejecting it.[21] Second, his own new suggestion that "some preferences reflect will more than others do in a way that bears on justice" seems itself to require the assumption he wrongly attributes to me and rightly rejects. It could matter for justice whether a voluntary act reflects a willed preference only if responsibility for the consequence of choice does depend on responsibility for the "situation" in which it is made.

Third, my argument that his "cut" among expensive tastes is and remains illusory in no way depends on any such assumption. It depends on a much simpler point:[22] that among the wholly uncultivated expensive tastes that many people have, which cause them frustration or some other welfare cost if they are not satisfied, are second-order tastes like a taste for gambling in the cultivation of other tastes, snobbish tastes, and the fateful ambitions that welled up in the young Gatsby as he watched the blinking lights across the water. Of course people with such tastes could choose not to develop the more concrete tastes for Kobe beef, Titians, and beautiful West Egg houses that Cohen has in mind. Their decisions whether to cultivate these more concrete expensive tastes are certainly subject to their "will." But if they did not develop these more concrete tastes they would suffer a "welfare" deficit: buzzes of pain, perhaps, at their continued and disappointingly plebeian tastes.

Their situation is perfectly parallel to that of their colleagues in Cohen's menagerie who love photography or opera or baseball and find those tastes expensive to satisfy. Someone who loves photography can certainly choose not to indulge his taste: he can grit his teeth and go fishing instead. Cohen is "indulgent" toward him not because he could not choose not to photograph, but because he would feel some welfare loss if he did make that choice. But that is just as true of the snob, the gambler, and the Bourbon prince who has a taste for expensive tastes. They could choose not to act as their tastes dictate, which would include not developing the concrete expensive tastes Cohen imagines, but they would suffer welfare loss if they did. If their welfare for that reason fell below that of others, the "flagship" formulation would demand extra resources to save them from that fate, because that formulation insists on compensation for expensive tastes that "they could not have helped forming and/or could not now unform without violating their own judgment." (Cohen's use of "judgment" tracks my own;[23] he means that people should be compensated for expensive tastes that they judge to be desirable.) There is no mention of relative force of will here, and no space for Cohen's distinctions. The woman who gambles by eating steak every night, the snob who wants to be different from the hoi polloi, and the Bourbon prince who cultivates expensive tastes just because they are expensive certainly all judge that these second-order tastes are desirable attributes of their personality. They could not "unform" these second-order tastes without violating their own judgment. Cohen still has no way of distinguishing his view from what he thinks are cruder and implausible forms of welfare equality.[24]

U-turn?

Cohen thinks that I have changed my mind on some crucial issue – made a "remarkable and consequential U-turn" which is in effect a "volte-face" – without acknowledging it, and that this 180-degree silent switch makes a "large" concession to my critics. He repeats that suggestion several times and plainly thinks it important. The issue on which I am supposed to have changed my mind is this: does equality require compensation for what we might call raw expensive tastes –

tastes, like those dictated by one's physical constitution, that have not been deliberately cultivated but that are relatively expensive to satisfy?

In what Cohen calls my 1981 essays I imagined a community in which resources were equally distributed in the manner and sense I defined, and I then asked under what circumstances resources should be transferred from that equal division to compensate for handicaps of different kind. I said that transfers were not justified just because, given the equal distribution, some people were able to obtain less welfare under some particular conception – more pleasure buzzes, for example – than others because their ambitions and tastes were more expensive to satisfy. I said that expensive tastes do not in general count as handicaps even if they are raw rather than cultivated. But I also said that some properties that someone might classify as expensive tastes do count as handicaps. I offered this test for that important distinction: someone's "taste" is actually a handicap if, given an equal distribution of resources, he would prefer not to have that taste. In effect, that is, I said that bad preference luck though not bad price luck is sometimes eligible for compensation. (It is eligible, roughly, when it would be unreasonable not to expect someone who would prefer not to have the taste to insure against having it if resources were equal and insurance rates the same for all.) I gave, as an example of handicaps so defined, cravings or obsessions that people struggle to overcome and would prefer to lose. I have not abandoned or changed any even minor part of this account, let alone made a "remarkable and consequential U-turn." Why does Cohen think I have?

His original criticism cited an unfortunate man who cannot move his arms without great pain, though this disability in no way limits his ability either to earn income or to engage in other projects. He can carry on as he otherwise would and just suffer the constant pain. Cohen said, in 1989, that my general account of equality could not justify providing funds to that poor man for expensive medicine that would alleviate his condition. I replied that, on the contrary, my view of equality would certainly recommend compensating him: he suffered from what was without any doubt a very serious handicap. He would be compensated, I said, not in order to make his overall welfare on some conception less unequal to that of others, but because he has a handicap that he would prefer not to have and that we may presume he would have insured to alleviate had insurance been available to him on proper terms. This is the reply that Cohen thinks reveals a dramatic change in my view, because I here recognize what he thinks I earlier denied: that equality may require compensation whose purpose is to improve someone's well-being or welfare rather than to improve his ability to gather wealth or pursue projects. My supposed concession, that is, lies in my conversion not to equality of welfare as a goal of justice but to a use of the "currency" of welfare in some other way.

Cohen says that the crucial issue in the argument between us at this point is not about whether justice requires people's welfare to be equal but whether justice requires "aiming at remedying a deficiency in welfare" or "aiming at remedying a deficiency in something else" (p. 10). The contrast between these two "aims" is confusing. First, the contrast suggests what is plainly wrong: that the two aims it supposedly distinguishes are mutually exclusive. Cohen's man in pain has what Cohen would call "deficiencies" of both kinds: he needs extra resources to buy medicine, and he needs medicine because he is in pain. A community that supplies those resources could be said to aim at remedying his lack of resources or at helping him relieve his pain or, most naturally, at both. The two aims are certainly not exclusive, though one description might seem more illuminating in some circumstances.[25]

The contrast is confusing in another way, moreover, which is more germane to Cohen's indictment. He apparently assumes that I meant to avoid any mention or use of the idea of well-being in my account of equality of resources. But, on the contrary, I have always insisted that people want resources out of concern for, among other things, their own well-being.[26] Indeed, I argued that equality of resources is to be preferred to other theories of distributive justice because it better fits a more attractive account of what well-being really is.[27] In particular I emphasized, in my original account of the crucial phenomenon of insurance, that people buy insurance not to improve their resources but to improve their welfare.[28]

My claim was and remains only that welfare cannot supply a metric for equality or justice. It is certainly open to me to say that handicaps, including constant pain, are generally bad for their victims and that compensation based on hypothetical insurance would probably enable them to live better lives. But (to return to Cohen's contrast) I would not say that the point of such compensation is to cure a welfare "deficiency." That phrase is essentially comparative. It suggests what I reject: that the ground of such compensation is the bare fact that the victim's well-being is less than it might be, or is less than that of someone or anyone else, or falls below some stipulated minimum of well-being. Compensation is appropriate not whenever someone's welfare falls below some stipulated benchmark, but when he is worse off for some reason of particular significance to justice: that reason, in the case of the man in pain, is a physical handicap that he would cure if he could and against which it seems plausible to suppose he would have insured under appropriate conditions.

So Cohen is wrong about the issue between us. The issue is only, as he says it is not, the issue of justice. Ideas about human well-being – what counts as a successful life – are of the greatest importance to ethical, moral, and even political reflection. But these ideas cannot furnish a metric of distributive justice, either in the shape of utilitarianism or welfare egalitarianism or welfare "priority" or any other welfarist goal. Tiny Tim's welfare level, on any conception Cohen thinks pertinent, may already be higher than Scrooge's. We would not deny Tim his crutch even so. Nor would we tax the Cratchits to give Scrooge even greater resources if he had an uncultivated, insatiable, and misery-making second-order ambition to be the richest man in London.

Cohen uses three new examples to reinforce his claim about my new concession. A man suffers from a physical condition that makes ordinary tap water but not expensive bottled water taste unbearably sour. A woman must eat plovers' eggs because she gags at chicken eggs. People have suffered certain brain lesions and in consequence crave fine food. He apparently thinks that I would be contradicting my earlier opinions if I allowed the heroes of any of these stories compensation. But that is wrong. Each of these "tastes" would count as a handicap as I defined this if, as seems almost certain in at least the first two cases and likely in the third, the victim regretted the disability.

Cohen says:

> Now people who find chicken's eggs disgusting may not regret having that reaction *as such*: they might even approve of it. If they wish that they did not have it, that is probably because the alternative to which the reaction drives them, namely, plovers' eggs, are so expensive. But that hardly qualifies their desire for plovers' eggs as a *craving*, either in the ordinary sense of that word or as Dworkin intended his use of it. And if regretting the special expense that one of my tastes imposes on me *did* make that taste a craving, then virtually *all* expensive tastes would attract compensation under this widened understanding of Dworkin's compensate-for-cravings proviso. (p. 8)[29]

There are two misunderstandings here. First, I cited cravings only as an example of what might seem to be tastes but are really handicaps. I agree that it would be odd to classify gagging at eggs as a craving, but it is even odder to classify it as a taste of any kind, and it is even more plainly a handicap than a craving is. The second misunderstanding is more serious: Cohen appears here to misunderstand the distinction between bad preference and bad price luck. As I explained, someone has had bad preference luck if he wishes, given his actual resources, that he did not have the preference in question and would take costless steps to lose it. The fact that he has that wish because the preference is difficult or expensive to satisfy rather than for some other reason makes no difference. After all, people with certain diseases that can be wholly and easily controlled with expensive medicine might regret their condition mainly or even entirely because of the expense. It is of course true, as I said, that almost everyone with expensive tastes wishes his tastes were less expensive. But that does not mean that "virtually all" expensive tastes would constitute bad preference luck eligible for compensation on this account, because people have bad preference luck when they regret that they have the tastes they do, perhaps because their tastes are expensive, not just that their tastes are expensive. Many people with expensive tastes believe that these tastes contribute to their well-being in spite of their expense.[30] That is certainly true of those who cultivate or refine such tastes, and it is also true of those who, in spite of any added expense, would prefer to keep rather than lose their raw tastes, as Cohen apparently wants to keep his surprising taste for Coca-Cola.[31] When we rectify these two misunderstandings, there seems no challenge left in his new examples. Presumably almost everyone for whom tap water tastes sour or who gags on chicken eggs would prefer to lose those vulnerabilities. I am less clear about gourmand syndrome. No doubt many of its victims would prefer to have their brain lesions healed, but some, who delight in their new rapture at fine cuisine, might not. The former are handicapped, but the latter are not.

Cohen closes his essay in chief with a climactic reductio-ad-absurdum of my opinions. He quotes the editor of this collection, Justine Burley, who said in a letter to him that ". . . when it comes to reproductive capacities for example, the greater financial burdens imposed on women by virtue of their unique biological endowments probably will not be compensated on Dworkin's view [unless] there is penis envy as it were. . . . To demand that a woman *want to be a man* to support compensation is simply ridiculous." I wish Burley had specified what "financial burdens" she has in mind, because compensation for handicaps is only one aspect of equality of resources, and the burdens she has in mind might be alleviated through other principles. Women suffer no financial disadvantage just in virtue of their reproductive "endowments." In a just society women like men are guaranteed an equal share of a community's resources with which to make decisions about, among other important matters, whether they wish to procreate, and no discrimination against women is permitted in the structure or background of an economic market.[32] If a woman becomes pregnant she needs special medical care, but she is no more responsible, morally or legally, for that care than her sexual partner is. She has, moreover, the benefit of the communal health care that equality of resources provides, which includes pregnancy and childbirth coverage.[33] A just society provides obstetrics care, and also provides child support for parents who need it, including maternity and paternity leave, out of concern not just for the health of the mother, but for the health and well-being of a child who will be or has been born. Public goods considerations play a role as well. Women need not wish not to be women to be eligible for help justified in any of these ways. Reproduction does raise special problems and some of these are discussed with great sensitivity by Paula Casals and Andrew Williams in their contribution to this collection. But penis envy plays no part in that story either.

Miriam Cohen Christofidis

I argued in *Sovereign Virtue* that if people's labor was auctioned as a commodity in the kind of auction I describe to illustrate equality of resources in a simple situation, then people with great talent would be in effect "slaves" to those talents.[34] Miriam Cohen Christofidis insists that this is not so plain as I suppose. She suggests, in fact, that though a labor auction of that kind would indeed produce violations of the envy test *ex post*, these might not be as serious as the *ex post* violations that I concede my hypothetical low wage auction would produce. She adds that I am wrong to suppose that highly talented people would always be able to purchase their own labor, thereby avoiding literal slavery, in that labor auction.

I am not persuaded of any of these claims. It is true that Deborah, the beautiful and talented actress I imagine, who could generate a fabulous income in films, might not be able to purchase control of her labor out of her initial endowment, and also that a consortium of would-be film producers could purchase that control by pooling their initial resources. But Deborah could, if she wished, borrow enough to purchase control of herself. Imagine two consortia. The first wishes to purchase control of Deborah outright, but the price it is willing to pay of course takes into account the expenses and uncertainties of directing someone else's labor, which are significant. The second wishes to lend money to Deborah to allow her to buy control of her own labor, under a loan agreement with constraints and other provisions satisfactory to minimize the risk of default. The second consortium would presumably be willing to loan a sum greater than the first would be willing to pay, because it is less expensive to monitor debt service than it is constantly to ensure that an employee is working to the exact limit of her high-production endurance. If so, Deborah could purchase her own labor no matter how potentially productive she is.

In either case, however – whether the first consortium buys control of her or she borrows enough from the second consortium to outbid the first – her life is the life of a slave, either to slave-owners or creditors. She does not have the option that Cohen Christofidis assumes she does: of trading off income beyond what she otherwise needs for survival for leisure or for an occupation less lucrative but more satisfying to her. A consortium that has outbid all others, including her, for control of her labor must force her to work as hard as she is physically capable of working, and at the most lucrative occupation she can perform, in order to avoid loss and maximize profit from its extravagant investment. If she has outbid all such consortia by borrowing she will have to work just as hard at her most lucrative occupation to meet debt service. Cohen Christofidis is right to emphasize the theoretical importance of the question whether people's talents should be treated as part of a community's stock of resources, but her particular response to my answer to that question is not successful.

Philippe Van Parijs

In his engaging and witty essay, Philippe Van Parijs assumes that insurers in a hypothetical insurance story would each make insurance decisions so as to maximize some function of his "utility," according to some particular conception of what that is, and that the collective results would tend to match some specified function of utility in the community of insurers overall. This assumption seems wrong, and arguments based on it (including the argument of John Roemer that equality of resources collapses into equality of welfare, which Van Parijs discusses) seem misconceived.

Most people make decisions about their future on a mix of considerations that cannot be reduced to any single conception of utility that permits comparisons or summing across people. Even if these manifold considerations could be captured in a conception of utility for some people, this would not be the same conception for all, and any overall utility calculation would be frustrated for that reason. My reservations follow from more general arguments against welfarism,[35] and are elaborated in a response to arguments of Marc Fleurbaey's that are similar to those of Van Parijs and Roemer.[36]

Though Van Parijs mentions a variety of objections to different possible versions of the insurance scheme, he finally poses, as his own objections to the scheme I proposed, only those he mentions under the title "Four Objections to Dworkin" (pp. 52–5). He says first that the insurance scheme will not satisfy the envy test *ex post*. I agree: as he says, it is designed to satisfy that test *ex ante*.[37] He says, second, that the test is biased against compensation for people like Lonely who lack "nonlucrative talents" like a talent for flirting. But the insurance device permits, in principle, insurance against lacking any advantage including cosmetic advantages. (Others have, in fact, criticized me because the scheme does permit such insurance.[38]) It is true that insurance against bad looks would be unavailable or prohibitively expensive in practice. But that in itself suggests that it is not an injustice that ugly people receive no welfare payments on that account.[39] His third objection is less easy to identify, but I believe it charges me with inconsistency because, though I concede that people often tailor their ambitions to their talents, I do not notice how far their decisions about the seriousness of some potential handicap are also sensitive to their ambitions and talents. But I explicitly suppose that people know both their ambitions and talents in deciding how much and what kind of accident and health insurance to buy.

Van Parijs's final objection is that my account, after all, "rewards" people with expensive tastes. He thinks that if you and I are both inept oboe players, and I insist on trying to succeed at that profession while you abandon it, I will do better under the insurance scheme than you will. That is a misunderstanding. Low wage insurance insures against being unable to earn at the level the insured party specifies in the insurance contract. If we both specify the same earning level, if we both have the same talents, and if these talents do not enable us to earn at the stipulated level, then we will both collect the same indemnity in spite of my stubbornness about the oboe. True, if I stipulate a higher level, and pay the higher premium that level demands, I may collect more than you do. But that has nothing to do with my stubbornness in sticking to the oboe.

Michael Otsuka

Michael Otsuka fears that my treatment of estate or inheritance taxes betrays a conflict of the kind I deny between two technical desiderata of equality: the envy test and the principle of abstraction. This is also, he believes, a conflict between the twin political virtues of equality and liberty that I claim to be so interwoven with one another that conflict of that kind is ruled out. His argument is based on a passage in my article, "Sovereign Virtue Revisited," which is a response to critical articles collected in an issue of *Ethics*. In that passage I describe a conflict internal to equality.[40] On the one hand, equality demands that people start their careers of production and consumption, so far as this is possible, with equal resources. That is the requirement captured in the envy test: it seems to recommend a prohibition against people giving or bequeathing resources to their children (or to anyone else) because the beneficiaries of such gifts start with an advantage.

But, as I put it in that passage, it is also "inegalitarian for government to prohibit or tax differentially the different choices that people make about how to spend what is rightfully theirs, and therefore inegalitarian even separately to tax gifts and bequests," let alone prohibiting such gifts altogether. That objection follows from the abstraction principle I defend in chapter 3 of *Sovereign Virtue*. In the end I defend a tax on gifts and bequests, though at less than 100 percent rate, provided that the tax is modeled on a hypothetical insurance policy against being born into a relatively poor family. Otsuka believes that this defense amounts to a compromise between the envy test and the abstraction principle and therefore concedes what I otherwise deny, which is that these two ideas, the former of which represents equality and the latter liberty, are sometimes in conflict.

My brief account of this particular issue, in the passage of "Sovereign Virtue Revisited" that Otsuka cites, is compressed. It presupposes other discussions of the envy test in *Sovereign Virtue* and earlier in that article, and it refers to the longer discussion of the specific problem of gifts and bequests in chapter 9 of *Sovereign Virtue*. These, taken together, explain why Otsuka's conclusions are not justified. I stress throughout both the book and the article that the envy test must be applied *ex ante* the resolution of the various risks against which people are permitted to insure. It aims that no one envy the resources of others *ex ante* such risks: it is therefore not a violation of the envy principle that even after compensation is paid to those who are unemployed or fall ill, for example, in accordance with hypothetical insurance assumptions, they are still worse off than those in employment and healthy. I also stress, throughout the book and the article, that taxing someone is not a taking of property that is "rightfully" his if the taxes are modeled on a hypothetical insurance market in which he is properly presumed to have traded. On the contrary, we need to calculate the impact of taxation so modeled in order to determine what someone's rightful property is.

The reconciliation of the two demands of equality described in chapter 9 of *Sovereign Virtue* therefore does not produce any conflict between the envy test and the abstraction principle. It supposes, as I explained there, that the most attractive form of insurance against bad luck in family economics would fix the premiums one pays for the benefits of such insurance as a percentage of the gifts one makes in one's own lifetime or at one's death. Provided such a scheme of taxation is in place, and the proceeds of such taxes are used in the way I described in chapter 9, the envy test is not violated when some people nevertheless start ahead of others, because that taxation and expenditure policy satisfies the *ex ante* test. (I need hardly add that tax policy in the United States, particularly following the sharp reduction and planned elimination of gift and estate taxes, is certainly condemned by the envy test.) Nor do such taxes violate either the abstraction principle or liberty rightly construed: they are measured by gifts, but justified as an insurance-efficient retroactive premium for insurance, and so do not constrain the use of resources rightfully those of the insured.

Otsuka would not even have been tempted to see a conflict with the abstraction principle, moreover, had I given a somewhat different (and I now think better) description of gift and inheritance tax as insurance premium. On this different account, such taxes fall not on the donor, as my discussion assumed, but on the recipient of the gift or bequest.[41] It is plainly no violation of the abstraction principle when income is taxed on a hypothetical insurance model, even if one type or level of income attracts a different rate, justified under that model, from others. There is, however, no difference in principle between my description in *Sovereign Virtue* and this different and better one: in each case a tax is imposed on the hypothetical beneficiary of insurance, and freedom, understood as I propose, is in no way curtailed or compromised.[42]

Richard Arneson

I am very grateful to Richard Arneson for a powerful critique of a whole range of my claims and ideas. I cannot do full justice to all his criticism here; I will limit my response to the set of claims that he identifies as most important in his conclusion. He distinguishes, first, between a praiseworthy or admirable and a choice-worthy or desirable life: he believes that a life that is more admirable, at least according to my "challenge" model of ethics, may nevertheless be less desirable. He points out that someone whose decisions about how to live are exemplary may nevertheless have bad luck and a worse life in consequence. But I argue that someone's life is successful to the degree he succeeds not only in identifying but in meeting the right challenge, and I acknowledge that he may fail to meet the right challenge through no fault of his own for a variety of reasons: he may not have a fair share of resources available to him, for example, or he may be cut down young by disease. It goes without saying, I should have thought, that he can also fail to meet the right challenge through other forms of bad luck.

Arneson next declares that the "impact" model with which I contrast my favored "challenge" model of ethics is so implausible as to make the superiority of the challenge model to it pointless. I am surprised, because so many of those who have commented on my essay have declared their preference for the impact model, which holds that the success or value of a life consists in the degree to which the world is a better place for that life having been lived. Arneson's dismissal may be encouraged by his failure to notice a distinction important to my argument: between people's interests in having what they happen to want from a life, day by day, and their interest in having what is in fact a successful or valuable life. I assume that the man in his example, who picks gum off the floor, thereby averting a nuclear holocaust, does so in full knowledge of this consequence and with the intention of realizing it. It is hardly ludicrous that he would take great pride in his decision and that he would tell his grandchildren (or, if his assumed misery included having no descendants, himself) that it had all been worthwhile because of that one devastatingly important act. If so, it is hardly ludicrous to think that he did, in fact, have the good life he thinks he had.

I should not further defend a view I finally reject, but I should comment on Arneson's apparent preference for a different ethical ideal, which he calls the "objective list" model. Of course, each of the two models I discuss requires further judgments about the importance of particular achievements and experiences: someone who thinks the value of a life lies in its meeting a challenge or in making an impact must decide what life meets the challenge well or makes the right impact, and that decision will require some judgment about which experiences and achievements are valuable. It will require what Arneson calls an objective list. Arneson means his objective list to provide not a concrete elaboration of some more general ethical ideal, however, but a distinct ideal on its own. He thinks it possible to construct a list of merit badges of achievement and experience such that a life decorated with those particular badges is a good one no matter whose life it is and no matter what he himself thinks of the badges' value or importance. That seems deeply implausible. Whether someone lives well cannot be just a question of how many tick marks he scores, one by one, on some long list – how could that matter just on its own? – but of what his life as a whole *comes to*, of whether it has achieved, in the common phrase, a *meaning*, and this must be a matter of integrating discrete experiences and achievements in some way that he himself finds to have value in some dimension.[43]

Arneson's third conclusion summarizes a long and complex discussion of tolerance and paternalism. He thinks that the principle of ethical integrity that I defend is "wrongheaded" because it requires that "the slightest loss in integrity should outweigh any threatened loss of any size in any other value." I do not know how to make sense of "lexical" ordering in this context. But it is in any case not what I meant by insisting on the "priority" of integrity. "Someone has achieved ethical integrity," I wrote,

> when he lives out of the conviction that his life, in its central features, is an appropriate one . . . If we give priority to ethical integrity, we make the merger of life and conviction a parameter of ethical success, and we stipulate that a life that never achieves that kind of integrity cannot be critically better for someone to lead than a life that does.[44]

My contrast is not between lives that achieve slightly different levels of integrity (however Arneson thinks integrity might be calibrated) but between lives that have and those that have not achieved an overall "merger of life and conviction." I gave, as an example of the latter, someone who yearns for a religious life that the law prohibits, who becomes a successful politician but goes to his grave thinking his life wholly spoiled because it did not have the religious direction he thought essential to its success.

Arneson offers a counterexample. "If cultural achievement is a great good," he says, "it is doubtful that a person who writes a great novel nonetheless fails to achieve a great good just because that person has eccentric philosophical beliefs that rank cultural achievement as of no value" (p. 87). It is unclear why someone with this person's eccentric beliefs would bother to write a novel at all. In any case, however, the question is not whether she has achieved a "great good," which on the stated assumption she clearly has: her life has been good for others in virtue of her achievement. But the question is whether it has been a good life for her, in virtue of that, if she counts writing a novel worth nothing. On the impact model that Arneson says he rejects, her life is indeed better for the achievement, no matter what she thinks, and perhaps Arneson is more susceptible to the lure of that model, at least as a component of ethical value, than he thinks. But once we reject that model, it is hard to see how doing what a person despises could make his life better for him as distinct from better for others. Would you want someone you particularly love to lead a life in which he finds no fulfillment but in which he produces much that you admire?

Arneson next observes that my "rigid antipaternalism" is "extreme and illiberal;" in his earlier discussion he says that there is nothing wrong with forcing people to try chocolate ice cream because they might come to like it, in which case the experiment would add pleasure to their life. But I specifically reject any "rigid" antipaternalism: "It overstates the point to say that the challenge model rules out any form of paternalism, because the defect it finds in paternalism can be cured by endorsement, provided that the paternalism is sufficiently short-term and limited so that it does not significantly constrict choice if the endorsement never comes."[45] Presumably those conditions are satisfied by Arneson's chocolate ice cream example and by the other examples of permissible paternalism he has in mind. I offered the perhaps more realistic example of compulsory liberal education.

Section V of Arneson's chapter summarizes his earlier objections to my account of equality of resources as an ideal of distributive justice: these include the objection that my account requires leveling down and other forms of economic irrationality. But he is wrong in each of his claims about what equality of resources requires, as I had hoped was plain from *Sovereign Virtue*,[46] and from the pertinent passages of "Sovereign Virtue Revisited."[47] Equality of resources is drawn from and must be interpreted in the light of the more basic ideal that a community must collectively, in politics, treat each of its members as individuals with equal concern and, as I said, "It seems as obvious as anything could that equal concern does not mean forcing some people to starve when that will do no one else any good."[48] Arneson insists that justice requires helping people who are in absolute terms very badly off, rather than seeking equality, which is a relative matter, however measured. But a community that accepts the demand of equal concern must have some answer to the question why its laws and policies allow some people to secure lives of greater excitement, interest, and achievement than others can, even when no one is starving or even badly off measured historically. Equal concern is essentially a comparative concept.[49]

The second part of section V refers to Arneson's complex but compressed earlier discussion of the bearing of ethics on distributive justice. I argue that if we accept my "parameter" thesis that the success or goodness of a life depends on the fairness of the distribution of resources in the community in which the life is lived, then we cannot accept any welfarist theory of fair distribution of resources such as utilitarianism or equality of welfare. Any welfarist theory requires some measure of how good people's lives are under alternate distributions, and would therefore require, if the parameter thesis is sound, some other, nonwelfarist account of distributive justice. Arneson replies that even if the parameter thesis were true, a two-stage calculation would solve the problem and permit welfarist theories of justice. At the first stage, the welfarist government calculates what Arneson calls "nonmoral" good – what is good for a person apart from moral considerations – and distributes resources so as to achieve its welfarist function of that good. It distributes resources so that, for example, the average level of happiness is as great as it can be. At the second stage, "we correct the computation of people's welfare by taking at a discount the fulfillment of their interests that conflict with the moral rules developed in stage one" (p. 92).

I do not see how this helps; indeed I find it mysterious. If the parameter thesis is right, then we cannot calculate the "nonmoral" good of persons: what is good for them to have depends too much on what they would have under a fair distribution. (This is not just a matter of how much they would have of some designated commodity, but of which kinds of lives, built around what kinds of commodities, they should aim to live.) That is the nerve of the problem I raise for welfarist theories. If they could somehow solve that problem, then they could insist that the distribution of "nonmoral" good at the first stage, in accordance with the designated welfarist standard, would be finally just. There would be no need for a second stage, let alone further stages of distribution. A second stage would make sense only if it appealed to principles of justice different from the welfarist principles enacted at the first stage. But perhaps I have misunderstood Areneson's argument here.

The closing remarks of this section refer, I take it, to the more general remarks with which he closes his earlier substantive argument. He says that equality of resources oddly supposes that what matters "morally" is resources as such, rather than what people can do with resources. (I take it that he is here using "morality" to include what I called ethics.) That is wrong. Of course what matters fundamentally to people is the success they can make of their lives, not the resources they have available for that purpose. But the question of what part of the responsibility for achieving that success belongs to individuals one by one, and what part belongs to the community collectively, is plainly a different one, as Arneson himself immediately recognizes. It does not contradict the assumption that it is successful lives that finally matter to insist that the community's role is to make resources available, not to identify and pursue that success for individuals itself. Arneson next says that equality of resources would require distributing resources to someone who will make no use of them to benefit anyone including himself. I assume he means that this person will not use his resources to benefit himself even in his own eyes; in that pathological case he seems a candidate for paternalistic help which, as I have emphasized,[50] equality of resources hardly rules out. It would be a different case if he were to use the resources in a way that he, but not the rest of his community, thought beneficial to him.

Arneson's section VI is of great interest. He suggests that I am wrong to link the challenge model of ethics to equality of resources in the way I do. The challenge model is equally consistent, he says, with a welfarist theory that requires government to distribute resources so as to make everyone equally successful at meeting the challenges specified in an objective list of valuable experiences and achievements. Suppose that the right objective list identifies only one item: it declares that meeting the challenge of living consists, for everyone, only in playing football well. In that case, someone who accepts the challenge model could consistently accept that government's duty is to arrange, so far as this is possible, that everyone has an equal opportunity to play football well.

But the challenge model is explicitly constructed to reflect the more fundamental ethical principle that people must take special responsibility for the design as well as performance of their own lives: the challenge of living includes, as I emphasized, the challenge of deciding what meeting the challenge requires.[51] So people who accept the challenge model could not accept what is implicit in Arneson's suggestion that the community has the power and responsibility to impose one objective list on everyone: to distribute resources only so as to equalize football ability, for example, a talent some of its members might think of no value or importance at all. Of course, he has in mind a much more complex objective list of what contributes to a good life, a list that must somehow indicate not only what experiences and achievements count, but also "what weight any level of achievement on any dimensions of achievement of any entry should get . . ." (p. 94). But people can disagree about all of that. Even if they all agree that "friendship" counts for something, for instance, which is unlikely, they will nevertheless disagree about how much it counts, and what other values or achievements it should be subordinated to or trump. It is wholly inconsistent with the challenge approach that such decisions should be made collectively for all, rather than individually by responsible agents one by one. That approach demands a resource-based rather than a welfare-based metric of distributive justice.

Matthew Clayton

Matthew Clayton provides an excellent account and a probing critique of my opinions about ethics, and about the connection between ethics and concrete political controversies, including the abortion question. He questions, for example, whether the challenge model of ethics I endorse is sufficiently widely accepted in contemporary democracies to allow what I call a partnership democracy, in which citizens see themselves as "joint authors" of collective decisions, to embrace a scheme of justice that presupposes that model. The answer seems to me to depend on whether I am right in claiming that the challenge model is "ecumenical" in the required sense and degree for that: I believe it is.[52] But, in any case, as Clayton recognizes, I argue in *Sovereign Virtue* that even though people who embrace the challenge model have special reasons for also accepting equality of resources, the latter theory does not presuppose that conception of ethical value, but rests independently on the much more widely accepted ideals of equal political concern.[53]

Clayton also suggests that I endorse a version of perfectionism, because I accept that officials may attempt to persuade citizens, in various ways, to pursue one rather than another vision of what makes a life successful. But I would not allow government to go beyond persuasion; in particular I reject the use of fines, taxes, or other forms of positive or negative subsidy as prods or inducements toward particular lives.[54] I also reject the use of what I called "cultural paternalism," which I defined as "the suggestion that people should be protected from choosing wasteful or bad lives not by flat prohibitions of the criminal law but by educational constraints and devices that remove bad options from people's view and imagination."[55] As Clayton recognizes, moreover, I distinguish between coercive measures such as reasonable mandatory delays that government might adopt to encourage citizens to make certain important ethical decisions with care, which seem to me permissible, and other coercive measures aimed at inducing them to make one rather than another decision, which I do not consider permissible. I would therefore not regard myself as a perfectionist though, as Clayton also points out, labels are unimportant.

His most powerful challenge asks me to justify the distinction I draw between government's responsibility in matters of ethics, which does not include authority to coerce particular behavior, and its responsibility to identify and enforce requirements of justice, including distributive justice, which does. The distinction, he suggests, is more problematic because on my view each person must have views about justice in order to have the right kind of ethical convictions. Why must government leave him free to follow his own considered views about how he should live, within the set of resources that justice allows him, if it does not leave him free also to decide what justice does allow him? Conversely, if government imposes a collective view about justice on individuals, why should it not impose a collective view about other matters of great ethical importance? Government may properly enforce laws against theft even against those who disagree that taking another's property is unjust. Why, then, may government not use the criminal law to impose a particular view about the ethics of abortion? How is the difference to be explained and justified?

Clayton does not challenge, as others have, the distinction I draw between ethical convictions that are central to personality, like convictions about abortion, and other convictions, like ecological opinions, that I think are not. His challenge is different and more interesting: he challenges the more profound distinction I draw between justice and all matters of ethical conviction. I have defended that distinction, however, in the following way.[56] Rules and decisions that fix property and define at least part of what people otherwise owe to each other must in the nature of the case be formed and enforced centrally: they must apply uniformly to all. Otherwise government could not provide essential services, including the service of allowing individuals to design their lives on confident assumptions about their resources. That is not true of ethical convictions in general: government may leave these to individual decision without failing in any of its cardinal responsibilities. It is true that government could not achieve certain ambitions its leaders might have, including an ambition to protect detached values like art and endangered species, if it had no power to act beyond a power to enforce justice. But these ambitions are not central to its legitimacy, and it is therefore appropriate to limit government's powers to safeguard detached values when there are particularly strong reasons to protect individual freedom of choice, as there are in the case of abortion.[57]

Part II

Will Kymlicka

Will Kymlicka raises a set of fascinating questions about government support for the distinct cultures of certain minorities who have been absorbed into a larger political entity by conquest or other involuntary means – Native American, Inuit, and Quebequois cultures in North America, for example. He does not argue that the government of that larger entity has a responsibility to support such cultures as compensation for past injustice to the ancestors of present minority members. He appeals instead to the needs of everyone to an adequately rich culture, needs that members of a linguistic minority may not be capable of fulfilling if their ancestral culture atrophies or disappears. He does not describe any particular measures that government might take to meet that need in this essay, though he has done so to great effect in much other writing.

We must take care to distinguish, as he does, a variety of issues. He does not argue that members of minorities are entitled, as a matter of equality of resources, to a cultural background equally as rich as that available to the majority of their fellow citizens. Culture is not an impersonal resource that can be shifted from person to person, and we have, in any case, no useful metric of cultural richness. But government does have two further responsibilities that Kymlicka cites. It has a responsibility first to protect the detached value of worthwhile literature and other forms of art, and second to provide all citizens, so far as it can, with a sufficiently rich cultural background to allow them properly to exercise their own responsibilities to design and lead a chosen life. These further responsibilities of government cannot be quantified, however, and it must be a question of circumstance and judgment, case by case, whether a government better acquits these responsibilities by safeguarding or improving the access of a cultural minority to their ancestral culture or by making the majority culture more fully available, through education and encouragement, to those minorities.

That choice may depend, among much else, on the means available to protect the ancestral culture. Strategies that include coercion, or that dampen the opportunities of individuals within the minority culture to embrace the majority culture as their own if they wish, are plainly less eligible. So we should consider, in the light of the two responsibilities just identified, a less invasive option. When would it be right for government to use general revenue to protect and enhance the special linguistic and other culture of a minority within its dominion, for example by subsidizing its literature and art, or providing for the education of minority children in their ancestral language at their parents' option? If the goal is to protect detached value, the answer must depend, principally, on the value of this particular culture and on how well it flourishes elsewhere: there would be little point in striving to add to the richness of Hispanic culture by necessarily limited endeavors in Miami when that culture thrives throughout so much of the world.

If, on the other hand, the goal is to provide an adequately rich cultural background for a cultural minority, then the answer must depend principally on the difficulties of opening the general national culture to that minority. If, as must often be the case, it is to the long-term advantage of members of the minority to become assimilated to that general culture, the sooner that process begins the better. We must recognize, of course, that many individual people prefer to retain a link to their own ancestral culture in spite of the fact that another at least equally rich culture is available to them, and a fair government will respect that ambition as it respects all others. It will permit individuals to use and pool their resources to that end, as they wish, so long as this is done within a system of liberty for all, including members of the same cultural minority who do not share that ambition.

Lesley Jacobs

"Universal access to health care exists," according to Lesley Jacobs, "when all citizens . . . are assured access to a certain set of basic or 'medically necessary' health care services and products"

(p. 134). He believes that universal health care is only achieved, however, when such services and products are provided directly, in kind. Suppose someone suffering from AIDS will only live a short time even with the most expensive care. He might sensibly prefer, instead of that care, the money it would cost, which he can spend on realizing other ambitions in the short time he has left. Jacobs thinks that it would be inconsistent with the underlying justification for providing universal access to allow him that choice, however. He can refuse the care, of course, but cannot have even a discounted share of the money the health care system would then save.

I cannot follow Jacob's argument. He says that it is part of the point of universal access that there be no competition among patients for health care. I agree that in some circumstances the effect of cash benefits that could be used to purchase medical services would have competitive consequences. Suppose, for example, that government paid a lump sum to everyone who contracted appendicitis, no matter how rich or poor, but regulated health care provision in no way. Patients would then bid for the services of the best abdominal surgeons, forcing up the price and insuring that those patients who were wealthier anyway would get the best care. But how could competition possibly be the result in the case Jacobs discusses? If government itself provided state-of-the-art care for dying AIDS patients, but allowed a patient to opt out of such care and receive a cash payment instead (which, as Jacobs points out, would have to be somewhat less than the cost of that care), that patient would of course not then attempt to buy the services he could have had free under the plan. He would have been mad to ask for the money if that had been his intention.

In any case Jacobs argues that I can find no arguments, within the general scheme of equal resources that I defend, for denying citizens the right to opt out of government health care plans and take cash instead, and he concludes that I cannot support universal health care as this is now understood. He is careful to point out various arguments I have made that could justify insisting on in-kind benefit in some circumstances. But he says that I could not use those arguments to justify a total prohibition of substituting cash for in-kind provision in all cases. I would not want to justify a flat prohibition. In some circumstances a cash rather than an in-kind indemnity would be preferable, and many actual health insurance markets provide such payments.[58] But many arguments are available, under the general scheme of equal resources that I favor, for quite extensive substitution of in-kind provision for cash. Jacobs does not mention the strongest and most obvious of these, which we can identify by noticing that the bulk of the private health care plans that now flourish in the United States, which hardly aim at eliminating competition in medical care, do not allow beneficiaries to substitute cash for medical care any more than government health services do.

These private plans reimburse beneficiaries for approved medical expenses already incurred, or they pay doctors for approved medical services directly. A major reason for that universal policy is moral hazard. Patients often ask for medical treatment they do not really need – insurers must guard against this, to the degree they can, in other ways – but patients are obviously much more likely to exaggerate if they can receive cash instead of the expensive treatment they claim to need. Much private medical insurance is paid for, at least in part, by the insured's employer, moreover, and employers have a direct and further reason for insisting that benefit be in kind. Sick or disabled employees are in many ways expensive.

Both these reasons hold for state-provided as well as private insurance, though the second takes a somewhat different form in public provision. Government plans make health insurance mandatory by financing it through taxes. One reason for mandatory insurance is the paternalism that Jacobs describes. People responsible for their own health insurance may make bad decisions: they may irresponsibly pass up insurance they could and should buy. But another reason is externality: sick citizens are as expensive to the community's overall economy as they are to their private employers, and they are particularly expensive to a community of decent people who will not let the indigent die or suffer for lack of medical care. These grounds for mandatory health insurance would of course be subverted if beneficiaries were allowed to pass up the care that taxation provided for cash instead.

These are all among the reasons I gave why a government that is committed to the general principles of resource equality may nevertheless constrain choice in some circumstances.[59] And the health care scheme I defended in *Sovereign Virtue* does not allow beneficiaries to substitute cash for treatment.[60] It might seem cruel to deny Jacob's AIDS victim the choice he wants. But if a universal care program has been designed to match sensible hypothetical insurance assumptions, the program would already, in effect, have made the choice he wants. It would provide less expensive care in the few months known to be a patient's last, and therefore more resource for that person's life when he was healthy.

Paula Casal and Andrew Williams

I found Paula Casal's and Andrew Williams's discussion of procreative autonomy instructive and intriguing. They ask whether it is fair to require people who choose to have no or fewer children to share in the costs – of education, for example – of raising the children of other people who choose to have larger families. They consider that issue from what we might call a single-generation perspective: they assume that the procreative decisions of members of one generation affect other members of the same generation in ways that raise issues of fairness. We might, however, consider the same problem from a different and more dynamic perspective: we might suppose that the procreative decisions of members of one generation affect members of following generations, and consider whether any issues of fairness arise when we look at the matter that way.

As the authors point out, the procreative decisions of members of one generation affect the resources available to each member of the succeeding generation. But no member of that succeeding generation can sensibly complain that any injustice has been done to him by the preceding generation's decision to have more rather than fewer children. Each person in each generation must treat himself, as it were, as a member of a freshly shipwrecked population that must take its total numbers as it finds them.[61] If we adopt this different perspective, then the problems of fairness that seem pressing from the authors' original perspective no longer arise.

The difference between these two perspectives is stark. In the static perspective the authors use, members of an original generation absorb the costs of succeeding ones, and the distribution of those costs among those original members raises issues of fairness. In the different dynamic perspective I describe, each generation treats the procreative decisions of the preceding generation as givens it must accept. Each of the two perspectives is artificial: the real world, in which generations are not organized as discrete cohorts, is not fully captured in either. I am not persuaded, however, that the static perspective is the more useful of the two. The costs or benefits of increasing or decreasing population levels are borne principally by the generation whose size is in question, not by the preceding generation whose decisions produced that size, and questions of justice seem most important within the former rather than the latter. Someone's available resources are usually more affected by the wealth and other benefits his family has made available to him, compared to the wealth and benefits others in his generation have received, than by how many siblings he or they have, though of course the number of his siblings may in different ways affect his inherited or donated wealth. It may be that these disparities in initial resources are best addressed (as I said in my reply to Otsuka in this response, and in the material cited in that reply) through taxation falling on the subject generation, rather than on anything in the nature of an excise tax on procreation in the earlier one. Of course, I do not mean to deny what the authors skillfully point out: that population levels raise important issues of public policy that are quite independent of questions about fairness to individuals, and that wise policy may require incentives or disincentives to procreation. These are, however, quite different issues.

Justine Burley

Justine Burley offers an interesting and thorough discussion of my views about the moral and political implications of recent advances in genetic science and technology. She makes two main claims. She says, first, that some of my suggestions about the implications of the new genetics are exaggerated. Her second claim is more arresting: she says that my exaggerated claims are provoked by my own fear, which she believes justified, that recent advances in genetics "sound the death knell" for my own theories about distributive justice. I am wrong, she says, to suppose that people generally would be in moral free-fall if the most speculative and dramatic predictions of genetic engineering were realized: the only fall in prospect is my own.

She supports her second claim with three distinct arguments each of which rests on an assumption about my own views. First, I believe, she thinks, that people should be compensated for handicaps of various sorts only when these are the result of natural forces but not of social conditions or decisions. Genetic advances may mean that more handicaps are preventable and therefore, when not prevented, are social rather than natural in origin. It would follow that many handicaps would, on my view, no longer be compensable, which seems heartless and implausible. Second, I believe that claims of compensation should be measured by, and limited to, what people could reasonably be expected to have insured against if wealth had been equal and insurance had been available to all on equal terms. But no insurer would insure against a parental decision not to engage in genetic engineering or repair, so I would be committed for this different reason as well to a heartless denial of compensation. Third, if genetic repair and engineering, including radical designer procreation and cloning, became feasible then it might seem wise and fair for the state to mandate the use of these techniques in some circumstances and forbid it in others. But a variety of my views would "hamstring" me in considering those measures: I could not support them without abandoning fundamental parts of my general ethical and moral, as well as political, theories.

Free-fall?

The first claim depends on taking my claim about moral "free-fall" to have a much wider scope than I intended. I asked a diagnostic question: why do people react so irrationally to the prospects of dramatic genetic engineering? I suggested that they sense that if the most fantastic dreams of genetic engineering were realized, that would cause a seismic shift in the boundary between chance and choice on which many of our deepest ethical and moral convictions – about pride, shame, blame, and personal and intergenerational responsibility – rest. It is not yet clear which common attitudes would be revised if the most dramatic claims for the new genetics were ever realized, but people nevertheless sense, I think, that many would have to be revised. The range of properties and achievements in which people could sensibly take pride, for example, would be likely to shrink, and the scope for intergenerational resentment would sharply increase.

But this is not the claim about "free-fall" that Burley discusses; indeed she does not mention any of the particulars of ordinary ethics and morality that I actually discussed.[62] She suggests that my claim is exaggerated because she assumes that I meant to include, as further candidates for obsolescence, widely accepted principles of political morality including principles about bodily integrity and reproductive freedom, and she believes that though those principles might need substantial amendment if the most dramatic promises of genetic engineering were realized, they would not have to be wholly abandoned. But these are not principles that depend crucially on the chance/choice boundary I discussed, they do not figure in most people's ethical and moral experience, they played no part in my diagnostic suggestion, and I said nothing about their being swept away. On the contrary, I said that if genetic advances do someday force changes in our everyday moral and ethical convictions about responsibility, pride, resentment, and shame, we must rely on "a more critical and abstract part of our morality," which includes the deep political principles of ethical individualism, to decide how far and in what way these everyday convictions should be revised.[63]

Social and natural?
Burley's first argument for her "death knell" claim depends, as I said, on the surprising assumption that I do not believe that people should be compensated for disadvantages that are caused by social rather than biological phenomena. She cites only chapter 2 of *Sovereign Virtue* as authority for that attribution, but I find nothing in that chapter that supports it, and much there and in the rest of the book that rebuts it. The low-wage insurance discussed in that chapter presupposes, among the causes of unemployment and low wages, a host of social factors including technological change. Chapter 3 is largely devoted to argument that justice condemns certain kinds of social disadvantages, including those arising from discrimination of various sorts, and in the chapter Burley mainly discusses I suggest, describing popular attitudes that might shift as genetic technology improves, that "we feel a *greater* responsibility to compensate victims of industrial accidents and of racial prejudice, as in both cases victims, though in different ways, of society generally, than we feel to compensate those born with genetic defects or those injured by lightning or in those other ways that lawyers and insurance companies call 'acts of God.'"[64] I do indeed distinguish between someone's "brute" bad luck for which he is not responsible, which include his genetic inheritance, and his bad "option" luck, that is, his luck in gambles that he chooses to run. Burley suggests that it follows from my distinction that disadvantages that parents might have prevented through genetic engineering "are more properly regarded as instances of *noncompensatable* bad brute social luck because they can be traced to parental choice" (p. 179). But the fact that someone's genes have been designed by others, rather than chance or nature, and are in that way "social," does not convert his genetic structure into option luck for him. Nor does it make his genetic defects in principle noncompensable for any other reason.[65]

Insurance?
Burley's second argument for her apocalyptic claim depends on the details of the hypothetical insurance model I suggest to ground compensation for handicaps and disabilities. If genetic engineering permitted parents to repair genetic defects in their children, certain groups of parents including those of a particular religious ideology might not take advantage of the new technology, and their children would suffer in comparison to the children of those parents who did. But, she says, hypothetical insurers would not offer insurance against defects or failings that parental attention could have prevented so my scheme, which conditions compensation of counterfactual

insurance, would leave some children unprotected. In that way, she fears, my theory would mimic libertarianism.

Burley apparently has in mind, in this part of her discussion, serious physical and mental defects that are not now preventable and so would plainly be covered by hypothetical insurance now. If so, she is wrong about the shape that a hypothetical insurance market would take if such defects became preventable. It seems likely, as Burley insists in her third argument for the death knell claim, that the community would force prospective parents to accept testing and repair out of concern for the child who will be born. Even if this does not happen, the overall incidence of such defects would markedly decline from present levels, and premiums attributable to those defects would correspondingly fall. Insurers would have no greater reason to exclude coverage than they have now. True, they would have to predict roughly what the new incidence of defects would be, and they would have to take into account not only parents who refused therapy, if the law did not require it, but also cases in which the therapy for some reason failed, which might include cases of medical negligence or misadventure. But prediction would be in principle no more difficult, under the changed circumstances, than it is now: new experience would yield new data. Insurers, we should note, could not selectively refuse insurance to children of parents of partic-ular religious convictions (for example) because the hypothetical model requires community premium rating.

Suppose Burley switched her attention to a different possibility: not genetic repair but genetic enhancement. Some parents, including those who would be anxious to protect their children against obvious physical or mental handicaps, might nevertheless refuse new techniques that became available to enhance their children's intellectual or physical powers – they might refuse, for example, to make them cleverer or finer in musical appreciation – even though other parents take advantage of this opportunity.[66] Any sharp disadvantage in earning power that resulted would be cushioned by low-wage insurance: nothing in the theory or structure of such insurance would deny indemnity to people whose parents had refused available enhancements.[67] Handicap insur-ance would probably not be available to someone who wished his parents had given him a more discriminating musical taste than they did. But it is not inconceivable that some particular genetic enhancement would become so routine that people who had not been enhanced in that way, either because the technology had failed or because their parents refused to permit it, would indeed be deemed to be handicapped, and insurance against that fate would develop. That would not be pos-sible, however, unless there were sufficient agreement within the community about the importance of enhancement in that direction. The insurance model is sensitive to such opinion: in this context, as in others, its decisions are not accidents or gimmicks, but have roots in principles of political morality.[68]

Hamstrung?

Burley insists that dramatic advances in genetic engineering might require communities to impose various requirements and constraints on procreation: they might, for example, require pregnant women to undergo testing and if necessary at least certain kinds of genetic repair, and they might prohibit or regulate cloning. But she thinks that my own "liberal" position "hamstrings" me in accepting these steps. In any case, she believes that my views as so far published would provide no ground on which they might be justified.

Much of her argument focuses on what she calls the "nonidentity" problem. She imagines that medicine allows parents to eliminate certain of their own genes, which might produce a geneti-cally damaged child, before conception. (The example is outré: the nonidentity problem would not arise in the most likely cases of state regulation of genetic engineering.[69]) Can we construct arguments why parents with dangerous genes should take this step? Arguments why a state would be justified in requiring them to do so? We cannot say that they should choose to or be made to modify their genes in order not to injure a child they might create. If they do not modify their genes they might produce a damaged child, but they do not help that child by modification, because the result is that it will never exist. So we need some other kind of reason why the parents should take this step, and Burley says that I cannot provide one consistently with the rest of what I have said.

I should begin my response by pointing out that I did indeed offer an argument for regulation that might well be thought to apply to this case. I discussed the "nonidentity" problem at some length. I said that people should take steps to prevent having a damaged child not out of concern for any particular person's interests, but in order to protect what I called the "detached" value of future people's lives going well.[70] So Burley must think that this proposal is inconsistent with more general aspects of my moral, ethical, or political opinions and, in fact, she cites a variety of those opinions. She cites my endorsement, first, of what I call two principles of ethical individualism.[71] The first is a principle of value: it holds that it is objectively important that any human life succeed once it has begun. She says I cannot rely on that principle to support measures to improve the lives of future people, whose lives have not yet begun. That is not quite right: I might defend a decision by parents not to conceive a damaged child by calling attention to the interests of other people who do exist – children they already have, for example, or members of their community who will share the various costs of raising the damaged child. But in any case the first principle hardly exhausts the political values I have endorsed, and provides no reason why I cannot also appeal to a different principle of detached value: that it is wrong or in any case undesirable to bring a child into the world whose life will be painful and frustrating, not out of concern for that child, or necessarily for anyone else, but just as something undesirable in itself.

The second principle of ethical individualism imposes on each person a special responsibility for the design and success of his or her own life. Burley thinks that any regulation of procreation would contradict that principle. But a state that requires a pregnant woman to undergo genetic testing and repair acts not to impose on her a design for her own life, but to protect the detached value I described. Burley says that my arguments for a prochoice political position about abortion and euthanasia assume that the principle of special responsibility outlaws any regulation of procreation that is based on detached value.[72] But I did not rely on the general principle of special responsibility to ground a political right to an early abortion or to euthanasia in certain circumstances; I relied instead on the much more concrete and targeted argument that is described and discussed in Eric Rakowski's chapter in this collection, and in my response to that chapter below, an argument that would not apply to mandating genetic repair or forbidding cloning.[73] I did not say that a state may never rely on considerations of detached value to regulate choice, even in matters of procreation. On the contrary: I argued, for example, that states may impose reasonable regulations designed to improve deliberation about abortion or suicide.[74] I explicitly endorsed legal constraints that protect the welfare of future generations, which is a matter of detached not derivative value,[75] and I cited, as a reason many women have for choosing abortion, that they think it is wrong – a detached wrong – to bring a doomed child into the world.[76]

Burley provides an important hint that might help to explain her misunderstanding of my views about genetics and procreation. She says (in a passage similar to some of G. A. Cohen's comments in his contribution to this collection) that I would reject any argument that appeals to the detached value of the lives of future generations going well, of the kind I have in fact embraced, because any such argument "smacks of welfarism," and she adds that I "deny the legitimacy of positing any objective measure of welfare for individuals" (p. 184). But I do not deny that we may take an objective view of human well-being: an important part of *Sovereign Virtue* defends such a view.[77] Nor, as I said in my response to G. A. Cohen's contribution to this volume, do I deny the sense or importance of all judgments of human well-being or welfare. In particular I accept what is obvious: that human beings of some future generation will be better off – lead better lives – if they do not suffer from terrible poverty or disease than people would be who did suffer from such diseases. I object only to using welfare as the metric of distributive justice, and to what I called "critical paternalism: that a person's life can be improved by forcing him into some act or abstinence that he thinks valueless."[78] It is not paternalistic to adopt strategies of conservation, research, and control aimed at allowing people who live later to live with abundant resources, in an environment that has not been poisoned, and free from wracking handicaps and diseases. It would be a different matter if a state directed mass genetic enhancements on more controversial assumptions about what lives are desirable to lead.[79] But I do not believe that Burley would endorse regulations of that character; nor would I.[80]

Part III

Seana Valentine Shiffrin

How should we respect the autonomy of a person who has become seriously and permanently demented? What is in the best interests of such a person? We must confront a preliminary but crucial metaphysical and ethical issue. Is a person suffering from serious and permanent dementia the same person as the competent person who became demented? If someone remains the same person after dementia, then we must ask about the autonomy or interests of that single person, and we must consider every part of that person's life as bearing on any such question. If, on the other hand, we accept that the person after serious dementia is a different person from the competent person that existed before, then we have two sets of questions about autonomy and interests to answer. In either case, we have to resolve conflicts, but the character of the conflicts is different.

If only one person is involved, we have to decide what is in his overall best interests when he has different and competing interests at different stages of his life. That is a familiar sort of conflict that everyone has to resolve: is it in my interest overall to sacrifice exciting travel now in order to prepare for a career that will flourish only later? Dementia may make the conflict more searing or even tragic, because the interests in question may be more antagonistic. But it does not make the conflict different in character. If serious dementia ends the life of one person and begins the life of another, however, then any conflict is between the autonomies and interests of two people, and raises questions of fairness. We might have to consider whether granting a certain form of autonomy to the competent person is cheating the demented person of his or her own autonomy, for example, or whether it is fair or unfair to act in the interests of one person at the cost of damaging the interests of another. These, too, are familiar questions in more pedestrian conflicts. They are questions of justice however, and though dementia may also make these questions more agonizing, they remain questions of justice rather than, as in the case of a single person, questions of intrapersonal balance.

I believe that the competent person and the demented person are the same person: the same, single object of ethical inquiry. The life of each is part of the life of the other, and only one person's autonomy and overall best interests are at stake. My arguments in *Life's Dominion* about the treatment of seriously demented people begin with that assumption. In her tightly argued and powerful chapter in this volume, Seana Shiffrin says that she is willing, for purposes of her discussion, to assume that I am right in this. In fact, however, much of her argument seems to me to reject the single-person assumption, and to depend for its force on rejecting it.[81] She speaks throughout of P_1 and P_2: the first is a person P before, and the second that person after, serious dementia. The distinction between the two Ps might, of course, be only a device to distinguish different stages of the same person's life. But the distinction actually plays a much more important role in her argument than that.

Shiffrin discusses at length my example of a Jehovah's Witness who calls for a blood transfusion when she becomes temporarily deranged. Shiffrin agrees with me that it would be an insult to the Witness's autonomy to perform the transfusion, but she insists that this is because such temporarily deranged people "will, or can, in time, return to their senses and will have to live with our action" (p. 202). But in the case of permanent dementia, she says, the competent person will not have to live with the consequences of what happens to the demented person, because the competent person will have disappeared, never to return. "P_1 may be the more capable decision maker, but P_2 will have to live with the consequences of the decision, not P_1" (p. 202). She repeats the point later: "Unlike the Jehovah's Witness case, a self with an altogether different will is not going to have to live with the results of the action undertaken" (p. 206). Soon after she states that she accepts, for the sake of argument, my assumption that personal identity is preserved after dementia, she directs readers' attention to "the interests of demented people" (p. 209) as if that could be considered separately from the interests of those people when competent. Indeed, she wonders whether "P_1's interests concerning P_2 are *relevant* to our beneficent concern for P_2," (p. 208, italics added) and calls it "odd" for me "to say that the life of the demented cannot be made valuable enough for it to be in the demented person's critical interest *qua* demented person for it to continue" (p. 208). She says that P_1's interest in P_2 "may be entirely understandable" since they "share a body, a history, and some psychological features and habits; they are the same person" and since "P's circle of friends and family may transfer their attachment to P_1 to include concern for P_2 as well" (pp. 209–10). But, however understandable, P_1's concern for P_2 is "by analogy," it is like the concern someone might have for his or her "doppelganger," and "we would not be compelled to give much weight to an understandable interest P_1 might take in her doppelganger, given the inevitable connections others might make between them, if our aim were to act beneficently toward the doppelganger" (p. 210). None of this is consistent with taking seriously the ethical identity of the people she calls P_1 and P_2. Questions about the autonomy or interests of a single person must be resolved within the life of that person. As I said, there are not two autonomies or the autonomies of two different people to balance or adjudicate, and though it does make sense to speak of the different interests of that single person at different times, these are all necessarily relevant to the further, inescapable, question of what is in the person's best interests overall.

Shiffrin's repeated remark that P_1 need not "live with" events in P_2's life is particularly striking and, I believe, misconceived. I distinguish, as she acknowledges, between two kinds of interests people have – critical interests and experiential interests. People's experiential interests are their interests in enjoying or avoiding certain kinds of experience: their interests in having pleasure, for example, and avoiding pain. Their critical interests are their interests in having a life that is a good one judged as a whole. Of course experiences that occur in a person's life after he has become seriously demented are not experienced by that person in a competent state. But it does not follow, and it is opposed to most people's own judgment, that what happens to someone after he become demented cannot affect his critical interests.

That distinction is evident when we consider how a person's interests are affected by events after his death. Experiential interests end with death: burial or cremation is not either in or against the experiential interests of the deceased. But, as I assume throughout *Life's Dominion*, a person's critical interests can be and often are affected by what happens after his death. It was against Hector's interests that his corpse was dragged around the walls of Troy, for instance, and it would make an author's life less successful if his entire oeuvre was destroyed after his death. People often take steps to guard against ignominy or to secure or protect their reputation after their death, and they think they are acting in their own, not other people's, interests.

A person's experiential interests also end if he falls into the state I discussed in chapter 7 of *Life's Dominion*: a permanent vegetative state. But most people think their critical interests survive that event and become, if anything, more dramatic. Some think it important that they be kept alive as long as possible in a vegetative state, and others think it crucial, in their own interests, that they die as soon as possible. That is why some people make "living wills" providing that life support be terminated in that event, and why the Supreme Court insisted that such wills, if properly executed, be respected.[82]

It seems *a fortiori* plain, therefore, that a person's critical interests survive even serious and permanent dementia. A competent person looking ahead to impending dementia may be concerned about the quality of experience he will have: these experiences will, after all, be happening to him. That concern may affect the wishes he expresses about how he is treated then. Shiffrin is of course right to say that he is no longer competent when he is having demented experiences; in that sense, she is right to say that P_1 does not "live with" what happens to P_2. But since the critical interests of P_2 and P_1 are the same, P_1 (which is simply one of P's three names) certainly does "live with" those events in a more important sense: in one way or another they affect what kind of a life he or she will have had. People's dread of and preparation for dementia would be inexplicable without that assumption. They do not dread and prepare for events in the life of a doppelganger, but in their own lives; they act not in someone else's interests but in their own.

Now consider the Jehovah's Witness case again. Shiffrin says she agrees with me that it would be wrong to give a fervent Witness a blood transfusion when she is deranged even if she then asks for it. I said, in constructing the example, that the Witness's derangement is temporary; Shiffrin says that fact is crucial, but not because she may later regret that we complied with her deranged wishes. After all, she might later regret that, and writhe in agonized shame, even if she asked for it in a fit of weakness while still competent: our prediction of regret would not be enough to justify refusing her the transfusion in that moment of weakness. The fact that the derangement is temporary is crucial, Shiffrin says, because it means that the competent Witness will have to "live with" the fact of the transfusion. But since she does not mean that the Witness will have to live with it in the experiential sense – the experience of transfusion will not have occurred in a competent moment – she must mean that the Witness has to live *through* it: that it is a fact in her life that has, at least as she judges it when she is competent, soiled that life. That is exactly true of the person who dreads living on in dementia: he dreads that a stage of his life that he lives through will soil that life. He knows, or strongly believes, that that stage will occur; that is why he tries to guard against it. He cannot know that it has occurred, and in that way he is different from the Witness in my example. But the kind of pain he might feel at contemplating his dementia does not depend on whether that experience occurs before or after the event. In any case, Shiffrin says that the difference has nothing to do with any such sensations or experiences, and it is therefore hard to see why it matters at all. In both cases, someone's life goes worse as he judges it because his competent wishes have been disobeyed. Shiffrin's argument does not sustain her claim of disanalogy.

She has two further arguments against my position, but these, too, depend on not taking seriously enough the identity of a person before and after dementia. First, she says that my understanding of the point of autonomy is too narrow. Autonomy does serve the "integrity" value I describe, she says, and that value, she agrees, is not available to someone while he is seriously demented. But autonomy also provides a value that she thinks is available then, which is "the basic value of being in control of one's experience and in not having experiences forced or imposed on one when one's will is to the contrary" (p. 202). Elsewhere she says that "the simple exercise of control over one's experience reinforces the special relation one has to one's experience" and confirms "the uniqueness and separateness of persons" (p. 203).

There are difficulties in this idea: autonomy alone is hardly enough to guarantee that experience will not contradict will, and control over one's experience is certainly not necessary to the personal distinctness of experience, which is, after all, never more evident than in torture. It is unclear, moreover, how far recognizing this part of autonomy's value is simply recognizing the experiential satisfaction of having one's own way and the badness of frustration. These are the values that best explain the deference to the wishes of young children that Shiffrin cites, and they are values that I mention in explaining why we should often allow demented people to do as they wish even when their acts seem pointless or inconsistent.[83]

I see no harm in treating these experiential interests as among autonomy's benefits on at least some occasions, however, even though I did not recognize them in that way. That would still leave open the question of how we best respect a single person's autonomy overall and we might still think, as I do, that we best respect this by giving powerful weight to an exercise of what I called "precedent" autonomy, that is, the autonomy exercised by a person when most competent to exercise it. After all, someone who is fully competent must feel frustration and a sense of lack of control when he is told that he cannot guard against what he regards as the coming savage indignity of dementia, that he cannot bring his life under the control of his will in that way. If that frustration counts distinctly at all, under the title of autonomy, then it counts as least as much in favor of precedent autonomy as in favor of the paler and dubious autonomy, grounded only in that way, that he might be able to exercise after deep dementia sets in. This is not a matter, to repeat, of justice: not a matter of cheating one person of autonomy to aggrandize the autonomy of another. It is just a matter of deciding what set of policies do best to protect a single person's autonomy overall.

Shiffrin believes, finally, that I confront a dilemma when I speak of that single person's best interests as distinct from his autonomy. How can I judge that it would be in the best critical interests of someone in serious and permanent dementia to die as soon as possible without taking sides, as I say I do not, on the controversy about whether suicide does in fact make the life of such a person go critically better? But I do not offer that judgment. I say that respecting the precedent autonomy of a patient who has expressed a clear wish to die in those circumstances does not conflict "with her critical interests as she herself conceived them when she was competent to do so."[84] I said that those called upon to act as she requested might have a different opinion, but that insisting on their own opinion would be "an unacceptable form of moral paternalism."[85] So I am not taking sides on the underlying ethical issue. We often defer to the judgments of competent people, about where their interests lie when we aim to act in their interests, as a fiduciary does, for example.

That deference does not collapse the distinction between beneficence and autonomy, because respect for autonomy requires us to follow someone's directions that are not even intended to be in his own interests.

I close by trying to guard against a possible misunderstanding. I did not say, as some of some of Shiffrin's comments might be read to suggest, that it would be all things considered right to deny a demented patient life-saving treatment or to kill him if he had requested this while competent. Since the point is important I shall repeat what I said:

> We might consider it morally unforgivable not to try to save the life of someone who plainly enjoys her life, no matter how demented she is, and we might think it beyond imagining that we should actually kill her. We might hate living in a community whose officials might make or license either of those decisions. We might have other good reasons for treating [a demented person] as she now wishes, rather than as, in my imaginary case, she once asked. But still, that violates rather than respects her autonomy.[86]

F. M. Kamm

F. M. Kamm's characteristically ingenious essay is a revision of an article previously published to which I have previously responded.[87] There is much new and interesting material in her revision, and though I repeat some of my previous response, I concentrate on certain parts of the new material. Her initial discussion of abortion is usefully divided into headed subsections, and I can reply to that discussion most easily by tracking her headings.

Does Dworkin really have a theory of the intrinsic value of life?
People have indeed used "intrinsic," "extrinsic," and "instrumental," as well as related terms like "constitutive," in various ways. It doesn't matter, so long as it is clear what each writer means. In any case, I mainly relied, not on "intrinsic" and "extrinsic," but on a new distinction I thought more illuminating: I said that the value of the sacred is detached rather than derivative: independent of human interests, that is, rather than derivative from such interests.

Does the value of life respond to changes in its cause in the way that Dworkin describes?
Kamm suggests that something's value must be independent of the history of its production: Rembrandt's picture would have been as wonderful if he had painted it under coercion. True, but a perfect copy produced mechanically, even if absolutely identical, is not wonderful at all. In the revised version of her essay she agrees, but adds that a clone, which might be considered a mechanical copy, still is wonderful. I suppose so, but I think it important that the clone, unlike a copy of a painting, is produced from and is in that sense a continuation of the original. The testing case would be a copy of a human embryo produced from scratch from chemicals rather than through cloning. One mustn't trust intuitions about such (so far) fantastic possibilities, but my initial reaction is that a fully mechanical copy, as distinct from an organic clone, would not have intrinsic value (except, perhaps, as a scientific marvel) from the start. It could be destroyed, though only immediately, without compunction.

Can an intrinsic value be nonincremental?
My claim is that once a human life has begun it is important that it go well. That does not entail, nor do I believe, that the more lives that go well the better. I do not think that a discovery that

twice as many people as we thought had led satisfactory lives in some earlier period would be, on its own, good news.

Is Dworkin's use of "inviolability" correct?
I think it a matter of substance not definition whether inviolability is absolute. But, once again, nothing turns on the verbal point.

Is the investment waste thesis correct?
In my response to Kamm's original paper, I said that nature's investment in a fetus is not just a matter of gestation time, but of complexity of development as well. In the revised version of her paper she worries that this comment threatens to undermine my claim that intrinsic value depends on investment, because "[g]iven any property the entity has (for example, consciousness) that one can describe without any knowledge of the entity's history, Dworkin's view (based on his response) seems to be that we can automatically say that there was investment in it of that property. We need no knowledge independent of the entity's properties to describe an investment history for it." I don't think this right, however. The value of an investment does depend not just on time or effort but on the character of the result. But it does not follow that it does not also depend on the history of production. A mechanical copy of a quick Picasso sketch has all the elegance of the original, and the original has value in virtue of its elegance and not just the time it took Picasso to create it. But it doesn't follow that the sketch has the value of the original, or, indeed, any intrinsic value at all. We do need historical knowledge independent of contemporary properties to define the character and value of an investment.

Kamm also now considers a different objection to my suggestion that the idea of investment must figure in accounting for the kind of intrinsic value I discussed. She says that on my view it would be worse – presumably all else being equal – if a woman in whose life a great deal has been invested, by herself and others, declines an abortion than if a woman in whose life little has been invested does. It is also true in this case, however, that much less of the natural and human investment in the unlucky woman's life has been realized, and the case that she ought to attempt to make something of her own life now is in that way stronger. It would be difficult, and seems quite unnecessary, to decide which of them has a stronger moral case for abortion.

Is Dworkin's account of conflicts between values (with and without consideration of rights)
sufficient to account for the permissibility of abortion?
Kamm adds a new discussion of the importance of the distinction between aiding something with intrinsic value and not destroying it. I do think that responsibilities not to destroy – a valuable painting one owns, for example – are generally stronger than responsibilities to aid. But the latter may be strong too: people have a responsibility to conserve and protect works of art they own, and the community may have a collective responsibility to aid them – by subsidizing owners of historically important buildings, for example, or by buying and protecting important works of art. I do not think, however, that we should count the law's permitting a woman to have an abortion as aiding her, out of respect for the intrinsic value of her own life going well, at the cost of destroying the fetus. The law permits her to have an abortion out of respect for her freedom, not because the community approves her decision as right.

In the balance of this part of her chapter, Kamm argues that the fact that a fetus imposes on a pregnant woman must be part of any successful case justifying abortion. She has in mind, perhaps, her own arguments, and those of Judith Jarvis Thomson, that abortion is permissible even if a fetus does have full rights of its own because people have a right not to be imposed upon: for example, a woman who finds that doctors have connected her body to that of a distinguished violinist, to save his life, may disconnect the tubes even though that means his death. I have argued against this analogy: if we were to assume (and make sense of the idea) that a fetus has rights, then a pregnant woman might have responsibilities to it that people do not have to strangers. Kamm resists my argument that because a fetus has no interests, it has no rights either. She says that some rights exist – she gives the example of free expression – not to protect the interests of the right-holder but the interests of others. I agree that some legal rights are derivative from the interests of others, though I do not agree that the right of free speech is best explained in that way. However, it is hard to imagine how a fetus could be thought to have rights derivative in that way – whose interests would such rights protect? In any case the antiabortion movement claims that the rights of a fetus are not derivative but fundamental: how else could such rights justify forbidding abortion altogether?

Is Dworkin correct to describe opinions on abortion as a matter of constitutionally protected religious belief?

Kamm thinks I mean to distinguish between religious and philosophical issues. But I certainly did not intend to make that distinction,[88] and of course I agree with her that many philosophers, including Kant, have studied the issues I call religious. The important distinction is between the issues I call essentially religious, which I believe to be part of the larger category of ethical issues, on the one hand, and issues of "morality, fairness and justice" on the other. I do not think, as she suggests I might, that essentially religious issues "connote an area of discourse that is not subject to rational proof." Proof is out of the question, of course, but I think she means rational argument, and I have tried to contribute to that kind of argument myself. I think religious convictions special not for the reasons she suggests but for those I described in *Life's Dominion* and that three justices of the Supreme Court identified in the important abortion decision I discuss in my response to Eric Rakowski's chapter below. Essentially religious convictions play a special role in defining personality. People of self-respect must insist on deciding such issues for themselves, and a fully legitimate political society will therefore not impose any single view collectively upon them.

Is Dworkin's hard-line view correct?

I need not repeat my reservations, which Kamm cites, about her claim that abortion would still be permissible even if (whatever that would mean) a fetus had the full rights of any person from conception. I have no considered opinion about the legal and moral responsibilities someone would have toward a creature manufactured from his or her genetic material, but it would certainly be pertinent whether he or she agreed to the construction. I do agree, however, that abortion becomes morally more problematic as a fetus develops.

Assisted suicide

The bulk of Kamm's essay is devoted to the different issue of assisted suicide. She disagrees with the treatment of certain issues in "The Philosophers' Brief" submitted to the Supreme Court in two assisted suicide cases on behalf of six philosophers including myself. I said, in a published comment on the brief, that it supposes that the "common sense" distinction in point is not the distinction between acts and omissions that cause death and those that do not, but between acts and omissions that are designed to cause death and those that are not. I should have made plainer that I limited that claim to its context. Kamm agrees that the distinction between acts and omissions is not morally relevant in the familiar kinds of assisted suicide cases that the brief discusses, and I agree with her that the distinction is sometimes morally important in other, very different, cases. I cannot now discuss her interesting remarks about several of these cases.

I do not, however, agree that all doctors, including, for example, Catholic doctors who believe it a sin, are morally required to assist terminally ill patients who ask their help in suicide, and I must therefore confront the "duty argument" that she constructs in the final section of her chapter (pp. 236–7). A doctor has no duty to provide treatment that he believes is against the best interests of his patients. He may believe that it is against the interests of a terminally ill patient in great pain to relieve that pain through medicine that will advance death. In that case he does not have even the duty cited in Kamm's paragraph (1b). It is a further question whether medical boards should license doctors who have convictions about their patients' best interests that orthodox medical opinion condemns.

Eric Rakowski

In *Life's Dominion*, I argued for a somewhat different approach to moral, political, and legal controversies about abortion and assisted suicide than those that have become familiar. I said that the freedom of women to choose abortion in early pregnancy, and of terminally ill patients to choose death as relief from pain and indignity, should be regarded as part of more general rights to religious freedom. Eric Rakowski calls my argument "unusual" and adds that it "has little force," for two reasons. He says, first, that only a small number of women who seek abortions or of patients who want help in suicide act out of religious motives, and, second, that my understanding of religion stretches the shared understanding of our political traditions out of recognition.

The first of these objections confuses the motives of those whose liberty is constrained with the assumptions presupposed in the legislation that constrains them. (In terms familiar to constitutional lawyers, it confuses First Amendment "exercise" and "establishment" claims.) Many people who seek abortions or euthanasia do act out of a religious conviction in the broad sense I described: they think it dishonors important values to bring a life into the world with very dim prospects, for example, or wrong to struggle to keep oneself alive when life no longer has point. Many others act more passively out of convictions I take to be religious in character: they would not seek abortion or euthanasia if they did not think or assume this to be consistent with the right conception of the value of life.

But, as I emphasized, my argument does not suppose that everyone who wants an abortion or euthanasia acts out of or even has convictions of that kind. It rather supposes that a prohibition of early abortion or a flat prohibition of assisted suicide could reasonably be justified only on the basis of such convictions, and that government should not appeal to essentially religious positions to justify imposing constraints on individuals that seriously impair those individuals' lives. Rakowski therefore misunderstands my argument when he reports that I appeal to the same reasons as those that deny government the power to "force a church or a mosque to shut its doors." That would be unjustifiable almost no matter what kind of reason justified the government's decision; my argument is different.

He also objects, as I said, to my understanding of an "essentially religious" conviction, which is built up in the following way. I distinguish, first, between two kinds of justification for government intervention: protecting people's interests and protecting intrinsic value. Rakowski complains that this distinction truncates the idea of intrinsic value because it supposes that laws that prohibit murder do not protect something – human life – that has intrinsic value. He has misread the text again, however, because I say explicitly that the two kinds of justification can overlap. I say that human life has all three kinds of value I distinguish: that it is subjectively and instrumentally valuable, and that laws prohibiting murder are therefore justified because they protect people's interests of different kinds, and also because they protect something intrinsically valuable.[89]

An essentially religious conviction, in my view, is a special kind of conviction about intrinsic value. Only certain intrinsic values are essentially religious: I define these to include all convictions about whether, how, and why human life is important, whether or not these convictions are drawn from assumptions about a supernatural god. I then use that broad view of essentially religious conviction to frame the following principle of political morality: "A state may not curtail liberty, in order to protect an intrinsic value, when the effect on one group of citizens would be special and grave, when the community is seriously divided about what respect for that value requires, and when people's opinions about the nature of that value reflect essentially religious convictions that are fundamental to moral personality."[90]

Rakowski declares that this account "defines religiously motivated action more broadly than our tradition of toleration approves." That is certainly true, since toleration of abortion and assisted suicide is hardly traditional. But we must, as citizens as well as lawyers, interpret and restate our traditions so as to display them as principled rather than only as a set of historical compromises: we must reformulate our traditions to try to capture what is really of value in our values.[91] As the Supreme Court has held, an interpretation of our legal tradition of religious freedom that limited religion to orthodox superstition would be unprincipled: it would leave religious freedom parochial and arbitrary. That is why the Court declared a conception of religion, for the purpose of interpreting the draft exemption for conscientious objectors, that is similar to the account I defend: a scruple is religious for that purpose, it said, if it has "a place in the life of its possessor parallel to that filled by the orthodox belief in God of one who qualifies for the exemption."[92] Someone who objects to all wars acts out of such a scruple, the Court held, though someone who distinguishes the justice of different wars does not.

Rakowski offers a much narrower interpretation, based on his assumption that the central point of religious freedom is to protect public order and to forestall self-defeating attempts to convert people to religion by force. But though such justifications of religious toleration were indeed popular in the seventeenth century, they are inapposite as justifications of our present law and practice. Civil order would no more be threatened by a mandatory period of prayer in schools, for example, than it would be by prohibition of abortion.

My account of "essentially" religious freedom defines a special area of conviction – about the meaning and importance of human life as such – that plays a distinct and personality-defining role in people's lives. It is particularly important to someone's self-respect that he decide such issues for himself, and it is that role in the structure of personality, as the Supreme Court said, that explains the need for special protection. Though Rakowski objects that earlier versions of my argument have had little influence in constitutional law, my account is very close to that given in the crucial opinion in the Supreme Court's most important recent abortion case. Three justices said that "at the heart of liberty is the right to define one's own conception of existence, of meaning, of the universe, and of the mystery of human life." A society committed to freedom, they said, must leave such decisions to individual conscience because "beliefs about such matters could not define the attributes of personhood were they formed under the compulsion of the state."[93]

Rakowski objects to a different facet of my argument as well. I said that though many opponents of abortion insist that abortion is murder, and that a fetus has from conception as powerful a right to live as any other person, the full range of their more detailed convictions suggests that their opposition does not really reflect that set of beliefs. (I did not mean that people dissemble, or that I know what is in their minds better than they do, but that people's convictions, like much else that they create, need interpretation, particularly when they concern the subjects of heated political argument.) It would be inconsistent with the idea that a fetus has full rights to suppose, for example, as many abortion opponents do, that abortion is permissible when pregnancy arises from rape. I suggested that the fierce opposition to abortion is better explained by supposing that opponents express an often inarticulate conviction that abortion dishonors the intrinsic value of human life, a conviction that is essentially religious in the sense I had defined. Rakowski offers a third possibility: they may believe that a fetus has a right to life but, in spite of their rhetoric, actually think that it has a weaker right to life than people do after birth. It is unclear, however, what such a belief would consist in. If people think a fetus has a right to life because it is a full person at the moment of conception, then how can they think its rights are weaker than other people's rights? Do they think it is something between a person and not-a-person? Or that it has only the lesser rights that might be attributed to a nonhuman animal? These suggestions are as hard to reconcile with people's beliefs, though for different reasons, as the supposition that they think a fetus has full human rights.

Rakowski concludes the initial part of his argument with two odder points. He says, first, that my question whether an early fetus has interests of its own – I argue that it does not – "depends on how 'interest' is defined." That is certainly true, but he does not suggest that he disagrees with my definition, or with my answer. He then denies that my argument about abortion exactly parallels my argument about assisted suicide. That is true as well: the two arguments are not mirror-images, though they are indeed closely related in the ways I suggest.

He next declares that my distinction between the justification government has for protecting people's interests and its justification for protecting intrinsic value "has at best modest significance" because we can frame no general principle limiting the range of the latter justification, but must instead decide on a case-by-case basis. This seems a non sequitur: the distinction would be helpful even if we could not find a general principle, because it would suggest that the kinds of considerations that figure in detailed studies of the two kinds of justification would be different, as they evidently are. I am unsure, however, why Rakowski is so confident that no useful general principles can be defended, particularly since he later announces that he is himself committed to a particularly dramatic example of exactly such a principle – that government is never justified in restricting liberty to protect intrinsic value, but only to protect people's interests. He suggests that any such principle could only be defended by induction, but, as many philosophers have noted, this is not possible because we need principles of some kind even to decide issues "case by case." How could we decide whether government has the right to protect historic buildings from destruction without some general idea of the kind of interest government is or is not entitled to protect, at the cost of what kind of constraint?

Much of the rest of Rakowski's argument – apart from his valuable instruction that I should have written about many more issues than I actually took up in *Life's Dominion* – asks how I distinguish early abortion and assisted suicide for dying patients from other controversial issues of political morality. I rely on the principle of political morality that I described above, which, for the reasons I gave, Rakowski's objections do not impugn. Much of his argument toward the end of his chapter is spoiled by another, particularly unfortunate, misreading, however. He reports that I believe that a state may legitimately outlaw abortion at some time before a fetus acquires interests of its own – that it might outlaw it "much sooner" – because most women would have a fair opportunity to decide on abortion before that time. If I had made that statement it would, as he says it does, undermine much of my argument. But I never made it. I did say that once it is conceded that a state may outlaw abortion after six months of pregnancy, the question naturally arises why it cannot outlaw it sooner: "after five months? Four? Three?"[94] But I immediately answered that question as I had answered it earlier in the argument: I said that the state cannot outlaw abortion until the point at which a fetus has interests that the state can claim a derivative responsibility to protect, and that though this point might be said, on the embryological evidence, to be "somewhat" earlier than the sixth month of pregnancy that the Supreme Court had chosen, it could not be said to be "much" earlier.

Part IV

Leslie Green

Many philosophers think that all genuine moral obligations rest on consent, and they worry about the implications of that view for political obligation – the obligation most people in a just state think they have, at least in principle, to obey its laws. Few people have actually consented to any such duty. Almost all of them were born into their political community, and were simply expected, from the start, to obey its laws. So these philosophers worry that, in spite of most people's assumption, political obligation is an illusion. Some of them try to avoid that threat by showing that, in spite of first appearances, people actually do consent, at least in some attenuated or hypothetical way, to an obligation to obey the law. Some of them say, for example, that people who live in a political community "tacitly" consent to that obligation by not leaving it and moving elsewhere.

Leslie Green's ambitions seem entirely different. He does not hold the popular view that obligations can arise only from consent. On the contrary he accepts the idea of what I have called "associational obligations": that people have obligations in virtue of being members of certain kinds of communities, even though they have not chosen that status or role. But he denies that political obligation can arise from membership in a political community: that kind of obligation, he insists, does require consent. His aim, in this unusual combination of opinions, is not to save political obligation but, on the contrary, if not actually to annihilate it, at least to show that it is rarer than is commonly supposed. So he need not argue that people actually do consent to that form of obligation; in fact, if I am right in my reading, he must think that almost no one ever does.

In this chapter he sets out to rebut my own argument that political obligation is a species of associational obligation.[95] I began my argument by offering examples of less controversial associative obligations – the obligations of family, for example – in order to rebut the general view I mentioned that obligations can be acquired only by consent. Once we abandon that general view, I said, we can try to define the circumstances in which it would be plausible to treat political obligation as an associational obligation of the same sort. I had two aims. I hoped, first, to find a general principle that would match the circumstances under which many people already suppose themselves to have political obligations of different kinds and, in particular, obligations to obey even laws they think unwise or unfair. I wanted, that is, to achieve what – following John Rawls – is now often called a "reflective equilibrium" between general principles and more concrete convictions or "intuitions." Second, I wanted to support those principles through an interpretive argument that explains the point of distinct values, like political obligation, by finding their place in a larger network of interconnected and mutually supporting values.[96] I tried to show such interpretive connections among a variety of values: equality as a sovereign virtue of political community, democracy as a paradigm of fair political process, integrity as an independent feature of legal structure, and the mutual concern of individual citizens tied together in true community.

Green believes that my argument is unsatisfactory in various ways. He says that it is necessary, in order to accept that a particular kind of association carries obligations, to see some point or value in obligations being created in that way. We may agree, but with some care: his claim is not tantamount to the very different claim that associative obligations are only valid if we would have sufficient reason to accept them in the absence of the practice that constitutes the association. The "bare" facts of a social practice – the obligations that it identifies for its members – count in fixing what obligations its members actually have. Members of a neighborhood have an obligation to play their part in various improvement schemes the neighbors have in some fair way adopted, even though they would otherwise have no obligation to do what the scheme provides, and perhaps no obligation as neighbors to create any improvement scheme at all.

Of course there are constraints both on what kind of an association can generate obligations and what kind of obligation any association can generate. As I said, only true political communities can generate political obligations, and, as Green says, neighborhoods cannot create an obligation to vote Republican. We might well accept, however, what must be Green's point here: that no association can generate obligations if the association is wholly without value to its members. I believe that my account of true community satisfies that condition for political obligation; in any case the interpretive claim I made depends on satisfying it. But of course Green does not mean to claim either that political community is without value, or that it is of no value to members of true political communities that membership carries a general obligation to abide by collective decisions that are fairly reached.

Green next argues, as I understand him, that the other cases of associational obligation I mention do not involve, as political obligation does, obedience: "One *thanks* a benefactor, *respects* the wise, *defends* a friend. But one does not *obey* them as an expression of the relationship. For Locke, obedience is out of place in all these contexts, whereas it would be fitting in the relationship of Creator and created, or of parent and child" (p. 273). (Green then questions whether political authority can properly be seen as like the authority of a parent over a child.) Some of his examples, including the relationship between benefactor and beneficiary and the wise and the not-so-wise, are not examples of involuntary associations or even genuine obligation: one is normally free to reject the gift and the gratitude, and there is no relation of association or obligation at all between the wise and the dull.

In nonpolitical cases that are clearly associational, however, like friendship, family, and neighborhood, the discrete acts required are indeed matters of obligation. I am obliged to defend my friends and help my siblings in certain ways and to cooperate in appropriate neighborhood schemes. True, it would be odd to speak of obedience in some of these cases: the obligations of friendship are not usually obligations to do as a friend says. In some cases they are, however: you might well feel obliged to go along with a friend's declarations about where you should spend a vacation together, and in that case it would not be odd to speak of bowing to his will. Of course that kind of deference or obedience is a much more characteristic feature of political obligation, for obvious reasons, but that does not make political obligation wholly different in that dimension.

It is also true, however, that any requirement of obedience that might arise in nonpolitical associations would not be fundamental but derivative: your underlying motive for accepting your
friend's decision about a vacation is not based on any general requirement of obedience to him,
but on more complex requirements of friendship from which that duty might be thought to follow
on some specific occasions. It is therefore particularly important to see that the same is true, in
spite of Green's suggestions to the contrary, of the requirement of political obedience. He asks
whether my account of associative obligation is sufficient to "accommodate the *state's* claim to
authority," and adds that "Surprisingly, Dworkin does not explicitly address the point and his
central example [he means my analogy to the obligations of siblings] counts against it" (p. 271,
italics added). My entire argument, however, aims to show that an obligation of obedience to collectively enacted laws is derivative from the more basic attitudes, which are not themselves attitudes of obedience, that hold among the citizens of a true community. The association I describe,
to which obligations of different kinds attach, is an association of individuals in political community, not an association to which the state, which I insist is only a useful personification, is a
party.

This is a convenient point at which to report Green's extended discussion of a particular
example I used. I said that associations that display the egalitarian virtues of true community
might nevertheless generate expectations of obedience that should be rejected, but that leave, as
many overridden claims of obligation leave in other contexts, good reason for residual regret. I
imagined an otherwise egalitarian community whose shared and long-standing social practices
required daughters to accept the decision of their fathers about a suitable marriage. "The fact that
a true community's practices require this of daughters," Green says, "does nothing to justify it"
(p. 273). But the pertinent question is different: whether the practice generates a more diffuse
responsibility of concern for defeated expectations. I said that it might do that in the right kind
of community in which disobedience, while justified, nevertheless brings embarrassment and
perhaps shame to others whose beliefs and attitudes are honorable. Green may be right to say that
the obligation to obey a father's wishes in marriage, considered on its own, is not even a *prima
facie* obligation. But the residual responsibilities I described may nevertheless exist only in communities that in general generate associational obligations.

Green continues by discussing what he calls "the centerpiece" of my argument for political
obligation as associational, which he takes to be some argument involving integrity, that is, a principled coherence within law. He apparently thinks that I think that integrity is on its own a ground
for obligation, because he roundly declares that, "Secondly, and this is the main point, integrity
creates no duty to obey those who display the virtue" (p. 275). Of course it doesn't: I have no
obligation to obey the decisions of the Geneva parliament no matter how much integrity the law
of that canton displays, and I would have no obligations to obey the government of my own territory if it were wicked, no matter how coherent its wickedness. My remarks about integrity that
he cites are not the "centerpiece" of any argument for political obligation, but rather part of my
interpretive argument connecting political obligation with other political virtues. Integrity, at some
level, is a necessary condition of true community, and in that way contributes to legitimacy and
obligation. But it does so only as a necessary, and certainly not sufficient, condition.

I should add, however, that in the course of this part of his discussion Green offers a variety
of highly critical but bewildering comments about my views on law more generally. The most
important of his mistakes is an argument that supposedly shows that I am committed to a solip-
sistic theory of law that "turns principled civil disobedience into obedience to true law" (p. 276)
and that claims that "the law's requirements are, for each individual, simply his or her own best

interpretation." Green here confuses my comment that each person has a "protestant" responsibility for identifying law's requirements for himself, in an interpretive style, with the very different, indeed inconsistent, claim that there is no right answer to that interpretive question but only different answers, so that each person's answer is right for him. I have argued for many years against that latter, skeptical view.[97]

I shall close my response to Green with some comments about his own account of a consensual basis for political obligation. This is pertinent because we must ask whether the associational account I defend provides a more satisfactory account of our political convictions and experience than any more skeptical account that makes political obligation hostage to consent. It is unclear what acts he thinks constitute the requisite consent. He rejects the tacit consent theory I described as an "embarrassment" to liberal theory (p. 279). He also rejects the opposite idea: that the requisite consent consists in a datable performative act of fealty. The required consent, he says, "may be assumed by actions, by omissions, and by a series of actions and omissions that collectively amount to the deliberate assumption of a role" (p. 279).

But what acts and omissions do constitute a "deliberate" assumption of political obligation, and why? If someone does not believe that his various acts and omissions have the force of consenting to political obligation (surely that thought would not occur to more than a tiny number of people) does it follow that the acts and omissions do not have that force? Perhaps Green thinks that acting in a particular way amounts to accepting the role of political obligation even if one doesn't know that that is the upshot of acting in that way. But that makes "deliberate" obscure, and sounds like tacit consent all over again. He does say that one may undertake obligations, in virtue of accepting that role, that one doesn't know are part of that role, and he agrees that a person can assume a role and its attendant obligations – become a friend or lover, for example – without realizing that that is what one is doing. But if self-consciousness is not required, after all, then why is this a *consent* theory?

One passage suggests a possible answer. Green may think that people have given the requisite consent if they remain in the community and do not positively "reject" political obligation (p. 279). But what constitutes such a rejection? Is a datable act necessary – declaring rejection in a special public place or newspaper notice, for example? Or is it enough to reject authority in one's heart? In either case, where on this hypothesis does the obligation come from that one has if one does not reject it, and retains until one does? Must there be some earlier act of consent before rejection becomes necessary or appropriate? Then we return to the question of the form that earlier consent must take.

The possibility of rejection is surrounded by its own mysteries, moreover. Why should anyone *not* reject political obligation, or refuse to accept it? There seems no price to pay for rejecting it. Rejecters "may, for example, remain in the country, participate in its affairs, obey the law when conscience so counsels, but reject the moral authority of the state. Those who comply in such a peaceful and principled fashion will, in a reasonably just state, support the government and avoid sanction, but the law will create no obligations for them" (p. 278). It seems a no-lose option. It might also seem, however, that though there is nothing to be lost by rejection, there is very little to be gained either, for Green insists that a reasonably just government will still be entitled, at least on some occasions, to coerce people's obedience even though they have no general obligation to obey. The government could not rely on any general political authority to justify such coercion, to be sure, but it could rely on a variety of more limited justifications appropriate on different occasions. "It may be justified in coercing those who murder in order to protect those at risk, in coercing those who break contracts in order to protect valued social practices, and in coercing those who negligently harm others in order to establish a public framework for reciprocity, and so on."

In fact, however, there would be distinct advantages in rejecting political authority and, particularly if most others rejected it as well, it would be foolish for anyone not to do so. The citizen who rejects the moral authority of the state has no duty to obey laws that do not capture his genuine moral obligations. He may think he has no duty to respect a complex system of securities regulation, for example, or of financial regulation aimed at improving the gross national product. He may agree that he has a moral obligation to protect valuable social practices, but disagree that the securities market is valuable or that the gross national product matters. Or he may agree that these institutions and goals are important, but disagree that the scheme of law in force is well-conceived to protect them. Or he may disagree that he has a moral obligation, even in principle, to protect valuable social practices. He may also think that he has no moral reason to defer to the state in enforcing what he takes to be the obligations of others: that he has no duty, that is, not to take the law into his own hands when he can do so efficaciously. So on many occasions on which he would think he has a duty of compliance if he had accepted the political authority of the state, he will feel no duty, and no reason beyond prudence, since he has rejected that authority.

The moral authority of the state to coerce those who have rejected its authority is also limited, in a different but potentially very significant way. If officials accept that they have no general moral justification to enforce the law, but only discrete justifications in particular circumstances, then they will believe that they lack authority to enforce laws when there is no persuasive case for enacting those laws at the moment when they are asked to enforce them. A political administration bent on radical revision of the laws regulating securities transactions would think it had both responsibility and adequate justification for enforcing the present regime of laws, before the revisions were enacted, against violators who had accepted the state's political authority. But it would not think it had any justification for enforcing those laws against people who had rejected that authority.

Green believes that almost all of the familiar political practice of modern states would survive a general abandonment of the idea of a distinct political obligation; that is the premise, as I suggested, of his attempt to show that someone's consent is necessary in order that he have such an obligation. He believes that political obligation is in fact a rare phenomenon, and not a particularly useful one. In fact, as this last discussion shows, many of the most familiar and important of our political assumptions and expectations would have to be sacrificed in a reductive reconstruction of political practice that appeals only to independent moral obligations and never to a distinct political obligation. But it is indispensable to our political life that citizens have a duty, in principle, to obey the law because it is the law and that government is justified, again in principle, in enforcing the law because it is the law.

We might try to save a reductive reconstruction by supposing that people do have a standing and independent moral obligation to yield to the collective judgment of a fair political process, as that judgment is recorded in the published laws of their community, and that officials are justified in using coercion to enforce just that moral obligation. Citizens who think they have no such moral obligation and officials who think they have no such justification for coercion, we might say, are simply wrong as a matter of moral fact. But this would not be reconstructing political practice without political obligation: it would be a roundabout attempt to justify political obligation itself. For it is just that general moral obligation that citizens who "reject the moral authority of the state" reject.

Joseph Raz

I am very grateful to Joseph Raz for his painstaking examination of my writings about the nature of law and adjudication. His contribution to this volume is only the edited version of the Appendix to an earlier and much longer article about the role of coherence in legal theory which also discusses my views, but which could not be reprinted here in full.[98] In the version of the Appendix that appears here he mainly takes up an interpretive question: what role does coherence play in my own account of law in *Law's Empire* and elsewhere? It is difficult to understand the interpretive issue he has in mind, however, or to gauge its importance from that section alone, and in this response I will draw and comment on the larger article.

Not very constructive interpretation

In the Appendix Raz mainly discusses whether I endorse the "strong monistic coherence" of law, which he defines in the larger article as the view that all legal principles "follow from one of their number."[99] He says that my account of legal interpretation commits me to monism so defined because I describe constructive interpretation as "imposing purpose on an object or practice in order to make of it the best possible example of the form or genre to which it is taken to belong" (p. 285).[100] But "purpose," used in the singular, need not mean a single overriding ambition; someone acts with purpose even if his ambitions are complex and competing so that he must sometimes neglect one to serve another. Any suspicion that I had "monism" in mind should have been put to rest by the dozens of examples of constructive interpretation I gave that involve complexity and competition, and by several more theoretical discussions in which I said that interpretation often requires fitting a complex justification composed of independent principles to unruly data. Raz might have attended, for example, to my discussion of skeptical arguments associated with critical legal studies, in which I emphasize that the best overall interpretation of a branch of law may appeal to principles that are "independent" and "competing";[101] my discussion of "local priority," which argues that an overall interpretation of law, which must respect the practice of legal compartmentalization, may for that reason be forced to assign different, even contradictory, principles to different areas of the law;[102] and my discussion of the distinction between "inclusive" and "pure" integrity, which begins by stating that "Law as integrity therefore not only permits but fosters different forms of substantive conflict or tension within the overall best interpretation of law."[103] He offers four bare page citations to support his charge of "monism" against these plain rejections of it, but none of them does offer any support.[104] He can't make up his mind whether it is uncertain whether I am a monist or certain that I am.[105] I am not a monist, however, and I do not think my writings leave any room for doubt. I do agree with his conclusion: that my account of interpretation leaves open, in the way the passages I just quoted say, how much coherence (in different senses of that complex ideal) a successful interpretation of any part of any particular legal system can achieve.

Raz offers three other interpretations of my work that I am anxious to correct. First, he apparently subscribes to the opinion that I think that the two dimensions of interpretation I distinguish – the degree to which an interpretation "fits" the data and the degree to which it confers "value" on the data – are independent, and that the second dimension comes into play only when two interpretations are "tied" in the first dimension.[106] Though I did once introduce the distinction in that way, I took care to say that this account of the relation was a heuristic construction, and that a full analysis would show the two dimensions interdependent and neither prior to the other.[107] I summarized my actual view in this way: a judgment of integrity

> is structured by different dimensions of interpretation and different aspects of these. We noticed how conviction about fit contest with and constrain judgments of substance, and how convictions about fairness and justice and procedural due process contest with one another. The interpretive judgment must notice and take account of these several dimensions . . . But it must also meld these dimensions into an overall opinion; about which interpretation, all things considered, makes the community's legal record the best it can be from the point of view of political morality.[108]

We have no reason to think, in advance of case-by-case analysis, that the various strands are incommensurate, or that an overall judgment must be defeated for some other reason.[109] However, Raz does identify a sentence in *Law's Empire* that, as he says, seems to suggest that integrity is a matter of fit alone.[110] He is right and generous to say that this sentence is inconsistent with everything else I say about the matter, and so "it seems best to disregard it" (p. 288).

Second, Raz believes that my discussion in *Law's Empire* of the dilemma judges face when they regard the law as profoundly immoral suggests a striking change from opinions I had earlier expressed. He says that I once thought that a theory of law is equivalent to a comprehensive theory of judges' legal, practical, and moral responsibilities, so that if it is morally right to think that a judge ought sometimes to lie – declare that the law does not require what he actually thinks it does require – then the law does not after all require him to decide as he thinks it does. I do not find that view even intelligible, however; in any case I have never held it. I do think that a theory of law is a theory of adjudication, but that is not surprising because I mean, by the latter, a theory of how judges should identify and enforce people's legal rights, that is, how they should acquit their institutional duty to apply the law.

Raz also says that I once denied "that courts are ever legally required or permitted to do anything other than apply the law." But, on the contrary, I insisted that the law often gives judges discretion: for example in sentencing those convicted of crimes.[111] It is crucial for any competent theory of law or of adjudication, however, to distinguish between a judge's situation and responsibilities when the law allows him discretion of that sort and when it does not. Morality requires him to ignore what the law does require – when the law requires him to return escaped slaves or to enforce an apartheid regime, for example, and morality forbids this. Raz ignores that distinction when he asks why I do not recognize that the law itself grants a discretion to ignore the law when it is grossly immoral. He says that "in all common-law countries courts, both judges and juries, have a legally recognized discretion to refuse to enforce a clear law on grounds of equity, or because it violates fundamental constitutional doctrines."[112] This formulation hides the crucial distinction: it equates the legal power that the traditions and practices of some legal systems give judges to overrule precedent by appeal to more general principles, on some occasions, with the moral responsibility of judges to ignore unjust law even when the traditions and practices of their system explicitly deny them that power. We may disagree about whether the former power is a power to alter the existing law or is rather part of the complex of principles and practices through which a judge determines what the existing law is. I do disagree with the legal positivists Raz names – H. L. A. Hart and Hans Kelsen – about that issue. But it would be false and fatally confusing to call the latter responsibility a legal as well as a moral responsibility. The dilemma judges face in such cases is posed only when we understand that the law does *not* allow any discretion for freeing escaped slaves or acquitting blacks who have violated the pass laws. I dare say that Hart and Kelsen would not have disagreed with me about that.

Third, Raz describes what he calls the argument for integrity from loyalty to the community, but though he says he intends to describe my own argument for integrity, he does not.[113] He says my argument begins by supposing that "the law is the organized voice of the community." I do not understand the argument he constructs from that start, but I believe my own argument to be very different and it is, in any case, not refuted by what he describes as a refutation of the argument he constructs. I argue, not that the law is the voice of the community personified, but that the practices of the community recognize a general obligation to obey its law. The crucial step in my argument is the claim of "associational obligation"; the claim, that is, that someone is subject to obligations established in the practices of communities to which he belongs (though only under certain conditions and subject to certain limitations) even though he has not chosen those obligations or chosen to belong to those communities.[114] That is the claim properly identified in Leslie Green's contribution to this volume; I responded to Green's criticism of my claim earlier in this chapter.

Authority, intention, and politics
In the end, Raz says in his contribution here, the interpretive questions he considers do not much matter, because the argument he makes against my appeal to the idea of integrity as a distinct political virtue are sound whether integrity appeals to coherence or not. His argument, he says, "relies on one feature of integrity only: that it advocates acting on principles that may never have been considered or approved, either explicitly or implicitly, by any legal authority, and that are inferior to some alternatives in justice and fairness" (p. 289).

This rather cryptic statement is amplified in his main article. In fact Raz relies on two distinct claims: first, that judges should not pursue integrity in their decisions because that would compromise their ability to secure fair and just decisions and, second, that integrity cannot be the key to law because law is a matter of authority and integrity subverts authority. The first of these claims assumes that if the judges of a community aim to decide new cases in the light of the principles that provide the best justification of the law as a whole they will reach decisions over time that are less just than if they sought justice in each case without regard to integrity. It is true that a judge who is bent on integrity may therefore be required to reach a decision contrary to what he thinks a more abstract judgment of justice would require. It is also true that people with political convictions would often prefer, as Raz says he himself does, compromises that would provide what is, in his opinion, "half a loaf" of justice instead of none. That is why I insist that integrity is a distinct political virtue that might conflict with justice and other such virtues.

But it certainly does not follow that a legal system that accepts integrity as a distinct and controlling virtue will produce decisions that are on the whole less just over time, even considered one by one, than alternative decisions would have been. Judges and other legal actors disagree about justice, and the decision that one judge reaches because he deems that solution just will seem unjust to others. Citizens deciding behind a veil of ignorance who are concerned only to improve the justice of discrete judicial decisions in the long run might well stipulate that judges should be bound by integrity, and not try to serve their own individual opinions about justice save as these are disciplined by integrity, because citizens might think that individual judicial decisions are less likely to be just if they depart from principles reflected in the decisions of many legislators, judges, and lawyers over time.

I must be careful: I do not mean that my case for integrity as a virtue depends on some two-level assumption that judicial decisions will on the whole be closer to what justice requires, if judges aim at integrity rather than justice. My arguments for integrity, in *Law's Empire* and elsewhere, do not rely on any such assumption. I only object to what I take to be the opposite assumption that Raz and other critics of integrity seem to make. They have no ground for that opposite assumption, so it can be no objection to integrity that the results it dictates are "inferior to some alternatives in justice and fairness."

Raz's second claim, about authority, is more complex and takes us deeper into his own opinions about the nature of jurisprudence and law. I have written at length about those opinions recently;[115] I argued that his conception of authority is eccentric and unhelpful, and that the positivistic view of law that he bases on that conception is counterintuitive and implausible. I will not summarize my arguments here. But Raz's essay about coherence, from which his contribution to this volume is taken, offers fresh clues as to the genesis of his conception of authority which we might now explore. In a striking passage he properly warns against a bad argument for legal positivism. It does not follow from the assumption that "the law is a function of human acts and social practices" that the intentions of lawmakers are decisive over the content of the law they create, he says, because the answer to the question of what law legislators create by their performative utterances depends on the further question of *what* that function is. We might accept the assumption that law depends in some way on what people with legislative power do and still say, as advocates of integrity do say, that the law that legislators create includes the principles that provide the best justification of enacting the statutes they do: that still describes law as a "function" of the statutory text that a majority of legislators have enacted.

However, Raz seems himself later to ignore his own warning, and to make the very argument he earlier said was a bad one. First, he argues that because legal standards "emerge from the activities of authoritative institutions" and such institutions "are subject to a requirement of acting with deliberation, in good faith, and for cogent reasons," it follows that "we must assign considerable importance to the intentions of legal authorities and to their reasons for acting as they do when we interpret the law and establish its content." He then concludes that "because the law is meant to be taken as a system based on authority its content is to be determined by reference to the intention of legal authorities and their reasons, and, therefore, that, given the vagaries of politics . . . there is no reason to expect the law to be coherent."[116]

But this simply brushes aside the possibility that though law in some sense "emerges" from the activities of parliaments, courts, and other legal actors and institutions, the law that these activities actually create is not fixed by the crude "function" of these activities that Raz here assumes, which makes the law only what the lawmakers intended it to be, but a more complex function that puts into play principles that provide the best political justification of what they have done. Raz argues for this choice of "function" that "Otherwise, it would be a mystery why legal institutions are invested with authority in the first place, and why they are required to exercise it on the basis of reasons."[117] Elsewhere he asks why, unless legislators' intentions fix the law, "we care whether a Democrat or a Republican is elected to the Senate?"[118] There are good answers to these questions if we choose an "integrity" function, however, because what legislators do matters crucially to what the law becomes even if their intentions do not fix the limits of the changes their acts make. Even if the law consists in the best interpretation of the words of a statute instead of the interpretation the lawmakers would put on their own work, even if the words of a statute might change not only the law they aim to change but law in other areas as well because the initial change has gravitational force, it still matters devastatingly what the words of the statute are, and we still have every reason to care who makes those words and the reasons they have for doing so.

In fact, Raz himself does not accept the view that a statute or other law-making act changes the law only in the way its author intended, which he calls "unsustainable." He rejects that view because "What we need is a way of regarding the law as the function of the activities of legal authorities in general, that is, a way of seeing how its content is a function of various activities, and layers of activities, in continuous interaction, rather than as a function of a single act, fixed once and for all."[119] I find this statement as promising as it is mysterious. The nerve of integrity is exactly the idea that we must interpret the acts of various kinds of legislative bodies over time "in continuous interaction" rather than as a function of each act fixed once and for all. Raz may have something very different in mind, but I cannot imagine what it might be.

He also makes the bad argument he warns against when he says, in different ways, that "the rough and tumble" of politics leaves law "untidy" and that theories of law that appeal to integrity "attempt to prettify it and minimize the effect of politics." That seems brazenly to beg the jurisprudential question of how law should be identified. The political history of legislation and adjudication is of course untidy – or worse. No one could deny that. But it does not follow that the law that this history is taken to have made must be equally untidy. It does not follow, that is, that the "function" we must impose on political history to fix law is one that transfers politics' untidiness to law. That is what the jurisprudential arguments about the adequacy of legal positivism are all about.[120]

Raz proposes, however, two general jurisprudential theses to support his choice of a narrowly positivistic "function" for deriving law from politics. (I set his promising and mysterious remarks aside.) The first is methodological. He says that this narrow function helps us better to understand "the processes shaping our social environment, e.g., that the existence of social authorities is important."[121] It is, however, unclear what form of explanation of social processes Raz and others who describe the positivist's methodology have in mind.[122] As I just said, any function that makes what lawmakers do critical hopes to explain the fact that "the existence of social authorities is important." Raz says that his methods are not evaluative in any political or moral sense. But it is a crucial aspect of our social "processes" that we reflect and argue about what the law is, and take the answer to have great consequences. Any successful analysis of the concept of law must not only show how such reflection and argument is possible, but must also guide our use of the concept within that part of our experience. It is hard to see how an analysis that separates explanatory from political evaluation could conceivably provide that guidance.

Raz's second argument for preserving the untidiness of politics in our account of what law our politics have made is, at least in a negative way, political. He says that "in countries with decent constitutions" there is no reason why the historical contradictions should not be reflected in an account of what the law now requires. Even this negative claim seems overstated. A general theory of law cannot restrict its application only to legal systems that its authors take to have decent constitutions. Judge Arthur Chaskalson, who is the President of the South African Constitutional Court, has recently written that recognizing integrity as part of a sound conception of law was of great importance to lawyers and judges who struggled against injustice during the apartheid regime in that country.[123] Integrity is also crucial, however, in countries with decent constitutions. Judges have no power in such countries to overrule legislation just because they believe it morally wrong: they must find grounds in existing constitutional law. Advocates of "original intention" constitutional interpretation, who embrace legal positivism, do insist that historical untidiness means constitutional untidiness as well. But they want to restrict constitutional rights, and that is a goal that itself needs a political defense.[124] Lawyers who care more about rights do not want to "prettify" history, which would be mendacious. They are drawn to a conception of law that struggles against what is bad in history, which is not mendacious but humane.

Gerald Postema

I believe Gerald Postema's thorough and provocative exploration of the ideal of integrity very valuable indeed, and I am grateful to him for seeking further grounds for defending the distinctness and importance of that ideal. I agree with almost all of what he says. I agree that integrity is a distinct political virtue, even though it is rooted in the other main political virtues of justice, fairness, and due process; that integrity would be redundant among people whose concrete conceptions of these virtues are and have been identical, but it is needed as a distinct virtue by people who disagree about political morality but aspire nevertheless to work together toward a common vision of justice, fairness, and process in the right relation; and that though what I called "inclusive" integrity requires lawyers and citizens to recognize some "mistakes" as nevertheless part of the community's law, it also requires doctrines for isolating those mistakes – for institutionally, in Postema's apt phrase, "regretting" them.

I also agree with him that the pursuit of integrity is in essence a collective enterprise. He worries, however, that my endorsement of a "protestant" attitude toward law, "while rightly highlighting individual responsibility, ignores the interactive, public character of the practical reasoning demanded by integrity" (pp. 295–6). I meant that description not to deny that public character, however, but to deny one way in which people might suppose that the public character must be realized. I do not believe that citizens must accept either that they must all hold the same beliefs about what their law requires, or that they must accept any person's or institution's statement of what it requires as automatically correct. Integrity requires that people reason about law together, and also that each aim at an understanding that states principles to which he believes all are committed through a shared history. But it does not require consensus or cognitive as distinct from political deference to the conclusions of any group or institution.

Postema agrees with at least much of the general defense of integrity that I offered in *Law's Empire*: "One might maintain," he says, "that [integrity] is required by a principle of treating each other as equals or according each other equal respect, or perhaps the reason is simply that we desire such a community."[125] But he thinks that more can and must be said to provide an adequate defense: "However, the more fundamental reason to pursue a common conception of justice is that it is required by structural features of justice itself" (p. 301). He rightly regards that claim as offering a distinctive further justification for integrity as a political virtue. He does not mean simply what I noted in my comments on Raz's essay: that we have no reason to think that a community whose judges aim at integrity rather than justice, when they believe these to conflict, will produce more injustice in the long run for that reason. Nor does he mean only that there is a broad sense of "justice" that collapses together into a single, comprehensive political virtue, fairness, due process, integrity, and justice in the narrower sense I distinguished. He means that in practical political circumstances the search for justice in that narrower sense must take the form of a search for integrity.

He says that this is true only in what Jeremy Waldron has called the "circumstances of integrity"; and I take it, in view of that qualification, that Postema has in mind only justice within a political community. He does not mean that justice between the peoples of different nations requires integrity. But even if we think only of domestic justice, the claim seems troubling. In *Law's Empire* I described the choice a legislature might face if it found that it was politically and financially feasible to enact a scheme of strict liability rather than negligence for certain defective products, but not for all those products to which its rationale for that change would equally apply.[126] It makes sense, I think, to suppose that justice might be improved by that change – half a loaf, I said, is sometimes better than none – even though the choice would impair the law's integrity. There is a much stronger case, which I tried to make, for judges preferring inclusive integrity to justice in the narrow sense.[127] But Postema emphasizes that he is discussing integrity as a political virtue, not distinctly in its legal role.

Jeremy Waldron

It is pleasurable that Jeremy Waldron's particularly illuminating essay should end this fine collection. His purpose is expository: he puts a question to me, and reports the answer that he believes implicit in my work as a whole. Government respects the rule of law when it establishes appropriate procedures – like courts, prosecutions, and civil suits in which each party has a right to argue for its own view – for identifying and enforcing people's legal rights, and when it takes no action against individuals except as justified by or consistent with those rights so determined. Much legal philosophy is devoted to the question of what these legal rights are: to the question of what makes a claim of legal right true when it is true. In my view this is an objective matter: there are right answers to the question of what the law permits or requires on particular occasions. Lawyers and judges may get this wrong, even if they all follow the stipulated procedures and even if they agree on the answer.

Does it matter, however, what procedures are stipulated, so long as these are well designed to reach the right answers? Are there any requirements on procedure, drawn from the very idea of legality, that go beyond accuracy? Requirements that might even justify accepting less accuracy? Suppose we somehow discovered that radically different procedures from those familiar to us now – bizarre techniques of divination or augury, for example – were more accurate in identifying legal rights. Would the rule of law nevertheless require us to retain procedures much more like those we have?

That question, Waldron suggests, forces us to distinguish between a "proceduralist" conception of the rule of law, which identifies legality with our familiar institutions of legislation, adjudication, and the rest, and an "objectivist" conception that defines legality as conformity to the institutional and political rights that people actually have. He finds a "very substantial" proceduralist element in my own conception of the rule of law, and believes that this proceduralist element, which is "at times . . . ascendant over the objectivist element," would lead me to reject radically different methods of identifying law even when these would produce results more in congruence with the rights people actually have.

I do not find his questions easy to answer, however, because I take questions of proper legal procedure to be themselves questions of political morality that themselves have right answers. I am, that is, an objectivist about procedures. I tried to show the importance of that position for legal theory in *Law's Empire* – in my discussion of "inclusive" and "pure" integrity, for example.[128] So I could not come to think that radically different methods of administering a legal system were more effective in identifying right answers to questions about individual rights unless I had first changed my mind about the right answers to some of these questions: about the rights people have to particular procedures. I cannot imagine what evidence would cause me to doubt, for example, that people whose fates are at stake in a legal decision should have an opportunity to participate in that decision.

I do not mean to deny the importance of Waldron's distinction. It is certainly intelligible to think that some substantive legal issues have no independently right answers – that the only "right" answer is the answer that the institutions we happen to have happen to have given. Many legal philosophers have indeed held something like that view. But those who think, as I do, that substantive legal issues do have right answers that are independent of the procedures through which we try to answer them cannot sensibly deny that questions about proper institutional structure also have right answers that are independent of the substantive decisions that a given institution is likely to produce. That is why, as I put it, inclusive integrity and pure integrity diverge. Waldron is right that the interplay between substantive and procedural ideals is, in my view, a complex one: inclusive integrity, which is what fixes what the law now is, must weave both together in an interpretive resolution.

There is a subplot in Waldron's discussion: he believes that my "right answer" thesis plays less of a role in my view of law, or in any case a rather different role, from what many writers, including me, have thought. I do indeed insist that disagreement is different from and no evidence for indeterminacy, and that genuine disagreement is possible only among those who agree that there is something for them to disagree about. I do try to call attention to the value of officials struggling in good faith to find right answers to legal puzzles even when they disagree with one another, and even when we think that the struggle has produced, on occasion or even often, the wrong answers. But I do not sense, in any of this, any compromise or weakening of the philosophical position that I have defended on other occasions: that "external" skepticism about right answers, which purports to be based on metaphysical rather than ordinary moral or legal argument, is misconceived.[129]

As Waldron says, I am as critical, in the same way, of external "realism," that is, the view that the possibility of right answers can be established through metaphysical rather than ordinary moral or legal argument. When I rejected the "transcendental strongbox" theory of right answers in my early essay on civil disobedience,[130] I meant only to reject one particular version of external realism: the idea of a privileged perspective from which one could absolutely verify moral claims in an authoritative manner.[131]

I did prescind in Law's Empire, as Waldron says, from some of these philosophical issues: I said that I would not on that occasion consider whether what I called "external" skepticism is right.[132] But that was in the course of insisting that the important question for the right answer thesis is whether a global "internal" skepticism about law is plausible, and I said it is not.[133] I would not myself say that "the right answer thesis is notable by its absence" in the arguments of Law's Empire. On the contrary, that thesis "underwrites," in a phrase Waldron uses elsewhere, all the arguments I make about judges' responsibility to pursue legal issues in depth, and citizens' responsibility to judge those issues for themselves. If there were not right answers to find, that dedication would be delusional. Still, Waldron is right to insist that the importance of these responsibilities does not depend on any assumption that any judge or any citizen will find the right answer on any occasion; still less on the deeply improbable assumption that they will all agree about what the right answer is.

Notes

1   Note that all page references in the text and notes refer to page numbers in this volume, unless otherwise specified.
2   Ronald Dworkin, *Sovereign Virtue* (Cambridge, MA: Harvard University Press, 2000), p. 47ff.
3   See, for example, ibid., chapter 6: "Equality and the Good Life."
4   G. A. Cohen, "On the Currency of Egalitarian Justice," *Ethics*, vol. 99, 1989, p. 914.
5   Cohen supposes that my discussion of expensive tastes was meant to supply an argument against welfare equality that is wholly distinct from my argument about the ambiguity of welfare and the implausibility of making people equal in any distinct conception of welfare. It was not. I rather assumed (wrongly) that no one would wish to defend transferring resources to people with expensive tastes, and my discussion was devoted to showing that it was not possible to embrace the general thesis of equality of welfare without also embracing that counterintuitive implication. See *Sovereign Virtue*, op. cit., p. 48ff.
6   See Cohen, "On the Currency," op. cit., p. 909:

> Of the many readings of "welfare" . . . I am interested in two: welfare as enjoyment, or, more broadly, as a desirable or agreeable state of consciousness, which I shall call hedonic welfare; and welfare as preference satisfaction, where preferences order states of the world, and where a person's preference is satisfied if a state of the world that he prefers obtains . . .

7   See *Sovereign Virtue*, op. cit., chapters 2, 8, and 9, and "Sovereign Virtue Revisited," *Ethics*, vol. 113, 2002, pp. 106–43.
8   Cohen makes this suggestion in response to my objection, to his claim that people have had bad luck for which the community should compensate when their tastes are expensive because either too many or too few others share their tastes, that people must take the tastes of others as they find them. That, I continue to think, is an important and decisive objection to his position, even though I elaborate it in a different form later in this response. Cohen says that if I were right that people must take the tastes of others as they find them, constitutions protecting individual rights would be objectionable. That hardly follows: as I have emphasized repeatedly, individual rights are part of the background against which a fair market must be taken to operate. That is the main burden of *Sovereign Virtue*'s chapter 3.
9   See the extended discussion in *Sovereign Virtue* at pp. 155ff.
10 I said that it is not unjust, for example, that the community not compensate for putative handicaps that no one would insure against in a fair and efficient insurance market.
11 See "Terror and the Attack on Civil Liberties," *New York Review of Books*, November 6, 2003 on rights and terrorism.
12 I argue for this view of equality in the Introduction to *Sovereign Virtue*, op. cit., and in "Sovereign Virtue Revisited," op. cit.
13 See *Sovereign Virtue*, op. cit., chapter 7.
14 Cohen thinks it surprising that I did not press the same argument against the bad-price-luck version that I made against the bad-preference-luck version: he thinks I must have abandoned the argument, which he calls the "alienation" argument, half-way through the chapter. "And that confirms," he says, "the utter irrelevance of the alienation motif for our dispute" (p. 13). Though the "alienation" objection seems decisive against the bad-preference-luck argument, it is indeed irrelevant against the bad-price-luck argument, which is why I made it only against the former.
15 Some of the passages that suggest Cohen means to appeal to bad preference luck might be just unfortunate choices of phrasing, as when, on page 926 of "On the Currency" he describes expensive tastes quite generally as "tastes which hamper the individual's life," or when he says, of someone who prefers expensive photography to inexpensive fishing, that "Paul's problem is that he hates fishing." Other statements rely more argumentatively on the idea of bad preference luck. He says, for example, on

page 922 that we should not "draw a line between unfortunate resource endowment [like physical hand-icaps] and unfortunate utility function," adding in a footnote that "An unfortunate utility function could itself be regarded as a resource deficiency. . . ." He offers as an example of people with "expen-sive tastes" those who "need costly heavy sweaters and a great deal of fuel to achieve an average level of thermal well-being" (I assume that such people would gladly take a pill to cure themselves of this physical condition) and he says, on pages 936–7, that we should suppose that the misfortune of a reli-gious crank who feels guilt at not building monuments to his god lies not in the expense of the mon-uments but in the bad luck to have the false convictions that fuel the guilt he feels. Finally, toward the end of his article, he dramatically amends the view he had set out earlier in the article, that justice requires compensating people for all the expensive tastes they did not deliberately cultivate, to insist that it requires compensation only "for disadvantages which are not traceable to the subject's choice *and* which the subject would choose not to suffer from." He insists, that is, on compensation only for those who suffer bad preference luck and not those who suffer bad price luck. The bad-price-luck argument is in his essay as well – most explicitly on page 927 – but the two arguments are not well distinguished, and are sometimes, as in the last quotation just offered, at odds. I do not know how much of his earlier argument he means to abandon in now insisting that the bad-price-luck argument is the only one he intends to make.

16 In a crucial paragraph he says that "What matters is whether I have the bad luck to be saddled with tastes that are more expensive to satisfy than, on the whole, other people's tastes are," and elsewhere that "Egalitarians like me . . . are correspondingly obliged to highlight the misfortune of those who are saddled with expensive tastes." No one who is comfortable with his tastes, and would not wish to abandon them even if they are costly to satisfy, would think he had been "saddled" with them.

17 Earlier in the essay (p. 5) he seems to agree with my argument, in chapter 1 of *Sovereign Virtue*, that justice cannot require equality in any conception or dimension of welfare that people value differently.

18 Cohen says there might be such an argument: he says that justice might require equalizing welfare under some particular conception or in some particular dimension in spite of the fact that this con-ception or dimension does not match or exhaust people's understanding of their own well-being. But he must explain what conception or dimension this is, and why justice nevertheless requires that it be equalized. Nothing he says seems even to try. He cites Thomas Scanlon's discussion of well-being from chapter 3 of his *What We Owe to Each Other* (Cambridge, MA: Harvard University Press, 1998), which Cohen says supports the view that "welfare, *even* buzz-and-tick-defined, might be a good metric of just equality even if it isn't the right metric by which to run one's life" (p. 15). Scanlon does say that benefactors aiming to help someone will have that person's own well-being in mind, even though he himself sometimes acts either ignoring or contrary to his own well-being, as when, for example, he acts in the interests of others. But Cohen's immediate question, which he must answer positively to save the bad-price-luck argument, is not whether justice aims to make people equal in their own well-being in spite of the fact that they themselves sometimes disregard or are unaware of their own well-being, but whether justice requires making people equal in their own well-being on an understanding of that idea that they themselves reject as an account of their own well-being. He could answer the latter question positively if he deployed an objective conception of well-being that allowed interper-sonal comparisons; he could then say, for example, that true well-being is a matter of pleasure buzzes, that most people are wrong in not understanding this, and that justice requires making people equally well off in pleasure buzzes because that is the best even though not the most popular understanding of true well-being. But buzzes and ticks seem hopeless as an objective account of well-being, as does anything else that might permit interpersonal comparisons. In any case, Cohen rejects the idea that justice seeks equality in some objectively right conception of welfare (see his "On the Currency," op. cit., p. 909, fn. 4).

Cohen also appeals to my own views: he says, correctly, that I believe that a community should aim to distribute resources rather than success in life equally, even though people want resources only as a means to making their life successful, and he reminds me that I pressed that position in response to

Amartya Sen in fondly remembered Oxford seminars long ago. But I have an argument to explain that choice of metric: I urge a division of responsibility between the community and its individual members so that the community is responsible for distributing the resources people need to make successful lives, and individuals for deciding what lives to try to make of those resources, that is, what lives to count as successful. It is a premise of this story that people value resources equally in what I called the abstract, that is, in a mode that allows them to have, so far as is feasible, their equal share of resources in whatever form is most congenial to their own ambitions. Scanlon, in the pages Cohen cites, describes John Rawls's distributive metric of primary goods in much the same way. He says that Rawls uses primary goods in spite of the fact that people finally want goods only to improve their lives because Rawls draws a "line between those aspects of individuals' situations that are the responsibility of social institutions and those that are properly left to individuals themselves" (Scanlon, *What We Owe to Each Other*, op. cit., p. 139). But Cohen cannot think that people aim to make successful lives out of pleasure buzzes, which should therefore be distributed equally as a kind of primary good. See chapter 7 of *Sovereign Virtue*, op. cit.

19 This particular example is troubling. In a world in which resources were transferred to compensate for deliberately cultivated expensive tastes, no one would need to gamble about having enough resources to satisfy whatever tastes she cultivated.

20 On the contrary, he says, this distinction "in material part imitates our quotidian treatment of responsibility in more familiar domains" (p. 21). He does not mean that common sense endorses his view about expensive tastes; shortly thereafter he concedes that people "no doubt" agree with John Rawls that individuals with expensive tastes, no matter whether these arise from upbringing or choice, must take responsibility for their costs (p. 23).

21 See *Sovereign Virtue*, particularly chapter 7; "Sovereign Virtue Revisited," op. cit.; and "Equality, Luck and Hierarchy," *Philosophy & Public Affairs*, vol. 31, Spring 2003, pp. 190–8.

22 I can put this point in the quasi-formal way that Cohen often prefers. (1) People should be compensated for expensive tastes that they have not deliberately cultivated when a failure to compensate would mean lower than average welfare for such people because they cannot satisfy those expensive tastes to the degree others can satisfy less expensive tastes. (2) People's second-order tastes for expensive tastes are expensive tastes that they have not deliberately cultivated. (3) People who have lower than average welfare because they cannot satisfy their second-order tastes for expensive tastes to the degree others can satisfy less expensive tastes should be compensated.

23 See *Sovereign Virtue*, op. cit., chapter 7.

24 In fact Cohen lists three replies to my suggestion that his view collapses into equality of welfare. He says, first, that his and that view would not be identical in meaning – his view would not be equality of welfare under a different name – even if they were coextensive in practical force because no one in fact ever exercised will in forming his preferences. But as I said in the text, his purported distinction among expensive tastes does not turn on amenability to will: it is not just a contingent fact that people who choose to develop expensive concrete tastes are choosing to indulge expensive second-order tastes. He says, second, that my objection ignores the fact that "we can . . . distinguish relevantly different *degrees* of care and choice in preference formation." But, as the text points out, that is not in fact relevant to my objection. He says, finally, that in any case he commends not equality of welfare but equality of opportunity for advantage. As I pointed out earlier, his comments about "advantage" do not yield a distinct theory.

25 Suppose he has enough money to buy the medicine, and would certainly do so, but would then have less money left for other uses. We might then say that we aim at restoring his resources. But suppose he cannot afford the medicine at all, and so would be doomed to pain but for our help: we might then say we aim at stopping the pain. Neither description would be wholly out of place in either circumstance, however, and, as I said in the text, it would often be most natural to say that we aim at both goals.

26 Cohen recognizes this in another part of his argument. See p. 26.

27 See *Sovereign Virtue*, op. cit., chapter 6.

28   Ibid., pp. 95–6.
29   It is unclear why the egg-gagger is driven to plovers' eggs. Protein is available in other, less cholesterol-threatening, forms. Never mind: I assume she has a general desire for eggs of some kind.
30   See *Sovereign Virtue*, op. cit., p. 50ff.
31   I should take note of another passage in Cohen's new essay:

> Note that one may identify with a preference (by which I here mean, roughly, be glad that one has it), disidentify with it (by which I here mean, roughly, wish that one did not have it), or possess neither attitude. In Dworkin (1981) you pay for your preference *unless you disidentify with it*, in which case it qualifies as a handicapping craving. But in Dworkin (2000) you pay for your preference *if you identify with it*, and not if you neither identify nor disidentify with it, this last being the condition of typical haters of tap water and hen's eggs. (p. 9)

That description of the change in my views seems anticlimatic given Cohen's "U-turn" and "volte-face" rhetoric. But it is in any case inaccurate. I am not fond of Cohen's "identify" vocabulary: it makes one's relationship to one's tastes and ambitions sound like patriotism. But my test has been and remains the same: a "taste" is a handicap if one would prefer not to have it. The last clause in this quotation ceases to be amazing when one notices the endnote Cohen attaches to it. He concedes that people for whom tap water tastes sour would indeed wish to lose that property, but only because it puts them to great expense. So he simply repeats here the mistake about bad preference luck that I identified in the text.

32   See *Sovereign Virtue*, op. cit., chapter 3.
33   See ibid., chapter 8.
34   See ibid., chapter 2.
35   See ibid., chapter 1.
36   Dworkin, "Sovereign Virtue Revisited," op. cit., pp. 129–36.
37   See "Sovereign Virtue Revisited," passim.
38   See, e.g., Elizabeth Anderson, "What is the Point of Equality?" *Ethics*, vol. 109, 1999, p. 287.
39   See my reply to Anderson's objection in *Sovereign Virtue Revisited*, op. cit., pp. 113–18.
40   "Sovereign Virtue Revisited," op. cit., p. 125.
41   The difference is not just terminological: if a gift is treated as income to the donee, it is taxed at rates determined by his not the donor's economic status. Liam Murphy and Thomas Nagel, in their recent book on justice in taxation, argue that this would be fairer. See Murphy and Nagel, *The Myth of Ownership: Taxes and Justice* (Oxford: Oxford University Press, 2002). Many nations (though not the United States, whose practice I was uncritically following) do tax gifts and bequests in that way.
42   For my account of liberty see *Sovereign Virtue*, chapter 3; "Do Liberal Values Conflict?" in Ronald Dworkin, Mark Lilla, and Robert Silvers (eds.), *The Legacy of Isaiah Berlin* (New York: New York Review of Books, 2001), and my "Do Liberty and Equality Conflict?" in Paul Barker, (ed.), *Living as Equals* (Oxford: Oxford University Press, 1996), pp. 39–58.
43   Cf. the discussion of objective list accounts of welfare in chapter 1 of *Sovereign Virtue*, op. cit.
44   *Sovereign Virtue*, op. cit., p. 270.
45   Ibid., p. 269.
46   See particularly the Introduction to *Sovereign Virtue*, op. cit., and chapters 2, 8, and 9.
47   See particularly pp. 122–5.
48   "Sovereign Virtue Revisited," op. cit., p. 125.
49   For an elaboration, see *Sovereign Virtue*, op. cit., pp. 1–2, and my recent article, "Equality, Luck and Hierarchy," op, cit., pp. 190, 198.
50   In *Sovereign Virtue*, op. cit., chapter 6 and in "Sovereign Virtue Revisited," op. cit.
51   See ibid., chapter 6.
52   See ibid., pp. 281–2.
53   See ibid., Introduction.

54 See ibid., chapters 2 and 3.

55 Ibid., p. 272.

56 Ibid., chapter 3.

57 I describe these special reasons in *Life's Dominion* (New York: Alfred Knopf, 1993).

58 Critical life cover, for instance, pays stipulated amounts rather than providing medical treatment. I am grateful to Justine Burley for pointing out that example to me.

59 See, for example, *Sovereign Virtue*, op. cit., chapter 3.

60 See ibid., chapter 8.

61 Just as each must take the preferences of other members of his generation as given rather than as grounds for complaint of injustice. See ibid., p. 298.

62 She does say that conventional morality rests on assumptions about social as well as biological chance. I agree: I have emphasized that myself (see *Sovereign Virtue*, op. cit., chapter 6). But the former assumptions are already built into conventional morality, and there is no comparable shift in social technology on any horizon.

63 See ibid., p. 448.

64 Ibid., p. 446. Italics added.

65 Burley also cites my remark that people are not entitled that other people have any particular mix of tastes, preferences, and ambitions. I made that observation in the course of arguing that it is not unjust that what people want is expensive because others want it too (see *Sovereign Virtue*, op. cit., p. 298). But of course people can complain when others injure them or fail in their responsibilities toward them, and it is no answer that others may act out of convictions that they believe justify the injury.

66 This is different matter from the question of equality I raised in *Sovereign Virtue*: whether sophisticated genetic engineering, which will presumably be expensive, be prohibited if only the relatively rich can afford it. See *Sovereign Virtue*, op. cit., pp. 436ff.

67 For a description of low-wage insurance, financed through general taxes, see ibid., chapters 2 and 9.

68 See, e.g., "Sovereign Virtue Revisited," op. cit., pp. 108–29, passim.

69 Requiring a woman to undergo testing for serious physical handicaps in an existing fetus, and to repair any damaged genes discovered, would not threaten the identity of the person the fetus became. Forbidding cloning could not be justified as in the interests of the potential clone, but no one would be tempted to offer that justification anyway.

70 *Life's Dominion*, op. cit., pp. 77–8.

71 I have described and discussed these two principles in various places. See, for example, *Sovereign Virtue*, op. cit., p. 448.

72 See my *Life's Dominion*, op. cit., p. 199.

73 This is the argument developed in *Life's Dominion*. Burley may have conflated my argument about abortion in that book with my account of liberal individualism in *Sovereign Virtue*. She quotes from an account of the former as an explication of the latter. See p. 180.

74 *Life's Dominion*, op. cit., p. 151ff.

75 See ibid., p. 76ff.

76 See ibid., pp. 97–8.

77 See, in particular, chapter 6 of *Sovereign Virtue*, op. cit.

78 Ibid., p. 269.

79 See the discussion of "cultural" paternalism in *Sovereign Virtue*, op. cit., p. 273.

80 Burley ends her discussion by recommending theories of distributive justice that she believes to be better suited to an age of genetic engineering than mine is. In particular she recommends applying to handicaps a proposal that G. A. Cohen once made with respect to expensive tastes. He argued that people with expensive tastes should receive extra resources, but not if they had "deliberately cultivated" those expensive tastes. I note that Cohen has abandoned that distinction, on which Burley places such emphasis, in his own contribution to this volume. See chapter 1, and my discussion of Cohen in this response.

81   Shiffrin says that "where there has been substantial involuntary psychological change, maintenance of metaphysical personal identity may not be what is relevant from the normative, beneficent viewpoint" (p. 210). But metaphysical and normative issues cannot be distinguished in that way (see my article, "Objectivity and Truth: You'd Better Believe It," *Philosophy & Public Affairs*, vol. 25, 1996, pp. 87–139). I have a special interest in what happens if I should become demented, not just because the demented person is still metaphysically me, but because I am responsible for my own life. If I came to think that some part of the career of a person inhabiting my body lay outside the bounds of my responsibility and my interests, I would not think that person was me.

82   See *Cruzan v. Director, Missouri Department of Health*, 497 U.S. 261, discussed in chapter 7 of *Life's Dominion*, op. cit. The Supreme Court affirmed a state court's refusal to honor the alleged prior desire of a woman in a permanent vegetative state to die in that circumstance, but most of the justices insisted that a properly executed living will to that effect must be respected.

83   See *Life's Dominion*, op. cit., p. 222.

84   Ibid., p. 231.

85   Ibid.

86   Ibid., pp. 228–9.

87   See Kamm, "Ronald Dworkin on Abortion and Assisted Suicide," *Ethics*, vol. 5, 2001, pp. 200, 221–40 and my article, "Replies to Endicott, Kamm and Altman," ibid., pp. 265–6.

88   Kamm cites, as evidence that I distinguish religious and philosophical issues, two pages of *Life's Dominion*: pp. 93 and 156. I find no pertinent distinction on page 93. On page 156 I distinguish between religious convictions and "more secular convictions about morality, fairness and justice." These latter convictions do not exhaust philosophical interest about ethics and "the meaning of life."

89   *Life's Dominion*, op. cit., p. 72ff.

90   Ibid., p. 157.

91   See my book *Freedom's Law* (Cambridge, MA: Harvard University Press, 1996), Introduction and chapter x, and "Hart's Postscript and the Point of Political Philosophy," forthcoming in the *Oxford Journal of Legal Studies*.

92   *United States v. Seegar*, 380 U.S. 163 (1965).

93   *Planned Parenthood v. Casey*, 112 S. Ct, 2791 (1992).

94   *Life's Dominion*, op. cit., p. 170.

95   See *Law's Empire*, op. cit.

96   For a description of this methodological aim, see *Law's Empire*; the Introduction to *Sovereign Virtue*, op. cit.; and, particularly, my article, "Hart's Postscript and the Point of Political Philosophy," op. cit.

97   See citation to *Law's Empire* and to "Objectivity and Truth: You'd Better Believe It," op. cit. Some of Green's other comments are equally mysterious. See his endnote 20: "Stripped of rhetoric and dubious claims, the only important difference between Dworkin's methodological claims for the 'plateau' and Hart's account of the concept of law is that Dworkin explicitly limits the range of his theory to Anglo-American common-law systems." That is wrong in several ways. For Hart's own comments about the differences between us, see H. L. A. Hart, "Postscript," in *The Concept of Law* (Oxford: Oxford University Press, 1994). Green seems himself to disagree with this judgment in his next endnote and its accompanying text, in which he notes how controversial my views are. I explicitly deny, incidentally, that my account is limited to Anglo-American systems.

98   See chapter 13 of his *Ethics in the Public Domain*, rev. edn. (Oxford: Oxford University Press, 2001).

99   Ibid., p. 290.

100 Citation is to my *Law's Empire*, op. cit., p. 52.

101 Ibid., p. 268ff.

102 Ibid., p. 250ff.

103 Ibid., p. 404.

104 He cites page 67 of *Law's Empire*, on which, discussing disagreements about the best interpretation of the simpler social practice of courtesy, I say that people might not reflect but just "see . . . a purpose or aim in the practice." The purpose people "see" may be complex, composed of different goals and

principles, or they may on some occasion "see" only one of these goals as particularly in point without denying that there may be others, or, if they do deny that, they may be wrong. He then cites passages in which I speak of the "point," in the singular, of a practice. But these passages are fully consistent with the thesis I later develop: that identifying the point of some part of legal practice may require appealing to a mix of values. In one of the passages he cites, moreover, I say explicitly that it *does* involve a mix of values. See *Law's Empire*, pp. 94–5. I say first that each of the three paradigm theories of law I propose to discuss assigns a "point" to law as a whole, and I say of "conventionalism" that it claims the "point" of law to be predictability and procedural fairness, which are, of course, two goals not one.

105 In adjoining sentences he says both that "as we saw above, interpretation must, according to Dworkin, be not only coherent but monistic," and that, "Dworkin's commitment to a monistic view of interpretation must itself be questionable" (p. 287). He also says that my discussion of interpretation, "to be any good, must be understood to lead to a strongly, monistically coherent view of interpretation" (p. 286). He doesn't say why the discussion would be no good at all if construed the way I intended it to be.

106 See his discussion at p. 286. He says that I am subject to an objection that is analogous to the objection he makes to the view described in the text. In fact I am not, because my view is sufficiently different from that view so as to avoid the objection altogether.

107 See *Law's Empire*, op. cit., pp. 139, 230, 231, 239, 255, 257, 410–11.

108 Ibid., pp. 410–11.

109 See "Objectivity and Truth: You'd Better Believe It," op. cit.

110 I said that, "an interpretation is *pro tanto* more satisfactory if it shows less damage to integrity than its rival" (*Law's Empire*, op. cit., pp. 246–7). I should have said "less damage to one dimension of integrity."

111 See, e.g., my book, *Taking Rights Seriously* (Cambridge, MA: Harvard University Press, 1977), chapter 8.

112 Raz, *Ethics in the Public Domain*, op. cit., p. 304, fn. 41.

113 Ibid., p. 397ff.

114 See *Law's Empire*, op. cit., p. 195ff.

115 See "Thirty Years On," *Harvard Law Review*, vol. 115, 2002, pp. 1655–87.

116 These various passages are from Raz, *Ethics in the Public Domain*, op. cit., pp. 299–300.

117 Ibid., p. 300.

118 Ibid., p. 293.

119 Ibid., p. 300.

120 Raz's point about history and untidiness was at the center of the once-powerful "critical legal studies" movement in American and other law schools. See my discussion in *Law's Empire*, op. cit., pp. 271–4.

121 Raz, *Ethics in the Public Domain*, op. cit., pp. 300–1, fn. 35.

122 I explored this difficulty in "Thirty Years On," op. cit.

123 Chaskalson, "From Wickedness to Equality: The Moral Transformation of South African Law," *International Journal of Constitutional Law*, vol. 1, 2003, pp. 590–609.

124 See *Sovereign Virtue*, op. cit., chapter 14; "Sex, Death and the Courts," *The New York Review of Books*, August 8, 1996.

125 See *Law's Empire*, op. cit., p. 200.

126 Ibid., pp. 217–8.

127 Ibid., p. 404ff.

128 See ibid., p. 404ff.

129 See my "Objectivity and Truth: You'd Better Believe It," op. cit.

130 See my *Taking Rights Seriously*, op. cit., p. 216.

131 See my discussion of moral particles or "morons" in "Objectivity and Truth: You'd Better Believe It," op. cit.

132 See *Law's Empire*, op. cit., p. 80.

133 See ibid., p. 266ff.

Bibliography of Ronald Dworkin's Works

Essays are organized chronologically (in descending order, by year), by subject – the choice of umbrella subject for those essays falling into more than one category was necessarily a matter of editorial choice. The original place of publication for all included essays is given. Whenever an essay was revised and/or reprinted under a different title, or appears in a more readily accessible publication, the second, and sometimes third source of the essay is also indicated.

Attempts were made to compile here as complete a bibliography as possible of Ronald Dworkin's oeuvre. Omissions below are both unintended and solely the editor's responsibility.

Where the symbol . . . is shown, the piece is available electronically, *gratis and in full*, and the web address is supplied. Web addresses are not provided for other listed articles which may only be obtained electronically with an appropriate subscription.

Monographs

Etica Privada e Igualitarismo Politico (Barcelona: Paidos Iberica, 1995).

Life's Dominion: An Argument About Abortion, Euthanasia and Individual Freedom (New York: Alfred Knopf, 1993).

A Bill of Rights for Britain: Why British Liberty Needs Protecting (London: Chatto & Windus, 1990); the basis of "Does Britain Need A Bill of Rights?" in *Freedom's Law*, pp. 352–72.

Law's Empire (Cambridge, MA: Belknap Press, 1986).

Taking Rights Seriously (London: Duckworth, 1977); rev. edn. includes "Reply to Critics" (Cambridge, MA: Harvard University Press, 1978).

Collections of Essays

Sovereign Virtue: The Theory and Practice of Equality (Cambridge, MA: Harvard University Press, 2000).

Freedom's Law: The Moral Reading of the American Constitution (Cambridge, MA: Harvard University Press, 1996); (Oxford: Oxford University Press, 1996); (Bridgewater, NJ: Replica Books, 1997).

A Matter of Principle (Cambridge, MA: Harvard University Press, 1985).

Edited Books

A Badly Flawed Election: Debating Bush v. Gore, The Supreme Court, and American Democracy (New York: New Press; distributed by Norton, 2002).

The Philosophy of Law (London and New York: Oxford University Press, 1977).

Coedited Books

(with Mark Lilla and Robert B. Silvers) *The Legacy of Isaiah Berlin* (New York: New York Review of Books, 2001).

Introductions to Books

Nunca Más: The Report of the Argentine National Commission on the Disappeared (by Elias Canetti) (New York: Farrar, Strauss, and Giroux, 1986).

Articles in Journals, Reviews, and Books (Chronologically, by Subject)

Moral theory

"Reply by Ronald Dworkin," in Symposium on "Objectivity and Truth: You'd Better Believe It," *BEARS in Moral and Political Philosophy:* (75322.3100@compuserve.com), posted 4/9/97.

"Objectivity and Truth: You'd Better Believe It," *Philosophy & Public Affairs*, vol. 25, Spring 1996, pp. 87–139; (http://www.nyu.edu/gsas/dept/philo/faculty/dworkin/papers/objectivity.html).

"Ethical Theory: Character and Virtue," *Midwest Studies in Philosophy: Special Issue*, vol. 12, 1988.

"What Moral Philosophies Can Learn from the Law," *University of Maryland Law Forum*, vol. 7, 1977, p. 115.

Legal theory

"Thirty Years On," *Harvard Law Review*, vol. 115, 2002, pp. 1655–87.

"Darwin's New Bulldog," *Harvard Law Review*, vol. 111, 1998.

"Indeterminacy and Law," in Stephen Guest (ed.), *Positivism Today* (Burlington, VA: Dartmouth, 1996).

"Reply to Paul Ricoeur," *Ratio Juris*, vol. 7, 1994, p. 287.

"Jurisprudence and Constitutional Law," in Leonard Williams Levy, Kenneth L. Karst, and Adam Winkler (eds.), *Encyclopaedia of the American Constitution* (New York: Macmillan, 1991).

"Pragmatism, Right Answers, and True Banality," in Michael Brint and W. Weaver (eds.), *Pragmatism in Law and Society* (Boulder, CO: Westview Press, 1991), p. 359.

"On Gaps in the Law," in P. Amselek and N. MacCormick (eds.) *Controversies About Law's Ontology* (Edinburgh: Edinburgh University Press, 1991).

"Equality, Democracy, and Constitution: We the People in Court," *Alberta Law Review*, vol. 28, 1990, p. 324.

"Posner's Charges: What I Actually Said," (http://www.nyu.edu/gsas/dept/philo/faculty/dworkin/papers/posner.html), 1990.

"The Tempting of America: The Political Seduction of the Law," *University of Chicago Law Review*, vol. 57, 1990, p. 479.

"Legal Theory and the Problem of Sense," in R. Gavison (ed.), *Issues in Contemporary Legal Philosophy: The Influence of HLA Hart* (Oxford: Oxford University Press, 1987).

"A New Link in the Chain," *University of California Law Review*, vol. 74, 1986, p. 103.

"The High Cost of Virtue," Review of *Morality and Conflict* by Stuart Hampshire, *The New York Review of Books*, October 24, 1985.

"Law's Ambition for Itself," *Vanderbilt Law Review*, vol. 71, 1985, p. 173.

"A Reply to Critics," in Marshall Cohen (ed.), *Ronald Dworkin and Contemporary Jurisprudence* (Totowa, NJ: Rowman and Allanheld, 1984; London: Duckworth)

"Law as Interpretation," *Texas Law Review*, vol. 60, March 1982; revised under the title "Please Don't Talk About Objectivity Any More," *Critical Inquiry*, vol. 9, 1982, pp. 179–200; published by W. J. T. Mitchell (ed.), in *The Politics of Interpretation* (Chicago and London: University of Chicago Press, 1983); forms the basis of "Interpretation and Objectivity," in *A Matter of Principle*, pp. 167–80.

"Natural Law Revisited," *University of Florida Law Review*, vol. 34, 1982, p. 165.

"Principle, Policy, Procedure," in *Crime, Proof and Punishment: Essays in Memory of Sir Rupert Cross* (London and Boston: Butterworths, 1981), p. 193; reprinted in *A Matter of Principle*, pp. 72–103.

"The Forum of Principle," *New York University Law Review*, vol. 56, May–June 1981; reprinted in *A Matter of Principle*, pp. 33–71.

"Political Judges and the Rule of Law," *Proceedings of the British Academy*, vol. 64, 1978; reprinted in *A Matter of Principle*, pp. 9–32.

"No Right Answer?" *New York University Law Review*, vol. 53, 1978; revised and reprinted in P. M. S. Hacker and J. Raz (eds.), *Law, Morality and Society: Essays in Honour of H. L. A. Hart* (Oxford: Oxford University Press, 1977), pp. 58–84; reprinted under the title "Is There Really No Right Answer in Hard Cases?" in *A Matter of Principle*, pp. 119–45.

"Is Law a System of Rules?" in R. Dworkin (ed.), *The Philosophy of Law*; also appears as chs. 2 and 4 of *Taking Rights Seriously*.

"Hard Cases," *Harvard Law Review*, vol. 88, 1975; revised and reprinted in *Taking Rights Seriously*, pp. 81–130.

"Social Rules and Legal Theory," *Yale Law Journal*, vol. 81, 1972, p. 855; reprinted under the title "The Model of Rules II," in *Taking Rights Seriously*, pp. 46–80.

"Morality and the Law," Review of *Punishment and Responsibility: Essays in the Philosophy of Law* by H. L. A. Hart, *The New York Review of Books*, May 22, 1969; reprinted under the title "Jurisprudence" in *Taking Rights Seriously*, pp. 1–13.

"The Model of Rules," *University of Chicago Law Review*, vol. 35, 1967, p. 14; reprinted under the title "Is Law a System of Rules?" in R. Summers (ed.), *Essays in Legal Philosophy* (Oxford: Blackwell, 1968), p. 25; and as "The Model of Rules I," in *Taking Rights Seriously*, pp. 14–46; and in R. Dworkin (ed.), *The Philosophy of Law*, p. 38.

"The Case for Law – A Critique," *Valparaiso Law Review*, vol. 1, 1967, p. 215.

"Lord Devlin and the Enforcement of Morals," *Yale Law Journal*, vol. 75, 1966, p. 986; reprinted under the title "Liberty and Moralism," in *Taking Rights Seriously*, pp. 240–58; and in R. Wasserstrom (ed.), *Morality and the Law* (Belmont, CA: Wadsworth, 1971), p. 55.

"Philosophy, Morality and Law – Observations prompted by Professor Fuller's Novel Claim," *Ethics*, vol. 13, 1965, p. 47.

"Does Law Have A Function? A Comment on the Two-Level Theory of Decision," *Yale Law Journal*, vol. 74, 1965, p. 640; retitled from "Wasserstrom, 'The Judicial Decision',", *Ethics*, vol. 75, 1964, p. 47.

"The Elusive Morality of Law," *Vanderbilt Law Review*, vol. 10, 1965, p. 631; shortened version of "Philosophy, Morality and Law – Observations prompted by Professor Fuller's Novel Claim."

"Judicial Discretion," *Journal of Philosophy*, vol. 60, 1963.

Political theory

"Hart's Postscript and the Character of Political Philosophy," pp. 24–28, forthcoming in the *Oxford Journal of Legal Studies* (available on-line at:
http://www.law.nyu.edu/clppt/program2001/readings/readingshart/rdhartcolloquium2.pdf).

"Equality, Luck and Hierarchy," *Philosophy and Public Affairs*, vol. 31, Spring 2003, pp. 190–8.

"Sovereign Virtue Revisited," *Ethics: Symposium on Ronald Dworkin's 'Sovereign Virtue'*, vol. 113, 2002, pp. 106–43.

"Playing God: Genes, Clones and Luck," *Prospect Magazine*, 1999; reprinted in *Sovereign Virtue*, pp. 427–52.

"Do Liberty and Equality Conflict?" in Paul Barker (ed.), *Living As Equals* (Oxford: Oxford University Press, 1996), pp. 39–58.

"Ethik und Pragmatik des zivilen Ungehorsams," in *Widerstands Recht in der Demokratie* (Germany, 1994).

"Gleichheit, Demokratie und die Verfassung," in *Zum Begriff der Verfassung* (Frankfurt am Main: Fischer, 1994).

"Constitutionalism and Democracy," *European Journal of Philosophy: Colloquium on Law and Morality*, vol. 3, 1994.

"Svobada, Rovnost, a Pospolitost," in *Liberalni Spolecnost* (Prague, 1993).

"Foundations of Liberal Equality," in G. B. Petersen (ed.), *The Tanner Lectures on Human Values, vol. XI* (Salt Lake City: Utah University Press, 1990); reprinted in: S. Darwall (ed.), *Equal Freedom* (Ann Arbor: Michigan University Press, 1995), pp. 190–206; revised and reprinted in *Sovereign Virtue*, pp. 237–84.

"Liberal Community," *California Law Review*, vol. 77, 1989, pp. 479–504; reprinted in *Sovereign Virtue*, pp. 211–36.

"What is Equality? – Part 3: The Place of Liberty," *Iowa Law Review*, vol. 73, 1988, pp. 1–54; reprinted in *Sovereign Virtue*, pp. 120–83.

"What is Equality? – Part 4: Political Equality," *University of San Francisco Law Review*, vol. 22, 1987, pp. 1–30; reprinted in *Sovereign Virtue*, pp. 184–210.

"Art as a Public Good," *Art and the Law*, vol. 9, 1985, p. 143.

"To Each His Own," Review of *Spheres of Justice: A Defense of Pluralism and Equality* by Michael Walzer, *The New York Review of Books*, April 14, 1983; reprinted under the title "What Justice Isn't," in *A Matter of Principle*, pp. 214–20.

"Civil Disobedience and Nuclear Protests," talk delivered in Bonn, September 1983; adapted and published in *A Matter of Principle*, pp. 104–16.

"In Defense of Equality," *Social Philosophy and Policy*, 1983, pp. 24–40.

"'Spheres of Justice': An Exchange," *The New York Review of Books*, July 21, 1983.

"Equality First," *The New York Review of Books*, May 12, 1983.

"Why Liberals Should Believe in Equality," *The New York Review of Books*, February 3, 1983; reprinted under the title "Why Liberals Should Care About Equality," in *A Matter of Principle*, pp. 205–13.

"What Liberalism Isn't," Review of *Social Justice in the Liberal State* by Bruce A. Ackerman, *The New York Review of Books*, January 20, 1983.

"What is Equality? – Part 1: Equality of Welfare," *Philosophy and Public Affairs*, vol. 10, 1981, pp. 185–246; reprinted in *Sovereign Virtue*, pp. 11–64.

"What is Equality? – Part 2: Equality of Resources," *Philosophy and Public Affairs*, vol. 10, 1981, pp. 283–345; reprinted in *Sovereign Virtue*, pp. 65–119.

"Is Wealth a Value?" *Journal of Legal Studies*, vol. 9, 1980, pp. 191–226; reprinted in *A Matter of Principle*, pp. 237–66.

"Why Efficiency?" *Hofstra Law Review*, vol. 8, 1980, pp. 563–90; reprinted in *A Matter of Principle*, pp. 267–92.

"Three Concepts of Liberalism," *New Republic*, April 14, 1979, pp. 41–9.

"Liberalism," in S. Hampshire (ed.), *Public, Private Morality* (Cambridge, UK: Cambridge University Press, 1978), pp. 113–43; reprinted in *A Matter of Principle*, pp. 181–204.

"Did Mill Go Too Far?" Review of *On Liberty and Liberalism: The Case of John Stuart Mill* by Gertrude Himmelfarb, *The New York Review of Books*, October 31, 1974; revised and reprinted under the title "Liberty and Liberalism," in *Taking Rights Seriously*, pp. 259–65.

"On Not Prosecuting Civil Disobedience," *The New York Review of Books*, June 6, 1968; revised and reprinted under the title "Civil Disobedience," in *Taking Rights Seriously*, pp. 206–22.

Rights

"Terror and the Attack on Civil Liberties," *The New York Review of Books*, November 6, 2003.

"Taking Rights Seriously in Beijing," *The New York Review of Books*, September 26, 2002.

"Do We Have a Right to Pornography?" *Oxford Journal of Legal Studies*, vol. 1, Summer 1981, pp. 177–212; reprinted in *A Matter of Principle*, pp. 335–72; and under the title "Rights as Trumps," in J. Waldron (ed.), *Theories of Rights* (Oxford: Oxford University Press, 1984), pp. 153–67.

"The Rights of Myron Farber," *The New York Review of Books*, October 26, 1978; reprinted under the title "The Farber Case: Reporters and Informers," in *A Matter of Principle*, pp. 373–80.

"The Rights of M. A. Farber: An Exchange," *The New York Review of Books*, December 7, 1978.

"Seven Critics," *University of Georgia Law Review*, vol. 11, 1977, p. 1201.

"Social Sciences and Constitutional Rights," *The Educational Forum*, vol. XLI, 1977, p. 271.

"Rights and Interests," *The New York Review of Books*, March 11, 1971.

"A Special Supplement: Taking Rights Seriously," *The New York Review of Books* December 17, 1970; (http://www.nybooks.com/articles/10713); reprinted as chapter 7 of *Taking Rights Seriously*, pp. 184–205.

Affirmative action

"The Court and the University: An Exchange," *The New York Review of Books*, August 14, 2003; (http://www.nybooks.com/articles/16529).

"The Court and the University," *The New York Review of Books*, May 15, 2003; (http://www.nybooks.com/articles/16271).

"Affirming Affirmative Action," Review of *The Shape of the River: Long-Term Consequences of Considering Race in College and University Admissions* by William G. Bowen and Derek Bok, *The New York Review of Books*, October 22, 1998; reprinted under the title "Affirmative Action: Does it Work?" in *Sovereign Virtue*, pp. 386–408.

"Is Affirmative Action Doomed?" *The New York Review of Books*, November 5, 1998; reprinted under the title "Affirmative Action: Is it Fair?" in *Sovereign Virtue*, pp. 409–52.

"How to Read the Civil Rights Act: An Exchange," *The New York Review of Books*, May 15, 1980.

"How to Read the Civil Rights Act," *The New York Review of Books*, December 20, 1979; reprinted in *A Matter of Principle*, pp. 316–34.

"Begging the Bakke Question," *The New York Review of Books*, September 28, 1978.

"The Bakke Decision: Did It Decide Anything?" *The New York Review of Books*, August 17, 1978; reprinted under the title "What Did Bakke Really Decide?" in *A Matter of Principle*, pp. 304–15.

"The Bakke Case: An Exchange," *The New York Review of Books*, January 26, 1978.

"DeFunis v. Sweatt," in Marshall Cohen, Thomas Nagel, and Thomas Scanlon (eds.), *Equality and Preferential Treatment* (Princeton, NJ: Princeton University Press, 1977).

"Why Bakke Has No Case," *The New York Review of Books*, November 10, 1977; reprinted under the title "Bakke's Case: Are Quotas Unfair?" in *A Matter of Principle*, pp. 293–303.

"The DeFunis Case: An Exchange," *The New York Review of Books*, July 15, 1976.

"The DeFunis Case: The Right to Go to Law School," Review of *DeFunis versus Odegaard and the University of Washington: The University Admissions Case, The Record* edited by Ann Fagan Ginger published in *The New York Review of Books*, vol. 23, February 5, 1976; review revised and reprinted under the title "Reverse Discrimination," in *Taking Rights Seriously*, pp. 223–39.

Free speech

"Free Speech, Politics, and the Dimensions of Democracy," in E. Joshua Rosencrantz (ed.), *If Buckly Fell* (New York: Century Foundation, 1999); reprinted in *Sovereign Virtue*, pp. 351–385.

"We Need a New Interpretation of Academic Freedom," in Louis Menand (ed.), *Academic Freedom and Its Future* (Chicago: Chicago University Press, 1996), published under the title "Why Academic Freedom?" in *Freedom's Law*, pp. 244–60.

"The Unbearable Cost of Liberty," *Index on Censorship*, vol. 24, May–June 1995, pp. 43–6.

"Pornography: An Exchange," *The New York Review of Books*, March 3, 1994; Dworkin's letter reprinted as Addendum to "MacKinnon's Words," in *Freedom's Law*, pp. 239–43.

"A New Map of Censorship," *Index on Censorship*, vol. 23, 1994.

"Women and Pornography," Review of *Only Words* by Catherine A. MacKinnon, *New York Review of Books*, October 21, 1993; reprinted under the title "MacKinnon's Words," in *Freedom's Law*, pp. 227–43.

" 'Free Speech and its Limits,' by George Brunn, Reply by Ronald Dworkin," *The New York Review of Books*, November 19, 1992.

"The Coming Battles over Free Speech," Review of *Make No Law: The Sullivan Case and the First Amendment* by Anthony Lewis, *The New York Review of Books*, June 11, 1992; reprinted under the title "Why Must Speech be Free?" in *Freedom's Law*, pp. 195–213.

"Liberty and Pornography," *The New York Review of Books*, August 15, 1991; based on "Two Concepts of Liberty," in Edna Ullman-Margalit and Avishai Margalit (eds.), *Isaiah Berlin: A Celebration* (Chicago: University of Chicago Press, 1991).

"A Harmful Precedent," *Index on Censorship*, 1991; reprinted under the title "No News is Bad News for Democracy," in *The Times*, 27 March, 1991; and under the title "A Compelling Case for Censorship, the Addendum to "Pornography and Hate," in *Freedom's Law*, p. 223–6.

"Devaluing Liberty," *Index on Censorship*, vol. 17, 1988.

"The Press on Trial," Review of *Reckless Disregard: Westmoreland v. CBS et al.; Sharon v. Time* by Renata Adler, *The New York Review of Books*, February 26, 1987; reprinted in *Freedom's Law*, pp. 167–94.

"Is the Press Losing the First Amendment?" *The New York Review of Books*, December 4, 1980; reprinted in *A Matter of Principle*, pp. 381–97.

The court

"The Moral Reading of the Constitution," *The New York Review of Books*, March 21, 1996.

"Mr. Liberty," Review of *Learned Hand: The Man and the Judge* by Gerald Gunther, *The New York Review of Books*, August 11, 1994; reprinted under the title "Learned Hand," in *Freedom's Law*, pp. 332–47.

"One Year Later the Debate Goes On," *The New York Times Book Review*, October 25, 1992; reprinted under the title "Anita Hill and Clarence Thomas," in *Freedom's Law*, pp. 321–31.

"The Reagan Revolution and the Supreme Court," Review of *Order and Law: Arguing the Reagan Revolution – A Firsthand Account*, by Charles Fried, *The New York Review of Books*, July 18, 1991; reprinted under the title "Gag Rule and Affirmative Action," in *Freedom's Law*, pp. 147–62.

"Justice for Clarence Thomas," *The New York Review of Books*, November 7, 1991; reprinted under the title "The Thomas Nomination," in *Freedom's Law*, pp. 306–20.

"Revolution in the Court," *The New York Review of Books*, August 15, 1991.

"La Cour Supreme," *Pouvoirs*, 1991.

"Bork's Jurisprudence," *University of Chicago Law Review*, Vol. 57, 1990; reprinted under the title "Bork's Own Postmortem," in *Freedom's Law*, pp. 287–305.

"From Bork to Kennedy," *The New York Review of Books*, December 17, 1987; reprinted under the title "What Bork's Defeat Meant," in *Freedom's Law*, pp. 276–86.

"'The Bork Nomination' by Nathan P. Glazer, Reply by Ronald Dworkin," *The New York Review of Books*, November 5, 1987.

"'The Bork Nomination': An Exchange," *The New York Review of Books*, October 8, 1987.

"'Reckless Disregard': An Exchange," *The New York Review of Books*, September 24, 1987.

"The Bork Nomination," *The New York Review of Books*, August 13, 1987; reprinted in the *Cardozo Law Review*, vol. 9, 1987, p. 101; and appears under the title "Bork: The Senate's Responsibility" in *Freedom's Law*, pp. 265–75.

"Time's Rewrite," *The New York Review of Books*, April 9, 1987.

"Time's Settlement," *The New York Review of Books*, March 12, 1987.

"Reagan's Justice: An Exchange," *The New York Review of Books*, February 14, 1985.

"Reagan's Justice," *The New York Review of Books*, November 8, 1984.

"An Exchange on William O. Douglas," *New York Review of Books*, May 28, 1981.

"Dissent on Douglas," Review of *Independent Journey: The Life of William O. Douglas* by James F. Simon and *The Court Years, 1939 to 1975: The Autobiography of William O. Douglas* by William O. Douglas, *The New York Review of Books*, February 19, 1981.

"A Special Supplement: The Jurisprudence of Richard Nixon," *The New York Review of Books*, May 4, 1972; (http://www.nybooks.com/articles/10204); reprinted under the title "Constitutional Cases" in *Taking Rights Seriously*, pp. 131–49.

Contemporary politics

"The Trouble with the Tribunals," *The New York Review of Books*, April 25, 2002; (http://www.nybooks.com/articles/15284).

"The Threat to Patriotism," *The New York Review of Books*, February 28, 2002; (http://www.nybooks.com/articles/15145).

"'A Badly Flawed Election': An Exchange," *The New York Review of Books*, February 22, 2001.

"A Badly Flawed Election," *The New York Review of Books*, January 11, 2001; (http://www.nybooks.com/articles/13954).

"The Phantom Poll Booth," *The New York Review of Books*, December 21, 2000.

"Philosophy and Monica Lewinsky," Review of *An Affair of State: The Investigation, Impeachment, and Trial of President Clinton* by Richard A. Posner and *The Problematics of Moral and Legal Theory* by Richard A. Posner. *The New York Review of Books*, March 9, 2000.

"A Question of Ethics," *The New York Review of Books*, May 25, 2000; (http://www.nybooks.com/articles/79).

"'An Affair of State': An Exchange," *The New York Review of Books*, April 27, 2000.

"The Wounded Constitution," *The New York Review of Books*, March 18, 1999.

"A Kind of Coup," *The New York Review of Books*, January 14, 1999.

"The Curse of American Politics," *The New York Review of Books*, October 17, 1996.

"Court of Appeal: The Black Community Speaks Out on the Racial and Sexual Politics of Clarence Thomas vs Anita Hill," *The New York Times*, October 25, 1992.

"The New England," Review of *Mrs. Thatcher's Revolution: The Ending of the Socialist Era* by Peter Jenkins, *The New York Review of Books*, October 27, 1988.

"Report from Hell," *The New York Review of Books*, July 17, 1986.

"Some Views of Mrs. Thatcher's Victory," *The New York Review of Books*, June 28, 1979.

"Soulcraft," Review of *The Pursuit of Happiness, and Other Sobering Thoughts* by George F. Will, *The New York Review of Books*, October 12, 1978.

"There Oughta Be a Law," Review of *The Lawyers*, by Martin Mayer, *The New York Review of Books*, March 14, 1968.

Health care

"Would Clinton's Plan Be Fair?: An Exchange," *The New York Review of Books*, May 26, 1994.

"Will Clinton's Plan be Fair?" *Health Security Act* 103d Congress, 1st Session *The New York Review of Books*, January 13, 1994, pp. 20–5; reprinted under the title "Justice and the High Cost of Health" in *Sovereign Virtue*, pp. 307–19.

"Justice in the Distribution of Health Care," *McGill Law Journal*, vol. 38, 1993, pp. 883–98.

Abortion and euthanasia

(with Thomas Nagel, Robert Nozick, John Rawls, Thomas Scanlon, and Judith Jarvis Thomson) "Brief of Amicus Curiae in Support of Respondents: Washington v. Glucksberg, No. 96–110, and Vacco v. Quill, No. 95–1858," Filed in the United States Supreme Court, Washington, DC; December 10, 1996.

(with Thomas Nagel, Robert Nozick, John Rawls, Thomas Scanlon, and Judith Jarvis Thomson) "Assisted Suicide: The Philosophers' Brief," *The New York Review of Books*, vol. 44, March 27, 1997.

"Assisted Suicide and Euthanasia: An Exchange," *The New York Review of Books*, November 6, 1997.

"Assisted Suicide: What the Court Really Said," *The New York Review of Books*, September 25, 1997; revised and published under the title "Sex, Death and the Courts," in *Sovereign Virtue*, pp. 453–474.

"'The Philosopher's Brief': An Exchange," *The New York Review of Books*, May 29, 1997; (http://www.nybooks.com/articles/1171).

"Assisted Suicide: The Philosophers' Brief," *The New York Review of Books*, March 27, 1997; (http://www.nybooks.com/articles/1237).

"Sex, Death, and the Courts," Review of the judicial decisions: *Compassion in Dying v. State of Washington, 79 F. 3d 790, United States Court of Appeals, Ninth Circuit (1996); Quill v. Vacco, 80 F. 3d 716, United States Court of Appeals, Second Circuit (1996); Romer v. Evans, 116 S. Ct. 1620, United States Supreme Court (1996);* published in *The New York Review of Books*, August 8, 1996; revised and reprinted in *Sovereign Virtue*, pp. 453–74.

"Death, Politics and the Sacred," *Case Western Law Review*, 1995.

"When is it Right to Die? Doctor-assisted Suicide for the Terminally Ill," *The New York Times*, May 17, 1994; reprinted as Addendum to "Do We Have A Right to Die?" in *Freedom's Law*, pp. 143–6.

"Tyranny at the Two Edges of Life: A Liberal View," *New Perspectives Quarterly*, Winter 1994.

"Feminism and Abortion," *The New York Review of Books*, June 10, 1993.

"Life is Sacred, That's the Easy Part," *New York Times Magazine*, May 16, 1993.

"Unenumerated Rights: Whether and How *Roe v Wade* Should be Overruled," *University of Chicago Law Review*, vol. 59, 1992, pp. 381–432; reprinted under the title "What the Constitution Says," in *Freedom's Law*, pp. 72–116.

"The Center Holds!" *The New York Review of Books*, August 13, 1992; reprinted under the title "Roe Was Saved," in *Freedom's Law*, pp. 117–46.

"The Right to Death," *The New York Review of Books* March 28, 1991; (http://www.nybooks.com/articles/3322).

"The Right to Death," *The New York Review of Books*, January 31, 1991; reprinted under the title "Do We Have a Right to Die?" in *Freedom's Law*, pp. 130–46, Addendum originally published under the title "When is it Right to Die?" *New York Times*, May 17, 1994.

"Taking Rights Seriously in the Abortion Case," *Ratio Juris*, 1990, p. 68.

"The Future of Abortion," *The New York Review of Books*, September 28, 1989; reprinted under the title "Verdict Postponed," in *Freedom's Law*, pp. 60–71.

"The Great Abortion Case," *The New York Review of Books*, June 29, 1989; reprinted under the title "*Roe In Danger*" in *Freedom's Law*, pp. 44–59.

"Philosophical issues concerning the rights of patients suffering serious permanent dementia," prepared for the Office of Technology Assessment, Congress of the United States (Washington, DC: Government Printing Office, 1987).

Index

Note: "n" after a page number indicates that the reference is to information in the endnotes.